When Law Was in the Holster

Robert H. Paul in 1884. Robert H. Paul collection.

When Law
Was in the Holster

The Frontier Life of Bob Paul

John Boessenecker

University of Oklahoma Press : Norman

Also by John Boessenecker

Bandido: The Life and Times of Tiburcio Vasquez (Norman, 2010)
Against the Vigilantes: The Recollections of Dutch Charley Duane (Norman, 1999)
Gold Dust and Gunsmoke: Tales of Gold Rush Outlaws, Gunfighters, Lawmen, and Vigilantes (New York, 1999)
Lawman: The Life and Times of Harry Morse, 1835–1912 (Norman, 1998)
The Grey Fox: The True Story of Bill Miner, Last of the Old-Time Bandits, (with Mark Dugan) (Norman, 1992)
Badge and Buckshot: Lawlessness in Old California (Norman, 1988)

Library of Congress Cataloging-in-Publication Data

Boessenecker, John, 1953–
    When law was in the holster : the frontier life of Bob Paul / John Boessenecker.
        p. cm.
    Includes bibliographical references and index.
    ISBN 978-0-8061-4285-2 (cloth)
    ISBN 978-0-8061-6193-8 (paper)
    1. Paul, Robert Havlin, 1830–1901. 2. Frontier and pioneer life—West (U.S.) 3. Law enforcement—West (U.S.)—History—19th century. 4. Peace officers—West (U.S.)—Biography. 5. Sheriffs—Arizona—Biography. 6. United States marshals—Arizona—Biography. 7. West (U.S.)—Biography. I. Title.
    F594.P28B64 2012
    363.28'2092—dc23
    [B]

                                                                    2012017569

The paper in this book meets the guidelines for permanence and durability of the Committee on Production Guidelines for Book Longevity of the Council on Library Resources, Inc. ∞

Copyright © 2012 by John Boessenecker. Published by the University of Oklahoma Press, Norman, Publishing Division of the University. Paperback published 2018. Manufactured in the U.S.A.

For Robert G. Paul and Robert H. Paul,
great-grandsons of Bob Paul

"Bob Paul, as fearless a man and as fast a friend as I ever knew."

—Wyatt Earp, 1896

Contents

Illustrations

Preface and Acknowledgments

Bob Paul was one of the great lawmen of the Old West. For half a century he cast a giant shadow across the frontiers of California and Arizona Territory. Today he is remembered principally for his friendship with Wyatt Earp and the stirring events both before and after the 1881 gunfight near the OK Corral in Tombstone, Arizona. But Paul had been a veteran lawman in gold rush California while the Earp brothers were still wearing knee pants. For almost fifty years he served, respectively, as a frontier constable, deputy sheriff, and sheriff in Calaveras County, California; as a Wells Fargo shotgun messenger and detective in California, Nevada, Utah, and Arizona; then, in the turbulent 1880s, as sheriff of Pima County, Arizona, and railroad detective for the Southern Pacific. President Benjamin Harrison appointed him U.S. marshal of Arizona Territory in 1890, and Paul ended his career as undersheriff in Tucson, a position he held until the eve of his death in 1901.

For five decades he enforced the law without fear or favor on two of the wildest frontiers of the Old West. From his breaking up the notorious Tom Bell gang in the California gold fields of 1856 to his desperate gun duel with the Larry Sheehan band of train robbers in old Mexico in 1888, Paul played a prominent role in some of the frontier's most dramatic events. He battled lynch mobs and tracked down horse thieves, cattle rustlers, murderers, and stage robbers. He fought several of the most noted gun battles of the Southwest, sending five dangerous outlaws to their graves. His shootout with the notorious Cowboys while riding shotgun on the

Tombstone stage sparked Arizona's infamous Earp-Clanton feud and its resulting OK Corral gunfight. His bloody gun duels with the Rancheria killers of the California gold rush and the Red Jack gang in Arizona almost twenty years later were as exciting as anything filmmakers could conjure. As novelist and historian Frank Waters wrote in 1960, "Paul was a big man in every way, utterly fearless, and one of Wells, Fargo and Company's most trusted men; a peace officer whose fabulous career has yet to be dug out of history for the plaudits of posterity."[1]

Though Paul legally hanged eleven men, he strongly opposed lynch law and saved at least seven prisoners from mobs. He was so hated and feared by Arizona's outlaws that Cowboy leader Ike Clanton helped engineer a crooked election in an effort to defeat him as sheriff. Despite living much of his life in tough masculine company on the edge of civilization, he was a devoted husband and father who eschewed rough manners and coarse language. At the same time he was a highly controversial figure in frontier Arizona. His friendship with Wyatt Earp earned him the ever-lasting enmity of prominent Democratic newspaper editors. They accused Paul of being an election rigger himself, as well as a Republican political tool of Wells Fargo and the Southern Pacific Railroad. In Tucson, news-paper stories of his heroic exploits were almost crowded out by personal and partisan editorial attacks by his political adversaries.

Though Bob Paul led a life of almost constant adventure, his story is more than just a western shoot-em-up, and he was far more than a blood-and-thunder gunfighter. His life transcends both local history and the six-shooter culture of Old West law enforcement. A self-trained profes-sional lawman, he performed complex investigative work, prepared cases for prosecution in court, ran jails, collected taxes, supervised deputies, communicated with fellow officers by telegraph and telephone, provided security for the courts, managed political campaigns, and maintained close relations with law enforcement authorities in Mexico. His life pro-vides an inside look at the rough-and-tumble world of frontier politics, electoral corruption, Mexican-U.S. diplomatic relations, border security, vigilantism, and western justice. His career mirrored and exemplified the creation and development of modern American policing. Issues important in Paul's career—illegal immigration, smuggling along the Mexican border, violent crime, youth gangs, racial discrimination, ethnic violence, police-minority relations—are still with us today. A study of his life is both timely and appropriate.[2]

No full-length biography of Paul has yet been written. Given that he was one of the most important peace officers of the American frontier, this is a remarkable omission, one that I seek to rectify. He was a man of bold actions and scant words. Though educated and literate, he left behind few letters and no diaries or memoirs. Humble and modest to the extreme, he infrequently spoke of his thrilling exploits, even to his friends, and he very rarely gave newspaper interviews. A Tucson journalist writing in the 1880s remarked, "The annals of Calaveras County, and the stories of the miners who lived there in those early days are the books wherein are recorded the many bold and successful deeds of Sheriff Paul with the criminal element of those lawless times." Were it only so. The fact is, there are no recorded annals of Calaveras County, and the gold rush miners who lived there have been dead a hundred years. Very few Calaveras newspapers of the 1850s and '60s survive, and even fewer court records exist. Fortunately for the historian, once Paul moved to Arizona in 1878, the territory's newspapers reported his activities in detail.[3]

Researching Paul's life has been extremely challenging. It had to be dug out, bit by bit, from timeworn newspapers, forgotten court files, scattered government records, and obscure memoirs. The job could never have been completed without the generous help of many friends and colleagues. First and foremost, I owe a profound debt of gratitude to Robert G. Paul of Newbury Park, California, and Robert H. Paul of San Carlos, California. Both are great-grandsons of Bob Paul; the first named is a grandson of John V. Paul, and the second named is a grandson of Robert J. Paul. They provided me with immeasurable help in the form of family history, genealogical information, newspaper articles, photographs, and, most importantly, their fellowship. It is only appropriate that this volume is dedicated to my pals, the two modern-day Bob Pauls.

Special thanks are due to my great friend William B. Secrest, author and historian, who almost thirty years ago explained to me that Bob Paul of Tombstone fame was the same man as Robert H. Paul, the pioneer lawman of the California gold rush. Prior to that I had never made the connection. Bill generously shared with me his own research into Paul's career. I am also greatly indebted to Casey Tefertiller, biographer of Wyatt Earp, who graciously allowed me to copy many Paul items from his files and answered countless questions over the past fifteen years. In addition, Casey Tefertiller and Bob Palmquist, Tucson lawyer and historian, kindly provided me with a copy of the long-lost trial transcript of the 1881

Paul v. Shibell election case, which was discovered buried in the files of the Arizona Historical Society by author Steve Gatto. Tom Gaumer of Tucson, a researcher par excellence, tracked down many Paul items for me; this volume could not have been completed without his unselfish help. Dr. Larry D. Ball, author of several fine books on Southwestern law enforcement, generously shared documents related to Paul's service as U.S. marshal. Bob Garamendi graciously took me on a tour of the Bob Paul Mine property. My son Robert Boessenecker, a scholar and artist, kindly prepared copies of many of the images herein.

I also owe thanks to Stuart M. Frank and Laura C. Pereira of the New Bedford (MA) Whaling Museum; Joan E. Barney of the New Bedford Free Public Library; the late Lorrayne Kennedy of the Calaveras Museum; Nancy Sawyer of the Arizona State Archives; Shannon Van Zant of the Calaveras County Archives; Kathleen Brewster of the Santa Barbara Historical Museum; and Bruce Dinges, Jill McCleary, and the rest of the helpful staff of the Arizona Historical Society in Tucson. Additional thanks go to Bob Boze Bell, Peter Brand, Jack Burrows, Bob Chandler, Don Chaput, Anne Collier, Paul Cool, Robert K. DeArment, Harold L. "Lee" Edwards, Bill Evans, the late John D. Gilchriese, Don Gordon, Jeff Isble, Troy Kelley, Bob McCubbin, Rick Miller, Jeff Morey, the late Kevin J. Mullen, Terry Ommen, Robert P. Palazzo, Pam Potter, Gary L. Roberts, Bill Sander, Bill Shillingberg, Chuck Smith, Nancy Sosa, Ben Traywick, R. Michael Wilson, and Roy Young.

I would like to thank my fellow members of the Wild West History Association for their fellowship and support. The association's bimonthly journal and annual rendezvous are highly recommended. Anyone interested in the history of the frontier West is encouraged to join this organization.

Finally, my gratitude extends to Bill Secrest, Gary L. Roberts, Robert G. Paul, Harold Weiss, and the late Jeff Isble, who were kind enough to read the entire manuscript and offer their advice and criticism. Casey Tefertiller critiqued the section on Tombstone. Thanks also to my editors, Alice Stanton and Kate Frentzel. Their comments have been more than helpful and are much appreciated. Any errors in this volume, however, are mine alone.

When Law Was in the Holster

CHAPTER ONE

Whaleboat and Gold Pan

On a balmy July afternoon in 1842, the whaleship *Majestic*, her bow slicing the foam, sails filled with the salty Atlantic breeze, beat slowly out of New Bedford's harbor. Peering over the stern was a rail-thin cabin boy, waving fond goodbyes to his tearful mother on the wharf. As the spires and hills of New Bedford gradually faded in the distance, the youth turned his thoughts to the journey just begun, a twenty-two-month whaling voyage around the world. Filled with nervousness and excitement, twelve-year-old Bob Paul could never in his wildest dreams have foreseen the life that, like the *Majestic*'s billowing sails, was about to unfold before him.

His extraordinary story of high adventure on the American frontier began inconspicuously in the milling town of Lowell, Massachusetts. Situated along the Pawtucket Falls, where the Merrimack River churned white-water on its way to the ocean, Lowell was once one of the nation's most important industrial communities. Beginning in the 1820s, America's largest textile mills were founded in Lowell. Wealthy Boston entrepreneurs invested fortunes to build huge mills and an elaborate system of canals to bring hydraulic power to the factories. People by the thousands poured into the city to find work in the booming textile industry. Workers lived in the shadow of the mills in rows of drab brick boardinghouses. This thriving mill town was, during the 1820s, the home of John and Mary Paul, a young couple of extremely modest means. They had emigrated from Newfoundland, Canada, undoubtedly drawn by economic opportunity. John Paul's small grocery store catered to the mill workers. In 1822 came their first son, John, followed by Thomas in 1829. Their youngest, Robert Havlin Paul, was born in Lowell on June 12, 1830.[1]

Little is known of the Paul family's life in Lowell. The booming factory town should have been perfect for a struggling merchant. Between 1830 and 1833 Lowell's population exploded from 6,500 to 15,000, with more than a third of citizens employed in the cotton mills. But in 1832, either due to John Paul's poor health or poor business acumen, he closed his grocery store and moved eighty-five miles south to the seaport town of New Bedford. There he and his wife appear to have run a boardinghouse at 20 South Water Street; later they lived at 20 South Second Street. In New Bedford, such boardinghouses, generally operated by widowed or married women, often catered to seafaring men who needed inexpensive lodging. In an era when it was considered degrading for a woman to work, lodging boarders was viewed as an extension of domestic life and was socially acceptable.[2]

New Bedford was a celebrated town, the preeminent whaling port in North America. In 1840 it was home to twelve thousand people and a large fleet of whaling ships. In the 1830s and 1840s the nation experienced an ever-increasing demand for whale oil, which was used as lamp fuel and to lubricate factory machines. The finest candles were made from valuable sperm oil, while whalebone was used to manufacture buggy whips, fishing poles, and women's corsets. As the whale population in the Atlantic was depleted, whalers broadened their search into the South Pacific and then the North Pacific. During Paul's childhood the New Bedford whaling industry flourished, in part because the harbor at the rival port of Nantucket was too shallow for the newest and largest whaling ships. In 1829 New Bedford had 94 whaleships employing 2,029 men; ten years later it boasted 232 whaleships and 5,679 crewmen. The whaling industry also supported people in other industries, such as candle makers, the coopers who formed whale-oil barrels, shipwrights, and ship chandlers, all of whom made New Bedford prosper. The picturesque town sported many houses with distinctive widow's walks, railed roof platforms that overlooked the sea.[3]

In *Moby Dick*, Herman Melville provided a memorable description of the New Bedford that young Paul knew in 1840:

> The town itself is perhaps the dearest place to live in, in all New
> England. It is a land of oil, true enough. . . . Yet, in spite of this,

nowhere in all America will you find more patrician-like houses; parks and gardens more opulent, than in New Bedford. Whence came they? . . .

Go and gaze upon the iron emblematical harpoons round yonder lofty mansion, and your question will be answered. Yes; all these brave houses and flowery gardens came from the Atlantic, Pacific, and Indian oceans. One and all, they were harpooned and dragged up hither from the bottom of the sea. . . .

In New Bedford, fathers, they say, give whales for dowers to their daughters, and portion off their nieces with a few porpoises a-piece. You must go to New Bedford to see a brilliant wedding; for, they say, they have reservoirs of oil in every house, and every night recklessly burn their lengths in spermaceti candles.

In summer time, the town is sweet to see; full of fine maples—long avenues of green and gold. And in August, high in air, the beautiful and bountiful horse-chestnuts, candelabra-wise, proffer the passer-by their tapering upright cones of congregated blossoms.[4]

But life was not so idyllic in the Paul household. The family's boarding-house appears to have been run by Mary Paul, which indicates that her husband probably was in ill health. Sometime in 1838 or early 1839 John Paul died, leaving Mary to raise their three sons alone. Mary Paul was soon living with her boys at 6 First Street, still taking in boarders. But she was unable to support her sons, and the eldest, John, now seventeen, was ready and willing to go to sea. For most young men, whaling was a romantic adventure, especially when it involved a voyage to the exotic paradises of Tahiti and Hawaii, where they might encounter pretty island girls freely offering up their Polynesian charms. John signed ship's articles with Captain Shubael Hawes, a noted whaler. His whaleship, the *Julian*, was a 356-ton, double-decked, triple-masted vessel, 110 feet from bow to stern, and she had made one prior voyage to the South Pacific. The *Julian* left New Bedford on September 28, 1839. Nine-year-old Bob no doubt watched wistfully from the wharf with his mother and brother Thomas as the ship passed down the Acushnet River into Buzzards Bay. John would be gone for more than two years on a whaling voyage that would take him to New Zealand and the South Pacific.[5]

New Bedford life on the brink of poverty was not easy for young Bob Paul. His mother was undoubtedly a stern, tough woman, for he grew up with strong Protestant values: loyalty to friends and family, strict honesty, an unfailing belief in fairness and justice, and a hard, stubborn New England work ethic. Yet considering that as an adult Paul was good natured, emotionally stable, had a fine sense of humor, and made friends easily, his boyhood was probably a happy one. In the public grammar schools, he learned to read, to speak in precise English and never in slang, and to write in an elegant, practiced hand. At the same time, an economically deprived childhood taught him to reach for things beyond his grasp, a characteristic that would be the hallmark of his adult life.[6]

Young Paul grew up in a culture steeped in whaling. Every boy in town dreamed of becoming a whaleman. Just a few doors north of the Paul home stood the Seamen's Bethel, immortalized by Herman Melville in *Moby Dick*. Whalers traditionally attended services here before embarking on a voyage. Paul, like all boys in New Bedford, played on the wharves, watching the whalemen at work. When no one was looking, they would climb a ship's rigging and explore its hold and forecastle, or row abandoned whaleboats in the harbor. An observer once called such boys "a distinctive class of juveniles, accustomed to consider themselves as predestined mariners. . . . They climbed ratlines like monkeys—little fellows of ten or twelve years—and laid out on the yardarms with the most perfect nonchalance."[7]

On October 21, 1841, the Paul family was filled with excitement as the *Julian* sailed into New Bedford for a joyful homecoming. Captain Hawes brought a small fortune in the ship's hold: 635 barrels of sperm oil and 2,300 barrels of whale oil. John Paul's "lay," or proportionate share, though just a few hundred dollars, was a godsend to his mother. John's stories of the sea, of hunting whales, and of the exotic world he had seen captivated his younger brother. Even at that early age, Bob yearned for a life of high adventure and no doubt pleaded with his mother for a chance to make his own whaling voyage.

Shubael Hawes was a fine man and role model, though he had a fondness for drink. Born in New Bedford in 1802, he was a master mariner and veteran of seven whaling voyages. Hawes had been almost constantly at sea since 1827. Nonetheless, he had managed to marry and father three children; in 1841, his wife, Nancy, was pregnant with their fourth. Shubael Hawes was no Captain Ahab. Though bold and daring, he was thoughtful, kind, and treated his crewmen well. A friend once described him as "warm hearted and generous." Mary Paul's faith in Hawes's ability to keep her sons

A whaler leaving New Bedford harbor. *Whale Fishery of New England*.

safe was exceeded only by her financial need. Bob was puny, even for his age, standing only four feet nine inches tall. But Mary Paul finally agreed to allow both John and Bob, now twelve, to accompany Captain Hawes on his next voyage. On July 18, 1842, an immensely proud Bob Paul was granted his seaman's passport. It was a day he would fondly recall for the rest of his life.[8]

Captain Hawes was part owner of the 103-foot-long whaleship *Majestic*, a 297-ton vessel with a crew of thirty-one. She boasted two decks, three masts, a square stern, three whaleboats, and one longboat. John Paul, now nineteen, signed on as a boat steerer, and Bob Paul enlisted as cabin boy. The *Majestic*'s crew was very young, even for a whaleship. Bob Paul was the youngest, and the eldest was twenty-six. Most of the crew were between the ages of sixteen and twenty-two. Two were African American, and three were Portuguese from the Azores. They were paid according to experience. Captain Hawes received the highest lay, $\frac{1}{15}$ of all whale and sperm oil brought home. John Paul, an experienced hand, was one of the highest paid at $\frac{1}{90}$. As cabin boy, Bob Paul's lay was the lowest, $\frac{1}{250}$. Hawes planned on recruiting additional whalemen in the Azores and Cape Verde Islands, where experienced whalers could be hired cheaply.[9]

The *Majestic* sailed on July 22, 1842, four days after Bob Paul got his passport. Passing out of the Acushnet River into the bay, she lay at anchor off the lighthouse until Captain Hawes and his first mate came aboard in a small boat. At 7:00 P.M. she was again under way, passing out of Buzzards Bay at three in the morning. By daybreak the *Majestic* had sailed around Gay Head, at the western tip of Martha's Vineyard, and into the Atlantic. The ocean crossing took six weeks, and Paul had plenty of time to learn his cabin-boy duties, which included serving meals to the officers, keeping the night lamps lit, cleaning the decks, and learning the whaleman's skills. The latter duty was important, for if a sailor was killed or injured, the cabin boy could be called on to replace him.[10]

Bob Paul became intimately acquainted with the *Majestic*'s whaleboats. Every whaleship had between four and seven oar-powered whaleboats, three on the port side, one on the starboard side, and sometimes several others on deck, and Paul became intimately acquainted with them. They were symmetrical, with pointed bows and sterns, so they could make a dash at a whale, and then pull back quickly. Their bottoms were flat, so that they drew little water and could be maneuvered quickly. Each was about twenty-eight feet in length, with one long steering oar in the stern and five rowing oars; many also had a sail to be used in the event that the whaleboat drifted far from the mother ship. In the bow were two seven-foot harpoons, which would be attached a line of manila rope two-thirds of an inch thick and twelve to eighteen hundred feet long. The rope ran from the harpoon, through a groove in the bow, to a coil in a box, and, from there, lengthwise along the floor of the boat to the stern, where it was looped around a sturdy post. From the post it went forward to the line tub, where most of the rope was left coiled. Whalers would say that the round tub "resembled a Christmas cake ready to present to the whales." A spare line was carried in a second tub. Whaleboats also carried extra harpoons, lances, spades, a hatchet to cut the line if necessary, a box of food, a keg of water, and a compass. A fully loaded whaleboat, without crew, weighed about twelve hundred pounds.[11]

At daybreak on August 6 the crew spotted a wrecked ship in the distance. Captain Hawes ordered the starboard boat lowered to investigate, but there were no survivors on the floating hulk. For young Paul, it was an ominous sign of the dangers inherent in his new calling. Three days later the *Majestic* was west of the Azores when the crew "raised a whale." Paul's heart pounded with excitement at the cry "There he blows!" Captain Hawes ordered the *Majestic* luffed to the windward side and lowered away all boats. Paul, as cabin boy, watched from the rail as the experienced whalemen and boat steerers chased the sperm whale across the open sea. It was dark when the harpooner in the lead boat managed to "fasten to" the behemoth. The crew let enough rope out for safety, then made it fast. The whale surged forward, trying to lose its pursuer. This was the most dangerous aspect of whaling, for the animal might dive and take the boat down or turn and attack the whaleboat. But in this case the whale sped onward at a tremendous rate, giving the whalemen what was called a "Nantucket sleigh ride." Finally the whale tired, allowing the crew to approach and kill it with repeated lance thrusts.

Then came the grueling work of towing the behemoth back to the *Majestic*. It was 2:00 A.M. before the whale was finally brought alongside the ship. The crew ate dinner, then set to work. The head of a sperm whale was its most valuable part because it contained the spermaceti organ, or case. This was a huge sac filled with spermaceti, a waxy oil used at the time to make the finest candles. The crew cut off the whale's head and, with block, tackle, and windlass, hauled it aboard and shoved it aft, onto the quarter deck. Then the ship's officers peeled off the blubber from the floating carcass with sharp spades. The crew hoisted huge slabs onto the deck, where they were thrown into the "blubber room" below decks. By 8:00 A.M. the "cutting in" was finished, and the whale's body, swarming with ravenous sharks, was "hove in" the sea. The crew in the blubber room cut the blubber into square chunks and threw it up onto the deck. The blubber was tossed into two large kettles, called try-pots, stoked with wood fires, and boiled down into whale oil. The oil was cooled in a copper tank, then ladled into casks and stored below. Next the case in the whale's head was opened, and a crewman reached inside and bailed out the white spermaceti with a bucket. The spermaceti was fluid while encased in the whale's head, but upon exposure to air it congealed quickly into a white, waxy mass. The spermaceti was poured into casks, each labeled "case" to signify its valuable contents. The whale's teeth, used for scrimshaw, were removed. Finally the head, or what remained of it, was wrestled to the gangway and heaved overboard.[12]

This backbreaking work took four days, with the crew working in six-hour watches. The mates and boat steerers supervised the try-pots, fed the fires, and ladled the oil into the copper cooler. Some crewmen operated a mincing machine, which ground up the blubber, while others rolled the casks onto the deck. The sight and stench was a shock to Paul. As one young whaler recalled,

The smell of the burning cracklings is too horribly nauseous for description. . . . Walking upon deck has become an impossibility. The oil washes from one side to the other, as the ship lazily rolls in the seaway, and the safest mode of locomotion is sliding from place to place, on the seat of your pantaloons. Moreover, everything is drenched with oil. Shirts and trowsers are dripping with the loathsome stuff. The pores of the skin seem to be filled with it. Feet, hands and hair, all are full. The biscuit you eat glistens with oil, and tastes as though just out of the blubber room. The knife with which you cut your meat leaves upon the morsel, which nearly chokes you as you reluctantly swallow it, plain traces of the abominable blubber. Every few minutes it becomes necessary to work at something on the lee side of the vessel, and while there you are compelled to breath in the fetid smoke of the scrap fires, until you feel as though filth had struck into your blood, and suffused every vein in your body. From this smell and taste of blubber, raw, boiling and burning, there is no relief or place of refuge. The cabin, the forecastle, even the mastheads, all are filled with it.[13]

Now it was the nauseated Paul's turn to clean the oil-soaked deck and blubber room. He found that whale oil washed off easily, but the smoke and cinders were harder to remove. After they had rested, the crew helped with the chore of scrubbing the decks, sides, bulwarks, forecastle, and cabin. Two days later, the *Majestic* was clean. Meanwhile, Captain Hawes had hoisted the sails, and on August 11 the crew spotted Flores Island, westernmost of the Azores. At 4:00 A.M. on the 13th Captain Hawes sent the bow boat ashore to look for recruits, and soon returned to report that there were plenty of willing hands. The following day the boat picked up several Portuguese crewmen as well as a load of hogs and potatoes. Then the *Majestic* turned south and three weeks later anchored off Sal, known to the whalers as Salt Island, in the Cape Verdes. An American brig bound for New York was lying at anchor, and Captain Hawes told the crew that she could bring their letters home. No doubt young Paul jumped at the chance to write to his mother.[14]

The next day, September 7, the *Majestic* anchored off Boa Vista Island. As was the custom for the more appealing ports, the crew was not allowed

on shore; Captain Hawes would not risk losing a single man to deser-
tion. Hawes himself went instead, unsuccessfully looking for experienced
whalers. The ship then sailed to Fogo Island, 120 miles southwest. There,
according to the ship's log, "Captain Hawes sold our Long Boat for hogs
and fowls. Sent the Long Boat on shore with 2 men." The captain also
dispatched his officers in two additional boats to pick up recruits, a number
of whom joined up. Cape Verdeans made excellent whalemen, and New
England ship captains liked to hire them because they worked cheaply.
Of African descent, the Cape Verdeans were young and impoverished and
jumped at the chance to join an American whaler. On board they were
steady and reliable, worked hard, and, like the African American and Azorean
crewmen, received equal treatment as their Anglo shipmates. A typical
whaling voyage became more and more culturally diverse as men left the
ship and replacements were recruited in foreign ports. This made a strong
impact on young Paul, as he learned to judge men by their character, not
by the color of their skin.[15]

As the *Majestic* continued south along the west shore of Africa toward
the Cape of Good Hope, Captain Hawes kept the crew busy painting the
ship and repairing the rigging and sails. It was winter when they rounded
the cape and entered the Indian Ocean. Sailing east, they finally reached
prime whaling grounds off the Crozet Islands, 1,400 miles southeast of
South Africa. Eleven other whaleships were there, and the hunting was good.
On January 10, 1843, Captain Hawes reported that they had captured seven
whales, and by mid-February the *Majestic* was carrying 1,400 barrels of
whale oil and 100 barrels of sperm oil. From there the *Majestic*, accompanied by the New Bedford whaleship *Lancaster*, commanded by T. S. Barker,
continued east to the Lacepede Islands off the west coast of Australia, where
that spring they took in another 800 barrels each. Then they sailed to
King George Sound on Australia's southwest coast, arriving May 5. From
there they cruised the waters south of Australia.[16]

In September, after three months of hunting, the *Majestic* and the
Lancaster sailed to Kangaroo Island on Australia's south coast to pick up fresh
water and supplies. By now six of the *Majestic*'s original crew had left the
ship, and Captain Hawes had to recruit replacements. The Paul brothers,
with the rest of the crew, got leave in nearby Port Adelaide. Both captains
were incensed that the collector forced them to pay taxes to enter the port.
Hawes and Barker wrote an open letter of complaint, which was

published in the Port Adelaide newspaper. The captains reported that rumors of the port taxes had spread among American whalers, preventing at least fifty whaleships from docking there that season. Their letter was given prominent coverage, for Port Adelaide was a new community and sorely needed the whalers' business.[17]

On September 18 the *Majestic* and the *Lancaster* set sail for New Zealand. From there the *Majestic* set out alone, her crew finding more whales in the South Pacific and finally sailing east to Cape Horn. It was slow going, for a heavily loaded, barnacle-encrusted whaleship could make only two or three knots. And if a whale was spotted, the crew would stop to hunt it, for no frugal Yankee whaler would eschew such a chance. The passage around the tip of South America was the most dreaded part of the journey, with enormous waves, treacherous currents, and howling winds. Rounding Cape Horn could take from twelve to thirty-seven days, depending on the weather. To Paul it was all part of the adventure. By May 3, 1844, they had reached Pernambuco, on the easternmost tip of Brazil, where the *Majestic* docked for supplies. The journey north was much quicker, and just a month later, on June 2, Paul was filled with anticipation as the hills and church steeples of New Bedford came into view. The twenty-two-month voyage had been a profitable one. In all, they had captured fifty-six whales and brought home twenty-four thousand pounds of bone. Whaling agent Dennis Wood inspected the *Majestic*'s cargo and reported that she "turned out 333 bbls. sperm & 2580 bbls. whale oil." Bob Paul's lay paid him about $250.[18]

The reunion of Bob and John Paul with their mother must have been an emotional one. Bob was now fourteen, but just as small as ever—he had not grown an inch. John had taken two whaling voyages, and for him, that was enough. He became apprenticed to a cooper and never again went to sea. But Bob had found his calling—he wanted a whaleman's life and all the freedom and adventure that went with it. And now he looked up to Captain Hawes as a father figure. Hawes, who had just greeted his wife and children, including a two-year-old daughter whom he had never seen, soon began planning another voyage. He and several partners paid $10,000 for the whaleship *Factor*, a 100-foot-long, 303-ton vessel. She was aging, built in 1822, but appeared seaworthy, and Paul was eager to enlist as part of her crew. As a journalist friend of Paul's said years later, "The first voyage so kindled his love of adventure that he embarked on another cruise." By now young Paul had graduated from cabin boy; he had enough experience to sign on as an able seaman with a $\frac{1}{165}$ lay. He had been home

The whaleship *Factor*, one hundred feet long with a thirty-man crew. Bob Paul served his second voyage on the *Factor* from 1844 to 1847. He left the ship when she was condemned as unsafe in Tahiti on July 8, 1847. Author's collection.

just four months when he had a second tearful parting with his mother. Little did he know when the *Factor* sailed out of New Bedford on October 1, 1844, that it would be more than fifteen years before he would see her again.[19]

The *Factor's* thirty-man crew was older than that of the *Majestic* and somewhat more diverse. Three crewmen were in their thirties and eleven in their twenties. The diminutive Paul was the second youngest, just a few years older than the ten-year-old cabin boy. Three of the crew were African American, five Azorean, and one Spanish. Captain Hawes intended to return to the Pacific, and this time he would go west, around Cape Horn. Six days out, their venture almost ended. A ferocious gale assailed the ship, which lost three whaleboats, bulwarks, and some of its sails. It was an ominous sign, and Hawes became concerned that the *Factor* might not withstand heavy seas. Undaunted, he ordered repairs and continued on. The prevailing winds took the *Factor* across the Atlantic to the Azores, where she arrived

November 1. Captain Hawes discharged one greenhand, who was sick, and picked up two Azorean whalers. Sailing south to the Cape Verde Islands, the *Factor* veered west on November 21, headed toward Cape Horn. They managed to round the horn without difficulty, and by February 7, 1845, they were plying the waters off the Juan Fernandez Islands, about four hundred miles west of the coast of Chile. Years of hunting by Yankee whalers had depleted the whale population, and the *Factor* had not taken in a single whale. Captain Hawes set off northwest toward Hawaii.[20]

On April 9 the *Factor*, still "clean" of oil, sailed into the whaling port of Lahaina, on the island of Maui, where the crew spent ten days resupplying and enjoying the town's pleasures. Yankee whaling captains preferred Lahaina over Honolulu: in Lahaina there were no steep anchorage charges, and provisions could be easily purchased. Lahaina itself was a collection of grass houses that stretched along the beach for three-fourths of a mile. Two decades earlier, Protestant missionaries had banned alcohol and prostitution there. But by the mid-1840s the grog shops, dancehalls, and brothels had reappeared, and Lahaina again became notorious. Captain Hawes had no objection to grog. On board he was sober, but in port he could be a heavy drinker. On one voyage Hawes got "in a drunken stupor" when his ship stopped at a South American port. His drinking was one habit that Paul did not emulate, for in later life he was only a social drinker and rarely imbibed to excess. At fourteen, under Captain Hawes's watchful eye, Paul was probably too young to participate in the whalers' pastime of drinking and whoring. But there was little else to do in the village of three thousand, except perhaps to enjoy the warm sand and water.[21]

The *Factor* sailed from Lahaina on April 19, and for the next six months she plied the frigid waters of the North Pacific, between Kamtchatka on the south coast of Siberia, and east to Kodiak Island in the Aleutians. Here the crew found good hunting, as the whale population had not been depleted. One day in September Paul was with the crew of an open longboat, pursuing a whale. They managed to harpoon the behemoth and secure the running line to the sternpost. In heavy fog and driving rain they lost sight of the whale, which turned and made an enraged attack on the small boat. The leviathan rammed the whaleboat, hurling it into the air and smashing it to splinters. The impact shattered Paul's right leg just below the knee and sent him plunging into the icy waters. The youth managed to stay afloat by seizing a piece of flotsam. In excruciating pain, bleeding from the compound fracture, and his wound tortured by salt water, he hung on for

The dangers of whaling: a whaleboat attacked by a whale. In September 1845 in the North Pacific, fifteen-year-old Bob Paul came close to death in such an attack. *Whale Fishery of New England.*

dear life. Captain Hawes promptly dispatched a second whaleboat to rescue the crewmen, but it was forty-five agonizing minutes before the bedraggled and half-conscious young whaler could be hauled from the frigid sea. According to one account, "His physical endurance at this time was the wonder of the whole ship's crew."[22]

Medical care on whaling ships was rudimentary at best, but Paul's tibia was reset and a splint attached to his lower leg. He made a quick and complete recovery. On October 16 the *Factor* returned to Lahaina for supplies. The cruise to the North Pacific had been successful, for the ship now carried 1,900 barrels of whale oil and 75 barrels of sperm oil. In Lahaina the lure of freedom was too great, and two crewmen sought and received discharge from Captain Hawes. He did not stay long in that notorious port, and four days later the *Factor* arrived in Honolulu. There, several dozen whaleships were in the harbor, and hundreds of crewmen took leave to visit the grog shops and bordellos. Hawes recruited four whalemen and resupplied the ship. After almost a month in Hawaii, the *Factor* set sail on November 12 for the Northwest Coast of America. Perhaps owing to the winds, Captain Hawes soon turned about and headed for the South Pacific.[23]

By March 5, 1846, the *Factor* was within five days' sail of Sydney, on Australia's east coast. On the trip south they had taken in one sperm whale. That spring and summer they cruised the whaling grounds between Australia and New Zealand. On August 5 the *Factor* sailed into Sydney for supplies, and Captain Hawes allowed the men shore leave. Paul found Sydney a rapidly developing community of about thirty-five thousand people. It was an important whaling port; forty-six American whaleships visited it that year. It was originally a penal colony, but transportation of convicts from England to New South Wales had been halted in 1840. Nonetheless Sydney was still a rowdy town, with plenty of gambling dens, saloons, and brothels catering to the whalemen. Such attractions again proved too much for some of the crew: five more of them obtained discharges from Captain Hawes, and five others simply deserted. The *Factor* spent six weeks in Sydney while Hawes worked to recruit a handful of replacements.[24]

On September 19, 1846, the *Factor* finally sailed out of Sydney harbor. The crew managed to take in a couple of sperm whales and a month later docked at Lord Howe Island in the Tasman Sea, 370 miles east of Australia. From there the *Factor* cruised the south coast of New Zealand. On January 8, 1847, the *Factor* began a leisurely voyage back to Sydney for supplies, arriving February 4. Ten days later she started out again. That spring the *Factor* sailed off the Bay of Islands on New Zealand's east coast. By June, having taken in many whales, Captain Hawes was ready to head home, and he set his course eastward toward Chile.[25]

The *Factor*, heavily loaded with more than 2,700 barrels of oil, did not get far. On June 21, twelve days after leaving the Bay of Islands, a horrendous typhoon assailed the ship. Crashing waves and spumes of whitewater tore away her sails, larboard bulwarks, the rail, two whaleboats, the deckhouse, and part of the deck. The hull and spars were damaged. The *Factor* was leaking badly, and the crew insisted that Captain Hawes take her into the nearest port. Hawes managed to sail the damaged hulk north to Tahiti, arriving in Papeete in early July. The journey had been perilous; Paul recalled simply that they limped into port "after many dangers." The *Factor* was one of only nineteen whaleships to call at Papeete that year. Paul must have been hugely impressed with the famous island paradise. Like all young whalers, he had heard many stories of the sexually compliant females of Polynesia. One whaleman, upon arriving in the islands in 1843, was "surprised to see about 30 to 40 girls all standing on the beach with their white tappa or cloth in their hands or thrown round their necks perfectly naked . . . [inquiring] if we were after girls."[26]

Captain Hawes had more important business at hand. He applied to the American consul for a marine survey, or inspection, of the *Factor*. The consul appointed a mariner, Captain Christopher J. Hall, who kept a general store in Tahiti. But Hawes was almost immediately suspicious of Hall. His survey was brief and desultory, and he failed to adequately examine the rotting timbers and cracked caulking in the ship's hull. When Hall concluded that the *Factor* could be made seaworthy with only minor repairs, Captain Hawes became convinced that he intended to make a profit by supplying the replacement materials himself. A British sloop of war, the *Calypso*, lay at anchor in the harbor, and Hawes had its officers and carpenter make a second survey. They found that the ship "was so old, rotten, and weak, that she was unseaworthy" and that the cost of repairs would exceed the value of the ship. Based on the second survey, Captain Hawes sold the *Factor* at auction for $1,200 and arranged for its cargo of oil to be shipped home. Three years later, an important maritime lawsuit resulted from this incident. When Hawes's partners refused to pay him, even though he had delivered the cargo of oil intact, he sued. The partners filed their own lawsuit against Hawes, alleging that he caused them more than $22,000 in damages. In the end, Captain Hawes was fully vindicated. The Massachusetts court awarded him $4,600 in damages and refused to give the owners a cent.[27]

Young Paul was not ready to go home. When Captain Hawes sailed out of Tahiti on another ship with his cargo of whale oil, Paul and some of the crew remained behind. For many crewmen, service on a whaler was a depressing life of relentless labor, foul and crowded quarters, detestable food, and miserly wages. Paul, on the other hand, had thrived on board. He had felt at home and secure in his faith in Captain Hawes. He loved the whaleman's life and even the diet. While most greenhands gagged on the taste of blubber, experienced whalers reveled in it. Paul developed a taste for whalemeat, which was highly nutritious and packed with calories and protein. Hard work, sea air, and ample food, coupled with a growth spurt, soon made him shed his boy's clothes.

During the voyage he had shot up more than a foot and a half. At first he was a gangly string bean whose tattered clothes could barely cover his slender limbs. But long hours of heavy toil thickened his muscles. His arms, chest, and legs exploded into a sinewy mass. Beneath his threadbare cotton shirt and patchwork woolen trousers bulged a powerful frame, six feet four inches tall and 240 pounds, all muscle and gristle. In an era when the average American male stood five feet seven, Paul was a giant. With heavily calloused, hamlike fists, massive shoulders, and a barrel chest, he became an imposing figure, towering over his shipmates, able to easily perform the hardest and most dangerous tasks. From the officers he admired on board, especially Captain Hawes, he had acquired the gift of good speech, a thirst for knowledge and education, and a strong belief in fair play and justice. He was developing into a remarkable young man, a striking combination of honesty, courage, and modesty.

Bob Paul was ready to set out on his own. A few weeks after the *Factor's* arrival, a New Bedford whaler, the *Nassau*, anchored in the Papeete harbor. Like the *Majestic* and the *Factor*, she was a three-masted vessel, but somewhat larger at 407 tons. The *Nassau* was a famous whaleship, and its captain, Hiram Weeks, a noted mariner. Nassau, in the Cook Islands, had been named after the ship, which had visited it in 1835. In 1842, the *Nassau* had rescued twenty sailors of the shipwrecked whaleship *Parker*, whose captain had earlier been killed by a whale. A year later, one of the *Nassau's* crew, Luther Fox, stabbed to death the first mate, and Captain Weeks brought him in irons to Honolulu. These events, coupled with the 1820 sinking of the whaleship *Essex* by an enraged whale, inspired Herman Melville's *Moby Dick*.[28]

Paul applied to Captain Weeks for a position on the *Nassau*. Though he was only seventeen, he had five years of valuable experience and was hired on and eventually promoted to second or third mate. The *Nassau* sailed from Tahiti in late July and by October was cruising the whaling grounds off the coast of Peru. By November 8 the ship docked for supplies at Callao, Peru's most important port, where it remained for almost a month. Here the crew was given shore leave, with plenty of time to visit the picturesque capital city of Lima, nine miles inland. On December 3 the *Nassau* began a four-month voyage to Hawaii, arriving off Honolulu on March 30, 1848. The ship lay in the waters off Diamond Head until a bar pilot came out in a small boat and guided them into port. Captain Weeks put the entire crew to work for two days, wrestling water casks ashore, filling them, then hoisting them below decks. For the next two weeks the crew took liberty in watches, while the rest painted and repaired the ship. On April 15 the *Nassau* sailed again, this time for the Sea of Okhotsk, off the coast of

Siberia. The whaleship later drifted south to the Sea of Japan and finally returned to Hawaii, anchoring at Lahaina on November 9, 1848. Her seven-month journey had been a fruitful one, for the *Nassau* was heavily laden with 900 barrels of sperm oil and 1,500 barrels of whale oil.[29]

As soon as they stepped ashore, Paul and the rest of the crew heard electrifying news. A rich gold strike had been made in California in January of that year. Due to California's isolation, the news had not reached Hawaii until June, and numerous ships filled with gold seekers had already sailed from Honolulu. The stories of gold were fabulous; miners were making in a day what a whaleman could earn in a year. Paul's heart thudded with excitement as he heard the stories brought by ship and read the reports in the *Honolulu Friend*: "Every week and almost every day the report comes that still richer mines of gold have been discovered. If gold, purer and in larger quantities, than is to be found in any other part of the world, is all men want, they can undoubtedly obtain it by going to California." He could barely restrain himself when he saw the accounts: "It is no exaggeration to report that the energies of the entire population of California are now directed to the collection of gold. . . . The towns of San Francisco and Monterey are nearly deserted, business has nearly ceased—newspapers stopped for want of readers—stores shut—mechanics fled—schools broken up—in fine, the rage is for *gold, solid gold!*"[30]

Paul was in a quandary. Now eighteen, he had been a professional whaleman for six and a half years. He was an officer on one of the best-known whaleships in the Pacific. He had even dared to dream of commanding his own ship. But now the thought of gold was quickly erasing the hopes and ambitions that had consumed him since boyhood. He was quickly overcome with gold mania. One young argonaut recalled how they felt: "A frenzy seized my soul. . . . Piles of gold rose up before me at every step; castles of marble . . . thousands of slaves bowing to my beck and call; myriads of fair virgins contending with each other for my love—were among the fancies of my fevered imagination. The Rothschilds, Girards, and Astors appeared to me but poor people; in short, I had a very violent attack of the gold fever."[31]

In Lahaina, Paul helped resupply the *Nassau*. Then Captain Weeks set sail for Honolulu, arriving on November 18. By this time young Paul had made up his mind. He asked for, and was granted, a discharge from Captain Weeks. On December 21 he set sail for San Francisco aboard the schooner *Catharine*. The journey took just five weeks, and the *Catharine* arrived off the Farallone Islands on the night of January 27, 1849. At daybreak Paul got his first glimpse of the Golden Gate and the rolling green hills beyond. Because word of the gold discovery had not reached the East Coast until late 1848, he was one of the earliest forty-niners to arrive in San Francisco. By then, hundreds of ships were departing from New York and other East Coast cities. That spring, Americans in the border states and in the Ohio and Mississippi Valleys would set out westward in trains of covered wagons. As gold fever spread around the world, emigrants soon flooded into California from South America, the Caribbean, Europe, Australia, and China. The California gold rush would be one of mankind's greatest mass migrations. None of these argonauts, however, would arrive for months.[32]

The San Francisco that Paul saw in early 1849 was a bustling tent camp of perhaps 2,000. Within a year it would explode into a roaring boom town of 25,000 living in canvas tents and wood-frame houses, with modern, four-story brick buildings sprouting up everywhere. At the time gold was discovered, California's population consisted of more than 100,000 American Indians and about 10,000 whites, most of them native Californians, known as Californios, plus a substantial number of American and European immigrants. By the time Paul reached San Francisco there were already 10,000 men laboring in the gold region; a year later the number would increase fourfold. Like Paul, they were overwhelmingly young and male, having left mothers, sisters, daughters, and sweethearts at home. California's non-Indian population exploded to 115,000 by the end of 1849, 90 percent of it male. By July 1850 more than five hundred vessels had been abandoned in San Francisco Bay, their crews having jumped ship and departed for the mines. Statehood was achieved the same year, and just two years later the population swelled to more than 255,000. Within ten years California's residents would number 380,000.

For Bob Paul and the tens of thousands of gold seekers who would soon follow, San Francisco was the jumping-off place for the mines. From there, one would cross San Francisco Bay and proceed by boat or land up the Sacramento River to Sacramento, gateway to the northern mines, or by boat on the San Joaquin River to Stockton, gateway to the southern mines. The mining region was vast and extended across much of the western foothills of the Sierra Nevada. In 1848 and 1849, prospectors swarmed through the region and located many rich diggings. The northern mines lay north of the Mokelumne River, an area drained by the Cosumnes, American, Bear, Yuba, and Feather Rivers and their many creeks and tributaries.

Placerville as Bob Paul saw it in the early years of the gold rush. The settlement was typical of California mining camps. Courtesy of William B. Secrest.

The southern mines constituted all of the country south of the Mokelumne River, including the Calaveras, Stanislaus, Tuolumne, and Merced Rivers.

Small settlements and tent encampments were already springing up at the most promising sites. The towns of Placerville, Auburn, Grass Valley, Nevada City, and Downieville soon became important centers of mining and commerce. Marysville, at the confluence of the Sacramento and Yuba Rivers and accessible by riverboat, became a second entrance to the northern mines, and its growth exploded. The southern mines saw gold hunters from Mexico and Americans who arrived by covered wagon through the Southwest pour into the Sierra Nevada foothills. There, Mariposa, Sonora, Columbia, Murphys, and Mokelumne Hill were among the principal camps.

Paul lingered in San Francisco just long enough to acquire some rudimentary mining equipment, then set off across the bay and up the Sacramento River for the mother lode. As an experienced sailor, he undoubtedly made the journey by boat; many crewmen simply appropriated whaleboats and other small craft and headed for the Sacramento or San

Joaquin Rivers. Paul found Sacramento a booming community of tents and rude wood houses; already several dozen stores lined the riverfront. The air crackled with excitement as men bought supplies and started expectantly for the mining country. Paul made his way up the American River and through the Sierra Nevada foothills to Placerville, situated in a deep, wooded ravine on Weber Creek. It was a cold, muddy camp that February, consisting of about fifty log cabins lining the ravine bottom. There, a month earlier, three robbers had been lynched in the mining region's first vigilante hanging. This earned Placerville its colorful but sanguinary nickname, Hangtown.[33]

Here young Paul first experienced placer mining. In the early years of the gold rush, surface, or placer, gold was found in rivers and creeks, where it had been washed loose from deeper deposits and bedrock. Miners used flat-bottomed pans to scoop sand and gravel from the streambeds, flushing and swirling the water in a circular motion that left the heavy particles of gold at the bottom of the pan. Soon miners adopted the gold rocker in which water and sand were mixed in a box that resembled a child's cradle. The cradle was rocked back and forth, allowing the muddy sand to pass out through a sieve at one end and separating the gold. From the cradle evolved the long tom—essentially a huge rocker, up to fifteen feet long, with water fed into it by a flume at the top. Later, sluice boxes, long wooden troughs with steplike slats, or riffle bars, became popular. Water was run through the sluice while river rock and sand were shoveled in at the top; the water rushed down, leaving particles of gold collected on the riffle bars. All such methods were common in placer mining.

Placerville did not have a great deal of water and in fact was first known as Dry Diggings. In dry camps, "coyoting"—a technique by which each man dug his own hole to reach the water level—or the use of flumes to bring in water to wash the dirt were prevalent. Winnowing, in which sand and gravel were placed in a blanket, then tossed in the air and caught again, was another method used to separate gold in the dry diggings. Gold dust was the common currency; miners carried their dust in small buckskin pouches called pokes.

Most gold seekers worked in small companies generally consisting of their traveling companions from home, and they lived in mining camps that were clusters of tents and log cabins precariously perched on the steep slopes of ravines and rivers. Summers were dry, hot, and dusty, with temperatures often reaching one hundred degrees. Winters were wet, muddy, and bitterly cold; snow flurries, ice, and hail were common. Life was primitive, comforts were few, and food and supplies were scarce. Without women, most miners were forced for the first time to perform all domestic chores for themselves: washing, cooking, housekeeping, and mending tattered clothing. And gold mining was backbreaking work. It was exactly the kind of life that Paul was used to. He loved it, and to his dying day he was exceedingly proud that he had been a forty-niner.

Because good claims were abundant, a spirit of cooperation and cama-raderie prevailed among the miners during the first year of the gold rush. But in 1849 and 1850 an avalanche of adventurous young men descended on California from the eastern states, Europe, Australia, South America, and China. Heavily armed because of the dangers posed by Indians, robbers, and claim jumpers, they flooded into the diggings, many carrying the newly invented pepperbox and Colt revolving pistols. Never before had so many armed civilians of such varied ethnic and religious backgrounds been thrown together. Tens of thousands of young men were away from their homes, many for the first time in their lives. Unrestrained by the settling influ-ences of home, family, women, and church, they became reckless in their newfound freedom and, fortified with alcohol, revolvers, and Bowie knives, lawless in their anonymity. They behaved in ways that would have brought disgrace back home. Gold hunters openly carried weapons, consorted with prostitutes, drank, gambled, and brawled. The increasing competition for good claims made men desperate. As argonauts sought instant fortunes, violence became increasingly common after the winter of 1849–50. As the editor of the *Sonora Herald* reported in 1850, "That firearms are neces-sary in a country like this, no one living here can doubt. It would not be prudent to travel without them, nor should they be thought useless under the pillow at night."[34]

Paul, confident in his ability to protect himself and his claim, paid little heed to such dangers. He labored in the placers along Weber Creek until early summer. On July 3, 1849, hearing that a huge patriotic celebration was to be held in Coloma, he left Placerville and walked sixteen miles south to join the festivities. Coloma was hallowed ground, for there, in January 1848, James W. Marshall had discovered gold in the tailrace of John Sutter's lumber mill. It was a fitting place to celebrate the nation's independence. On the Fourth, Paul found a huge, rowdy crowd congregated about the mill, drinking, gambling, fighting, and drinking some more. Pine trees were festooned with American flags and patriotic speeches were made, while drunken miners fired their pistols in the air. A handful of Chinese were present, among the first of their many countrymen who would flock to California in the months and years to come. Above the celebratory din Paul heard a terrified scream. Rushing forward, he saw a gang of heavily bearded American miners savagely beating a Chinese. The man's offense: he had accidentally spilled coffee on one of the miners. Years of living and working with Pacific Islanders had affected young Paul profoundly. To him, every man was an individual, irrespective of race or creed. Without a moment's hesitation, he instinctively dropped his head and plunged into the band of toughs. With his hamlike fists swinging left and right, Paul dropped the ruffians like pins in a bowling alley. The bruised and bloodied miners were no match for his massive size or for that strength and endurance born of two thousand days at sea. As one witness recalled years later, "It was a sight to see him save that Chinaman." Paul's actions that Fourth of July in 1849 were emblematic of his character and would be repeated countless times in the years to come.[35]

One of the argonauts present, impressed at Paul's ability to handle the band of roughs, offered him a job supervising men who were to erect the first dam on the Yuba River. The dam was to be built at Rose Bar, on the main Yuba, twenty miles above Marysville. Gold had been discovered there in June 1848, and a trading post had been established; within two years, two thousand miners were working the rich placers. During the late summer and early fall the river was at its lowest flow, and a company of fifty gold seekers was organized to build a timber cofferdam across the stream. The water would be diverted into a side channel, allowing miners access to gold in the dry riverbed. With Paul supervising, work on the Rose Bar dam began in September 1849, and by early October it had been completed, and the riverbed was exposed. Miners shoveled sand and gravel into sluices and long toms and washed it for gold. In just a few days Paul and the others had taken in about $1,000 each. This was more money than Paul had earned in all his whaling voyages combined. But the vagaries of gold mining were soon made clear to him. On October 8 an early rain started to fall, and the river began to swell. Two days later the surging stream poured over the top of the dam and washed it away.[36]

Discouraged but not defeated, Paul pocketed his earnings and took a riverboat from Marysville to San Francisco to spend the winter. It is possible that he had learned by letter from home that his friend and mentor Captain

Hawes was planning to leave Boston in charge of the ship *Harriet Rockwell*, jammed with argonauts. The *Harriet Rockwell* sailed in September, arriving in San Francisco on February 25, 1850, and Paul may well have been there to greet the captain. In San Francisco he found gold hunters pouring in from around the globe, and within a few months he returned to the mining region. A new camp, Auburn, had been founded in a ravine near the North Fork of the American River, thirty miles northeast of Sacramento. He found the area swarming with miners, and he did not stay long. From Auburn he headed to Downieville, seventy miles north, arriving in April 1850. Paul discovered a crowded camp of five thousand people, its tents and rough-plank houses clustered together between the steep canyon walls of the North Fork of the Yuba River. Fifteen hotels and numerous saloons and gambling halls catered to its transient populace. Paul headed five miles upriver to the area near Union Flat. There he worked the placers for a year and a half and at times was employed as a mine guard, watching over sluices and warding off claim jumpers.[37]

In October 1851 Paul left Downieville and drifted south to Mokelumne Hill, a trip of more than 140 miles. Located in Calaveras County, "Mok Hill" was one of the most important gold camps of the southern mines. The young forty-niner did not stay long in the crowded camp and soon pushed on to Campo Seco, eight miles southwest. First known as Turnersville, Campo Seco is Spanish for "dry field," a name given to the place by Mexican miners because it had no streams for gold washing. Most mining took place when the gullies flowed in the winter months. In summer, earth was hauled to the Mokelumne River, one mile distant, to be washed for gold. Paul found it a busy camp, with about 250 wood-and-canvas houses and a population of some two thousand people, largely male. Typical of the gold rush, its argonauts were of many ethnicities: Anglo, French, Italian, Mexican, Chileno, Chinese, and African American. [38]

Within weeks of his arrival in Campo Seco, a bloody bandit raid brought home the dangers inherent in the life of a gold hunter. On the night of November 14, 1851, a motley and multiethnic band of gold rush outlaws—four Mexicans, one Englishman, and an American—rode into a small miners' camp just outside Campo Seco. With knives and guns they shot and stabbed to death Christopher Olin and W. H. Boose and wounded two brothers, Jerome and Charles Steward. It developed that Olin had boasted about the large quantity of gold they had found. One of the killers, Domingo, was

Campo Seco in the 1890s, looking much the same as it did during the gold rush. Bob Paul lived here from 1851 to 1859 and served two years (1854–56) as constable. Courtesy of Patricia Pereira.

captured the next day and, after confessing his guilt, was promptly strung up. Another suspect, Manuel Rosas, was later jailed in Jackson, but he managed to escape by cutting his way out with a knife.[39]

Campo Seco had seen much violence, but this bandit raid was the worst. In February 1852, decrying the "many robberies and murders which have been committed at Camp Seco, and gone unwhipped of justice," local miners formed a vigilance committee. They drew up a constitution and bylaws and soon took action. On April 5 a Mexican suspect in the November raid was captured and tried by the vigilance committee, found guilty of the murders, and hanged in Campo Seco. These events no doubt profoundly affected Paul. Like most forty-niners, he supported the efforts of vigilantes to establish law and order. Gold rush judges and lawmen were often untrained, incompetent, and sometimes corrupt, and the few jails in the mining region were notoriously insecure; a state prison would not be built until 1854. The result was that many criminals escaped punishment. Between 1849 and 1853, California saw more than two hundred lynchings, the vast majority occurring in the mother lode country. In the next four years one hundred more took place in the state. Early vigilantes operated openly, held public trials, and made no effort to disguise themselves. Those convicted of theft were generally flogged and sometimes branded with an *R* for robber or *H. T.* for horse thief, while murderers were hanged. Vigilantes did not see their role as one in opposition to the established legal system, but in support of it, as indicated in the 1851 constitution of the vigilance committee in Sonora: "We are not opposing ourselves to the courts of justice already organized. We are simply aiding them or doing work which they should do, but which under the imperfect laws of the State, they are unable to accomplish." In the first few years of the gold rush, popular tribunals could even be difficult to distinguish from regular courts of law.[40]

Paul quickly learned that ethnic conflict was a hallmark of gold rush violence. What threatened to be one of the biggest racial confrontations in the mining region began on the Mokelumne River near Campo Seco in May 1852. Four companies of miners, one composed of Mexicans and Chilenos, another of Austrians, a third of Spaniards and Italians, and a fourth of Frenchmen, registered mining claims on the river. A company of Americans took up a claim just upriver. The "foreigners," as they were called, built a wing dam, which backed up the river and flooded the Americans' upstream claim. The Americans held a public meeting in Campo Seco, where a miner's court ordered that the dam be removed. The foreign miners appealed to the court in Mokelumne Hill, which ruled that their dam could remain. On September 7 their force of about one hundred men armed itself with double-barreled shotguns and six-shooters and prepared to defend the dam. The Americans, seeing they were outnumbered, called for assistance, and three hundred rifle-toting miners responded.

The foreign miners sent for reinforcements and mustered a force of two hundred. The scene was set for massive bloodshed. Citizens sent a frantic message to Mokelumne Hill, the Calaveras County seat, and the local militia unit, the Calaveras Guards, quickly set out for Campo Seco. The Calaveras Guards had been organized only a month earlier, with Charles A. Clarke, a dashing Mexican War veteran, as lieutenant. Led by Clarke, eighty strong, and with a huge silk flag flying, they arrived at the scene of conflict accompanied by the stirring music of pipe and drum. According to one account, "So brave and dramatic was their entrance that both sides involuntarily cheered and, forgetting their differences, rushed forth to bid them welcome." The foreign miners were disarmed, marched into Campo Seco, and ordered, "You have been expelled from Calaveras County for having taken up arms, and you have eight days to leave." Few, if any, of them, did so. The comic opera climax inspired a local theater troupe to produce a satirical play that lampooned the affair. Entitled *The Battle of Campo Seco; or, the Fall of the Six Nations,* it was a huge success and played to crowds in Campo Seco, Mokelumne Hill, and neighboring camps. The good-humored Paul no doubt enjoyed it immensely. At the same time he was hugely impressed by the gallant Charlie Clarke, who would soon become his good friend and mentor.[41]

That winter a rampaging band of Hispanic outlaws led by the infamous Joaquin Murrieta terrorized the southern mines. Many of the band's raids took place in Calaveras County. In January 1853, the gang robbed several Chinese mining camps near San Andreas, killing five Chinese and Anglo miners. Hunted by a posse led by Constable Charles H. Ellis from San Andreas, the brazen outlaws turned and charged their pursuers. After a sharp gunfight the desperadoes fled, then shot up Yaqui Camp and killed another miner. That night they raided the Phoenix Quartz Mill, shooting to death two miners. Amid great excitement a massive manhunt began, and soon a wounded bandit was captured, brought into San Andreas, and strung up. Vigilantes raided Yaqui Camp and Cherokee Flat, lynching two more suspects and shooting to death a third who tried to escape. The bandidos were undeterred, for they promptly robbed and killed two Chinese not far from San Andreas, then murdered three gold hunters near French Camp. On February 1, miners caught another suspect and lynched him near Angels Camp.

A week later Joaquin and two compadres forced a ferryman to take them across the Mokelumne River near Campo Seco. Justice of the peace E. T. Beatty of Campo Seco organized a strong posse and pursued them north into Amador County. There the gang robbed numerous miners' camps, murdering two more Chinese and an American. On February 15 yet another suspect was captured. After being identified by Chinese victims, he was lynched on Jackson's infamous hanging tree. The wildest excitement prevailed. Towns and camps were guarded, and bands of vigilantes took to the field. On February 18 Undersheriff Charlie Clarke organized a five-man posse in Mokelumne Hill and tracked the bandidos into Amador County, then back south to Campo Seco. Meanwhile, in their most brazen raid, the gang rounded up two hundred Chinese miners on the Calaveras River, robbing them all. They killed two Chinese and an American and wounded five more who tried to resist them. The next day, February 22, Undersheriff Clarke and his men caught up with the gang and engaged them in a running gunfight. Reported Clarke later, "We followed them all over the country, and, while we were on their trail, they killed and wounded 15 Chinamen and stole seven or eight thousand dollars. We got one or two chances at them but they were so well mounted that they beat us running all to hell."[42]

The pressure from posses and vigilantes in Amador and Calaveras soon drove the gang from the placers. Large rewards were offered, and the California Rangers, a state police force, were organized to break up the gang. Joaquin Murrieta was finally tracked down and killed by the California Rangers on the west side of the San Joaquin Valley on July 25, 1853. Though the flesh-and-blood Joaquin was dead, his legend was just beginning to come to life. The ever-modest Bob Paul, if he took part in the Calaveras manhunt for Joaquin's band, characteristically left no record of it.[43]

Campo Seco's gullies and ravines, as was customary in late spring, soon dried up, and mining was slow until the winter. Paul had been laboring in the placers for four years and decided to spend the dry months in San Francisco. Eager to return to the new metropolis, his poke filled with dust and nuggets, he set off. By now San Francisco had boomed to a city of forty thousand people, with modern brick buildings and many paved streets. It was the most important community in California, the center of shipping, business, and politics. Paul stayed there until October, when the rains returned, then went back to his mining claim in Campo Seco.[44]

Paul had frequent contact with the camp's large Mexican and Chilean population. During his early years in Campo Seco, he picked up an elemental familiarity with the Spanish language. Though he never became fluent, he was able to communicate without difficulty. There was a fundamental reason for learning the language. During the early years of the gold rush very few unattached English-speaking women came to California, and as a result the majority of single young females were Hispanic. If a virile young miner like Paul had any expectation of success with the opposite sex, he needed to learn Spanish. His ability to understand the language would serve him well in his official career.

Bob Paul had come of age during two of the most exciting epochs in American history. His experiences as a whaleman and gold miner would mark his character indelibly. First, he developed an absolute fearlessness; his perilous life on the high seas led to an almost total disregard of danger. At the same time shipboard discipline instilled in him a strong belief in fairness and justice. Combined, these traits imbued in him both physical and moral courage. And during his six-and-a-half years before the mast, he developed attitudes toward race and religion that were not shared by most nineteenth-century Americans. He had visited ports in Africa, Australia, the South Pacific, and South America, and had met people of myriad colors and faiths. On shipboard, he had bunked with New England Protestants and Portuguese Catholics, with African Americans, Azoreans, Cape Verdeans, Australians, and Hispanics. In ports he had rubbed elbows with South Americans, Pacific Islanders, and Asians. While Paul certainly did not possess modern-day notions of ethnic sensitivity, nonetheless he learned to measure men by their deeds and not by the color of their skin.

During the gold rush, the youthful miner witnessed firsthand an extraordinary amount of violence in Campo Seco and other mining camps. The crime and mayhem in the wild placer region affected him deeply. Early on he realized that his massive size and strength made him more than a match for even the toughest of bullies and ruffians. At the same time, he developed a lifelong love affair with gold mining. Many forty-niners could not stand a miner's heavy labor and hardships and spent only a short time in the diggings before realizing that the burgeoning new territory offered myriad opportunities in business, shipping, agriculture, and the trades. Paul, on the other hand, had long endured privation and hard labor. Backbreaking work, blistering heat, freezing rain, poor food, primitive shelter, and performing domestic chores—cooking, cleaning, and washing—were nothing new to him, nor were the rough, masculine society and the lack of women and other refinements. Just as he had done on the open sea, Paul thrived in the mines. Even if he did not strike it rich, he now earned far more than he ever could as a whaler. He loved the raw new society and enjoyed his new companions, many of them tough, hard-drinking, heavy-gambling, hard-hitting frontier types. Unlike many forty-niners, he had no interest in returning home. "I shall never go East," he once said, "unless it be as a sight-seer." And despite reaching manhood on the rough edge of civilization, he remained a gentleman—good natured, sober, thoughtful, and modest.[45]

These traits and experiences prepared him well. A long, extraordinary career of high adventure on the American frontier was about to begin.

CHAPTER TWO

Gold Rush Lawman

Bob Paul was a very popular figure in Campo Seco. His huge size, coupled with a genial and humorous disposition, made him highly visible and well liked. In personality, he was friendly, frank, and plainspoken. As a friend once said, "There was no sham about him." His leadership qualities and work ethic had been honed by his years on shipboard, yet at the same time he was humble and unassuming. One comrade called him "modest as a chaste woman, active, honest, and courageous to a fault." His lack of fear of the many hardcases and desperadoes who plagued Campo Seco was well known. His friends, probably among them Charlie Clarke, thought that he could win election as one of the camp's two constables. Paul had never considered law enforcement before, but now he decided to throw his hat in the ring.[1]

Calaveras County was then divided into nine townships. The county's chief lawman was the sheriff, who was elected for a two-year term. He enforced criminal laws and served as officer for the district court, which heard important civil and felony cases, and the county court, which handled less serious felonies and civil matters. He also acted as tax collector and was charged with enforcing the jingoistic Foreign Miners' Tax Law, which required all noncitizen miners to pay a license fee of twenty dollars a month. His second in command was the undersheriff, and he employed a number of full- and part-time deputies, as well as several jailers. Each township had one elected justice of the peace and two elected constables, who at that time served one-year terms.

At the general election in September 1854, Paul was elected constable of Campo Seco, Township 4 of Calaveras County. Paul's fellow constable was Mark McCormick, a thirty-two-year-old New Yorker who ran a general store in Campo Seco. The constables enforced criminal laws and acted as the court officers for the justice of the peace. Sheriffs and constables devoted much of their time and energy to performing civil duties: rounding up jurors, serving subpoenas and other civil papers, executing writs, and attaching property for sale to satisfy judgments. A month after the election, Charlie Clarke, now sheriff, appointed Paul a deputy so that he would have authority to make arrests anywhere in Calaveras County.[2]

The Calaveras mining camps that Paul and his fellow lawmen policed were extremely violent. Many men, and a few women, died in brawls, shooting scrapes, and bandit raids. A correspondent to the *San Andreas Independent* pointed out in 1860: "During the past two years, in traveling over the hills to the south and west of San Andreas, we have been shown many and many a little mound in lonely canon and on green hill-side, which were explained to us as the last rest of some unfortunate adventurer slain by the robber or assassin, for the gold it was supposed he possessed." His observation is confirmed by modern studies of gold rush–era homicide rates. In 1854, for example, there were 530 homicides in California; the next year there were 538. These were huge numbers for a state that had a population of about 300,000—the rate of homicide was more than thirty times the current national homicide rate. In Calavareras County in 1855, there were eighteen homicides; in 1856, 11; in 1857, 13; in 1858, 9; and in 1859, 14. The county's population at this time was no more than 16,000. These figures, when adjusted for population, result in annual homicide rates ranging from a low in 1858 of 56 per 100,000 to a high in 1855 of 112 per 100,000. By comparison, the current U.S. homicide rate is only about 5.5 per 100,000 people. The Calaveras rates of the 1850s were about the same or higher than those in current national murder capitals like New Orleans and Detroit. California as a whole, and Calaveras County in particular, was a dangerous place in the 1850s.[3]

American policing was then in its infancy. Prior to 1845, there were no organized, professional police departments in the United States; law enforcement was performed by watchmen at night and by constables during the day. Policing was not a profession, and many watchmen were volunteers.

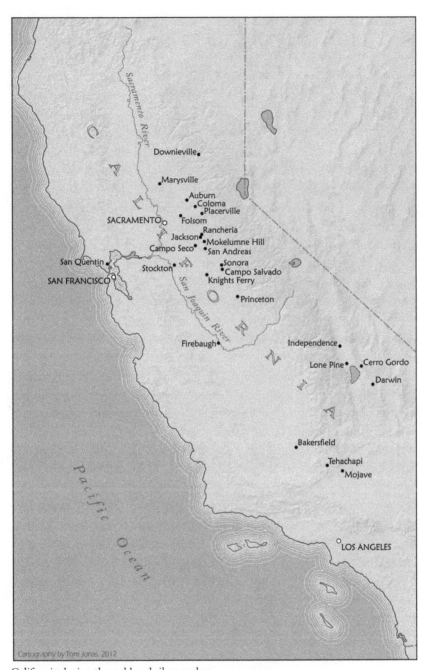

California during the gold and silver rushes

33

As East Coast villages turned into cities, the old system could no longer cope with the increasing crime, social unrest, and rioting that took place in the urban centers of the 1830s and '40s. New York City and Philadelphia were among the first cities to form full-time, twenty-four-hour police forces manned by paid officers. Soon these departments were divided into patrol divisions for the prevention of crime and detective bureaus for the investigation of crime. The result was a rapid rise in urban police professionalism, with older, experienced officers teaching new men the trade.[4]

Because of the unstable and transient nature of frontier communities, professional policing developed far more slowly in the American West. Only in San Francisco, where a small group of highly experienced career officers controlled its police department from the gold rush until the end of the century, did law enforcement reach a degree of professionalism by the late 1850s. Throughout the nineteenth century, most western policemen and deputy sheriffs were political appointees who, as a result of the spoils system, were replaced by successive administrations. Since an entire force might be fired every few years to make room for members of the new political party in power, few officers could obtain expertise. Some experienced East Coast policemen joined the gold rush and helped contribute to the development of professional law enforcement in California. However, Paul, like most frontier lawmen, had no choice but to learn his new job by trial and error. By diligent practice he also became expert in the use of rifle, shotgun, and Colt revolver.[5]

Charlie Clarke, who had been elected sheriff a year before, was a popular officer, as one of his comrades recalled: "A perfect gentleman; soft hearted as a child, but with courage that never flinched. He was the pride of all the gals on the Hill, and the terror of horse thieves." A thirty-three-year-old Canadian, Clarke had taken part in the Texas revolution, seeing action in the Battle of San Jacinto. Six years later, in 1842, he was a lieutenant in the ill-fated Mier Expedition into Mexico. Captured by Mexican troops, he escaped death in the notorious Black Bean Episode, in which one of every ten men who drew a black bean from a pot filled with white beans was executed by firing squad. Clarke's British citizenship eventually gained his release from a Mexican prison. He fought with the Texas Rangers in the Mexican War and joined the gold rush in 1849. After mining in Calaveras for two years, he was appointed deputy sheriff and elected county sheriff in 1853. Clarke and Paul worked together closely. Bob Paul's new duties included frequent official visits to Mokelumne Hill, bringing in prisoners and attending court. He became a familiar and well-liked figure on "the Hill." The courthouse was situated on the corner of Main and Lafayette Streets, next door to George Leger's hotel (the building, somewhat remodeled, is still standing as the Hotel Leger). Recalled one of Paul's friends, "We talked politics all day in front of the Union Hotel and Leger's place—at that time the finest hotels in the state. You could always see Judge Porter, Alf. Laforge, Bob Paul, Dan Lamphier, Al Dudley, Dr. Hepburn and Bill Inness in the crowd. We played euchre for drinks in the evening, after the stage had brought us the [San Francisco] Bay papers and the *Union*—the Sacramento *Union*."[6]

The courthouse was the former county jail. Early in 1854 a new jail was constructed near the intersection of Main and Center Streets, a block north of the courthouse. The Calaveras jail was more strongly built than most gold rush lockups. The walls were stone, and the floor had a top layer of thick wood planks, a middle layer of sheet iron, and a bottom layer of heavy planking. A journalist who examined the cells reported, "The floors, sides, and ceilings of the detention rooms are lined with three inch plank, covered with a double layer of heavy sheet-iron, and the rooms resemble iron safes."[7]

Within a few weeks the young lawman would have to assist in an unpleasant duty, one that he would perform many times in the future. The county jail held a twenty-nine-year-old Irishman named Dennis O'Brien, under sentence of death for murder. On July 10 he had stabbed and mortally wounded Michael Ryan in a brawl at James Bar on the Mokelumne River. At that time hangings were public, and Sheriff Clarke had a scaffold erected halfway down the deep ravine behind the jail. On the specified date, November 10, 1854, a huge crowd estimated at three to five thousand people gathered around the gallows. Clarke arranged for a local militia unit, the Jesus Maria Guard, to be on hand to maintain order. This company had been organized only two months previous, "for the purpose of protecting the citizens of Calaveras and community from violent acts of a large foreign population."[8]

Sheriff Clarke, Paul, and the other deputies brought the condemned man from the jail in a wagon. While the Jesus Maria Guard set up a cordon around the scaffold, the lawmen escorted O'Brien up the wooden steps. With his priest standing next to him, O'Brien sat on a chair while Sheriff Clarke solemnly read the death warrant. Then Clarke told him that "if he had anything to say to the people he might now address them." O'Brien

Mokelumne Hill in the 1860s. The large white building in the center contains the county courthouse on the left, with the Leger Hotel on the right. It is still standing. Library of Congress Prints and Photographs Division, Washington, DC, LC-USZ62-27359.

stood up and in a firm voice told the crowd, "Before you, good people, I have to confess committing the deed for which I am about to die." He insisted he had always been a good man: "I have always worked hard and honestly for my living," adding, "I die without any hard feeling for any man." He announced that he forgave the judge, jury, and prosecuting attorneys. Looking around the crowd, then glancing up at the bright midday sky, he concluded, "Sinful world, I bid you a last farewell."

Then O'Brien kneeled and for a few minutes prayed with his priest. Finally he arose and shook hands with Clarke, Paul, and the other deputies. The lawmen then bound his ankles and tied his hands behind him. Sheriff Clarke fastened the noose around his neck, being careful to place the knot under his ear, and then drew a black hood over his head. Then the officers and clergymen stepped down from the gallows, leaving O'Brien alone on the trap. A moment later the bolt was pulled, the trap door dropped open, and O'Brien plunged to his death. A local newspaperman present noted that the crowd "preserved the most respectful silence, and seemed to deeply sympathize with the unfortunate man."[9]

Paul quickly gained experience as constable of Campo Seco, which, like most mining camps, saw much mayhem. Though news coverage of the isolated camp was sketchy, the budding constable likely handled numerous murder cases. In March 1855, an African American barber named Brown, while entering his house, was shot dead. An investigation, probably by Paul, revealed that the woman he lived with had been involved with a Mexican, who had fled out the back door after shooting Brown. The woman was arrested, but she refused to say what had happened. A few weeks later a body was found in the Calaveras River. The unknown victim had been shot in the chest; a rope attached to a sixty-pound sack of stones was tied around his waist. Paul and fellow lawmen were unable to solve this murder. In June, a British sailor named Colebrook quarreled with two men, one a fellow Briton and the other a Mexican, and shot them both. He was arrested and held by Campo Seco officers. Although Colebrook vanished after posting bail, a year later his brother, also a desperado, was lynched for killing a doctor in Angels Camp. In another incident, a black former ship's steward named Frisbie Hood quarreled with his wife in their Campo Seco home. He pulled a pistol and shot her in the stomach, a mortal wound. Hood was arrested but seems to have escaped punishment. On another occasion, in Chile Camp, a few miles north of Campo Seco, a quarrel broke out between two groups of miners, one American and the other Irish. Hot words soon led to blows with stones and picks, and then to six-shooters. In an exchange of thirty shots, four miners were wounded. A fifth man was injured by a blow from a pick. The culprits were arrested and brought into Campo Seco; the mining claim they fought over was worth just one hundred dollars. Bob Paul undoubtedly played a leading role in these incidents. He was quickly becoming an able detective: examining crime scenes, interviewing witnesses, preserving evidence, cultivating informants, and identifying suspects.[10]

On the night of March 25, 1855, a ruffian named Wallace Stewart was playing three-card monte with John Flynn, a former San Francisco policeman, in a Campo Seco dance house. Stewart objected when Flynn won, and a brawl broke out. Paul broke up the fight and arrested Flynn, who was evidently the aggressor. Most mining camps had no jails, and it was customary for officers to lock their manacled prisoners inside a house or chain them to a log or a tree. Paul took Flynn to his room and ironed his ankle to the wood floor, intending to bring him to the Mokelumne Hill jail at daylight. As Paul was preparing to bed down for the night, Stewart crept up to the window. Leveling his revolver, he fired one shot at the ironed prisoner. The heavy ball tore through Flynn from side to side, killing him. Paul raced outside but could find no trace of the assailant. Flynn suffered in agony for several hours before he died, and Sheriff Clarke offered a $300 reward for Stewart's arrest. More than a year later, in August 1856, the fugitive was captured in Butte County. He was returned to Mokelumne Hill, convicted of murder, and sentenced to hang. His attorney appealed to the California Supreme Court, which granted a new trial due to a legal error in selecting the jury. Stewart was retried in June 1857, and, much to Paul's chagrin, he was promptly acquitted. The facts of the case are scanty, and it is unclear why the first jury convicted him while the second did not. Perhaps the evidence was mainly circumstantial, and Paul may have been too busy ducking for cover to get a good look at the assassin. In the end, the young constable could just as easily have been killed as his prisoner. This was but the first of many close brushes with death in Paul's long career as a lawman.[11]

Chinese miners continued to be a favorite target of robbers. In May 1855, three desperadoes rode into a Chinese mining camp near Greaser-town, east of Campo Seco. There was only one Chinese present, and the ruffians asked him for a drink. While he was handing over a cup of water, one badman drew his pistol and fired, wounding the Chinese in the hand. Unlike most Chinese miners, this one carried a revolver and knew how to use it. He jerked the pistol and opened fire, badly wounding his assailant. The three robbers fled. Paul suspected that the wounded man was Bill Link, a notorious ruffian from Campo Seco. His suspicions were heightened when Link failed to appear in Campo Seco for months. Finally, in December, Paul—apparently acting on a tip from an informant—located a grave in the chaparral on a hill not far from the scene of the shooting. He dug up the body, and, as one newspaperman wryly reported, "sufficient proof was found to identify it as the missing Link."[12]

On May 27, 1855, a miner named Caspar Sheppard quarreled with Jack Williams, a forty-year-old Welshman, over a paltry debt. In a confrontation in front of a Campo Seco billiard saloon, Williams demanded repayment of $2.50. Sheppard responded with curses and insults, then struck Williams a blow to the chin. Williams yanked his six-shooter and opened fire. Only one ball struck his target, tearing though the arm into the chest, but that was enough. Shephard died in excruciating pain at three o'clock the next morning. Paul arrested Williams, but spotted what a witness described as "an unusual number of hombres about." Fearing lynch law, at nine o'clock the young constable bundled his prisoner into a buggy, whipped up the horses, and raced for Mokelumne Hill. But he didn't get past the outskirts of town. The buggy careened around a corner too fast, spilling Paul and Williams into the street. An angry crowd surrounded the upturned buggy, yelling, "Hang him! Hang him!"

Constable Paul, with the help of several friends, managed to shove his way through the mob with Jack Williams in tow and take refuge in a nearby house. As the enraged mob surrounded the house, three local judges and two lawyers called for order and tried to calm the throng. But their voices of reason were drowned out in the din. A rope was produced, and the mob smashed open the doors and rushed inside. Paul and the volunteer guards put up a desperate struggle, but they were overpowered. A noose was draped around Williams's neck, and the lynchers seized the rope and started to drag him from the house. Someone—perhaps Paul or another of the guards—drew a knife and cut the rope, and the mob rushed outside with an empty noose. They quickly repaired the rope and dragged Williams to a tree a few hundred yards away. Its limbs were too high, so they hurried him to another tree. Now Paul and the other officials again confronted the mob. An eyewitness said that "by the faithful, fearless stand they took in the matter, in maintaining the majesty of the law, these few gentlemen succeeded effectually in disarming the multitude, and the prisoner was taken in charge back to town by Mr. Paul, and in a very moment he was en route for Mok-elumne Hill—greatly to the gratification of all the law-abiding citizens." Constable Paul lodged Williams in the county jail to await trial for murder.[13]

Two weeks later, in the morning darkness of June 12, a pair of horse thieves, William Freeman and Jim Neal, alias J. H. Simpson, drove a herd of forty to fifty stolen horses and mules toward the Mokelumne River at Winters Bar, just north of Campo Seco. They had stolen the animals from nearby ranches and mining camps. A 220-foot-long wire suspension bridge, just completed a few days before, spanned the river. The desperadoes started across, but the weight of the herd was too great, and the bridge collapsed. Twelve horses plunged to their deaths, including the animals ridden by the thieves. Eight others were badly injured but managed to swim to shore. Free-man and Neal fled on foot into the blackness. At daylight the crumpled bridge and dead animals were discovered. Paul was notified and started in pursuit with a small posse. He found that two of the recovered horses were saddled, and he deduced that the fugitives were on foot and may have been injured in the fall.

The next day, on the road to Mokelumne Hill, Paul caught up with the suspected horse thieves, one of whom had his arm in a sling. They were identified as having been in the area where the horses were stolen. Paul arrested the pair and brought them into Campo Seco, where they were recognized as notorious criminals. Freeman was identified as one of the men who had robbed Adams & Co. Express in Mormon Island two years before; Freeman had escaped but his partner, Dorsey, had been killed resisting arrest. Others recognized Neal as a notorious fugitive from Stockton who, while being taken by riverboat to San Quentin prison a year earlier, had leaped overboard and escaped.

A preliminary hearing was held before the justice of the peace the following day, June 16, and the two were held to answer the horse-theft charges. The huge crowd attending the hearing was enraged at the pair, whose status as fugitives illustrated the problems with lax gold rush era law enforcement. They decided to take matters into their own hands. The throng watched as Paul loaded Neal into a buggy, while a guard named Cosgrove put Freeman into a wagon. When Paul and Cosgrove started off for the Mokelumne Hill jail, the angry crowd surrounded them and seized the horses' bridles. In the melee Cosgrove's wagon overturned, and the mob snatched Freeman and headed toward the damaged bridge at Winter's Bar, intending to hang him there. At the same time the mob attacked Neal in Paul's buggy. They managed to get a rope around Neal's neck, but Paul's massive size and strength prevailed. He managed to fight off the mob and secure his prisoner.

Now Constable Paul and Deputy Sheriff J. B. "Six-Finger" Smith mounted horses and charged after the rest of the mob. They rescued Freeman and, bundling him into the buggy with Neal, raced to Mokelumne Hill. There Paul lodged them both in the county jail. Neal, instead of being charged with the horse theft, was promptly shipped to San Quentin to serve out his ten-year sentence. Freeman was convicted of grand larceny and sentenced to a year in the state prison. Both managed to get out in 1856. Freeman escaped, and, in a separate incident, Neal tried the same thing, but he was shot dead by prison guards.[14]

In less than three weeks, Paul had saved three men from lynch mobs. During the first years of the gold rush, when government and law enforcement were all but nonexistent, Paul had supported vigilantism. But those dramatic shortcomings no longer existed. By the mid-1850s the state's judicial system was becoming established. Most county seats and larger towns had jails, albeit poorly constructed ones, and a state prison had been established at San Quentin. None were particularly secure, for escapes occurred frequently until the mid-1860s. But as each year passed, there was less excuse for mob action, and it gradually became less common. Paul recognized that his duty was to resist lynch mobs, an ethic that would become a hallmark of his career.[15]

That summer the budding young lawman played a prominent role in one of the most important incidents of racial violence in the gold rush. It began on a sweltering August 6, 1855, when a violent gang of bandidos rode down Dry Creek in Amador County, robbing each Chinese mining camp they came across. The leader was reported to be Guadalupe Gamba, and his followers were Manuel Castro and Rafael Escobar, plus six others later identified only by their first names or nicknames: "Macemanio" (probably Maximiliano), Trinidad, California, Bonito, a Californio known as Paisano, and a red-bearded American named Gregorio, or Gregory. Frightened Chinese reported the raids to Amador County Deputy Sheriff George Durham, who got a tip that the bandits were hiding out near Drytown. At dusk, with Constable J. D. Cross, he made a search of Drytown's Hispanic quarter, known as Chile Flat. A Mexican woman was inside one of the houses, cooking, and the officers stepped inside and asked her if she had seen the robbers. She answered no, but then quietly pulled back a curtain to show the shadowy forms of several desperadoes who had hidden in a back room.[16]

As Durham and Cross backed out, the bandidos broke for the back door and raced for their horses in a corral behind the house. Durham and Cross, six-guns in hand, sprinted after them. At a distance of fifteen steps the outlaws opened up with a thundering barrage of pistol fire. The officers, aiming at muzzle flashes, emptied their revolvers at the robbers and thought they wounded two of them. After the bandits had fired some fifty shots they leaped into their saddles and escaped. While the two lawmen returned to the Anglo quarter to organize a posse, the bandidos rode three miles southwest toward the little mining camp of Rancheria. The camp had a hotel, store, livery stable, fandango house, and a water-powered quartz mill.

It was night when the freebooters galloped into Rancheria. Tethering their horses, they first stepped into the fandango house to get liquored up. Then, learning that there was considerable cash in town, they poured outside and, in two groups, burst into the store and hotel, shouting "Viva Mexico!" Six-shooters belching flame, bandidos in the hotel indiscriminately fired on everyone in sight. Several men seated at a table playing cards tried to take cover. A bullet tore Sam Wilson from his chair, killing him instantly. Another card player fell dead in a bloody pool. The hotel-keeper, Michael Dynan, was badly wounded at the bar. As his terrified wife, Mary, shoved their two children out a window, Rafael Escobar shot her in the back, killing her.

At the same time the second bunch of screaming outlaws broke into the Rancheria store. They shot and killed the clerk, Daniel Hutchens, and wounded the owner, Eugene Francis. Though bleeding heavily, Francis struggled with the robbers. A Mexican picked up an axe and chopped at his legs. Francis stumbled out the back door and collapsed. The bandits followed and hacked him to death. For good measure they also killed a local Indian who happened to be sleeping behind the store. The robbers broke open the store safe and stole $6,000. Then, after taking all the horses from the livery stable, they thundered out of town, repeating their battle cry, "Viva Mexico!"[17]

In one of the Old West's most murderous bandit raids, the gang left six dead victims behind. News of the "Rancheria Tragedy" created the wildest excitement. By morning hundreds of miners had poured into Rancheria. The killing of innocent people, including a woman, was beyond the pale, and while some men started in pursuit of the gang, others began rounding up local Mexicans. By afternoon, thirty-six had been herded into a make-shift corral, surrounded by two hundred armed guards. Three of the captives were identified as having been with the bunch that had run from the fandango house to the store; one of them had Mary Dynan's jewelry, and another had her husband's watch. They gave their names as Puertovino, Trancolino, and Jose. The infuriated mob marched all thirty-six captives to a large oak tree one hundred yards east of town. A motion was made that they all be immediately strung up. Cooler heads prevailed, however, and instead Puertovino, Trancolino, and Jose were given half an hour to pray and then were hanged from the tree.[18]

Now the mob turned its fury on Mexicans who they knew were innocent of the murders. Said one witness, "After the three were hung up, the citizens of Rancheria passed a resolution that no Mexican shall hereafter reside at the place; and every Mexican who shall be found at Rancheria after seven o'clock this evening should be requested to leave, and receive one hundred and fifty lashes in the bargain." Enraged miners then set fire to the fandango house and all the Mexican *jacales* (huts) in town. The fire got out of control and threatened to burn down the town before it was finally put out. The terrified Mexicans fled and took refuge in nearby Mile Gulch. Local Indians, angered by the death of their compadre and egged on by some of the mob, followed and attacked Mexican men, women, and children in the gulch. At least eight were slain as they tried to escape from the ravine. As one Mexican led his donkey out of the gulch, a trunk of clothes fell from its back. The Indians dropped their weapons, scrambled around the broken trunk, and started donning the clothes. This distraction alone saved the Mexicans from more slaughter. Scattered corpses were later found near the gulch, and hogs were spotted devouring bodies. How many were slain was never determined.[19]

Next the vigilantes descended on Gopher Flat, several miles from Rancheria. The mob had heard a report that one of the bandits was secreted there. He was found in a jacal, under a pile of clothes. Without ceremony, the lynchers hanged him from a makeshift scaffold formed by a pair of wagon tongues. Then the mob drove fifty Mexicans from the camp and destroyed their homes. Another mob torched Chile Flat in Drytown, burned the Catholic church to the ground, and sent the town's Chilenos and Mexicans fleeing. The day after the raid, the murdered Indian was turned over to his tribe for burial. Mrs. Dynan and the four Americans were all buried in a common grave. Said one who attended the funeral, "It was certainly a heart-rending spectacle, and many a stony heart gave way."[20]

While senseless mob violence was engulfing Amador County, its young sheriff, William A. Phoenix, was busy tracking the rest of the real bandits. He first struck a false trail north of Rancheria. Realizing his error, Phoenix led his posse back to Jackson, where he found that the gang had headed south and crossed the Mokelumne River into Calaveras County. The sheriff, with Deputy Durham and several other possemen, rode to Mokelumne Hill that night. There they met with Sheriff Clarke and began preparing for a joint manhunt in the morning.

Meanwhile, word of the tragedy quickly reached Campo Seco, twenty-two miles south of Rancheria. The morning after the raid, August 7, Bob Paul heard a rumor that "seven or eight men had been murdered by a band of Mexicans at Rancheria, in Amador County." This seemed improbable; as one Campo Seco resident explained, "At first the news that such a wholesale murder had been committed was scarcely credited." But soon afterward a miner came into town from the Mokelumne River and reported that at daybreak he had spotted seven armed riders going up the river. Later in the morning Joseph Petty rode into Campo Seco and reported that a band of seven or eight mounted men were riding south toward the Calaveras River. That was enough for Paul. He and Constable Mark McCormick organized a posse including Petty, Deputy Sheriff Six-Finger Smith, and David Wells. It took time to obtain good men, horses, and weapons, and it was three in the afternoon before Paul was ready to start in pursuit.

Spurring their horses, the posse galloped south six miles to Texas Bar on the Calaveras River. An Italian told them that a local Mexican, Manuel Castro, had been there "and boasted of killing six men and a woman at Rancheria." Paul and the others raced after Castro. They trailed him three miles down the river but lost his tracks in the rocky terrain. The officers rode on to the Don Manuel Rancho, where they learned that seven heavily armed horsemen had headed up the Calaveras River. The possemen now retraced their steps, going up the river and returning to Texas Bar, which they reached after dark. There they found Manuel Castro, a six-shooter in each fist, standing defiantly in front of a dancehall.

Constable McCormick stepped up to Castro, told him he was his prisoner, and seized him in a bear hug. With a desperate effort, Castro managed to wrench loose. As he started to run, several of the posse opened fire, but their shots went wide in the darkness. Paul and McCormick, six-guns in hand, raced after him. There were twenty feet between them when the fleeing outlaw threw his revolver over his shoulder and opened fire. Pistol muzzles flaming in the blackness, outlaw and officers exchanged fifteen shots in a running gunfight. Castro fired five times, McCormick four, and Paul "four or five," according to a witness. Finally one of the constables' bullets tore into the small of Castro's back, ripping completely through his body and just missing his spine. The bandido dropped like a stone.

The officers obtained a buggy and brought Castro to a doctor in Texas Bar. The physician opined that his wound was mortal. Castro, who spoke good English, was asked if he wished to make a dying confession. Though in great pain, Castro agreed, and his statement was taken down by the local magistrate and witnessed by the possemen. He said he had met the American, Gregorio, in Hornitos two or three weeks earlier. He gave full details of the Rancheria raid and identified five of his compadres, saying that he could not recall the names of the other two. He claimed that he had not done any of the killing, but had stood guard outside during the raid.[21]

Castro was a tough character, and it soon became evident that his wound was not fatal. Paul and the others brought their prisoner to Mokelumne Hill and turned him over to Sheriffs Clarke and Phoenix. The Amador sheriff detailed two of his possemen to return Castro to Jackson in a buggy. But no sooner had they appeared on the town's streets than a huge mob surrounded the buggy and drove it underneath the town's infamous hanging tree. A noose was already hanging from a limb, and it was fastened around the wounded Castro's neck. Then the horses were given a slap, the buggy jerked forward, and Castro was left swinging in the shadow of the hanging tree.[22]

Meanwhile, Sheriff Clarke, with Paul, Deputy Sheriff Ben K. Thorn, Sheriff Phoenix, George Durham, Six-Finger Smith, Constable McCormick, Edward Sherry, and several other possemen, set out on the outlaws' trail. At Jenny Lind they disarmed a large number of Mexicans and interrogated them, learning that the bandidos were camped near Reynolds Ferry on the Stanislaus River. By the time the posse arrived at Reynolds Ferry they found that the gang had fled south toward Tuolumne County. The possemen continued after them, searching Tuttletown, Sonora, and then Campo Seco, a different camp from the one in Calaveras, situated four miles southwest of Sonora. From there, they rode a mile north to Jamestown, where they recovered several of the horses that had been stolen from Rancheria. The animals were half-dead from exhaustion, and the lawmen now knew they were pushing the bandits hard.

On the morning of August 12, 1855, Paul and the rest of the posse rode back into Sonora. They found that the killers' trail led toward the settlement at Campo Salvado, ten miles south, and Clarke, Phoenix, Paul, and the other officers decided to search it. The lawmen rode into Campo Salvado at noon and arrested every Hispanic in the camp for questioning. Sheriff Clarke later said that "a more villainous looking set were never seen." However, Americans in the camp quickly came forward and provided solid alibis, declaring that all the men arrested were residents of Campo Salvado and had been there at the time of the Rancheria raid.

The lawmen were not ready to give up, and they split into two parties. One, consisting of Phoenix, Durham, Smith, and McCormick, entered a large adobe cantina to search it. Paul and the balance of the posse stood guard at various points around the camp. When a lone Mexican rode in, he was placed under arrest by one of the guards. At his request, several of the posse took him across a gulch just outside of town so that he could "obtain proof of good character." By this time Sheriff Phoenix and his three possemen, having searched the cantina, sat down to take a drink. They spotted a Mexican girl motioning toward someone outside the back door. Durham glanced outside and immediately recognized three of the gang.

"There they are!" he exclaimed to Phoenix. The sheriff and his men quickly stepped outside and approached the three armed Hispanics. Paul, alerted by the shout, ran toward the cantina in time to see Phoenix seize one of the suspects. One of the possemen cried a warning to Phoenix, "Shoot him—do not try to take him!"

But it was too late. The Mexican jerked loose and pulled his revolver. He and his compadres raced behind a picket fence, then all three wheeled to face Sheriff Phoenix. One bandido, the Californio known as Paisano, opened fire at close range, shooting the sheriff through the heart. As Phoenix went down, he managed to get off two pistol shots, slightly wounding one of the Mexicans. By now all the desperados had their six-shooters out, one of them with a revolver in each fist. Bob Paul, in one fluid movement, whipped his six-gun from its holster, thumbed the hammer, and took dead aim at Paisano. His weapon boomed and a pistol ball tore into Paisano's chest. Then Paul emptied his six-shooter on Paisano. The killer dropped into the dusty street, apparently dead, his neck and chest perforated by pistol balls. At the same time, Durham, Smith, and McCormick opened up with their revolvers, and another of the desperadoes dropped in a hail of six-gun fire, riddled with fatal bullets.

The third bandit, flourishing both six-shooters, fled into a nearby tent with the lawmen in pursuit. The gunfire brought the balance of the posse racing back into town. They surrounded the tent, but the outlaw kept them at bay with his pistols. Finally the officers decided to fire the tent and those adjoining it. As the flames burst forth the bandido rushed out, shooting as he came, right hand, left hand. The lawmen fired back, hitting him twice, but the wounds did not slow him down. When his revolvers were empty the desperado used them as clubs, fighting the officers like a tiger. Finally one of the lawmen, whose weapons were also empty, seized an axe and hacked him to death.[23]

Now the officers realized that the man Paul had shot was not dead. During the excitement Paisano had crawled off into the chapparal and

Rafael Escobar lynched on Jackson's notorious hanging tree, August 15, 1855. This lithograph is an exact copy of a lost daguerreotype. Courtesy of William B. Secrest.

disappeared. Sheriff Clarke and the rest of the posse left the two dead bandits to be buried in Campo Salvado and brought Phoenix's body into Sonora the following morning, where the Masonic fraternity laid him to rest that afternoon. At five o'clock, just after the funeral, Clarke, Paul, and the others started out after the balance of the gang. They were unable to find the wounded Paisano but picked up another suspect and headed back toward Calaveras. Passing through Columbia the next morning, August 14, they learned that local citizens had rounded up a dozen suspicious Mexicans. One of them, Rafael Escobar, had been found sleeping under a tree with two large six-guns under his blanket. Constable John Leary, an experienced lawman who had fought the Joaquin Murrieta band in 1852, identified him as a friend of Joaquin's. Sheriff Clarke and his posse were asked to visit the Columbia jail and look over the suspects.

Durham immediately identified Rafael Escobar as the man who had slain Mrs. Dynan. Escobar admitted to Clarke "that he belonged to the gang, and was at Rancheria—that they had all taken an oath to die rather than expose each other." Clarke, Paul, and the posse brought the bandido into Mokelumne Hill and lodged him in jail for the night. In the morning Durham bundled Escobar into a buggy and, with several of the posse as guards, started for Jackson. Once there, the scene involving Manuel Castro was repeated. An enraged mob surrounded the buggy and drove it under the hanging tree. An American who spoke Spanish was appointed to interrogate Escobar. Now he claimed that although he knew the members of the gang, he had not participated in the Rancheria Tragedy. He provided the first names and nicknames of four of the killers.[24]

The mob was determined to make him confess, as Jackson's newspaper editor reported: "The Mexican was 'run up' and held there for a short time, then lowered, when great difficulty was encountered getting the rope loosened from his neck. It was finally cut loose; in the meantime, he suffered excruciating pain, rolling his eyes about, throwing his head and body about at random, and making a loud gurgling noise with his throat. When the rope was taken from his neck he revived and asked for brandy and water and said he would like to talk, but it was no use, as the people would believe nothing he said, and he wished they would kill him outright. . . . He said if the Americans would arm themselves and take him with them he could point out every man that was connected with the Rancheria affair." But by this time the crowd would have none of it. They began to yell, "Run him up!" This was done, and Escobar was left dangling from the tree. A local photographer took a daguerreotype of the scene, which has long since been lost, but a lithograph made of the image still exists. Escobar was the tenth and last man to die on Jackson's infamous hanging tree.[25]

Paisano had managed to survive the wounds inflicted by Paul, for the gunpowder used in that era did not have the punch of modern weaponry. On August 27 an old Mexican came into Sonora and reported that the badly wounded desperado had come to his house in Algerine Camp for assistance. When Paisano threatened to kill the *viejo* if he did not help him, the old man hid the desperado in a nearby mineshaft. Durham and a posse accompanied the Mexican to Algerine Camp, where they approached the shaft and ordered Paisano to give himself up. The bandido responded that he "had five shots for the Americans and one for himself." The possemen then stuffed the shaft with dry brush and set a match to it. As the tunnel filled with smoke a single pistol shot rang out. Paisano had committed suicide rather than surrender. When the fire died down, they dragged out his body, which plainly showed Paul's bullet wounds in the neck and chest.[26]

Two more suspects were captured in Sonora in early September. They were brought to Jackson and given a vigilante trial on September 8. Strong evidence against them was presented, and both confessed their guilt. The next morning they were brought to Rancheria and publicly hanged before a large throng. These were the last deaths in the Rancheria Tragedy. At least twenty-five people had been slain. In terms of sheer brutality and senseless violence, both by Hispanic bandidos and Anglo mobs, few gold rush incidents equaled it. Offsetting the mindless brutality of the mobs, which punished the innocent as well as the guilty, were the lawful actions of the officers. They had diligently trailed the real killers and attempted to take them alive. Both Constable McCormick and Sheriff Phoenix had physically seized two of the armed outlaws, and Phoenix paid for his compassion with his life. Paul and the others only fired on the bandits after they were shot at first. The officers did not kill their captives, but instead brought them to face criminal charges in Jackson, where mobs overwhelmed them and lynched their prisoners. Paul's courage in helping track down the killers and in shooting two of them who resisted arrest was recognized by the voters of Campo Seco. In the election that month six candidates appeared on the ballot for township constable. Paul received the highest number of votes, 435, and his friend Mark McCormick polled 375. Both were reelected for one-year terms.[27]

The young lawman had gained valuable experience in his gunfights with the Rancheria killers. He recognized that he could remain calm under fire and wield his six-shooter with deadly accuracy. These skills would prove of utmost importance in the years to come. But now his attention was directed to less sanguine affairs. For any politician of the era, membership in either a fraternity or a volunteer fire company was essential. Both provided votes and financial support at election time. In February 1856 a meeting was held in Campo Seco to discuss formation of a Masonic lodge. This struck Paul's interest, for both Charlie Clarke and his undersheriff, David Mulford, were Masons. On May 8, Paul became one of the founding members of the Campo Seco lodge of Masons. Fraternal, benevolent organizations like the Freemasons and the Independent Order of Odd Fellows were very popular in the nineteenth century. Freemasons were distinctive in that membership was open both to Christians and Jews, though not to Catholics. As we will see, Bob Paul did not agree with the order's anti-Catholic views. His participation in the Masonic order reinforced his ethic of accepting men as individuals. This principle would become evident in later years, when Jews and Hispanics would number among his most faithful friends and deputies. Paul later joined another fraternity that was wildly popular in the gold rush, E Clampus Vitus. A facetious society, its members lampooned the established fraternities, often drank prodigiously, and hosted balls and benefits for charity.[28]

Soon Paul's opposition to lynch law was again in the news. On the evening of June 11, 1856, four Mexican bandidos entered the store of William Smith at Boston Bar on the Calaveras River. Drawing pistols and knives, they stabbed Smith seven times, killing him. Smith's clerk, Jose Sanchez, was overpowered, bound with rope, and blindfolded. After the robbers looted the store and fled, Sanchez managed to get loose and warn some American miners about the raid. A large posse from San Andreas, led by Deputy Sheriff C. H. Shrobel, started in pursuit, but it could not find the killers. The next day an inquest was held, and it was revealed that Smith often had on hand large sums in gold dust and coin, plus watches and jewelry. Local miners believed that Sanchez had set up the robbery himself, and a band of vigilantes proceeded to Smith's store, seized Sanchez, and brought him secretly into Campo Seco.

Paul and Undersheriff Mulford soon heard rumors of the vigilantes and set out to rescue Sanchez. They found him guarded by a mob in a house in Campo Seco. Evidently the vigilantes were trying to determine his guilt, for they had not yet decided to lynch him. The two lawmen confronted the mob and demanded that they turn over the prisoner. Out of respect for the officers' authority—or perhaps in fear of them—the vigilantes handed over Jose Sanchez. Paul and Mulford brought him to jail in Mokelumne Hill "to await judicial investigation." Sanchez was evidently released for lack of evidence.[29]

As constable of Campo Seco, Paul had rescued four men from lynch mobs, one of them Hispanic, a fact that underscored his firm belief in fairness and justice. In a very short time he had obtained a great deal of police and detective experience. So violent was gold rush society that he had frequently been called on to break up brawls, investigate murders, and ferret out thieves. He had played a leading role in tracking down the culprits in one of the bloodiest bandit raids of that era, shooting down two of them in desperate gun battles. He policed the most violent society in the history of peacetime America.

Paul's experiences as a gold rush lawman triggered a lifelong ethic of firm law enforcement coupled with compassion and devotion to justice.

The violence of the gold rush affected him deeply. As a journalist who interviewed him many years later wrote, "Once in the mining camps his experiences were varied. . . . He passed through many exciting periods and has seen hundreds of men killed or hung." Those early, turbulent, exciting years in Campo Seco set the stage for Bob Paul's half century of law enforcement on two of the West's wildest frontiers.[30]

CHAPTER THREE

The Tom Bell Gang

In the spring of 1856 the mining region was thrown into tumult by the raids of the Tom Bell gang. Tom Bell was the most notorious bandit to hit the gold fields since Joaquin Murrieta. Bob Paul learned that he was well educated and a natural leader of men and that he headed a motley band of desperadoes of assorted races and nationalities that reflected gold rush society in general. His gang included Americans from both Northern and Southern states, including at least two African Americans, and ruffians from Mexico, Chile, Canada, England, Germany, Sweden, and Australia. The gang, consisting of thirty to forty members, was so large that not all the members knew each other, and they used secret passwords and signs to identify themselves. This level of organization and close cooperation was very unusual and was testament to Tom Bell's intelligent leadership. His gang would commit some of the earliest and most daring express robberies of the gold rush.

Tom Bell's true name was Thomas J. Hodges. Born around 1826 to a respectable family in Rome, Tennessee, he was educated and had some medical training. In the Mexican War, he joined Colonel Frank Cheatham's Tennessee Volunteers, serving as a hospital orderly and accompanying the command south to the capture of Mexico City. There he hired a Mexican youth, Juan Fernandez, as a servant, and at the end of the war Hodges brought him home to Tennessee to work for his family. In 1850 Hodges came to California, and his Mexican servant, nicknamed "Spanish John," followed

David Mulford, carte de visite image taken in San Francisco, 1863–64. Undersheriff and sheriff of Calaveras County in the 1850s, Mulford was a dead ringer for bandit leader Tom Bell. Idaho State Historical Society, 249-28.

two years later. In California Hodges was a miner and gambler. He was tall and spare, standing six feet two, with long auburn hair, full beard, and a distinctive nose, broken and flattened in a boyhood accident. Ironically, he was a dead ringer for Undersheriff Dave Mulford.

Tom Hodges found no success in mining or gambling and soon became a robber. In 1851 he was arrested in Sacramento County for grand larceny and sentenced to five years in prison, which was then a converted ship anchored at Angel Island in San Francisco Bay. The following year he escaped, but he was soon recaptured and returned to prison. In 1854 all the state prisoners were moved into a new convict-built penitentiary at Point San Quentin in Marin County. The site was a spit of land that jutted into San Francisco Bay. In San Quentin prison Hodges met many of the men who would become principal members of his gang: Cyrus Skinner and his younger brother, George, both daring highway robbers; Ned Conway, from a respectable New Orleans family; and Jim Smith, a young, hard-drinking German. Bill Gristy, alias Bill White, highly intelligent, would vie for control of the gang, and Richard A. "Rattlesnake Dick" Barter would become almost as notorious as Tom Bell himself. [1]

On May 12, 1855, Tom Hodges, with Bill Gristy, Jim Smith, and several other convicts, escaped their guard while out on a wood-chopping detail. Soon after Tom Hodges became Tom Bell, the leader of a large band of highway robbers that operated in the mining country from the Kings River in the south to Marysville in the northern mines. His San Quentin colleagues, Gristy, Smith, Conway, and the Skinner brothers, formed the nucleus of the gang. Other key members were Rattlesnake Dick, Jim Webster, "English Bob" Carr, Montague "Monte Jack" Lyon, Adolph "Big Dolph" Newton, Nicanor Rodriguez (only seventeen years old, from a well-connected family in Chile), and his former servant, Spanish John Fernandez. Spanish John had, by his own account, been an honest miner and had not seen Tom Bell in California until he accidentally encountered him in Nevada City and was persuaded to join the band.

The gang had three main hideouts. One was the Mountaineer House, a stage stop made of rough-hewn logs eight miles below Auburn on the highway to Folsom. It was run by Jack Phillips, an ex-convict from the Australian penal colony, and his wife, Catherine, and their twenty-year-old daughter. Phillips regularly harbored the gang, spotted likely victims, and fenced stolen goods. Another hideout was the California House, a hotel and saloon run by John Gardner and a woman, Mrs. Cole, located on the road between Marysville to Camptonville. And last was the Osage Ranch, nicknamed "the Hog Ranch," a brothel on the road from Sacramento to Nevada City, owned by a widow, Elizabeth Hood. She had three daughters, and according to Bill Gristy, her oldest, fourteen-year-old Sarah, was Tom Bell's mistress.[2]

Unlike the depredations of Joaquin Murrieta, Tom Bell's gang did not murder wantonly, nor did they rob Chinese mining camps. Instead, they focused on express companies, teamsters, and travelers who were carrying gold. In July 1855, they held up the messenger of Langton's Express near Forest City and stole $3,000 in gold specie. George Skinner was arrested and lodged in the Downieville jail, but he soon filed off his irons and escaped. In December 1855 the gang made an unsuccessful attempt to rob a Rhodes & Whitney Express messenger on the trail between Shasta and Weaverville. The band also stood up numerous lone travelers and teamsters. During one raid, Tom Bell used his medical training to give first aid to a robbery victim who had been shot and wounded by Bill Gristy.

The Tom Bell gang's most successful raid was the Trinity Mountain pack train holdup of March 12, 1856. At that time there were no roads into the rich mining camps on the Trinity River in the northern mines. Supplies and gold shipments were packed on rough trails by mule train. The robbery was well planned. Bill Gristy, Cyrus Skinner, and Rattlesnake Dick stole thirteen mules for the raid. Then George Skinner, Big Dolph Newton, Nicanor Rodriguez, and another gang member, William Carter, rode north to the Trinity mines. On March 10, the pack train of the Rhodes & Whitney Express left Yreka for Shasta, 110 miles to the south. As the mule train headed up the side of Trinity Mountain, the masked robbers halted it at gunpoint, tied four men to trees, and made off with $17,000 in gold dust packed onto the stolen mules.

This was one of the biggest armed robberies of the gold rush, and it created a sensation. While posses searched for the highwaymen, reward notices were distributed throughout the mining region. In Chico, Carter was arrested after displaying some gold dust. He soon confessed, implicating George Skinner, Big Dolph, and Rodriguez. He said that they could be found with Gristy at their hideout near Folsom. Sacramento police detective Bob Harrison was notified and managed to capture Big Dolph and another gang member. Then, with two very capable lawmen from Marysville, Isaac Anderson and A. J. "Jack" Barkley, Bob Harrison raided the cabin hideout on April 22. Gristy, Rodriguez, and George Skinner were inside. In a blistering, close-quarters gun duel, George Skinner was shot to death and Rodriguez was wounded. Big Dolph, Rodriguez, and Carter were convicted of highway robbery and sentenced to ten years each in San Quentin.[3]

Gristy escaped and rejoined Tom Bell. By now every robbery in the northern mines was being blamed on the Bell gang, and lawmen in both the northern and southern mines were busy hunting the band. Said B. F. Moore, the youthful undersheriff of Placer County, "About the most vigilant officer cooperating with us was R. H. Paul, or 'Bob,' as most of us endearingly called him." Moore, one of the most active lawmen in hunting the gang, first met the gang's fence, Jack Phillips, at his roadhouse near Auburn in March 1856. At that time none of the officers suspected Phillips of involvement in the band. Moore recalled, "Although rough in speech and appearance, he was rather jolly; and, to his credit be it stated, had a wife and daughter—the latter about twenty years old—who seemed fairly well educated, and were quite lady-like in their deportment. . . . Jack at once began to regale me with a tirade abusing officers; that, with their connivance or neglect, highwaymen were allowed to roam around at will, to the detriment of good citizens." Moore listened patiently until he was through, then replied with a grin, "Why Jack, if I did not know you so well, I would judge you to be one of the gang, from the way you have been talking."

Phillips, stung by Moore's casual joke, immediately rejoined, "I didn't mean you."

"Present company excepted, always," answered Moore. "But one thing I can tell you, there will be ten on their hunt now, where one was before."[4]

One day in June Phillips spotted a Jewish peddler named Rosenthal passing the Mountaineer House and heading toward Folsom. He pointed out the peddler as a likely prospect, and soon Bell, Gristy, and several of the band saddled up and galloped after him. They forced Rosenthal a hundred yards from the road, took $1,250, and tied him to a tree. Then one of desperadoes killed him in cold blood. Gristy claimed later that Bell waited until they rode off, then returned and murdered Rosenthal. Gristy was unhappy with this turn of events, and he said later, "Tom Bell and I could not agree well together on our operations. We frequently quarreled, and on several occasions I have had to draw my pistol on him. The fact is, we would have separated long ago, but I could use Tom, and he thought he could use me. He wanted to make us all do as he pleased."[5]

On July 25, Bell and Ned Conway repeated this feat by robbing another peddler, David Lash, near the Mountaineer House. Lash fared better than their last victim and was left alive, bound to a tree in the woods. Bell then sold Lash's goods to Jack Phillips. On August 4 the gang stopped a stage near Folsom, which carried $60,000 in bullion, but, seeing numerous passengers and fearing a fight, they allowed it to proceed. The highwaymen then rode north to the California House run by John Gardner and Mrs. Cole, twenty-five miles below Camptonville. Bell sent one of the gang, Smith Sutton, to nose around Camptonville. He soon returned and reported that a large gold shipment would be sent on the down stage. On August 11, 1856, Bell, Gristy, Conway, Spanish John, Jim Smith, and English Bob Carr stopped the coach from Camptonville to Marysville. It was carrying a staggering $100,000 in gold dust (about $3 million today). Neither the express messenger nor the passengers were willing to be robbed. They opened fire, and forty shots were exchanged at close quarters. The outlaws riddled the stagecoach with pistol balls, wounding three men and killing a woman passenger. Bell was not prepared for such a fierce resistance, and his band pulled back while the stagecoach escaped.[6]

The audaciousness of the attack, coupled with the cold-blooded killing of an innocent woman, spurred lawmen throughout the mining region to even greater efforts to break up the gang. The Camptonville holdup was Tom Bell's last in the Northern Mines. The gang, accompanied by the brothel-keeper Elizabeth Hood and her three daughters, plus a pair of brothers, Fred and Warren Farnsworth, rode south to a spot on the San Joaquin River, six miles from Firebaugh's Ferry. Situated in the vast San Joaquin Valley, this spot was extremely isolated. Nearby were the Hispanic settlements of Las Juntas and Rancho de los Californios, both notorious hideouts for fugitives and cattle thieves. Bell's plan was to start a ranch and stock it with stolen horses and cattle, while he, Gristy, Conway, and Spanish John would, as Gristy put it, "take to the highway for cash to keep up expenses on the ranch."[7]

In the meantime Bob Paul and Sheriff Clarke were forced to stop hunting Bell and to deal instead with problems closer to home. In May 1856 the famous San Francisco Committee of Vigilance had been formed to rid the city of political ruffians, many of them graduates of New York City street gangs, who had corrupted the city's voting process. They hanged four murderers and banished more than forty men from California. Most were placed on outgoing ships, while a few fled inland to avoid arrest.

One of the latter was James Cusick, a notorious prizefighter, shoulder striker, and ward heeler. Cusick escaped to Sacramento, where he was almost captured by a posse of vigilantes. When he fled south to Mokelumne Hill, several citizens tipped off the vigilance committee in San Francisco. A posse of four vigilantes led by William Wolfe arrived in Mokelumne Hill on July 6. They found that Cusick was attending the horse races at the Mokelumne racecourse, surrounded by a crowd of gamblers and desperadoes. Cusick got wind of the vigilantes' arrival and turned himself in to Sheriff Clarke and his deputies. Wolfe and his vigilantes then demanded that Cusick be delivered to them. Like Paul, Charlie Clarke was adamantly opposed to vigilantism. Clarke calmly told the vigilantes that Cusick "was under his protection, and could not be obtained, except in a legal manner."[8]

Meanwhile, a crowd of 150 gamblers and blacklegs, armed with six-shooters and Bowie knives, arrived in town to protect Cusick. Several of them threatened to kill Wolfe. The San Francisco vigilantes were outnumbered, and one of them later recalled, "Seeing how matters were going, we . . . concluded not to raise a disturbance in a place where we were strangers." The vigilantes later claimed that they were supported by many of the leading citizens of Mokelumne Hill. Cusick's friends averred that Wolfe and the other vigilance men became terrified and sought help from Sheriff Clarke, who summoned his deputies to protect them. Clarke, Paul, and the other officers stayed up all night guarding Wolfe and his companions. In the end, the vigilantes returned to San Francisco empty-handed, while Cusick went on to a colorful career as a boxing trainer and prize-fight promoter.[9]

A few weeks later, in late July, a serious disturbance over water rights broke out in the hills southeast of Mokelumne Hill. Calaveras County then had a complex system of seventeen different ditch and flume systems, with a total length of 325 miles. The ditches and flumes were operated by private companies that supplied water to the mines and hydraulic-powered stamp mills. The Table Mountain Company drew water from San Antonio and Calaveritas Creeks and supplied it to the mining districts near San Andreas, Cave City, and French Gulch. For several weeks San Antonio Creek had been siphoned almost dry, angering the miners along the stream, who were mainly American, Irish, and French. With no water, they could not wash gold. To placate the miners, the directors of the Table Mountain Company offered to release water back into the creek for a few weeks while they repaired their ditch. This was only a temporary solution and did not satisfy the gold seekers. On July 25 a band of 160 exasperated miners set to work tearing down the company's flume. They removed the dam and demolished a mile of flume, splintering the lumber so that it could not be rebuilt. After working all day, they headed home.[10]

Three of the culprits were arrested and jailed in Mokelumne Hill. The next day Sheriff Clarke got word that a large group of enraged miners from San Antonio Creek was gathering to free the prisoners. He called together the townsfolk and arranged that on the banging of a gong, they would rush to the jail to help protect it. For several days miners trooped into Lower Calaveritas, and on the morning of July 28, the band, now numbering three hundred, marched on Mokelumne Hill. Half of them were American; the rest were French, Irish, Greek, and Spanish. A mile from town they sent a small committee to parley with Sheriff Clarke, the district attorney, and the county judge. The miners' committee warned that they would free the three prisoners either legally or by force. Proclaimed a dispatch from Mokelumne Hill that day, "Great excitement prevails. Business is entirely suspended."[11]

That evening a hearing was held before Judge William W. Porter in the courthouse on the charges of demolishing the flume. The prisoners were guarded by Clarke, Paul, C. H. Shrobel, and a posse of citizens. Outside, in a huge show of force, the armed gold seekers marched into town, led by twenty horsemen. The miners, to signify that they were not a lawless mob, followed a flag bearer waving the stars and stripes. They were also determined to demonstrate that they were united as a group, regardless of nationality. As the main body marched down Main Street, a troop of Irish miners led by a Frenchman came up Center Street toward the courthouse. At the same time a company of French miners, commanded by an American, took up a position in an alley behind the courthouse. Sheriff Clarke approached the last group alone and ordered them to disperse. When they refused, Clarke seized several of their guns, but he was knocked down. In a wild scuffle, one of the Frenchmen accidentally discharged his weapon directly at Clarke. Fortunately the sheriff was grasping a shotgun across his breast. The bullet struck the shotgun and glanced off harmlessly, saving his life. Paul and the others, alerted by the shot, raced to Clarke's aid. No doubt Paul's huge physique was instrumental, for in moments they arrested two Frenchmen, seized eight guns, and dispersed the mob behind the courthouse.

From inside the courthouse, Judge Porter watched the main band of 250 armed men march by. Declaring that he would not be intimidated,

Bob Paul in the late 1850s. Robert H. Paul collection.

he refused to release the prisoners. Clarke, Paul, Porter, and a small posse now started to return the three prisoners to the county jail. They encountered the mob at the corner of Main and Center Streets. It was a tense confrontation, as many of the miners held longarms and unholstered pistols. As Paul and the posse covered the mob with their own six-guns, the flag bearer exhorted his comrades to follow him and free the prisoners. But, explained the editor of the *Calaveras Chronicle*, "he had no backers . . . he raved, swore and cursed them, but it availed not; the prisoners were safely conducted to jail. It was lucky for the ensign he was alone in this matter; had a shot been fired he would have been riddled."[12]

That night Judge Porter released the three prisoners on bail of $1,000 each, which was posted by their fellow miners. Clarke and Paul set up a strong guard around the jail, but there was no trouble. In the morning the two Frenchmen who had attacked Clarke were released without charge. Later many of the Frenchmen called on Clarke and apologized for their rash actions. They "told him they had been compelled to join the mob, that they respected him as an officer and a brave man, and would heartily respond hereafter to any call he might make on them to aid him in support of the laws." In the end, Clarke and Paul, gold seekers themselves, must have sympathized with the miners' collective plight. The jurors who heard their cases also empathized by finding them not guilty of destroying the flume.[13]

On the first of August, three days after breaking up the mob, Clarke and Paul executed a much harsher punishment. Jack Williams, whom Paul saved from the Campo Seco lynch mob a year before, had been tried and convicted of killing Caspar Sheppard. His lawyer appealed to the California Supreme Court on grounds of juror bias. In April 1856 the supreme court reversed the conviction and ordered a new trial. In June Williams was retried and again convicted and sentenced to death. The scheduled date for his hanging was August 1, 1856. Williams looked upon his fate with utmost composure and asked only that his hanging take place in the early morning so that few people would witness it. The place of execution was the scaffold on the side of the steep ravine just north of the jail, the scene of several prior hangings, including that of Dennis O'Brien. The night before the execution, Williams stayed up until 1:00 A.M., good-naturedly chatting with visitors in his cell, then he slept soundly until daybreak. His last breakfast was a single cup of coffee. Then Sheriff Clarke presented Williams with a new black suit, but he refused to accept it, saying that "it was a useless expense." At 9:00 A.M. he was marched out of the jail, supported by Sheriff Clarke on one side and Jailer Dunbar on the other. But Williams did not get his last wish. A crowd of two thousand filled the ravine. Said one newspaperman, "We were sorry to perceive that quite a number of females were also present."[14]

Sheriff Clarke's deputies, including Paul, marched alongside, carrying muskets. Williams coolly smoked a cigar and chatted nonchalantly with onlookers. Arriving at the scaffold, the guards encircled it, and then Williams unhesitatingly climbed its steps. Sheriff Clarke read him the death warrant and asked him if he had any final words. Williams answered no, then stepped across the gallows, saying goodbye to friends in the crowd. Of one friend from Campo Seco he asked, "Did you know anything bad of me before this affair occurred?" "No, Jack" was the reply. Williams then retorted, "Tell those Campo Seco fellows that I would do the same thing and be hanged, rather than put up with an insult."

Then Williams took his place on the trap. Reported a journalist, "The prisoner stood facing the northward, perfectly cool, calm, and collected—not a nerve weakened." The officers affixed the black cap and draped the noose around his neck. At half past nine Sheriff Clarke gave the signal and Williams plunged through the trap, his neck broken instantly. He was allowed to hang for thirty minutes, after which physicians pronounced him dead. At Clarke's order his body was cut down, placed in a coffin, and buried at the foot of the gallows. Paul's feelings about the execution are unknown, but Clarke despised the duty. A friend recalled that the sheriff "felt as if he was murdering the man on his own account instead of carrying out the sentence of the law. Couldn't do enough for him before the execution."[15]

Within a few weeks Paul was back on the trail of the Tom Bell gang. On September 9, 1856, Gristy and Spanish John rode north from their ranch on the San Joaquin River, looking for potential victims on the roads from the diggings. They were afraid to rob freighters because, as Gristy said later, "We noticed that almost all the teamsters traveled in large companies." After several days they robbed two teamsters between Stockton and Mokelumne Hill, taking a meager fourteen dollars, and then stole a pair of horses from a nearby roadhouse. The same day they held up another teamster and a rider near Stockton. These robberies alarmed the populace, and vigilance committees were formed to hunt the bandits. On September 16, the two highwaymen were spotted hiding their stolen horses in a small gulch near Knights Ferry on the Stanislaus River. Three local men armed themselves and headed into the gulch, where they captured Gristy and Spanish John without a fight. They brought the prisoners into Knights Ferry, where the hotelkeeper, Major Thomas W. Lane, recognized Gristy as a convict he had once seen during a visit to San Quentin. A vigilance committee quickly formed and debated what to do with their prisoners. To save his neck, Gristy made a long and detailed confession of the crimes committed by the gang. The next day Major Lane left with Gristy to return him to San Quentin, and the vigilantes formed a people's court to try Spanish John.

By this time word of the capture was sent to the sheriff's office in Mokelumne Hill, fifty-seven miles distant. Paul wasted no time in swearing out an arrest warrant for Spanish John, then he mounted his horse and raced south to Knights Ferry. There he found that the vigilantes had convicted Spanish John and sentenced him to hang. Determined to prevent a lynching, Paul sought out the local Stanislaus County justice of the peace to endorse his warrant. According to an early account, "during Paul's temporary absence [Spanish John] was taken by the mob and had a rope around his neck when the resolute deputy reappeared on the scene." The *San Andreas Independent* provided a less dramatic version: "Deputy Sheriff Paul presented a warrant for the arrest of the prisoner and conveyed him to Mokelumne Hill."[16]

Spanish John was so grateful to Paul for saving his life that on the long ride back to Mokelumne Hill he made a full confession and provided the location of the gang's hideouts. Spanish John was arraigned in court and, after being provided with an attorney, agreed to plead guilty to highway robbery in exchange for leniency. He promised to help Sheriff Clarke and his deputies capture the entire gang. Spanish John told Paul that Jack Phillips had given Tom Bell a pistol ball marked with four crosses and four small holes for use as a secret sign when sending him messages. Paul had Fernandez make him an identical bullet, which the deputy intended to use to trap Phillips. Paul and Clarke carefully drew up plans to capture the entire gang. Clarke divided his men into two posses. One, consisting of himself, Paul, Deputy Sheriff George Shuler, and Constable Mark McCormick, would accompany Spanish John to the northern mines. The other, a five-man posse that included Undersheriff David Mulford, Deputy Sheriff John McNish, and three volunteers, would attempt to capture the gang members at the ranch on the San Joaquin.

Sheriff Clarke and his men, guided by Spanish John, arrived at a spot near the Mountaineer House at 2:00 A.M. on September 29. Paul went inside alone, awakened Phillips, and called for a drink. As the lawman later recalled, "I closed the front door and told him to close the one behind the bar. I then asked him if there was anyone who could hear us. He pointed to the ceiling and said, 'Talk low, there are people sleeping upstairs.'" Paul showed him the marked bullet, and Phillips examined it closely and asked, "Where is Tom?"

"I told him I did not know. I had not seen him," continued Paul. "I told him I got the bullet of Spanish John. I told him that Bill White [Gristy] and Spanish John were arrested, and that I had been under arrest and he, Spanish John, had given me the bullet to come and get some assistance, to try and get them out of jail."

Then the unsuspecting Phillips had Paul describe the details of the arrest. As Paul recalled, "I then asked him where Tom Bell was. He said he had not seen him since he went south. I told him White was sent to state's prison. He said they could not keep him long." When Phillips asked his name, Paul replied, "Bill Gleason." Said Paul, "I told him I had promised Spanish John to find Bell and I was determined to find him. He then asked me if I knew where to go down south. I told him I did not, but that I could find it. He asked if I knew the name to inquire for. I told him it was Farnsworth; he said that was right." Phillips explained that some time previous one of the Farnsworth brothers had brought him a letter from Tom Bell, asking for a horse, but he did not trust letters and refused. As he spoke, the crooked innkeeper held up the bullet and smiled, "There is nothing like these fellows."

Phillips then described a recent visit to the Mountaineer House by lawmen from Auburn in search of Tom Bell. "He cursed them," said Paul. "He told me he ridiculed their arms; that one had a five-shooter, and he wanted to know of them if they thought they could take Tom Bell or his men with such arms as those." The two had a long talk about local lawmen, and Phillips revealed that after one robbery "he came near being caught, while taking provisions to them back of the field." He admitted that Gristy, Conway, and Spanish John had stopped at the Mountaineer House to bid him goodbye as they headed south to the San Joaquin. Said Paul, "At one time, looking at the bullet, [he] said it was strange how Spanish John knew of the bullet; that he thought only he and Bell knew of it."

They had been talking for almost two hours, and liquor had thoroughly loosened Phillips's tongue. Said Paul, "He took up a candle and looking at the clock said it was a quarter to four . . . and asked me to take a drink and cigars." Paul took a last drink, then casually sauntered out into the darkness. At daybreak Paul and the rest of the posse returned to the Mountaineer House and arrested Phillips for robbery. The officers of Placer County were elated. As Undersheriff Moore recalled, "We all said, 'Amen!' and 'Long live Bob Paul!' He was certainly a wide-awake and efficient officer, and his record then and since justly entitles him to . . . the plaudit, 'Well done thou good and faithful servant.'"[17]

The Placer County lawmen had not been sleeping. They had rounded up several desperadoes whom they suspected of belonging to the gang. One of them turned informant and helped set up an ambush. The night after Phillips's arrest, Bell, Conway, and Perrie "Texas Jack" Owen headed back to the Mountaineer House. They were met in the road by Undersheriff Moore, Auburn Constable John C. Boggs, and several other officers. In a wild gunfight, Boggs shot Conway to death, while Bell and Texas Jack were unhorsed, barely escaping with their lives. The bandit chieftain stole a mount and fled south to his ranch on the San Joaquin River. There he felt safe, for he had no idea that Gristy and Spanish John had been captured.[18]

While Deputy Sheriff George Shuler took Jack Phillips by stage to Sacramento and then to the jail in Mokelumne Hill, Sheriff Clarke, Deputy Paul, Constable McCormick, and Spanish John rode to Marysville in search of more gang members. From there they headed twenty-eight miles into the mountains to the California House, arriving at daybreak on October 1. Everyone was asleep, and the lawmen had no trouble arresting the owner, John Gardner, and gang member Smith Sutton as accessories to the bloody attempted holdup of the Camptonville stage. Then the posse returned with their prisoners to Mokelumne Hill. The sheriff was exhausted, reported the *San Andreas Independent*: "In fact, the exposure and fatigue brought Sheriff Clarke to a sick bed, where his recovery for some time was very doubtful."[19]

In the meantime Undersheriff David Mulford was having equal success. He led his posse to the outlaws' ranch on the San Joaquin River, where they captured the Farnsworth brothers, Elizabeth Hood, and Hood's three daughters and recovered a herd of stolen stock. Mulford and one deputy took the prisoners into Stockton, leaving the rest of his men on the ranch in the hope that Bell or other gang members would show up. They were soon joined by a posse led by George Belt, the gunfighting former alcalde of Stockton. For five days the manhunters remained hidden in the willows near the river. Finally, on the morning of October 4, 1856, they gave up, riding home in different groups. Sheriff Clarke's deputies were long gone when one of Belt's possemen spotted a lone rider hiding in the riverbank willows a mile south of Firebaugh's Ferry. He quickly summoned the rest of the posse. They disarmed the well-dressed stranger, who coolly admitted he was Tom Bell. After tying his hands, they brought him into Firebaugh's, which, at that time and for thirty years after, was a predominately Hispanic settlement and a favorite stomping ground for fugitives. The bandit chief admitted being in the gunfight near the Mountaineer

House four days earlier, but claimed that he had not committed a robbery in two months. Belt had no intention of bringing Bell one hundred miles back to Stockton. It was getting dark, and he was concerned that more of the gang might be nearby. He told the outlaw to prepare for hanging. Bell was given pen and paper and allowed two hours to compose his thoughts and write letters to Elizabeth Hood and his mother in Tennessee. When the letters were finished he was led to a tree on the bank of the San Joaquin River, and moments later Tom Bell's body was swinging in the October breeze.[20]

CHAPTER FOUR

Sheriff of Calaveras

Sheriff Clarke, Bob Paul, and the other deputies were kept busy policing the mining camps, serving warrants, and hunting murderers, sluice robbers, and horse thieves. Unlike many lawmen of that wide-open era, Clarke's deputies did not take bribes. In 1856 the *San Andreas Independent* reported an incident in which "a thief was caught in the act of stealing. When arrested, he tried to buy off the officers, but failed, when he doggedly replied, 'You officers of Mokelumne Hill are not half the gentlemen those of Sacramento are; there I can buy any one of them for ten dollars.'" Of Clarke's deputies, Bob Paul and Ben Thorn were especially conscientious and exhibited sufficient skill and tenacity to allow their law enforcement careers to last the rest of the century. Thorn, a twenty-six-year-old former schoolteacher from Illinois, was a forty-niner. In 1855 he was elected constable at the mining camp of San Antonio, and soon after Charlie Clarke appointed him a deputy. He stood five feet eight, had a well-knit, muscular frame, was pugnacious by nature and a deadly pistol shot by practice. Thorn had many dangerous encounters with desperadoes during the gold rush, and he would later serve more than three decades as sheriff of Calaveras County. During the 1880s and '90s he became one of the most famous sheriffs on the West Coast.[1]

By the mid-1850s there were more than twenty thousand Chinese in California, most of them in the diggings. The vast majority were law abiding and industrious, though harsh conditions, unfair tax laws, and racial torment

Ben Thorn in the 1880s. He was Bob Paul's close friend and undersheriff. Author's collection.

at the hands of Anglo and Hispanic ruffians made their lives very difficult. Most belonged to Chinese fraternal societies, or tongs, which offered them some protection. In October 1856 members of two rival tongs, the Sam Yup and the Yan Wo, quarreled over a mining claim on the Stanislaus River, near Knights Ferry. The Sam Yup company was from Canton, and its members mined in Tuolumne County, while the Yan Wo company consisted of men from Hong Kong who mined in Calaveras. The Stanislaus River, scene of the trouble, separated the two counties. The Sam Yups issued a public challenge to the Yan Wos, which was published in the *Columbia*

Gazette. Members of the Yan Wo tong quickly responded and flocked to Campo Salvado, while hundreds of miners connected with the Sam Yup tong crowded into Chinese Camp, a mile to the west. The blacksmiths of the two camps were put to work making pikes, swords, shields, and helmets. Chinese miners purchased muskets, shotguns, and Colt revolvers and had them shipped from San Francisco. They paid American ruffians to teach them how to load and shoot the weapons.

The date for the battle was set for October 25, 1856, on a flat midway between the two camps. Some 5,000 Anglo miners gathered to see the spectacle. Tuolumne County Sheriff James Stewart sought the assistance of Calaveras lawmen, and Paul answered the call. When they arrived on the scene, there was not much the outnumbered posse could do. As the lawmen tried vainly to stop the fight, one of the deputies had his horse shot out from under him. The Yan Wos numbered about 900 to the Sam Yups' 1,200. Some witnesses put the total of Chinese combatants as high as 2,500. The Sam Yups had the foresight to hire 15 disguised Anglo gunmen, who dressed in Chinese garb and wore queues made of horsehair. The Yan Wos, on the other hand, had only 12 muskets. The stage was set for the biggest armed conflict in California since the Mexican War.

After much parading, posturing, and beating of gongs, the Sam Yups, with the larger number of firearms, poured a volley of lead into the Yan Wos, killing their leader and two others. One more Chinese was slain and seven were wounded before the Yan Wo fighters broke ranks and fled. Deputy sheriffs then went after the Sam Yups to disarm them, but they were fired on, and the officers managed to arrest only three. Sheriff Stewart, with Paul and other lawmen, rounded up 250 Yan Wos in Chinese Camp and seized their weapons. Most expressed regret and admitted they had been foolish to get drawn into the fight. All of them were quickly released. A correspondent to the *San Francisco Bulletin*, reflecting the cavalier and callous attitude toward violence that was so prevalent in the gold rush, commented, "It was perhaps a very bad battle as so few were killed."[2]

Soon the voters of Campo Seco Township rewarded Paul's successful work against the Tom Bell gang. In the general election on November 4, 1856, he was elected to a third term as constable of Township 4. A few months later, in February 1857, he returned to Placer County to testify in Jack Phillips's trial as an accessory to the robbery of the peddler David Lash. Paul and Spanish John were the star witnesses, and they told their stories in great detail. The jury deliberated only twenty minutes before finding the Australian innkeeper guilty. Phillips was sentenced to serve two years in state prison and to pay a $5,000 fine. Although this punishment seems surprisingly lenient, it was the maximum allowed under the law. Many members of the Tom Bell gang managed to elude the dragnet, but in later years they were either killed or imprisoned for other crimes.[3]

In early August Sheriff Clarke and his deputies began preparing for yet another hanging. The condemned man was John Phipps, a thirty-two-year-old miner. In San Antonio Camp in 1854, Phipps had engaged in a wild brawl in a saloon and fandango hall run by a Chileno, Juan Morales. Phipps was playing monte when he ran out of money and offered his pistol as collateral. Morales objected in profane terms, and Phipps struggled with Morales for the revolver, then struck him with a water pitcher. Other patrons joined the fray, which ended with Phipps picking up an axe and hacking Morales to death. A desperado, Phipps was greatly feared; at his preliminary hearing the witnesses were too scared to testify, and he was released. For several years he worked in the northern mines, then, incorrectly believing that double jeopardy would protect him, he returned to Calaveras County. He was soon arrested by Ben Thorn. Because he had never been acquitted by a jury, Phipps was charged with murder and convicted in June. He was sentenced to hang on August 7, 1857.[4]

At noon on the fateful day, Clarke, Dave Mulford, Paul, and Thorn took him from the jail to the nearby public gallows. He was accompanied by his minister and lawyer, to whom he confessed his guilt. Before a large crowd they climbed the scaffold, where Sheriff Clarke read Phipps the death warrant and asked him if he had any last words. Phipps faced the throng and responded in a firm voice, "My friends, I forgive all those in the world who have injured me, and ask the forgiveness of all whom I have injured. I owe some debts which I have not been able to pay; I ask those to whom I am indebted to forgive."

He then turned, stepped onto the trap, and kneeled. For two minutes Phipps prayed with his clergyman. He then arose, standing firm and erect, while the deputies bound his arms. Sheriff Clarke placed a black silk hood over his head and affixed the noose. Phipps never faltered, said a witness: "He . . . was, in the moment of death, as brave a man as ever died—without fear, without bravado." When Sheriff Clarke gave the signal Phipps plunged through the trap. His neck snapped, and he died quickly. Commented the editor of the *Calaveras Chronicle*, "Thanks to the progress of good breeding and good taste, not one American woman was present."[5]

Paul never recorded his feelings about the hangings he helped carry out. Though the duty was highly unpleasant, he had learned the fine points of capital punishment: how to first stretch the rope with weights so it would not expand; how to tie the hangman's noose so it would hold the rope tightly; how to coat the rope with tallow so it would slide easily through the noose; and how to place the large knot under the condemned man's left ear, which caused the head to snap to the right and break the neck. He learned that a drop of about five feet was sufficient to break the average man's neck, and if his neck was not broken in the fall, the condemned man would slowly strangle to death. Such bungled executions were as embarrassing to sheriffs as jailbreaks. Americans in that era strongly supported the death penalty and just as strongly disfavored cruel or botched hangings.

Meanwhile, Sheriff Clarke had decided not to run for reelection, and he threw his support behind his undersheriff. At the Democratic county convention in Angels Camp on June 30, 1857, a slate of candidates was chosen. In the general election on September 3, Dave Mulford was elected as sheriff of Calaveras County. He took office on October 5, the same day appointing the ever-faithful Paul as his undersheriff and Ben Thorn, Gordon E. Sloss, George C. Tryon, and J. F. Britton as deputies.[6]

Sheriff Mulford, like most lawmen of the era, had political and personal enemies. At two o'clock on the morning of March 2, 1858, a stranger wakened Mulford at his house and said that the jailer needed him immediately. The sheriff put on his gunbelt, which held two revolvers and a Bowie knife, and rushed to the jail. It was a bright, moonlit night, and he spotted two men in front of him. Suspicious, the sheriff awoke a friend, Martin Rowan, and handed him a pistol. Mulford instructed him to circle around one side of the jail, while he would check the other side, then the two would meet behind it. The sheriff reached the back of the jail first, and while waiting for Rowan, he was suddenly attacked by two knife-wielding desperadoes, one of whom stabbed him in the face, cutting a large gash on his forehead. Mulford, almost blinded by blood, grappled with his assailants and was slashed again, in the back of his head. The sheriff managed to get one hand on his six-gun and cock it. The weapon discharged harmlessly, but it startled the two ruffians, who released him and fled. Mulford lost a great deal of blood, but he was a tough customer and recovered in less than a week. Paul and the other deputies could not find the outlaws, and they were never identified. Paul and Mulford suspected, however, that the attack was motivated by revenge. As the *Sacramento Bee* reported, "it is supposed to have been some of the Tom Bell gang."[7]

That year the state legislature abolished public executions and mandated that they be held within the walls of a jailyard or other private place, with spectators limited to the sheriff and his assistants, a physician, the district attorney, twelve citizens, two ministers, and no more than five friends or family of the condemned. The first murderer to face the new law was Chung Lug, a forty-two-year-old miner from Hong Kong. On August 25, 1858, he had quarreled with a countryman over a woman in Mokelumne Hill. Chung Lug attacked his adversary with a large Chinese Bowie knife, stabbing him through the left breast and into the heart with a single thrust. He was promptly arrested, and in October he was tried and sentenced to hang.[8]

To comply with the new law, Sheriff Mulford had a scaffold erected in the jailyard. At eleven on the morning of November 26, 1858, Mulford, Undersheriff Paul, and their deputies led Chung Lug into the jailyard. The onlookers totaled just twenty-five, including lawmen, jail guards, newspaper reporters, several physicians, and a few citizens who had been invited by the sheriff. Chung Lug was resigned to his fate and "remained perfectly composed," according to one of the reporters, who added, "When he was ascending the scaffold in company with the sheriff he raised his hands as if in triumph." While the doomed man sat in a chair on the trap, Sheriff Mulford read the death warrant, which was translated by an English-speaking Chinese prisoner. At eight minutes past eleven the hood and noose were slipped on. Chung Lug gasped his last request: "that it might be done quickly." Three minutes later the trap was sprung and he plunged to his death. His body hung for another twenty-seven minutes, until the physicians pronounced him dead.[9]

Calaveras County had numerous Chileno desperadoes. One of the most dangerous was Pedro Ybarra, who had first achieved notoriety in San Antonio Camp in 1854. Ybarra had been living there with a prostitute named Juana, who left him and moved in with another man, Antonio. After stewing over this for two weeks, Ybarra barged into Juana's house and shot her and Antonio to death. A crowd raced to the scene, among them Ben Thorn, at that time a miner. Before she died, Juana told Thorn that Ybarra had shot them in a jealous rage. Ybarra vanished, but a shaken Thorn never forgot the killing. More than four years later he got a tip that the killer was hiding out with an American and four Mexicans in a cave in the Tuolumne River Canyon, now covered by Don Pedro Reservoir.

The notorious Pedro Ybarra, captured by Bob Paul's posse in 1858. This image was taken in 1878. Author's collection.

On October 20, 1858, Paul, Thorn, and Deputy Gordon Sloss rode to the hideout with a deputy sheriff from Stanislaus County. From the river's south bank the six outlaws saw the lawmen coming and splashed across to the cave. Paul and his posse cut them off, cornering Ybarra and a desperado named Simón. As Thorn leaped from his horse and seized Ybarra, Simón jerked his pistol and pointed it at the deputy's head. Before he could fire, Paul and Sloss grabbed him and pinioned his arms. Simón continued to struggle, so the lawmen knocked him out with a heavy blow to the head. At that, the rest of the gang fled on foot into the hills. Then Thorn took Ybarra into the cave to collect his valise, but the badman bolted and grabbed a six-gun. Thorn wrestled it away from him. The Stanislaus deputy took charge of Simón for assault, while Paul and his posse returned to Mokelumne Hill with Ybarra.

The desperado hired good lawyers, but when Ybarra was brought to trial in August 1859, a strong prosecution case was presented. Juana's deathbed statement to Thorn was the key testimony against him. Ybarra was convicted of murder and sentenced to death. While he languished in jail, his lawyers appealed to the California Supreme Court. In October 1860 his conviction was set aside on the grounds that the judge had given an erroneous jury instruction. Ybarra's lawyers, in preparation for a new trial, rounded up witnesses who claimed that one Juan Morena had admitted the double murder. Much to the disgust of Paul and Thorn, Ybarra was acquitted in 1862. Two years later he murdered a Chinese during a robbery, but again escaped punishment due to a racist law that prevented Asians and American Indians from testifying in court. Justice finally came in 1878 when Ybarra was convicted of stage robbery and sentenced to life imprisonment, due in large part to Thorn's detective work.[10]

Yet another Chileno outlaw was Jose Luis Cortes, whom the *Sacramento Daily Union* called "one of the most desperate characters in the state." During the summer of 1856 he had killed two men in Calaveras County—one in Mokelumne Hill and another in the mining camp of Jesus Maria. Cortes escaped, but in January 1859 Paul received information that he was holed up in a camp near Forest Hill, in Placer County. Paul set off alone after the fugitive, arriving on the morning of January 11. He located Cortes and an accomplice named Pantaleon, arrested them both without trouble, and brought them into Forest Hill. There word of the arrest quickly spread, and a crowd of Chilenos began to gather to rescue the prisoners. Paul raced out of the camp with his men before the mob could attack. He rushed into

Auburn, twenty miles east, where he got assistance from his friend, Constable John C. Boggs. Paul was still concerned about a rescue, so he and Boggs rented a wagon, loaded the two outlaws aboard, and set off for Sacramento, thirty-five miles down the foothills. As darkness fell the lawmen became increasingly alert, and at eight o'clock they thought they heard the pounding hooves of a mounted band in pursuit. As the officers whipped their horses into a run, the two desperadoes suddenly made a leap from the wagon. With a powerful hand, Paul seized Cortes by the coat and stopped him cold. Boggs grabbed Pantaleon by the hair, pulling it out by the roots. Pantaleon hit the ground running, and Boggs jerked his six-shooter and fired. The bullet winged Pantaleon, but he did not stop. He plunged into the chaparral and disappeared. Paul brought Cortes into Mokelumne Hill to stand trial. Commented the *Sacramento Union*, "It is nothing but just to note that the Sheriffalty of Calaveras has been remarkable for perseverance in the pursuit of criminals. . . . If all officers in the State should discharge their duty as faithfully as has Under Sheriff Paul . . . the State would soon be rid of the legion of rascals which infest it." Cortes was convicted of a lesser charge of assault with intent to commit murder and was sentenced to a term that was typically lenient for the wild and woolly 1850s: one year in San Quentin.[11]

All the while Paul still had the gold fever that had seized him ten years earlier. By the mid-1850s the surface gold in the mining region was gone, and the streams were panned out. But miners recognized that there were rich veins of gold-bearing quartz deep below the earth. Heavily capitalized mining companies began to appear, using sophisticated methods of extracting the gold. Hydraulic miners used giant water nozzles to wash away entire hillsides. Hardrock miners tunneled into the mountains, burrowing like gophers in search of veins of quartz gold. Lumbering thrived, as countless heavy beams were needed to shore up the tunnels. The stamp mill, by which rock and quartz were crushed to remove the gold, was invented. By 1857, $500 million in gold had been taken from the mother lode. Gold mining had become big business; the days of the wandering "sourdough" with his pickaxe and pack mule were drawing to a close.

Paul adapted to these changes. In 1859 he and several partners acquired a claim in Chili Gulch, about two miles south of Mokelumne Hill, which they operated as the Bob Paul Mine. In the next few years Paul would expend much of his earnings on men and equipment to construct drift tunnels through solid granite to locate the veins of gold deep inside. Eventually

Paul's company would drill and blast 2,600 feet of tunnels, erect a water flume, sluices, and a stamp mill, and employ numerous men in a large-scale gold mining operation. During the next ten years, the Bob Paul Mine would reportedly yield $160,000 in gold, but much of the earnings went toward expenses.[12]

During the 1850s, California politics were dominated by a furious struggle for control of the Democratic Party. Democrats were divided on the issue of slavery, exemplified by a bitter feud between the state's two most powerful lawmakers, Senator William M. Gwin, leader of the Democrats' proslavery wing, and Senator David Broderick, leader of the antislavery or "free soil" faction. In 1856 many Northern antislavery Democrats joined the newly formed Republican Party, and the following year the Democratic Party formally split into the Lecompton and anti-Lecompton factions. Lecompton Democrats supported the Kansas Lecompton Constitution, which would allow slavery in that territory, while anti-Lecompton members opposed slavery's expansion. Paul would become a Lecompton Democrat, despite the fact that as a New England Protestant he opposed slavery and that his close friend and mentor Charlie Clarke joined the anti-Lecompton wing.[13]

The Democrats were then in power in Calaveras, and elections were generally between the Lecompton and anti-Lecompton wings. In the spring of 1859 the county's Lecompton Democrats were extremely active in securing candidates for a host of state and local offices. Said one observer, "I never saw such a swarm of office-seekers before, in all my life, for the county and township offices." Their leader was Colonel Allen P. Dudley, a fiery lawyer who had switched over from the antislavery faction. John Shannon, editor of the *Calaveras Chronicle*, and Judge James H. Hardy were also prominent Lecomptons in Calaveras. Party leaders offered Paul support, and he agreed to join the Lecomptons and throw his hat in the ring for sheriff. His principal opponent for the Lecompton nomination was Joseph K. Doak, a rancher widely known as a "roaring Democrat." Doak was supremely confident that he would be nominated for sheriff. "This is just like an old-fashioned fox hunt," he boasted. "We're just closing in on them now."[14]

The Lecompton Democrat county convention opened in Mokelumne Hill on June 15, 1859, with a passionate crowd packing the town theater. The sheriff's position came up on the second day, and four men were nominated: Paul, Doak, W. H. Clary, a mine owner, and Paul's friend,

Constable Mark McCormick. The latter, undoubtedly in deference to Paul, immediately withdrew. On the first ballot, Paul received 62 votes, while Doak got 51, and Clary only 17. Since none of them had a majority, a one-hour adjournment was taken, during which Clary withdrew and threw his support to Paul. On the second ballot, Paul polled 74 votes to Doak's 56, and Paul was declared nominated. Doak was stunned, as one pioneer recalled: "But he didn't get elected, and he was so mad over it, he left the Democratic Party."[15]

Paul's opponent in the fall election was George C. Tryon, a former deputy sheriff and county assessor, who ran as an independent. In the election on September 7, 1859, Paul's popularity, coupled with his obvious abilities as a lawman, won the day. He polled 2,651 votes to 1,992 for Tryon, a comfortable margin. Such elections in the late 1850s were extremely bitter and laid bare the deep divisions that would soon result in the Civil War. This was made clear by events that soon followed. At a political meeting in San Andreas just before the election, a quarrel had taken place between Dr. Preston Goodwyn, a strong Southern sympathizer, and William Jefferson "Jeff" Gatewood, a prominent lawyer and anti-Lecompton candidate for district attorney. Dr. Goodwyn angrily called Gatewood a "Black Republican," a derogatory term for an antislavery man. After a sharp exchange of words, Gatewood felled Dr. Goodwyn to the ground. The doctor demanded satisfaction on the field of honor.[16]

During the gold rush, the conditions and attitudes that led men to embrace vigilantism were also responsible for the popularity of dueling; more formal duels took place in California between 1849 and 1859 than in any other place in the United States. Dueling had a special appeal to men living on a frontier where government was often rudimentary, courts were frequently ineffective, and men were expected to solve their own problems, to "kill their own snakes." Dueling, like vigilantism, represented a primal version of violent self-redress. Within days after the election rumors began spreading that a duel would be fought between Goodwyn and Gatewood. Seconds for the two antagonists drew up written articles; it was agreed that they would fight with rifles at forty paces. The arrangements were all made in secret, and early on the morning of September 16, 1859, five carriages left San Andreas with the participants, seconds, surgeons, and friends. The "affair of honor" took place on a flat five miles from town. At the command "Fire! One, two, three," Dr. Goodwyn's rifle misfired. Jeff Gatewood's did not, and the doctor collapsed with a mortal wound.

Bob Paul as sheriff of Calaveras County, carte de visite image taken in about 1860. Photograph used with permission of Wells Fargo Bank, N.A., 6552b.

Sheriff Mulford and Sheriff-elect Paul made no effort to prevent the duel. Given Paul's stern opposition to vigilantism, he could not have knowingly failed to take action. Mulford, on the other hand, was a friend of Gatewood's second, Martin Rowan, and must have had some knowledge of the pending affair. Perhaps as a lame-duck sheriff he did not want to offend the supporters of either man. Nonetheless, their failure to prevent the duel was a black mark on the records of both lawmen.[17]

Paul was sworn in as sheriff in early October. For both practical and political reasons, it was necessary for him to move from Campo Seco to the county seat. On October 19 he purchased a home from a prominent lawyer and politician, William H. Badgley, and his wife, for the then princely sum of $1,250. It was a fine wood-frame building situated next door to St. Peter's Catholic church at the corner of Lafayette and Marlette Streets in Mokelumne Hill. The house was ideal for his purposes. The lot was large, had a stable in the rear for his buggy and horses, and was situated just five hundred feet east of the courthouse, where he would spend much of his time on official business.[18]

The sheriff's offices in the mining region had been highly lucrative. The sheriff was also the county tax collector and received significant fees, especially for enforcing the Foreign Miners' Tax Law. In 1858 it was estimated that the sheriff of neighboring Amador County earned more than $20,000 a year. However, in March 1859 the state legislature stripped the sheriff of the duty of collecting the Foreign Miners' Tax, and that officer's income plummeted. Nonetheless, Paul would earn about $6,000 a year as sheriff, most of it in fees from handling civil and criminal cases and a lesser amount for collecting property taxes. For acting as tax collector, he received up to 10 percent of the amount collected. As sheriff, civil litigants paid him between 40¢ and $2 for each civil paper served, 50¢ for each witness subpoenaed, and 50¢ per mile one way for traveling. In criminal cases, he received $3 per arrest, plus 20¢ per mile. For summoning a grand jury, the fee was $15; for a trial jury, $6. He was paid $5 a day for attending court, whether he appeared in person or whether a deputy did so on his behalf. Remarkably, for executing a man under sentence of death, he received $50. Paul appointed as undersheriff Ben Thorn, as deputies J. P. Douglass and David Lampson, and as jailer George W. "Pink" Smith. Years later, Lampson boasted to an interviewer that he and Paul "rode thousands of miles in search of daring criminals of the worst character, and in the capture of some of the men showed undaunted bravery and fearless spirit. They succeeded in arresting and ridding the county of many of the worst men, and the lawless element of the community were thereby held in subjection."[19]

Charley Williams, alias Green, was part of that lawless element and one of the noted desperadoes in the southern mines. According to one early account, "He was a bold and bloody-hearted villain, without pity or remorse." In 1857 he robbed a teamster at Knights Ferry and was captured in a saloon in Columbia and sentenced to five years in San Quentin. He escaped and embarked on a robbery spree in Calaveras County. On the night of July 9, 1860, Williams and a comrade pulled an exceptionally brutal robbery at the West Point bridge tollhouse, on the North Fork of the Mokelumne River. The tollkeeper, John McDonough, and a friend, Gwin Raymond, were inside when two robbers crept up and leveled their pistols through an open window. They fired at point-blank range, hitting Raymond in the shoulder and McDonough in the right arm. Ignoring the bleeding victims, the robbers took $300 in toll receipts and vanished. A constable from West Point tracked the robbers and caught one, but his partner escaped. The prisoner confessed and named his accomplice as Charley Williams. Ben Thorn organized a twenty-man posse and scoured the mountains, but no trace of Williams could be found.[20]

Paul and Thorn kept up a "still hunt" for the outlaw and five months later got a tip that he was at Princeton (now Mount Bullion) in Mariposa County. Sheriff Paul and Thorn rode eight miles south to Princeton. On the way they picked up Charles M. Benbrook, constable of Hornitos. On December 6, 1860, the three lawmen rode up to a cabin near Princeton where two men were chopping wood some distance apart. While Paul and Constable Benbrook approached one man, Thorn rode up to the other. Thorn immediately recognized Williams.

Jerking his six-shooter, he ordered, "Stand!"

He then called to Sheriff Paul, "Come down. I have the right man!"

Williams instantly swung up his axe and charged the mounted deputy. When Thorn cocked and raised his weapon, Williams threw down the axe and fled toward the dense chaparral.

"Stop, or I'll shoot!" Thorn shouted twice, but the desperado only ran faster. Thorn fired and missed, and Williams plunged into the chaparral and vanished. The brush was too thick to follow on horseback, so the three lawmen galloped around to cut off the fugitive. They pulled up their horses just in time to see Williams burst out of the thicket with a large Bowie knife in his fist. Thorn, at a range of fifty feet, fired a single shot at the running outlaw. The pistol ball tore into Williams's left shoulder and pierced his lungs. The badman ran another thirty feet before he dropped. Throwing away his knife, he gasped, "I give up. You have killed me!"

Paul and Thorn borrowed a wagon, loaded the outlaw aboard, and drove him to the Mariposa jail, where a doctor treated his wound. Several newspapers lambasted Thorn for shooting a fleeing man. The *Mariposa News* said, "We are inclined to think that Thorn fired rather too quick," and the *San Francisco Bulletin* complained that Thorn "seemed to not be very scrupulous" in using his revolver. Paul promptly wrote a letter to the *Bulletin* in defense of his friend and undersheriff, insisting that "all others who know Mr. Thorn well are convinced that he is a man and officer of such discretion, circumspection and tried courage, as would disdain to use the full power placed by the law into his hands, save in case of extreme emergency." In the end the dispute was academic. Williams recovered within six weeks, and Paul brought him to the county jail in Mokelumne Hill. He was promptly tried, convicted, and sentenced to twelve years in prison.[21]

Williams and four other prisoners were held in a single large cell in the northwest corner of the jail. One of them managed to smuggle in a small pocketknife. Despite the fact that the flooring was made of thick planks layered with sheet iron, they managed to cut through a floorboard. Then they loosened and pried up the sheet iron. It took several weeks of labor, done mainly at night, but by the early morning of February 7, 1861, the prisoners finally had an opening large enough to slip through. Cutting through the bottom layer of planking, Williams and the others crawled into the basement. Once in the jailyard, they broke a hole through the outer wall and fled into the blackness. Paul was not amused when he found his charges gone and a sarcastic but ungrammatical letter left behind. Addressed to "Paul's house," it read, "Good bye we are a going to leave you going we hope to a better atmosphere. Don't grieve tis part of human nature to be ungrateful although you have watched us with the care of a tiger for her young. . . . Tis our sincere wish that we may never see you again. Adios senores although we have some doubts about your forgiveness let us hope you will not . . . . Good bye we are off." It was signed "We us & Co."[22]

Paul and Thorn made every effort to capture Williams, but without success. The fugitive surfaced six weeks later, on March 19, 1861, when he entered an Italian store with a band of Chilenos at Mount Ophir in Mariposa County. In a wild melee, Williams choked a woman and stabbed a Mexican before he and his compadres fled in a hail of bullets. But the desperado did not live long. He stayed in Mariposa County, where that fall someone shot him in the head and left his body to rot on a hillside near Princeton. His corpse was found and fully identified a few months later; the bullet from Thorn's six-gun was still in his shoulder blade.[23]

Sheriff Paul found that violent crime remained common in Calaveras during the 1860s. The county's population was fairly stable during the 1850s, averaging about sixteen thousand. In 1858, gold was discovered on the Fraser River in British Columbia. This new strike drew many miners from California, including much of the state's lawless element. Additional discoveries, most notably Nevada's Comstock Lode in 1859, Idaho in 1860, and Montana in 1862, further drained the mother lode of miners. After 1860 the Calaveras population steeply declined; by 1870 the county had lost almost half of its residents. Nonetheless, Calaveras County was still overwhelmingly male (84 percent), and the conditions that caused so much violence during the gold rush were still prevalent. During the 1860s, the county's homicide rate averaged forty-four per hundred thousand, vastly higher than the modern national rate. Sheriff Paul's bailiwick remained a tough and dangerous place to police.[24]

Paul sorely missed his family back in New Bedford. He had last seen his mother when he sailed on the *Factor* at age fourteen; he had not laid eyes on any of his family for more than fifteen years. His new sheriff's income made him very comfortable financially, and soon after the election he sent for them. In 1859 his mother Mary, along with older brother Thomas, his twenty-five-year-old Irish-born wife, Jane, and their three-year-old daughter, Anna, made the long sea voyage from New Bedford to San Francisco. His delight at seeing them and at meeting his niece and sister-in-law can only be imagined. They moved into a house in Mokelumne Hill. In April 1860 Jane gave birth to a second child, Robert E. Paul, who would be like a son to Bob Paul and who grew up idolizing his uncle. Paul employed his brother as a deputy sheriff and jailer. Tom Paul, who had been a shipwright and volunteer fireman in New Bedford, promptly joined Mokelumne Engine Company No. 1 and helped raise $1,250 to purchase the town's first fire engine.[25]

But Tom Paul was not cut from the same cloth as his younger brother. The jail held some twenty felons awaiting trial, including ten charged with murder. After the escape of Charley Williams, its most dangerous inmate was a killer, Jesus Villalobo. On February 5, 1860, L. L. Roberts, justice of the peace at Jenny Lind, had issued a warrant charging Villalobo with

Jesus Villalobo, 1861 wood engraving made from a photograph. Tom Paul failed Ben Thorn in a desperate struggle with the outlaw. Courtesy of William B. Secrest.

horse theft. When Roberts and his constable tried to serve the warrant at a fandango house, Villalobo drew a six-gun and mortally wounded Justice Roberts. A posse of citizens pursued him across the Calaveras River, and Villalobo was shot four times before he was captured. He was jailed in Mokelumne Hill, tried for murder, and sentenced to hang. Villalobo's lawyers appealed to the California Supreme Court, which upheld the death sentence. The date of his execution was set for March 19, 1861. Four days before that, at the pleading of Villalobo's mother, Thorn and Tom Paul took the killer from his cell and walked him to a nearby daguerreotype gallery to be photographed.[26]

Jesus Villalobo was a man of huge size and strength. On the way back to the jail, Tom Paul told Thorn he had forgotten something at the gallery and left the undersheriff alone with the unironed murderer. Thorn proceeded on, keeping Villalobo eight feet in front of him. As they neared the jail, the prisoner suddenly whirled, crouched, and charged Thorn. Seizing the officer in a bear hug, Villalobo snatched his pistol from its holster with one hand and his Bowie knife with the other. Thorn managed to force the knife from his fist, and it fell to the ground. As the two struggled desperately for the six-gun, the burly outlaw wrestled it from the much smaller Thorn. Fighting for his life, the undersheriff managed to throw Villalobo to the ground and straddle him, seizing his throat with one hand. Villalobo cocked the pistol and rammed it into Thorn's belly. Without a second to lose, Thorn knocked the six-gun away with his left hand and rammed the forefinger of his right hand into the desperado's nostril. It caused such instant and excruciating pain that Villalobo dropped the pistol, screaming in agony. Thorn held him tightly, shouting for help. Soon several of his friends appeared on the scene and helped Thorn overpower Villalobo and drag him to his cell. There the killer showed great remorse and apologized profusely. Thorn was incensed at Tom Paul for leaving him alone with the burly outlaw.[27]

Villalobo's attorneys had been fighting vigorously to save his neck, and two days later Bob Paul received a notice from the governor advising that he had commuted his sentence to life imprisonment. On April 8 Thorn took Villalobo to San Quentin prison. There, his apologies for attempting to escape proved hollow. Along with the notorious Tiburcio Vasquez, Villalobo was one of the leaders of the Big Break of 1862, during which two to three hundred convicts, almost half of the prison population, managed to escape in one of the largest prison breaks in American history.[28]

With the outbreak of the Civil War in 1861, Paul became a pro-Union Democrat. The Union Democrats supported Abraham Lincoln's war efforts; they were opposed by Peace Democrats, who favored the Union but were strongly against the war. In the September election Paul was challenged by three candidates, including his old boss, Charlie Clarke, who ran as an independent. Paul won, as the *Calaveras Chronicle* commented, "by a handsome plurality over all of his opponents." But he did not have long to enjoy his victory. On October 7 he was riding in a two-seat buggy near Angels Camp with a mine-owner friend, James Tate. Suddenly its coupling pole gave way, and the frightened horses broke loose. Paul and Tate were thrown violently from the buggy, Tate striking his head so hard his skull received multiple fractures. Tate lost consciousness for days, and doctors believed he would die, but eventually he recovered. Paul was luckier, though badly battered, with serious bruises on his face, neck, and side.[29]

It was about this time that there occurred one of the most important events in his life, one that had nothing to do with whaling, mining, politics, or bandits. In late 1861 the family of his sister-in-law, Jane Coughlan Paul, arrived in San Francisco by ship from New Bedford. Jane's family included her younger sister, Eliza, who was married to a tailor, Thomas Drady, and their two small children, plus Jane's youngest sister, Margaret, just sixteen. Paul went to San Francisco to meet Jane's family and bring them to Calaveras. Paul and his brother Tom had made arrangements for Drady to open a tailoring business in Mokelumne Hill. The Dradys quickly settled in, and by December Drady's tailor shop on Center Street was open to customers.[30]

Paul was particularly taken with young Margaret Coughlan. She was pretty and petite, with thick brown tresses and flashing green eyes. There can be little doubt that Margaret was swept off her feet by this strange brother-in-law about whom she had heard so much: dark complected from a life in the sun, physically imposing, and ruggedly handsome. The earliest photographs of him, taken in the 1860s, show what she would have seen: a craggy, weather-beaten face, tanned and worn by the fierce sun and bitter sleet of two thousand topside watches, creased and folded by six years of heavy toil with shovel, pick, rocker, and gold pan. He was rugged and tough beyond imagination, yet at the same time he was gentle and kind, educated and thoughtful. His affable personality and easy smile were augmented by a heavy beard and brown eyes that sparkled with humor. He had followed a life beyond her imaginings; he had traveled and experienced the exotic worlds of Africa, South America, Australia, New Zealand, Hawaii, and Tahiti. His years of hunting whales and digging gold fascinated her. He was nothing like any man she had ever met.

For his entire adult life, first on shipboard, then in the mining camps, Paul had lived in an environment that was primarily male. Many of the women he had encountered in seaports and in the mining country were wild and coarse, and many of them must have been prostitutes. His awkwardness around refined girls and women can only have been offset by clumsy but earnest attentions to Margaret. She had been born in Castlelyons, County Cork, Ireland, on January 24, 1845. As a child her parents immigrated with their brood to America, settling in New Bedford. But her father had died, and she was raised by her widowed mother, Ann Coughlan. Her sister Eliza had married Thomas Drady in New Bedford in 1854; Jane wed Tom Paul there the following year. Like Bob Paul, Margaret's deprived childhood had made her tough and had taught her the importance of

Margaret Coughlan Paul in the late 1860s. She married Bob Paul in 1862 at the age
of seventeen. Robert H. Paul collection.

keeping her family close. For Paul, Margaret's attractiveness, coupled with
the suddenness in which his own family had reentered his life, made him
think for the first time of marriage.[31]

Their differences, however, seemed almost insurmountable. He was
fifteen years her senior, and his huge physical bulk dwarfed the diminutive Margaret, who stood just five feet three. He was a Protestant, she was a
devout Roman Catholic who attended Mass every morning. He was easygoing,

with a soft-spoken, ironic sense of humor. Margaret was strong willed, opinionated, and sharp tongued, both flinty and resilient. She loved children, cooking, and domestic life and hated rough language, liquor, gambling, guns, and violence. Despite her youth, Margaret could quickly see beyond her brother-in-law's rough appearance. Though powerful and imposing, he was quiet and humble, a perfect combination of courage and kindness. As a friend said in later years, "Yet so modest and retiring is he that no one ever hears him boast of anything he has ever done; in fact, it is with great difficulty that one can get him to tell of any of his adventures." For Margaret, that was best, for his life both thrilled and terrified her.[32]

In those years California courtships were often brief. By 1860, even with all of the immigration during the previous decade, there was still a huge gender imbalance: the statewide population was 72 percent male. Accordingly there was strong competition for single girls and women. For men like Paul, who were over thirty, it was even tougher, for most single females were in their late teens, reflecting the fact that many families had migrated to California with their young daughters. If a man found an eligible female, he had to move fast. And that was exactly what Paul intended to do. But there was one impediment: Margaret would never marry outside of the Catholic Church. Unlike many argonauts, Paul was unconcerned about his potential mate's religious and ethnic background. He was relatively indifferent to religion, and he hesitated little before complying with her insistence that he be baptized in the Catholic faith. So on the evening of March 4, 1862, just five weeks after Margaret's seventeenth birthday and surrounded by their families, the couple was married by Father James Byrne in St. Peter's Catholic church in Mokelumne Hill. No doubt a large number of the popular groom's friends and supporters attended the wedding party in the sheriff's house.[33]

Paul's second term as sheriff was marked by newlywed bliss, offset by the bitter political divisions of the Civil War. Many Southerners had come west during the gold rush, and it was estimated that 10 percent of the state's population, about forty thousand people, were Confederate sympathizers. California gold and Nevada silver were essential in funding the war effort, and it was imperative that the state not fall into rebel hands. The state legislature passed emergency laws prohibiting the display of rebel flags and making it a crime to defend, endorse, or cheer subversion of the United States. Although there was scattered sectarian violence during the war, no rebellion ever materialized on the Pacific Coast. Nonetheless, antisedition laws were strictly enforced. The most famous treason prosecution was that of James H. Hardy, judge of the Sixteenth Judicial District, comprising Calaveras and Amador Counties.[34]

Judge Hardy, a Southern partisan, was strongly disliked by Unionists for his role in the famous Broderick-Terry case. Senator David Broderick, leader of the antislavery Democrats, had clashed with David S. Terry, chief justice of the state supreme court and a leader of the party's proslavery faction. Their bitter dispute climaxed in 1859, when they paired off near San Francisco in one of the most important duels ever fought in America. Terry killed Broderick and was charged with murder, but Judge Hardy dismissed the charges, incurring the wrath of Republicans and Union Democrats. The Broderick-Terry duel was a precursor of the bitter antagonism that resulted in civil war, and most Californians saw Senator Broderick as an antislavery martyr.[35]

In 1862, impeachment proceedings against Judge Hardy were initiated in the state legislature in Sacramento. There were numerous charges against him, from drunkenness to his ruling in the Terry case to his use of "seditious and treasonable language." It was alleged that in Jackson in 1861, soon after the war broke out, he offered a toast to "Jeff Davis and the Southern Confederacy" and while drunk shouted huzzahs for Davis. The next day, in Angels Camp, he exclaimed, on seeing an American flag, "That is an old woman's rag and ought to be torn down." Another time, after adjourning court in Mokelumne Hill, he proclaimed, "I am now off the bench. My mother was born in the South, and I am a rebel and don't care a damn who knows it." Amid huge fanfare, Hardy's trial began in the state senate on April 28, 1862.[36]

The impeachment trial lasted several weeks, and Paul and Thorn were among many witnesses called to Sacramento to testify in his defense. Dave Mulford was also present, because one of the charges against Hardy involved a civil lawsuit that Mulford had brought as sheriff. On the second day of trial Mulford quarreled with attorney Allen P. Dudley in the capitol building. Dudley had represented the ex-sheriff in the lawsuit, and on the witness stand he brazenly admitted that he had assisted Judge Hardy in writing the decision against Mulford, his own client, in order to obtain votes in an upcoming election. This disclosure enraged the former sheriff, and he confronted Dudley in the lobby. The pair came to blows, with Mulford knocking the lawyer down. One pulled a knife, but bystanders separated them before any blood was spilled. Mulford was fined fifty dollars for his part in the fray.[37]

As it turned out, Mulford's anger at Dudley was well directed. A few months earlier Dudley had won a lawsuit on behalf of an Italian client, Paolo DeMartini. Sheriff Paul collected about $400 on the judgment and handed it over to Dudley. Instead of giving it to his client, Dudley falsely told DeMartini that Paul was holding the money, which would be paid over in the next term of court. DeMartini later learned the truth from Paul. Outraged, DeMartini complained to the district court, which found Dudley guilty of "gross unprofessional conduct" and barred the dishonest lawyer from practicing in its jurisdiction.[38]

Unlike their old boss, Paul and Thorn liked Judge Hardy and evidently believed that he was being unfairly prosecuted. Both had been present in the courthouse in April 1862 when news arrived of the Union victory at the battle of Fort Donelson. Thorn, who took the stand first, testified that he had heard Judge Hardy praise the Union forces. Thorn also swore that he had never seen Hardy drunk, but when pressed on cross-examination, he admitted, "I suppose that he may be considered a tolerably good drinker." Paul's testimony was similar, though less humorous. He explained that although he was a Union Democrat, he was on friendly terms with the controversial judge. When asked if he had ever heard Hardy disparage the Union, Paul declared, "Judge Hardy came into my office ... and began speaking in high terms of the success of the Federal forces at Fort Donelson." When questioned whether he had ever seen Hardy drunk, Sheriff Paul replied, "Only once," and described how he was intoxicated one day as he came off the bench at the end of a trial. In the end, Judge Hardy was acquitted of every charge except that of using treasonable language, for which he was removed from office. This was the only time a California judge was impeached and removed by trial in the legislature.[39]

The newly domesticated Paul now spent much time at home with his bride and in his office handling civil matters and administrative duties. Increasingly the fieldwork and manhunting were done by Thorn. Paul also devoted much of his energy to managing his mine. He was becoming financially successful. When the county assessor appraised his property in 1863, he found that the sheriff owned bonds valued at $6,960, a house and stable worth $1,800, plus two horses, a buggy, and other personal property, with a total value of $10,040. By the time of the Union Democrat county convention in July, Paul had decided not to run for reelection. Former deputy George Tryon received the party's nomination and won the election in September. Paul would remain sheriff until his term expired the following March.[40]

Paul's newfound financial security gave him extra cash to invest. In February 1863 he had loaned $3,000 to a pair of German brothers, Augustus and J. C. Gebhardt, who owned the Mokelumne Hill Brewery. The terms were 2 percent a month, with all principal and interest due in nine months. The loan was secured by the brewery and by the Gebhardts' mining tunnel claim in Chili Gulch. J. C. Gebhardt was the Calaveras County treasurer, with a reputation for strict honesty. He was very popular and had recently been reelected to a third term. On February 11, 1864, he left town, claiming that he was going to Sacramento to make his regular settlement with the state controller. When he did not return after two weeks, Paul and other county officials became alarmed. They opened the treasury safe and found only $30 inside. A quick audit showed that $11,500 was missing. They sent a frantic telegram to the San Francisco police, who reported that Gebhardt had quietly sailed for Europe by steamer on February 13, accompanied by his two young sons. The Gebhardts's loan was still outstanding, and Augustus Gebhardt was unable to pay it off. As a result, Paul became the owner of the Gebhardts' brewery and their Chili Gulch mine. The Mokelumne Hill Brewery was highly visible, located in a large stone building on Church Street. Given the popularity of imbibing in the mother lode, it should have been the best investment he ever made. But Margaret was appalled by the fact that her husband made liquor. Undoubtedly due to pressure from his young wife, Paul sold the business nine months later, putting an end to his short-lived career as a brewer.[41]

The young couple was ecstatic when Margaret gave birth to their first child, John Vincent, on December 29, 1863. Paul's happiness was offset by the mixed feelings he must have felt when he turned the sheriff's office over to George Tryon two months later, on March 7, 1864. Yet things were looking up for him. To go along with his bride and infant son he had a new and potentially valuable gold mine. During the past year, the value of his holdings had almost doubled. In addition to the brewery, two mines in Chili Gulch, and his home, he owned bonds and other property with a total value of $19,480, a small fortune in that era. Bob Paul looked forward to a new life as a husband, father, and mine owner.[42]

CHAPTER FIVE

Shotgun Messenger

Bob Paul was now in a strong position to pursue his dream of becoming a wealthy mining entrepreneur. He sold his interest in his Chili Gulch mine, thereafter known as the Old Bob Paul Claim, and invested all of his money and energy into the tunnel claim he had acquired from the Gebhardt brothers. It was also situated in Chili Gulch, one mile south of Mokelumne Hill. With his brother-in-law, Thomas Drady; two friends, William W. Hopkins and Andrew W. Holbrook; and three other investors, he formed a mining partnership, R. H. Paul & Co. The partnership soon acquired a nearby tunnel claim in Indian Ravine, which became known as the Paul Consolidated Mine.

Paul and his partners spent $30,000 to blast and drill a new 850-foot tunnel through solid granite to get at the gold vein. The project took three years of constant work and was extremely dangerous; on December 1, 1864, a cave-in killed two of his miners, John McManus and Frank Jefferson. Once the tunnel was completed, tracks were laid and small ore carts brought out rocks and gravel. These were pulverized in a stamp mill, then sifted and washed to separate the gold. At first the mine was successful. In 1864, Paul's income totaled $8,860, and that of his partner William Hopkins was $9,300. They were two of the biggest taxpayers in Calaveras that year. By March 1867, the mine was producing $14 per cartload of ore, even though the main ore lead had not yet been reached. Reported the *Calaveras Chronicle*, "It will not only prove a fortune to its lucky owners, but also add greatly

A tunnel entrance to the Bob Paul Mine as it looks today. Photograph by Don Gordon.

to the wealth and prosperity of this section of the county. . . . The company are busily engaged in getting their dump-boxes, sluices, etc., in readiness for washing, and when their arrangements are completed the amount of gold extracted will be fabulous." Four months later Paul finally struck a lead of high-paying gravel. The *San Francisco Bulletin* confidently announced,

"The claim is undoubtedly one of the most extensive as well as the richest in the county."[1]

Meanwhile, Paul moved his family to Chili Junction, four miles south of Mokelumne Hill, along with his mother and the families of his brother Thomas and brother-in-law, Thomas Drady. Tom Paul worked for his brother. Bob Paul's partner, Andrew W. Holbrook, who had been a close friend since 1855, also settled in Chili Junction, moving in next door to the Pauls. The friendship between Paul and Holbrook would culminate tragically in Tucson more than fifteen years later. The Paul family was saddened when its seventy-eight-year-old matriarch, Mary, died at home on November 28, 1866. But within weeks, spirits were lifted. Five days after Christmas Margaret Paul gave birth to a healthy baby boy, christened Robert Joseph Paul. The couple had a relationship that was close and passionate, and they would be blessed with many more children in the years to come. A little more than a year later, on March 29, 1868, their first daughter, Agnes Loretta, was born in Chili Gulch.[2]

Though the former sheriff was happy at home, things were not panning out at the Paul mine. The ore lead quickly played out. Mining success was proving as elusive as supporting a family was expensive. He had sunk most of his money into his gold mining operations and found that his financial resources were rapidly dwindling. Accordingly, in May 1869 Paul announced himself as Republican candidate for sheriff. His old friend and former undersheriff Ben Thorn had been elected to the post in 1867, defeating the Republican incumbent James Oliphant. During the Civil War, Paul had again switched parties, finding that his political loyalties to the Union were more consistent with Republicans. Thorn had remained a Democrat. Even though the Republican Party now held a majority in Calaveras County, a feud had developed between Oliphant and former sheriff George Tryon. The result was a split in the Republican vote, allowing Thorn to be elected. Paul's financial straits trumped any loyalty he may have felt toward Thorn. The Republican editor of the *Calaveras Chronicle* immediately offered his support: "It is needless to say that Calaveras never had a better official than Mr. Paul, nor one who attained a greater degree of personal popularity. The Democracy will strain every nerve to retain the office, and if we hope to wrest it from their grasp, we must present a candidate who can poll every vote of the party." However, in the Republican county convention in August the nomination went to W. F. Colton, who had served as undersheriff under Oliphant. In the September election, Thorn was victorious.[3]

Large piles of tailings from the Bob Paul Mine, now abandoned. Photograph by Don Gordon.

Paul's fortunes continued to decline. In April 1870 he and his partners were forced to sell their Indian Ravine tunnel claim. That year the census taker found that he owned but $500 in real property and $3,000 in personal property. Nothing seemed to be going right. He had to lay off his brother Tom, who departed with Jane and their children to San Francisco. There they moved in with brother-in-law Thomas Drady, who a year earlier had sold out and opened a tailor shop in San Francisco. On July 3, 1870, the forty-one-year-old Tom Paul died of Bright's disease, a kidney ailment. Jane, now a widow with four children to support, stayed in San Francisco with the Dradys. Paul continued to work his other Chili Gulch mine, and in September he was elated when he struck a vein of rich gravel. In five days of work he took out fifty ounces of gold dust, worth about $950. The vein, however, quickly petered out. Paul's disappointment evaporated when daughter Anna was born on January 22, 1871, but three months later she suddenly died, for child mortality was very high in those years. Within a few months the grieving couple conceived another child, who would be born April 11, 1872, christened Mary, and nicknamed Mamie.[4]

Paul was desperate to regain the sheriff's office. In July 1871, at the Republican county convention, he was nominated for sheriff. Thorn, however, was highly popular and had made a fine record as the county's chief lawman. On election day, September 6, Thorn won by a large margin, 1,244 to 794. To add to Paul's bad luck, his mine claimed another victim. The day after the election, one of his partners, a Frenchman named Feat, entered a drift, or side tunnel, to get a pick that had been left behind. He collapsed after being overcome by poisonous fumes. Other miners found him, but he died shortly after they carried him from the tunnel. For Paul, this was evidently the last straw. He had squandered almost everything he had acquired since 1849. As Paul later said, he had "lost $60,000 and was dead broke." He and his investors sold their interest in the mine to a French company. His partner William Hopkins left for Santa Barbara. Perhaps on Paul's advice, Hopkins went into police work, serving until the turn of the century as Santa Barbara's capable night watchman, city marshal, deputy sheriff, and constable.[5]

Bob Paul sorely needed paying work, and a new job opportunity soon presented itself. His friend Lee Mathews, who had been a deputy sheriff under Thorn, was the Wells Fargo shotgun messenger on the stage route between Mokelumne Hill and Ione. Stagecoaches on this road carried a great deal of treasure from the mines. During the 1870s it was considered one of the most important stagecoach routes, and, as Paul later recalled, it had "always been regarded as the most dangerous in California." In November 1871 Mathews was appointed captain of the yard at San Quentin prison, and Paul sought and received the position of shotgun messenger in his place. The salary, $125 a month, was a fraction of what he had earned as sheriff, but it was enough to support his family. Compared with most jobs, this pay was in fact very good; the average monthly wage in the United States in the 1870s was only fifty dollars.[6]

Paul's decision to work for Wells Fargo would prove one of the most important of his life. Wells Fargo & Company's Express was a staple in early California. Founded during the gold rush in 1852, it competed with the U.S. Post Office to deliver mail and packages. Wells Fargo was faster and more reliable than the mail, and it made all losses good while the Post Office did not. For that reason the company actively investigated cases in which it was victimized by robberies, thefts, or embezzlements. During the 1850s and 1860s, Wells Fargo did not have a detective department. Instead, the company offered rewards and employed detectives from the San Francisco and Sacramento police departments on a case-by-case basis. As stage holdups increased after 1870, it became necessary to employ a full-time detective. James B. Hume, former sheriff of El Dorado County, got the job in 1873 and was Wells Fargo's chief special officer until his death in 1904. In 1875 Hume retained an assistant, John N. Thacker, ex-sheriff of Humboldt County, Nevada, who first worked part time, then full time during the 1880s. During their long careers, Hume and Thacker became the most famous express detectives in the West. Hume and Paul had much in common. They were close in age, and both were former forty-niners and California sheriffs. The two developed a fast friendship that lasted the rest of their lives.[7]

In addition to detectives, Wells Fargo employed numerous agents and messengers in California. The earliest Wells Fargo messengers carried letters by horseback to the gold rush mining camps; soon they brought treasure from the mines on riverboats to San Francisco. Sometimes these gold rush messengers were armed with revolvers, sometimes they were not armed at all. At first there were only a few such messengers, the best known being Pilsbury "Chips" Hodgkins, who worked for Wells Fargo from 1853 to 1891. During the 1850s, if a stagecoach carried a large shipment of bullion, the company's local Wells Fargo agent would act as armed guard. Contrary to myth, a Wells Fargo agent was not a detective or a secret agent. Generally he was a merchant who held the Wells Fargo franchise for his community and ran a Wells Fargo office in one corner of his general store. His primary job was to send and receive packages and letters for shipment; in later years Wells Fargo agents also took on banking duties. As stagecoach holdups became increasingly common in California after 1860, Wells Fargo authorized its local agents to hire armed guards to accompany treasure shipments. Because these guards carried sawed-off shotguns, they soon became known as shotgun messengers.

These messengers did not guard stagecoaches; they guarded Wells Fargo's express boxes. Most stagecoaches did not carry messengers; a guard would only be on board if there was a sizeable express shipment of money or bullion. Wells Fargo employed sixteen shotgun messengers in 1861. As holdups increased, so did the number of guards. The number also grew as Wells Fargo expanded its operations into other western states and territories. By the mid-1870s there were 35 shotgun messengers, a number of which grew to 110 in the early 1880s and then 200 by 1885. Of these men, Wells Fargo detective Jim Hume said, "In all my experience, there has never been an occasion when a regular shotgun messenger showed the white feather no matter what the odds against him or the promise of danger might be. They are the kind of men you can depend on if you get in a fix, with the certainty that they will pull you through or stay by you to the last." Messengers generally rode on the front seat of the stage, next to the driver, hence the modern term "riding shotgun."

For nine years Bob Paul's second home would be on the hurricane deck of a Concord coach. The big stage lines used the deluxe, heavy-duty coaches made by the Abbot-Downing Company of Concord, New Hampshire. The Concord stagecoach could carry up to eighteen people, ten inside and eight on top, including the "whip," or driver, and the shotgun messenger. The coach was pulled by six horses and traveled twenty-four hours a day, seven days a week, with the teams being changed every twelve to twenty miles at stage stations along the route. Many stagecoaches in California and the West were inexpensive and uncomfortable "mud wagons" built by local carriage makers and used on short stage routes. It has been estimated that only about one-fourth of all western stages were Concord coaches; the rest were mud wagons.[8]

Valuables were shipped in Wells Fargo treasure boxes made of pine, strapped with iron, and painted green. These were carried in the boot, under the driver's seat, and were the object of the highway robber's time-honored command, "Throw down the box." Some coaches had an iron safe with a cushioned top that also served as the rear inside passenger seat. After the completion of the transcontinental railroad in 1869, Wells Fargo messengers were also assigned to guard shipments aboard trains. Messengers on stages and trains carried a sawed-off, double-barreled shotgun and sometimes a revolver. During the 1860s and early 1870s, Wells Fargo shotguns were generally English-made, muzzle-loading percussion guns, purchased by company officials at its San Francisco headquarters from several of the city's firearm dealers. Percussion shotguns were difficult to load. In 1874 E. Remington & Sons began making reasonably priced breech-loading shotguns. These were easily loaded by moving a lever above the breech, which opened the barrels and allowed insertion of a pair of brass shells filled with buckshot. Wells Fargo first purchased Remington shotguns, followed in the 1880s by shotguns of various other makes, including Parker and L. C. Smith, all of them sturdy, twelve-gauge, double-barreled hammer guns. Contrary to myth, Wells Fargo shotguns were never known as "coach guns," which is a modern term coined by gun collectors. Instead, they were known as "cut-off shotguns" or "messenger's guns."[9]

Undoubtedly the most famous man to ride shotgun for Wells Fargo was Wyatt Earp, who once explained:

The Wells Fargo shotgun is not a scientific weapon. It is not a sportsmanlike weapon. It is not a weapon wherewith to settle an affair of honor between gentlemen. . . . The barrels . . . are not more than two-thirds the length of an ordinary gun barrel. That makes it easy to carry and easy to throw upon the enemy, with less danger of wasting good lead by reason of the muzzle catching in some vexatious obstruction. As the gun has to be used quickly or not at all, this shortness of barrel is no mean advantage. The weapon furthermore differs from the ordinary gun in being much heavier as to barrel, thus enabling it to carry a big charge of buckshot. No less than twenty-one buckshot are loaded into each barrel. That means a shower of forty-two leaden messengers, each fit to take a man's life or break a bone if it should reach the right spot. And as the buckshot scatters liberally the odds are all in its favor. At close quarters the charge will convert a man into a most unpleasant mess. . . . As for range—well, at 100 yards, I have killed a coyote with one of these guns, and what will kill a coyote will kill a stage robber any day.[10]

Shotgun messengers like Paul operated under the orders of local agents. In addition to guarding express shipments, they kept written records, or waybills, for all shipments. They received detailed instructions, which a few years later were printed in booklet form and distributed to all messengers on stages and trains:

- "Messengers on all important routes are required to travel armed for defense, in case of attack. Arms and ammunition can be procured by requisition."
- "In case a Messenger on a stage route leaves the coach, for meals, etc., he must retain possession of his fire-arms."
- "They must not drink intoxicating liquors of any kind when on duty."
- "They must never receive from strangers cigars, tobacco, or anything by which they might be drugged."
- "They must never show or mention the contents of their safes."
- "Safes must not be left unlocked longer than necessary, even when Messengers are alone; and money or valuables must never be lost sight of."
- "In going to and from depots, Messengers must accompany their safes or treasure boxes—never leaving them out of sight or reach;

A clean-shaven Bob
Paul, carte de visite
image taken in Stockton
in about 1871. Photo-
graph used with per-
mission of Wells Fargo
Bank, N.A., 6552a.

and money must never be carried to and from depots and offices
except in safes or treasure boxes; and hand safes or treasure boxes
must never be left in cars at end of routes."
- "All way-bills carried by Messengers must be entered on the
  Way-bill register, taking receipt in the usual form."[11]

A noted shotgun messenger in Nevada, Aaron Y. Ross, taught new guards
how to watch for trouble. He told them to "watch the pointer teams'
ears. When they stood erect, straining, with quick jerks backward, it was
the signal that there was danger ahead and high time to watch for movement on the ground and behind every rock." Paul would have plenty of
time to gain his own experience. His first two years as a shotgun messenger were on the route from Mokelumne Hill to Ione, and from time
to time he probably rode on other stage roads in the gold region as the
company required. As Jim Hume once explained, "Robberies are generally
committed on mountain roads on an up grade, and the driver is too busy
with his team to do any fighting." Margaret Paul was relieved that road

agents left her husband's stage alone and grateful that this local work allowed him to spend time at home with his family.[12]

A pioneer who knew shotgun messenger Paul recalled, "The sight of his dark, heavy face and thick figure on the box at the left of the driver always made the passengers feel better. It made the driver feel better too." His reputation was enough to ward off most highwaymen. As one would-be stage robber reportedly said to his comrades, "Let's skip her today, boys. Bob Paul's up!"[13]

In 1874 Paul was transferred to the Central Pacific Railroad, which had been completed five years earlier to connect California with the East. Each train carried a Wells Fargo express car, which was generally the first car behind the coal tender. In later years, a baggage car was coupled behind the express car; on some trains, the express and baggage were combined in a single coach. Paul guarded treasure shipments on the run from Sacramento across the Sierra and through the Nevada desert to Ogden, Utah. He had little to worry about from train robbers. Although Nevada had seen two train holdups in 1870—the first in the far West—no such attack occurred again on the Central Pacific until an attempted robbery at Cape Horn Mills in the Sierra Nevada Mountains in 1881. Paul's duties on this run were routine. On one trip to Ogden, he realized that it was the farthest east he had been since 1844. But although the assignment was relatively safe, he could not have been too happy with it, as it kept him from home for long periods. Just to get back to his family, he would have to travel by train to Sacramento and then board a stagecoach for the sixty-five-mile trip to Mokelumne Hill. From there he would have to walk or rent a horse or buggy for the final few miles to Chili Gulch. He was probably not home when Margaret gave birth to a daughter, Loretta, on April 5, 1875.[14]

That year Paul was detailed to ride shotgun on the stage route from Carson City, Nevada, to Bodie, California, and on the road between Virginia City and Pioche, Nevada. Other noted messengers on the Nevada routes included John Brent, Aaron Ross, Eugene Blair, "Shotgun Jimmy" Brown, and Martin "Mike" Tovey, a nervy thirty-four-year-old who was Paul's equal both in physical bulk and in courage and with whom Paul became fast friends. Tovey would later find fame as a messenger and would ultimately die a violent death from a bandit's bullet. Paul's duty was to go wherever large bullion shipments were sent: sometimes on the Central Pacific and sometimes on the high desert stage roads. John Brent, for example, later recalled how he was repeatedly transferred by Wells Fargo as demand required: from Montana to Nevada, back to Montana, again to Nevada, then Utah, California, Arizona, and back to California. Such constant traveling was hard on Paul, and he sorely missed Margaret and the children. Unlike Paul, many of the messengers were hard-drinking, single men who enjoyed their itinerant existence. In November 1876 Paul picked up his pay, just $86.66, at the train depot in Battle Mountain, Nevada. By Thanksgiving he had had enough, and he resigned from Wells Fargo. Quitting may have been the only way he could get leave to go home and spend the holidays with his family. Wells Fargo officials quickly persuaded him to accept a messenger's position guarding express shipments on the Southern Pacific Railroad. A corporate partner of the Central Pacific, the Southern Pacific had just completed its line through the San Joaquin Valley, connecting San Francisco with Los Angeles. From there Southern Pacific officials planned to connect with Tucson and, finally, El Paso.[15]

Because the new rail line was much closer to his home, Paul believed that it would allow him more time with Margaret and the children. But this was not to be. There were no train robberies on the Southern Pacific in California, and there would not be one until 1889. There was thus no need for a messenger of Paul's ability and courage. Instead, Wells Fargo now offered him an assignment guarding shipments on the stage lines running out of Visalia, in Tulare County. Visalia had long been the southern terminus for the Gilroy–Visalia stage route and the northern terminus for the Los Angeles–Visalia route. This was the main stage road connecting Northern and Southern California. The completion of the railroad into Los Angeles in 1876 greatly limited Visalia's importance as a transportation hub. Because it was still the principal stopping place for coaches in central California, Paul was initially assigned to guard stage shipments on the Visalia routes in January 1877. However, a series of daring stage robberies took him almost immediately to the mining country on the eastern side of the Sierra, straddling the line between California and Nevada.

Situated in the Inyo Mountains, between the Sierra Nevada to the west and Death Valley to the east, were the Cerro Gordo silver mines. Discovered in 1865 by Mexican prospectors, the mines produced silver, lead, and zinc. By the early 1870's the Cerro Gordo discovery sparked California's greatest silver rush. A San Francisco mining engineer, Mortimer W. Belshaw, had acquired one of the most important mines and constructed a toll road into Cerro Gordo. Belshaw and his partner, Victor Beaudry, built smelting furnaces at Cerro Gordo to reduce the cost of shipping the heavy ore.

The ore was smelted into eighty-five-pound bars, each the size of a long loaf of bread, to prevent thieves from carrying them off. Silver and lead bullion were then hauled by mule team from Cerro Gordo across the Mojave Desert to the Los Angeles port at San Pedro. It was an arduous three-week trip.

A number of mining camps sprang up in Inyo County. Two of the largest settlements were Lone Pine and Independence, the county seat. Twenty miles southeast of Cerro Gordo was the boomtown of Darwin, and further south stood the little camp of Coso. To the east, in the narrow and isolated Surprise Canyon, was another new camp, Panamint. Between 1868 and 1875, $13 million in silver and lead bullion was hauled from the mining region to Los Angeles, helping spur an economic and real estate boom that quickly transformed the sleepy adobe pueblo into an American city. Several thousand miners labored in the Cerro Gordo mines, many of them Hispanic. Among them were many gamblers and thieves. Bandidos found ripe pickings on the roads out of Cerro Gordo and its sister camps, and safe harbor among the Spanish-speaking miners. Early in 1874 the infamous Tiburcio Vasquez visited Coso, and soon after he robbed Mortimer Belshaw himself in a stage holdup at the Coyote Holes station. The following year Tiburcio's lieutenant, Clodoveo Chavez, terrorized the Cerro Gordo mines by leading an outlaw band that robbed stage stations, coaches, and travelers throughout the region.[16]

Paul could not have been pleased with his new assignment; after all, he had quit the Nevada service so that he could be closer to his family. But he needed work, and he had little choice but to go where he was ordered. Wells Fargo had sent him to the Eastern Sierra because of a series of raids by a gang of bandidos who had set out to emulate Tiburcio Vasquez. Santos Sotelo, twenty-five, and his brother, Francisco Sotelo, commonly known as Chico Lugo, eighteen, were Californios from Los Angeles, descendants of two pioneer families that had settled in California several generations earlier. Their father was a member of the prominent Lugo family, while their mother was from the Sotelo clan. Their older brother, Miguel Sotelo, had reputedly been a member of the Vasquez band; another brother, Guadalupe Sotelo, was a notorious horse thief. In June 1876 young Francisco Sotelo shot and killed one of his cousins in an ambush in Los Angeles. He fled east into the San Bernardino Mountains, where he was later joined by his brother Santos and another cousin, Jose Tapia. The three rode north to the Cerro Gordo mines.[17]

At two o'clock on the morning of August 28 the Sotelo brothers and Tapia stopped a stage twenty-five miles south of Darwin. They did not bother the passengers, but stole the Wells Fargo box. Riding hard, they fled back to Los Angeles County. On August 31 a posse tried to capture Francisco Sotelo near San Gabriel, but he escaped in a running gunfight.

On Friday night, January 5, 1877, the Sotelos and Tapia held up the southbound stagecoach from Darwin to Mojave in Red Rock Canyon, twenty-five miles north of Mojave. The only passengers were Robert M. Briggs, a well-known politician, and a young girl, Emma Martin. They ordered the driver to throw down the Wells Fargo express box, which, when smashed open, contained a measly twenty dollars. Turning their attention to the two passengers, they were frustrated to get little more than that from Briggs, who had furtively hidden his greenbacks and gold coin. The bandidos relieved the girl and the driver of their gold watches, then ordered the stage on.[18]

Before Paul could get on their trail, the three desperadoes again fled back to Los Angeles County. Officers there learned that Santos Sotelo sold one of the gold watches to a fence in Santa Monica. On the afternoon of January 20, 1877, the three bandidos posted themselves just west of Newhall on the stage road from Los Angeles to Ventura. As the stage approached, Santos Sotelo rode off, apparently fearful of being recognized. Francisco Sotelo and Tapia, armed with shotguns, allowed the coach to pass, then rode along leisurely behind it. Suddenly they spurred their horses and rode past the stage. As the coach reached an incline, they turned, one on each side of the road, and, leveling their shotguns, ordered the driver to halt. The driver and his two passengers were relieved of their watches and twenty-five dollars in cash. They broke open the Wells Fargo box and took another fifty dollars. It was a very poor haul.[19]

Los Angeles police officer Ramon Benitez, who had played a prominent role in the manhunt for Tiburcio Vasquez three years earlier, investigated the stage robbery and soon identified the Sotelos and Tapia as the bandidos. On January 31 he captured Tapia in Los Angeles. Tapia pled guilty to the robbery and was sentenced to seven years in San Quentin. The Sotelo brothers, fearing a similar fate, fled back to the Cerro Gordo mines. This was a mistake, for Paul had been investigating the Red Rock Canyon stage robbery for a month. He had managed to identify the Sotelos, either through an informant or a tip from Los Angeles lawmen.[20]

On February 7, 1877, Paul spotted Francisco Sotelo, alias Chico Lugo, in Lone Pine and placed him under arrest. Sotelo's friends hired a lawyer,

Francisco Sotelo, alias Chico
Lugo, the notorious stage
robber captured by Bob
Paul in Lone Pine in 1877.
Author's collection.

who filed a writ of habeas corpus in an effort to get the prisoner out of
jail. Paul was undeterred, and in a court hearing that day he produced
Robert Briggs, the passenger in the holdup. Briggs identified Francisco
Sotelo as one of the men who had robbed the stagecoach. The judge ordered
that Sotelo be brought to trial in Kern County, where Red Rock Canyon
is located. Now one of Sotelo's compadres named Diaz swore out a warrant
against Paul, charging him with impersonating an officer, evidently because
he was a private detective. Paul was arrested, but a sympathetic judge promptly
released him. The habeas corpus hearing was scheduled for the following
day, but Sotelo's lawyer failed to appear, and the bandido was remanded
into Paul's custody. To make sure he had no more trouble, Paul met with
his friend Tom Passmore, sheriff of Inyo County, who deputized him to
take the prisoner to Bakersfield. Local Hispanics believed that Sotelo was
innocent and were angered by these events, which exacerbated longstanding ill will between them and Anglos.[21]

Paul bundled Francisco Sotelo into a stagecoach and brought him in irons to Bakersfield. At his preliminary examination, the witnesses to the holdup could not or would not identify him. Robert Briggs, who had testified against him in Lone Pine, either was not present or recanted his prior testimony, perhaps due to fear of the outlaws. Sotelo was freed, much to the anger and dismay of Paul. The disgusted Wells Fargo man boarded a return stagecoach, crossing the Sierra Nevada to Mojave. There he learned that a large money shipment was to be sent north to Darwin, and he received instructions to guard it. Before he could board the northbound coach, Paul was notified that the shipment was delayed and that he would have to wait in Mojave until the next coach arrived. It was the luckiest day of his life. The driver, Billy Balch, left Paul at the stage station and started off with two passengers aboard. Paul's place next to the driver was taken by Jack Lloyd, a former shotgun messenger and unemployed whip who was looking for work on the stage line north of Darwin. It was an all-night trip, and Lloyd lay down in the front boot and went to sleep. Just before daybreak on February 14, 1877, as the coach was climbing the "big hill" thirty miles from Darwin, two bandidos rose up from behind the roadside brush, one on either side of the coach. Without any warning a shotgun roared. One of the bandits yelled, "Stop!" and Lloyd awoke and sat up in the boot. As he peered over the driver's footboard, a robber spotted him and fired his shotgun. The buckshot ripped into his head, splattering blood all over the boot and killing him instantly. The gunfire spooked the team, which bolted into a dead run up the hill. The other bandit fired again, and a lone buckshot pierced Balch's coat sleeve. The stage raced into Darwin with its bloody cargo.[22]

Reported the *Inyo Independent*, "It is very generally believed that the highwaymen intended this shot for R. H. Paul, the shot-gun messenger" in revenge for his "successful operations in corralling supposed stage robbers." Added the editor of the *Darwin Coso Mining News*, "Mexicans were greatly indignant . . . and we hear that threats were made that they 'would get even with him.' We shall expect to chronicle the death of Paul at any time unless these men are caught and punished." If the newspaper editors were correct, the killers were probably Francisco and Santos Sotelo.[23]

Wells Fargo and the state of California offered rewards of $800 for each of the murderers. Word of the murder was sent to Paul, who, along with the driver, Billy Balch, and Constable William Welch, set off on a manhunt

Santos Sotelo. He and his half brother, Chico Lugo, were suspected of laying a deadly ambush for Bob Paul in which another man was killed instead. Author's collection.

for the desperadoes. For more than a week they scoured the high desert, with no luck. To escape Paul's dragnet, the Sotelos fled back to Kern County. In the little Hispanic settlement of Panama, located three miles south of Bakersfield, they picked up a fellow desperado, Francisco Romero. Then the three embarked on one of the most reckless bandit sprees since the days of Tiburcio Vasquez. On February 23, 1877, near Tulare Lake, they robbed three riders, taking their horses and an extra mount, then continued on to the general store of Samuel A. Lobdell, on the west shore of the lake. They knocked down Lobdell, pistol-whipped him, and tied him up. Then they ransacked the store, stealing $200 in coin and goods, plus a valuable racehorse. Romero did not wear a mask, and Lobdell recognized him. The bandidos rode south, driving the horses in front of them. Soon they encountered three Italians and robbed them also. The next day, as the robbers rode by a camp of men who were building the West Side Canal, several laborers recognized the stolen horses. The workers pursued the band on horseback, and in a running gunfight the outlaws escaped.

The desperadoes returned to Panama, where they hid out in the bagnios and cantinas. After midnight on February 27 they stole a band of horses from the corral of an Anglo rancher near Panama, J. C. Crocker. With several of his hired hands, Crocker pursued them, but when the outlaws turned in their saddles and opened fire with pistols, Crocker and his men wisely gave up. Word was sent into Bakersfield, and a small posse led by Deputy Sheriff Harry Bludworth started after the robbers. Bludworth and his possemen caught up with the gang south of Bakersfield. In a blistering exchange of gunfire, Francisco Romero was unhorsed. He fled on foot into the brush and disappeared. The Sotelos, their saddle horses jaded from the pursuit, leaped onto fresh mounts and outran the posse.[24]

Deputy Bludworth returned the abandoned horses to Bakersfield and started out again after the gang the next day. First his posse found Romero hiding in the brush, and they sent him in irons to Bakersfield. Then they continued after the Sotelo brothers, spotting them the following day in a camp in the Tehachapi Mountains. Bludworth captured their horses and saddles while the brothers managed to escape on foot into the undergrowth. Searching in all directions, Bludworth's posse soon located boot prints and trailed the bandidos through the mountains to the ranch of George Reeg, a German farmer who lived four miles from the settlement of Tehachapi. No one in Reeg's cabin answered their call, so the posse followed the tracks south for another day. They lost the trail and returned to Reeg's ranch the next evening, March 3. Once again no one appeared to be home, but when one of the possemen discovered blood on the doorsteps, they broke into the locked cabin and encountered a horrific scene. The place had been ransacked, and Reeg lay dead in a back room, a bullet hole in his head.

Bludworth learned that one of the Sotelos had formerly worked for Reeg. Evidently the fugitives had gone there for shelter and had killed Reeg to get provisions and horses. Bludworth sent news of the murder to Tehachapi, then tracked the killers south across the Mojave Desert to the San Gabriel Mountains. He found that they had been at Elizabeth Lake, once a favorite hideout of Tiburcio Vasquez, and then had stolen three horses from the nearby ranch of Francisco "Chico" Lopez. The Sotelos rode into San Francisquito Canyon, which led through the San Gabriel Mountains to Los Angeles, then stopped and robbed a party of Chinese miners. By now Los Angeles lawmen were hunting the outlaws, so an exhausted Bludworth and his posse, after more than a week in the saddle, rode home to Bakersfield.[25]

Paul soon learned the fate of two of the gang. Southern California lawmen kept a lookout for them, and in April Francisco Sotelo, alias Chico Lugo, was captured in the San Bernardino Mountains. Because there were no witnesses to the murder of George Reeg, Francisco Sotelo was sent to Los Angeles to stand trial for the Newhall stage robbery. He pled guilty and got ten years in San Quentin. Francisco Romero was brought to Visalia and convicted of robbing Sam Lobdell in Tulare County. He received a five-year term in state prison. Santos Sotelo, for the time being, managed to elude the manhunt.[26]

Meanwhile, Paul recognized that the desolate and dangerous Cerro Gordo country was no place to raise a family. The nearest established town of any size was Visalia, and in May he moved Margaret and the children, John, Robert, Agnes, Mamie, and Loretta, from Calaveras two hundred miles south to their new home. In so doing, he left behind his friends and the community he had lived in for twenty-five years. But to Paul, his family came first, and he could not bear the long absences from home. Visalia, the oldest permanent inland settlement between Stockton and Los Angeles, was a pretty town of one thousand people with spectacular views of the snow-crested Sierra Nevada. It was situated in a massive oak grove watered by four large creeks that emptied onto the plain from the towering Sierra. Though Visalia had a red-light district, known as Spanishtown, the village was a booming center for business and agriculture. Much to Margaret's satisfaction, Visalia boasted churches and schools, clubs and societies. The congregation of the Catholic church there was a typical California mix, principally Irish and Hispanic. To the Pauls, it was a good place to raise children.[27]

After getting his family settled in, Paul returned to the Eastern Sierra. When he got a tip that Santos Sotelo had been spotted near Cerro Gordo, he and Constable Welch started in pursuit. They scoured Cerro Gordo, but Sotelo had many friends among the Mexican miners, who kept him secreted from the officers. Paul did manage to learn that Sotelo had a camp on the Owens River. He and Welch searched it that evening but found no trace of the fugitive. Sotelo, fearing capture by Paul, again fled back to Los Angeles County. A few weeks later, on July 6, he was spotted at Elizabeth Lake, on the edge of the Mojave Desert, by a young Californio, Rafael Lopez, who captured him at gunpoint. Sotelo was returned to Kern

County to face charges of robbing the stage in Red Rock Canyon. Paul interviewed him in the Bakersfield jail. Sotelo admitted that he had been hiding in Cerro Gordo at the time of Paul's search and that he rode to Los Angeles the morning after learning that Paul had located his camp. Eventually he pled guilty to the robbery charge. Unlike his brother, who had escaped punishment for the same holdup, Santos Sotelo received a fifteen-year jolt in San Quentin.[28]

While Paul rode the lonely stage roads of the Eastern Sierra, Margaret busied herself making a new home. But just three months later their two little girls, Mamie, now five, and Loretta, two, came down with whooping cough. The disease was highly contagious and little understood; no cure existed, and in most cases death resulted. Her husband was on the route between Mojave and Darwin, and she sent him an urgent wire. Paul rushed home by stagecoach, arriving in time for Mamie's death on June 20. Three days later little Loretta succumbed too. The couple's grief can only be imagined. Wrote the editor of the *Visalia Weekly Delta*, "Mr. and Mrs. Paul, although but recently settled in Visalia, are well known to many of our citizens, and by such highly esteemed for their excellent qualities; and we feel assured that many will extend with us the heartfelt sympathy which this bereavement awakens." The Pauls' marriage was strong, and soon, perhaps to make up for their loss, they conceived another child.[29]

Paul stayed with his grieving wife as long as he could, but in late July he had to return to the Eastern Sierra. His principal job now was riding shotgun on the Kern and Inyo Stage Company coaches between Darwin and the Southern Pacific depot in Mojave. This was a dusty, 125-mile, 22-hour trip on rough roads through high desert plains and mountains. The *Darwin Coso Mining News* recorded Paul's comings and goings on stages that fall and winter. Paul's other principal route was on the stage road between Lone Pine and Mojave. He happened to be stopping over in Lone Pine on February 10, 1878, when his friend, Inyo County Sheriff Tom Passmore, met a tragic fate. In a camp outside of town, a Mexican, Gumesindo Palacio, and several compadres attempted to rape a Paiute Indian woman. They were driven off by an Indian known as Dick. Then the outlaws rode into Lone Pine and took drinks in the saloon owned by Palacio's uncle, Frank Debeney. The barkeeper was a hardcase who had once been jailed for selling liquor to Indians; two men had been slain in gunfights in his saloon. After downing a few drinks, the desperadoes decided to kill the Indian, Dick, to prevent him from testifying against them. Palacio found the Paiute in a nearby cabin and, after calling him to the door, shot him dead. Dick had lived in Lone Pine for several years; he had worked as a hired man and had been well liked by the whites. Word of his death spread like wildfire, and soon a crowd of determined citizens, Paul among them, trapped Palacio and his compadres in Debeney's saloon.[30]

Lone Pine had no police or constable, but Sheriff Passmore happened to be in town. It was 10:00 P.M. when the townsfolk awoke him. Passmore elbowed his way through the crowd, but found the saloon door barricaded. As the sheriff broke it down, Debeney and Palacio gunned him down. Passmore died instantly. To Paul's consternation, the crowd, which had merely wanted to help arrest Palacio, now became an enraged mob. They opened fire and riddled the saloon with lead. After an hour-long siege, Debeney fled out the rear. He was captured and then summarily shot to death. Several hours later Palacio made a break, but before he could cross the street he was sieved with bullets and buckshot. At 4:00 A.M. another desperado showed his head, prompting another barrage of gunfire. Paul had no law enforcement authority to control the mob, and he was now busy preparing his waybills and loading bullion at the Wells Fargo office. By daylight the down stage was ready to leave, and Paul swung aboard. The saloon siege was still under way, and Paul saw that Debeney's body had been left where it fell in the street as a warning to outlaws. Two days later his stage arrived in Visalia, and Paul's account of the bloodshed was the first to reach the outside world. He later learned the story's postscript. Just after he left town, five Hispanics in the saloon surrendered. Three were peaceable customers, but two, Carlos Fermin and Eustacio Santoyo, were desperadoes. They were ordered out of town. At ten o'clock that morning a traveler came in and reported that their bullet-riddled bodies were in the roadside sagebrush four miles south of Lone Pine. In all, six men had been slain that bloody night.[31]

Two months later, on April 14, Margaret and her husband were overjoyed when she gave birth to a son, Thomas Alfred. Paul was across the Sierra when he received the news, and he was not able to return to Visalia for another six weeks. On May 26, Margaret, her husband, and their brood trooped to the Catholic church, where the baby was baptized by Father Valentin Aguilera, Visalia's Hispanic priest. Despite their delight, Margaret's stay in Visalia was not a happy one. She looked forward to a day when she could find a new home and leave the bitter memories of their dead daughters behind. Her husband's long absences, coupled with worry about his safety, were a constant strain.[32]

For more than five years Paul had dutifully obeyed instructions from Wells Fargo as the company sent him from one stage and rail line to another, from California to the high deserts of Nevada and Utah, and finally to the Eastern Sierra. He had transported millions of dollars in gold and silver bullion and had never lost an ounce. During the month of July 1877 alone, as Paul later pointed out, "the stages on which he was messenger carried out gold bullion valued at $670,000." Prominent Wells Fargo officials, including general superintendent John J. Valentine, assistant superintendent L. F. Rowell, and chief detective James B. Hume, considered him one of their best and most reliable men. Now, one final assignment from Wells Fargo would change his life forever.[33]

CHAPTER SIX

Wells Fargo Detective

On August 30, 1878, Wells Fargo's John J. Valentine penned a letter that would prove momentous for Bob Paul. Written in San Francisco and marked "confidential," it read: "Mr. R. H. Paul, Special Messenger, etc., Wells, Fargo & Co's. Express. Dear Sir: The enclosed documents relative to the Maricopa Wells and Picacho robberies explain themselves. The man who committed at least one of the Picacho robberies has since been killed by civil officers at Tucson. Please go to Arizona ostensibly as a stage employee or under any guise you may deem best, and look over the country Yuma to Tucson to see if Maricopa robbers particularly may be apprehended, and if future protection is possible. This letter with your signature hereon will identify and enable you to get money for expenses, when necessary, of our agents, and to insure their cooperation with your efforts. Copies to Yuma, Florence and Tucson agents which they must treat confidentially."[1]

To Paul, it was just another assignment from Wells Fargo. He packed his grip bag, his six-shooter, and his messenger's shotgun, kissed his wife and children goodbye, and caught a stage to Los Angeles. From there he boarded a train to the railhead at Yuma. The moment Paul crossed the Colorado River, he became the most experienced lawman in Arizona Territory. As was customary for railroad and express detectives in that era, he obtained an appointment as a deputy from Crawley P. Dake, Arizona's U.S. marshal, so that he would have the legal authority to make arrests throughout the territory. Prior to Paul's arrival, Deputy U. S. Marshal Joseph W. Evans had handled Wells Fargo detective work on a case-by-case basis. Evans's Wells Fargo assignments soon dried up. This made Evans very bitter, which, years later, would have severe repercussions for Paul.[2]

Arizona was a territory at the time, and it would not achieve statehood for another thirty-four years. Its craggy, arid mountains and vast deserts were home to less than ten thousand people in 1870, a number that grew to only forty thousand by 1880. Roads were poor and travel was difficult. There were no railroad lines until the Southern Pacific constructed a bridge across the Colorado River in 1877; the line to New Mexico would not be completed for three more years. Wells Fargo was a new commodity in Arizona Territory. The company had opened its first Arizona office, a stop on the Butterfield overland stage route, in Tucson in 1860. By 1870, there were only three Wells Fargo offices in the entire territory. During the next decade, gold and silver strikes, especially at Tombstone, brought rapid development and a need for increased express service. By 1881 the number of Wells Fargo offices in the territory had grown to thirty-six. In contrast to its operations in California, Wells Fargo did not run stagecoach lines in Arizona. Instead, the company paid a fee to independent stage lines for the right to transport its express shipments on their coaches. As Arizona's economic development rapidly increased, Wells Fargo carried more and more bullion shipments from the mining camps and brought in cash payrolls for the miners. Such shipments, in turn, invited the attentions of express robbers.[3]

Although California had suffered scores of stage robberies during the late 1850s and 1860s, the first such holdup did not take place in Arizona until 1875. The following year another occurred, but things really took off in 1877 and 1878, when the territory experienced sixteen. Arizona's boosters and businessmen were outraged. In May 1877 the *Prescott Weekly Arizona Miner* complained about the increasing stage robberies and expressed the fear that "travel in Arizona will be entirely suspended by capitalists." The following year, Arizona Supreme Court justice Charles Silent warned that "this lawlessness . . . is paralyzing business."[4]

Because stage robbers often robbed multiple coaches over a wide region, local officers could not always spend sufficient time, energy, and money to track them down. Manhunts were expensive, since lawmen had to eat, pay for lodging, obtain feed for their horses, and bribe informants. Some sheriffs were uncooperative, even mercenary. Once, after two stagecoach holdups on the Flagstaff–Prescott route, Wells Fargo's agent in Prescott appealed to Yavapai County Sheriff Joseph R. Walker. But, as the agent reported, "the sheriff . . . declined most positively to go out unless paid" and demanded $1,000 to hunt the bandits. By the summer of 1878 it was obvious to John Valentine that Wells Fargo needed a good man in Arizona. His two special officers, Jim Hume and John Thacker, had their hands full investigating holdups, thefts, and embezzlements in California, Nevada, Oregon, and Idaho. In August Jim Hume visited Arizona to look into a pair of robberies near Tucson. The case came to a quick close when the bandit, Bill Brazelton, was slain by a posse led by Sheriff Charlie Shibell. Hume, who loathed the desert heat and dreaded his visits to Arizona, undoubtedly pressed Valentine for Paul's appointment.[5]

Lawmen with more than ten years of experience were uncommon on the American frontier, and officers like Paul, with three decades of law enforcement under their gunbelts, were then unknown in Arizona Territory. In Arizona, as in California and other parts of the West, most local sheriffs were either public-spirited citizens or politicians using the position as a stepladder to higher office. Few sheriffs served more than a couple of two-year elected terms. In addition, there was no formalized police training during Paul's time, and lawmen had to learn on the job. As sheriffs, deputies, and police drifted in and out of office, few acquired the experience necessary to become a successful officer and detective. On the Arizona frontier, the work was made even more difficult by the great dangers faced by lawmen. Almost every man carried a gun; most arrests, therefore, were of armed suspects. Because courts and juries treated those who resisted arrest very leniently, lawmen were frequently met with violence. Manhunts took place in wild, desolate country, with little access to water or food. On one such desert manhunt, Paul would come close to death. The wilds of Arizona attracted tough men: miners, soldiers, adventurers, gamblers, cowboys, fugitives, and desperadoes, to say nothing of Apache Indians. Policing such a frontier was more than difficult.[6]

In this atmosphere, Paul found that his main role as Wells Fargo detective was to assist inexperienced local officers in investigating robberies and tracking down suspects. He did not operate alone, repeatedly teaming up with sheriffs, city marshals, and constables. His frank, good-natured, and humorous personality won him friends quickly. Many of the Arizona settlers had come from California, and if they did not know Paul personally, they knew his reputation. Paul's willingness to cooperate with local officers and his vast experience also created fellowship with Arizona lawmen. Before long, "Detective Paul," as the newspapers called him, was one of the best-known peace officers in Arizona.

Paul's assignment in Arizona was twofold: to ride shotgun on coaches carrying heavy treasure shipments and to investigate holdups. His official title was "special officer." Wells Fargo paid him the same salary as detective that he had earned as a messenger, $125 a month. But now he had additional expenses: lodging; hiring horses, wagons, and guides for manhunts; printing wanted posters; and paying informants. These costs ranged from $50 to $300 per month and were reimbursed by Wells Fargo.[7]

Paul arrived in Tucson in early September 1878. At first he may have believed that his Wells Fargo assignment would be short-lived, for he left Margaret and the children behind in Visalia. He had no way of knowing it then, but Tucson, the Pima County seat, would be his home for the rest of his life. Sprawling across a sun-baked desert valley overlooked by craggy peaks, Tucson was watered by the Santa Cruz River, a shallow stream that ran north from Mexico. Tucson's long, narrow streets were lined with hundreds of single-story adobe buildings. The thick mud-brick walls of the houses kept out much of the extreme summer heat. Seven miles northeast of town was Fort Lowell, one of the Southwest's principal army posts.

Tucsonans rose late, took siestas in the afternoon, and retired even later. For many of its male citizens, drinking and gambling were the principal pastimes. The southern end of town was the red-light district, known as El Barrio Libre (The Free Neighborhood). Although gringos would eventually become dominant, the Old Pueblo, as Tucson had long been known, was Mexican in look, language, and culture. During the 1870s, Tucson's native Hispanic population was augmented by a significant influx of Sonorans. Many came to Arizona to find work and to escape the political instability and Apache troubles of northern Mexico. These Mexican immigrants were assiduously courted by officials of both the Democratic and Republican Parties, who encouraged them to become naturalized citizens and register to vote. Only a minority did. Tucson's population was almost 64 percent Spanish speaking. Although the arrival of the railroad in 1880 meant that Anglos began to dominate politically and socially, as late as 1891, a writer for the *San Francisco Chronicle* called Tucson a "decidedly foreign town, foreign in its looks, in its habits, its population . . . it is no more American than

Meyer Street in Tucson as Bob Paul first saw it in 1878, showing many typical adobe dwellings. Courtesy of the Arizona Historical Society/Tucson, 14843.

the northwest province of British India is European." By 1900, Tucson was still almost 55 percent Spanish speaking. Paul, familiar with both the culture and language, was very much at home in the Old Pueblo.[8]

As John Valentine had explained in his letter to Paul, there had been a recent rash of stage robberies on the roads between Tucson and Phoenix. The lone bandit Bill Brazelton had held up coaches north of Tucson on July 31 and August 14. Five days later he was slain by a posse led by Pima County Sheriff Charles Shibell. Three more stage robberies had also taken place on the night of the 14th. Five Anglo road agents armed with shot-guns had robbed a coach near Maricopa Wells, south of Phoenix. Four Mexican bandits had stopped both the northbound and southbound stage-coaches near Desert Station, twenty-eight miles north of Tucson. Embar-rassingly, Joseph W. Evans, the one-armed Wells Fargo detective and deputy U. S. marshal, had been the sole passenger in the second coach. Evans had been wakened from a sound sleep and robbed by the bandidos. The fact that he had not put up any resistance was undoubtedly a factor in Valentine's

ordering Paul to Arizona. Wells Fargo officials were desperate to put a stop
to the robberies. Wrote an exasperated L. F. Rowell, the company's assistant superintendent in San Francisco, "We have lost nearly $16,000 in
the past six weeks."[9]

In Tucson, Joseph Evans, accompanied by a small posse, started on the
trail of the Mexican bandidos who had robbed him. He crossed the border
into Sonora, where he wisely obtained permission from Mexican officials
to continue the hunt. A detachment of cavalry was assigned to assist him.
When heavy rains wiped out the tracks, Evans returned to Tucson on
September 1, having made an eighteen-day ride. Reported the *Tucson Arizona
Star*, "It is a difficult matter to catch criminals in Sonora, as they are aided
by their kind from place to place and concealed from the authorities."
The next day yet another stage was robbed, this one twenty miles west of
Maricopa Wells, on the route from Phoenix to Yuma. The robbers were two
Mexicans and an ex-convict from Nevada, James Rhodes. They stole several
bars of silver, which Rhodes cut up into small pieces and used to pay his
way toward New Mexico. This made it relatively simple for Evans to track
him, and the Wells Fargo detective managed to arrest Rhodes near Camp
Thomas. Evans brought his prisoner into Tucson on September 16.[10]

By this time Paul had arrived in Tucson and gathered information on
the Mexican suspects, who were in hiding across the border. Contrary to
Valentine's suggestion that he adopt a disguise, Paul worked openly as a
Wells Fargo detective. He found that the leader of the band was Guada-
lupe Celaya, a notorious desperado from Sonora. His gang was extremely
dangerous. On September 2 five of them had murdered Captain John H.
Adams, former sheriff from San Jose, California, and his mining partner,
Cornelius Finley, in Davidson Canyon, about twenty miles southeast of
Tucson. Adams was a famous lawman, widely known as the nemesis of
Tiburcio Vasquez. His murder created a public uproar, and a posse of private
citizens pursued the killers into Mexico. Now Paul started for the border
in a rented wagon and team. Like Evans, Paul sought and received the
cooperation of Mexican authorities. He was completely unfamiliar with
both Arizona and Mexico, so he hired a guide and managed to trace the
stage robbers to Altar. There he arrested one of the gang, Joaquin Franco,
and lodged him in the local *calabozo*.[11]

Because Franco was a Mexican citizen, the officials in Altar were reluctant to hold him. Paul wired Wells Fargo headquarters in San Francisco
for assistance. Assistant superintendent Rowell promptly dispatched a

letter to the U. S. Consul at Guaymas, Mexico: "Paul has one under arrest in Altar and is endeavoring to induce the Mexican authorities to hold him until proper papers can be procured from the government of Arizona, but it is extremely doubtful if they will do so. Will you please try and induce the governor of Sonora to issue the necessary order to the prefects on the border to deliver up these marauders to our officers on a proper showing being made of their guilt? We will be obliged to withdraw our express from Southern Arizona unless we can put a stop to the frequent robberies by these brigands from a sister republic."[12]

The result was an exchange of diplomatic correspondence between Vicente Mariscal, governor of Sonora, and the American consul. Under Mexican law, only that country's president could order a Mexican citizen extradited. While Governor Mariscal attempted to obtain extradition authority, he ordered a general roundup of the Guadalupe Celaya band. His officers captured two of the killers of Adams and Finley, Gregorio Arce and Florentino Sais, and jailed them in Magdalena. A troop of Mexican soldiers tracked six of the gang to their hideout in the mountains near Campas, killing one, wounding another, and capturing the rest. The wounded bandit confessed that he and the dead man had helped kill Adams and Finley, while the other four had been responsible for robbing several of the stages north of Tucson. Another of the band, Nestor Estrada, was arrested and jailed in Arizpe. Several months later, in January 1879, gang member Antonio Rodriguez was slain in a shootout with citizens in Tubutama. Finally, on February 2, 1879, Mexican border guards shot and killed the leader, Guadalupe Celaya, in a gunfight near Magdalena. But despite diplomatic efforts by American officials, none of the captured outlaws was ever extradited to the United States to face charges of stage robbery and murder. In the spring of 1879, Governor Mariscal was deposed in a coup and, apparently as a result of the political unrest, the imprisoned gang members were all set free.[13]

Paul gained valuable experience on his manhunt in Mexico. He found that its officials were generally willing to assist him, provided that he obtained permission to cross the border and complied with Mexican laws and customs. He also made important contacts and friendships with Mexican officers. At the same time, he found that Sonora was in a period of civil strife, and its criminal justice system was exceedingly lax. In the years to come, Paul would make many manhunts into Mexico, and the lessons he learned on his first trip south of the border would serve him well.

Back in Tucson, Paul was soon dispatched on another manhunt for stage robbers. On November 11, 1878, two road agents stopped the Prescott–Yuma stage six miles north of Date Creek Station. Seizing the Wells Fargo box, they shook it and found it so light they did not bother to break it open. They searched the coach for bullion but did not rob its two passengers. Paul started an investigation, and Jim Hume traveled from California by rail and stagecoach to assist. When Hume's train reached Yuma, he dashed off a wry note to his future wife, Lida Munson: "This is the most God forsaken place I ever saw. The buildings adobe, the streets sand, and the air full of dust. Not ten righteous persons in the place. One-third the population is Mexican. Business places are mostly saloons. The streets are lined day and night with Indians. Males and females are nearly nude, but pretty good looking."[14]

Hume boarded a coach for the grueling forty-eight-hour ride to Date Creek, sixty miles southwest of Prescott. From there he continued on to Prescott, where he met Paul. The two Wells Fargo detectives suspected that the stage robbers were a pair of suspicious strangers who were camped in the mountains forty miles west of town. Paul started for their hideout, followed by Hume the next day, Thanksgiving. Hume spent the night in a lonely cabin in the mountains thirty miles west of Prescott. He wrote to his fiancé, "Special Officer R. H. Paul and myself had information of two fellows camped in these mountains, upon whom we looked with suspicion as stage robbers. Their camp was ten miles from this cabin. Paul reached here last night and learned that our fellows broke camp yesterday and 'lit out.' Paul started at daylight this morning in pursuit, leaving a note advising me to remain here until I heard from him. So I am in the greatest state of anxiety and uncertainty. . . . If I could determine the direction Paul has taken I should undertake to join him."[15]

Hume ate a simple Arizona Thanksgiving meal of pork, beans, and coffee. "I had a very good supper," he wrote. "Was hungry and enjoyed it." That night Paul rode in with one of the suspects in tow, as a relieved Hume recounted: "Paul has just come in with one man, the other is thought to have gone toward Prescott. I take this one in to Prescott and Paul will go in pursuit of the other. We start at daylight. Think they are the men who stopped the stage the 11th, but doubt about being able to convict." After several days of searching, Paul managed to capture the second man and jailed him in Prescott. Contrary to Hume's private doubts, the detectives

Bob Paul's friend and colleague
James B. Hume, chief detective
for Wells Fargo, in 1879.
Author's collection.

told the local newspaper editor that they were "confident that they are
the roosters who made the attempt." However, at their preliminary examination on December 4, Justice A. O. Noyes ordered the pair released for
lack of evidence.[16]

Paul and Hume, much disappointed, returned to Tucson, where Hume
penned another letter to his fiancé: "I do so dread the three hundred
miles of staging from here to Yuma. I am almost tempted to say, 'damn
Arizona, and damn the staging.'" Much as he disliked Arizona, Hume
shared Paul's fondness for Tucson: "This is a pretty nice town. Would not
mind living here. The place contains some six to seven thousand inhabitants,
four-fifths of whom are Spanish or Mexican. Some terribly nice looking
Spanish women. . . . The buildings are all one story and built of adobe.
Roofs are flat and covered with brush and earth. Not a half dozen houses

in town have floors." Hume returned to California, but he would be back in Arizona with Paul sooner than he would have expected or wanted. Meanwhile, the *Tucson Citizen* reported that "Robert Paul has been appointed by Wells Fargo & Co. chief detective in this [Arizona's] department."[17]

During the next year Paul made numerous visits to Prescott, a picturesque mountain town one hundred miles north of Phoenix, which served as the territorial capital until 1889. There he became acquainted with Virgil Earp, a Prescott constable, John H. Behan, former county sheriff, and the notorious gambler John H. "Doc" Holliday. Virgil Earp, the elder brother of Wyatt Earp, had settled in Prescott a year earlier with his Irish-born wife, Allie, running a sawmill and driving stagecoaches before being elected constable. Behan had been in Arizona since the early 1860s. A popular Democratic politician, he served as deputy sheriff in Prescott, then was elected successively as Yavapai County recorder in 1868, sheriff in 1871, and member of the territorial legislature in 1873. Doc Holliday made extended visits to Prescott in the fall of 1879 and during the following year. All three men would play prominent roles in Paul's life.[18]

In the early morning hours of May 5, 1879, as the Maricopa stage was three miles south of Phoenix, it was halted by a lone highwayman who appeared from the blackness. He demanded the express box, then ordered the stage on. At daylight lawmen rode out from Phoenix to investigate, but no trace of the road agent was found. Paul was in Phoenix investigating this holdup when he got word from Margaret that their thirteen-month-old son, Thomas Alfred, had suddenly fallen ill with meningitis back in Visalia. Paul rushed back to California by stagecoach and train. By the time he arrived in Visalia the baby was gone, having died on May 23. This was the third child the couple had lost in less than two years, and they were overcome with grief. For Margaret, Visalia was a horrible place that had taken three of her beloved children. She refused to spend another day there. The Pauls promptly packed two of their children, Robert, age twelve, and Agnes, ten, and their belongings onto a stagecoach for the long journey to the wilds of Arizona. Their oldest son, John, age fifteen, was then living with his aunts in San Francisco and attending Heald College, a business school. For the younger two children, the trip to Arizona must have been the adventure of a lifetime. Though the springtime desert was in bloom, stagecoach travel was slow, hot, dusty, and arduous, and, once in Arizona, there was always the threat of an Apache raid. Margaret's thoughts when they reached Tucson can only be imagined. The dusty, sun-baked adobe pueblo was a far cry from the winding streets of New Bedford or even the oak-encrusted hills of Calaveras. For Margaret, Tucson's one saving grace was its Catholicism. Since the Old Pueblo was predominately Mexican, it had a large Catholic population and an active church. Paul's grieving wife could still attend Mass daily.[19]

The Pauls moved into a rented house at 501 Stone Avenue South, and Margaret enrolled young Robert and Agnes in school. Agnes attended St. Joseph's Female Academy, a large, single-story adobe building next door to San Agustin Church, where she soon distinguished herself as an honor student. Paul liked Tucson and, despite Margaret's misgivings, they decided to stay. Margaret was willing to follow her husband anywhere, as long as her children could be raised safely and receive a good education. Her spirits were lifted when John graduated from Heald College in December 1879. The boy was a few weeks shy of sixteen—four years older than his father was when he started out on his own. Paul no doubt expected John to begin working as a clerk in one of the big San Francisco business houses. But Margaret had other ideas. A strong-willed woman who never shirked from influencing her children, she missed John terribly. It was no surprise that the youth was soon in Tucson, living with his parents. John followed in his father's footsteps by going to work as an expressman in Wells Fargo's Tucson office.[20]

No sooner had Paul moved his family to Tucson than he faced a new wave of stage robberies. On June 10, 1879, a coach left Prescott and proceeded three miles before it was stopped by a lone robber wearing a barley-sack mask. After securing the Wells Fargo box, the masked bandit ordered the driver to go on. Ten days later, on the night of June 20, a road agent stopped the southbound stagecoach at the same place it had been robbed on May 5. This time the driver was line superintendent Jim Stewart, famous for his exploits on the old Overland Stage Line in Wyoming. The highwayman, after ordering Stewart to throw out the strongbox and mail pouch, allowed the stage to proceed. In each case local officers could find no trace of the robber.[21]

Paul was in Prescott when he got word of the June 20th robbery. He investigated it and the two previous holdups and concluded that the same man had perpetrated them all. Three weeks later, on the night of July 10, the southbound coach left Phoenix. Its treasure shipment was guarded by Wells Fargo messenger Billy Blankenship. Seven miles out of town Blankenship spotted two men in the moonlight, crouching behind a fallen tree. The two stood up and ordered the driver to halt. Blankenship swung up his sawed-off shotgun and fired one barrel. He missed, and the highwaymen turned loose their shotguns. Blankenship reeled on the seat, riddled with buckshot. Although both hands were wounded, he managed to fire again. One of the road agents yelled out an oath, and the messenger thought he hit him. But Blankenship was too badly wounded to fight any more. The bandits, covering the driver, directed him to throw down the mail pouches and the express box, which he did. Then they ordered the stage on. Unknown to the robbers, eighteen bars of bullion worth $30,000 were on board. The stage soon met the northbound coach, and the wounded messenger was loaded aboard and brought back into Phoenix for medical treatment.[22]

Maricopa County Undersheriff Hiram C. McDonald immediately rode out to the scene. A hundred-yard trail led to the broken express box and mailbags. The mail was scattered about, and horses' tracks led two miles west, where another mail sack was found. The loss was $700 cash plus $25,000 in checks and drafts, which were not negotiable and were discarded by the bandits. McDonald and a posseman found and then lost the bandits' tracks. McDonald worked up the case for two days and learned that just before the holdup, two Phoenix youths, Lafayette Price Hickey and Frank Mayhew, had mounted their horses and headed south toward the holdup scene. He found that Hickey's horse had a defect in the left front hoof that matched identically the track left by one robber's horse. McDonald arrested Hickey and Mayhew on July 12 and lodged them in the Phoenix jail. Hickey, not quite eighteen, was one of the many children of farmer Isaac Hickey. Frank Mayhew was Price Hickey's brother-in-law.[23]

Bob Paul immediately headed for Phoenix to assist in the investigation. He was joined by J. H. Mahoney, a special agent for the for the U.S. Post Office. Paul interrogated both Hickey and Mayhew but was unable to get any admissions from them. The pair insisted that they had been asleep in the Hickey family farmhouse the night of the holdup. Although both admitted borrowing a rifle, ammunition, and a saddle prior to the robbery, they insisted that they were preparing for a deer hunt. The two were brought into court to face charges, and their preliminary hearing lasted a full week. Numerous witnesses testified, providing a substantial chain of circumstantial evidence against them. Henry Garfias, the noted Phoenix lawman, swore that Hickey's mount made one set of tracks found at the crime scene. Both Hickey and Mayhew took the stand in their own defense, and several witnesses, including Hickey's parents, provided them with alibis. The judge found that there was probable cause to hold them to answer, and he released them on bail to await action by the grand jury. But when the case went before the grand jury in October, that body refused to indict the pair. A chagrined Paul learned a lesson about the influence of express companies and railroads in frontier Arizona. Although Wells Fargo and the Southern Pacific wielded tremendous political and economic power, average citizens were suspicious of these large corporations. That distrust, coupled with the circumstantial nature of the evidence and the alibi testimony, was enough to convince the grand jurors to set Hickey and Mayhew free.[24]

Within two weeks after the Phoenix preliminary hearing, Paul was again on the trail of a stage robber. On the night of August 8, 1879, the southbound coach was held up by a lone highwayman three miles outside of Phoenix. This was the same general area as the prior three holdups. The driver handed over the Wells Fargo box, which proved to be empty. The bandit was unlucky; the stagecoach on the previous night had carried twenty large bars of gold bullion valued at $29,000. Paul was still in Phoenix and quickly got word of the holdup. He immediately set out for the robbery scene and trailed the bandit for more than a mile across open fields, finding the broken express box. At a spot near the Salt River the tracks joined the dusty highway, where they were obliterated. Paul brought the express box back to Phoenix, raised a posse, and set off again after the highwayman. His efforts were in vain, and he returned to Phoenix empty-handed. Jim Hume soon arrived from California to assist him, but they could not crack the case. Whether the bandit was Hickey or Mayhew, then free on bail, or someone else altogether, they could never determine.[25]

These repeated stage robberies alarmed the territorial government. On August 12, acting governor John J. Gosper issued a proclamation declaring that "the forcible stopping of stages . . . is becoming alarmingly frequent" and offering a $300 reward for the arrest and conviction of stage robbers and $500 for each bandit killed in the act of holding up a stagecoach. This dead-or-alive reward had little effect. On November 19, 1879, a coach was held up near Skull Valley, fourteen miles west of Prescott, by two bandits, Thomas Francis and William Morgan, alias David Williams. Three days later Sheriff Joseph Walker got a tip that two men matching the robbers' descriptions were living in a cabin in Thompson Valley. He raised a small posse, including Al Sieber, the famous chief of scouts, and Prescott City Marshal James Dodson, that arrived at the hideout the night of November 23. Instead of attempting the arrest at night, the lawmen went to a

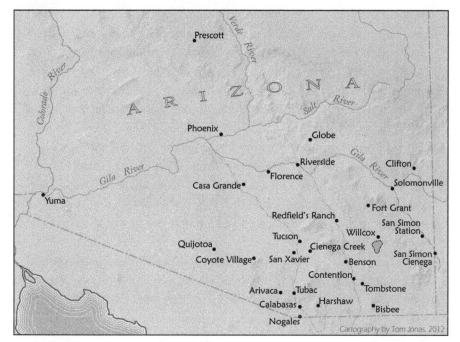

Bob Paul's Arizona

neighboring cabin and stayed there until the following day, when the two desperadoes rode up unexpectedly. Sheriff Walker ordered them to surrender, and Francis wheeled his horse and went for his six-shooter. City Marshal Dodson shot him out of the saddle, killing him. Morgan wisely raised his hands skyward. The posse brought Morgan into Prescott, leaving Francis's body at the ranch. Paul soon arrived in Prescott, and he and Sieber rode out to Thompson Valley to attend the inquest into the fatal shooting. "Mr. Paul is anxious to see the corpse," reported the *Prescott Arizona Miner*, "and may be able to tell . . . from what penitentiary the deceased escaped." But Paul was apparently unable to further identify the dead bandit. His fellow highwayman, Morgan, was convicted of robbery and sent to the territorial prison at Yuma.[26]

A few days later Paul was called on to investigate an extremely violent stage holdup. On the night of November 27, the southbound coach left Prescott with William C. Ayers at the ribbons and only one passenger, Billy Thomas, former superintendent of the Tip Top Mine located near Gillett, about fifty miles north of Phoenix. The coach was stopped two miles north of Gillett by three Mexicans, Fermin Fimbres,

Gumecindo Moraga, and Demetrio Dominguez. The latter was a youth, about seventeen years old, who carried a grudge against Thomas for firing him from his job as a woodcutter. As the coach climbed a hill, the three ran forward, two on the right side and one on the left. One of the robbers, in advance on the right, shoved his pistol through the window and fired at Thomas point-blank, setting his clothes on fire. Another bandido opened fire on Ayers, while the third seized the wheel lines and ordered the unscathed driver down. At that the bandit on the left fired into the stage at Thomas, then drew a bayonet and, leaning into the window, stabbed him. Dominguez climbed into the stage and dragged out the desperately wounded Thomas, dumping him into the roadway. Dominguez pointed his six-gun at the prostrate victim's head, but before he could fire he was stopped by his compadres.[27]

The highwaymen ordered Ayers to turn over his pistol, watch, and money. Then they had him take down Thomas's trunk, which they looted, taking three watches. After emptying the mail sacks they went through Thomas's pockets, removing his pocket watch and valuables. When the driver asked why they had shot Thomas, one responded, "Este hombre no es bueno" ("That man is no good").[28]

The outlaws unhitched the stage horses and rode off toward Prescott. The badly wounded Thomas was brought into Gillett, where he died the next day. News of the brutal murder created public outrage. A four-man posse led by Johnny Behan immediately left Gillett, while two other posses, one from Prescott and another from Phoenix, also started out. Paul was in Phoenix and promptly headed north to Prescott, where he met with Al Sieber, one of the finest trackers in the Southwest. With a small posse, Paul and Sieber trailed the killers across the Verde River six miles from Fort McDowell, then to the Salt River ten or twelve miles above its confluence with the Verde. From here they tracked the outlaws to an Indian camp, where they found hoofprints from four horses heading south toward the border. Soon a heavy winter rainstorm wiped out all traces of the animals.[29]

Paul and Sieber had been on the trail for several days, and now, low on food, they rode back to Fort McDowell for supplies. There they heard a rumor that the killers had been trapped near Tempe on the Salt River. This rumor, which proved false, took them on the wrong trail, and they returned to Prescott empty-handed. But Paul wasn't close to giving up. He got good descriptions of the bandits and learned that one was very young, with a dark, hairy mole on his chin. The detective kept up his hunt, and in early February 1880 he got word that a Mexican youth matching that description had been seen in Maricopa. From there Paul traced him to the Empire mining district and on February 3 found that he was in Tucson. After making what one newspaper called a "considerable search," Paul learned that the wanted man had left Tucson in a wagon with David Harshaw, a noted Indian fighter and miner for whom the town of Harshaw would soon be named.

Paul quickly hitched up his buggy and started after them, racing south on the road toward the Patagonia mining district. The lawman caught up with his quarry twenty miles south of Tucson. The wagon's driver proved to be Demetrio Dominguez. Harshaw had no idea he was in company with a much-wanted fugitive. Paul searched Dominguez and found one of the watches taken from Billy Thomas (the Wells Fargo detective had obtained detailed descriptions of each of Thomas's watches from a Prescott jeweler who had repaired them). Paul brought his young prisoner into Tucson that night. In the morning he managed to get Dominguez to admit being with the gang. The youth claimed that Fimbres and Moraga had forced him to participate in the holdup and that they, not he, had slain Billy Thomas.[30]

The next day Paul bundled his heavily ironed prisoner into a stagecoach and took him north to Prescott. There Ayers, the stage driver, identified Dominguez as one of the killers. It was later determined that the murder had actually occurred in Maricopa County, and in July Dominguez was taken to Phoenix to stand trial. In October he was convicted of the murder of Billy Thomas and sentenced to death. The young desperado was publicly hanged in Phoenix on November 26, 1880. Before Dominguez died he made a long confession, admitting his participation in the holdup but insisting that he was innocent of murder. Although there had been four previous lynchings in Phoenix, his was the first legal hanging in Maricopa County.[31]

Meanwhile, Paul teamed up for a quick manhunt with Pete Gabriel, a noted Arizona sheriff. Gabriel, like Paul, had been a peace officer in California, serving as a deputy sheriff in Los Angeles, where he played a prominent role in hunting the notorious Tiburcio Vasquez and lost a lung in a gunfight with another desperado. In January 1880 Gabriel captured a New Mexico horse thief named Hall, who promptly tunneled out of the county jail in Florence. Gabriel trailed him south and concluded that he was headed for Altar in Mexico. Stopping in Tucson, Gabriel enlisted Paul's help, and the two started for the border in a buckboard. Not far from the Mexico line they spotted a man on foot in the distance, and Gabriel recognized the fugitive. With Paul at the reins, they drove close. Gabriel suddenly leaped out with Winchester in hand and ordered Hall to surrender. At the same time Paul swung up his sawed-off shotgun, and Hall wisely raised his hands. When the lawmen brought their prisoner in, the *Tucson Citizen* heaped praised on them, saying, "Gabriel and Paul deserve great credit . . . in the capture of this offender, who is evidently one of an old cowboy gang, lately in New Mexico." This manhunt marked the beginning of a long friendship between Paul and Gabriel.[32]

During 1880 one of Paul's principal assignments was riding shotgun on the stage route between Tombstone and the railroad depot at Benson. In early June, when Wells Fargo's agent in Tucson resigned, Paul was appointed acting agent. But his expertise was in the field, not behind a desk, and soon he was in Florence, investigating yet another stage robbery. On the night of July 11, the northbound coach from Florence to Globe was held up by three highwaymen at Cane Springs Summit, near Riverside Station (now Kelvin), twenty-five miles from Florence. The bandits did not open the mailbags or bother the five passengers, but they took from the Wells Fargo box several packages valued at only ninety dollars. Paul joined local officers in a fruitless hunt for the road agents. He was not helped by citizens' descriptions, as witnesses alternately identified them as Mexicans and Americans. The next day he was in Globe, where $60,000 in bullion was being readied for shipment to Florence. Due to his concern about a second attack, Paul arranged for three private guards and a deputy sheriff to help him protect the stage. Before it left on July 13, eight adventurous passengers, including three women, clambered aboard. Paul and the four guards, heavily armed with shotguns and rifles, were ready for an assault, but it never came. Passengers and bullion arrived in Florence without incident. Then Paul joined Pinal County Sheriff Gabriel for another hard but fruitless hunt for the stage robbers in the mountainous country south of Globe.[33]

By this time Bob Paul had made many warm friendships in Arizona. His work had taken him often to the territory's far-flung mining camps, and in Prescott, Phoenix, and Tucson he had met many of Arizona's leading journalists, businessmen, and political figures. Newspapers gave him a great deal of favorable publicity for his Wells Fargo detective work. Miners from California repeated tales of his courageous exploits during the gold rush. Now leaders of the Republican Party in Tucson concluded that Paul would make an excellent chief lawman, and in June he announced himself as candidate for sheriff of Pima County. It was the beginning of the most dramatic and controversial period of his life.

CHAPTER SEVEN

Paul v. Shibell

As a newcomer to Arizona, Bob Paul had very little political clout. But he had a level of experience that no man in the territory could match. At the same time, he recognized that the sheriff's job would give a tremendous boost to his sagging finances. His Wells Fargo salary of $125 a month was a pittance compared with the sheriff's income. In Arizona the county sheriff was also tax collector and assessor, and instead of a fixed salary, he received fees for performing sheriff's duties and a portion (as much as 5 percent) of the taxes he collected. In 1880, a journalist estimated that the post was worth up to $25,000 a year, from which sum the sheriff would have to pay some expenses of his office.[1]

Paul knew that victory would be a daunting task. The county sheriff, Charles A. Shibell, was hugely popular and well respected. One of the most established Anglo residents of Pima County, Shibell had arrived in Tucson in 1862 at age twenty-one. He married a Mexican woman, raised a family, served one term as deputy sheriff, and was elected sheriff in late 1876. Shibell was a reasonably competent lawman. In 1878 he led a posse that ambushed and killed the highway robber Bill Brazelton. But Sheriff Shibell was more of a politician and administrator than a hard-bitten detective and manhunter, and he left much of the actual police work to his deputies. Owing to his marriage and long residence in the county, Shibell had strong ties to both the Anglo and Hispanic communities. Defeating him would not be easy.[2]

Charlie Shibbell,
Aug. 1, 1877

Charles A. Shibell, sheriff of Pima County and Bob Paul's political adversary. Author's collection.

Arizona politics were defined at the time by Arizona's status as a territory. Because Arizona was not a state, many of its officials, including the governor, U.S. marshal, and judges, were appointed by the president. Often such appointees were not even residents of the territory, and Arizonans considered them carpetbaggers. Therefore the federal government was looked upon with distrust, and its most visible arm, the U.S. Army, was frequently criticized for its perceived inability to protect the citizenry from hostile Apaches. Arizonans' animosity toward the federal government extended to large corporations such as the Southern Pacific Railroad, Wells Fargo, and mining companies, as well as to cattle and sheep barons. The Republican Party was identified with such institutions, whereas Arizona's farmers, small ranchers, miners, and laboring men generally belonged to the Democratic Party. Because Arizona's citizens lacked the power to elect important territorial officials, they focused their concerns on local politics.[3]

Prior to 1880, the territory's politics had been generally nonpartisan. Although Arizona's governors were mainly Republican and most locally elected officials were Democrats, strict party lines had not existed. The territory's political, business, and social leaders were primarily concerned with promoting economic development, suppressing lawlessness, and achieving statehood. They recognized that a nonpartisan coalition was the best method to attain unity in the sparsely settled territory. Republican leaders, in the minority, often played down their party name and called themselves Unionists or independents. But by the late 1870s Arizona's demographics began to change. In 1877–78 rich silver deposits were discovered in southern Pima County, particularly in Tombstone, setting off a great mining rush. In 1877 the Southern Pacific Railroad line was extended from California across the Colorado River to Yuma, reaching Tucson on March 17, 1880. Miners, settlers, and railroad workers, many of them Republicans from California and elsewhere, flooded in. As a result, the first party lines were drawn in Arizona Territory in the political campaign of 1880, and both Democrats and Republicans held territorial conventions and elected slates of candidates.[4]

One of Arizona's most influential Democrats was Louis C. Hughes, who founded the *Arizona Star* in 1877 and was its editor for thirty years. Hughes had settled in Arizona in 1871, and, after a stint as a private lawyer and territorial attorney general, he jumped into journalism and politics, which would eventually lead him to the governor's mansion. Standing just five feet five, with a partly bald and somewhat pointed dome, he was derisively called "Pinhead" Hughes by his enemies. Hughes has been treated kindly by historians, who have judged him a progressive and reform-minded leader. But in many ways, Hughes was hardly different from the countless opportunistic lawyers, hack politicians, and yellow journalists who flocked to America's frontier regions in the nineteenth century. His honesty was hardly above reproach; in 1873 he was removed from office as Arizona's attorney general for attempting to extort a $5,000 bribe. As editor, he was repeatedly charged with demanding money in exchange for political support, and his journalism was partisan to the point of mindlessness. He lambasted Republicans for the very things for which he praised Democrats. Unable to moderate his positions or compromise with his opponents, he quickly alienated Arizona's Republicans. His extremism finally earned him the hatred of his own party, resulting in a spectacular downfall.

What stood Hughes apart were the progressive convictions that he acquired from his well-bred and well-educated wife, Josephina Brawley Hughes, who became popularly known as the Mother of Arizona. She impressed upon him notions that were decidedly unpopular in frontier Arizona: opposition to liquor and gambling and support of women's suffrage. Though he was supposedly happily married, in the mid-1880s Hughes was accused of consorting with prostitutes. Hughes's reputation as a reformer persists, despite his support of lynch law as well as his nativist editorial campaigns to expel Chinese from Arizona and to strip Hispanic citizens of ranches granted to them generations before by Spain and Mexico. In 1906 President Theodore Roosevelt referred to Hughes as "a fussy person of no consequence." Oddly enough, his elder brother Sam Hughes was a prominent Republican politician in Tucson and a friend of Paul.[5]

Although Louis Hughes recognized Paul's experience and courage, once calling him "Pima County's brave sheriff," he took an instant dislike to Paul's politics. Hughes would soon become his most ardent and outspoken opponent. The fact that Paul was genial, popular, and respected by men in both parties only seems to have aggravated the ill-tempered Hughes, who threw his support behind Charlie Shibell. Paul was fortunate to have the backing of Tucson's Republican newspaper, the *Daily Citizen*. Its influential founder and editor, John Wasson, liked and respected Paul and provided staunch support until the journalist moved to California in 1882. Subsequent publishers and editors of the *Citizen*, including R. C. Brown, William C. Davis, and Herbert Brown, would strongly support Paul for the rest of his official career.[6]

In contrast to Shibell, Paul had lived in Tucson for less than two years, and had other disadvantages. In addition to his Wells Fargo employment, he had strong connections with the Southern Pacific Railroad Company, and both companies supported his candidacy with votes and campaign funds. However, though new to Arizona, the Southern Pacific was already a reviled monopoly in California. There it was accused of land grabbing, fixing extortionate rates, evading taxes, exerting an unholy influence in state politics, and using that influence to extend its economic power. Just a month earlier, on May 11, 1880, a hostile land dispute between the Southern Pacific and farmers in Tulare County led to the infamous Mussel Slough Tragedy. In a pitched gunfight between settlers and railroad agents, seven men had been slain, and the Southern Pacific's reputation was permanently blackened. Arizonans looked upon the new railroad with equal degrees of anticipation and dread, while many Democrats in Pima County came to see Paul as a Republican carpetbagger and a tool of the railroad and express companies.[7]

The new sheriff—whoever he turned out to be—would face a daunting task. Pima County, one of the four original counties in Arizona, was one of the largest bailiwicks in America, consisting of much of the current counties of Pima, Cochise, Graham, Santa Cruz, and Greenlee. It stretched 300 miles from New Mexico east to Yuma County, and from the Mexican border 150 miles north to the Gila River. Its 23,000 square miles were almost the same size as the state of West Virginia and more than twice the size of Paul's home state of Massachusetts. The town of Tombstone was settled in 1878, and soon afterward such mining camps as Contention City, Charleston, Bisbee, and Harshaw sprang up. By 1880 the county's population had boomed to 20,000, with about 7,000 people living in Tucson, the county seat. It was a vast region of parched deserts and numberless mountains, interspersed with scattered mining camps, settlements, and ranches. Its remoteness attracted fugitives, bandits, and desperadoes of every stripe. Pima County was then one of the most violent regions in the United States. The county experienced 25 murders between October 1879 and October 1880. When adjusted for population, this converts to a rate of 125 homicides per 100,000, which is twenty-two times higher than the modern national rate. In 1881, Pima County, which by that time no longer included what are now Cochise and Graham Counties, with a population of about 17,500, experienced at least 8 homicides, for a rate of 45 per 100,000. In 1882 there were at least 18 murders, with a resulting rate of 103 per 100,000. When killings in Apache warfare are included, the county's homicide rates were even higher. By comparison, in 2008 Tucson had a rate of 14 per 100,000, which was considered very high and made newspaper headlines.[8]

During the early and mid-1870s much of the banditry along the Arizona-Mexico border was caused by outlaws from Mexico raiding and rustling cattle on the American side. However, in 1878 things changed. Fugitives from New Mexico began congregating across the border in northern Chihuahua and Sonora. They included former members of the gangs of the notorious New Mexico outlaws Jesse Evans and John Kinney, as well as gunfighters and desperadoes who had taken part in the El Paso Salt War in late 1877 and the Lincoln County War in 1878. Robert E. Martin, a notorious cattle rustler and friend of Jesse Evans, emerged as the leader of this motley, disorganized band. His lieutenant was Curly Bill Brocius. By all accounts, Curly Bill was a colorful and swashbuckling rogue. A contemporary described him thus: "His rude makeup of rough pants stuck in his boots, blue shirt, flaming red necktie and great sombrero added to a bad countenance much that is picturesque. He had a knife in his boot, two six-shooters stuck against his waist and was ready for a frolic at any time, even at the risk of life." On May 21, 1878, Martin and Curly Bill attempted to rob a U.S. Army ambulance north of El Paso. They riddled the ambulance with bullets, wounding two soldiers, then fled across the border with a posse of Texas Rangers in pursuit. Both were captured in Mexico, returned for trial, and sentenced to five years each in the Texas state penitentiary. But in November, while their case was on appeal, the pair managed to break out of jail and escape back to Mexico.[9]

During the next two years, Martin and Curly Bill were joined by a host of badmen and fugitives, including such desperadoes as John Ringo, Cactus Bill Graham, Pony Deal, Sherman McMaster, Jim Wallace, Billy Leonard, Jim Crane, Harry "the Kid" Head, Luther King, Joe Hill, Pete Spence, Jimmy Hughes, and Dick Lloyd. The loose-knit gang consisted of approximately one hundred outlaws operating in small bands on both sides of the border. They were dubbed "Cowboys" by the newspapers and "Tejanos," or Texans, by Arizona's Hispanics. They were an 1880s incarnation of modern youth gangs. Except for a certain camaraderie there was little unity or organization among them. Sometimes they raided ranches in Sonora and Chihuahua and drove the stolen cattle north for sale; at other times they rustled American stock and sold it in Mexico. Their constant raids alarmed the governments of the United States and Mexico, and diplomatic dispatches from both sides of the border repeatedly identified Bob Martin as the leader of the rustling and smuggling bands. In the southern part of Pima County, the rustlers joined forces with established local ranchers, most notably Newman H. "Old Man" Clanton, his sons Ike, Fin, and Billy, and brothers Frank and Tom McLaury. Some of the Cowboys, such as

Bob Martin, Joe Hill, John Ringo, George Turner, and Billy Leonard, claimed government rangeland in southern Arizona and southeastern New Mexico, where they grazed stolen cattle. By late 1880, Martin, who at age forty-five was much older than most of the Cowboys, had become somewhat domesticated, with a wife and child living on George Turner's ranch on the New Mexico side of the San Simon Valley.[10]

John Ringo, on the other hand, became ever more notorious. Born in Indiana in 1850, his family had crossed the plains to California and settled in San Jose. Ringo left home in 1871, drifting into Texas, where he took part in the bloody Mason County War. There he met Joe Hill, and the two became close friends. Ringo took part in a number of gunfights connected to the feud, killing one man. In 1876 he broke jail, but was later elected constable by supporters. He arrived in Arizona in 1879, where he shot a man in the neck for refusing to take a drink. Ringo made his headquarters with Hill and other cattle rustlers in the San Simon Valley, and he established a reputation as one of the most dangerous gunmen in Arizona.[11]

The Cowboys' favorite resort was Tombstone, the principal mining camp in southern Arizona, located seventy miles southeast of Tucson and just thirty-five miles from the Mexican border. By 1880 Tombstone boasted a floating population of five thousand people, including many miners and gamblers from Nevada's silver and gold camps. Tucson would become the seat of the new county of Cochise, formed in February 1881 from the southeastern portion of Pima County. Among the newcomers to Tombstone were the Earp brothers—Virgil, Wyatt, and Jim—who arrived with their wives in December 1879. They were later joined by younger brother Morgan and Wyatt's close friend, the tubercular gambler John H. "Doc" Holliday. Virgil, having served as a constable in Prescott, had recently received a commission as deputy U.S. marshal. Wyatt had worked for several years as a police officer in the Kansas cow towns of Wichita and Dodge City. In late July 1880 Sheriff Charlie Shibell appointed him a deputy sheriff for the Tombstone area. At the same time, on the recommendation of Paul, Wells Fargo agent Marshall Williams hired Wyatt as shotgun messenger on the route between Tombstone and Benson, an important stop on the Southern Pacific Railroad. Wyatt rode shotgun only for the month of August, trading duties on the coaches with Paul. By late August Paul had to return to Tucson to begin his campaign for sheriff. Presumably because of the press of Wyatt's deputy sheriff duties, the messenger job was turned over to his brother Morgan, who covered the run full-time until February 1881 and occasionally thereafter. Wyatt would soon prove himself an aggressive and no-nonsense lawman.[12]

The people of Pima County's boom camps needed beef, and the rustlers saw a new market. Crooked butchers in Tombstone and elsewhere were willing to buy cheap cattle with no questions asked. The rustlers also dealt in stolen horses. Deputy Sheriff Billy Breakenridge recalled that one of the outlaws brought a horse from New Mexico to sell in Tombstone. When asked about the animal's legal ownership, he wisecracked, "The title is good west of here but don't take him into New Mexico."[13]

By 1880 Curly Bill Brocius and John Ringo had emerged as the most prominent of the Cowboys. Virgil Earp described the Cowboys thus: "The most of them are what we call "saddlers," living almost wholly in the saddle, and largely engaged in raiding into Sonora and adjacent country and stealing cattle, which they sell in Tombstone. . . . When cattle are not handy the cowboys rob stages and engage in similar enterprises to raise money. As soon as they are in funds they ride into town, drink, gamble, and fight. They spend their money as free as water in the saloons, dance houses, or faro banks, and this is one reason they have so many friends in town. . . . The saloons and gambling houses . . . receive them cordially and must be called warm friends of the cowboys. A good many of the merchants fear to express themselves against the criminal element, because they want to keep the patronage of the cowboys' friends."[14]

Despite the fact that the Cowboys had caused a series of diplomatic incidents, Charlie Shibell seems to have taken little action to curb their rustling and smuggling activities before his appointment of Wyatt Earp as resident deputy in Tombstone. The notable exception was when the Cowboys shot innocent people, after which Shibell's deputies arrested several of the desperadoes. Perhaps Shibell's lax attitude was owing to the fact that most of the Cowboys were Democrats who supported him for sheriff. At the Democratic county convention in Tucson on August 31, Shibell was formally nominated to run for his third term. A measure of the Cowboys' interest in the election is reflected in the fact that John Ringo attended the convention and objected that he was not given a seat as delegate from the San Simon precinct. The San Simon Valley was the headquarters of the Cowboys. Situated in southeastern Arizona, close to the New Mexico line and running north and south, it was a hundred miles long, surrounded by the craggy spires of the Chiricahua Mountains on the west and the Peloncillo Mountains on the east. It was watered by the San Simon River, which ran north from its New Mexico headwaters into a marshy area straddling the Arizona line called the San Simon Cienega, and finally emptied into the Gila River seventy miles distant. Profuse desert grasses made the San Simon Valley ideal for raising cattle. The valley's principal settlements were Solomonville, near the San Simon's confluence with the Gila, and San Simon Station, a freight stop on the new railroad, with a store, restaurant, saloon, and about twenty inhabitants. The San Simon Valley was notorious as a resort for rustlers; local ranches owned by Bob Martin, George Turner, Ike Clanton, and Joe Hill served as hideouts for the Cowboys. Nestled in a mesquite-choked canyon in the nearby Chiricahuas was the tiny and short-lived silver camp of Galeyville, which soon became celebrated as the Cowboys' watering hole.[15]

On September 20, three weeks after Bob Paul returned to Tucson, the Republicans met there and chose a slate of candidates, among them Paul for sheriff. The Wells Fargo man, though a newcomer, was very popular, especially among the settlers from California, who knew his reputation for fearlessness. And for those who were unfamiliar with him, the *Tucson Citizen* described his long career as a lawman in California, adding, "road agents fight shy of Bob Paul." Proclaimed editor John Wasson, "Cool and collected under all circumstances, his indomitable courage has been tested on many trying occasions, and he has always 'been there.' His integrity is unimpeachable, his bravery a proverb. Such a man we want for Sheriff of this county." Wasson was impressed by Paul's sobriety, commenting that he "does not make acquaintances over saloon bars, or buy men's votes for the 'drinks all around.'" Tombstone's Republican newspaper, the *Epitaph*, raved about the selection: "No man in the Territory of Arizona has had the experience that Mr. Paul has had in that particular kind of service incidental to the office of Sheriff. This experience has run through a long series of years, and has grown as the man has advanced in life. He commenced his work of this kind a long while ago in California, where he was known as one of the best Sheriffs in the state." To many voters it was clear that Charlie Shibell could not hold a candle to his opponent. At the same time, Wells Fargo and the Southern Pacific provided political and financial support for Paul's budding candidacy.[16]

Sheriff Shibell's critics believed that he spent too much time behind his desk. On September 29, the *Tombstone Epitaph* issued an anti-Shibell broadside:"The people of Pima County want a fearless man, one who will say come boys instead of go boys, when danger menaces. Any good clerk can do the civil work in a sheriff's office. A sheriff's duties are in the field and not in his office. The people pay a sheriff for taking chances, and when he thinks his hide is too good to stop bullets in the line of his duty he ought to be relegated to some other sphere in life. Shibell does not possess one qualification for a sheriff. Paul possesses and has demonstrated the fact while sheriff of one of the, at the time, most lawless counties in California, namely Calaveras, that he was the right man in the right place."[17]

Such sentiments did not sit well with William Sanders Oury, one of the Democratic political bosses of Pima County. Bill Oury was an old and famous pioneer. Born in Virginia in 1817, he came to Texas on his own at sixteen. Family sources claim that he was one of the defenders at the Alamo and that he had been sent out as a courier a week before the climactic battle, a circumstance that saved his life. In fact, Oury enlisted in the Texas army eight months later, and in 1840 he rode with Jack Hays's Texas Rangers against the Comanches. He claimed to have taken part in the ill-fated Mier Expedition into Mexico of 1842, escaping death in the notorious Black Bean Episode. However, his name does not appear on any of the official rosters. Oury served with the Texas Rangers in the Mexican War, and in 1849 he took a Mexican bride. Oury and his wife promptly joined the California gold rush, later drifting into Arizona and settling permanently in Tucson in 1856. Oury raised cattle and served as mayor of Tucson in 1865 and as Pima County sheriff from 1873 to 1877. He was self-educated, highly intelligent, literate, and eloquent. His temper was legendary; he killed two men in duels in Tucson. His ironhanded approach to fighting Mexican soldiers and Indians extended to the way he battled Republican politicians.[18]

In 1880 Oury was clerk of the Pima County Board of Supervisors. A close friend of Charlie Shibell, he took very seriously the threat posed by Bob Paul. Oury's younger brother, Granville, likewise an important Arizona pioneer, was running for a seat in Congress, and Bill Oury was determined to see a Democratic victory. Oury was also a good friend of Old Man Clanton and his son Ike, the latter of whom owned a ranch with the notorious Joe Hill in the San Simon Cienega. Oury wanted to make sure that the San Simon voting went Shibell's way. To accomplish that, he needed the help of the Cowboys.

At that time the only year-round water source in the San Simon Valley was the San Simon Cienega, situated about ten miles south of the San Simon railroad station on the Arizona–New Mexico line. The cienega was one mile wide and three miles long. It was occupied by only six ranches, all located along the streambed. The northernmost ranch was owned by forty-five-year-old John Magill, a former soldier who, with his wife and two children, lived in an adobe house and raised corn and a small herd of cattle. Half a mile south was the ranch of Nick Hughes, and another half mile beyond that was a ranch known in 1880 as "the Missouri boys' place." Below that, across the New Mexico line, was the one-room house and spread owned by Joe Hill and Ike Clanton. A short distance farther was George Turner's ranch, and the southernmost ranch belonged to A. H. Thompson. This was isolated country; below Thompson's ranch there was not an inhabited dwelling until one reached Cloverdale Springs in the New Mexico boot heel, forty miles to the south.[19]

Most of the ranchers in the San Simon Cienega were associated with the Cowboys. The most infamous was Joe Hill, whose true name was Joseph Olney. A thirty-one-year-old Texan, he had taken part in shooting scrapes and cattle rustling and had been embroiled in the Mason County War, one of the West's deadliest feuds. There he met fellow feudist John Ringo. The two became fast friends, with Olney once helping Ringo to escape jail. After killing a deputy sheriff in 1876, Olney fled to New Mexico and adopted the alias of Joe Hill. When a warrant was issued for him there, he fled to the San Simon Cienega, where he settled in 1879. He met Ike Clanton, and the two ran a cattle ranch together, Clanton dividing his time between San Simon and his father's ranch located south of Charleston on the San Pedro River. Hill employed as a drover Dick Lloyd, a notorious member of the Cowboys. Hill's neighbor, Nick Hughes, was a thirty-nine-year-old Irishman who had come to New Mexico as a young cavalryman. There he married a Hispanic woman, Josefa Armijo, and they had four children. The eldest, Jimmy, was handsome and reckless. Known as the Sweetheart of the San Simon, Jimmy, though but sixteen, was soon riding with the Cowboys. Nick Hughes was a cattleman, a Democrat, and a notorious livestock thief. His neighbor and fellow Cowboy George Turner was a cattle rustler and hardcase who had once shot up the settlements of Maxey and Safford with John Ringo, Ike Clanton, and Joe Hill. Rancher A. H. Thompson, a cattle thief, had recently sold a small herd to the beef contractor at Fort San Carlos; the cattle turned out to be stolen.[20]

The notorious Joe Hill of the Cowboys. His true name was Joseph Olney. Joe Hill, Ike Clanton, and William S. Oury were the ringleaders in the ballot-box stuffing at San Simon Cienega. Courtesy of David Johnson.

Bill Oury undoubtedly knew that the Cowboys, whose rustling and smuggling activities had been all but ignored by Sheriff Shibell, were eager to see Paul defeated. In mid-October, the board of supervisors—presumably at Oury's urging—designated Joe Hill's house as the polling place for the San Simon precinct and appointed Ike Clanton as election inspector and John Ringo and A. H. Thompson election judges. Republicans became alarmed at Oury's actions. Complained the editor of the *Tombstone Epitaph*, "The meeting of the Board of Supervisors held on Tuesday to establish voting precincts and appoint election officers must have been a queer arrangement. . . . Sheriff Shibell, Treasurer [Robert] Leatherwood, and Clerk Oury appear to have run the machine." The board denied a petition to establish a polling place near the Tombstone Company's mine and the Grand Central mine, which employed large numbers of Republican miners. The *Epitaph*'s editor also charged that they established the polling place at San Simon "to give the Texan cow-boys, who last year turned Lincoln County, N. M., into pandemonium, a chance to vote the Democratic ticket." In a long, rambling reply published in Tombstone's Democratic paper, the *Daily Nugget*, Oury sidestepped the charges and thundered, "If it is a crime to vote the Democratic ticket, then our lawgivers should place upon the statute books a law prohibiting it."[21]

In late October Oury boarded a train for San Simon Station, carrying with him a list of San Simon voters from the Pima County Great Register, blank ballots, and blank certificates of registration. He also brought a barrel of whiskey, for in those years it was customary to supply prospective voters with free liquor. From the railroad Oury made his way south to Hill and Clanton's ranch. There he met with Ike Clanton and gave him the copy of the Great Register list and the ballots and registration certificates. Oury later claimed, improbably, that he did not give Clanton the barrel of whiskey and that although there were a number of Mexicans and Americans present, he did not know their names. Oury told Ike that his house would be the polling place for the San Simon Cienega precinct, and he swore in Clanton as election inspector and Ringo and Thompson as precinct judges.[22]

The Great Register list of voters for San Simon Cienega precinct that Oury brought with him was fraudulent. Despite the fact that there were only three or four citizens of voting age in the entire precinct, his Great Register list contained 192 names, many of them wholly fictitious. The roll included some of the most notorious of the Cowboys, among them Bob Martin, Ike and Fin Clanton, Bill and George Graham, Billy Leonard, Dick Lloyd, John Ringo, George Turner, Nick Hughes, and Joe Hill. It also included a number of other men who actually lived in New Mexico, as far away as Lordsburg and Cloverdale. The date of registration for all of the voters was the same, October 21, 1880, a few days before Oury's visit to Ike Clanton's ranch. As clerk of the board of supervisors, Oury had the necessary documents and expertise to create the phony list. And because it contained the names of many of the Cowboys as well as other settlers on the Arizona–New Mexico line, it is evident that Ike Clanton, John Ringo, or one of their cohorts who knew the local men had helped him create it.[23]

After setting up the highly suspect polling location, Oury returned to Tucson to continue his energetic campaigning. When William C. Davis and other Republican leaders learned that he had chosen the Clanton-Hill house as the polling place, and that Clanton and Ringo were to run the election, they became gravely concerned. They quickly demonstrated that Clanton's house was actually in New Mexico, and they had the board of supervisors move the polling place to John Magill's house, which was a mile inside of the Arizona border. In the meantime, Clanton had been busy creating a phony poll list of voters' names. Three or four days before the election, he came into Tucson by rail to visit Curly Bill, who was then in jail. While he was there, Ike learned that the polling place had changed, thus necessitating a new poll list. Clanton obtained a packet of printed ballots and returned to his ranch house in San Simon. There he and Bob Martin created a new poll list and a tally sheet containing one hundred phony votes. In making up the fake poll list, Clanton and Martin included several dozen actual residents of southwestern New Mexico, but, apparently believing that number was not enough, they added many names from the Great Register list that were entirely fictitious. They also filled out numerous ballots in favor of Charlie Shibell and other Democratic candidates.[24]

In a century-old myth, it was Curly Bill Brocius who engineered the San Simon election fraud, and just before the polls closed, he supposedly declared, "Boys, this election has gone too one-sided to suit me, and just to show them fellers down at Tucson that there is no coercion in this camp I am going to give Bob Paul one." Yet another oft-repeated account, this one from Arizona pioneer James C. Hancock, claimed that "on the morning of election day, John Ringo, Curly Bill, Milt and Billy Hicks, Joe Hill and a few others rode into the little station of San Simon . . . on the Southern Pacific Railroad, and took possession of the voting precinct and all of them proceeded to vote, and to make sure that none had been left out or overlooked, they voted several times over again; then they got all the white people of the little place—men, women, and children, probably eight or ten in all—and voted them in the same manner, then they rounded up the Chinese and Mexican section hands and voted them two or three times over, then they voted all their horses and a dog or two and a stray cat, and finally to make sure no one was neglected and not been given a chance to cast his ballot, they voted every one over again."[25]

These stories are fiction. Curly Bill Brocius was then a prisoner in the Pima County jail. On the night of October 27, six days before the election, he embarked on a drunken spree in Tombstone and shot and mortally wounded City Marshal Fred White. The Cowboy chieftain was disarmed and arrested by Wyatt Earp. Four Cowboys, including Dick Lloyd and James K. Johnson, were with Curly Bill, and Wyatt and his brothers jailed them on firearms charges. The next day the four Cowboys were fined and released, but Wyatt brought Curly Bill into Tucson and locked him up in the Pima County jail to await trial for murder. Lloyd and Johnson wisely left Tombstone immediately and rode east to the Clanton-Hill ranch. When Johnson reached Clanton's house, he found ballots scattered all over the bed and the washstand. He helped Ike Clanton and Bob Martin prepare their phony poll list and registration certificates. Martin "Bud" Stiles, a saloonkeeper from Lordsburg, also helped out. As Stiles later said, "We were all partly full of whiskey."[26]

For some reason Ike Clanton decided that he needed more ballots. He made another quick trip to Tucson by train and returned with them the day before the election. He and Martin marked up the additional ballots until they had one hundred for Charlie Shibell and other Democrats. When Jim Johnson stopped by the ranch, he found Ike Clanton struggling to put together the phony poll and tally lists. The Cowboys, Cactus Bill Graham in particular, found enormous fun in the scheme. Cactus Bill, also called "Cactus Root" Graham, was described by Jim Johnson: "I have always known him by the name of Cactus Root, the boys call him that because he is a comical genius." "Cactus root" was a colloquial term for peyote, the hallucinogen found in the root of the peyote cactus widely used in religious ceremonies by Native Americans of the Southwest. The Cowboys had seen or heard of the effects of the cactus root and applied it to their humorous comrade. Johnson later said that Cactus Bill and the other Cowboys laughed and joked about the crooked election. John Magill, whose house was to serve as the polling place, must have heard the talk, for when the Cowboys asked him to act as an election inspector, he refused.[27]

At daybreak on election day, November 2, Ike and Fin Clanton, with Bob Martin, Jim Johnson, Cactus Bill Graham, Layman "Lem" Ball, and Ed "Duke" Raymond, rode over to Magill's ranch. By the time the Cowboys reached his adobe, Magill had made sure he was long gone, harvesting his corn crop. Neither John Ringo nor Nick Hughes was present; the latter was in a Mexican jail on a charge of stealing sheep. But Bud Stiles, the saloonkeeper, was there to help. As Jim Johnson recalled, they went inside and immediately "commenced counting the certificates out to correspond with the ballots and put them in the box." While Magill's wife tended to her children and household duties, the Cowboys rigged the election. It took them an hour and a half. As several Cowboys read the names from the registration certificates, Martin wrote each one down on the tally list. Then they folded the ballots and put them in the ballot box with the certificates. In addition to entering the names of nonexistent voters, Johnson signed the poll list as "Henry Johnson," Duke Raymond voted as "George M. Perkins," and Cactus Bill voted using his brother's alias, George Ross. After stuffing the ballot box, the Cowboys loitered about Magill's adobe, but no actual voters showed up. "We laughed and joked one another . . . about the affair," recalled Johnson. At 11:30 A.M. they swung into their saddles and made the ten-minute ride back to Clanton's to eat lunch.[28]

In the meantime William C. Davis had asked Randolph B. Kelly, a Republican who lived in Willcox, to be a poll watcher at the San Simon Cienega. It would not be an easy task. The afternoon before the election, Kelly mounted his horse and started for San Simon, fifty-four miles distant. He stopped to rest at Fort Bowie, the halfway point, but by the time he left it was eight P.M. Fifteen miles from Fort Bowie, Kelly got lost in the dark and decided to wait until daylight. Dismounting, he hobbled his horse and went to sleep, but upon waking, he discovered that his pony had wandered off. Kelly was forced to hike the remaining fourteen miles across the San Simon Valley until he finally stumbled onto James Magill, who agreed to take him to the polls in his wagon. The two stopped at Clanton's house, where the Cowboys were finishing their noonday meal. Kelly had brought some Republican ballots, which he displayed while explaining that he had been sent there as a poll watcher. The Cowboys invited Magill and Kelly to eat, but the latter was anxious to get to the polls. Magill, Kelly, a man named Smith, and the two "Missouri boys" clambered into the wagon and headed toward Magill's house.[29]

The Cowboys were alarmed, and, fearing that Kelly would discover the fraud, they mounted up and raced back to the polls, galloping past Magill's wagon on the way. When Magill, Kelly, and the others arrived, half a dozen Cowboys were inside the adobe, pretending to run a legitimate election.

The notorious Ike Clanton, one of the leaders of the Cowboys. In 1880 he helped engineer the crooked balloting in San Simon Cienega in an effort to prevent Bob Paul's election as sheriff of Pima County. Wild West History Association.

Kelly was instructed to step up to a window on the front porch, where he handed over his certificate of registration and was allowed to vote. Kelly found Cactus Bill Graham and Layman Ball acting as election judges, Bob Martin and Duke Raymond as clerks, and Jim Johnson as inspector. Kelly later reported that some twenty-five people were there, including Magill's family, and about eight of them cast ballots. These were the Cowboys, making a show of voting in hopes of fooling Kelly. When the polls closed that evening and the votes were counted, Kelly was surprised to learn that the box contained 104 ballots. All of them were for Charlie Shibell, excepting his own vote for Paul. Upon Kelly's return to Willcox, he wrote to William C. Davis that the San Simon election was a fraud. "My suspicions were aroused at the large number of votes cast there and I suggested means by which it might be detected," he later explained.[30]

Through Davis and other Republican leaders, Paul quickly learned of the ballot-box stuffing. Although the early vote counts put Paul ahead, he was not surprised when his luck turned after the San Simon count came in. By November 6, four days after the polls closed, it was evident that Shibell had the most votes. The final count was 1,726 for Shibell and 1,668 for Paul. Charlie Shibell had won by the slimmest of margins: 58 votes out of a total of 3,394 ballots cast. A downcast but angry Paul visited Tombstone that day. After climbing down from the stagecoach, he spotted Wyatt Earp in the crowd. As Earp later recalled, Paul stepped close and growled, "Wyatt, I've been robbed."

Earp promptly responded, "I know it, Bob. But you can win yet." Wyatt later said that he and Paul discussed the election result for an hour. Even without Kelly's disclosure, they knew it was impossible for the tiny San Simon precinct to have polled 104 votes. The two lawmen also understood that most of the inhabitants of the San Simon Cienega were associated with the Cowboys, and to prove fraud they needed one of the election riggers to confess. Earp later related that he talked with several of Curly Bill's friends in Tombstone and offered to testify that the Marshal White shooting was an accident, provided that one of them came clean about the election fraud. Curly Bill had already sought help from Wyatt; on the way to jail he had asked Earp to recommend a good lawyer. Brocius had a strong defense to the murder charge: Marshal White had foolishly seized the barrel of Curly Bill's gun, causing it to discharge; before White died he swore that the shooting was not intentional.[31]

Earp's biographer, Stuart N. Lake, claimed that Wyatt told Curly Bill, "Come through about the . . . votes, and I won't dispute White's dying statement. Otherwise I'll swear you shot White as he reached for your gun. If the law doesn't hang you on that, Fred White's friends will." It has since been discovered that Lake recreated, and in many cases invented, his quotes from Earp, whom he met personally only a few times. But in this case, substantial evidence exists that Earp did indeed assist Paul in uncovering the election fraud. Wyatt had openly supported Paul in the election campaign, and on November 9 he resigned as deputy sheriff, probably at Shibell's demand. Earp was promptly replaced with the politically connected Johnny Behan, former legislator and ex-sheriff of Yavapai County. Though Earp had lost his badge, he had gained a lifelong friend in Paul.[32]

Ike Clanton was one of the Cowboys to whom Paul and Earp spoke about the crooked balloting. Paul also met with Jim Johnson in Tombstone. Paul had first met Johnson a few weeks before the election. Johnson had worked as a butcher in San Jose, California, then drifted to the mining camps in Nevada and the Black Hills, finally landing in Arizona during the great silver rush. Though nominally a miner, he had bought horses and cattle—probably stolen—from Ike Clanton and Curly Bill and sold them in Tombstone. He had also been accused of assisting Pony Deal and Sherman McMaster in the theft of U.S. Army mules. Johnson agreed to tell Paul the truth. He cooperated because he and Ike Clanton were eager to help Curly Bill, but neither had the money to pay for his attorney. Therefore Clanton offered Paul a deal: if Paul would loan Johnson $250 to pay for Curly Bill's defense, Johnson would testify to the San Simon election fraud. Paul agreed and turned over the $250, and Johnson in turn paid Curly Bill's attorney in Tucson. For his part of the bargain, Wyatt appeared at Curly Bill's preliminary hearing in December and testified that the shooting was an accident. Curly Bill was released from jail to wreak ever more havoc on the border. In the end, Bob Paul had made a deal with the devil. Although entirely justified, it was the most unsavory compromise he had ever undertaken. It was also his introduction to the rabidly partisan world of Arizona politics.[33]

On November 15 the Pima County Board of Supervisors met, certified the final election results, and officially declared Charles Shibell as sheriff. Four days later, Paul appeared before the board and requested copies of the poll lists for the San Simon, Solomonville, Turkey Creek, and Benson precincts. Shibell also appeared and asked for copies of the same poll lists. It was obvious to all that an election contest was brewing. Paul believed that he was not the only candidate who had been cheated. His actions would ignite a long and acrimonious feud with the ambitious William Kidder Meade, later U.S. marshal of Arizona. As Paul later recalled, "I found that . . . W. K. Meade, who was the nominee for the legislative council, was fraudulently counted [and] elected, by thirty-five votes. I went to Richard Gird, Marshal Meade's opponent on the Republican ticket . . . and wanted him to contest the election with me and three others of the nominees for the legislature, as it would be very expensive to them and the probability was that the legislature would adjourn before the contest would be decided. They declined but insisted on my making the contest and they would assist me financially. I met Mr. Meade about that time for the first time. He was very indignant that I should presume to advise Mr. Gird to contest his election, and he done all he could to defeat me in my contest and I made him my personal and political enemy."[34]

On December 18, Paul filed his election contest, *Paul v. Shibell*, in the district court in Tucson. In addition to allegations of fraud at San Simon, based upon the confession of Jim Johnson, Paul's lawsuit also claimed election fraud at the Tombstone and Tres Alamos precincts. He alleged that in the Tombstone count, a man named Burdett had erased Paul's name from twenty-seven Tombstone ballots and that twenty-three Paul votes had been ignored. He charged that the Tres Alamos count of seventeen Paul votes to five for Shibell was never included in the final tally. Under territorial law, election contests were tried by the court, not a jury, and Judge C. G. W. French set the trial for December 28. That day, Shibell's lawyers appeared in court, seeking more time to prepare their case, and Judge French continued the trial to January 17, 1881. The importance of the case was underscored by the array of attorneys who represented the two sides. Paul had six lawyers, among them Warner Earll, Alex Campbell, and John Haynes. Not to be outdone, Shibell retained six attorneys himself, among them some of the most prominent in Arizona: former judge Charles Silent, pioneer Benjamin H. Hereford, James A. Zabriskie, later U.S. attorney of Arizona, and James C. Perry, who had successfully defended Curly Bill.[35]

From the outset, Shibell's lawyers knew they would have great difficulty in getting the Cowboys to come to Tucson to testify, thus putting the sheriff at a distinct disadvantage. Bob Martin, for one, had already cashed in. Three weeks after the election, on November 22, 1880, Martin quarreled with fellow rustlers over a herd of stolen cattle. Four Cowboys—two of whom were apparently Billy Leonard and Luther King—ambushed and killed Martin at Stein's Pass, just east of the Arizona–New Mexico line. None of the other Cowboys had any interest in testifying. Paul, in his capacity as deputy U.S. marshal, went to the San Simon Cienega to serve subpoenas. To get there he had to take a train to Lordsburg, New Mexico, where he rented a horse and buggy and drove thirty miles southwest on rough roads. He tried to locate Layman Ball, but the latter had disappeared. Paul did manage to find Jim Johnson and John Magill and serve them both. Meanwhile, Shibell sent a telegram to Johnny Behan, his new deputy in Tombstone, instructing him to subpoena Ike Clanton. The inept Behan had no idea where the Clanton place was located and was forced to ask Virgil Earp, who told him that the ranch was near Charleston. Behan rode out in a buggy with a fellow deputy, Leslie Blackburn, and a third man.

In Charleston, Behan ran into Wyatt Earp and Doc Holliday, who said they were looking for a stolen horse. Instead of serving the subpoena himself, Behan sent it with a messenger to the Clanton place, with the result that Ike was not served. Behan said that he was later told by Ike that Wyatt Earp had warned him of the subpoena and that Clanton had armed his men and would have forcibly resisted Behan if he had tried to serve it. Behan later claimed that this incident caused him to revoke an offer to make Wyatt his deputy when he was appointed sheriff in newly formed Cochise County. It is evident that part of Clanton's deal with Bob Paul and Wyatt Earp was that they would not call him to testify, which is why Earp had warned him about the subpoena.[36]

The election lawsuit created a public sensation, and on the morning of January 17, 1881, the trial began in the crowded adobe courthouse situated on the corner of Court and Ott Streets. Paul's lawyers led off with John Magill, who testified in detail about the few residents of San Simon Cienega, though he professed to have little knowledge about the voting fraud. Paul's counsel next called their star witness, Jim Johnson, who admitted frankly that he was not registered to vote. He described the scheme in great detail and explained the leadership roles played by Ike Clanton, Bob Martin, and Cactus Bill Graham. One by one he was read the names of all 104 voters, and he confirmed that almost all of them were either fictitious or lived in New Mexico. On cross-examination, Shibell's incredulous lawyers asked him, "You knew you were acting a fraud?"

"No sir," Johnson replied. "I never had anything to do with any other election in the world."

"You thought ballot box stuffing was all right?"

"I never knew anything about it. I never voted but once in my life and that was for Horace Greeley." Johnson explained that he had joined in the scheme as a favor to Ike Clanton.[37]

The testimony from Paul's witnesses took two days. On January 19 Paul took the stand and explained that ten or twelve days after the election, he had toured San Simon Cienega to determine its population. He visited the ranches of John Magill, Ike Clanton and Joe Hill, Nick Hughes, and George Turner and found only a handful of settlers along the river. On cross-examination, Shibell's lawyer Charles Silent attempted to show that there were numerous transients in San Simon who could have voted. Silent demanded, "Is it not a fact that San Simon is notorious for being the rendezvous of what is called the 'cowboys'?"

Paul replied, "It used to be," and explained that since the election the Cowboys had stopped gathering there. After questioning him closely about his work for Wells Fargo, Silent asked, "Your business has been then that of a special officer, to look after robbers and robberies?"

"Yes, sir," Paul replied.

"And all classes of criminals?"

"No, sir."

"Have you not of your own volition looked after all classes of criminals?"

"I do sir. I think it is in their [Wells Fargo's] interest."

"But outside of cases where they were specially interested, where they were not specially interested?" Silent insisted.

"I think they are specially interested in any parties who might commit any crime."

"Well, didn't you look after some of the 'cowboys'?"

"No, sir. I never was down there [San Simon] before the election."

"Is it not a fact that these people called 'cowboys'—a great majority of them—have no fixed place of habitation—that they are here one day and then some place else another day—and migrate over the country?"

"Yes, sir."

"Tombstone tomorrow, Charleston another day, Tucson the day following, and so on?"

"Yes, sir," Paul replied. "They generally drive cattle—vaqueros as we call them."

"They have no fixed habitation?"

"A great many of them have not."

"It is a fact that . . . there were a great many of those 'cowboys' in and about the San Simon country at and before the election?"

"I don't know," Paul responded. "I was never out there before. I don't know whether that is a fact or not."

Though it was common knowledge that San Simon Cienega was the headquarters of the Cowboys, Paul truthfully said he had no firsthand knowledge of that fact. In the end, Silent's line of questioning backfired, because all he had done was demonstrate to the judge that San Simon was full of desperadoes who, if anything, were capable of committing election fraud.[38]

Then Paul's lawyers attempted to show irregularities at the Tres Alamos precinct, but they had no specific evidence of fraud. Finally, they rested their case. Spectators were flabbergasted at the clear evidence of ballot-box stuffing at San Simon. Even Louis C. Hughes remarked in the *Star*, "Some very singular evidence was brought out yesterday. . . . There has been some big cheating somewhere. . . . The evidence is very straightforward and to the point . . . that out of one hundred and four votes cast at San Simon, about one hundred were fraudulent."[39]

Now Shibell's lawyers tried gamely to refute the San Simon fraud. They called Randolph B. Kelly, the Republican poll watcher. He testified that he had seen twenty-five to thirty people around the polls all day, of whom only eight or ten voted. He said that one man had been forcibly ejected when his ballot was rejected. But this testimony fell far short of explaining how 104 votes ended up in the ballot box. Shibell's only chance to offset those phony ballots was to show that Paul's supporters had committed fraud in Tombstone. His lawyers called Leslie Blackburn, a saloon-keeper and deputy sheriff. At first blush, Blackburn's testimony appeared very damaging to Paul. He testified that it had taken four days to count the Tombstone votes and that he had been an observer at the polls the entire time. He claimed to have stood behind the judges as they counted the ballots on a table. Blackburn swore that sixty to seventy votes had been erroneously tallied for Paul instead of Shibell. On cross-examination, however, Paul's counsel asked him, "In what relation do you stand to Paul, are you a friend or an enemy of his?"

"I don't believe either one of us have any love for the other," Blackburn replied. When asked if Shibell had promised him a deputy's job before the election, he denied it.

"Did you ever ask Paul for the same office?"

"I was in the convention that nominated Paul. He came to me and—" Before he could finish, Paul's attorney demanded, "I ask you if you ever asked Mr. Paul for the office of deputy sheriff?"

"No sir, never directly," Blackburn responded. Pressed further, his answers became argumentative and evasive. When asked if he had once been a friend of Paul's and had pledged to support him in the Republican convention, Blackburn denied it. He testified that Shibell had personally asked him to monitor the Tombstone vote. Under close questioning, Blackburn admitted that the miscount in Tombstone was actually twenty-five to thirty votes. He first said he had not kept a written tally of the votes, but in the next breath he claimed to have made written notes. When requested to produce his tally, Blackburn said he had thrown it away. Asked why he would do that, Blackburn replied lamely, "I saw what they [the judges] were doing and got tired."

Sensing blood, Paul's counsel honed in for the kill. "Were you not asked after the election the reason you went against Mr. Paul and for Mr. Shibell and you replied because you had asked for an appointment as deputy sheriff of Mr. Paul and Mr. Paul refused it?"

"I don't think that I ever did," Blackburn responded.

"Are you positive about it?"

"I don't recollect ever making such a remark."

"Are you willing to swear you did not?"

Blackburn started to waffle: "I might have made the remark but I don't think I did."

"You are not willing to swear that you did not then?"

"No, I would not say positively whether I did or not. I might have done it. Somebody might have asked me the question, being a Republican, and I might have made that remark. . . . Probably I have. I would be liable to make that remark. . . . Very likely that I did."[40]

Deputy Blackburn's shifting, inconsistent testimony and his admission of bias against Paul was hardly helpful to Shibell's cause. Shibell's lawyers then called George Atwood, one of the election judges, who claimed that an error was made in the tally, giving Paul eight or ten votes to which he wasn't entitled. Shibell's next witness was Marshall Williams, Tombstone's Wells Fargo agent. Williams testified that after the votes were counted, they were placed in the ballot box, which was next wrapped in paper. He then affixed Wells Fargo wax seals, using the company's public sealer. Shibell's lawyers needed this testimony to show that the box had not been tampered with so that its ballots could be admitted into evidence. But their strategy backfired. When Williams was asked to examine the box, he found that it had been tampered with. The ballot box had been opened and the inside string broken, and then it had been resealed with a different color wax that did not have the impression of Wells Fargo's seal.[41]

Judge French then adjourned court for the evening to consider Shibell's request that the ballot box be admitted into evidence and the votes counted. In the morning, on January 22, he ordered the box admitted, despite the obvious tampering. The ballots were removed and counted in open court. The result was hardly surprising. Instead of the original vote of 453 for Paul and 339 for Shibell, the box now contained 402 ballots for Paul and 354 for Shibell. Another thirty-seven ballots had Paul's name erased from them. It was evident that Shibell's supporters had opened the box and changed some of the Paul votes.[42]

That afternoon Paul was recalled and cross-examined by Shibell's attorney Charles Silent to try to prove that he had bribed Jim Johnson for his testimony. Paul admitted that he had loaned $250 to Johnson: "I let him have some money on another person's request."

"Did you give him the money yourself?" asked Silent.

"I did."

"Personally?"

"Yes, sir."

"Whereabouts?"

"Here in town."

"At whose request did you give it to him?"

"Ike Clanton."

The answer stunned the audience, but Silent asked no further questions about Clanton's involvement. Paul's counsel, eager to dispel any notion that Johnson had been paid to commit perjury, asked him on redirect examination, "What did you let Mr. Johnson have that money for?"

"I let him have it at the request of Mr. Clanton," Paul replied.

"Did you let him have it for any evil purposes in this case?"

"No sir."

Not surprisingly, Shibell's lawyers failed to further explore this line of questioning. After all, Jim Johnson gave Paul's money to Curly Bill's attorney, James C. Perry—one of the very lawyers defending Shibell in the trial. That embarrassing disclosure would hardly have been helpful to Shibell.[43]

In the meantime, Paul and his lawyers became concerned that Bill Oury, who had religiously attended the trial, had been absent from court for several days. Oury had been shocked by Jim Johnson's testimony and could not understand why one of the Cowboys was cooperating with Paul. When Oury returned to the courthouse, Paul's attorneys called him to the stand. The old warhorse was hotheaded, arrogant, and not used to having his authority challenged. When Paul's counsel asked where he had been, Oury was evasive and argumentative, finally admitting he had gone to serve Ike Clanton with a subpoena at Old Man Clanton's ranch near Charleston. When asked what he discussed with Ike, Oury snapped, "That is none of your business, that is my matter." Oury was then asked whether Shibell had sent him after Ike Clanton. He responded, "I told him [Shibell] that if I saw Mr. Clanton I would tell him I thought he ought to come in."

As Paul's counsel pressed him for details, Oury became enraged. Judge French admonished him, "Keep cool."

Asked again why he went to see Ike, Oury barked, "That is none of your business."

"Keep cool," the judge repeated.

"Well, it's none of his business," Oury responded plaintively.

Asked once again, Oury exclaimed, "Well, I won't tell you."

"I want an answer."

"You won't get it," Oury retorted contemptuously.

After more sparring, Oury finally relented: "I will tell you what I went there for. He was a friend of mine, and he had been accused of wrong-doing by one of the witnesses here that was examined. I did not feel that he had but if he could get himself out of any such predicament that he should free himself from any imputation of wrongdoing. . . . I felt that it was his duty to come here and free himself of that aspersion."

When asked if he had any other object in meeting with Ike, Oury again snapped, "That is none of your business."

"Did it take a subpoena to do that?"

"No, sir. Mr. Shibell gave me the subpoena. I never looked at it. I don't know that I had a subpoena for him."

"You do know and you don't know?" asked Paul's incredulous counsel.

"I don't know that I had it, only Mr. Shibell told me."

Oury admitted that he had been upset by Jim Johnson's testimony. When the old frontiersman was asked where the Clanton ranch was situated, he became even more evasive, first claiming he did not know how to measure distance in miles, and finally saying, "It might have been four, two, or six miles" from Charleston. Oury eventually explained that when he got to the ranch, Old Man Clanton told him that Ike and one of his brothers "went out after some cattle" and that he met with Ike after he rode in. Oury's antagonistic demeanor, his evasive testimony, and his self-confessed connection with a notorious Cowboy did nothing to advance Shibell's case. It was undoubtedly only his stature in Tucson that kept him from being cited for contempt or from being questioned any further about his role in the San Simon frauds. Oury's trip to the Clanton ranch had been in vain. Ike Clanton never came to Tucson to testify, and the reason for this is evident. He had already made a deal with Paul and Wyatt Earp and had double-crossed Oury. He knew that Paul would not subpoena him, and he had no reason to testify for Shibell. If he did come to court, he would have to explain why he had stuffed the ballot box, and he might face criminal charges for election fraud.[44]

William S. Oury, Democratic warhorse and Bob Paul's bitter enemy. Author's collection.

The next day Paul's counsel began calling rebuttal witnesses, systematically dismantling Deputy Blackburn's claims of fraud and miscounting in Tombstone. Several of the election officers testified that the count had been done carefully in front of numerous observers representing both Paul and Shibell, including Wyatt and Virgil Earp. They insisted that any mistakes were promptly corrected. Others testified that Blackburn could not have stood behind the election officers, because they all sat in chairs backed up to a wall. Then Paul was recalled and described how, two weeks before the election, Blackburn had approached him and asked to be appointed a deputy if Paul became sheriff. Paul's testimony was confirmed by Ike Brokaw, city marshal of Tucson, who swore that a few days after the election Blackburn told him "he had asked Paul for a place in the [sheriff's] office and that he had given him no satisfaction and the consequence was that he turned around and worked against him." This combined testimony had the effect of nullifying Blackburn's account of fraudulent vote counting.[45]

Paul's counsel then rested, and Shibell called his final rebuttal witness: Johnny Behan. The deputy had acted as one of the election judges and testified that there had been room for an observer to stand behind the table. He said Blackburn had complained about a discrepancy in two tally lists, but Behan offered no testimony to support Blackburn's claim of sixty to seventy false votes for Paul. Behan was the last witness. The testimony had lasted eleven days. On January 26 and 27 the lawyers made long closing arguments, then, after considering the evidence for two days, Judge French rendered his opinion. To no one's surprise, he declared that all 103 votes cast for Shibell at San Simon were invalid. He found no fraud at Tres Alamos and upheld the count: 17 for Paul and 5 for Shibell. At Tombstone he found Marshall Williams's testimony credible and ruled that the ballot box had been tampered with, presumably by Shibell's partisans. He refused to accept any recount of the Tombstone votes. Judge French found that the final vote was 1,684 for Bob Paul and 1,628 for Charlie Shibell. Judge French ruled, "Robert H. Paul was duly elected sheriff."[46]

The case was the most celebrated election contest of frontier Arizona. It had also been expensive. Paul's court costs alone, which included mileage fees for numerous witnesses, amounted to almost $700, a large figure in that era. The attorney fees must have been thousands more. There was so much at stake that Shibell's lawyers promptly filed an appeal to the Arizona Supreme Court. As a result, Shibell remained sheriff until the appeal was decided. Paul was confident that he would prevail. His spirits were given a further boost when Margaret gave birth to a healthy baby boy, Walter, on January 26, two days after her thirty-sixth birthday. His mother-in-law, Ann Coughlan, had arrived in Tucson from New Bedford soon after the railroad was completed, to live with the Pauls and help Margaret with the infant. After the bitter loss of so many children in California, the new baby instilled hope and vitality in the Pauls' lives. In the meantime, Bob Paul went back to riding shotgun on the territory's lonely stage roads. It was that service for Wells Fargo that would soon draw him headlong into one of the most dramatic episodes of the American frontier.[47]

CHAPTER EIGHT

Death Rides the Tombstone Stage

A few weeks after the election trial, Bob Paul made a sensational arrest that had nothing to do with stage robbers, Cowboys, or frontier desperadoes. Instead, his target was Joseph Goldwater, a pioneer Jewish merchant. During the 1860s Goldwater and his older brother Mike had established mercantile stores on the Colorado River, and in time their family became extremely important in Arizona's political and business life. In January 1881 Joe Goldwater purchased on credit $80,000 worth of goods—six railroad cars full—from some of San Francisco's biggest wholesale merchants and shipped them to Isaac Lyons, a storekeeper in Yuma. When payment was not received, the San Francisco wholesalers became alarmed and obtained a warrant for Goldwater's arrest. The warrant was given to Captain A. W. Stone of the San Francisco police. In that freewheeling era, San Francisco policemen frequently performed private detective work while on duty, and Stone had previously worked on cases for both Wells Fargo and the Central Pacific. Captain Stone entrained for Yuma, where he found that the goods were all in the store of Isaac Lyons and that Goldwater was with him—despite wild rumors that he had fled to Mexico. He also learned that Goldwater had many friends in Yuma who would assist him in resisting or evading arrest and that the local officers were all sympathetic to him.

Captain Stone proceeded to Prescott, where he obtained an extradition order from Governor John Charles Fremont. Then he wired Paul in Tombstone and Sam Deal, chief of detectives for the Central Pacific Railroad, in Sacramento to meet him in Yuma. Although Paul was a deputy U.S. marshal, it was undoubtedly his connection with Wells Fargo that prompted Stone to call on him for assistance. Paul arrived in Yuma on February 12, and an hour later Deal came in on the eastbound train. After meeting with Captain Stone, they decided that they would have to spirit Goldwater out of town fast. Deal arranged with the Southern Pacific to have a special train on standby at the depot. Then all three lawmen stepped into Isaac Lyons's store, where they learned that he and Goldwater were eating dinner at Lyons's nearby home. While Deal waited in the front yard, Paul and Captain Stone entered the house and found Goldwater, Lyons, Deputy Sheriff Ira Mabbitt, and Probate Judge Isaac Levi in the dining room. Addressing Goldwater, Paul announced, "I am a deputy United States marshal and have a warrant for your arrest."

Goldwater replied that he would go with him, but made no move to get up from the table. Instead, he motioned to Levi, who quickly slipped out the back door. Lyons invited the lawmen to sit down and eat dinner, but they declined. Again Bob Paul told Goldwater to come with him, and again the merchant agreed to cooperate but failed to stand up. Paul picked up Goldwater's hat and placed it on his head, then he and Stone yanked him to his feet. Paul and Captain Stone dragged the struggling Goldwater out the front door. As Deal opened the gate, Levi dashed up and demanded to know where they were taking him. Stone replied that they were going to the railroad depot. At that, Judge Levi exclaimed, "I am an officer, and will not allow you to kidnap Goldwater!"

Levi seized Captain Stone, who jerked his pistol and ordered him back. Then the three officers marched Goldwater to the train. Deputy Sheriff Mabbitt raced to the sheriff's office for help. As Paul climbed the steps of the lone passenger car, Levi again tried to free Goldwater by pulling him back. Paul drew his Colt Lightning revolver and warned, "I am a deputy United States marshal and Goldwater is my prisoner." Levi wisely let go of Goldwater. Before Mabbitt could arrive with help, the train steamed out of Yuma. As soon as they crossed the Colorado River bridge into California, Paul turned the prisoner over to Captain Stone. Goldwater was taken back to San Francisco, where he was quickly released on $5,000 bond. Three weeks later Deputy U.S. Marshal Joseph W. Evans arrived in Yuma and attempted to seize the disputed goods from Lyons. He was met with an armed force of Lyons's friends, including guards from the Yuma prison. Evans arrested several of them and seized all of the disputed merchandise, which was shipped back to San Francisco. The criminal charges against Joe Goldwater were dismissed after the goods were returned. But for years the incident would remain a black spot on the reputation of the Goldwater family.[1]

Paul was now spending much of his time riding shotgun on the stage route between Tombstone and the railroad depot at Benson. Tombstone was the county seat of newly created Cochise County. The Anglo California Bank in San Francisco made a number of large shipments of coin to Tombstone, and Wells Fargo's assistant superintendent, L. F. Rowell, assigned Paul to guard the route. It was a wise decision, for by this time some of the Cowboys had graduated from stock theft to stage robbery. On the night of February 16, 1881, the stage from Globe to Florence was stopped by two masked road agents near Dripping Springs. Finding the Wells Fargo box empty, they looted the U.S. mailbag and disappeared. Paul investigated and some months later found evidence that the bandits were Pony Deal and Sherman McMaster, a former Texas Ranger. A week after the Dripping Springs holdup, newly formed Cochise County experienced its first stage robbery. Tombstone was connected to the railhead at Benson by a twenty-eight-mile stage road that ran west from Tombstone ten miles to the San Pedro River and then followed the river north past Contention City to Benson. On February 25, a stagecoach was held up and robbed near Contention City, but the highwaymen found only $135 in the Wells Fargo box. Because the shipment had been so small, Paul had not been aboard. The road agents did not molest the passengers or the U.S. mail, and they were never caught.[2]

Doc Holliday was a good friend of one of the Cowboys, for he had known Billy Leonard in Las Vegas, New Mexico. Leonard was a jeweler by trade but a thief and morphine addict by avocation. He had fled Las Vegas to escape charges of carrying deadly weapons and shooting a man. He drifted to the southwest corner of New Mexico, where he claimed good ranch land near Cloverdale Springs. Like the other Cowboys who could easily make the hundred-mile ride in less than two days, Leonard enjoyed regular visits to Tombstone. In March 1881 Leonard, Harry Head, Jim Crane, and Luther King were staying in a house at the Wells, two miles north of Tombstone. Doc Holliday was in the habit of occasionally renting a horse and riding out to visit them, probably to play cards. On the afternoon of March 15, 1881, Doc Holliday did exactly that. While he stopped at Leonard's house, Paul was at the Kinnear & Company stage office in Tombstone. He swung his massive frame onto the front seat of the Benson bound stage with no idea that the events that night would set off one of the most remarkable sagas of the Old West—the street gunfight near the OK Corral and the ensuing Earp-Clanton vendetta.[3]

At the reins of the Concord coach was twenty-seven-year-old Eli "Bud" Philpott, a popular whip who hailed from Calistoga, California, where his young wife and son lived. An experienced reinsman on the line between Calistoga and Lakeport, Philpott had been awarded a gold watch by Wells Fargo in 1877 for foiling a stage robbery. He had been in Arizona for a year. Wyatt Earp, who had ridden next to Philpott as shotgun messenger, admired "the accuracy with which he would flick a sandfly off the near leader's flank or plant a mouthful of tobacco juice in the heart of a cactus as we jolted past it." His coach carried six passengers. Inside the Wells Fargo strongbox was $26,000 in bullion. It was early evening when the stage rattled out of town. The air was cold, and Paul huddled in his heavy overcoat, sawed-off shotgun resting on his knees. Two miles west, at Watervale, the stagecoach stopped and picked up a pair of young Canadian miners, Peter Roerig and his partner, Davis. The latter took a seat inside, while Roerig climbed onto the rear dickey seat on top of the crowded coach.[4]

In a memoir written in 1913, Billy Breakenridge claimed that when the stage halted at Watervale, "Doc Holloday [sic] who was there on horse back brought out a drink of whiskey and wanted Paul to take it but Bob refused telling him he never drank while on duty, afterward he had every reason to be thankful he had refused because undoubtedly it was drugged." While Holliday was certainly in the area, it is most improbable that he would have attempted to drug Paul, who was Wyatt Earp's good friend and ally.[5]

The highway to Contention was a rough one, as Wyatt Earp later recalled: "The worst part of the road was where it skirted the San Pedro River. There the track was all sandy and cut up, which made traveling about as exhilarating as riding a rail." The trip was uneventful as the stage stopped to change horses at Contention, shortly after sundown, then proceeded toward Drew's Station, two miles beyond. Two hundred yards before reaching the stage station, the road crossed a dry, ten-foot-deep wash that drained the hills to the east. The stage road dropped into the wash, followed the sandy streambed for a short distance, and then climbed up a low spot in the opposite bank. As the coach swayed along the middle of the wash, Paul suddenly spotted four men with rifles, two each on the ten-foot-high embankments on both sides of the road. The full moon kept the landscape well lit, and, according to one report, Paul recognized the form of Billy Leonard outlined against the night sky. One of the figures briskly stepped into the road from Paul's right and shouted, "Hold!"

"I don't hold for anybody!" Paul thundered.

Simultaneously, two bandits on each side of the stagecoach opened fire with Winchesters. Paul threw his sawed-off shotgun to his shoulder and emptied both barrels. Two buckshot slammed into Billy Leonard's belly, and he staggered, painfully wounded. The robbers poured a volley of fire into the stagecoach. One bullet passed through Paul's seat cushion, and two bullets tattered his clothing. A rifle slug ripped into Bud Philpott's left arm, above the elbow. It tore through his arm, shattering the bone, entered his left side through the ribs, cut the aorta, and severed his spinal column. The driver pitched forward, and Paul seized him with one hand. But the messenger's great strength was not enough to keep Philpott from falling over the footboard. Paul almost lost his seat as the driver dropped between the wheel horses and landed heavily on the road, dead. The horses, crazed by gunfire, broke into a dead run. The outlaws riddled the fleeing coach with bullets, mortally wounding Peter Roerig, who was completely exposed at the rear of the coach. Some twenty shots were fired before the uncontrollable stage thundered past Drew's Station. Paul, unable to retrieve the reins, worked the brake for a mile until he finally brought the runaway team to a halt. Looking back for the first time, he saw Peter Roerig slumped on top of the coach, desperately wounded.

The gunfire roused the hostlers at Drew's Station. They ran to the scene and, in the bright moonlight, found Philpott's body in the road and saw the bandits fleeing into the distance on horseback. At eleven o'clock, Paul brought the stagecoach into Benson, where Peter Roerig died a few minutes later. Paul telegraphed news of the attack to Marshall Williams, the Wells Fargo agent in Tombstone. With four local men, Paul raced back to the holdup scene, where he found that the robbers had built brush blinds for concealment on either side of the road. Thirteen expended Winchester shells and two unfired cartridges were found on the roadside, along with three cloth masks covered with frayed rope to simulate long hair and whiskers. The tracks of four horses headed east; blood droppings showed that Paul had wounded one of the bandits.[6]

The double murder of two innocent men during the course of a robbery was not taken lightly in nineteenth-century America. In addition to the standing rewards of $300 offered by the Territory of Arizona and Wells

The author standing at the site of the attack on Bob Paul's stage near Drew's Station. Photograph by Alan Blanchette.

Fargo & Company, the governor and Wells Fargo offered another $300, making the aggregate bounty $1,200 each for the fugitive bandits. Paul's quick actions during the holdup were widely praised. Reported the *Tombstone Epitaph*, "There were eight passengers on the coach, and they all united in praise of Mr. Paul's bravery and presence of mind."[7]

In Tombstone, Marshall Williams promptly raised a posse of capable lawmen: Virgil, Wyatt, and Morgan Earp and their good friend William Barclay "Bat" Masterson, the noted gambler and lawman. Arthur Cowan, Wells Fargo agent in Contention, recruited a posse of almost thirty local men. Paul met the posses at the holdup site. Explained Virgil Earp, "The night was so dark we could not follow the trail and had to lie there until daylight, when Sheriff Behan came down" (Johnny Behan had recently been appointed Cochise County's first sheriff). Of the volunteer possemen from Contention, Virgil said, "Twenty-five or thirty men offered their services to pursue, and he [Behan] told them all he wanted was the Earp boys and Bob Paul."[8]

At 5:00 A.M. the Earps, Paul, Masterson, Behan, and Williams set out on the killers' trail. It led east toward the Dragoon Mountains, where a party of woodchoppers told the lawmen that three riders had passed by, heading east toward the San Simon Valley. Paul and the rest followed their sign for several miles, when the tracks suddenly turned westward to the San Pedro River and crossed the stream below Tres Alamos, then headed up the river valley. The outlaws rode single file and employed every trick they knew to outwit their pursuers. They double-backed on their trail and rode for miles on solid rock. At one point they went a long distance in the river, then rode out into the brush, then back into the stream, then along a bar of rocks, and finally up a steep rocky bank out of the river. This last trick threw the posse off the track, but Paul and the others finally picked up the trail again. It led to William Wheaton's ranch on the San Pedro River, which the posse reached on March 18 after three days and 150 miles of hard riding. There they found a broken-down horse, its back raw from saddle sores.

The outlaws' tracks were completely wiped out by the stock on the ranch, so Paul and the posse continued north along the river to the next ranch, owned by Hank Redfield. Redfield assured the lawmen that no riders had passed his ranch. Morgan Earp, however, found fresh sign nearby, which the posse followed four miles down the river to the ranch of Len Redfield. The Redfields' ranches were located near present-day Redington, about forty miles northeast of Tucson. Paul later learned that Len Redfield had lived in Arizona since 1875 and hailed from Tulare County, California, where his family was prominent. The brothers had borne good reputations in California, but their San Pedro ranches would become known as hangouts for robbers and cattle rustlers. It later developed that Len Redfield was a friend of both Pony Deal and Curly Bill; the latter was a regular visitor to the Redfield ranch. Paul would have good reason to remember the Redfield brothers.[9]

As the officers rode up to Len Redfield's place, they spotted a figure milking a cow in the corral. Suddenly he leaped over the corral fence and ran for the underbrush. Wyatt and Morgan Earp raced after and collared him. The man proved to be Luther King. He carried a Winchester rifle, two six-guns, and a heavily loaded cartridge belt. Paul and Wyatt Earp grilled him closely, and he soon admitted that the worn-out pony found by the officers belonged to him. King made a number of conflicting statements about how he happened to be at Redfield's ranch. Len Redfield told the lawmen that King worked for him and that he had previously been a cowhand. What methods of persuasion Paul used on King can only be guessed at, but he soon broke down and admitted his guilt. King named Leonard,

Crane, and Head as the other robbers, and he offered the time-worn excuse that he had only held the horses while the others did the shooting. King told the lawmen that Leonard, Crane, and Head were camped near Hank Redfield's place and that Hank had supplied them with fresh mounts that morning. The officers had unwisely allowed Hank Redfield to leave the ranch. By the time the posse located the outlaws' camping place, Hank Redfield had warned the killers, and they had fled.[10]

By this time the posse had not been heard from for three days, and the officers' friends feared the worst. Wire reports from Tombstone the next day, March 18, declared, "Grave fears are expressed that they have fallen into the hands of the desperadoes. . . . If no word is received here from the pursuers before morning a large expedition will be organized to go at once to their aid, or to avenge them if they have met with an ill fate." However, later that day Johnny Behan and Marshall Williams returned to Tombstone with Luther King while Paul, Bat Masterson, and the Earps started out again in pursuit of the murderers. Paul and the others picked up the trail of the three killers and followed it west toward the Santa Catalina Mountains. As night fell, they found a freshly extinguished campfire, proof that they were close behind their quarry. Paul was too old a hand to make camp with the outlaws so close; he decided to return to Redfield's ranch for the night, where he believed there would be less chance of an ambush. In the morning, March 19, the officers again started on the trail. They were at a severe disadvantage: their horses were tired, while the outlaws had been supplied with fresh mounts by the Redfields.[11]

For six days they tracked the outlaws through the Tanque Verde, Rincon, and Santa Catalina Mountains, through the Oracles and Canada del Oro, east through the Santa Cruz Mountains, across the San Pedro River, and back toward the Dragoons. They learned that the outlaws had stolen eight horses at Charles Helm's ranch, near the middle pass in the Dragoons, northeast of Tombstone. At a telegraph station on the railroad they sent word to Sheriff Behan to meet them with horses and supplies at Helm's ranch. "We telegraphed to Behan for fresh horses, as ours were played out," said Virgil Earp. "Behan met us where we expected to get the horses but he did not bring them. That night Bob Paul's horse laid down and died. Wyatt's and Masterson's horses were so used up they were left at the ranch and the boys had to hoof it in eighteen miles to Tombstone."[12]

Wyatt Earp and Bat Masterson walked back to Tombstone, while Paul sent instructions for wanted circulars to be published announcing an aggregate $3,600 reward for Leonard, Crane, and Head. The reward notice offered detailed descriptions of the three robbers. Paul described Billy Leonard as thirty years old, slender, with "long, dark, curly hair when cared for hanging in ringlets down to shoulders; . . . small, sharp, and very effeminate features; . . . left arm full of scars caused by injecting morphine; . . . chews tobacco incessantly; speaks good Spanish; good shot with rifle and pistol; a jeweler by trade." Jim Crane's description was "American; about 27 years old; about 5 feet, 11 inches high; weight 175 or 180 pounds; . . . talks and laughs at same time; talks slow and hesitating; illiterate; cattle driver or cow-boy." Paul listed Harry Head as the youngest of the bunch: "About 18 or 20 years old; . . . chunky and well built; dark complexion; dark hair and eyes; rather dandyish; almost beardless; . . . good rider, and handy with rifle and pistol."[13]

It was March 24 when Sheriff Behan, his deputy, Billy Breakenridge, and Buckskin Frank Leslie, a noted Indian scout, met Bob Paul and Virgil and Morgan Earp at Helm's ranch. Once again they took up the fugitives' trail, but now the posse was several days behind. The tracks led east twenty-five miles to the Sulphur Spring Valley, then across the Chiricahua Mountains near Fort Bowie toward the San Simon Cienega. Believing that their quarry was headed for Galeyville, a small mining camp and notorious outlaws' hangout on the east slope of the Chiricahuas, the possemen cut directly across the mountain range in an effort to head them off. Virgil Earp was riding the same horse he started the hunt with, and Paul's and Morgan Earp's mounts were badly worn out. Behan, Breakenridge, and Leslie, on fresh animals, rode far in front of the others. In Galeyville the officers learned that Billy Leonard owned a stock ranch near Cloverdale Springs, across the line in the southwest corner of New Mexico. They rode on to Joe Hill's ranch at the San Simon Cienega, where they spent the night.[14]

Joe Hill was willing to feed the posse, but he would not betray his Cowboy friends. The lawmen asked him for directions to Cloverdale Springs, but they were foolish to have trusted him. Breakenridge later explained, "As none of us had ever been in that part of the country before, we had to inquire the way to Cloverdale, and were directed wrongly as we ought to have expected." Hill sent them due east, through the Stein's Pass Range, instead of southeast toward the New Mexico boot heel. After a hard forty-mile ride, they came that night to a deserted ranch house called the Double Dobe, situated on Double Adobe Creek, about fifteen miles south of present-day Animas, New Mexico, and a good twenty miles north of Cloverdale. With only water from a spring for nourishment, they spent a

$3,600 00 REWARD.

ARREST THE MURDERERS!

ABOUT 9 o'clock Tuesday evening, March 15, 1881, the stage bound from Tombstone to Benson was attacked by three men armed with Winchester rifles, at a point about two miles west from Drew's stage station, and Budd Philpot, the driver, and Peter Roerig, a passenger, shot and killed.

The attack was no doubt made for the purpose of robbery. The Territory and Wells, Fargo & Co. have a liberal standing reward for the arrest and conviction of persons robbing or attempting to rob the Express. In addition, the Governor and Wells, Fargo & Co. have each offered $300 for the arrest and conviction of each of the murderers of Philpot and Roerig, so that the rewards now offered amount to $1,200 or $1,400 each.

It is believed that the attempted robbery and murders were committed by Bill Leonard, Jim Crain and Harry Head, described as follows:

BILL LEONARD.

American; about 30 years old; about 5 feet, 8 or 9 inches high; weight, 120 lbs.; long, dark, curly hair, when cared for hanging in ringlets down to shoulders; small, dark, boyish mustache, otherwise almost beardless; teeth very white and regular; dark eyes; small, sharp and very effeminate features; rather weak voice; left arm full of scars caused by injecting morphine; is subject to rheumatism; chews tobacco incessantly; speaks good Spanish; good shot with rifle and pistol; a jeweler by trade; is known in Silver City, Otero and Los Vegas, N. M.

JAMES CRAIN.

American; about 27 years old; about 5 feet, 11 inches high; weight, 175 or 180 lbs.; light complexion; light, sandy hair; light eyes; has worn light mustache; full, round face, and florid, healthy appearance; talks and laughs at same time; talks slow and hesitating; illiterate; cattle driver or cow-boy,

HARRY HEAD.

About 18 or 20 years old; 5 feet, 4 or 5 inches high, weight, 120 lbs.; chunky and well built; dark complexion; dark hair and eyes; rather dandyish; almost beardless; small foot and hand; good rider, and handy with rifle and pistol.

All mounted, and well armed with rifles and pistols, and the last trace of them they were going toward San Simon Valley.

If arrested, immediately inform Sheriff Behan and the undersigned by telegraph at Tombstone, A. T.

R. H. PAUL,
Special Officer of W., F. & Co.

Tombstone, A. T., March 23, 1881.

Reward poster issued by Bob Paul for Billy Leonard, Jim Crane, and Harry Head. Author's collection.

hungry night in the adobe dwelling. The next day, completely lost, they pushed on fifty miles due east, hoping to find a ranch where they could get food and water. The country was desolate and isolated. They were now on a wide-open plain, with no trees or water in sight. They made a dry camp and slept in the desert. The officers spent half of the next day search-ing in vain for a spring, when Virgil Earp's horse dropped dead from exhaustion caused by two weeks of hard riding. Morgan dismounted and packed his brother's saddle and traps on his mount, and the Earps con-tinued on foot. Paul, who at age fifty-one was by far the oldest member of the posse, remained on horseback. The posse now started back to the Double Dobe, as it was the only place that they knew had water.[15]

They reached the abandoned ranch by nightfall, half-dead from thirst and hunger. The posse had now been sixty hours without food and thirty-six hours without water. In the morning, Behan, Breakenridge, and Leslie headed back to San Simon Cienega, with Paul and the Earps follow-ing as best as they could. Buckskin Frank kept their spirits up, as Billy Breakenridge later related: "That was my first trip with Frank Leslie. He was the life of the party; he had a good voice and sang well, told good stories, never complained of being tired, was always ready to go. He was a much better companion than he was in town."[16]

At Joe Hill's ranch Sheriff Behan sent Hill's hired hand back with provisions and water for the other three. He met the famished Paul and the Earps at two o'clock that morning. In four and a half days they had eaten nothing except a single quail that they had managed to shoot. After eating and resting, the posse joined together and returned to Galeyville in search of fresh horses. Although Paul and the Earp boys had almost died in the desert, they were unwilling to give up the chase. But in Galeyville they could not get horses, and the possemen were in such physically weak condition that they reluctantly agreed to give up the pursuit. Paul returned to his home in Tucson, and the rest arrived in Tombstone on April 1. Bob Paul and the Earp boys had been continuously on the trail for seventeen days and had ridden more than five hundred miles across some of the most rugged terrain in the Southwest. The *Tucson Arizona Star* did not exaggerate when it pointed out that their ride "will pass into our frontier annals—more especially as regards Bob Paul and the Earp Boys," for the manhunt is remembered by western historians today as one of the most relentless of the Old West.[17]

This manhunt marked the beginning of hard feelings between Johnny Behan and the Earp boys. Behan had promised to appoint Wyatt undersheriff of Cochise County, but he reneged. To add injury to insult, Behan failed to pay the posse members. Complained Virgil Earp, "Behan brought in a bill against the county for $796.84. We supposed it was to pay expenses for the whole party, but he rendered it as a private account. I went before the Supervisors but they said Behan must vouch for us. This he refused to do, saying he had not deputized us. Everybody but my brothers and myself were paid, and we did not get a cent until Wells Fargo found it out and paid us for our time. From that time our troubles commenced, and the cowboys plotted to kill us." Wells Fargo records bear out the accuracy of Virgil's statement, as the company's general cash books of June and July 1881 show a total payment of $208 to Wyatt, Virgil, and Morgan Earp and Bat Masterson for "expenses in search of stage robbers."[18]

Upon his return to Tucson Paul was shocked to learn that Luther King had escaped from Sheriff Behan's jail. Wells Fargo detective Jim Hume had arrived in Tombstone on March 19 to help investigate the stagecoach murders. On March 28, a few days before Paul's return, Hume warned Behan's undersheriff, Harry Woods, to guard King closely because an attempt would be made to help him escape. Virgil Earp later explained, "Hume got Wyatt to go with him to the Sheriff's office to notify them, and they asked for a favor to put King in irons. He promised to do so, and fifteen minutes afterward King escaped, going on a horse that was tied back of the Sheriff's office." In an unguarded moment, King had picked up a deputy's revolver, walked out the back door, and rode off on a waiting horse. Bob Paul, given the several breaks from his leaky jail in Mokelumne Hill, would normally have been the last person to fault Johnny Behan. But Paul's escapes had all been due to poor jail construction, not inept jail-keeping. No doubt he was furious and believed, like most citizens, that Behan and Woods were grossly negligent. This would not be the last time that Behan's competence as a lawman would be questioned.[19]

Paul's thoughts now turned to his election lawsuit. Charlie Shibell's appeal to the Arizona Supreme Court had been pending for several months. On April 11, Paul appeared in the supreme court in Phoenix with his attorney, Alex Campbell, for the hearing on Shibell's appeal. Campbell made a motion to dismiss the appeal for lack of jurisdiction. The justices considered the motion and the next day issued an order dismissing the appeal and sending the case back to the trial court for further proceedings. Why the justices believed they had no jurisdiction is not explained in court documents. Declared the editor of the *Phoenix Herald*, "This makes Paul Sheriff of Pima County."[20]

But Shibell hung on desperately to his sheriff's badge. The next day he left with two prisoners for the California state insane asylum in Stockton, which then housed Arizona's mentally ill convicts. Paul returned to Tucson and made a demand upon Undersheriff Henry Ward for possession of the sheriff's office and its papers and effects. Ward refused on the ground that there was no order from the district court that Shibell vacate the office. The *Star* reported that Shibell planned on appealing to the U.S. Supreme Court. For more than two weeks Shibell stubbornly held on. Wrote *Star* editor Louis Hughes: "Mr. Shibell still retains possession of the office . . . and will continue to do so until he is removed by due process of law." Paul ignored Shibell's intransigence and filed his bonds as assessor with the county recorder. At the same time Shibell filed his own bonds, contending that he was still sheriff and assessor. When one of Shibell's deputy assessors attempted to exert his authority, an exasperated Paul arrested him for impersonating an officer and brought him into court for arraignment. Lawyers for Paul and Shibell spent the entire day arguing the matter before justice of the peace W. J. Osborn. Commented Hughes, "It is to be hoped that this case will settle the vexed question one way or the other." Finally Justice Osborn found that there was sufficient evidence to hold the deputy for trial and remanded him to Paul's custody as sheriff. Editor Hughes conceded that "the court by this action [was] virtually recognizing Paul as Sheriff of the county."[21]

In an editorial, Hughes put aside his partisanship long enough to urge Shibell to give up for the public good: "There is growing impression in this community, and particularly among the adherents of Mr. Shibell, that the public interests would best be conserved by the final abandonment of what seems to be a hopeless claim, and a graceful yielding to the apparently inevitable. Until this contest is finally and effectually settled, a feeling of doubt and distrust as to the legality of the acts of the chief executive officer of the county must prevail, and such feeling can but deleteriously affect the public welfare." Shibell followed this advice, and on April 27 he formally turned over his office to Paul. Within a few days John N. Thacker was appointed to take Paul's place as Wells Fargo detective in Arizona.[22]

The veteran lawman immediately appointed James J. Coleman his undersheriff. His first deputies were John W. Evarts and Agustin Caballero, the latter a well-known Mexican American who had been active in Republican politics. Paul named Isaac E. Brokaw as jailer, the duties of which included supervising an assistant jailer and two guards. Ike Brokaw was a noted character. He had served as a lawman on Nevada's Comstock Lode in the early 1860s. In San Francisco in 1870 Brokaw killed a gambler, "White Headed" Bob Evans, for sleeping with his wife. Sentenced to sixteen years in San Quentin, he was pardoned in 1875 and drifted to Arizona Territory, where he became city marshal of Tucson and served as deputy under Charlie Shibell. Paul believed that Brokaw had reformed, and, in recognition of his police experience, the sheriff had no qualms about making him jailer. Paul strove to hire men of experience, although most of his deputies served only a year or two before moving on. He had little concern for their political, religious, or ethnic status. When James Coleman resigned in May 1882 to become a Cochise County deputy sheriff under Johnny Behan, Paul appointed Henry Ward as undersheriff. Though Ward had been Shibell's loyal undersheriff, Paul did not hold that against him, for he recognized that Ward had the experience needed to perform the office's civil duties.[23]

Because Pima County had such a large Hispanic population, Paul wanted officers who spoke Spanish. Alfredo E. Carrillo, a thirty-six-year-old Californio who had settled in Tucson, first worked for Paul as a jail guard and was later promoted to deputy sheriff. One of the sheriff's most loyal deputies was Nathan B. Appel, a German Jew and early pioneer who had settled in Arizona in 1858 and took a Hispanic wife. Appel would act for many years as constable, deputy sheriff, and chief of police of Tucson, finally serving fourteen years as a policeman in Los Angeles. He was fluent in English, Spanish, French, and German, had long worked as a freighter on the Arizona frontier, and had been wounded in several battles with Indians. Thomas D. Casanega was a Serb who lived in Southern California before coming to Arizona. Because of his last name, dark complexion, and fluency in Spanish, many Anglos thought he was Hispanic. Tom Casanega served as a deputy under Paul from 1882 to 1884. Sheriff Paul would also work closely with James Speedy, who for many years was a deputy sheriff and constable in Nogales. Speedy's father was English, his mother was Chileno, and he too spoke Spanish fluently.[24]

One of Paul's first jobs was to inventory the meager equipment of the Pima County sheriff's office. The property included office furniture, account ledgers, law books, legal forms, and assorted tools, lamps, and even a well bucket and rope. For the jail, there were tables, blankets, dishes, eating utensils, twenty-seven pairs of iron shackles, eight pairs of handcuffs, and five padlocks. As was customary in that era, Paul and his deputies had to furnish their own guns, ammunition, saddles, tack, and horses. If they needed buggies or wagons to transport witnesses or prisoners, they had to buy or rent them. But the sheriff's income was substantial, and Paul soon acquired a stable of fast horses for manhunting.[25]

Paul's new duties as sheriff differed little from those he had in Calaveras. He ran the county jail, served civil process papers, provided security for the courts, and rounded up reluctant jurors for both civil and criminal trials. Under territorial law, the sheriff also acted as ex officio county assessor and tax collector. He employed three deputy assessors whose duty was to travel throughout the county and affix taxable values to real property and the improvements thereon (houses, barns, wells, and mines) and also to value such personal property as cattle and horses. The latter was especially difficult, as roving stockmen would move their herds from one jurisdiction to another to evade assessment. The sheriff's final duty as tax collector was even more onerous. While small property owners and ranchers might try to duck the collectors, railroads and mining companies would resort to the more sophisticated tactic of litigation to delay or avoid collection. Tax collecting was also a political minefield, for it brought the sheriff into conflict with otherwise law-abiding citizens, and it had the potential for creating hard feelings and enemies at election time.[26]

One of Paul's first actions as sheriff revealed his depth of experience and knowledge of civil law. Learning that a Tucson merchant was about to move a large stock of goods from the city to avoid paying taxes on them, he promptly assessed the merchandise and demanded the taxes owed. The merchant refused and said that he had already shipped the goods. Paul knew every trick that businessmen used to evade taxes, so he went to the railroad depot, located the shipment, and seized it. The outraged merchant had no choice but to pay up. Despite his bitter opposition to Paul, Editor Hughes of the *Star* was impressed: "While this proceeding may be somewhat new to our people, yet it is strictly in accordance with the law, and it is a good point for Paul." As a warning to other recalcitrant taxpayers, Hughes then published the statute that Paul had invoked. Soon after, the new sheriff began another aggressive effort to collect taxes by ordering the assessment of all ore found in the dumps of Pima County's mines. Commented Editor Hughes, "Although this may be a hardship to some of our mine-owners it is nevertheless in accordance with the law."[27]

Nor was the powerful Southern Pacific immune from Sheriff Paul's aggressive tax collecting. Perhaps because the company claimed it was exempt under federal law from paying taxes, Shibell had overlooked much of the property owned by the new railroad. Paul, on the other hand, had his deputy assessors make a thorough valuation of Southern Pacific property, which they completed in July 1881. Then Paul levied an assessment against the Southern Pacific for everything it owned in Pima County: sixty-eight miles of track bed, its telegraph line, all of its land and buildings in Tucson, its property at the Rillito, Papago, and Pantano stations, and its "rolling stock, materials, fuel, furniture, fixtures, tools, trucks, scales and all other personal property." To the dismay of Southern Pacific officials, the total assessment was just over $202,000. They promptly appealed to the county board of equalization (made up of two members of the board of supervisors), which instead of decreasing the assessment actually raised it by another $189,000. When the Southern Pacific refused to pay, Sheriff Paul advertised the railroad's property for public sale. After the company filed suit against Paul in 1882, the county board of equalization reduced the assessment by $100,000. However, Southern Pacific attorneys pressed forward with their lawsuit. When the case came to trial in 1883, they proved that the act of Congress that authorized the building of the railroad made it exempt from local taxes for six years after the line was completed. The Pima County district judge set aside the assessment and issued an injunction prohibiting Paul from collecting the taxes. Although Bob Paul would often be accused of being a tool of the Southern Pacific, his actions in this case show otherwise.[28]

The greatest financial risk to a county sheriff involved mistakes in the attachment of real and personal property to satisfy court judgments. To guard against this, and to provide financial protection for those who might be damaged by an officer's actions, a sheriff was required to be bonded. In those years such bonds were not issued by surety companies, but instead by friends of the sheriff who pledged their own property as security, in the same way a bail bond was made. If it turned out that the property seized and sold by the sheriff was actually owned by a third party, the sheriff and his bondsmen could be personally liable for the damages. For Paul, this problem would surface almost immediately.[29]

Tucson's largest mercantile establishment was Lord & Williams. It had been founded twelve years earlier by Tucson's postmaster, W. W. Williams, and his partner, Charles H. Lord, a physician who had come to Arizona as a military surgeon. They prospered, running a bank and selling goods and livestock to citizens and the government. Dr. Lord was a controversial figure who for years lived lavishly, far beyond his means. In 1881 the firm failed spectacularly, with debts estimated at $200,000 to $400,000. Dr. Lord fled to Mexico and tried to convince his life insurance companies that he was dead. One of the firm's creditors obtained a writ of attachment, which was handed to Sheriff Paul for execution. In order to enforce the writ, Paul seized and sold the firm's entire $35,000 stock of merchandise in its store on Congress Street. However, unknown to Paul, months earlier Lord & Williams had sold the stock to another merchant, Henry Cullum. An incensed Cullum brought a lawsuit against Paul, demanding return of the merchandise or $35,000 in damages. This case would alternately linger and be litigated in the courts for many years and would later have severe financial repercussions for Paul.[30]

In May 1881 Tucson joined the ranks of modern cities by getting local telephone service. The telephone headquarters were established in a building next to the post office, poles and lines were erected, and telephone receivers were set up at various businesses in town. There was no residential service yet, but for public-safety purposes, telephones were installed in the houses of Sheriff Paul and City Marshal Adolph G. Buttner. This was undoubtedly one of the earliest examples of police telephone use in the Southwest, and it illustrates Paul's forward-looking approach to law enforcement.[31]

Soon after taking office, Sheriff Paul learned that wild rumors were circulating in Tombstone that Doc Holliday had been one of the highwaymen at Drew's Station. Doc's close friendship with Billy Leonard, coupled with his visit to the robbers' house just before the attack, created suspicion. The rumors came to fruition early in July when Holliday's paramour, "Big Nose" Kate Elder, after a drunken spat and at the urging of Sheriff Behan, swore out an affidavit accusing Holliday of complicity in the murders of Bud Philpott and Peter Roerig. The district attorney made an investigation and reported that "there was not the slightest evidence to show the guilt of the defendant." He dismissed the charges. Elder's affidavit was the basis for oft-repeated claims that Holliday and the Earp brothers were behind the stage robberies in Southern Arizona. But as Jim Hume later commented, "Doc Holliday, although a man of dissipated habits and a gambler, has never been a thief and was never in any way connected with the attempted stage robbery. . . . The statement that he was present on the occasion of that robbery was put forth by the cowboys and their friends to throw further discredit upon the Earp brothers and their friends." This incident caused even more hard feelings between Wyatt Earp and Johnny Behan. To make things worse, Behan's former paramour, the beautiful Josephine Sarah "Sadie" Marcus, turned her attentions to Wyatt.[32]

Wyatt Earp wanted to be sheriff of Cochise County, and he approached three of the Cowboys, Ike Clanton, Frank McLaury, and Joe Hill, behind the Oriental Saloon and made them an offer. If they would put him on the track of Leonard, Crane, and Head, and Wyatt could capture or kill them, he would give them the entire $3,600 reward. All Earp wanted was the publicity, which he hoped would result in his election as sheriff. Wyatt said he also wanted to help his friend Holliday: "I told Ike Clanton . . . that there were some parties here in town who were trying to give Doc Holliday the worst of it by their talk, that there was some suspicion that he knew something about the attempted robbery and killing of Bud Philpott, and if I could catch Leonard, Head, and Crane, I could prove to the citizens that he knew nothing about it." According to Earp, Clanton agreed. Clanton later denied making such a deal, but he admitted that Earp had approached him and made the offer. For the time being, however, Wyatt's plan remained a secret.[33]

In the end, Earp's scheme came to naught. On June 17, 1881, Sheriff Paul received a message from Deming, New Mexico, that Billy Leonard had been slain. It turned out that after eluding Paul's posse, Leonard, Head, and Crane went to Leonard's claim near Cloverdale Springs. Leonard and Head had been trying to take over a neighboring ranch owned by two brothers, Ike and Billy Heslet, and had threatened to kill them. On June 11, Leonard and Head were at the general store in the mining camp of Eureka (now called Old Hachita), New Mexico, looking for the Heslet brothers, who were working at a nearby mine. Leonard told bystanders that he was going to shoot the Heslet boys on sight. Leonard was still suffering from the wounds inflicted by Paul's shotgun and said "that he wished someone would shoot him in the heart and put him out of his misery, as he had two big holes in his belly that he got when he tried to rob the stage at Tombstone."[34]

The Heslets got wind of the threats, and the next day they set up an ambush. As Leonard and Head rode up to the general store, Ike and Billy Heslet opened fire from an adjacent corral, killing them both. Their shooting down two of the Cowboys proved a fatal mistake. Four days later, on the night of June 16, the Heslet boys were playing cards in a Eureka saloon when a band of fifteen or twenty Cowboys led by Jim Crane burst in with guns blazing. Both Heslet boys and a fellow card player were riddled with bullets and instantly killed. Crane fled to Mexico, but he did not live long. On July 27 a band of Cowboys made a stock raid in northern Sonora and killed several Mexicans who pursued them. A troop of Mexican cavalry started after the Cowboys and came across the camp of the probable suspects on the night of August 13. The soldiers opened fire, killing six men, including Crane and Old Man Clanton. This left Luther King as the sole survivor of the four Cowboys who had killed Bud Philpott and Peter Roerig. It was rumored a few days after his escape from the Tombstone jail that Cowboys had lynched him in the Huachucas in revenge for squealing on his fellow robbers. According to other accounts, he was murdered in Mexico. Some writers have suggested that he was the rustler Sandy King, who was lynched with "Russian Bill" Tettenborn at Shakespeare, New Mexico, on November 9, 1881. Either way, Luther King was the last of the Cowboys who battled Bob Paul on the Tombstone stage.[35]

CHAPTER NINE

Wyatt Earp

Wyatt Earp is one of the most illustrious figures of the Old West and the most famous lawman in American history. But for most of his life he was a controversial character, best known for his role in the inaptly named "Gunfight at the OK Corral." During his waning years several writers discovered the dramatic significance of Earp's life, and after his death in 1929 a flood of books, novels, films, and television programs firmly cemented his place in legend. But the real Earp needed no fictional embellishments, for by any measure his story was an extraordinary one. He saw adventure on one frontier after another: first in the cattle towns of Kansas, then on the successive mining frontiers in Arizona, Idaho, and the Klondike. He counted as close friends some of the most colorful and romantic characters of the Old West—Bat Masterson, Doc Holliday, and Luke Short—and his brothers, especially Virgil and Morgan, achieved both fame and notoriety in their own right.

Born in Illinois in 1848, Wyatt Earp served briefly as a constable in Missouri and eventually drifted to the Kansas cattle frontier. In Wichita he was a policeman from 1874 to 1876 and made a good record until he was fired for brawling with a fellow officer. During the next two years he worked off and on as a deputy city marshal in Dodge City. In July 1878 he and Jim Masterson, younger brother of Bat, shot and killed a cowboy who resisted arrest. Although later writers invented deeds and exaggerated his importance in Wichita and Dodge City, Earp served ably as a lawman and acquired valuable experience that would serve him well in Tombstone.

Raised on the frontier, Wyatt Earp was a product of his environment. Early in life he absorbed the frontier ethic of self-redress with the six-shooter and of quick money from a faro bank, a roulette wheel, or a winning hand. Earp was ambitious; a quest for easy money would be the foremost driving influence in his life and explains much of his behavior. As a young man he engaged in farming, freighting, and manual work, but after the age of twenty-two he assiduously avoided manual labor. He found that policing paid a decent wage, allowed him time to gamble, and kept his hands uncalloused.

Wyatt was an enigmatic figure. Capable of great bravery and moral courage, at the same time he could be petty and vindictive. Loyal to his brothers and friends to a fault, he was a bitter and unrelenting enemy. He always lived on the outer fringe of respectable society, and his closest companions were gamblers and sporting men—racetrack touts, racehorse owners, prizefight promoters, saloonkeepers, faro dealers, and mining speculators. At the same time he was respected and befriended by reputable attorneys, lawmen, journalists, and politicians. His third (perhaps fourth) wife, probably a common-law relationship, was Josephine Sarah "Sadie" Marcus—grasping, suspicious, secretive, bitter, and a compulsive gambler. That Earp remained loyal to her for forty-seven years, until his death, speaks volumes both of his tolerance for her unattractive personality as well as his own secretive, suspicious, and grasping nature. Wyatt never set down roots in any one place: when the money stopped coming in or his problems became too great, he would pull up stakes and move on to the next boomtown. This was a pattern he would repeat until his final years. Perhaps Earp's greatest failing was his greatest skill—gambling. For his entire life was a gamble, an effort to make money without working hard for it, to succeed quickly without ever settling in for the long haul.

Despite his reputation today as the West's greatest peace officer, Earp spent only a few years behind the badge. He lived most of his life as an itinerant frontier gambler, racehorse manager, saloonkeeper, and mining speculator. Because he routinely associated with the saloon and gambling element, his ethics and morals were elastic at best. His life was repeatedly tainted with strong accusations of criminal behavior. In 1871, while serving as constable in Lamar, Missouri, Earp was charged with embezzling the paltry sum of $20; he skipped town before he could be tried. That same year he was indicted for horse theft in the Indian Territory, once again

Wyatt Earp in 1883. He called Bob Paul
"as fast a friend as I ever knew." Courtesy
of Robert G. McCubbin.

fleeing before he could be brought to trial. In 1872 in Peoria, Illinois, he
was arrested several times—and convicted—on charges of pimping and
prostitution. In 1885 he was accused of illegally entering a gambling parlor
in Hot Springs, Arkansas to mark and switch cards. In 1896, as referee of
the Sharkey-Fitzsimmons prizefight in San Francisco, he was accused of

accepting a $2,500 bribe to throw the fight. In 1911 an aging Earp was charged with taking part in a bunko scheme to swindle a Los Angeles man out of $2,500.[1]

These events provide substantial evidence that Wyatt was, at best, somewhat unscrupulous and, at worst, fundamentally dishonest, at least in financial matters. Wyatt lived with a prostitute, Sally Haspel, in Illinois and Kansas, and his second wife, Mattie Blaylock, was also a bawd. His common-law wife, Josephine Sarah Marcus, was rumored to have been a prostitute before she took up with Earp. Several of his brothers also married prostitutes. Earp gravitated to the frontier boom camps, where he was accepted socially as a gambler and fighting man. In later life, Earp would be vilified in the press for his actions, some dishonest and some not, and would be deeply wounded by the criticism. When his last boom—Alaska—was over, Wyatt returned to California and lived a nomadic life, drifting from the San Francisco–Oakland Bay Area to Los Angeles and to his mining property in the Mojave Desert. He never achieved social, professional, or political prominence and, for the most part, lived quietly. He achieved enduring fame with the release of Walter Noble Burns's hugely popular *Tombstone* in 1927 and Stuart N. Lake's bestselling biography, *Wyatt Earp: Frontier Marshal*, in 1931, two years after his death.

Despite a perennial quest for fast and easy money that led him into numerous controversies, Earp nonetheless had a myriad of fine qualities: dogged loyalty to his brothers and friends, an iron-willed determination to enforce the law, extraordinary courage, and superb skill with firearms. He was a strong leader of men and a highly capable lawman. Where others faltered from fear or lack of resolve, he pressed on, stubbornly and relentlessly. Earp was a man of extremes: his faults were severe, and his good qualities attracted a host of faithful comrades. As Charles Bartholomew, Tucson police officer and Wells Fargo shotgun messenger, said of him in 1888, "I never saw a braver nor a more efficient man than Wyatt Earp. He was gentlemanly and kind in his conduct."[2]

Bartholomew's thought was echoed twenty years later by Bat Masterson: "Wyatt Earp, like many more men of his character who lived in the West in its early days, has excited, by his display of great courage and nerve under trying conditions, the envy and hatred of those small-minded creatures with which the world seems to be abundantly peopled, and whose sole delight in life seems to be in fly-specking the reputations of real men.

I have known him since the early seventies and have always found him a quiet, unassuming man, not given to brag or bluster, but at all times and under all circumstances a loyal friend and an equally dangerous enemy."[3]

Bob Paul became a close friend of Earp. Wyatt and his brothers were very much like the footloose miners and gamblers he had known and liked during the gold rush and in the mining camps of Nevada and the eastern Sierra. At the same time, they were very different from him. None except Virgil were stable family men with the longtime careers necessary to support a wife and children. For the Earps and Doc Holliday, gambling was not a pastime, but an addiction. Paul, on the other hand, limited his gambling to risky mining ventures and worked hard to support his wife and children. And while some of the Earp wives and paramours had been prostitutes, Margaret Paul was a devout Roman Catholic, a devoted spouse, and a doting mother.

Paul's feelings about the Earps and Holliday are shown in two statements he would make to the newspapers. In one interview with a Denver journalist, he was asked his opinion about "the Earp gang." Paul quickly corrected the reporter, saying that the Earps were a faction, not a gang. He explained that Holliday was not regarded as a desperate character: "He was always decently peaceable, though his powers when engaged in following his ostensible calling, furthering the ends of justice, made him a terror to the criminal classes of Arizona." A second reporter who interviewed the sheriff at the same time wrote that Paul "is evidently in favor of Holliday and the Earps. . . . The cowboys, who represent the worst element of Arizona, were Democrats to a man. Holliday and the Earps represented the Republican element of Tombstone and the best class of citizens."[4]

Unlike the good-humored Paul, Wyatt Earp was quiet and serious, even dour. But Paul had great respect for Wyatt and Virgil and their abilities as peace officers. Johnny Behan, however, was cut from another cloth entirely. Unlike Wyatt, he was charming, fun, and highly sociable—all qualities that made him a natural politician. But like many western sheriffs, Behan was a politician, not a lawman. Although he had served a two-year term as sheriff in Prescott, he was at best inexperienced, and at worst incompetent. In his zeal for popularity and political capital, he befriended almost everyone, including many of the Cowboys. Even given the freewheeling social atmosphere of the frontier, Sheriff Behan's associations with the Cowboys were especially troubling. Wyatt Earp, who despised Behan, once said, "He stood in with this tough element, the cow boys and stage robbers and others, because they were pretty strong and he wanted their vote."[5]

As Paul pointed out, the Cowboys were mainly Democrats, for many of them were from the Southern states, particularly Texas. Behan was also a Democrat, while the Earps were staunch Republicans. Just as in Pima County, political divisions were deep and bitter in Cochise County. Tombstone's competing newspapers, the Republican *Epitaph* and the Democratic *Nugget*, were partisan in the extreme, and in both editorials and reporting, they stirred the cauldron. When Virgil Earp was appointed city marshal of Tombstone in June 1881, the feud between the Cowboys and the Earps intensified.

In the meantime Paul settled into his new duties as sheriff. On the afternoon of June 19 he was called on to investigate a murder near Warner's Mill, situated a mile southwest of Tucson. When a Yaqui Indian, Dolores Romero, got into a brawl with a fellow Yaqui, Matias, and a Mexican named Tiburcio, the latter two killed Romero and fled. That night Sheriff Paul got a tip that the murderers were still in the area. With City Marshal Adolph Buttner and police officer John Moore, he set out for Warner's Mill. Just east of the mill was an old convent, a massive two-story adobe built by the Spanish padres eighty years earlier. It was now abandoned and in ruins. Paul's little posse set up an ambush behind a low adobe wall in the convent gardens, halfway between the mill and the crumbling convent. It was midnight when several figures crept silently up to the wall and looked over. Spotting the dim forms of the crouching officers, they jumped back and opened fire. Bob Paul and his possemen leveled their weapons over the wall and responded with a barrage of gunfire. As the gunmen tried to flee in the blackness, Paul and his men charged after them. After a short pursuit, the assailants dropped their weapons and surrendered. Paul was flabbergasted to discover that they were not the killers, but instead a band of Yaqui Indians out to avenge the death of their compadre. Sheriff Paul no doubt gave them an angry lecture in Spanish before releasing them. He soon found some humor in the incident, as a local journalist commented: "Had the moon been up somebody would have been killed; as it was, the incident created a good deal of fun."[6]

One of the tasks Paul inherited from Charlie Shibell was to officiate at Pima County's first legal execution. Although the county had seen vigilantism over the years, most notably in an 1873 quadruple lynching in Tucson, there had never been a judicial hanging. The condemned man was Tom Harper, one of the Cowboys and a close friend of Curly Bill Brocius. On September 19, 1880, Harper had shot and killed an unarmed teamster, John Tolliday, in Ramsey Canyon in the Huachuca Mountains during a quarrel over thirty-five dollars that Harper owed to his victim. Harper fled for the border on horseback, but he was quickly captured and lodged in the Tucson jail. Just a month later the young desperado was tried, and although he claimed self-defense, the jury convicted him of murder. He was quickly sentenced to death. While Paul's election was being litigated, Harper's conviction had been on appeal to the territorial supreme court. When the trial verdict was upheld by the supreme court, Harper was scheduled to be hanged on July 8, 1881. Because the murder had taken place in Pima County before its split with Cochise, responsibility for the execution fell on Bob Paul.

Paul had assisted in four hangings in Calaveras, and his experience was evident to newspaper reporters and other observers. Sheriff Paul personally designed the gallows and supervised its construction in the jailyard. Eleven steps led to the platform, which was ten feet high and allowed the condemned man a drop of five to seven feet. The trap door was secured by a lever and bolt, and a spring mounted below the door prevented it from banging against the dangling body. The length of the drop was set according to a convict's weight and, if measured properly, would result in a broken neck and near-instant death. Like any experienced lawman of that era, Paul was careful to avoid a botched hanging by strangulation. Many bungled executions took place in the nineteenth century, and the cruel sight of a condemned man writhing and strangling to death inflamed the public and embarrassed sheriffs.

While the eerie sound of pounding hammers rattled through the jail, Harper received visits from Tucson's energetic Catholic priest, Father Antonio Jouvenceau, and several nuns. Due to a previous escape attempt, Sheriff Paul kept Harper ironed with a ball and chain. The desperado gave an interview to a newspaperman and insisted that he had killed Tolliday in self-defense: "He had told me he was heeled, and sworn to kill me before morning." Harper was fast losing his nerve and kept calling for liquor, but Paul allowed him only a little wine. Among Harper's last thoughts were those of his pal, Curly Bill. He left him a long letter, cautioning, "Curly, I want you to take warning by me. Do not be too handy with a pistol. Keep cool and never fire at a man unless in the actual defense of your life. You must stand a heap from a man before you kill him. Words do not hurt, so you must never mind what is said to aggravate you. . . . Give my kind regards to any of my old friends whom you may chance to meet, and tell them to take a warning by me. I bear no man ill will, and think I am going to die in peace."[7]

The next morning, July 8, carpenters were still finishing the scaffold. Harper's dying requests were to be allowed to inspect the gallows and to be photographed for his family and friends. Paul granted both wishes. At 2:30 P.M. the sheriff, accompanied by Undersheriff Ward and two of his deputies, Tucson City Marshal Buttner, and Father Jouvenceau, brought Harper into the jailyard. As was the custom, a crowd of 150—almost all the jailyard could hold—had been issued invitations to witness the hanging. Paul and Buttner, one on each side of the condemned man, helped Harper up the scaffold stairs. Sheriff Paul read aloud the death warrant, then asked Harper if he had any last words. In a low, mumbling tone, Harper replied that he had nothing to say. Then, spotting in the throng J. H. Martin, a Tucson policeman for whom he had once worked in Texas, Harper asked him to ascend the gallows. Martin did so, asking, "What is it, Tom?" The condemned man answered, "I want you to write my brother and send my picture."

Martin promised to do so. Harper requested another drink, which was given to him. He then called for a glass of cold water, but Paul, thinking he was trying to delay the inevitable, refused. Harper took his place on the trap, with the fatal noose draped around his neck, and called out, "Good-bye to the United States." Then, shaking hands with Undersheriff Ward, he said, "Boy, I always liked you." As the priest prayed, Harper readjusted the noose. Paul stopped him, placing the knot under his ear, and Harper complained, "That won't do. That's wrong." As the sheriff and his deputies strapped his legs and arms, Harper exclaimed, "Boys, well here goes." Paul dropped a black hood over his head, and the condemned man's muffled voice called out, "I have something to say before I die." He was drowned out by a distant peal of thunder that echoed ominously from the east. Sheriff Paul gave the signal, and Harper plunged through the trap, his neck broken by the fall. His body was taken to the Catholic church and, after a funeral service, was buried in Tucson's Catholic cemetery.[8]

Despite Sheriff Paul's determination to have orderly legal executions, lynch law was still common in frontier Arizona. On March 15, 1881, a few weeks before he became sheriff, two Mexicans named Jose Orduna and Rafael Salcido stole a band of horses on the Gila River in newly created

Graham County. A posse of Hispanic and Anglo ranchers pursued them down the San Simon Valley and captured both. Jose Orduna was strung up. In June a woman friend of Orduna wrote to the Mexican consul in Tucson, complaining about the lynching. He contacted Sheriff Paul, who looked into the incident and then replied to the consul:

> A large number of horses and mules was stolen on the 15th of March, 1881, from the ranches on the Gila River, in the neighborhood of Safford and Solomonsville, in Graham County. The owners of the stolen animals, to the number of about twenty, two thirds of whom were natives of Mexico, followed the trail and pursued the thieves. They succeeded in capturing Jose Orduna and Rafael Salcido, who had disposed of the animals and were returning to the Gila River. Jose Orduna, who was recognized as a horse and cattle thief, was hung by the pursuing party, and Salcido was compelled to go with them and show them where they had hidden the animals. He took them to the Valley of San Simon, and almost all the animals were found through the information given by him. The party returned to the Gila River, bringing Salcido with them, and I have as yet received no positive information as to what they did with him.
>
> I think, however, that I shall be able to give you positive information in a few days. The south-eastern portion of the Territory has been under the control of the worst and most desperate class of outlaws, both American and Mexican, and an example was needed in order to put an end to so deplorable a state of affairs. I do not know of a single instance in which an innocent person has been hung or killed by good law-abiding citizens.[9]

The lynching resulted in a minor diplomatic incident. Manuel de Zamacona, the Mexican ambassador in Washington, made a formal complaint to James G. Blaine, U.S. secretary of state. Blaine instructed Arizona's acting governor, John J. Gosper, to personally investigate, and the governor in turn interviewed Paul for further details. Paul told the governor that "the citizens of the Gila whose horses had been stolen were as certain that the two men whom they had captured were regular horse thieves as though they had been tried in court and regularly proven as such; that they did not intend to take the life of Orduna, only intending to let him hang long enough to compel him to give information of the whereabouts of the stolen animals, and by mistake let him hang too long." Governor Gosper, while admitting that Orduna was hanged "without due process of law," said that the Mexican consul agreed that Orduna and Salcido "were probably outlaws." Gosper concluded that even if the lynchers were arrested, "it was doubtful if there could be found a witness . . . to testify against them."[10]

Secretary Blaine, in his response to the Mexican government, quoted Governor Gosper: "While it is true Americans on our side of the line . . . are often guilty of murder and theft upon citizens of Mexico, it is equally true that Mexicans on their side of said line are equally guilty with Americans in the matter of murder and theft; and until recently, since the cow-boy combination along the borders for plunder, the crimes committed by citizens of both the Government of the United States and Mexico along the border were, for the most part, committed by citizens of Mexico." Blaine concluded by again quoting Gosper: "I think the civil authorities of the Government of Mexico are sometimes more sensitive over crimes committed by Americans than circumstances in particular cases would justify." In other words, Mexican authorities, while rightfully condemning the depredations of Cowboys and other lawless Americans, often overlooked the raids by Mexican bandidos into the United States.[11]

The concerns of violence on the border were all too real. On May 13, 1881, George Turner and a band of Cowboys had stolen a herd of cattle in Mexico. Juan Vasquez, a Mexican ranchero, and his vaqueros caught up with the Cowboys near Fronteras and, in a pitched gun battle, killed four of them, including George Turner. Sensational but unfounded news reports claimed that the Cowboys intended to raid Fronteras and clean out the town in revenge. A few weeks later were the gunfights in which Billy Leonard, Harry Head, Jim Crane, Old Man Clanton, and other Cowboys were slain. But these deaths, coupled with the hanging of Tom Harper and the lynchings of Jose Orduna and several other Mexicans, had no salutary effect on the Cowboys.

Paul had been searching for Pony Deal and Sherman McMaster as suspects in the Dripping Springs stage robbery in February. When he learned that McMaster was regularly visiting Tombstone, Paul advised City Marshal Virgil Earp not to arrest him until Pony Deal could be captured first. On September 7, 1881, one of Paul's deputies, John W. Evarts, collared Pony Deal in the mining camp of Harshaw, ten miles north of the border, and brought him to jail in Tucson. Two days later Johnny Behan returned to

Tombstone after a visit to Tucson and told Virgil Earp that Sheriff Paul had Deal in custody. Earp went immediately to the telegraph office and wired Paul: "Do you want McMaster? Answer tonight."

While waiting for a reply, Virgil wandered down the street and engaged the unsuspecting McMaster in idle conversation. Later he returned to the telegraph office, where he learned that John Ringo had just come into town and had joined up with McMaster. In the meantime Paul had received Earp's telegram, and he sent a reply to Wells Fargo agent Marshall Williams: "Tell V. W. Earp, to-night, that I want McMasters [sic]." After some delay the telegram was finally delivered to Virgil Earp, who, with his brother Jim, set off in search of McMaster. The outlaw saw Virgil coming and leaped out of his hiding place in a clump of brush on the outskirts of town. As he fled into the darkness, Virgil emptied his six-gun, but McMaster escaped. Paul immediately came under criticism from the *Tombstone Epitaph*: "Had Sheriff Paul telegraphed direct to the Marshal, McMaster would now have been in custody and safely reposing in the County Jail." The *Nugget* directed its criticism at both Paul and Virgil Earp: "The worst mistake was in Paul not telegraphing immediately to Earp, or the Sheriff, and the error was in the officers not arresting him when they first saw him on the street."[12]

Meanwhile, a posse including Wyatt and Morgan Earp was hunting two bandits who had robbed the Tombstone–Bisbee stage on September 8, escaping with $2,500. Within a few days they arrested two suspects, Frank Stilwell and Pete Spence. Stilwell was one of Behan's deputy sheriffs and was the younger brother of the noted scout "Comanche Jack" Stilwell. Pete Spence, whose true name was Elliot Larkin Ferguson, was a former Texas Ranger. The two were released on bail. On October 8 the stage from Benson to Tombstone was halted by five bandits north of Contention. Several days later Wyatt and Virgil Earp rearrested Frank Stilwell and Pete Spence. Although it was first reported that they were picked up for the Contention robbery, in fact the Earps arrested them on federal mail robbery charges connected with the Bisbee holdup. Stilwell and Spence had close ties to the Cowboys, and soon Ike Clanton, the McLaury brothers, and John Ringo were threatening to kill the Earp brothers. At the same time, the Earps and Sheriff Behan were in open conflict. When Governor John Gosper visited Tombstone to look into the Cowboy troubles, he reprimanded both and demanded that they cooperate. He also lambasted the *Epitaph* and the *Nugget* for taking sides to gain political benefit.[13]

Meanwhile, Paul had his own encounter with one of the Cowboys. Jerry Barton was a desperado and friend of Pony Deal. Born in New York in about 1849, he drifted as a young man into Arizona Territory, where he made his living mainly as a saloonkeeper. A contemporary described him as "a man of wonderful physique" whose "reputation rested mainly upon the forceful blows he could deliver with his fist." It was later reported by newspapers that he had killed twelve men, a gross exaggeration. Barton first came to prominence by beating a man to death during a quarrel in Phoenix in 1876. A year later he was in New Mexico and accompanied a band of hardcases into West Texas, where he took part in the El Paso Salt War. There he evidently first met the notorious Pony Deal. By 1878 he was back in Arizona, running a saloon in Globe; Pony Deal was his bartender. That same year Barton severely beat a Mexican, who managed to escape the fate of his first victim. By 1880 he was running a saloon in Charleston, a favorite hangout of the Cowboys. Despite Barton's unsavory reputation, he served as constable in Charleston, where at the same time he associated with desperadoes like Curly Bill and Frank Stilwell. Barton, a bigot who spoke with a stutter, was once asked how many men he had killed. He mulled it over a moment and replied, "Do you co-co-count M-M-Mexicans?"

On October 10, 1880, Barton shot and killed a young cowboy, E. G. Merrill, in his saloon. He was released on bond and disappeared. In May 1881 he was incorrectly reported to have been killed by Curly Bill in Shakespeare, New Mexico. Instead, he returned to his saloon in Charleston, where on October 9, 1881, he quarreled with a Mexican patron, Jesus Gamboa, and shot him in the shoulder. It was a dangerous, but not fatal, wound. Barton was arrested and released on bond, but on the night of October 12 he fled Charleston. Paul was immediately notified by telegraph, and he suspected that Barton might come into Tucson on the railroad from Benson. At daybreak, armed with a double-barrel shotgun, he took up a position near the Southern Pacific machine shops, well southeast of the train depot. As the morning train approached and slowed, Paul spotted a burly figure leap down from the cars. Shouldering the shotgun, the sheriff barked, "Throw up your hands!"

Barton was taken completely by surprise. He had thought he could evade detection by jumping from the train before it reached the station. He raised his hands, and Paul ordered him to march to the depot. It was quite a hike, and several times Barton lowered his muscular arms to rest them. But at gunpoint Sheriff Paul forced him to keep his hands high until they reached the station. There he handcuffed Barton and lodged his notorious prisoner in the county jail. The *Tucson Citizen* reported, "He has a slight impediment in his speech, and when he gets through with the courts he will likely have a serious impediment in his neck—a fate he richly deserves." Barton was sent to Tombstone to stand trial for shooting Jesus Gamboa. But Cochise County justice was exceedingly weak and ineffective, and not one of the Cowboys had been sent to prison by its courts, a fact that rankled Paul and infuriated the Earp brothers. The case against Barton was dismissed, and in February 1882 he was sent to Tucson to face charges for killing the young drover, E. G. Merrill. Because that shooting had taken place before Cochise County was created, the proper jurisdiction was in Pima County. Paul put Barton in jail to await a grand jury hearing. Barton was tried and acquitted on grounds of self-defense.[14]

By October 1881 the conflict between Ike Clanton and the Earps had reached fever pitch. One night, while drinking, Wells Fargo's Marshall Williams told Clanton that he knew about his deal to betray Leonard, Head, and Crane. Ike believed that Wyatt had deliberately leaked the information so that other members of the Cowboy gang would kill him as a traitor. Clanton cornered Wyatt and accused him of telling both Williams and Doc Holliday. Wyatt denied it. At one point Clanton and Frank McLaury approached Virgil Earp and angrily told him that they "could not live in this country an hour if Leonard's friends learned that they had plotted against him." On the night of October 25 a drunken Clanton confronted Holliday, but their oath-filled quarrel was broken up by Virgil Earp. The next morning Clanton made threats against Virgil and Holliday, then armed himself and roamed the streets looking for Holliday. Virgil took Clanton's Winchester, and when the Cowboy tried to pull his revolver, the marshal knocked him down with his six-gun. Virgil, Morgan, and Wyatt brought Clanton to court, where Ike declared, "Fight is my racket, and all I want is four feet of ground." After a heated confrontation, Wyatt exploded, "You cattle thieving son of a bitch, and you know that I know that you are a cattle thieving son of a bitch, you've threatened my life enough and you've got to fight." Wyatt stormed out of the courtroom and collided with Tom McLaury. In another angry exchange, McLaury exclaimed, "If you want to fight, I will fight you anywhere." Earp pistol-whipped him and stormed off.[15]

Ike Clanton was released after paying a fine for carrying weapons in town. It was just past noon when Frank McLaury and Billy Clanton rode into town. Although Billy wanted to take his brother home, rumors reached the Earps that all four of the Cowboys were after them. Virgil Earp stepped into the Wells Fargo office and borrowed a messenger's shotgun. With each passing minute, townsfolk brought word to the Earps of more threats made by the Cowboys. Sheriff Behan heard the rumors and was warned by citizens that the Clantons and McLaurys were on Fremont Street behind the OK Corral and that he must disarm them. Behan found Virgil Earp and asked him what the problem was. Virgil spat, "Some sons of bitches have been looking for a fight and now they can have it." Behan told Virgil that it was his duty to disarm them. "I will not," Virgil replied. "I will give them their chance to make a fight."

After more discussion, Behan agreed that he would disarm the Cowboys. Yet the Cowboys had no fear of Johnny Behan. While Ike Clanton and Tom McLaury told him they were unarmed, Frank McLaury and Billy Clanton refused to surrender their pistols. It was about three o'clock when Behan spotted Virgil, Wyatt, and Morgan Earp, with their friend Doc Holliday, coming down the Fremont Street sidewalk at a brisk pace. Holliday was carrying a Wells Fargo shotgun under his coat. Behan first warned the Cowboys to leave town, then rushed toward the Earps and begged them not to go any further. Behan told them, "I have been down there to disarm them."

Virgil Earp pushed by him. As city marshal, he was responsible for enforcing the law within city limits, not Behan. Despite his previous threat to fight, Virgil's temper had cooled and now he intended to arrest the Cowboys. The Earp-Holliday party found the Clantons and McLaurys with another Cowboy, young Billy Claiborne, in an empty lot on Fremont Street behind the OK Corral. Virgil shouted, "Throw up your hands, boys. I intend to disarm you." What happened next has been debated in courtrooms and newspapers, in saloons and around campfires, and in books, magazines, and films for more than a century. At close quarters, each side opened fire. Frank McLaury, Tom McLaury, and Billy Clanton were shot to death. Virgil Earp dropped with a bullet in his lower leg, another pistol ball passed through Morgan Earp's back, and Holliday was grazed in the hip. Ike Clanton, whose loud threats had ignited the confrontation, fled at first fire, as did Billy Claiborne. Thirty shots had been exchanged in thirty seconds in what would become the most famous gunfight of the Old West.[16]

Three days later Ike Clanton swore out a complaint charging the Earps and Holliday with murder. While Morgan and Virgil were still recovering, Wyatt and Doc were arrested. After a month-long preliminary hearing,

Tombstone justice of the peace Wells Spicer found that there was insufficient evidence to hold them for trial. Wyatt had been defended by Thomas Fitch, a noted attorney and orator. Spicer strongly criticized Virgil for bringing partisans with personal grudges against the Cowboys to the OK Corral. In fact, Virgil had several police officers who could have assisted him instead. However, Virgil undoubtedly wanted men of unquestioned loyalty who he knew would stand with him and face gunfire if necessary. Despite Spicer's criticism, given the desperate and lawless nature of the Cowboys, as well as what happened in the street fight and what was about to happen, Virgil Earp's judgment was appropriate under the circumstances.[17]

If anything, tensions were now even greater, and the Cowboys threatened repeatedly to kill the Earps. On the night of December 14, gunmen opened fire on the Tombstone–Benson stage in what may have been an attempt to assassinate John Clum, Tombstone's mayor, editor of the *Epitaph*, and staunch Earp supporter. Two weeks later, in the darkness of December 28, while Virgil Earp was walking to his hotel, three men with shotguns opened fire on him from ambush. Virgil dropped, riddled with buckshot. Doctors amputated part of his arm and saved his life. Virgil had seen Frank Stilwell in the area earlier, and Ike Clanton's hat was found at the scene. By telegram Wyatt Earp immediately requested and received an appointment from U.S. Marshal Crawley Dake to act as deputy marshal, with authority to select his own possemen. Wyatt swore in his brothers Morgan and Warren, plus Doc Holliday and three men who had been associated with the Cowboys: Sherman McMaster, Texas Jack Vermillion, and Turkey Creek Jack Johnson. Wyatt Earp later revealed that Johnson, whose true name was John Blount, had defected from the Cowboys and acted as his informant. McMaster, the hunted stage robber and partner of Pony Deal, probably had the same motive. These men and several others would act as the Earps' bodyguards and posse.[18]

Two more stage robberies in Cochise County, one on January 6, 1882, and another the next day, showed that the Cowboys were as brazen as ever. In the first holdup, bandits apparently led by Pony Deal riddled the Bisbee coach with bullets and forced the Wells Fargo messenger to surrender $6,500. In the second, James B. Hume, Wells Fargo's chief detective, was relieved of two fancy revolvers on the Contention City–Tombstone stage. Wyatt Earp suspected Curly Bill and Pony Deal. Wyatt, with McMaster and Johnson, trailed the Cowboys to Len Redfield's ranch on the San Pedro. They were evidently accompanied by some U.S. cavalrymen. As Redfield's nephew, Frank Carpenter, later said, "I have seen Curly Bill at Redfield's many different times. I was at Redfield's when the troops came there looking after the Bisbee robbers. They asked me if I had seen the men they were after." Carpenter implied that Curly Bill and Pony Deal were the Bisbee stage robbers and declared that he told the posse, "Gentlemen, you cannot scare or bribe me into telling where they are." Wyatt was unable to capture the Bisbee holdup men.[19]

The Earps and Holliday should have left Tombstone, but running from their enemies was unthinkable. Wyatt swore out warrants for the arrest of Ike and Fin Clanton and Pony Deal, charging them with shooting Virgil. The Clantons surrendered, but were released when seven men testified that they had been in Charleston at the time of the shooting. Ike Clanton retaliated by bringing new charges against the Earps and Holliday for the murder of Billy Clanton and the McLaurys, but this case was also dismissed.

On the night of March 18, 1882, Morgan Earp was playing pool with Bob Hatch in the rear of the latter's saloon, as Wyatt, Sherman McMaster, and another friend watched. Suddenly gunmen fired through a window, mortally wounding Morgan and just missing Wyatt, then fled into the blackness. A distraught Wyatt sent his brother's body to their parents' home in Colton, California. The next day, March 20, Wyatt and a group of body-guards took the still-recovering Virgil and his wife, Allie, to the Tucson train depot so they could be sent to Colton in safety. Wyatt was accompanied by his youngest brother, Warren, as well as by Doc Holliday, Sherman McMaster, and Turkey Creek Johnson. Wyatt was warned that Ike Clanton, Frank Stilwell, and two other Cowboys were near the depot, watching for them. At 7:15 P.M., just before the train departed, Wyatt spotted Stilwell and a man he believed was Ike Clanton. In the darkness Stilwell started to run, but Wyatt filled him with buckshot. At that, Doc Holliday, Warren Earp, Sherman McMaster, and Turkey Creek Johnson stepped up, and some or all of them riddled Stilwell's body with their shotguns and Winchesters.

Several railroad hands raced to the scene, but they were warned off by the Earp band. The shooting took place within earshot of Sheriff Paul's house at 501 Stone Avenue. He was later criticized for not bothering to investigate the gunfire. However, the townsfolk thought the gunshots were fired in celebration of the city's new gaslights. At daybreak Stilwell's body was found in the railyard. Stilwell and Ike Clanton had been under sub-poena as witnesses in Jerry Barton's murder trial. Clanton later claimed that he and Stilwell had only been in Tucson to testify for Barton and that they had not been stalking the Earps. As Paul recalled, that was only partly true:

> Ike Clanton and Frank Stilwell came to Tucson and about two weeks later the Earps came on the train as an escort to Virgil Earp, who had been shot . . . and was on his way to Colton where his father and mother lived, for medical treatment. While the train was standing in Tucson, Frank Stilwell was seen standing on a gravel car peeking in the window of the car that Virgil Earp was in. Wyatt Earp and the balance of the escort started after him, overtook him and killed him. . . . The train pulled out before the shooting was over. The Earps then started on foot for Benson, where they left their horses. A freight train overtook them about eight miles from Tucson. They made signals and the train stopped and took them to Benson, where they got their horses and were in Tombstone before daylight.[20]

That same day in Tombstone a coroner's jury heard evidence in the murder of Morgan Earp. Pete Spence's estranged wife gave testimony that implicated five men, among them Spence, Stilwell, and Florentino Cruz, alias Indian Charley. Meanwhile, in Tucson, a warrant was issued for the arrest of Wyatt and Morgan Earp, Doc Holliday, Sherman McMaster, and Turkey Creek Johnson, charging them with the murder of Stilwell. A coroner's jury took testimony for two days. Among the witnesses were Johnny Murphy and Dave Gibson, both noted Tucson gamblers. Murphy was a friend of Stilwell's, and he and Gibson would soon play prominent roles in the career of Sheriff Paul.

Bob Paul later recalled that the morning Stilwell's body was found,

> a warrant was sworn out and placed in my hands. . . . Judge Alex Campbell was district attorney. We went to the telegraph office together and wired the warrant to Behan, and when Behan received the message all of the Earp party that were in the killing of Stilwell were upstairs in Bilicke's hotel. As soon as they heard that Behan had a warrant for them they sent to Montgomery's stable in the block below where their horses were to have them saddled, which was immediately done. When informed that their horses were ready they walked to the stable, mounted and rode out of

town. Behan had collected all his deputies and Dave Neagle, who afterwards killed Judge Terry, was city marshal, and Behan had Neagle and all the police at the door of the hotel as the Earps passed out. Behan said: 'Wyatt, I want to see you,' and Wyatt without stopping, said, 'You might see me once too often.' There was no further attempt made to arrest them.[21]

Before riding off, Wyatt told Behan, "I will see Paul." But he had no intention of seeing Bob Paul. As a deputy U.S. marshal, Wyatt had the legal authority to arrest the men who had shot Virgil, a federal officer. However, he had no authority to hunt the killers of Morgan, as that murder was a territorial, not a federal, offense. Wyatt, blinded by rage and grief, was unconcerned with such fine points of the law. He was not interested in bringing any of the suspects to the bar of justice. With his brother Warren, Doc Holliday, Sherman McMaster, Texas Jack Vermillion, Turkey Creek Johnson, and two others as his federal posse, he set off after the rest of Morgan's killers. Wyatt knew that Pete Spence ran a woodcutting camp in the Dragoon Mountains and that Florentino Cruz, alias Indian Charley, was one of his workers. The next day, March 22, Earp's posse rode into the camp. Failing to find Spence, they located Cruz nearby and shot him to death.

In the meantime Behan had raised a large posse of his own to track down the Earp party. Surprisingly, he included a number of the Cowboys, including John Ringo, Fin Clanton, George Hill (younger brother of Joe Hill), and Johnny Barnes. As Behan's deputy, Billy Breakenridge, later said, "He took those men knowing that the Earp party would resist arrest, and, on account of the feud between them, he believed the cowboys would stay and fight." Behan's decision to use such desperadoes as his possemen proved an even bigger blunder than Virgil's bringing partisans to the Tombstone street fight. It convinced many that Sheriff Behan was in league with the Cowboys and was engaged in a private feud with the Earps, and it would permanently damage Behan's reputation.[22]

Paul later recalled his movements with Sheriff Behan after Stilwell was killed: "The next day I started for Tombstone and met Behan and his posse about five miles this side of town. One of Behan's deputies gave me his horse and I went with the posse. We went to Contention that night, and next day we went to Tombstone. As I had had no sleep since leaving Tucson I went to sleep in the express office and told Behan where I could be found.

He agreed to call me if he heard where the Earps were as I wished to go with him. . . . I had a horse engaged to go with Behan and he agreed to call me if he started out again, but he did not do it and I returned to Tucson." Paul believed that Behan left him out because he intended to kill the Earps.[23]

Paul was publicly critical of Johnny Behan's methods, telling one newspaperman that Behan "persists in cloaking the most notorious outlaws and murderers in Arizona with the authority of the law. I will have nothing to do with such a gang." To a correspondent of the *San Francisco Chronicle*, who described the Pima sheriff as "a warm friend of Wyatt Earp," Paul declared that "the Earps will never surrender to the Behan posse." The newspaper said, "Paul also says he is confident the Earps would not resist him, but would surrender immediately without bloodshed." The *Tucson Arizona Star* added, "Sheriff Paul . . . says that he did not go in pursuit of the Earps because the posse selected by Sheriff Behan of Tombstone were mostly hostile to the Earps and that a meeting meant bloodshed without any probability of arrest. Sheriff Paul says the Earps will come to Tucson and surrender to the authorities." But the Earps did not surrender, and Paul's prediction of bloodshed proved all too correct. Two days after killing Florentino Cruz, Wyatt and his men rode into isolated Cottonwood Springs in the Whetstone Mountains and unexpectedly encountered a band of Cowboys that had been hunting them. In a pitched gun battle, Wyatt Earp killed Curly Bill with a blast of buckshot from a double-barrel shotgun.[24]

This marked the end of Wyatt Earp's vendetta. He and his men rode to Henry Hooker's Sierra Bonita ranch to wait for $2,000 in traveling money donated by Wells Fargo and a prominent mining man. Sheriff Behan arrived there on March 28, as Paul later related: "He got his posse of rustlers and brought up at Hooker's ranch, where the Earp party had been. They told Hooker where they were going to camp and that if Behan and posse came there looking for them to tell them where they were, as they intended to remain four or five days. When the Behan posse arrived at the Hooker ranch, Hooker told them where the Earp party was, but Behan did not want them." Wyatt and his men then rode out of Arizona Territory, arriving in Silver City, New Mexico, on April 15. They made their way north by stage and train to Colorado. There Wyatt knew they could get help from Bat Masterson, who was city marshal of Trinidad. And Holliday, who had lived in Denver, had many friends in the city's sporting community.

Doc and Wyatt quarreled in New Mexico, and Holliday proceeded to Denver alone while the Earps and Texas Jack went to Gunnison. By this time the so-called Cowboy troubles had long been a prominent story in the national news. The conflict was bitterly debated in the press, with Republican editors assailing the Cowboys and blaming Sheriff Behan for the lawlessness, and Democratic journals labeling the Earps and Holliday as outlaws, murderers, and stage robbers. The apex of publicity was reached on May 3, 1882, when President Chester A. Arthur issued a Proclamation Respecting Disturbances in Arizona, authorizing U.S. troops to enforce federal law and demanding that outlaws "disperse and retire peaceably to their respective abodes." Of course, that was impossible, for the Cowboys were not an organized band. But the president's action indicated how serious the situation was.[25]

In the meantime Sheriff Paul had been called to Los Angeles on business, arriving there on April 1. A reporter for the *Los Angeles Times* interviewed him about the troubles in Arizona, saying that "in and around Tombstone a feeling of insecurity, almost a reign of terror, exists . . . and it is telling very severely on the business interests." The journalist explained, "The cutthroats and cowboy desperadoes seem to have just about captured the country," "but feeble efforts are being made to suppress the lawless element." Based on Paul's statements, the reporter concluded, "The cowboy gang do not exceed fifty, but they have accomplished already about as much injury . . . as an army with banners. They are the most reckless of the dime novel description."[26]

It is clear that southeastern Arizona in 1881–82 was an unstable society. The law enforcement of Sheriff Behan was ineffective and partisan; he was in open conflict with the Earps, who were federal officers. The silver rush economy was of the boom-and-bust type; its citizens were primarily interested in making money and tended to neglect civic affairs. Its courts and juries did not deal effectively with violent crime, and politics were influenced by criminal interests, exemplified by gamblers and the Cowboys. These conditions gave rise to the Cowboy troubles, but they were not unique to Arizona. They occurred at various other times during the frontier period, most notably in San Francisco's vigilance movements of 1851 and 1856; the Roach-Belcher feud of Monterey, California, in the mid-1850s; Montana Territory's vigilante uprising of 1863–65 involving outlaw-sheriff Henry Plummer and organized banditry; and New Mexico's Lincoln County War of 1878–79. Such conditions combined to create a vacuum

John H. "Doc" Holliday, a dentist
by profession, a gambler and gunfighter by avocation. This image
shows him in Prescott in 1879,
when Bob Paul first knew him.
Courtesy of Craig Fouts.

of moral and legal order. In some cases, vigilantes stepped in to fill this
void; in others, violent feuds resulted.[27]

On May 15, a self-styled detective named Perry Mallen arrested Doc
Holliday on a Denver street. Although Mallen turned out to be more confidence man than sleuth, he succeeded in imprisoning the dentist-gunman
in the county jail. News of the arrest was telegraphed both to Sheriff Paul
in Tucson and Sheriff Behan in Tombstone. On May 18 Paul received a
telegram from the city marshal of Gunnison, Colorado, advising that the
Earps were there and asking whether he should arrest them. Although Paul
immediately wired an affirmative response, neither Wyatt nor Warren Earp
was arrested. Johnny Behan wanted desperately to capture Holliday and the
Earps; he had offered a $500 reward for the fugitives from his own pocket.
But the warrant for Doc had been issued in Pima County, and Behan had
submitted a controversial $2,600 bill to the Pima County Board of Super-
visors for his expenses in hunting the Earp-Holliday band. Pima County
officials appealed to Arizona's new governor, Frederick Tritle, to have their own
sheriff, and not Behan, designated to serve the requisition and indictment
papers in Denver. Tritle agreed, and Paul entrained for Colorado, arriving

in Denver on May 19. By that time Holliday's friends, including Bat Masterson, had concocted a clever scheme to keep him in Colorado. They trumped
up a swindling charge against Holliday, and a court in Pueblo issued a
warrant for him. If charges were pending against Doc in Colorado, he
could not be extradited to Arizona.[28]

Holliday's arrest caught the attention of newspapers throughout the
Southwest. Interviewed in the Denver jail, Doc expressed his fear of
returning to Arizona: "If I am taken back to Arizona, that is the last of
Holliday. We hunted the rustlers, and they all hate us. John Behan, Sheriff
of Cochise County, is one of the gang, and a deadly enemy of mine, who
would give any money to have me killed. It is almost certain that he instigated the assassination of Morgan Earp. Should he get me in his power
my life would not be worth much." When Doc was asked if Sheriff Paul
could protect him, he answered, "I am afraid not. He is a good man, but
I am afraid he cannot protect me. The [Tucson] jail is a little tumble-down
affair, which a few men can push over, and a few cans of oil thrown upon
it would cause it to burn up in a flash, and either burn a prisoner to death
or drive him out to be shot down. That will be my fate." Bat Masterson
disagreed, telling the *Denver Republican* about Paul: "That's the kind of man
. . . who will take Holliday back and you bet they will have to kill him
before they kill his prisoner."[29]

On Friday, May 26, Paul wrote to his undersheriff, Henry Ward, in Tucson:
"Holliday's friends are doing everything in their power to get him off,
and will appear before the Governor and fight the requisition. He has three
lawyers and all the sporting men in his favor; the District Attorney is
attending to the case for me. Wyatt and Warren Earp are in Gunnison and
I may go up there if the Governor grants the warrant. The United States
Marshal came from Gunnison yesterday. He says some of the [Earp] party
were there, but they kept hidden while he was there. He says they have a
great many friends there. There is more feeling over the Holliday affair
here than there is in Tucson, and all in his favor; but I do not think I will
have any trouble if he is turned over to me."[30]

On Monday morning Sheriff Paul met with Governor Frederick Pitkin, a Republican. Paul later described what happened in the meeting:

> After examining the papers he said that another charge had been
> made against Holliday at Pueblo, that of swindling a man in a
> confidence game out of $150. He also said that he had been

informed by prominent citizens of Denver that if Holliday was placed in my custody he would be murdered by cowboys before reaching Tucson. I told him that on my way to Denver I had made every preparation for any attack from cowboys; that I had reliable men at Willcox, Bowie, and Deming who were to notify me by telegraph of any cowboy demonstration at those places, and posses would be at those points to render assistance in case of an attack. Also that Deputy Sheriff Dan Tucker, at Deming, had agreed to meet me in New Mexico with a strong guard to travel as far in my company as I desired, should I think additional guard necessary. I felt no uneasiness about bringing the prisoner by the southern route, but should the Governor prefer, I would take Holliday by the northern road, by way of San Francisco.[31]

The governor had scheduled a hearing that afternoon, which was attended by Paul, the district attorney, Holliday's lawyers, Bat Masterson, and several others. After listening to arguments by counsel, Governor Pitkin stated that the law required that the requisition must contain language that certified that the copy of the indictment attached to the requisition was authentic. He then ruled that the Arizona requisition failed to contain that language and was therefore defective. This was plainly untrue, as an extant copy of the requisition shows. It states that "Doc Holliday, Wyatt Earp, Warren Earp, Sherman McMaster and John Johnson have been accused of the crime of murder committed in the County of Pima," that they had "taken refuge in the State of Colorado," and that the Colorado authorities should have them "arrested and delivered to R. H. Paul who is the duly appointed agent of the Territory of Arizona to receive said persons and return with them to this Territory where they will be dealt with according to law." Most importantly, it contained the statement that the murder indictment that was attached to the requisition was "a duly authenticated copy of an indictment against said parties." The requisition was signed by Governor Tritle and was properly dated, witnessed, and sealed with the territorial seal. The copy of the indictment was properly authenticated, and, contrary to Pitkin's assertion, the requisition had no legal defects that would make it unenforceable.[32]

The governor also ruled that Holliday could not be extradited because he had to be held on the Pueblo warrant. The gunfighting gambler was released and then promptly rearrested by the city marshal of Pueblo on the swindling charge. On May 31, Paul, Bat Masterson, and a deputy sheriff took Doc by train to Pueblo, where he was arraigned in the swindling charge. Holliday posted $300 bail and was released. Since Paul's requisition papers had been rejected by Governor Pitkin, he did not bother to go to Gunnison after the Earps. Governor Pitkin's claim that Paul could not protect Holliday was as specious as his reasons for rejecting the requisition. Doc could have easily and safely been extradited to Arizona after the swindling charge was disposed of. It seems clear that business and political interests—primarily Wells Fargo and the Republican Party—put pressure on the Republican governor of Colorado to protect Holliday. For the same reason, Wyatt and Warren Earp were never arrested in Colorado for the Stilwell murder. As Louis C. Hughes wrote in the *Tucson Arizona Star*, "The Republican officials could not afford to have the Earps or any of their crowd returned for trial; and of course the papers were defective. It was the easiest way out of the difficulty."[33]

Although Paul sympathized with the Earps, he could neither understand nor accept this manifest circumvention of the law. He knew there was nothing wrong with the requisition. He also recognized that he, not the governors, would bear the brunt of criticism for failing to bring the fugitives back. A Denver newspaperman interviewed an unhappy Paul and reported, "Sheriff Paul says he has done all he can in the matter and will now of necessity be forced to let the prisoner go. He naturally feels bitter, however, at the action of Governor Pitkin, and wonders how Colorado will succeed in getting any of its fugitive murderers away from Arizona when they take refuge there." Another Denver newspaper reported that Paul "gave Governor Pitkin a piece of his mind yesterday in strong but temperate language."[34]

Paul returned to Tucson, disappointed and chagrined. Questioned by a local reporter about Holliday, Paul explained: "He says he intends returning here for trial voluntarily when court opens. He does not either deny or acknowledge the killing of Stilwell. He however states that when his party were at the depot in this city some of them were standing on the rear platform of the train. Two men approached. One he was sure was Stilwell, and the other it was presumed was Ike Clanton. The latter leveled their guns at the Earp party, when he and his friends dodged into the cars, procured guns and jumping from the train started down the track after the other two. At this point Holliday stopped his story and would not say what happened afterwards."[35]

Paul was not ready to give up. He sent a wire to Governor Tritle in Prescott, asking him to issue a new requisition. On June 9 the governor's office complied. The new extradition paper was virtually identical to the first one, but, to address the purported defect found by Governor Pitkin, it contained additional language certifying the attached indictment. Governor Tritle had left for Washington, D.C., to discuss lawlessness and the Cowboy troubles with President Chester Arthur. In Tritle's absence, his secretary, H. M. Van Arman, signed the requisition as acting governor. Not surprisingly, Governor Pitkin also ignored this new requisition. He gave Arizona officials the same baseless excuse: that he "did not consider it possible for any agent to deliver the parties named in safety to Tucson."[36]

As expected, Pima's sheriff received a great deal of bad press from the Democratic newspapers over his failure to bring the fugitives back for trial. Even before Paul could serve the requisition papers, a wire report originated by political enemies in Tombstone referred to him as "notorious for his friendship with the Earps, and whom common rumor says connived at their escape from the Territory." Louis C. Hughes of the *Tucson Arizona Star* had initially supported Paul, saying, "The impression shared by many that Sheriff Paul will not bring the Earps to Tucson but will permit them to escape in transit, the *Star* considers an injurious suspicion which is not justified by the high reputation of the officer." But now Hughes was outraged: "Our next sheriff will be a Democrat, and he will not be deterred from arresting criminals by the fear of compromising his party." The *Tombstone Epitaph*, formerly a supporter of the Earps but now under Democratic management, was equally harsh: "The friendship of Paul for the Earps is notorious, and it is a well known fact that he has made no effort to effect their capture." The *Epitaph*'s editor crowed, "Mr. Paul has placed himself in a ludicrous position, and afforded the people of the Territory a subject for derisive laughter, long and loud."[37]

Paul never arrested Holliday or the Earp brothers, and they were never brought to trial for killing Frank Stilwell or anyone else in Arizona. Wyatt Earp did many wrong things in his life, but in Tombstone, at least, he had been in the right. Nonetheless, for years Arizona's Democratic newspapers would refer to the Earp brothers and Holliday as stage robbers, murderers, and "fleeing deputy U.S. marshals" and would use the Cowboy troubles to give Paul a political black eye. But in the end such judgments were confirmed neither by public perception, collective memory, nor history. Wyatt Earp, under extraordinary provocation, had certainly crossed the line into lawlessness. But he would not be remembered for that. Instead, his memory would be cemented into a legend of enormous proportions, crystallized by the lyrics of the 1950s television theme song: "Wyatt Earp, Wyatt Earp, brave, courageous, and bold. / Long live his fame and long live his glory, and long may his story be told."[38]

CHAPTER TEN

Apaches and Gunfighters

Conflict between Apache Indians and settlers was endemic in frontier Arizona. As early as 1672 the warlike Apaches had resisted the incursions of Spanish explorers and colonists into northern Mexico. Warfare continued after Mexico won its independence from Spain in 1821 and into the American period following the Mexican War. Such Apache war chiefs as Mangas Coloradas (1793–1863), Cochise (1815–74), and Geronimo (1829–1909) furiously resisted encroachment into their tribal lands and battled Mexicans and Americans on both sides of the border. Tucson was situated in the middle of Apacheria, and its citizens were particularly vulnerable to Indian raids. Early in 1871 a series of thefts and killings by Apache marauders rocked the Old Pueblo. Tucsonans blamed the depredations on a band of Apaches that had been allowed by the army to settle near Camp Grant, on the San Pedro River fifty miles northeast of Tucson. Jesus Maria Elias, a Tucson pioneer and rancher, had suffered heavily from Indian raids; several years earlier one of his brothers had been slain by Apaches. Elias was a noted Indian-fighter, tracker, and leader of the Mexican American community in southern Arizona. He and William S. Oury organized a band of 6 Anglos, 48 Mexican Americans, and 94 Papago Indians, deadly enemies of the Apache. On April 28, 1871, they attacked the Apaches near Camp Grant, killing 144 people, all but 8 of them women and children. Twenty-seven children were captured alive and sold by the Papagos into slavery in Sonora. The Camp Grant Massacre was one of the darkest events in Arizona's history. The perpetrators were tried for murder in Tucson, but a sympathetic jury acquitted them. Oury was rewarded by Pima County voters, who elected him sheriff in 1873.[1]

In 1877 the Apache war chief Geronimo was captured by U.S. soldiers. He was later moved with his band onto the San Carlos Reservation, 120 miles northeast of Tucson. There he and his people remained for a time, but in April 1878 they fled to Mexico, accompanied by the famous Chief Juh. Both Geronimo and Juh took part in the Victorio War of 1878, when, under Chief Victorio, the Eastern Chiricahua Apaches at San Carlos fled the reservation, frustrated with the poor living conditions and extreme summer heat. After pillaging and murdering on both sides of the border, Victorio's band was finally tracked down and killed by Mexican troops in October 1880. By this time Juh and Geronimo had surrendered and, with their bands, were moved to the San Carlos Reservation. The following year Juh and Geronimo jumped the reservation with their people and crossed the border to the Sierra Madre Mountains in northern Chihuahua.

Among the Indians left at the reservation was a band of Chiricahua Apaches under Chief Loco. On April 18, 1882, in the most daring raid in Apache annals, Juh, Geronimo, and the war leader Naiche returned to the San Carlos Reservation with sixty warriors. They forced the remainder of the Chiricahuas under Loco, forty warriors and three hundred women and children, to leave San Carlos and accompany them to their stronghold in Mexico. The raid was a bloody one. After two Indian police were slain on the reservation, the Apaches fled east, closely pursued by cavalry. The Apaches killed three prospectors, stole all the livestock they came across, and at one ranch massacred ten people, sparing not even two small children. Near Clifton they killed five teamsters and ran off sixty mules. As they crossed into New Mexico in scattered bands, riding south to the border, they slaughtered more than fifty prospectors, teamsters, and settlers, both Anglo and Hispanic, and burned numerous ranches.

These brazen raids created panic in much of the Southwest. Newspaper editors railed about the inability of the military to keep the Apaches on the reservations and the army's perceived ineptness in tracking them down. As one newspaper reported, "The military in this, as in other outbreaks, have proved entirely inadequate to the occasion, and much dissatisfaction is felt and expressed on all sides." Nonetheless, on April 24, U.S. troops caught up with some of the Indians in the mountains near Stein's Pass, just across the New Mexico line. In a pitched battle, five soldiers and two Apaches were slain, and others were wounded. On April 28 another cavalry detachment attacked Loco's band east of Cloverdale, New Mexico, wounding Loco and killing a dozen Apaches, including one of Loco's sons.[2]

Many of the Apache raids had taken place in Pima County, and its terrorized citizens clamored for protection. Bob Paul met with Tucson's prominent citizens, and it was proposed that he form a huge posse to track down the Apaches. Informal local militias had been used to fight Indians in the past, but Paul, cognizant of the Camp Grant massacre, wanted any posse to have full legal authority and to be recognized by both the courts and the governor. He agreed that a volunteer force of fifty special deputies would be led William J. Ross, a noted Indian-fighter. Ross had served in the U.S. Army during both the Civil War and the Apache Wars. In one encounter he saved the life of the Apache Chief Loco, and in another he saved General George Crook from death by an Apache bullet. Mustered out as a lieutenant in 1875, Ross settled in Tucson, engaged in business, and served as undersheriff for Charlie Shibell.[3]

The Old Pueblo's citizens quickly raised $11,000 to mount and arm the posse, which was dubbed the Tucson Rangers. The group consisted of thirty-six Anglos and fourteen Hispanics, of whom the best known was Jesus Maria Elias of the Camp Grant Massacre. Only one of Sheriff Paul's regular deputies, Alfredo E. Carrillo, joined the rangers. On April 27, Hugh Farley, district attorney of Pima County, swore out a warrant before a Tucson judge for the arrest of Juh, Naiche, and Geronimo, charging them with murder. He immediately handed the warrant to Sheriff Paul "for service and execution." Two days later Paul swore in Bill Ross as a deputy sheriff of Pima County. It was done with all legal solemnity: the appointment was in writing, with Ross signing an official oath, notarized and recorded. Paul, concerned about acting as a rogue sheriff, sought additional authority from the county board of supervisors to appoint such a large force of deputies. No doubt he also wanted to be sure that in the event that the $11,000 war chest was exhausted, the county, and not he, would foot the bill. The board met on May 1 and again on May 3 to debate the issue. Finally they agreed to authorize Paul to appoint the fifty special deputy sheriffs to track down the Apaches. On May 9, Governor F. A. Tritle provided additional authority by appointing Ross a captain of the territorial militia. Tritle authorized Ross to proceed to "the southeastern border of Arizona, to prevent the incursions and encroachments of hostile Apache Indians upon the citizens of the Territory."[4]

After procuring horses and Springfield rifles for each man, the Tucson Rangers rode out of town on May 10, 1882. They headed due east, and while Sheriff Paul was in Colorado attempting to extradite Doc Holliday, the rangers spent more than two weeks searching fruitlessly for the Apache marauders. Finally, on May 28, they met a patrol of U.S. cavalry who told them that Mexican troops had the Apaches surrounded near Casas Grandes, about eighty miles south of the border in Chihuahua. The Mexican commander had asked for help. Ross and his men made a hard ride south of the border, finally linking up with sixty Mexican National Guard troops under Captain Ramirez on June 2. For the next two days the combined forces guarded the country north of Casas Grandes to prevent the Apaches from escaping back into the United States. Probably at the urging of Captain Ramirez, Ross sent a courier to the Mexican colonel in command, advising of his presence in Mexico and offering his services. At the same time, Ross sent several of his men into the border town of Janos to purchase supplies. The courier was intercepted by General Bernardo Reyes, who was in charge of all operations against the Apaches. Reyes, later an important figure in Mexican politics, ordered both the courier and the rangers in Janos placed under arrest. Then, with 650 infantry and cavalry, he moved toward Casas Grandes and captured Bill Ross and the Tucson Rangers.[5]

Ross displayed his deputy sheriff's commission signed by Paul and insisted that they were private citizens hunting Apaches. But General Reyes produced a copy of a three-year-old U.S. Army register that listed Ross as a commissioned officer. With great difficulty, Ross finally convinced the general that he was no longer with the army. Ross believed that the rangers' lives were in danger and that "if he had not been able to produce his commission as a deputy sheriff . . . they would all have been shot." For several days the rangers made camp with the Mexican troops, each group warily watching the other. Military courtesies were observed, with Ross and the Mexican officers alternately dining with one another. Under Mexican law, U.S. troops could not cross the border without first obtaining permission from the president of Mexico. During the past few weeks the U.S. Army, in pursuit of Apaches, had done so twice without proper authority. On June 5 General Reyes decided to take action. He ordered Ross and the Tucson Rangers to leave Mexico and declared that Ross's "troops would be relieved of all their arms." The stunned Americans had no choice but to obey. Ross led his dejected men on a ride of almost three hundred miles through Apache-infested country. He had each man cut a short pole and carry it across his saddle, so at a distance it would appear they were armed.[6]

Their humiliating return to Tucson created a significant diplomatic incident. Governor Tritle had authorized the rangers only to proceed to the southeastern border. Although a treaty existed between the United States and Mexico that allowed the forces of each to cross the line when in pursuit of hostile Indians, the requisite official permission had not been obtained. The Americans were perplexed by their inhospitable reception by General Reyes, but, given his country's prior experience in the Mexican War and in dealing with American filibusters who invaded Mexico in the 1850s, the general's reaction was predictable. However, his sending the Arizonans home unarmed through hostile Apache country was vindictive and inexcusable. To Paul's relief, the rangers' guns were eventually returned and the incident soon forgotten. But Tucson's sheriff had been reminded of the importance of obtaining permission to enter Mexico, a lesson that would serve him well in the years to come.

Paul now faced a different kind of problem. The *Tombstone Epitaph*, under new and Democratic management, reported a horrendous crime on the railroad spur line where it crossed the Igo Ranch in what it claimed was "the southern extremity of Pima County." According to the *Epitaph*'s story, which was eagerly reprinted by Louis Hughes in the *Star*, a party of drunk Americans made an unprovoked pistol-and-knife attack on Mexican railroad laborers: "When the smoke of battle cleared off seven Mexicans were found dead and several wounded." The *Epitaph* concluded with a slap at Paul: "It is perhaps in order to suggest . . . that the sheriff of Pima County take some steps to bring the Igo ranch murderers to justice. If any assistance is necessary the officers of Cochise County will gladly cooperate with Mr. Paul." Yet not only was the story of seven dead Mexicans a canard, the ranch of V. H. Igo was located in the Huachuca Mountains, and it was not clear whether the purported crime occurred in Pima or Cochise County. Paul needed to develop a thick skin, for such baseless and politically motivated attacks would be used against him with increasing frequency by Democratic newspapers.[7]

Yet another problem was brewing much closer to home. Margaret Paul appreciated the fact that her husband's new job allowed him to spend more time at home with her and their children, but she had trouble with the summer heat in Tucson. Margaret missed the milder climate of California, and, like many Tucsonans, she often left town with her children, spending summer months on the coast to escape the extreme desert temperatures. As one Tucson newspaperman explained, it was "the fashion for our ladies to skip off to California as soon as the warm weather sets in, leaving their husbands here to shift for themselves." Margaret especially liked visiting San Francisco. Her sisters, Jane, the widow of Bob's brother Thomas, and Eliza, married to the tailor Thomas Drady, still lived there, as did her brother, Daniel Coughlan. Margaret and the children would often stay with them in the summertime. Undoubtedly her husband obtained free railroad passes for the family on the Southern Pacific. Paul missed them, and whenever business would allow it, he made trips to San Francisco to visit. In Tucson, Margaret was active in social circles and the Catholic church. At the Catholic Fair held in Levin's Park, ladies opened booths featuring floral displays, Mexican food, and even ice cream; Margaret ran the booth that sold fancy provisions. All the proceeds from the fair went to charity. Margaret also enjoyed trips into the desert during the spring, and she did not hesitate to join such excursions when her husband was busy. On a Sunday in March, with a group of ladies and gentlemen, she visited the W. B. Livingston ranch near Contention City. Recounted an observer, "The guests supplied themselves with a bountiful lunch, which was enjoyed under the waving branches of the mesquite which throws a welcome shade around Mr. Livingston's cabin." Margaret and her friends returned home by twilight, serenading the Mexican ranchos they passed on the way.[8]

While the Tucson Rangers were hunting Apaches in Mexico, the Old Pueblo was having its share of problems with gamblers and gunfighters. That spring James H. Leavy (often misspelled Levy), one of the Old West's noted man-killers, arrived in Tucson. Leavy was a forty-year-old Irishman. Like many Western gamblers, he drifted from one mining frontier to another, following the money. In the silver camp of Pioche, Nevada, in 1871, he took part in a wild shootout with Mike Casey and Dave Neagle, later a lawman in Tombstone. Leavy shot and killed Casey, but was wounded in the jaw by Neagle. At White Pine, Nevada, he went after an enemy with a pitchfork, but did not kill him. In 1873 he was arrested for killing Thomas Ryan in Pioche, but was not prosecuted. In 1876 Jim Leavy joined the gold rush to the Black Hills, and a year later he engaged in a celebrated duel in Cheyenne, Wyoming. There, following a drunken quarrel with fellow gambler Charlie Harrison, the two shot it out in the street until Harrison dropped with a fatal wound. Leavy's exploits were widely talked of on the mining frontier. Wyatt Earp reportedly called him "an outstanding six-gun artist" and "a topnotch gun-wielder."[9]

Leavy next drifted into Arizona Territory, visiting Tombstone late in 1880. There he associated with Wyatt Earp, Doc Holliday, and other well-known gamblers. His old enemy Dave Neagle was also in the camp, which may have precipitated Leavy's move to Tucson a few months later. Leavy was not long in Tucson before he fell afoul of Johnny Murphy, one of the Old Pueblo's most noted gamblers. Murphy, who had settled in Tucson seven years earlier, ran a faro table in Eli B. Gifford's popular Fashion Saloon at 23 Congress Street and was active in Democratic politics. His partner was Bill Moyer, a well-known cardsharp. Murphy and another gambler, Dave Gibson, had been credited with discovering the Silver Hill mining district, twenty miles due west of Tucson, in 1880. Murphy and Gibson had been friendly with Frank Stilwell and were among the last to see him before he was slain by Wyatt Earp. Early in May 1882, Leavy lost heavily at the Murphy-Moyer table and claimed he had been cheated. He and Moyer exchanged words, and two weeks later Leavy threatened to kill both Murphy and Moyer and "waltz on their layout and shoot their checks from the table."[10]

On the evening of June 5, 1882, a drunken and unarmed Leavy entered the Fashion Saloon and sat down at Murphy's faro table. Leavy soon accused Murphy of being a cheat, and an enraged Murphy unleashed a torrent of oaths. Leavy told Murphy and Moyer, "You have been making a talking fight. Now you've got to fight." Leavy calmly offered to settle the matter in a formal duel across the border in Mexico. Murphy promptly agreed, and the two put up thirty dollars to pay for a wagon to take them and their seconds across the frontier in the morning. Soon Tucson's city marshal, Adolph G. Buttner, arrived and foolishly concluded that neither man was serious. Instead of arresting them for proposing a duel, he simply persuaded Leavy to go home. Buttner then telephoned Sheriff Paul and warned him that a duel might be fought the next day. The marshal's failure to act was a fatal blunder. Leavy walked to his lodgings at the Palace Hotel on Meyer Street. Murphy, Moyer, and Gibson, thinking that Leavy was going for his gun, followed him at a discreet distance. In moments Leavy came back out of the hotel. Murphy later claimed that he saw Leavy reach for his gun. However, the best witness of the event was the prominent sheriff of Pinal County, Pete Gabriel, who happened to be standing across the street. Gabriel said that Murphy grabbed Leavy's coat, then Murphy and Gibson

The Palace Hotel on Meyer Street in Tucson in about 1880. The gunfighter Jim Leavy
was shot to death by Johnny Murphy, Bill Moyer, and Dave Gibson directly in front of
the hotel. Courtesy of the Arizona Historical Society/Tucson, 7268.

jerked out their revolvers and opened up with a barrage of pistol fire.
Leavy started to run, crying out, "My God! Don't murder me, I'm not armed."

His assailants, including Moyer, who joined in, paid no heed, riddling
the gambler with five balls. Leavy crumpled onto the sidewalk and in
minutes was dead. Marshal Buttner rushed to the scene with three policemen and Paul's undersheriff, Henry Ward. They found no weapon on the
body. Buttner arrested Murphy, who told him, "Well, he got it good. I did
it and don't deny it." Soon Moyer and Gibson were also under arrest. Moyer
had told a bystander, "The damn son of a bitch is dead; he's been threatening my life for the past two weeks."

In jail, the three argued brazenly over who would take credit for killing
the notorious gunfighter. Moyer told Marshal Buttner, "I finished him."

To that, Gibson responded, "No, I did it," then Murphy retorted, "I done it." Explained Buttner later, "Each claimed the honor of doing it." Old Tucson had seen one of its most famous shootings, and the only man killed had been unarmed. Had Marshal Buttner done his job, the killing would not have occurred—at least, not that night. Unfortunately, Leavy's death would, in the near future, cause Paul no end of trouble.[11]

The ill-fated expedition of the Tucson Rangers had taught Sheriff Paul a valuable lesson. Ever the astute diplomat, he sought to establish good relations with officials in Sonora and conducted numerous manhunts south of the border without any interference from Mexican officers. One such hunt, in July 1882, involved several unrelated crimes. In the first, an anti-Chinese mob went on a rampage in Calabasas, located eight miles north of Nogales. The mob, which included some of the town's merchants, was angered by the recent opening of an opium and gambling den. Fueled by alcohol and fortified by a force of local ruffians, they barged into the opium den, ransacked everything inside, and set it on fire. Next they destroyed a second opium den, tore down some of the Chinese tents, and broke open their chests, taking money and valuables. In the morning the leaders of the mob sobered up and remorsefully offered to pay a settlement to their victims. The Chinese were in no mood to compromise and swore out warrants for the members of the mob. The principal leader, storekeeper Frank W. Girard, and another of the mob, Tom Smith, promptly fled across the border. An arrest warrant for them was placed in Sheriff Paul's hands.[12]

At the same time a teamster named Jem Baldy, who ran freight between Calabasas and Tucson, hired Mike Nichols, known as Old Nick, to drive his team. Nichols went on a spree in Calabasas, drank up fifty dollars of Baldy's money, and, after sobering up, recognized that he was in trouble. With a friend named Graham, he headed for the border in Baldy's wagon, but the Mexican customs officers would not let them across unless they first deposited seventy-five dollars in cash. Unwilling to go back and face Baldy, Old Nick left the wagon as security and went south with the six-mule team. In the pueblo of Magdalena, fifty-five south of the border, he and Graham sold the mules and disappeared. Baldy tracked down his mules, recovered them, and reported the incident to Sheriff Paul, who headed into Mexico after four fugitives: Old Nick, Graham, Frank Girard, and Tom Smith.[13]

In the meantime, on July 5, a ruffian named Frank Morton shot and killed an old miner, Carl Roberts, at the mining headquarters of Hacienda de Santa Rita, just north of Calabasas near the abandoned mission at Tumacácori. Morton was brought before a justice of the peace in Tubac, where he claimed self-defense and was released. However, witnesses who had been too afraid to testify now came forward and revealed that Morton had slain the old prospector in cold blood. By this time the killer had fled across the border into Sonora. A warrant was issued for him and sent to Paul in Mexico, along with formal papers giving him authority to enter Mexico on official business. Now he was hunting five wanted men south of the border.[14]

The sheriff wired Charles H. Vosburg, his resident deputy at Calabasas, for help. At this time the Sonora Railway was nearing completion, and by October it would connect the brand-new border town of Nogales with the Mexican harbor at Guaymas, 250 miles to the south. The connection north to the Southern Pacific line at Benson would also be completed in October. On a tip that Frank Girard and Tom Smith had gone to Guaymas, Paul and his deputy rode south to the railhead, where they boarded a train and followed them to the coastal town. On hearing that Sheriff Paul was looking for them, the two American fugitives promptly surrendered. Paul and Vosburg took the pair back on the railroad to Hermosillo, capital of Sonora, where the sheriff left the train to resume his manhunt for Old Nick, Graham, and Frank Morton. Vosburg continued on with his two prisoners, but when he reached the end of the line, sixteen miles from Magdalena, Smith jumped from the train and escaped into the night.

Old Nick managed to give Paul the slip and escape back to the United States. Graham and Morton were not so lucky. Paul returned to Magdalena, where he located and arrested Graham. The sheriff learned that a gringo matching Morton's description was camped outside the pueblo. He sent an Indian to scout the camp; the scout reported that it was deserted and that tracks headed north toward the border. Sheriff Paul sent a posse of Mexicans after Morton on the road north to Calabasas, while he took Graham and followed the trail northeast to the mining camp of La Noria (now Lochiel), on the international line. Paul found Morton there and arrested him without trouble. He brought his two prisoners into Calabasas on the night of July 17. His undersheriff, Henry Ward, was waiting there to help guard them.[15]

In Calabasas, Paul discovered that two desperados, one named Joe Casey, had just held up and robbed a prostitute and her customer in a local brothel. Then the bandits proceeded to a saloon, lined up its occupants, and relieved them of their money. Casey spent his share of the loot in another saloon. In the morning the sheriff found that Casey was still in town, and he arrested him. From the saloonkeeper Paul confiscated a ten-dollar bill that Casey had taken from the prostitute and used to pay for his drinks. Calabasas had no jail, so Paul locked Casey and his other two prisoners in the basement of the Hotel Santa Rita, which was then under construction, and set off to find the robbery victims. While the sheriff was gone, Casey managed to squeeze through a window and escape. The local justice of the peace, G. W. Atkinson, cornered the badman and covered him with a double-barrel shotgun. Uncowed, Casey snarled, "You damned son of a bitch, I will take that gun away from you and shoot you with it."[16]

But before he could act, help arrived, and the robber was soon in custody. Leaving Casey and Graham with Undersheriff Ward to await a preliminary hearing the next day, Paul took the accused murderer, Frank Morton, to Tubac, fourteen miles north, for a second preliminary hearing before the pueblo's justice of the peace. This time the witnesses, seeing Morton in irons and comforted by Bob Paul's imposing figure, cooperated and testified that the killing of the old miner, Carl Roberts, was not done in self-defense. After a hearing that lasted until the next day, July 19, Morton was held to answer on a charge of murder. Word of Morton's arrest had spread, and by the conclusion of the hearing, angry friends of the murdered Carl Roberts had gathered in Tubac, intent on lynching the killer. Paul realized he needed to get Morton out of town and into the Tucson jail as quickly as possible. He bundled Morton into a two-seated buckboard, making the killer ride in front with one hand ironed to the seat. Sheriff Paul sat behind him holding the reins, a sawed-off shotgun in his lap.

The leader of the mob, identified in one old-timer's recollections as "John C.," was a good friend of the sheriff's. The vigilantes hid inside a building that served as a combination store and saloon, which Paul would have to pass on his way out of town. The mob posted a boy on top of an old building to watch the street. Their plan was simple: when Paul approached the store, his friend John would step out and shake hands, then seize the sheriff while the vigilantes poured outside to lynch Morton. The young lookout, after a long wait, called out that a buckboard was approaching. The men inside the store became too curious, and several heads popped out and then back in again. The ever-alert Paul spotted them and was immediately suspicious. Gently slapping the reins across the backs of the horses, he shifted the shotgun on his lap and smiled at his friend John, who had

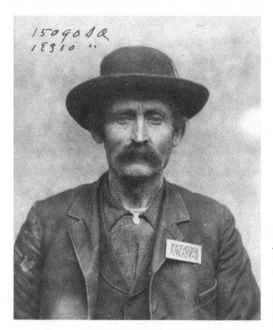

Frank Morton, murderer and jailbreaker, in his 1893 San Quentin mug shot. Bob Paul captured him in Mexico in 1882 and saved him from a lynch mob in Tubac. California State Archives.

stepped into the street. Seeing that Paul did not intend to stop, John rushed forward, his hand extended for a shake, and called out, "Hello, Bob!" The sheriff's smile broadened into a grin as he snapped the reins and the horses broke into a trot. In an instant he had left the would-be lynchers behind and, with a jaunty wave of his hand, sped north to Tucson and safety.[17]

Sheriff Paul's manhunt south of the border had been authorized by the Mexican government. Paul later praised the help he had received from Governor Carlos Ortiz and other Mexican officials, saying that they gave him "every desired assistance, as did also the officers of the [Sonora] railroad." On a manhunt into Sonora a few months earlier, the sheriff had received similar assistance from Governor Ortiz, and Paul's praise of the Mexican officials had been widely reported in wire-service accounts. Paul made numerous trips to Mexico over the years without diplomatic controversy. He worked well with its country's police and customs officers. His Spanish, rudimentary as it was, proved of immense help in connecting and communicating with people along the border. He was well aware of the historically strained relationship between the two governments and was careful to respect Mexican customs and to comply with Mexican laws. He cultivated friendships in Mexico that helped him greatly in tracking fugitives from the United States.[18]

The professionalism Paul displayed was, unfortunately, uncommon. In the nineteenth-century West, when a capable, professional chief lawman and the officers he trained left office, their accumulated experience often vanished. Such lawmen were usually succeeded by political opponents who were new to the job and who lacked their predecessors' expertise. Given the political turnover so common to that era's rural police and sheriffs and the resulting transitory nature of their jobs, there was little chance that long-term, institutionalized professionalism could be sustained in frontier law enforcement. The result on the U.S.-Mexico border was that incompetent, tactless, and even belligerent police practices would continue to crop up for another century, causing unnecessary ethnic conflict and violence. Bob Paul, in his relations with the Mexican government and its people, proved to be far ahead of his time, and his actions as sheriff were a model of diplomacy and professional law enforcement.

CHAPTER ELEVEN

Jailbreakers

Joe Casey was held to answer the charge of robbery in Calabasas, and on the evening of July 20, 1882, Bob Paul and his deputies lodged Frank Morton and Casey into the Tucson jail. Since 1868, Tucson's courthouse had been a single-story adobe at the corner of Court and Ott Streets. Next to it was a two-story jail, its lower floor built of stone blocks, which through age had deteriorated and loosened. The most dangerous prisoners were kept in two large cells. The upper story, made of adobe, was reached by two rickety wood staircases on the outside of the building; it also contained two cells. One was for those held on minor charges, and the other was for trusted prisoners, or trusties, who were considered unlikely to dig out through the mud-brick walls. Behind the building was the jail-yard, called the corral, surrounded by an adobe wall eighteen feet high. Of the adobe calaboose, L. C. Hughes, editor of the *Tucson Arizona Star*, opined: "Our jail is a miserable hut, illy constructed; no security and the seat of disease."[1]

Sheriff Paul was a humane and perhaps overly kind jailer. Despite the fact that his leaky jail held nine murderers out of a total of thirty-one prisoners, he allowed them to have liquor and other small luxuries. Four days after Casey and Morton were locked up, Paul let a newspaperman in to talk with the prisoners. The reporter found that Johnny Murphy, Bill Moyer, and Dave Gibson all occupied the same cell. "Murphy and Gibson do not eat with the other prisoners," the newsman reported, "but have their meals brought to them from the Palace Hotel, for the reason, Murphy jokingly remarked, that he did not want to owe Pima County for anything except room rent and the jewelry [shackles] he wore." Despite his small kindnesses to the prisoners, Sheriff Paul required that the felons wear leg irons after dark.[2]

Late on the night of August 14, Joe Casey, Frank Morton, and three other prisoners used a smuggled knife to saw off their shackles. Their cell floor was dirt, and they easily dug through it to the foundation. Removing some of the large stones, they managed to tunnel through. But just as the first escapees were wriggling out, a barking dog alerted the jailers, who captured them all. At Paul's direction, Casey, Morton, and the other three were placed in the adjacent cell, which had a wood floor. Heavy irons were attached to their legs and bolted to the floorboards. Editor Hughes, who had been a consistent critic of the unsafe jail, now accused Paul of "harsh and cruel treatment" of the escapees and declared, "There is no excuse for chaining men to the floor and loading their legs with heavy irons. That is simply unadulterated cruelty." Hughes ignored the fact that there was no other method by which to secure the prisoners. Hughes's extreme partisanship was exemplified by such diatribes, which would become increasingly common.[3]

Tucson's was not the only unsafe jail. On August 23, in response to an urgent wire from the sheriff of Gila County, Sheriff Paul ordered a special engine to rush him and his deputies north on the railroad to the Casa Grande and Globe stage road. A mob in Globe was threatening to lynch three prisoners in the Gila County jail. Three days earlier Lafayette Grimes and Curtis Hawley had robbed a pack train near Globe, killing the popular Wells Fargo messenger Andy Hall and another man. Grimes and Hawley were quickly arrested, along with Grimes's brother, Cicero, who had helped plan the holdup. They confessed and were locked in the Globe jail. Rumors of lynching were rampant, and at 2:00 A.M. on the 24th, before Paul and his men could arrive, a mob broke into the jail. Cicero Grimes, who had not taken part in the murders, was left alone, but, in one of Arizona's most famous lynchings, Lafayette Grimes and Curtis Hawley were strung up to a sycamore tree that stood in the middle of Globe's main street.[4]

No sooner had Sheriff Paul returned to Tucson than he had more trouble in his jail. On the afternoon of August 28, Frank Morton was unchained and allowed to wash himself in the jailyard. While the jailer was distracted, several prisoners helped him scale the adobe wall. Paul was furious and set out after Morton with two of the best trackers in Tucson, Jesus Maria Elias and Ascension Rios, chief of the Papago Indians. They trailed him to the Rillito River, which ran north of town, and found where he had dug for water in the dry sandy streambed. His tracks doubled back and then headed across rocky terrain, where the trail was lost. It later turned out that he had hid in the brush and that Paul and his trailers had passed within six feet of him. Morton then walked south for three days, finally arriving half-starved at the Total Wreck mine, forty miles south of Tucson. There he asked a friend for a meal. Pretending to go for food, the friend instead returned with a deputy sheriff, who arrested Morton and brought him back to Tucson in irons.[5]

That summer Bob and Margaret Paul were occupied with acquiring a new home. They had been renting the property at 501 Stone Avenue, but Margaret no doubt wanted her own house. Apparently their lease had expired, for Paul asked a Tucson real estate agent, Richard Starr, to find another rental house for his family. Starr suggested that he buy a home instead and showed him an adobe located at 146 East Pennington Street. Though small, with only three rooms, it had a large lot, a well, and a stable in the back for his horses. It was also conveniently located midway between the courthouse and the train depot and was a short walk to each. A typical Tucson adobe, its tile roof and thick mud-brick walls kept out much of the summer heat. Margaret must have liked it. They bought the house for $2,900, paying $1,100 cash and assuming a $1,800 mortgage. They would own this home for almost twenty years.[6]

In contrast with Bob Paul's adventurous life, his domestic affairs were quiet. He was a stern but fair father, gentle with his daughters and strict with his sons. Honesty was especially important to him, and once, after repeatedly catching one of his teenage boys in a lie, he thrashed him soundly with a switch. Although Margaret was a fine cook, Paul insisted on having a simple bowl of hot soup every day for lunch, no matter how high the temperature got in Tucson. After dinner, Margaret would clear the massive dining room table, and Paul would pull out a well-worn deck of cards and play solitaire, often for hours. Sometimes friends would drop by, and he loved to engage them in games of chess and cribbage. On such occasions the children would have to play outside or else remain in silence.[7]

The Pauls' eldest son, John, had graduated from the Heald business college in 1879, when he was sixteen. He returned to Tucson and followed in his father's footsteps, working for Wells Fargo. In 1882 John started his

The Pima County courthouse in about 1884. The county jail is the two-story wing attached to the left, or rear, of the courthouse. Courtesy of the Arizona Historical Society/ Tucson, BN205699.

own express business, Paul's Transfer Co., picking up packages and letters and delivering them to and from the train depot and other locations in Tucson. He ran advertisements in the *Citizen*, offering "cheap rates and prompt work. Orders may be left at Telephone Headquarters over City Marshal's office." John Paul also appears to have contracted with Wells Fargo to handle some of their Tucson delivery business. But Bob and Margaret Paul desired a better life for their son. Neither had more than a grade school education, but they were progressive and wanted more than the rudimentary schooling in Tucson could provide. In August 1882 they enrolled him in Santa Clara College (now Santa Clara University), located a few miles north of San Jose, California. It was one of the few colleges on the Pacific Coast, and it had lodging for out-of-state students. Margaret also liked the fact that her sisters in San Francisco were a short train ride away. John Paul proved an excellent student and studied at Santa Clara College for three years, returning to Tucson each summer.[8]

Pima County had long needed a larger courthouse and a safer jail. In 1881, with a construction budget of $75,000, the board of supervisors hired a young Tucson architect, A. W. Pattiani, to design it. The next year a two-story brick building was erected at the northwest corner of Pennington and Court Streets. With a stone foundation, two side wings with gable attics, and topped by a towering cupola, it was the most impressive public building in Arizona Territory and remained in constant use until it was demolished in 1927. The offices of the county officials, as well as those of the U.S. attorney and U.S. marshal, were all located on the first floor. On the second floor were the courtrooms, judges' chambers, and court clerks' offices. Its northern wing, separated from the rest of the structure by a passageway, served as the county jail. It also had two stories, each measuring forty by fifty-two feet, and it connected to the courthouse by one door on each level. Each floor of the jail had eight cells, capable of holding four prisoners apiece. The cells, built in two rows back to back, faced a pair of inner corridors that were connected by locked gates to an outer corridor. Next to the cell building was a large jailyard surrounded by a high brick wall. The architect, Pattiani, had submitted his plans to the board of supervisors in May 1881, just two weeks after Paul took office. For the jail design, Pattiani did not consult with the county's newly elected sheriff. The result was that the one man in Tucson with extensive experience in jail management had no input into its design. This would prove a deadly mistake.[9]

On September 12, 1882, Paul and his deputies moved all the prisoners, including Joe Casey, Frank Morton, Johnny Murphy, Bill Moyer, and Dave Gibson, into the new jail. The following day Paul settled into his new office on the first floor of the courthouse. Sheriff Paul employed a head jailer and three guards. Two had the day watch and two the night watch, each working a twelve-hour shift. Trusties did the cooking in the jailyard, and at seven each morning the prisoners were released from their cells into the outer corridor for breakfast. Paul's night jailer was George W. Cooler, a noted Arizona pioneer. Though Cooler was a Democrat, Paul admired him as a typical frontiersman. Cooler had enlisted in the army in 1852 at age twenty-one and had acquired extensive experience during Indian campaigns in Texas, Kansas, Utah, New Mexico, and Arizona. During the Civil War he was a civilian wagon master for the army in New Mexico. In 1865 he was accused of taking part in a massacre of Yavapai Indians. After service as a civilian scout, he settled in Tucson and opened the Gem Saloon. In 1882 Paul put him to work as jailer, but Cooler's closeness to Tucson's saloon and gambling element would throw into question the sheriff's judgment in hiring him.[10]

Johnny Murphy, Bill Moyer, and Dave Gibson had been causing trouble even before they were transferred to the new jail. A week earlier, Deputy Sheriff Nat S. Fullmer, who was in charge of the chain gang—the petty criminals who maintained the courthouse grounds—reported, "I encountered the most violent abuse from the prisoners Murphy, Gibson, and Moyer, the murderers of Levy, who applied to me every epithet of vile abuse their voluble tongues could command, and among other things asserted that they would 'fix me' when they got out." Fulmer said that the three were drunk in the jail at the time and were "permitted the most extraordinary latitude; are supplied with choice food from the Palace Hotel; have plenty of whisky and other liquors, and are often intoxicated. Visitors are permitted to see and talk with them at any and all times and they often have high old times with female visitors in the jailer's room."[11]

Undersheriff Henry Ward responded to Fullmer's charges, saying, "I have never known them to be drunk while in jail. I have seen them supplied with one drink at a time, which was given them by the jailer." Regarding female visitors, Ward explained, "Mr. Gibson has a wife and child, who visit him every day regularly. She has always behaved in a manner becoming a lady. Mr. Moyer has a wife also who calls to see him every day, and who evinces the true spirit of a wife. I have never seen anything indecorous going on in the jail, nor has any such thing been allowed." Deputy Sheriff Jimmy Hersey, who was in charge of the jail during the daytime, also disputed Fullmer's allegations and affirmed that Murphy, Moyer, and Gibson had behaved themselves: "They have given us no trouble since they were put in jail."[12]

Despite the public denials of Ward and Hersey, there were indeed problems in Sheriff Paul's jail. Many of them were caused by Paul's failure to rein in the night jailer, the aptly named George Cooler. Murphy, Moyer, and Gibson were all friends of Cooler's. Murphy had served for several years on Pima County's Democratic committee and shared political sympathies with Cooler, who in turn allowed the prisoners extraordinary liberties. At that time, Paul was preparing for another hotly contested election, and the campaigning distracted him from the brewing problems in his jail. On September 20 he was nominated by acclamation at the Republican county convention. His Democratic opponent, Eugene O. Shaw, a thirty-two-year-old miner, cattleman, and freight-line owner, had no law enforcement experience whatsoever. But Paul was taking no chances, and he aggressively canvassed the county for votes.[13]

In the meantime Louis C. Hughes began to rewrite history. Despite his published acknowledgment of Democratic fraud in the last election, he now claimed that "Sheriff Paul obtained the place to which Mr. Shibell was legally elected" as a result of "the frauds by which the Republican party obtained the Sheriffalty of this county." It was an outrageous falsehood that Hughes would often repeat in the coming years. While Hughes published items supporting Shaw in the *Star*, the *Citizen* countered: "Do you want such a state of affairs established as existed in Cochise County last winter? If you do, then elect an inexperienced man for sheriff; if not, re-elect Paul."[14]

Soon Paul had a firsthand experience with Hughes's political machinations. The incumbent Republican recorder was Charles R. Drake, and he was opposed by William S. Read. Paul recalled:

> Some time in the month of October, about three weeks before the election, L. C. Hughes approached Mr. Drake and myself and wanted to meet us privately. . . . I told Mr. Hughes that we would meet him at 7 o'clock that evening at my office in the Court House. At the hour designated we met and all three going into my private office I locked the door. Mr. Hughes then offered to support Drake and myself for the respective positions of Recorder and Sheriff in lieu of Read and Shaw, the regular Democratic nominees, for $500 each. After talking awhile we offered him $300 each. He said it was not enough; that his being a Democratic newspaper the sum would not remunerate him for the losses he would suffer by the withdrawal of Democratic patronage. We told him we would give no more and he finally said he would take the offer under consideration and then left. The negotiations were not resumed.

This was neither the first nor the last time Hughes was accused of soliciting bribes. And while Paul was honest in admitting that he had negotiated with Hughes, his offer of money for the *Star*'s support was uncharacteristic. Perhaps he had been browbeaten by Hughes's constant editorial attacks. Nonetheless it was a black mark on Paul's otherwise unblemished official record.[15]

While the campaign simmered, Murphy, Moyer, and Gibson were jailed in the same cell, this one on the ground floor. On October 23, 1882,

Paul was at home, suffering feverishly from an attack of malaria. In the evening he was roused from his sickbed by an extraordinary report. The jailer, Cooler, claimed that Murphy had feigned illness and begged to let him use the water closet, located at the end of the inner corridor. Cooler had unlocked the door to the corridor, then opened Murphy's cell and released him. Murphy spent about five minutes inside the bathroom, then called Cooler to let him back into his cell. Cooler reported that as he unlocked the cell, Murphy seized him and clapped his hand across the jailer's mouth, whispering, "I am sorry, George, but I have to do it."

Gibson, so Cooler said, leaped onto the hapless jailer and dragged him into the cell. The three desperadoes gagged him with a towel, then thrust his arms through the bars and tied them together with another towel. The jailer carried a revolver, which Moyer found in his back pocket. Taking Cooler's keys, they locked him in their cell, then quickly unlocked the other three cells in the corridor, releasing Joe Casey, Frank Morton, a killer named Tim Hurley, and three robbers, D. A. Westfall, Pat Mahoney, and Charles French. The nine prisoners then passed through the unlocked corridor wicket, entered the jailer's office, found the key to the outside door, and slipped out the back of the jail. Murphy, Moyer, Gibson, and Morton immediately separated from the others and walked quickly to Gibson's house on Court Street. After a brief visit with Gibson's wife, they headed toward the gas works on South Meyer Street. There two Mexicans were waiting with four horses, each with a blanket strapped behind the saddle and a brace of revolvers, a Winchester rifle, and cartridge belts looped over the pommel. The jailbreakers mounted up and fled. Joe Casey and Tim Hurley quietly slipped out of town on foot.

Cooler eventually emerged from the jail, calling to assistant jailer George Hand, "Murphy and the boys are all gone. They gagged me, locked me up, and left." Paul, unable to leave his sickbed, ordered Undersheriff Ward to organize the manhunt. But by then the escapees had vanished. Almost immediately suspicions were raised about Cooler's role in the escape. The *Citizen* pointed out that Sheriff Paul had given Cooler explicit orders to never enter the inner corridors unless another jailer first locked the door behind him. After describing the political relationship between Cooler and Murphy, the *Citizen* made the inflammatory charge that Democrats had conspired to engineer the jailbreak to embarrass Paul: "Occurring at this time, just on the eve of the election, it will be used for all it is worth against the re-election of Sheriff Paul." Two days later, as suspicions against

Johnny Murphy in a typical Arizona gambling scene, taken in Bisbee in about 1908. Murphy is the dealer, second from the right. Author's collection.

him mounted, Cooler was arrested by City Marshal Buttner on a warrant charging him with permitting the prisoners to escape. Unable to post the $3,000 bail, he was locked in a cell in his own jail.[16]

Cooler's preliminary hearing began on October 27. At his lawyers' request, it was held behind closed doors. When he was held to answer, his attorneys brought a habeas corpus petition in an effort to get him out of jail. That hearing was public, and the testimony shocked the citizenry and enraged Paul. Assistant jailer William M. "Billy" White testified that before leaving for dinner, he put fresh water and clean chamber pots in each cell and told Cooler he had done so. Thus there was no reason for Cooler to let Murphy out of his cell to use the water closet. Undersheriff Ward took the witness stand and stated that he had given Cooler written instructions against opening any of the cell doors when he was alone. Most damaging was the statement of George Hand, assistant jailer and courthouse janitor. He said that immediately after the break, Cooler emerged from the jail with a towel tied with a single loose knot around his neck and a second towel clenched in his teeth. Though both hands were free, he called on Hand to remove the towel from his neck. It was evident that he had not been bound and gagged. Cooler was kept in jail and eventually released on bond. In June 1883, facing strong evidence of his guilt, he pled guilty to assisting in the escape and, apparently due to his long service in the Indian wars, was let off with a $500 fine. For Paul, it had been one of the most embarrassing and discouraging incidents in his career. He sent out wanted flyers offering a hundred-dollar reward for each of the jailbreakers, and he vowed to track down every one of them.[17]

The election took place on November 7, 1882, and while Paul was awaiting the results from the county's far-flung polls, he attempted to find the escapees. Murphy, Moyer, and Gibson had many friends in Pima County. They had headed into the Santa Catalina Mountains, just north of Tucson. The desperadoes had not been there long when they heard a rumor that Sheriff Paul had discovered that they were in the mountains and had sent to the San Carlos Reservation for twenty Indians to track them down. They immediately saddled up and rode north to the White Mountains, some two hundred miles distant. On election day the three fugitives loped up to the ranch of T. J. Hazan, twenty miles from Fort Apache, and asked to buy barley for their horses. They were armed with Winchester rifles and six-shooters and led several pack animals. Hazan and Murphy knew each other, and Murphy told him they were camped in the White Mountains and were waiting for their friends in Tucson to "square things" regarding the Leavy killing. Murphy claimed they had killed Leavy in a fair fight, and he warned that if anyone tried to arrest them, "hell would pop." He boasted, "We three are about as hard a game as you can find anywhere, and if we are driven to desperation we will kick up the damndest muss ever raised in Arizona."[18]

The trio wintered in the White Mountains, and Paul later learned that they were "plentifully supplied with provisions by friends." In February 1883 they rode west to the Dripping Springs Mountains south of Globe, where they made a new camp not far from Riverside (now Kelvin). When Johnny Murphy and Bill Moyer quarreled, the latter headed south for Mexico. On the night of March 2, 1883, two masked men held up and robbed the stagecoach from Globe to Florence near Dripping Springs, but they got little for their efforts. On April 16 the same highwaymen robbed the Globe stage in the same spot, but the express box contained nothing of value. The presence of Johnny Murphy and Dave Gibson in the area, according to a Globe newspaperman, "led many persons to think that these parties were the perpetrators of the robberies." While possible, it seems more probable that the bandits were Red Jack Almer and his gang. Off and on, Murphy and Gibson showed up at the ranch of Len Redfield on the San Pedro River. Redfield was as ready as ever to shield outlaws, and for a time the pair hid out in the hills near his ranch. Explained Tucson pioneer William C. Davis, who later bought the Redfield ranch, "Food was supplied by Redfield. He used to take it some distance from the camp of the fugitives and leave it where they could come for it. He made these trips twice a week."[19]

Joe Casey had no such connections, so he and Tim Hurley fled east to El Paso, Texas. A few weeks after the escape, Paul received a wire that Casey had been captured in El Paso. The sheriff boarded an eastbound train and found Casey locked up in El Paso's adobe jail. He also learned that Tim Hurley had been in town the day before, but had crossed the border into Chihuahua. After paying the El Paso officers the hundred-dollar reward, Paul headed across the Rio Grande into El Paso del Norte (now Ciudad Juarez) in search of Hurley. He left instructions that Casey should be carefully watched, and he even offered to pay for an extra guard, a proposal that was declined. Unable to trace Hurley, the sheriff returned to El Paso and was chagrined to learn that Casey had again escaped. Despite the fact that Casey and another prisoner had been chained to a two-hundred-pound rock, they had tunneled through the adobe jail wall. Two other prisoners helped them carry the rock across the jailyard and hoist it over a ten-foot-high outer wall. The escapees stole an axe and were busily chopping their chains when they were discovered and dragged back to the jail. That night, despite an extra guard being posted, Casey obtained a smuggled file, cut through his chain, and escaped into the darkness. A disgusted Paul returned to Tucson empty-handed.[20]

Despite the fears of his supporters that the jailbreak would be used to defeat him at the polls, Paul made a respectable showing in the election. Though it took several weeks to complete the ballot count, in the end he achieved a narrow victory of 954 votes to 874 for Eugene O. Shaw. Several years later, Louis Hughes charged that "a fraud of over one hundred votes had been committed, and although Mr. Shaw was made aware of the fact, he with his advisors concluded to let the matter rest." Hughes offered no proof, and it can be safely assumed that if there had been any evidence of fraud, the Democrats would not have hesitated to file an election lawsuit. Paul's position was secure for another two years.[21]

Sheriff Paul now faced a new version of an old problem. Raids by the Cowboys into Mexico had greatly diminished, but in their place an organized gang of Mexican stock thieves was operating on both sides of the border. Its leader was one of the West's most dangerous outlaws, Procopio Bustamante, also known as Procopio Murrieta. Tall, handsome, and ruthless, he was the nephew of the infamous Joaquin Murrieta. After committing

The notorious Procopio Bustamante. Bob Paul could never
capture him. Author's collection.

several California murders in 1862 and 1863, Procopio shot and wounded
a constable who was trying to arrest him for cattle theft. He was captured
and sentenced to a term in San Quentin. On his release he joined the
Tiburcio Vasquez gang, which terrorized California in the early 1870s.
Arrested in San Francisco in 1872 by Sheriff Harry Morse, Procopio was
sent back to San Quentin for a five-year stint. In 1877 he led a series of
bandit raids in the San Joaquin Valley. Five of his gang were captured and
lynched in Bakersfield. After killing a pursuing posseman, he fled to Baja
California, where he reportedly headed of a gang of bandits. In the fall
of 1878, several of the band were captured, and Procopio was next heard of
in his boyhood home of Hermosillo, Sonora. There he became a city police
officer, but in 1882 he shot and killed a popular actor in a brothel and fled.[22]

Within months Procopio's band of horse and cattle thieves was operating extensively on both sides of the border. Among the members of his
gang were Francisco "Chino" Lopez, Canuto Soto, and two brothers, Antonio and Anselmo Bustamante (probably relatives of Procopio). Soto had
murdered a man in Yuma in 1872 but had escaped and was still a fugitive

ten years later. In December 1882 three of Procopio's gang drove a herd of sixty cattle north to Tucson for sale. When asked by Tucson butchers to prove their title to the animals, they produced a bill of sale from Procopio. Paul reported this to Tucson businessman Demetrio Velasco, who operated a stage line to the border, asking him to obtain proof from Mexico that the cattle were stolen. But Velasco was unable to learn anything about the cattle, and without evidence, Paul could not arrest the suspects. Instead, he trailed the three as they drove the herd north to Pioneer, near Globe, where they sold them to a less than honest butcher.[23]

Just before Christmas Sheriff Paul managed to nab one of Procopio's band. Francisco "Chino" Lopez was a notorious desperado who reportedly had once belonged to the Tiburcio Vasquez gang. Lopez, a fugitive from Southern California, had fled to Arizona, where he had been stealing horses along the border with Procopio. Paul got a tip that he would be at the Tucson racetrack for the festivities on Christmas Eve. The sheriff made sure he was there too, along with City Marshal Buttner. When Lopez rode up, heavily armed and magnificently mounted, Paul stepped forward and seized the bridle of his horse. The animal spooked and bucked so desperately that Lopez was thrown from the saddle. The outlaw had no chance against the brawny sheriff, and in a heartbeat Lopez was in handcuffs and on his way to jail. Sheriff Paul returned him to California to stand trial. In San Bernardino, Lopez was convicted of grand larceny and sent to San Quentin.[24]

In the meantime Paul continued his search for Procopio. In early February 1883 his gang brought a second herd of stolen cattle across the border and sold them in Benson. Then they brazenly rode into Tucson, where the Mexican consul, Antonio V. Lomeli, learned of the sale and asked Sheriff Paul to arrest them. Paul had no evidence that the cattle were stolen and told Lomeli that he "could not act without a warrant." For reasons that are not entirely clear, Lomeli refused to swear out a warrant. The *Citizen* claimed, improbably, that Lomeli refused to appear in court "through fear of compromising his official dignity" and "imagined himself above the law." Lomeli instead sent a telegram to Governor Tritle in Prescott, who wired back advising him to go before a Tucson judge and "have the proper warrants issued." The consul may have been under orders from Mexico not to appear in American courts. But because the owners of the stolen cattle were in Mexico, Lomeli was the only person who could have brought the criminal charges. Sheriff Paul assured the *Citizen* that "he holds himself in readiness to execute a warrant as soon as possible after its issuance." But no warrant was ever issued, and Procopio's men were never arrested. Later that year Procopio was reportedly caught near Tucson by Pete Gabriel, but it turned out to be a case of mistaken identity. In 1886 Deputy U.S. Marshal H. D. Underwood captured gang member Canuto Soto near Tucson and sent him to Yuma prison to serve out his original sentence for murder. But Bob Paul never laid a glove on the chief of the bandits. Procopio stayed mainly in Mexico, marrying in Hermosillo in 1884 and fathering two daughters. He was reportedly slain by Mexican police near Hermosillo in about 1894.[25]

In December 1882, Paul's friend, stage-line owner J. D. Kinnear, swore out a warrant for Dan "Dutch Henry" Moore, charging him with arson. In a dispute with Kinnear over possession of an adobe ranch house, Dutch Henry had burned the roof so that it could not be occupied. Kinnear and Paul rode to Moore's ranch in the Whetstone Mountains. As they approached the ranch, situated in a deep canyon, Paul spotted Moore on a rise in front of them. Dutch Henry was on horseback and promptly levered a round into the chamber of his Winchester. Paul and Kinnear closed to within fifty yards before Moore demanded their names and business. Paul answered, but Dutch Henry threw up his rifle and threatened to kill them if they came any closer. Paul paid no heed. In the face of Moore's yawning gun barrel, the sheriff rode directly toward him, then jerked the rifle from his grasp. Paul and Kinnear brought the blustering Dutch Henry to jail in Tucson, where he was later convicted of arson and sentenced to a year in Yuma.[26]

For every step forward, Paul must have felt that he took another one back. On New Year's Day in 1883, two burglars named Davitt and Sullivan, whom the sheriff had brought in from Los Angeles to stand trial in Tucson, used pieces of firewood to pry their cell door loose from its hinges. Jailer Billy White tried to stop them, but they attacked him with firewood clubs, beating him mercilessly across the arms, head, and face. Leaving the unconscious jailer in the corridor, they slipped into the jail-yard, scaled the wall, and vanished. White recovered, but promptly resigned as jailer. Paul's anger and frustration can be gleaned from a simple note in the diary of jailer George Hand: "Sheriff Paul is red hot." Two weeks later, his deputy in Calabasas, Charles H. Vosburg, while on a manhunt in the Patagonia Mountains, made camp for the night with his horse picketed a hundred yards distant. While he was in a sound sleep, thieves crept in and stole his horse, saddle, bridle, and spurs. Vosburg tracked them on foot for twenty miles, but they, like the jailbreaking burglars, vanished.[27]

More bad news came that month in the form of a smallpox epidemic in Tucson. Dr. John C. Handy, the county health officer, ordered that the populace be vaccinated. During the outbreak, fourteen-year-old Agnes Paul became deathly ill. Her worried parents called in Dr. Handy and a private physician, Dr. C. P.V. Watson. The doctors became embroiled in a very public but highly unprofessional dispute. Dr. Handy insisted that Agnes had smallpox, while Dr. Watson said she did not, and he offered to wager $500 that he was right. Dr. Handy, who was very popular but quarrelsome, took up the bet, which ended up as fodder for the newspapers. The doctors then began quibbling over the terms of the wager. Dr. Watson backed out, and the dispute was never resolved. Whatever the ailment, Agnes recovered, but her bouts with illness had only begun.[28]

In the meantime, Joe Casey, after escaping from El Paso, beat his way on the Texas & Pacific Railroad to Big Spring, Texas, 350 miles to the east. Casey was a died-in-the-wool desperado. He claimed to have been born in Rochester, New York, in 1858; his true name was reportedly Thomas Reed. In 1880 he enlisted in the Sixth U.S. Cavalry and was stationed at Camp Thomas and Fort Bowie. In a soldier's quarrel at Fort Apache, he was shot and wounded in the foot. Discharged in 1882, he drifted to the border, where he was suspected of several robberies before Paul captured him. After his arrival in Big Spring, Texas, he pulled a holdup and was arrested and lodged in jail to await trial. The county sheriff suspected that the prisoner might be Casey from the wanted notice issued by Paul, and he transferred him to the jail in Colorado City for safekeeping. There Casey made yet another break, which he later described: "I caught the jailer and tried to take his pistol away from him. I grabbed the stock and he held on the muzzle. He grabbed me around the waist and called to a [Texas] Ranger downstairs, who pointed his gun at me and I gave up. They then chained me down to the floor.... Til Paul came they fed me on bread and water." The Texas lawmen were only too happy to be rid of Casey, and on March 17, 1883, Paul returned him to Tucson.[29]

Sheriff Paul was not taking any chances with Casey. He ordered that the badman be ironed with two sixteen-pound Oregon boots, one on each foot. The Oregon boot, formally known as the Gardner shackle, had been patented by the warden of the Oregon State Penitentiary in 1866. It consisted of a heavy iron clasp that locked around the upper ankle. This thick band was supported by iron braces that attached to the heel of the boot. Unlike leg irons, which could be cut with a saw blade or even the bale of a water bucket, the Oregon boot was almost impossible to remove without a key. But Paul's best efforts could not compensate for a shoddily constructed jail. Although the jail specifications called for the bars and gratings to be made of chilled iron, they were instead built with softer wrought iron. That is why the prisoners Davitt and Sullivan had been able to pry their cell door loose. The bars should have been deeply embedded into the stone walls, but instead they were placed in sockets less than an inch deep. The jail walls should have been reinforced with an inside layer of sheet iron, but by design they were made only of stone, brick, and mortar. As the *Tucson Citizen* later reported, "Men of practical experience with this class of building condemn the general plan and the construction in very strong terms. The arrangement was such that unless a large force of guards was maintained, there was but little chance of keeping the prisoners in security."[30]

To replace George Cooler as jailer, the sheriff offered the job to his old friend and mining partner in Chili Gulch, fifty-two-year-old Andrew W. Holbrook. Holbrook was an experienced officer, having served as a special policeman in San Francisco. Joe Casey was assigned to a cell with Harry Sinclair, a deserter from the Sixth Cavalry who was awaiting trial for his part in a robbery and murder in La Noria, on the border. Directly above the cells was an open area where the prisoners were allowed to exercise. On the evening of April 28, 1883, Casey and Sinclair were on top of the cells when, as Casey later recalled, "We discovered that a bar in the grating leading to the corridor was loose. I said to Sinclair that I thought it was a good chance to pull the bar out and effect our escape. The next morning between eight and nine o'clock, while the jailer was in the backyard, the jail guard out in the courthouse, with trusties cleaning up, and [Deputy Sheriff] Vosburg asleep upstairs, we sprung the bar, and Sinclair went out first and I followed. I went immediately into the office, and while looking around for the key of the cupboard that contained the keys to the Oregon boots that were on my legs I discovered three pistols on a small cot."[31]

Casey and Sinclair had been followed into the outer corridor by another prisoner, Lorenzo Lopez. Casey handed one of the revolvers to Sinclair. The door from the corridor into the jailyard was held open by a rope tied to an iron grating. The escapees cut it, and the door swung shut. The unarmed

Holbrook, who was in the jailyard supervising the breakfast cleanup, heard the door close and hurried to investigate. Opening the door, he stepped into the corridor and, seeing no one, entered the jailer's room. He was shocked to see Casey with a Colt .44 pointed at him. Casey barked, "Throw up your hands!"

Holbrook, armed with more courage than common sense, charged Casey and seized his six-shooter. The desperado fired, and the muzzle flash powder-burned Holbrook's left hand as the bullet ricocheted harmlessly into the cells. As the two struggled for the gun, Holbrook caught a glimpse of Harry Sinclair a few feet away, standing next to the bed with a cocked pistol in his hand. Now Holbrook's better judgment took over, and he fled back to the door, with Casey in pursuit. Holbrook snatched up a coal shovel and, swinging wildly at Casey with the shovel in one hand, opened the door with his other. Casey, determined to get the jailer's keys and stop him from giving the alarm, fired a second time as Holbrook tried to open the door. The .44 caliber slug ripped completely through Holbrook, entering the lower back, slicing through his hipbone and intestines, and exiting near his navel. With a Herculean effort, the jailer pulled himself through the doorway and slammed the heavy door shut. As he desperately grasped the knob to keep his prisoners from escaping, Holbrook shouted for help.

The jail guards, Alfredo E. Carrillo and Miles H. Gifford, were in the courthouse when they heard the shots. They ran to the main door, but it was locked from the inside. Racing around the building, they climbed through a window of the sheriff's office that overlooked the jailyard. Lowering a stepladder through another window into the jailyard, they hoisted the wounded Holbrook into Paul's office. Then Carrillo climbed down into the yard and cautiously entered the jail door. Casey and Sinclair were nowhere in sight. Carrillo found two of Holbrook's revolvers on a shelf in the corridor and, after some searching, discovered that Casey had wriggled back through the bars and was crouching in the rear of the exercise area above the cells. Knowing that one pistol was still missing, Carrillo covered him with his six-gun and ordered him to come down. Instead, Casey, weighed down by the Oregon boots, climbed down a ladder at the back of the cells and staggered into the water closet. Carrillo fired four pistol shots through the wood door, but Casey lay flat on the floor and ducked the bullets. Finally the desperado came out and surrendered. He showed Carrillo where he had hidden the third pistol, under the sink. Then Carrillo and Gifford locked Casey, Sinclair, and Lopez back in their cells.[32]

Interior of the Pima County jail, 1910. The two figures at the right are standing in the outer corridor where Joe Casey murdered Deputy Holbrook. At the top right is the exercise area above the cells. At left, prisoners inside the inner corridor. Courtesy of Jane Eppinga.

By this time a huge crowd, attracted by the gunfire, had surrounded the courthouse. From his home, Paul raced to the jail and helped load his desperately wounded friend into an ambulance. They rushed to St. Mary's Hospital, where Dr. John C. Handy told the grief-stricken sheriff that Holbrook could not last more than a few hours. While Paul stayed at his bedside, the leading citizens and businessmen called for an "indignation meeting" at Levin's Park. A reporter for the *Arizona Star*, perhaps Louis Hughes himself, attended, reporting, "A chairman was elected, and one prominent citizen moved articles of indignation be drawn up, expressing the feelings of the community at the murder. One of our leading merchants said that the people of Tucson were indignant enough without any formal resolutions to that effect being passed, and if they were going to do anything about it, now was the time to do it. . . . It was then resolved to hang the murderer, and prominent gentlemen were appointed to supervise the good work."[33]

It was now 10:00 A.M., and the crowd agreed to meet en masse at 11:30 A.M. at the corner of Pennington Street and Maiden Lane. At the ringing of the fire bell, they would march to the jail and demand the prisoner; if refused, they would storm the jail. Said the *Star*, "The sentiment of the citizens of all classes was to rid the community of the murderer at all hazards." But ten minutes before the appointed time, an impatient vigilante telephoned the firehouse with instructions to sound the alarm. The mob leaders were not yet present, and what the *Star* called "a motley crowd of men and little boys" rushed the courthouse, where they grappled with Undersheriff Thomas Cordis and several deputies. The mob stormed into the hallway that led to the jail, but were stopped by the grated door. A messenger on horseback was sent to the hospital for Sheriff Paul, and he rushed to the courthouse. Forcing his way through the armed and angry crowd to his office, Paul retrieved his revolver and stepped out to confront the mob. By this time George Hand, the janitor and night watchman, had a brilliant idea. He uncoiled an indoor fire hose and turned a powerful stream of water onto the mob. This forced them out, and, the *Star* reported, "a grand stampede ensued." The vigilante leaders had now arrived, and they demanded that the sheriff hand over Joe Casey. Bob Paul had never lost a prisoner to a lynch mob, and he was not about to start now. He told the mob that he "could not give the prisoner up for execution in this summary manner." He explained that his "duty as an officer prohibited it" and that he would protect Casey, "let the results be what they might."

The leaders of the mob—either due to respect for Paul or in fear of him—gave up, and the crowd drifted away. But, as the *Star* reported, that night "there were threats and curses loud and deep to be heard on every side. It was generally supposed that the jail would be attacked and the prisoner hung." At 7:00 P.M. Holbrook died. Paul was there, and, as a newspaperman later reported, "the loss was as severe to the sheriff as if he had lost his own brother." Although in great agony, Holbrook had been alert, and Paul had him give a deathbed statement about the shooting and attempted break. Sheriff Paul placed a strong guard at the jail and made ready for the worst. But by morning no attack had come, and the lynching sentiment gradually dissolved. By April 30 tempers had quieted down sufficiently for Holbrook's funeral to take place in the courthouse.[34]

Paul's grief and anger can only be imagined. The issue of the jail's poor construction once again surfaced. In response to public criticism, the contractor, John Hanlon, asserted that there was "nothing in the specifications, plan, or contract calling for a railing above the top of the cells. When I finished the ironwork . . . then the architect and [board of] supervisors saw the necessity of closing in the space between the top of the cells and the ceiling. . . . The architect then ordered a railing from San Francisco. . . . I then employed two men to set it in place and that was all I had to do with it." But Hanlon ignored the fact that he had installed the railing so poorly that Casey was able to remove a loose bar. The circumstances of Holbrook's death plainly rested on the shoulders of Hanlon, architect A. W. Pattiani, and the Pima County Board of Supervisors, who designed, approved, and constructed a jail that was inherently unsafe.[35]

Pima County's district attorney wasted no time in bringing Casey to trial for killing Holbrook. The trial took place on June 15, 1883, and lasted but one day. A huge crowd packed the courtroom. Paul and his deputies and jail guards were on hand to preserve order. One of them told a reporter that "he had never before witnessed such interest as the people took in this trial." The evidence against Casey was overwhelming. Two fellow prisoners described the jailbreak and swore that Casey had shot the jailer. Holbrook's deathbed statement, which had been recorded in the hospital by justice of the peace Charles Meyer and witnessed by Paul, was read to the jury. Guards Carrillo and Gifford testified that Casey told them where he hid the murder weapon. They said that Casey had admitted the killing, but claimed it was an accident. The crowd was quiet until a drunk in the back yelled out, "Hang the son of a bitch!"

Sheriff Paul and his deputies quickly restored order. Then Casey took the stand and testified in his own defense, claiming, "My pistol went off accidentally as I stumbled over a stove. Holbrook then ran to the door. I followed to get his keys when he struck back at me with the shovel, which may have struck the pistol and caused it to go off." The jury didn't buy it. At 6:00 P.M. they began deliberations, reaching a verdict of first-degree murder in little more than an hour. Shooting a lawman in the back was not looked at lightly in frontier Arizona. One of Casey's lawyers told him, "Well, my boy, we've done the best for you we could."

The desperado answered glumly, "Yes you have done the best you could under the circumstances. They've made a neck-tie party of it." On June 19 Judge A. W. Sheldon sentenced Casey to death by hanging. His attorneys immediately appealed to the Arizona Supreme Court, and Casey remained in Paul's jail while the appeal was pending. Harry Sinclair had been charged as an accessory to Holbrook's murder. Rightly fearing that he too would be sent to the gallows, Sinclair elected to plead guilty to second-degree murder and throw himself on the mercy of the court. Judge Sheldon, never one to mince words, told him, "You have been a terror to the communities where you have resided, and have been regarded as a desperado and outlaw. Such men as you have retarded the growth and prosperity of Arizona and placed the lives and property of its citizens at jeopardy." The judge sentenced him to life in Yuma prison.[36]

Paul undoubtedly felt at least a modicum of satisfaction in the convictions of Casey and Sinclair. Due to Alfredo Carrillo's courage and cool thinking in the jailbreak, Paul promoted him from jail guard to deputy sheriff. In the meantime the sheriff continued his search for the other missing jailbreakers. Bill Moyer had drifted south into Sonora. There he eked out a living as a gambler, finally making a big haul in Magdalena. With his winnings he boarded a train for his parents' home in St. Louis, Missouri. From there he went to Denver, where a Tucson gambler recognized him, and word soon got out that he was in town. On July 18, 1883, Moyer visited the office of Tom Fitch, the noted attorney who had successfully defended the Earps on charges of murdering the Cowboys in Tombstone. Fitch was now practicing law in Denver. Acting on a tip, David J. Cook, head of the Rocky Mountain Detective Association, arrested Moyer in Fitch's office. Paul was notified by telegraph and brought a requisition to Governor Pitkin. This time the governor, unlike in the Doc Holliday affair, chose to cooperate with Paul. The sheriff brought Moyer back to Tucson to stand trial for killing Jim Leavy. Paul kept Moyer in manacles and leg irons, and when the train pulled into the depot, he saw that a large crowd was waiting to glimpse the prisoner. Moyer, thinking he was about to be lynched, leaped from the car and, despite his chains, rushed for a hack that the sheriff had waiting. Paul had difficulty keeping up with him and had to shove his way through the throng. The crowd caused no trouble, however, and Paul locked Moyer up in the jail, leaving on his leg irons as an added precaution.

The next morning Sheriff Paul, accompanied by a reporter for the *Tucson Citizen*, visited the fugitive in his cell. "Well, Moyer, how do you feel this morning?" Paul asked.

"I don't feel very well," Moyer grumbled.

"Well, here is a reporter who wants to see you," continued the sheriff.

"I don't know as I want to see one."

Turning to the reporter, Paul remarked, "Well, do what you can with him," and left the journalist alone with Moyer.

The newspaperman tried to elicit a story from Moyer, saying, "The boys in town would like to know how you liked your trip for the last year, and where you have been."

Moyer loosened up and replied, "Oh, I've been around pretty much everywhere. I don't know as I care to tell just where all I was. These shackles hurt my legs, and I have no drink. I was down in the Sierra Madre most of the time."

He gave a rambling account of the jailbreak, admitted visiting Tucson several times at night to get provisions from friends, and claimed he had seen nothing of Johnny Murphy or Dave Gibson. Of Joe Casey's murderous escape attempt, Moyer said he had read about it in the newspapers, remarking, "He made a fool of himself; that was a bad break." The interview ended when a friend of Moyer's entered the jail, with Paul's permission, and gave him a bottle of whiskey. Moyer would languish in jail while awaiting trial.[37]

The murder of his old friend Andrew Holbrook was surely one of the most traumatic events in Bob Paul's life. But Paul's actions that day spoke volumes of his character. Despite intense grief and anger, he went to great lengths to protect the killer from a lynch mob. It was the toughest day, and the brightest moment, of his professional career.

CHAPTER TWELVE

When Law Was in the Holster

"Red Jack" Almer was a desperado long before he landed in Arizona in the late 1870s. Born in Italy in about 1850, his true name is unknown. He used several aliases, among them Jack Elmer, Averill, and Boreman, and had reportedly been a miner in Montana during the 1870s, before vigilantes ran him out of the territory for robbing sluice boxes. Red Jack was not a big man, measuring five feet seven and weighing only 140 pounds. Nor was he handsome; a contemporary described him as having "a repulsive countenance." He walked with a limp caused by an old gunshot wound in his right hip. He was well known in Tombstone, Benson, and San Simon. By 1883 Red Jack had settled in the new town of Johnsonville (now Johnson) in the Little Dragoon Mountains. The *Tucson Citizen* called Johnsonville "a prosperous mining camp" with "a large lot of thieves and cutthroats" and later reported that Red Jack Almer and his compadre, Charley Hensley, were "two of the worst desperadoes in the camp." Hensley, a twenty-five-year-old Missourian, had once lived in Tucson and worked as a teamster in Tombstone. Unlike Red Jack, Hensley was handsome, with a drooping mustache, and tall, standing a shade over six feet and weighing a muscular 170 pounds. A sheriff who knew him later described him thus: "He is not a good horseman, sits slouchy in the saddle, and when he talks uses the phrases and localisms common to Missouri."[1]

Red Jack and Hensley frequented the Johnsonville home of a crooked rancher named Hartzel. There the two concocted a plan to hold up the stage that ran between Florence and Globe. They persuaded a friend, Joe "Old Man" Tuttle, to join them. Joe Tuttle was a fifty-four-year-old former saloonkeeper and stagecoach driver in Florence. He had once been justice of the peace in Florence and had formerly run a store at Fort Thomas. The trio knew they could count on help from Len Redfield, whose ranch was still a resort for outlaws and road agents. Redfield was the same rancher who had harbored Luther King and the other stage robbers who had slain Bud Philpott two years earlier, as well as the Bisbee stage robbers and the killers of Jim Leavy in 1882. Leonard G. Redfield had been born in New York in 1834. His brother, Henry T. Redfield, known as Hank, four years younger, followed the harness-making trade. Len Redfield had come to California as a young man, settling in Tulare County, where he raised horses, in 1858. Ten years later he was joined by his brothers, Hank and Leroy J. Redfield. Hank brought along his wife, Malvina, and their one-year-old son. The Redfields' sister, Euphrasia, with her husband, A. B. Carpenter, joined them in 1875. The family was highly respected. Leroy J. Redfield was elected to the Tulare County Board of Supervisors, and his brother-in-law, Carpenter, served as postmaster of the town of Poplar, California.[2]

That same year, 1875, Len and Hank Redfield pulled up stakes and moved to the San Pedro River in Arizona. The Carpenters' son Frank, the eldest of their five children, rode to Arizona with his uncles. The ranches of Len and Hank were only four miles apart. Len, who never married, built a large adobe house near the river. The brothers set up a post office and asked that it be named Redfield, but the government rejected the name, so they chose Redington instead. Hank served as postmaster, and his son later recalled that they "struggled along for several years, making corn do three meals a day and living in fear of the Indians. When the Indians came too close, the family fled to Tres Alamos, nine miles south." Eventually the brothers prospered, as a friend recalled: "[Len] Redfield was as nice a man as you could ever meet; that is, in appearance. . . . Len Redfield could have lived in comfort all his life without resorting to crime. He had a valuable ranch, well supplied with cattle and other stock. He was considered one of the most prosperous men in that part of the Territory. But he led a double life." Before long, the Cowboys found that they were welcome at Len's ranch. In addition to Curly Bill and Pony Deal, the Clanton brothers were friends with the Redfields. In an embankment on the San Pedro River, Len even built a small smelter, which was used to melt down stolen jewelry and bullion. At the same time Len was active in politics, serving on Republican Party committees in Pima County. For the time being, his double life was a well-kept secret.[3]

On August 1, 1883, Red Jack Almer, Charley Hensley, and Joe Tuttle rode into Len Redfield's ranch. Red Jack was riding a mare he had stolen, and he led a purloined buckskin horse. After discussing their robbery plan with Redfield and his twenty-seven-year-old nephew, Frank Carpenter, the outlaws displayed an old, broken hatchet with which they intended to break open the stage's express box. Redfield told them, "You better take my hatchet. . . . It is new and has never been used before." As the three left his ranch, Redfield cautioned them, "Take good care of your horses, as they are your main dependence." They rode toward Florence and on August 8 made camp in the brush just east of town. At that time the stage road went east to Riverside Station (now Kelvin), twenty-five miles from Florence, where it crossed the Gila River and circled the Dripping Springs Mountains to Globe.[4]

Red Jack spent the next two days loitering about the stage office. Since the three had no money, he sold his stolen mare and gave Hensley ten dollars to buy supplies. Their plan was for Charley Hensley and Joe Tuttle to set up an ambush in a big wash two miles west of Riverside Station. Here they would stop the evening coach as it slowed to cross the wash. Red Jack would wait in Florence until a large Wells Fargo shipment was sent. He would board the stage as a passenger, sit on top wearing a red shirt and white neckerchief, and sing loudly as a warning when the coach approached the wash. On two successive evenings Hensley and Tuttle rode out to the ambush site. While Tuttle minded their horses out of sight, Hensley kept watch for the stage, but each time Red Jack was not aboard. Finally, on August 10 Red Jack spotted a large treasure shipment being loaded onto the Globe-bound coach. The Wells Fargo box was so heavy it took two men to lift it into the boot. Red Jack promptly bought a ticket for Riverside and climbed aboard with his saddle. He told bystanders that he was headed to the mines, looking for work. It was late afternoon when the coach rolled out of town, driven by Watson Humphreys, a longtime whip. The Wells Fargo messenger was young John H. Collins, armed with a sawed-off shotgun and a six-shooter. There were numerous passengers, and Red Jack squeezed into the dickey seat on top of the coach.

It was still daylight when Hensley saw the stage approaching. However, by the time he spotted Red Jack aboard, the coach had crossed the wash and proceeded on. Hensley rushed back to the horses and told Tuttle,

Bob Paul, center foreground, in front of the office of the *Florence Weekly Enterprise*, early 1880s. Courtesy of the Arizona Historical Society/Tucson, 18112.

"The stage got by before I saw Jack." Tuttle later claimed that he got cold feet and said, "Let's not go. Let's stop this." But Hensley responded angrily, "You come along." Tuttle recalled, "I knew if I did not go he would shoot me." But his immediate actions showed that he was in fact a willing participant. Hensley and Tuttle jumped on their horses and raced up the road. When the coach stopped to change the horses at Riverside Station, Hensley and Tuttle circled widely, forded the Gila River, and set up an ambush two miles down the road.

Red Jack, thinking that his partners had abandoned him, was worried when the coach pulled into Riverside Station. Here all the passengers got off, and Red Jack asked the station keepers whether two men had left a horse there for him. When the answer was no, he became enraged. He was in an isolated area with no money, no ticket, and no horse. The stage rolled out of Riverside without Red Jack. Its only passenger was one of the station keepers, Felix LeBlanc. Two miles down the road, at the foot of the slope leading out of the Gila valley, Hensley and Tuttle were waiting. Hensley, hidden in the roadside brush, was armed with a Winchester rifle; Tuttle, concealed on the opposite side of the road, clutched a shotgun. Both wore masks made of red calico. As the stage approached, they stood up and opened fire without any warning. A blast from Tuttle's shotgun struck Messenger Collins in the throat, killing him instantly. Hensley levered seven shots from his Winchester, striking Collins in the neck, killing one stage horse, and wounding another. Finally the driver, Humphreys, yelled out, "For God's sake, stop shooting! You have killed one man. What more do you want?"

The two robbers ordered Felix LeBlanc out of the stage and took his money. Then they told him to climb into the boot and hand down the Wells Fargo box. It was so heavy that LeBlanc could not lift it, so the bandits ordered Humphreys to help. Humphreys asked if he could remove the dead messenger from the boot, but one of the desperadoes answered, "Let him lie where he is and get that box out at once, or we'll put holes through you sons of bitches."

LeBlanc and Humphreys struggled with the express box and dropped it into the road. The bandits gave LeBlanc their hatchet and ordered him to break open the strongbox. Then they ordered the passenger and driver to walk up the hill and not return on pain of death. Hensley and Tuttle removed two bags of silver coin, weighing sixty pounds each and worth $2,000, plus $620 in gold coin, and packed it onto one of the stage horses, overlooking a packet of $60 in bills. Then they mounted up and, leading the packhorse, rode south along the Gila River toward Dudleyville. In their haste and excitement, the outlaws foolishly left behind a belt and knife belonging to Red Jack, Tuttle's saddlebags, and Redfield's hatchet. The silver was so unwieldy that they stopped and buried it near the riverbank, then rode hard all night along the San Pedro River road to Len Redfield's ranch. Redfield, on hearing their story, ordered his nephew, Frank Carpenter, to ride back down the river, find the stranded Red Jack, and bring him in.

Meanwhile, LeBlanc and Humphreys continued up the road in the dark for several miles until they met the Globe–Florence buckboard stage. Fearing another attack, they spent the night camped by the road with the driver and sole passenger. At daylight they returned to the abandoned coach, with Collins's body still in the boot, and the shattered Wells Fargo box a few feet away. They loaded the dead messenger into the stage and brought him into Florence. There, George A. Brown, the Wells Fargo agent, immediately wired the news to the company's general office in San Francisco. He received a prompt reply that detective John N. Thacker would be sent to investigate. Wells Fargo, Arizona Territory, and Pinal County offered rewards totaling $1,500 each for the killers.[5]

By now Arizonans were used to stage holdups, but cold-blooded murder was another matter. Johnny Collins had been very popular in Florence, and an urgent manhunt was quickly under way. The county's most experienced lawman was its former sheriff, Pete Gabriel, who happened to be in Riverside on mining business. When Gabriel learned that Red Jack had been hanging around the Florence stage depot, had left town aboard the fatal stage, and had been angry that no horse had been left for him at Riverside Station, he immediately became convinced that Almer was one of the gang. Soon Sheriff A. J. Doran, Undersheriff G. J. Scanlan, and several local officers, plus the editor of Florence's weekly newspaper, arrived in Riverside and, with Pete Gabriel, they started south on the river road after the bandits. In Dudleyville they found that several people had seen two riders heading south, leading a packhorse. Next, the possemen learned that Red Jack had paid a youth ten dollars to take him on horseback to Len Redfield's ranch, forty-five miles south. Farther on they met the boy, who had returned from his errand. He told the lawmen that on the way south he and Red Jack had encountered Frank Carpenter on the trail. Red Jack and Carpenter had dismounted, then stepped aside and talked privately. Red Jack then mounted Carpenter's horse and went on toward Redfield's ranch, while Carpenter headed north to Dudleyville on foot. The lawmen knew Len Redfield's reputation, and were certain they were on the right track.

In the meantime Hensley and Tuttle made camp in the hills near Redfield's house, where they were soon joined by Red Jack. Redfield fed them and promised to provide alibis, but insisted that they go back and dig up the stolen loot. He burned their masks, wrapped Tuttle's shotgun in gunnysacks, and buried it in his stable under a pile of manure. Then Redfield took the stage horse into a mountain ravine and shot it. The robbers agreed that Redfield would receive an equal share of the loot and that he and Tuttle would go by wagon and recover the booty on August 14. Red Jack and Hensley left for a hideout in the mountains, while Tuttle, Redfield, and Carpenter stayed on the ranch, certain that no pursuing lawmen would suspect them. But they did not reckon with the tenacity of Pete Gabriel. He and his possemen arrived at the Redfield ranch at seven o'clock on the night of August 12, two days after the holdup. From a distance they spotted Redfield, Tuttle, and several ranch hands. Gabriel and Sheriff Doran decided to wait for daylight to raid the ranch.[6]

At dawn they charged in and arrested Redfield and Tuttle without incident. The pair claimed innocence, and Redfield was confident that nothing could be proved. When shown the hatchet, knife, belt, and saddlebags found at the scene, they denied having ever seen them before. But the officers made a careful search and noticed that the manure pile in the stable had been disturbed. Digging into it, they found the shotgun and a U.S. mailbag. Though the mail had not been taken in this holdup, there had been other stage holdups in which mailbags had been stolen. With this evidence and their two prisoners, Sheriff Doran and his posse started for Florence. Gabriel continued on alone to search for Red Jack and Hensley. When the sheriff's posse passed through Dudleyville, they ran into Frank Carpenter. Undersheriff Scanlan had Tuttle's saddlebags draped across his horse. Carpenter, seeing them, turned toward his uncle and foolishly blurted out, "Len, these fellows have got your saddle bags." Len Redfield snapped back, "Shut up!"[7]

That was enough to convict them both, but Tuttle and Redfield held fast. With Carpenter, they were brought into Florence and lodged in jail. Bob Paul was monitoring the case, and a telegram was sent to him in Tucson advising of the arrest of Redfield and Tuttle. For the time being, he took no action and left the case to local officers. Wells Fargo detective John Thacker arrived in Florence but had little luck interrogating the two suspects. Finally the cagey Redfield began negotiating a civil settlement with the express company, in which he proposed to pay $400 for the three stage horses that had been lost and $2,000 for the stolen coin. But he denied any guilt and apparently hoped that Wells Fargo would secure his release in exchange for the money. On August 27, Tuttle, after repeated questioning, finally broke down during his preliminary hearing in court and made a full confession. He then led a small group including Thacker and Sheriff Doran to the spot where the loot was buried, and it was returned to George Brown, the Wells Fargo agent in Florence. Tuttle's confession implicated Redfield, and local citizens were outraged. Wrote the editor of the *Florence Enterprise*, "Public sentiment runs unanimously in favor of hanging the robbers. . . . Justice through our courts is too uncertain." Tuttle, Redfield, and Carpenter were held in jail to await further court proceedings.[8]

In the meantime Red Jack Almer, Charley Hensley, and a third desperado whose name is unknown were hiding out on the east side of the Rincon Mountains, near the confluence of Sycamore Canyon and North Creek, thirty miles east of Tucson. Here they built a stone fort and waited for the manhunt to die down. Their crooked friend Hartzel owned a mining claim with a partner, Dan Dougherty, several miles away in Sycamore Canyon.

Agents of W., F. & Co. will NOT post this circular, but place them in the hands of your local and county officers, and reliable citizens in your region. Officers and citizens receiving them are respectfully requested to preserve them for future reference.

Agents WILL PRESERVE a copy on file in their office.

$1,600.00 Reward!

ARREST STAGE ROBBER

On the evening of August 10th, 1883, the stage running from Florence to Globe was stopped near Riverside, by two masked highwaymen, W., F. & Co.'s messenger killed, and the box rifled of $2,620—$2,000 being in U. S. silver dollars and $620 in gold coin. Wells, Fargo & Co. have a standing reward of $300 each for the arrest and conviction of the robbers, and the Governor offers a reward of $1,000, making a total of $1,600.

DESCRIPTON OF ROBBERS:

An American, true name Charley Hensley, a Missourian by birth, 24 or 25 years of age, six feet one inch in height, weighing 160 or 170 pounds, slightly stoop-shouldered, dark complected, black hair and black eyes, has long black moustache, a low forehead sloping back to a point, generally combs his hair down over his forehead, dosen't use tobacco at all and drinks very little, wears a No. 9 or 10 boot, had on when last seen cork soled boots, a light colored broad-brimmed hat, light colored cheviot shirt, light colored coat with dark diagonal stripes. He is not a good horseman, sits slouchy in the saddle, and when he talks uses the phrases and localisms common to Missouri, he is rather striking in appearance. He has driven teams about Tombstone and is well acquainted at that place, Benson, Russelville and on the San Pedro river.

Jack Elmer, an Italian by birth, is from 33 to 35 years of age, 5 feet and 6 or 7 inches in height, weighs about 140 pounds, lame in right hip (lameness caused by gunshot wound), when last seen his hair was clipped close and when it grows out it is very curley and black, has a repulsive countenance and is very talkative. Passes under the aliases of Red Jack, Jack Avery and several other aliases. Is well known at Tombstone, Benson, San Simon and on the San Pedro river.

If arrested telegraph to

Sheriff A. J. DORAN.
FLORENCE, Pinal County, A. T.

Or to J. N. Thacker, Special Officer of Wells, Fargo & Co., San Francisco, Cal., or to L. F. Rowell, Assistant Superintendent of Wells, Fargo & Co., San Francisco, Cal.

Wanted poster for stage robbers Red Jack Almer and Charley Hensley. Author's collection.

The outlaws stayed for several days at the cabin owned by Hartzel and Dougherty, telling them of the robbery and murder. Hensley talked Dougherty into riding into Benson, twenty-eight miles distant, to buy them a supply of bacon and fresh ammunition. Then the three outlaws, ever cautious, rode eight miles up to the summit and hid out at an old wood-cutters' camp. Dougherty, while in Benson, talked freely and foolishly of his errand. He said that his visitors were coming to his cabin in three days to pick up the supplies. No sooner had he left town than his story reached the ears of George H. Davis, the Wells Fargo agent in Benson. Davis immediately suspected that the strangers in the Rincons were the wanted killers. That day, August 26, he sent a telegram to Sheriff Paul in Tucson.

By the next morning Paul and his friend Pete Gabriel were in Benson. They obtained horses and, with the Wells Fargo agent and another posseman, started off for the hideout in Sycamore Canyon. A hard ride brought them to the cabin by evening, and they hid nearby, where they could watch the cabin without being seen. Unknown to the posse, the outlaws were camped near North Creek, three-quarters of a mile distant. Paul and the others kept watch all night, never catching sight of the outlaws. In the morning, August 28, Hensley got into a quarrel with Dougherty and threatened to kill him. Dougherty got away from Hensley and walked up a hill about halfway between the cabin and the bandits' camp to chop firewood. While he was busy with his axe, Hensley suddenly appeared with drawn gun. Dougherty dropped his axe and raced down the hill toward the cabin, screaming that Hensley was killing him.

Paul and his possemen grabbed their guns and raced up the hill. Hensley heard them crashing through the brush and ran toward his camp. Sheriff Paul spotted the fleeing outlaw, threw up his Winchester, and sent three shots flying after him. Hensley disappeared into the brush, just as Davis, the Wells Fargo agent, fired at him, but missed. His compadres had been lying on their blankets in the camp, Red Jack leisurely reading the latest issue of *Harper's Monthly*, while Hartzel perused an account of the deadly stage robbery in the *Tombstone Republican*. Hearing the shooting, they grabbed their guns and fled on foot up Sycamore Canyon to Deer Creek, followed by Hensley. Paul's posse pursued them carefully, fearing an ambush. They tracked the desperadoes several hundred yards up Deer Creek and finally lost their sign on the bare granite ledges. Then Paul and the others returned to the robbers' camp, where they recovered two horses, blankets, and provisions. They also found Red Jack's hat; inside was a copy of the reward poster that had been issued for them.

Sheriff Paul sent one man to Benson to telegraph a request to General George Crook for two Apache scouts. After taking the bandits' horses and supplies to the miners' cabin, he and the rest of the posse rode to the old wood camp at the summit, but found no trace of the bandits. Paul and his possemen spent the next four days scouring every canyon in the Rincons. The Apache scouts arrived on September 1, but by then the killers were long gone. The sheriff and his posse spent one more day in the mountains, but their horses were worn out, and official business called Paul back to Tucson. The posse made it only as far as Pantano, where their unshod horses were too footsore to go any farther. There Paul boarded a westbound train for home.[9]

When the sheriff got back to Tucson, he learned some stunning news about Len Redfield and Joe Tuttle. Redfield's family had hired an attorney, who sought a writ of habeas corpus from Daniel H. Pinney, a federal judge in Phoenix, on the grounds that the Florence jail was not safe from vigilantes. The judge issued the writ, which ordered that Redfield be brought to the Phoenix jail. In the meantime, on September 1, Tuttle made a second and even more detailed confession, which further inflamed public opinion against the robbers. At three o'clock the next morning, Joseph W. Evans, the one-armed deputy U.S. marshal, arrived in Florence with a seven-man posse, including a heavily armed Hank Redfield. Evans woke up Undersheriff Scanlan at the jail, delivered the writ, and demanded that Len Redfield be turned over to him. Scanlan refused, saying he had to first consult with the sheriff and district attorney to determine whether the order was legal.

Word spread like wildfire, and soon a mob of a hundred armed men surrounded the jail to prevent Evans from taking the prisoners. One of Evans's posse, apparently a friend of Redfield, warned the mob that they "could have forty cowboys on the ground at short notice to enforce the writ." Hank Redfield and a friend then hired a team and raced out of town. The townsfolk believed that he was on his way to gather the Cowboys to free his brother. When Deputy Marshal Evans threatened to declare martial law, a wild rumor spread that he had sent for soldiers to free Len Redfield. This caused even more excitement, and the leaders of the mob, which included most of the town's prominent citizens, decided to take matters into their own hands.

At 9:00 A.M. they quietly entered the jail, overpowered Undersheriff Scanlan and the jailer, and removed Redfield and Tuttle from their cells. Ropes were thrown over a beam in the jail corridor, nooses were fastened around the prisoner's necks, and moments later they were both dead. The vigilantes then took the terrified Frank Carpenter from his cell and showed him the dangling corpses. They interrogated him at length, but he steadfastly denied any involvement in the robbery and murder. Immediately after the hanging, several hundred Hispanic men and women flocked to the jail. Reported the *Florence Enterprise*, "It had been the common complaint among our Spanish population that nothing but Mexicans and Indians could be hanged here and they could hardly believe that they had been mistaken, till they gazed upon the evidence of the fact."[10]

The vigilantes held a meeting to determine Carpenter's fate. He was briefly released from jail and made a statement to the district attorney and several of the vigilantes. Though still professing innocence, Carpenter said that Red Jack told him that Johnny Murphy and Dave Gibson had committed the stage robbery and murder. Carpenter admitted that Redfield had harbored outlaws, and he added that Curly Bill had often visited the ranch. Finally one of the vigilantes told him, "You may thank your stars, Frank, that you were not hanged with Joe and Len." To that, Carpenter replied, "Yes. I fully expected it." Carpenter was returned to his cell to stand trial as an accessory to robbery and murder. He was released on bail, but two months later he died. It was widely believed that he suffered nervous prostration because the lynchings had scared him to death, but in truth he probably succumbed to inflammatory bowel disease.[11]

Although previous vigilante threats had been made against Redfield and Tuttle, they had been safely held in the Florence jail for more than two weeks, and no efforts had been made to lynch them prior to Evans's arrival in Florence. Judge Pinney had exceeded his authority by issuing the writ. The purpose of a writ of habeas corpus is to determine whether an arrest or detention was lawful, not to remove a prisoner from jail for safety reasons. Nor did Pinney in his capacity as a federal judge have any jurisdiction over a local murder case, which was a state—or, in this case, a territorial—offense. The federal officer, Deputy Marshal Evans, had used poor judgment in bringing Hank Redfield with him and by threatening martial law. The citizens believed that Len Redfield, through his money and political connections, would escape punishment in Phoenix. In the end, the actions of the federal judge and his deputy marshal inflamed the people of Florence and helped precipitate the lynching.

Paul had no intention of giving up the hunt for Red Jack Almer and Charley Hensley. But his work on the case was interrupted by good news from Texas: a man matching the description of the escaped killer Tim Hurley had been spotted in Fort Worth. Sheriff Paul made a trip by train to Fort Worth, where he found the fugitive working on a sewer line. Paul arrested Hurley without trouble, returning to Tucson with his prisoner on September 15, 1883. The next day a miner, Pete Mathews, spotted Red Jack and Charley Hensley near the Page Ranch, on the eastern slope of the

Arizona's famous lawman Pete Gabriel. Courtesy of Judy Pintar.

Rincon Mountains, six miles southwest of Oracle. Mathews rode south to Pantano, where he telegraphed a message to Paul. The lawman quickly recruited Pete Gabriel and Deputy Sheriff George McClarty, who owned a valuable bloodhound, and set off on September 17. They met Pete Mathews at Pantano, then rode north to the Page Ranch, where they learned that a shady miner nicknamed "Prospector Bob" had been taking provisions to two men in the mountains. For five days the little posse quietly watched Prospector Bob's movements until Sunday, September 23, when they learned that he was to meet the two strangers at Big Springs, near the summit, the next day.[12]

Paul recruited six more volunteers at the Page Ranch and set off for Big Springs, arriving late at night. Big Springs was in a deep canyon with only two approaches. Paul and part of the posse guarded one approach, while the rest of the men, under Gabriel, watched the other. Sheriff Paul ordered all of the possemen to stay hidden until the outlaws appeared in the morning. By 11:00 A.M., they had not shown up, and one of the posse, a Mexican, got impatient. He came out of his hiding place and started looking around the big rocks near the spring. Suddenly Charley Hensley appeared on horseback, headed toward the spring. He spotted the Mexican and called out, "Hello, stranger. What are you doing there?"

The Mexican yelled, "Halt!" and threw his rifle to his shoulder. Hensley leaped from his horse, jumped behind the rocks, and vanished. Paul, furious that his orders had been disobeyed, took half of the men to cut off the fugitives' flight, while Gabriel and the rest followed his trail. They pressed the two desperadoes so closely that they abandoned their horses, blankets, and food. McClarty released his bloodhound, but the animal did not return and was presumed to have been shot by the badmen. Paul and his men spent three days hunting for the outlaws, but once again they made good their escape. Gabriel became separated from the rest, and Paul finally gave up the chase and returned to Tucson after eleven days in the saddle. Having received no word from him, his friends and family, especially Margaret, had feared the worst. Margaret's relief at having her husband back was matched by Paul's, who was comforted when Gabriel showed up late that night, and McClarty's bloodhound later appeared at the Page Ranch, hungry but unharmed.[13]

But Paul was indefatigable. One of his deputies, Thomas D. Casanega, was then in Hermosillo, Mexico, attempting to extradite a pair of horse thieves back to the United States. At his hotel, Casanega met an old prospector, J. M. Jeffries, who claimed to know both Red Jack Almer and Charley Hensley. Jeffries said he was going to Willcox and would let Casanega know if he heard anything about the fugitives. After a long delay in Hermosillo, Casanega returned to Tucson with one of the horse thieves. On October 2, Deputy Casanega received a telegram from Jeffries in Willcox: "The programme is filled. Your men are here. Come get them. If you want them." Casanega later recalled, "I immediately walked . . . to the sheriff's office and met Mr. Paul. As he was always sending and receiving telegrams trying to get track of those stage robbers, I showed him the telegram from Mr. Jeffries. . . . Then he said, 'I'll go down to the express office and try to find out more about it.'"[14]

At the Wells Fargo office, Paul spoke with the agent, George Martin, who sent a telegram to Willcox. The reply confirmed Jeffries's report.

Recalled Casanega, "Mr. Paul returned, well assured, and asked if I was able to take the trip, and so we went and got prepared to take a special train to Willcox." The special train was an engine with a tender, and at 7:00 P.M. Paul, Casanega, and Deputy Sheriffs George McClarty and Alfredo Carrillo crowded into the cab and on top of the coal car for a fast eighty-mile ride into Willcox. Recalled Casanega, "When we arrived in Willcox, Mr. Paul told us to go to supper, but not to go together, and to talk to no one. His instructions were to me, 'Go find my men, and ask no one about them.'" Casanega soon located Jeffries, who told the deputy that he had seen Red Jack and Hensley at the house of L. J. Moore, who ran a freight line between Willcox and Globe. The outlaws had told Moore that they "were left afoot and had stolen two horses" and asked for provisions and rifle cartridges. They said that they intended to dig up the loot they had buried on the San Pedro River, unaware that Joe Tuttle had already led the officers to it. The badmen boasted that "Sheriff Paul and posse were after them, but they couldn't get anything but dead bodies" and that they would "never be taken alive, but would fight to the death."[15]

Jeffries told Deputy Casanega that L. J. Moore had left that morning with his freight teams for Henry Hooker's ranch at the north end of the Sulphur Springs Valley, twenty-two miles above Willcox. Moore had agreed to supply the outlaws there. Recalled Casanega, "As soon as I heard this story I started out to hunt for Mr. Paul. . . . I introduced Mr. Jeffries and we went together into a livery stable . . . and got a spring wagon." Then, with his deputies and Jeffries, Paul drove out of Willcox that night. Twelve miles north they passed the cattle ranch of brothers Jim and Hugh Percy, where Moore and his freighters were camped for the night. The posse continued on to Henry Hooker's Sierra Bonita Ranch, arriving there at midnight. At daybreak there was no sign of the outlaws, so Paul sent Deputy Carrillo to nearby Fort Grant, as he said, "to prospect for information." Leaving Deputies Casanega and McClarty to guard the Hooker ranch, Sheriff Paul and Jeffries rode back to the Percy ranch. It was pouring rain, and the roads were too soggy for the heavy freight wagons to travel. Moore was still there with his two freight teams, waiting for the storm to pass. Paul, accompanied by Jeffries, approached the freighter and told him he knew about his deal with the outlaws. Moore became enraged, as Deputy Casanega recalled: "He immediately reached for his gun to kill Mr. Jeffries for having betrayed him. Mr. Paul stepped between them, and

Thomas Casanega, a deputy
sheriff under Bob Paul.
Courtesy of the Arizona
Historical Society/Tucson,
14293.

told Mr. Moore to be very careful that he better not make any bad breaks;
that he, [the] sheriff, was there to get those robbers dead or alive and that
Mr. Moore could help us out."[16]

Casanega said that after some persuading, Moore "finally gave in and
offered to help." Moore admitted that he was carrying supplies for Red

Jack and Hensley and that he was to meet them that night. Moore claimed, "They called me out of my house and . . . they had firearms in their hands," adding, improbably, "They compelled me to give them provisions." Paul recruited the ranch's co-owner, Jim Percy, and two local men, John McCluskey and John Laird, to assist him. Sheriff Paul described what happened next: "Red Jack and Hensley were to come and get provisions from the wagon trains. There were two strings of wagons near Percy's house. Four wagons were in one train. Alongside was another train of four more wagons. The trains were about thirty feet apart. They were to get their provisions from the tail board of one of the wagons. I put Laird and McCluskey under one train and Percy and myself were underneath the other."

It was dark and still raining heavily. As was his custom, Paul wanted to give the outlaws a chance to surrender. He recalled, "A little after nine o'clock Red Jack and Hensley approached the tail board, and I halloed, 'Stop.'" The outlaws were on foot, having tied their horses to a telegraph pole four hundred yards away. Red Jack was in the lead, twenty-five yards in front of Hensley. The two desperadoes had not been bluffing when they said that they would never be taken alive. They were each armed with a .44 caliber Winchester Model 1873, and at the sound of Paul's order they swung up their rifles and levered a stream of lead at the wagons. Paul and his men instantly returned the fire. As the sheriff told it, "The whole posse fired a volley in the dark, and the men were heard to fall." However, the badmen continued to shoot, and the posse aimed at their rifle flashes. John McCluskey put a charge of buckshot into the pit of Red Jack's stomach, and an instant later a ball from Sheriff Paul's Winchester struck the killer just under the right eye, a mortal wound. A lone buckshot tore into Hensley's groin. The outlaws stopped shooting, and Paul yelled at his men to hold their fire. Everything was silent, but suddenly one of the desperadoes fired, and a bullet struck posseman John Laird in the leg.

The shooting had lasted about five minutes. Henlsey managed to crawl twenty-five yards to where Red Jack was lying. Hensley's Winchester had been disabled by the posse's bullets; one slug had torn off its hammer. Hensley crawled up to the dying Red Jack, took his rifle, and retreated four hundred yards on his stomach to their horses. The gut-shot killer climbed painfully into the saddle, then headed south. Sheriff Paul, ever cautious, ordered his men to stay put. He sent a messenger to Hooker's ranch for Deputies Carrillo, Casanega, and McClarty, who rode in at 2:00 A.M. Red

Jack had been moaning in agony for five hours. At first light they found him dead, riddled with lead and an empty six-shooter at his side.

Paul quickly scratched out a note to be sent to the telegraph operator in Willcox: "Percy's Ranch via Willcox, Oct. 4. Last night we came upon Jack Elmer and Charles Hensley. Elmer was killed and some one should come here to hold an inquest. Hensley escaped in the darkness, badly wounded. We start immediately on his trail. [Signed] Paul, sheriff."

Now Bob Paul set off after Hensley. With him were Deputies Carrillo, Casanega, and McClarty, John McCluskey, and two volunteers, Otto Moore and a vaquero from Hooker's ranch named Jimmie. They trailed the wounded outlaw three miles south through the Sulphur Springs Valley, then another five miles into the mountains. His tracks led into a deep canyon, across a ridge, and then into another large canyon and along its sandy bottom. The sheriff was concerned that they were following too closely and could be ambushed. He had his men stay high on the sloping canyon walls. As Paul later explained, "I told the boys to trail, while I kept a lookout ahead. I was ahead on the right hand side of the canyon as we went down it. I saw Hensley's horse with bridle and saddle on standing between us and a pile of rocks. I halloed to the boys to circle around on the other side of the canyon."

Casanega and McCluskey were with the sheriff; the rest were opposite them. Suddenly a volley of shots rang out, and a bullet whined past Paul. He caught a glimpse of Hensley behind a scrub oak, sixty yards distant, where a waft of gunsmoke drifted upward. Hensley was prone behind the tree, firing his Winchester rapidly at the sheriff. A bullet struck Paul's horse in the belly and the animal bucked wildly. Paul leaped from the saddle, dropped to his knees, and opened up with his Winchester. Deputies Carrillo and McClarty, from the ridge above Hensley, unloosed their guns. Paul and the rest sent a blistering barrage of rifle and shotgun fire into the outlaw, killing him instantly. Then Carrillo crawled down the canyon wall toward the body, yelling to Paul, "Don't shoot, he's deader'n Hades."

The sheriff called back, "Don't go near him, he might shoot you." But Carrillo ignored the warning. He found Hensley face down, Winchester still clutched in his hands. Carrillo and McClarty rolled the body over and took the weapon. The rest of the posse gathered around. Hensley's body was perfectly white, showing that he had lost a tremendous amount of blood. The officers counted ten balls in him, one shot from the night before and nine more from his last fight.

Paul and his men brought the bodies of Red Jack and Hensley into Willcox for burial. An inquest was held and, after hearing testimony from L. J. Moore and Deputy McClarty, the coroner's jury found that the killings were justifiable. The possemen were effusive in their praise of the sheriff, said the *Tucson Citizen:* "All speak in terms of the warmest admiration at the bravery which Paul manifested while under fire." News of the successful manhunt hit the wire services and was published widely. The *San Francisco Alta California* commented, "Too much credit cannot be accorded to Paul for his untiring energy and bravery in hunting down the red handed murderers." Added the *Tombstone Epitaph*, "The reputation as a brave and efficient officer, which preceded Bob Paul from old Calaveras to Arizona, has been nobly sustained, and the people of Pima County and the whole Territory will not soon forget it."[17]

For his part, Paul was grateful for the assistance of the posse. His sheriff's income was so sizeable that he elected to waive the rewards for himself, and his possemen had the utmost faith in his ability to divide them fairly. On October 12, Paul wrote to Wells Fargo's L. F. Rowell in San Francisco: "On the day I left Willcox, I had a talk with the parties interested in the rewards, and I told them ... that I did not claim any of the rewards for myself and would do everything I could to get the rewards for them, and it was agreed that I should get the different rewards and divide it as agreed upon by all parties interested, as I did not want any trouble or growling hereafter. If the money is sent to either Mr. Martin your agent here or to me it will be satisfactory. As regards the expense of the engine we used, I think it would only be right for the Rail Road Company to stand that, as both Hensley and Elmer had told several parties they would not leave the country until they had taken a train in."[18]

Newspaper accounts of the Red Jack gang and the resulting shootouts and lynchings were published nationwide, both embodying and emphasizing the territory's notoriety. Arizonans wanted statehood and the self-rule that accompanied it. To achieve that, they needed to attract eastern capital to invest in the territory's mineral and agricultural wealth, and they needed to encourage corporations like Wells Fargo and the Southern Pacific to operate in the territory. They also had to lure settlers, for the minimum population required for statehood was sixty thousand, and in 1880 the territory held only forty thousand people. Arizona, however, continued to have a fearsome reputation as a forbidding land populated by wild miners, dangerous outlaws, and savage Indians. Settlers and capital could not be had without first establishing law and order and suppressing the Apache danger. But Arizonans had mixed feelings about capitalists. They invested in mining, cattle, and railroads, creating jobs that lured settlers into the territory. At the same time their wealth bought political control, which was bitterly resented by the average Arizonan.

In the coming years Louis C. Hughes would repeatedly criticize Paul for acting on behalf of Wells Fargo by pursuing the Red Jack gang far from the borders of Pima County. Hughes accused the sheriff of being a Republican tool of Wells Fargo and later of the Southern Pacific. In his criticism, the Star's editor presaged historian Richard Maxwell Brown's modern concept of the "Western Civil War of Incorporation," a conflict in which industrial, urban, and corporate forces, supported by the Republican Party, "incorporated" the frontier. Wells Fargo and the Southern Pacific exemplified the drive to incorporate the West into the "corporation-dominated industrializing and urbanizing structure of America." The result was civil strife between, on the one hand, capitalists who were generally Republicans, like mine owners, express companies, railroads, and cattle barons, and, on the other, rural forces such as small farmers, cowboys, miners, and laborers, who were often Democrats. The Western Civil War of Incorporation manifested itself in such diverse incidents as Arizona's Cowboy troubles, California's Mussel Slough Tragedy, Wyoming's Johnson County War, and innumerable mine labor disputes in the American West. Brown posits that politically conservative Republican "incorporation gunfighters" used force to support property rights and to eliminate opposition to settlement. Sheriff Paul would fit the concept of the incorporation gunfighter.[19]

Bob Paul may not have recognized it, but he was playing an important role in a much broader conflict. In many ways, he was part and parcel of the forces that modernized the American frontier.

CHAPTER THIRTEEN

The Executioner

The pride Bob Paul felt in breaking up the Red Jack gang was soon eclipsed by his delight in a new addition to his family. On October 21, 1883, Margaret gave birth to a baby girl, Edith Margaret. The old lawman was ebullient. A reporter noted that he was one of "the three happiest men in Tucson today. Brand new babies are the cause." The Pauls were determined to provide the best education for all their children. They sent their second son, Robert, popularly known as Bob Paul, Jr., to join his brother John at Santa Clara College. The Pauls were forward thinking and believed that their daughters were just as deserving of a higher education as their sons. A year or so later they enrolled the eldest daughter, Agnes, in Notre Dame College in San Jose, the oldest women's college on the Pacific Coast. Agnes was frail and began to suffer from a chronic cough, which would later be diagnosed as tuberculosis. Despite her illness, she excelled in college, achieving high honors. Margaret spent summers in San Francisco with her sisters and visited her children often, while John and Robert returned to Tucson each summer to spend time with their father.[1]

The sheriff's domestic life was a far cry from the outlaw trail. While Paul had been tracking down Red Jack's bunch, another gang of desperadoes had been terrorizing neighboring Graham County. The newly formed county's oldest and wealthiest settlement was Clifton, nestled in the mountains about thirty miles from the New Mexico line. First prospected by Mexican miners in the 1860s, copper had been discovered there in the early 1870s, and the town was established in 1875. The county's other principal settlement, Solomonville, had been settled by Jewish pioneers a year later. Numerous Mormons drifted in from Utah and established farms and villages along the Gila River. Graham County was organized in 1881 from the eastern portion of Pima County and the southern part of Apache County. The county seat was first located in Safford, then moved five miles east to Solomonville (now Solomon) in 1883. George "Little Steve" Stevens, county political boss, was its first elected sheriff, and though he was extremely popular, he would prove corrupt and incompetent. Instead of aggressively hunting outlaws, he relied on the longstanding enmity between Texans and Mexicans to resolve problems. If a Mexican was wanted for a crime, Stevens would send a posse of Texans after him, knowing that they would probably kill their Hispanic quarry. On the other hand, if the wanted man was from Texas, he would dispatch a Hispanic posse, recognizing that no Texan would submit to arrest by a Mexican, and he would therefore be slain. In the election of 1882 he was accused of ballot-box stuffing. In 1889 Stevens embezzled $7,000 in public funds and fled to Canada.[2]

Due to its remote location, mining wealth, ineffective law enforcement, and closeness to old Mexico, Clifton in 1883 was a paradise for robbers, rustlers, and fugitives from justice. An estimated thirty to one hundred desperadoes made the camp their headquarters, drifting in and out in small bunches. Prominent among them was thirty-three-year-old John Heath, a troublemaker from a respectable family in Terrell, Texas. According to a contemporary, as a youth Heath was "suave in manner and glib of tongue" but "ever of a wayward disposition." He married in 1875, but his wife left him when he became involved in horse theft and cattle rustling. Heath moved to Dallas, thirty miles west, where in January 1879 he was charged with theft and forgery. Six months later he was indicted for another theft, jumped bond, and fled the state. Captured in Hot Springs, Arkansas, in April 1880, Heath was returned to Dallas but escaped punishment. He became a hack driver, an occupation that often went hand in hand with pimping. In June 1881 Heath was arrested for robbing a patron in the Long Branch, a notorious dance house and brothel in East Dallas. That year several prostitutes in Dallas were arrested bearing the surname of Heath; it was common for such girls to use their pimp's last name as an alias. By now Heath was well known to the Dallas police, but he always managed to worm his way out of trouble. Commented the *Dallas Herald*, "He has been charged with so many violations of the law, been arrested, imprisoned, bonded, tried, acquitted, etc., etc., that he has achieved the reputation of being . . . the slyest, smartest rogue extant." In March 1882 Heath was arrested by the famous man-hunter Jack Duncan for burglarizing a house, but he was again released on bond. By this time he had graduated to running the Long Branch, and in June he was indicted for keeping a disorderly house.[3]

Heath's close friend James "Tex" Howard, alias Texas Red, ran a rival bordello, the Red Light. By the end of 1882 Heath and Howard, having experienced enough run-ins with the Dallas police, set out together for Arizona Territory. The pair landed in Clifton, where Heath was conspicuous for wearing a pair of ivory-handled six-shooters. He opened a saloon with a prostitute, Emma Mortimer, and it quickly became the headquarters for some of the camp's most dangerous desperadoes. One was William E. "Billy" Delaney, the black sheep of a prominent family from Harrisburg, Pennsylvania. His brother, John C. Delaney, was the state senate librarian. After an 1880 theft in Harrisburg, Billy Delaney's family sent him to the Arizona frontier to escape arrest. Another of Clifton's toughs was "Big Dan" Dowd, who had been a buffalo hunter out of Fort Griffin, Texas, and later a teamster in Cochise County. In Clifton, Heath, Howard, Delaney, and Dowd closely associated with John C. "Yorky" Kelly, Omar W. "Red" Sample, and Doc Baker. The latter had reputedly ridden with the James-Younger gang in Missouri. A desperado named Kid Lewis was reported to be the leader of the Clifton ruffians, which also included the unrepentant Ike Clanton and such colorfully named but now obscure outlaws as Shoot-'Em-Up Dick, Mormon Bill, Two-Belt Johnny, Kid Vance, Cherokee Kid, and Sixto Garcia. According to Billy Breakenridge, who had been a deputy under Sheriff Behan, some of the Clifton outlaws (such as Ike Clanton) had been Cowboys in Cochise County.[4]

During the spring and summer of 1883, these desperadoes committed numerous robberies and murders in Graham County. The citizens were too terrorized to oppose them, and the outlaws became increasingly bold. Late on the night of April 29, two of the bandits attacked a Clifton merchant, Charles Reed, knocking him senseless and escaping with $500. A few days later, road agents held up the Clifton stage. On the night of May 22, three masked bandits held up and robbed the Fraissinet store in Clifton. In June the well-known Catholic priest of Tucson, Father Antonio Jouvenceau, visited Clifton. Red Sample and Big Dan Dowd plotted to rob him when he rode back to Tucson. For some reason they did not, perhaps because two of the gang, Billy Delaney and Yorky Kelly, were Catholics. The most heinous attack took place on the morning of August 24, when two coaches left Clifton, headed for the railroad terminus at Guthrie. The first stage held five passengers; it was closely followed by a mud wagon with seven Chinese miners and driver Henry Fowler at the reins. On their way to breakfast, Big Dan Dowd, Doc Baker, and a ruffian named Big Dave spotted the Chinese passengers and recognized easy victims.

Mounting up, they followed the coaches four miles west to Big Hill. As the mud wagon reached the summit, the bandits rode forward. They were so brazen they didn't bother to wear masks, and Fowler recognized them all. Without provocation the outlaws opened fire on the coach, seriously wounding Ah Chong, Ah Hoy, Sam Tang, and Ah Lin. One of the Chinese carried a Winchester rifle, and he fired back, wounding Big Dave. After taking $500 from the passengers, the road agents ordered the stage on. The wounded Chinese were brought by train to Lordsburg, where three of them died. It was one of the Southwest's bloodiest stagecoach holdups. A month later, as rumors spread that the gang was guilty of the attack, they rode into town and demanded a hearing. In court, they and their armed comrades intimidated the witnesses. When Henry Fowler was called to the stand, he claimed that he did not recognize any of the killers, and the suspects were released. Six years later, Fowler was a prominent witness in the trial of the Wham payroll robbers, and, under cross-examination, he admitted that he had lied because his life had been threatened.[5]

Bob Paul could only have wondered in amazement at Sheriff Stevens's failure to suppress the outlawry. On September 4, less than two weeks after the bloody stage robbery, Billy Delaney shot and killed Henry Sawyer in a close-quarters pistol duel in a Clifton gambling hall; two bystanders were wounded. Delaney was arrested and lodged in the county jail, which had been carved out of a rock wall on the edge of town. He and Big Dan Dowd, who was also in jail, soon escaped. On September 24, a posse led by Constable Nicolas Olguin tracked down Kid Lewis, who was wanted for several murders, and killed him in a wild gun battle. His saddle partner, Kid Vance, fled on horseback but was captured later that day. Red Sample, not to be outdone, took part in a stage holdup and horse theft and was later indicted for both offenses by the county grand jury. Territorial judge A. W. Sheldon railed against the lawlessness. When a jury returned a verdict of simple manslaughter in a case in which Herman Chavez murdered his wife and her lover, Judge Sheldon angrily called Graham County "a foul blot upon the map of Arizona and a disgrace to the civilization of the age." In rebuking the jury, Judge Sheldon accused its citizens of being "hampered by ignorance, controlled by prejudice, influenced by fear . . . [and] governed by sympathy [for outlaws]." For his tirade, Judge Sheldon was threatened with death by John Heath's gang.[6]

On November 23, 1883, Heath, Dowd, Sample, Kelly, and Howard were in Clifton, waiting for the stage from Solomonville. The coach held a large number of passengers who had appeared as witnesses in court. As the passengers climbed out, the brazen desperadoes looked them over carefully to determine whether any of their victims had gone to Solomonville to testify against them before the grand jury. Then they rode leisurely out of town, met up with Billy Delaney and Doc Baker, and headed south out of Graham County. The next afternoon they reached San Simon Station, where they spent the night. In the morning, while talking with the section boss, they learned that the previous day a train at Gage, New Mexico, seventy-five miles to the east, had been wrecked and robbed, and its engineer had been murdered. The desperadoes jokingly told the station agent, "We want you to bear witness that we had no hand in this robbery. If the rewards are sufficient, we might take a hand in capturing the robbers, as we are well fixed for that kind of business." Their little joke backfired. The incident became garbled in the retelling, and it was later widely reported that the desperadoes had told the station agent about the robbery first, before the wire had been received. As a result, the gang soon became suspects in the Gage holdup.[7]

The next day John Heath and Tex Howard rode up to the ranch of Frank Buckles, situated in White Water Draw in the Sulphur Springs Valley. Billy Delaney had been working there, on the lam from the murder charges in Clifton. That night Big Dan Dowd and Red Sample rode in, and soon Yorky Kelly joined them. Doc Baker had wisely left the bunch. Heath and Howard went on ahead to Bisbee, the bustling copper-mining camp situated twenty-three miles south of Tombstone. The next day the others rode to the ranch of an old man named Lucien Pardee, ten miles distant, in the Chiricahua Mountains. There, in front of Pardee, they brazenly discussed their plan to raid Bisbee.

Soon after arriving in Bisbee, Heath, with his paramour, Emma Mortimer, arranged to open a dancehall and scouted the town for prospects. Heath learned that when the Copper Queen Mine made its payroll, the town was flush with cash. Bisbee had no bank, and many of its townsfolk were in the habit of depositing their savings in the safe at the Goldwater and Castaneda store, run by the very Joe Goldwater whom Bob Paul had arrested in Yuma in 1881. Goldwater and his partner, Jose M. Castaneda, had opened their general merchandise business in 1883. The Copper Queen miners were paid by check, which, for a fee, they cashed at the store. Thus, on payday Goldwater and Castanega kept a large amount of cash on hand. To Heath, the store was ripe for picking.

On the morning of December 8, 1883, Heath rode out of Bisbee and met with the rest of the gang in their camp near town. That evening Tex Howard, Big Dan Dowd, Billy Delaney, Red Sample, and Yorky Kelly, all heavily armed, rode leisurely into Bisbee. Dismounting, they loitered briefly about the streets and saloons. Howard and Dowd were both known in Bisbee and were recognized by several townsfolk. Then Howard, Kelly, and Sample entered the Goldwater and Castaneda store. All but the brazen Tex Howard wore masks. Dowd and Delaney stayed out front, grasping Winchesters and watching the street. The robbers quickly forced Goldwater to empty the till. Red Sample found Castaneda sick in bed in a back room, and he took cash and a gold watch hidden under his pillow. Then Yorky Kelly forced Goldwater to open the safe and began emptying it.

In the meantime Dowd and Delaney forced several bystanders into the store. J. C. Tappenier, an assayer for the Copper Queen Mine, happened by and was also ordered inside. He panicked and tried to flee. Dowd and Delaney cut him down with Winchester fire. Hearing the shots, Deputy Sheriff D. T. Smith approached Dowd and Delaney and announced, "I am an officer." His reply was a rifle bullet in the head. The gunfire attracted onlookers, and Dowd and Delaney, accustomed to dealing callously with anyone who opposed them, opened fire indiscriminately. One of the towns-folk, J. A. Nolly, dropped with a bullet in his chest, a mortal wound. As Mrs. Annie Roberts, eight months pregnant, looked out of her doorway across the street, a bullet slammed into her midsection, severing her spine. Both she and her unborn child were killed. One of the shooters burst into the store and demanded fresh ammunition. Tex Howard replied, "That's right. Pump out the old shells and put in the new. We'll teach these God damned sons of bitches that we are running this town for a few minutes."

Deputy Sheriff William A. Daniels, who was also a Bisbee saloonkeeper, rushed to the scene, and he and several citizens opened fire on the bandits. Red Sample was the only one hit, receiving a minor wound in the back. The desperadoes leaped onto their horses and thundered out of town, firing wildly. In one of the most brutal bandit raids of the Southwest, they had taken $3,000 and five lives: three men, one woman, and an unborn child. It would ever after be known as the Bisbee Massacre.[8]

Deputy Sheriff Daniels quickly formed a posse. His first volunteer was none other than Heath. He had escaped punishment so often in Dallas and Clifton he was certain his involvement would not be suspected. Since Tex Howard and Big Dan Dowd had been recognized, Deputy Daniels knew the names of two of the gang before he started in pursuit. Daniels was immediately suspicious of Heath, since he had often been seen in the company of Howard. However, Heath had been in his saloon at the time of the murders, and to all outward signs he had not been involved in the crime. On the ride out of Bisbee, Heath told the posse that he did not think Howard was one of the killers, explaining that none of the hoof-prints matched those of Tex's horse. Daniels's posse followed the trail east-ward to a spot fifteen miles from Tombstone. Here, although the tracks vanished, Heath claimed that he could see hoofprints leading in the direction of Tombstone. Heath and two others left the posse and rode into Tomb-stone, while Deputy Daniels and the rest continued after the outlaws. At the ranch of Frank Buckles they learned of the bandits' prior visits and that Heath was one of the gang. The outlaws had returned to the ranch and boasted to Buckles, "We have raised hell." Daniels sent one of his men back to Bisbee, where Heath was promptly arrested and lodged in the county jail in Tombstone.[9]

By now the gang had split up. Dig Dan Dowd and Billy Delaney rode south into Mexico, while Tex Howard, Red Sample, and Yorky Kelly continued on toward Clifton. While camping near Galeyville, in the Chiricahua Mountains, they were spotted and fired on by a posse out hunting the Gage train robbers. The three outlaws escaped in a snowstorm. At San Simon Station, Kelly separated from the others, boarding a train for Deming, New Mexico. Soon after arriving in Clifton, Howard and Sample boasted brazenly about the raid, showed off their loot, and said that Kelly had gone to Deming. Howard and Sample left town in the middle of the night, but in the morning, on December 14, they were followed by a large posse that included the deadly constable and expert tracker Nicolas Olguin. They trailed Howard and Sample forty miles to the Blue River and captured them both. In the meantime officers in Deming picked up Yorky Kelly, and all three were soon behind bars in Tombstone.[10]

By this time Jim Hume and Southern Pacific detective Len Harris had arrived in Deming, New Mexico, to investigate the Gage train robbery.

Paul was working with them to identify the suspects in the train holdup and the Bisbee raid. Most lawmen believed that the same gang had pulled both holdups. From Deming, on December 11, Hume wrote a detailed letter to Sheriff Paul, addressing him "Dear Friend" and saying, "On the night of November 24th Big Red Sample, John Kelly, alias Yorky Kelly, John Heath, Joe [*sic*] Howard, and Big Dan Dowd took supper at San Simon R. R. Station and slept in the section house. They were riding two iron-grey horses, two white-grey, and one bay. They [returned and] took breakfast there Sunday morning [December 9] and then separated, Yorky Kelly going to Bowie and the other four going south, telling Kelly that they were going to Old Mexico. Since then the four have not been heard from. Yorky has been to Tucson and is here [in the Deming jail] tonight, talks freely, and says they are the outfit who did the shooting at Clifton and were talked of as threatening to take in the court at Solomonville and releasing the prisoners."[11]

The Wells Fargo detective and Sheriff Paul had been keeping track of various hardcases who were suspects in the train robbery. As Hume wrote Paul, "Peter Spence and Dan McCan were in Deming when the robbery occurred and probably knew nothing about it. Long Neck Charlie *was* in Johnson. Cab Kingsley was in Lordsburg. Chub Hayes and Bill Price were in Clifton. *None* of the above named was at the robbery. One-armed Price and Jake Rafael left Eureka the morning of the 20th and returned the evening of the 27th, claiming to have been in the Animas Mountains hunting. They say that good citizens can prove that they could not have been at the scene of the robbery. If so, the principal rustlers in the region could not have participated in the act."[12]

Although several writers have reported that Paul took part in the horseback manhunt for the Bisbee killers, his role is not mentioned in contemporary newspaper accounts. But given that Paul was friendly with Jerome L. Ward, Cochise County's new Republican sheriff, it does seem plausible that he would have gone to Tombstone to assist the inexperienced lawman in organizing the manhunt. However, Sheriff Paul's role could have only been a short-lived one, for on December 14 he got word that the long-missing Johnny Murphy and Dave Gibson had been arrested earlier that day. Gibson's wife had moved from Tucson to Downey, California, a small town twelve miles south of Los Angeles. The two fugitives were in the habit of visiting her, and for several months they had been living near the little railroad stop of Fenner, thirty-five miles west of Needles in the Mojave

Desert, on the recently completed Santa Fe Railroad. The two used assumed names, and Gibson had been working as a stage driver. As he and Murphy were walking out of a Fenner hotel, a pair of deputy sheriffs recognized them. Upon being arrested at gunpoint, Murphy exclaimed to Gibson, "Paul will make you sweat."

"You seem to know where you are going," interjected one of the deputies.

"We know all about it," they answered.

The fugitives were jailed in San Bernardino, and a wire was sent to Paul, who boarded a westbound train, arriving at the jail on the morning of December 16. Visiting the prisoners in their cell, Paul told them, "Well, boys, I want you to come back with me."

"Let's go then," replied Gibson. "The sooner it is over the better." They waived extradition, and Paul, after chaining the pair together with a pair of leg irons, loaded them onto an eastbound train. A large crowd gathered to greet them at the Tucson depot, among them a newspaper reporter, who noted, "As the train halted a large number gathered at the first car expecting Sheriff Paul would emerge there. Suddenly the cry was heard, 'There are the boys,' and the crowd surged in the direction of the second car, where two men of medium size, well dressed in black, were coming down the steps. The well known form of Sheriff Paul was seen above them, and then everybody knew they were Murphy and Gibson. . . . As they passed through the crowd they were greeted by many, and often halted a step to shake hands with one more eager than the rest."[13]

To a reporter, they denied robbing any stagecoaches after their escape. Gibson admitted that he was "in a tight fix," but was confident he could beat the case, saying he could "knock it all down stairs." A week earlier, Bill Moyer, after languishing in the Tucson jail for five months, had finally been brought to trial for killing Jim Leavy. The star witnesses in the case were Pete Gabriel and Adolph Buttner, and Moyer was convicted of second-degree murder. Judge A. W. Sheldon, who had presided over the Graham County murder cases, sentenced Moyer on December 20. Sheldon, known for his tough words and tougher sentencing, remained appalled at Arizona's bloody record of violence and its negative effect on business, commerce, and development. After Paul led the gambler into the courtroom, Judge Sheldon intoned: "Moyer, the cheapest thing in this territory today is human life, and as long as men of your character are allowed to go unrestrained and unpunished it will be held at its present low estimate. . . . The crime for which you were indicted and convicted is one of the gravest known to the law, and yet from the frequency with which it is committed in Arizona it might be inferred that it was a trifling offense."

Warming to his task, the judge termed Jim Leavy's murder "a cold-blooded, cowardly assassination, and in the manner of its conception and execution would have done credit to a Russian Nihilist or an Apache Indian." Railing with anger—both at Moyer and at jurors who treated murder lightly—he thundered, "You are a dastardly assassin in the eyes of the law. . . . The highest penalty which the law imposes is not an adequate punishment for the outrageous crime of which you stand convicted. The sentence of the court is that you be confined in the territorial prison at Yuma for the period of your natural life. Mr. Sheriff, remove the prisoner." Although Judge Sheldon's frustration was palpable, it had little effect on juries, the public, or politicians. Arizona was a raw frontier where, for another generation, violence would be widely condoned as a tool to solve personal problems. Not surprisingly, after Moyer served less than five years of his life term, he was pardoned by Governor C. Meyer Zulick.[14]

On Christmas Day 1883, Bob and Margaret Paul were visited by Jim Hume and Len Harris. The latter had concluded that the Bisbee killers were the same men who had wrecked and robbed the train at Gage, but Hume disagreed and managed to prove that the Bisbee bandits were in San Simon at the very time the train was stopped. Hume, a grumpy, fifty-seven-year-old bachelor, still disliked Arizona and missed his young, vivacious fiancé, Lida Munson, who was only twenty-five. On one trip to Phoenix he had written to Lida, complaining, "Ye heathen Gods! How I dread it! Ah, Maricopa, mercury up to 112 at midnight!" But Hume enjoyed his visit with the Pauls. He boasted to Margaret about his fiancé's cooking, but admitted in a letter to Lida, "It came nearer to being one of your dinners than anything I have seen." Margaret went all out, serving roast beef, mashed potatoes with gravy, boiled turnips and beets, celery, coleslaw, and, for dessert, cake, pie, and custard, all washed down with red wine.[15]

The next day Sheriff Paul joined Hume and Harris on a train trip down to Sonora, Mexico. The detectives had received a tip that two of the Gage train robbers were in the picturesque seaport town of Guaymas. Paul was hopeful that he could help capture Dig Dan Dowd and Billy Delaney, who he believed were hiding out in Mexico. The three lawmen enjoyed their visit to Guaymas, but Hume and Harris soon found that they were on, as one newspaper called it, "a false scent." The Gage train robbers were actually still in New Mexico. Paul paid a visit to the governor of Sonora in

Hermosillo and gave that official copies of the *Tucson Citizen*, *Clifton Clarion*, *Tombstone Epitaph*, and *Tombstone Republican*, all of which contained detailed accounts of the Gage and Bisbee robberies and descriptions of the suspects. Paul reported that the governor "disseminated the information to all the state officials." Then Sheriff Paul and the two detectives returned to Tucson. The information Paul provided to the Sonora governor would soon prove important to the Bisbee manhunt.[16]

Meanwhile, Arizonans' lenient attitude toward violence resurfaced in the trial of Johnny Murphy, which had begun a few days earlier. The testimony took a week and was much the same as that during Moyer's trial. Murphy took the stand in his own defense, claiming, "I saw him drop his hand to his side and thinking that such movement of his hand indicated an intention of drawing a pistol, drew my own and fired two shots." Even though none of the impartial witnesses saw Leavy reach for a gun, the jury deliberated only three hours before acquitting Johnny Murphy on December 31. Judge Sheldon was flabbergasted by the result, but checked both his tongue and his temper. He cautioned Murphy, "I believe you will profit by this lesson, and trust that you will conduct yourself in the future as never again to fall within the meshes of the law. . . . You might not be so fortunate the second time."

To that, Murphy stood up and thanked the judge for his comments, adding, "I have lived all my life on the frontier. . . . I have been amongst rough men all my life, have stopped many a bad fight, and have never before been in any trouble." Much to Paul's disgust, he left the courthouse with a throng of friends and well-wishers. Murphy's pal Eli B. Gifford gave him back his old faro table at the Fashion Saloon. Johnny Murphy remained a fixture in Tucson sporting circles for decades, drifting in and out of trouble until his death there in 1926.[17]

In the meantime Paul learned that Deputy Sheriff Daniels had good luck in his hunt for the last of the Bisbee gang, Big Dan Dowd and Billy Delaney. In addition to the information Paul gave to the Sonora governor, reward notices offering $7,500 for the Bisbee killers had been printed in English and Spanish and were widely distributed on both sides of the border. Daniels, acting on information that Dowd and Delaney had been spotted in Mexico, rode out of Bisbee the day after Christmas. An expert tracker, Cesario Lucero, accompanied him. The officers first went to Fronteras, in Sonora, and then to Bavispe, where they found that the two fugitives had split up and left town. Daniels located Dowd in Coralitos on New Year's

Day and arrested him. To avoid the legal headaches of extradition, he locked the prisoner in a railroad express car and brought him to El Paso. Daniels and Deputy Sheriff Bob Hatch then returned to Mexico, seeking Billy Delaney. On January 15, 1884, they located their man at Minas Prietas, then the largest gold camp in Sonora and now called La Colorada. Daniels and Hatch returned Delaney to Tombstone, and now all six killers were behind bars.[18]

The desperadoes were quickly indicted for first-degree murder. John Heath hired William Herring, a noted and skilled attorney. Herring obtained an order severing Heath's case from the others. The trial of Delaney, Dowd, Sample, Howard, and Kelly began on February 9, just two months after the Bisbee Massacre. The evidence against them was overwhelming, and after a trial lasting just three days, they were convicted and sentenced to hang on March 28. Heath's trial began on February 16 and took five days. Heath testified at length in his own defense and insisted that he was innocent. The other outlaws also testified for him, claiming that he had nothing to do with the raid. The jury was correctly instructed that if they found that Heath had planned and instigated the crime, he was just as guilty as the perpetrators. Because he had not actually killed anyone, the jurors wanted to spare him the gallows and convicted him of second-degree murder. Heath was sentenced to life in Yuma prison. This result enraged the people of Tombstone, and on February 22 a mob stormed the jail, took Heath from his cell, and hanged him from a telegraph pole on Toughnut Street. Before he died he asked the mob to tie his handkerchief around his face. His last words were, "Boys, I have only one request to make. Don't fill my body with bullets when I am dead." Before he was cut down, a famous photograph was taken of him dangling from the rope.[19]

Sheriff Ward was determined not to lose another prisoner, and he placed a strong guard at the jail. Ward, age fifty, had been elected sheriff in November 1882. His sons Fred and Will served as deputies. A rancher and freighter by profession, Ward had served in the Civil War and then emigrated to San Diego, where he opened a commission mercantile business. In 1872 he established a freight line to Arizona, shipping goods to the mining camps. Eventually he moved to Tombstone, where he became active in politics. Sheriff Ward had no law enforcement experience whatsoever and had certainly never hanged anyone. He promptly sought help from Paul.[20]

Sheriff Ward had a special scaffold built for the hanging. Paul undoubtedly had a hand in its design, as a Tombstone newspaperman commented:

The lynching of John Heath in Tombstone marked the end of his long criminal career in Texas and Arizona. Author's collection.

"What Bob don't know about 'working off' a man neatly and artistically wouldn't make a very large book." The gallows was similar to the one he had built in Tucson, but was much larger to accommodate the roping of five men. The gibbet's platform was eight feet high, twenty feet long, fourteen feet wide, and provided for a five-foot drop. It was topped by a crossbeam eight feet above the platform. Its long trapdoor was held in place by metal bolts, which in turn were attached to a 250-pound weight suspended by a cord. When the cord was cut, the weight would yank the bolts free, and the trap would open. Sheriff Ward issued one thousand invitations to the hanging, as that was the maximum number of people who could fit into the jailyard. The yard's thirteen-foot-high walls would prevent outside onlookers from viewing the hanging. This angered citizens, many of whom believed the hanging should be public. Some hotheads even threatened to tear down the jailyard wall. As a result, W. M. Constable, a Tombstone speculator, hired carpenters to build a large grandstand capable of sitting up to six hundred people just outside the jail walls and announced that he would charge an admission fee to view the hanging.[21]

Local Catholic priests, Father Patrick Gallagher of Tombstone and Father Antonio Jouvenceau of Tucson, regularly visited the condemned men. Delaney and Kelly were Catholics and were administered the last rites of the church. Dowd, Sample, and Howard at first rejected the ministrations of the clergymen, but as their final hour approached, they agreed to be baptized and to receive the final sacraments. The day before the execution, strangers flooded into Tombstone, filling up the hotels and boarding-houses. Some of the townsfolk objected to the grandstand next to the jailyard, and at four thirty on the fatal morning of March 28, a band of 150 miners marched to the courthouse, threw ropes over the structure, and jerked it to the ground. Nellie Cashman, the "Angel of Tombstone," already famous as a friend and caregiver to the miners, had reportedly encouraged them to tear it down.

Paul was in the Tombstone jail that morning, assisting Sheriff Ward with the preparations. A barber entered and gave each man his last shave. Sheriff Ward then presented each of the condemned men a new black broad-cloth suit. Billy Delaney looked his over carefully and remarked, "Well, boys, if we haven't lived like gentlemen we'll die like them, anyhow." Then Fathers Jouvenceau and Gallagher, accompanied by Nellie Cashman, spent the morning with them in prayer. Although the five desperadoes were determined to die bravely, they were plainly shaken, and none had slept during the night. At noon the jailyard gate was thrown open, and a huge crowd flocked in. An estimated two thousand people, including many women, were on hand, many of them clustered on rooftops surrounding the jail-yard. Just before one o'clock Sheriff Ward read the death warrant to the men in their cells, then said, "Boys, you have requested the privilege of going to the scaffold free from straps and manacles. This privilege I grant you, but each of you will be taken by the arm by an officer."

At that, Red Sample snapped, "I'd rather be strapped than packed up to the scaffold."

"So would I," echoed the other four. But Ward and Paul ignored their protests. At 1:10 P.M. they slowly filed out of the jail. In the vanguard was Sheriff Ward, followed by Fathers Jouvenceau and Gallagher. Next came Paul. As a reporter described: "Very little time elapsed before the familiar form of Sheriff Bob Paul, of Pima County, was seen approaching and having a hold of Red Sample's arm. Arm in arm the two men descended the steps

Bob Paul's friend Jerome L.
Ward, the inexperienced
sheriff of Cochise County.
Wild West History
Association.

leading into the jail yard, and crossing the slight space between the stairs
of the two structures, ascended the steps of the scaffold. Not a blanch of the
cheek, not a quiver of a muscle, nor a falter in the step of the condemned
as he, keeping step with the sheriff, ascended the stair. A stranger could
not have told from the demeanor of the two men which was the prisoner.
Upon reaching the platform, Sheriff Paul accompanied his charge to the
extreme right of the scaffold, where the prisoner sat down on a chair."[22]

Tex Howard, Big Dan Dowd, Billy Delaney, and Yorky Kelly followed,
guarded by Deputy Sheriffs Billy Daniels and Bob Hatch and several other
officers. They climbed the nine steps to the gallows, then sat down next
to Sample on chairs placed on the trapdoor. If the crowd thought that
these hardened desperadoes would falter, they were mistaken. Sample,
Delaney, and Kelly spotted friends in the vast throng and called out cheerfully, "Good-bye!"

EXECUTION OF

DANIEL KELLY, OMER W. SAMPLE, JAS. HOWARD, DANIEL DOWD and *WILLIAM DELANEY,*

AT THE COURT HOUSE, TOMBSTONE, ARIZONA,

March 28, 1884, at ..*1*.... O'clock p. m.

Admit Mr. G. F. Swain

J. L. Ward

NOT TRANSFERABLE.   SHERIFF.

Invitation to the hanging of the Bisbee murderers, issued by Sheriff Ward. Author's collection.

Paul, Sheriff Ward, and the other lawmen then shook hands with each of the condemned men. Then Ward ordered, "Stand up, boys." Sample stood next to Paul and announced in a loud voice, "I have a few words to say. I am innocent of the crime for which I am being hung. John Heath was innocent, too, so far as I knew. He never put up any Bisbee job with me. I want a Christian burial, and die a Catholic." The others made similar statements, with Delaney adding, "I am entirely innocent of the crime of which I was convicted, and if I had a fair trial I would not be here to hang today." The outlaws' brazenness knew no bounds, for even though they had made confessions to the priests and had been administered last rites, they continued to adhere to that rough ethic that barred them from "squealing" and "peaching."

The deputies quickly strapped the prisoners' arms and legs. As Paul and Sheriff Ward draped nooses around their necks, Dowd remarked, "This is a regular choking machine." Then the sheriffs dropped black caps over the prisoners' heads.

"Let her go," exclaimed Kelly in a muffled voice. At that Sheriff Ward, with a quick movement, cut the cord. The heavy weight fell, yanking the bolts loose, and the trap door fell with a heavy thud. All five men plunged, and the entire scaffold shivered and groaned under the weight of the condemned. All died of broken necks except Dowd, who struggled briefly, his body convulsing, but within minutes he strangled to death. Doctors soon pronounced them all dead, and they were allowed to hang for half an hour before being cut down.[23]

The Bisbee Massacre resulted in part from weak and incompetent law enforcement. For almost a year the deadly gang had been allowed to run roughshod over the citizens of Graham County. The desperadoes became increasingly bold and came to believe they could get away with murder in Bisbee because they got away with it in Clifton. Sheriff George Stevens had done little to rein in the gang, and it was no wonder that Graham County's jurors were afraid of them. If lawmen could not, or would not, control the ruffians, then jurymen could hardly be expected to. It was only when the gang left Graham County and entered Cochise did anyone stand up to them. And only after a large reward was offered could Graham County deputy sheriffs be induced to hunt down the outlaws. The vacuum created by peace officers who were unwilling to enforce the law without fear or favor was never so evident in frontier Arizona.

Paul returned to Tucson to begin preparations for yet another hanging. Joe Casey, his most dangerous prisoner, had been kept under careful guard. At all times he had an Oregon boot fastened to each leg, and his hands were ironed in front, even while he was in his cell. After he had been sentenced to death the previous June, his attorneys had taken an appeal to the Arizona Supreme Court. That court affirmed his conviction. On April 8, 1884, Casey was brought for resentencing into the courtroom of Judge William F. Fitzgerald, the replacement for Judge Sheldon, who had died two months earlier. Reported the *Citizen*, "When the court room doors were opened there was a general rush and in a very short time every seat in the room was occupied." Those who could not find seats jammed the corridor. Paul was on a trip to California, and in his absence Casey was brought into court by Undersheriff Thomas Cordis, Deputy Sheriff Nathan B. Appel, and two jailers. The *Citizen*'s reporter noted, "The prisoner walked erect and after taking a seat, leisurely patted his left foot and looking upon those he knew smiled as cheerfully as though the occasion was one to mark his liberation."[24]

Judge Fitzgerald recounted the procedural history of the case, then told Casey, "It now becomes my duty under the law to enquire if you know of the existence of any legal reason, or if you have anything to say, why sentence of death should not be passed on you."

"I have not," Casey responded sullenly. "I don't think it would be of any use."

At that, the judge intoned, "The sentence which the law prescribes for murder in the first degree, and the court awards, is that you be taken hence to the county jail of this county, to be safely kept in close confinement until Tuesday, the 15th day of April 1884, and said 15th day of April 1884, you be taken from the said jail by the sheriff of Pima County, and within the yard or the enclosure around said jail if there be such, and if not to the place of execution, and there between the hours of ten o'clock A.M. and four o'clock P.M. be hanged by the neck until you are dead. And may God have mercy upon your soul."

Casey, with an ironic grin, replied, "Thank you, sir, for what you have said."

An observer reported, "In the court room he wore the same unconcerned air that has characterized him throughout his entire imprisonment." Back in his cell Casey recognized the difference between Judge Sheldon and Judge Fitzgerald, telling a reporter, "That judge is pretty much of a gentleman. He don't abuse a man when he is down."

As Casey sat on the edge of his bunk, puffing a cigar, the newspaperman remarked, "You have not succeeded very well in the escaping business."

"Well, no, damn it," the desperado responded. "I have had hard luck in that line, and I guess I will now have to give up to these damned stranglers here in Tucson."[25]

Paul was in San Francisco when he learned that Casey had been sentenced to death. He immediately boarded a train for Arizona, via Los Angeles, but his trip home was anything but easy, and it illustrated the vagaries of western train travel. Due to landslides in the Tehachapi Mountains, he was delayed for a full day in Sumner, now part of Bakersfield. Reboarding the train, he made it just twenty-five miles to Caliente, where he lost a second day due to another slide that closed the tracks. At Mojave he was forced to spend the night because of more track problems. Finally arriving in Ravenna, north of Los Angeles, the train halted again. Desperate to get back to Tucson on time, Paul rented a livery team and raced twenty-one miles into Newhall, where his Southern Pacific connections got him a special locomotive into Los Angeles. There he boarded an eastbound train to Tucson. The usual day-and-a-half trip had taken four.[26]

Casey's courtroom show of nonchalance had been a sham. For weeks he had been quietly working on another escape. From a necktie he had removed a steel pointer, with which he laboriously sawed into one of the soft wrought iron bars of his cell. Filing surreptitiously for eight weeks, he finally managed to cut through the bar on the night of April 10, just five days before his hanging. He crawled through the bars into the inner corridor, and then slipped inside the water closet. There he worked all night, digging the mortar loose with the steel pointer and the handle of a toothbrush. In the morning he returned to his cell and replaced the iron bar. That night he slipped out again and brazenly walked down the corridor, shaking hands with the other prisoners though their cell bars. Then he stepped inside the water closet and resumed his work. The prisoners sang loudly to drown out the noise of his work. Casey had cut halfway though the outer wall when Ned Boyle, one of the night guards, entered the locked corridor and was surprised to find the badman in the water closet busily digging into the bricks, Oregon boots, handcuffs, and all. Boyle dragged Casey into a locked cell, where he and the other guards watched him closely all night.

Paul was beside himself when, on his return to Tucson, he learned of the escape attempt. Reported the *Tucson Citizen*, "Sheriff Paul was considerably excited, on going to the office this morning and learning the facts, and expressed some very uncomplimentary remarks regarding the architecture of the jail. He has all along contended that instead of the wainscoting the walls should be barred by heavy boiler iron and that a more secure caging should be arranged for the cells. As it is the iron rods are easily lifted from their sockets, and being only three-fourths of an inch in thickness are easily twisted and dislocated." Paul ordered that the jailers check Casey's cell every fifteen minutes. The outlaw boasted to a reporter, "I had a good kit of tools, and if let work for two hours more, I would have made it stick. There was a horse or two near by, and after getting out, I would have gone to the blacksmith shop down near Zeckendorf's and got tools to cut off my Oregon boots, but I would not cut them off there; I would have rode all night, and cut the boots off in camp the next day."[27]

The gallows that Sheriff Paul had designed three years earlier for the hanging of Tom Harper had been taken apart and put in storage. On April 14, Paul had the scaffold brought out and set up in the jailyard. He issued two hundred invitations to the hanging. Sheriff Ward of Tombstone, in gratitude for Paul's earlier assistance, came to Tucson to help, as did Paul's friend Len Harris, detective for the Southern Pacific. Casey spent his last night playing cards with his jailers. To a reporter for Tucson's *Arizona Mining Index* he complained, "I was punished in the most cruel manner possible. I was kept, in February, for 42 hours without anything to eat, not even bread; but they were kind enough to give me water. I don't want to mention the name of the jailer and guards who did this. . . . But let me say right here, that our present jailer had nothing to do with this. Since he has been here, he has treated me like a gentleman." Casey wore a new black funeral suit, given to him by a friend. He made a confession, absolving Harry Sinclair of any guilt in the killing of Holbrook. Incredibly, Casey claimed that he had shot in self-defense when the deputy came at him with the coal shovel. He said that he fired the second shot, which killed Holbrook, while under "great excitement and impulse of the moment. . . . It never entered my mind for a moment to do Mr. Holbrook any injury or bodily harm." Casey seemed to have forgotten that he had shot Holbrook to get his keys and prevent him from giving the alarm.[28]

The next morning large crowds clustered around the courthouse, but none could see over the jail walls. Casey asked Paul if he could inspect the gallows, and the sheriff allowed him a peek out the jail door. Arms folded, with a cigar clenched in his teeth, Casey looked over the scaffold carefully. Referring to the lynching of John Heath, he remarked, "I want the job done well. I want no Jim Crow business in mine."

Father Jouvenceau and two Catholic nuns visited Casey and prayed with him until noon. Then he was served a hearty lunch of roast beef, chicken, pie, and hot tea, which he devoured with relish. At one o'clock Sheriff Paul entered his cell and read him the death warrant. Then Paul, with Deputies Vosburg and Appel, Len Harris, Sheriff Ward, and Father Jouvenceau, filed out of the jail. As they passed Dave Gibson's cell, Casey shouted, "Good bye, Dave." Gibson made a reply that bystanders could not hear, to which Casey loudly responded, "You'll all think so if you have to turn your toes up."

The little procession passed into the jailyard. The small yard was jammed with two hundred spectators, who watched in silence as Casey climbed the gallows stairs and then sat on a chair on the trap. He took the cigar butt from his lips and carelessly tossed it away. When Paul asked him if he had any final words, Casey replied curtly, "Go on with your work and I'll say what I want to."

As Sheriff Paul began strapping his legs and arms, Casey announced in a loud voice that he had killed Holbrook "on the impulse of the moment" and repeated his statement that Sinclair was innocent and should be pardoned. He concluded, "I die a Catholic and my body will be cared for by the church. . . . We all got to get here sometime, boys. We all have to get to the jumping off place." Paul instructed him to stand, then fastened the noose around his neck. The desperado had not lost his sense of humor nor his bravado, and he wisecracked, "This is a very uncomfortable necktie."

As the black cap was dropped over his head, he shouted, "Good bye, boys. Turn her loose!" Then Paul cut the pulley cord, and Casey plunged eight feet through the trap, breaking his neck. He hung unconscious and was pronounced dead by doctors in twelve minutes. Casey's body was removed to Smith's undertaking parlor, where hundreds of gawkers filed in to see the corpse. A reporter visited Paul's office after the hanging and watched him tear open an envelope. Taking out a greenback, he remarked, "There is the ten dollar bill that Casey took from the woman at Calabasas." The sheriff explained, "Got it from the saloon keeper next morning after the fracas. Casey had spent it the night before." Paul had carefully preserved the note as evidence in the robbery case.[29]

Sheriff Paul took no pleasure in executing men. But where other officers flinched from this painful duty, he did not. Some sheriffs paid special deputies to spring the gallows trap, but Paul never delegated any unpleasant duty he would not perform himself. Joe Casey was the eleventh man— and the last—that Bob Paul hanged.

CHAPTER FOURTEEN

Another Election Battle

Sheriff Paul had little time to ruminate over the hanging of Joe Casey, for he needed to make preparations for the trial of Dave Gibson, the last of Jim Leavy's killers. Gibson was represented by highly capable counsel: Tom Fitch and Charles Silent. On April 25, 1884, jury selection began, but it was difficult to find jurors who did not already know about the case. An amusing incident illustrated this problem. One prospective juror admitted reading the newspaper accounts of Leavy's shooting, but said he did not believe them. When asked why not, he replied, "I don't believe anything newspapers say."

"Then why do you read them?" asked the incredulous lawyer.

"Oh, for diversion and to see what big yarns them newspaper men can tell without resting."

"Do you know of any other reason which might disqualify you from sitting as a juror in the trial of this case?"

"Yes," he responded. "I don't believe lawyers any more capable of telling the truth than newspapers." Amid howls of laughter from the audience, the juror was excused by Judge William F. Fitzgerald.[1]

Twelve jurors were eventually chosen out of 128 examined, and after five days of testimony and arguments, the jury was hung: nine in favor of acquittal, and only three for conviction. Once again, most of the jurors had accepted the claim of self-defense. The case was set for retrial in October, and Paul endeavored to select a venire of impartial jurors. But by this time, everyone in Pima County was thoroughly familiar with the case, and an unbiased jury could not be found. As a result, Judge Fitzgerald ordered a change of venue and sent the case to Pinal County for retrial. In May 1885 jurors in Florence emulated the verdict of Johnny Murphy's Tucson jury and acquitted Dave Gibson. In the end, only one of Leavy's murderers was punished, which would soon result in strong criticism of Sheriff Paul.[2]

On May 15 a party of Mexicans had a fiesta on the Santa Cruz River just outside of Tucson. Amid much carousing and imbibing of mescal, a desperado nicknamed El Negro ("the Dark One") quarreled with Marcos Cruz, and a general melee broke out. El Negro jerked a six-shooter and shot Cruz in the face, killing him instantly. Whirling to face the crowd, he fired point-blank at Loreto Higuera, wounding him in the chest. El Negro then fled across the fields on foot. A warrant for the killer was sworn out and given to Sheriff Paul. Within two minutes he started out with a posse including Deputy Sheriffs Charles H. Vosburg and Nathan Appel, the latter's twenty-one-year-old son, Horace, and Constable Martin W. Brady. Constable Brady was a former Southern Pacific brakeman and conductor and a close friend of Paul's. The lawmen made a determined search for the killer but were unable to find him. On a tip that El Negro had fled to Florence, Deputy Appel and his son searched for him there and at Casa Grande, without luck. Vosburg made a nighttime hunt for the badman in the desert, but Horace Appel later charged that the deputy had been sent on a wild goose chase by the fugitive's friends. Paul's failure to capture El Negro would soon come back to haunt him.[3]

A month later, on Saturday night, June 15, 1884, a ruffian named H. N. Twoner terrorized South Meyer Street. According to the *Citizen*, Twoner "filled himself with bad whiskey and had driven out a number of women and children from their homes and was having things all his own way." Sheriff Paul and Constable Brady rushed to the scene and arrested Twoner without trouble. Since he agreed to accompany them back to the jail, neither officer handcuffed him. But as the trio reached the top of the courthouse steps, Twoner suddenly braced one foot against the landing and threw himself backward. All three of them tumbled in a heap to the sidewalk. Before Twoner could break loose, Paul struck him a terrific blow on the jaw with his hamlike fist. The force of the punch knocked Twoner off the sidewalk and onto the courthouse lawn. Before the ruffian could get to his feet, Brady leaped onto him and seized his throat in an iron grip. Twoner wisely gave up and allowed the officers to lock him in a jail cell.[4]

Paul's manhunting skills were again called into question two weeks later. On the night of July 1, Fred Keister was murdered on the Con Ryan ranch near Harshaw. Ryan and Keister ran a general store and saloon in the ranch's adobe headquarters. Earlier that day Keister had run off several Mexicans and an American railroad section hand who had been drunk and boisterous. Just after dark a masked man, armed with a pistol and Bowie knife, entered the adobe through a rear door. Seizing a saloon patron by the shoulder, he pointed his revolver at Keister. The patron wrenched loose and fled, but Keister was not so lucky. As he tried to run, the assailant stabbed him in the shoulder and back. As Keister staggered out the back door, the masked desperado shot him in the back. He collapsed, gasping, "Oh, I'm dead! I'm dead! I'm dead!"

Two men who were camped near the corral ran to the railroad to get help, but the gunman escaped. Sheriff Paul was notified and took a southbound train to the scene. He tracked down the Mexicans and the American section hand, but all were able to provide alibis. At first Paul was unable to solve the crime, which was undoubtedly a robbery attempt, as $1,800 was missing. Three months later, he arrested Thomas Castro and Keister's partner, Con Ryan, but the charges did not stick. Paul's failure to crack this case would soon bring him trouble. But he remained popular in Tucson. The Old Pueblo threw a huge celebration on the Fourth of July. Most of the businesses closed, and all the fraternal and military societies turned out in full uniform for parades that began at daybreak. Paul served as grand marshal for the affair.[5]

Four days later an even more brutal murder took place. On July 8, 1884, a Mexican youth, Francisco Quinones, was found hanging from a tree on the San Rafael Ranch, in the Huachuca Mountains, six miles north of the U.S.-Mexico line. This affair created an uproar along the border. Mexicans were outraged, as were Americans who considered Francisco Quinones "a well behaved Mexican boy." At first it was reported that the murder had been committed in Pima County. When Paul heard the news, he was handling court and grand jury duties in Tucson, and the judge would not excuse him. In his stead the sheriff dispatched Deputy Nathan Appel, who determined that the crime scene was actually in Cochise County and offered to assist Sheriff Jerome Ward. An investigation revealed that young Quinones, whose father ran a mescal distillery just across the line, may have witnessed the theft of a rifle. It was thought that he had been slain to keep his mouth shut. Local Mexicans believed that a nearby rancher, Jim Rafferty, knew who did the lynching. But there was no firm evidence, and during the summer the investigation stalled.[6]

During the hot weather, Paul was in the habit of riding down to Silver Lake to swim. The lake, situated about two miles south of Tucson, had been created by a manmade dam on the Santa Cruz River. It was a popular resort, with a new hotel, two bathhouses, and a saloon. On a visit there that summer, the sheriff met a pair of prospectors, one of whom approached him, saying, "Paul, we are going out to the Cababi on a prospecting tour. We have our grub, tools, and everything we need, but no money with which to buy water. Can't you give us a little money to buy water?"

The old forty-niner had a soft spot for prospectors, and, digging into his pocket, he pulled out three dollars, saying, "I guess that would do." Paul then took a dip in the lake and, while swimming, was chagrined to see the two miners drinking in the saloon. When he got out of the water, the other prospector approached and asked for money to buy water. The sheriff replied that he had already given his partner three dollars, to which the miner explained that they had used it to buy the drinks. Paul turned over the rest of his change, $2.50, and rode back to Tucson. He would later have reason to regret his kind treatment of the two prospectors.[7]

Paul had long been unhappy with the performance of his deputy, Charles H. Vosburg. He had been furious with Vosburg for sleeping on duty at the time Deputy Holbrook was slain, and he had been embarrassed that Vosburg's horse was stolen while he had been asleep at camp in the Patagonias. Paul was further rankled by Vosburg's attempt to work simultaneously as a deputy sheriff and a deputy U.S. marshal. The final blow took place when *El Fronterizo*, Tucson's Spanish-language newspaper, charged that Vosburg had savagely pistol-whipped a Mexican suspect who had not resisted arrest. When a jury divided as to whether the man was guilty of larceny, Vosburg failed to appear for the retrial. Paul promptly demanded and received the deputy's resignation. Vosburg nurtured a bitter grudge against his former boss.[8]

As the summer waned and the fall election campaign approached, the *Star* began a steady drumbeat of harsh attacks on Paul. It started on August 30, 1884, when editor Louis C. Hughes published a broadside against the veteran lawman: "The term of Bob Paul has been one of fearful extravagance and reckless waste. . . . The debts which has been loaded upon the county during his administration is fearful to contemplate. His incompetency is fully established in the many jail deliveries, in his failure to bring to justice criminals who committed outrageous assassinations in our streets; in his unjust and unequal property assessments; in the hardships he has visited upon our citizens in forcing questionable processes against them and their property, causing wreck and financial ruin. . . . Mr. Paul has rendered much service to Wells Fargo & Co. and other corporations, but the tax payers of Pima County want a sheriff who will serve them."[9]

Much of the *Star's* criticism was thoroughly misplaced. There had been no "fearful extravagance" or "reckless waste" during Paul's tenure. In fact, the 1884 Pima County grand jury, which annually examined the branches of county government, found "everything satisfactory" with the sheriff's office. The grand jury found that Paul's fees for 1883 totaled $25,000, which included sheriff's, assessor's, and tax collector's fees. From these fees Paul paid for "a portion of the jailors and deputies." These were not debts "loaded upon the county," as Hughes charged; property owners and civil litigants paid the majority of the fees. The *Citizen* countered, "The sheriff's office is worth only from $7,000 to $8,000 per year, by close and careful management; but when a man like Paul fills it—a man who is lenient about collecting fees in civil cases, it is not worth more than half that amount." Though its estimate of Paul's income seems significantly understated, the *Citizen* correctly pointed out that civil fees were generally paid by litigants at the end of a lawsuit, by which time the parties often had no money left. The grand jury recommended that the office of tax collector and assessor be separated from the sheriff's office and that these positions be salaried. It found that such a change "would be a handsome saving to the county and the taxpayers." Paul himself claimed that his income "did not exceed $4,000 per annum," which was also a marked understatement. There can be little doubt that the Pima County shrievalty was a rich plum and that Paul earned a substantial income. However, the grand jury found fault with the fee system, set in place by territorial law, and not with Paul's management of the office. As a result the legislature passed a bill in 1885 that fixed the Pima County sheriff's salary at $7,500 a year, payable quarterly. Later, an 1897 law provided for separation of the offices of sheriff and tax collector.[10]

The *Star's* claim that Sheriff Paul was incompetent due to the many jail escapes was also a canard. The George Cooler jailbreak was caused by a conspiracy between a corrupt jailer and his Democratic Party cronies, a fact that Hughes conveniently ignored. The other escapes were the result of the faulty jail construction, something about which Paul had repeatedly complained to the county board of supervisors. The charge of Paul's alleged

Louis C. Hughes, founder and editor of the *Tucson Arizona Star* and governor of Arizona from 1893 to 1896. He was Bob Paul's most bitter political enemy. Courtesy of the Arizona Historical Society/ Tucson, 139.

"unjust and unequal property assessments" was both false and misleading. Citizens who believed that their property value had been assessed too high could and did appeal to the local board of equalization, which had the power to reduce the sheriff's valuation. Hughes's claim that Paul enforced "questionable processes" was equally specious. A sheriff is charged with the duty to enforce civil judgments by seizing and selling property. This ministerial duty leaves the sheriff with no discretion; he is strictly obligated to carry out the orders of the court. Paul could not voluntarily choose to execute some judgments and ignore others. Hughes, as an experienced attorney, knew that, and this charge against Paul was an outrageous misrepresentation of both the law and the facts.[11]

Hughes was on firmer ground when he alleged that Paul had favored Wells Fargo and did not "bring to justice criminals who committed outrageous assassinations in our streets." This charge referred to Paul's failure to arrest the Earps and Doc Holliday for murdering Frank Stilwell. When the killers Johnny Murphy, Dave Gibson, and Bill Moyer escaped from his jail, Paul went to extraordinary efforts to recapture them. But Paul made no such efforts with regard to Holliday and the Earps. After his initial visit to Colorado and his request for a second requisition for Holliday, he never made any further attempts to arrest any of them on the Stilwell murder warrant, and instead he maintained a close friendship with Wyatt Earp. It was that relationship, combined with his belief that the Cowboys got what they deserved, that blinded Paul's sense of duty. His partiality toward Wells Fargo and the Southern Pacific was widely talked of in Pima County. But while he indeed had made great efforts to track down the Red Jack gang, who had killed a Wells Fargo messenger, he had also gone to Globe to try to protect Hawley and Grimes, who likewise had murdered a Wells Fargo messenger. Nonetheless, Sheriff Paul's perceived favoritism toward these powerful corporations proved his greatest political weakness.

Louis Hughes was such a rabid partisan that he could not restrain himself from increasingly vitriolic attacks. He repeatedly insisted that it was unfair for any elected official to serve a third term, forgetting that he had previously supported Democratic third-termers, like Charlie Shibell. In an anti-Paul editorial he argued that "two terms are sufficient for any one man to fat and greed upon" and that "Pima County has been taxed during the last four years to pay a large part of the detective expenses of Wells Fargo & Co." Hughes demanded, "What has Bob Paul done to entitle him to keep the fat office of sheriff?" The editor even criticized Paul for failing to secure a jury in the Dave Gibson trial, ignoring the fact that it had been impossible to find impartial jurors in Pima County. Hughes complained that "all the witnesses will [have] to be taken to Florence at the expense of this county" and the cost "cannot be less than five thousand dollars, which the taxpayers of Pima County will have to meet." The *Citizen* fired back, "Had Sheriff Paul continued his efforts to secure a jury in this county, the entire term of Court would have been consumed in the fruitless effort." The *Arizona Mining Index* added the obvious: "The judge alone has the power to order a change of venue, not the Sheriff."[12]

Paul received strong election support from several newspapers. The editor of the *Arizona Mining Index* declared that "an Arizona sheriff has to carry his life in his hands and never wince when duty compels him to face criminals in their hiding places. Sheriff Paul has earned for himself a name for bravery and efficiency which will go down in the as yet unwritten history of the suppression of crime and cowboy rule in Southern Arizona." The *Nogales Express* also offered its support to Paul: "What is the matter with Pinhead Hughes; and what is the golden reason he has for his attempt at blackmailing honest, sturdy, reliable, fearless and conscientious Bob Paul, the man of iron and the man of nerve? If Pinhead opposes him politically, well and good, it is his right, and the spirit of a free press will uphold him; but let him do so honestly, without malice; let him fight him with the weapons of an honorable journalist."[13]

The sheriff's perceived political weakness encouraged Eli B. Gifford, a Tucson gambler, saloonkeeper, and politician, to challenge him as the Republican candidate. Gifford, like his brother Miles, had been a deputy under Paul, and before coming to Arizona, he had served as a deputy sheriff in San Diego, California. He was a close friend and gambling partner of Johnny Murphy, and Paul's dogged efforts to bring the killer to justice may have earned Gifford's enmity. Complained the *Citizen*: "Knowing the strength of R. H. Paul with the people, the Democrats and the *Star* have combined to defeat him at the primaries, if they can." The day before the Republican primary election in September, the *Citizen* charged that "the Democratic paper and leading Democrats are hard at work to beat him. . . . The fight between Paul and Gifford should not be interfered with by Democrats."[14]

Paul was strongly supported by John A. Muir, superintendent of the Southern Pacific in Arizona. Mose Drachman, then a teenager and the son of Tucson's pioneer merchant Philip Drachman, claimed that underhanded methods were used by Muir and the railroad company to secure votes in the 1884 primary: "Paul was the choice of the S. P. Railroad and in those days, the S. P. practically was the whole thing in Arizona, as well as in California politics. The Superintendent at that time in Tucson was John Muir, a very fine man. He surely liked politics and did everything he could to elect Paul in the primary fight. One of the plans upon which they decided was to have Paul's tickets printed on paper which was green on one side and white on the other. They bought up all this paper there was in Tucson which was not difficult in a place of its size. This enabled them to ascertain quickly if a railroad man was voting for Paul or not. No man who worked for the S. P. would dare to vote against him, for if Muir found it out he would certainly lose his job. That was before the days of the Australian [secret] ballot system."[15]

The *Arizona Mining Index*, however, explained that the reason for the green ballots "was to have a straight Paul ticket that could not be imitated" by Gifford's partisans. Paul, however, was sensitive to the criticism, as the *Index* reported: "Mr. Paul, as soon as he saw the tickets, ordered them to be burned, and we saw all of them burned except for a few which had got out about town, which down-town Republicans voted as a novelty. . . .

The green tickets were not used among the Railroad people as has been alleged." The newspaper also revealed that "Gifford's brother undertook to find that same kind of paper, and visited the *Index* office for that purpose. The presumption is that their intention was to counterfeit the ticket if green paper could be found." On the primary election day, August 30, both candidates had brass bands parade the streets of Tucson and sent carriages laden with supporters in search of voters. In the end the ballot controversy did not matter, for Paul soundly defeated Gifford by a vote of 443 to 253.[16]

The Democrats again nominated Eugene O. Shaw. A Tucson newspaperman who supported Shaw later said that he was "a big, simple-minded, good-natured cowboy, who had been induced by his friends to run for the same office two years previously, and in that campaign had blown in most of his means, so that he was then quite poor, as far as money is concerned, although he possessed a great wealth of warm friends." The journalist recalled that Shaw had only "$2 in his pocket on the morning of election day," but his supporters financed the campaign. The *Citizen* called Shaw "a good citizen" and refrained from attacking him, other than to point out that he had no law enforcement experience. Commenting on his career as a cattleman and teamster, the *Citizen* remarked, "No one doubts that Mr. Shaw understands the cattle business and that he can manage a freight train. But does that qualify him for the position of sheriff of the most populous and wealthy county of Arizona?" Added the *Arizona Mining Index*, "The best thing that can be said about Shaw is that he is a young, handsome, good-natured fellow, who knows how to mount a bronco and round up cattle." The *Star* responded with a letter detailing an incident ten years earlier in which Shaw had tracked down a band of stolen mules and recovered them in Mexico. It could hardly compare with Paul's thirty years of manhunting.[17]

The relentless and often petty attacks on Paul were exemplified by an incident that took place during the Republican primary election. The sheriff was busy campaigning on Tucson's dusty streets when he spotted one of the prospectors he had grubstaked at Silver Lake. He was surprised to see that the miner was electioneering for Gifford. Paul stepped up, tapped him on the shoulder, and angrily demanded, "What are you kicking about? I hope I'll meet you on the desert again when you are without water." Eugene Shaw heard about the encounter, and in a campaign flyer he published Paul's angry remarks without explaining what led to them. It was left

Eli B. Gifford, Tucson gambler, Republican candidate for sheriff of Pima County, and strident opponent of Bob Paul. University of Arizona Libraries, Special Collections.

to the *Citizen* to print an account of the whole story. But once again Paul was put on the defensive and was forced to respond to every trivial attack.[18]

On September 14 Paul attended a political convention in Tombstone. He took a train from Tucson and through Benson to the railhead at Fairbanks. As the cars approached Contention City, some passengers prevailed upon the sheriff to point out the place where Bud Philpott was killed. Paul obliged and indicated the spot, which was plainly visible from the tracks. Commented the *Arizona Mining Index*, "The scene revived the memory of the reign of ruffians in Arizona, now happily suppressed by the one who fortunately escaped the deadly bullet at that very place."[19]

As the campaign heated up, the murder of young Francisco Quinones near Jim Rafferty's ranch in the Huachucas became an election issue. A few days before the primary, Rafferty had come into Tucson and met with the Mexican consul, Antonio V. Lomeli. Rafferty said he knew who the murderers were and that they had been at his house just before Quinones was killed. Rafferty declared that he was afraid to disclose their names unless he was assured they would be arrested. Lomeli met with Sheriff Paul, who told the consul that the murder had taken place in Cochise County. Lomeli claimed that Sheriff Ward "believed it was committed in Pima County," which was certainly not correct, for Ward's own deputies had investigated the Quinones murder.

Then, on October 3, 1884, Sheriff Paul received a wire from Colin Cameron, the wealthy and politically connected owner of the vast San Rafael Ranch, with the electrifying news that four people had just been murdered on Rafferty's place: Joseph Raymond, Winfield S. Fritz, his wife, Mary, and Jim Rafferty himself. This was the worst murder in southern Arizona since the Bisbee Massacre, and it was far more mysterious. Theories as to who did it abounded. Some thought that the killers were Mexican bandits. Others believed that Rafferty and the rest were slain by the Quinones lynchers because Rafferty was about to reveal the killers' identities. Local Mexicans believed that Rafferty himself had instigated the murder of Quinones and that friends of the Quinones family had come up from Mexico and taken revenge against everyone at Rafferty's ranch. In later years many suspected Colin Cameron, who was accused of numerous underhanded acts in trying to expand his holdings and drive off opposing claimants. Although Cochise County officers arrested a number of local ranchers, no one was ever convicted of the Huachuca murders.[20]

Paul's opponents wasted no time in seizing on the latest murders to attack him. On October 18, Hughes leveled his most vitriolic assault yet on Paul. Although first acknowledging that the Huachuca murders had taken place in Cochise County, he jumped to the conclusion that the killers were the same who had hanged young Quinones. And even though it had been established that Quinones had also been slain in Cochise County, Hughes averred: "Quinones was hung in Pima County. Sheriff Paul was informed of that fact, and yet he never made any effort to find out the perpetrators of the deed." From that false premise, Hughes concluded that the quadruple murders were Paul's fault: "Had he done his duty then, we do not believe the horrible butchery would have been committed in the Huachucas." Hughes reminded his readers that lack of jurisdiction had not stopped Paul before, pointing out that "he has been known to spend weeks in trying to apprehend criminals for offenses committed in other counties against Wells Fargo & Co." Acknowledging that Sheriff Paul "is a brave, courageous man," the editor charged that if Wells Fargo had been the victim, "Sheriff Paul would not only get on their trail before it was cold, but that he would have taken the offenders."[21]

Such a concoction of truths, half truths, and outrageous lies was difficult, if not impossible, to contradict. The editor of the *Arizona Mining Index*
railed against the *Star*'s "glittering generalities, far-fetched insinuations and
downright lies" and explained that "Paul has no use for the bummers hanging around Shaw—hence their animosity." While the *Citizen* attempted
somewhat futilely to answer the false charges, Paul steadily made the rounds
to campaign in the county's far-flung mining towns and cattle camps. On
the morning of October 25 he boarded the stage for Quijotoa, a new
mining camp ninety miles west of Tucson. Also aboard were his rival, Eugene
Shaw, and two other Democratic candidates for county office. What would
have been an awkward, uncomfortable trip was made significantly easier
when one of the Democrats—possibly Shaw, who reportedly was a heavy
drinker—produced a wicker-bound demijohn, and its contents were drained
on the way to Quijotoa. On their arrival Paul found the camp about evenly
split between him and Shaw. According to the *Star*, Paul angered the camp's
Democrats by approaching a party leader and offering him a deputy sheriff's
commission in exchange for his support; the Democrat declined.[22]

After two days of campaigning, Paul continued on to the mining camp
of Gunsight, forty-five miles to the east. Shaw had been there earlier in
the day, and his supporters gave speeches in front of the mine office. When
Sheriff Paul arrived that evening, he had his own supply of whiskey, and
he spoke next to a bonfire at the mine office. Wrote one Democratic critic,
"He brought a demijohn of the real fighting article and after getting most
of the men full, left in the midst of a general free fight, in and in front of
the office. Guns and knives were drawn. The men acting like so many devils,
and yet he made not the slightest effort to quell the riot, but on the contrary left us to take care of ourselves. Had it not been for some eight or
ten and determined good men . . . who came down and put a stop to the
fight, it is hard to say what might have been the result." Louis C. Hughes
eagerly printed the correspondent's account in the *Star*. Its accuracy, however, was put into question by another letter from Gunsight published in
the very same issue. That writer, also a Democratic critic of Paul, detailed
the electioneering and pointed out that "the Republican liquor . . . did
not help matters, and the few Republicans here will not cast their votes
for him." But he said nothing of a riot with guns and knives.[23]

Paul's past performance as sheriff continued to provide rich fodder for
his political enemies. On October 22 the *Star* published another long
anti-Paul broadside, written by an anonymous correspondent. It started

innocuously enough, saying, "Personally I admit Bob Paul is a nice gentle-man," and then it promptly accused him of serving two masters, "Wells Fargo & Co. and the Southern Pacific Railroad corporation on one side, and the people of Pima County on the other." Next its author rehashed the murder of Frank Stilwell, "a man shot down in cold blood, right in the heart of our city, almost if not quite within hearing of the Sheriff's own house." Paul's friendship with the Earp brothers was explored, the edito-rialist reminding readers that "the Earps were old employees of Wells Fargo & Co. The whereabouts of the Earps has been no secret for the past two years. Mr. Paul knows the indictments still stand against them. Why are no efforts made to bring them back to answer before the law?" Referring to Paul's inability to solve the recent murders in Pima County, the author asked, "Again, what has Mr. Paul done to ferret out the murderers of Marcus [sic] Cruz, killed in broad daylight . . . or of poor old Fred Keister, killed on the Sonoita last June, or of the poor Mexican boy Quinones?"[24]

While Francisco Quinones had not been killed in his jurisdiction, the other criticisms were entirely valid. Paul received heavy support from Wells Fargo and the Southern Pacific. He had conducted brief manhunts for the killers of Marcos Cruz and Fred Keister, but they had not been the extraordinary efforts he had made in other cases, such as his relentless pursuit of the Red Jack gang. His failure to bring in the Earps and Holliday was especially damning, though it is certain that Republican leaders did not want them returned to Tucson for an embarrassing trial.

When the *Star* claimed that Paul had charged exaggerated mileage fees, the editor of the *Arizona Mining Index* countered: "They have been proved to be lies by the investigations made by three successive grand juries, who examined the sheriff's office for the very purpose of ascertaining if such things have occurred. Furthermore, none of these grand juries, even when the sub-committees assigned to investigate the sheriff's office have been headed by Democratic politicians, have found anything wrong in that office."[25]

The 1884 campaign was one of the most bitter of Arizona's territorial period. As one journalist later recalled, "The whole county was stirred up over the fight, which indeed aroused attention throughout the Territory." William S. Oury called it "one of the most exciting and absorbing political campaigns which has ever convulsed this Territory." On election day, Novem-ber 4, Hughes peppered his columns with attacks on Paul: "Remember, Paul is not the candidate of the citizens of Pima County, but of corpora-tions." "Shaw has no money to buy votes, he is running on pure merit."

"The people have a mighty battle to fight today. The Southern Pacific Railroad and $10,000 will be used to aid Bob Paul's election." "There are 96 railroad employees registered. Yet it is claimed they will poll 200 votes in Tucson and Pantano." As usual, however, Hughes offered no evidence in support of his inflammatory allegations.[26]

Paul and his supporters continued to campaign energetically all day. Among the most active campaigners were Constable Martin W. Brady, Deputy Sheriff Nathan Appel, and his son, Horace, later a prominent attorney in Los Angeles. Another was Lou Rickabaugh, a noted gambler and business partner of Wyatt Earp. One of Paul's staunchest supporters was a thirty-four-year-old Tucson barber, Harry Barron. In about 1881, he and several of his brothers had come from San Francisco to Tombstone, where Harry opened a popular bathhouse and barbershop on Allen Street. That is where Paul undoubtedly first met him. Barron later moved with his wife and children to Tucson. Paul frequented his barbershop and helped him out with occasional small loans, and in turn Barron campaigned for him.[27]

The election was an exciting one, as a witness recalled: "When the day of election came, a tremendous vote was brought out, embracing about the total voting population of the county, and perhaps a few more. The corridors of the Tucson courthouse, where the ballots were counted, were thronged with a surging crowd who stayed all night, many of them keeping tally of the vote as it was called out." Harry Barron, Lou Rickabaugh, Len Harris, and Deputy Appel all watched the ballot counting, with Appel and Barron both making a private tally. Democrats later charged that Len Harris had been at the polls to compel railroad workers to vote for Paul. The Tucson vote count was done in the office of the board of supervisors and took two full days to complete. After the final tally was made, W. A. McDermott, one of the judges, began slipping the ballots together on a string in preparation for packaging them. Deputy U.S. Marshal Charles Connell watched McDermott and thought that he was drunk. Connell walked down the hallway to Paul's office and announced, "McDermott is fixing up those ballots and the string is broke and they are flying all over the office. I think he is tight."[28]

As Paul later explained, "I went into the supervisors' office and said, 'Mac, you had better seal those up.' He first tried a half dollar [seal] and then a dollar, and it did not seem to make an impression, and then Mr. Connell went out and brought in one of the recorder's seals, and he then sealed it with that. I then stated that they ought to be sealed more securely, and suggested Wells Fargo's office, and he said he was not acquainted there, and I said I was and I would go down with him, and we went down and I got Mr. Groseclose to put on their seal." William B. Groseclose was Tucson's Wells Fargo agent. The sealed package of ballots was then taken to the nearby hardware and grocery store owned by one of the judges, Douglass Snyder, where his clerk, Marcus Katz, placed it in a drawer for safekeeping. Snyder, a Republican and former state legislator, was a political opponent of Paul. These seemingly benign events would later become of crucial importance.[29]

As usual, it took several days for the rest of the ballots to be gathered from the county's far-flung settlements and mining camps. It was an extremely tight race, and the *Citizen* was not optimistic: "If Eugene O. Shaw is the man that the people of Pima County have elected sheriff, we assure him that he will find no truer or stronger support than will be extended to him by the *Citizen*." The tally lists were delivered to the Pima County Board of Supervisors, which met on November 17 and made a formal count. Of the 1,715 votes cast for sheriff, Paul received 854 and Shaw 861. Paul had lost by just seven votes. It was surely one of the biggest disappointments of his life.[30]

Bill Oury, on the other hand, was delighted, writing to his daughter, "In our county matters we were more fortunate having won the shrievalty, the Probate Judgeship, Dist Atty and a fair share of the Legislative ticket, losing Supervisor, Recorder and Treasurer; the weight of the fight, in fact the point on which all interest was centered was the contest for Sheriff, this was a square fight between the people and the SPRR and we won a glorious victory over all the power of that tremendous engine." As usual, Oury was convinced that Democrats were pure and Republicans corrupt: "I can scarcely realize that such is the case in view of the fact that we had arrayed against us all, the vast power of the Federal Gov backed by all the monied monopolies of the land; how the people could win against such fearful odds is simply wonderful, but it gives proof that there is still life in the old land, and that corruption sooner or later is rebuked by American freemen."[31]

An ebullient Eugene Shaw was handed the certificate of election. A week later he filed his bonds and was sworn in as sheriff, with his term to begin the first day of the new year. The private tallies made by Appel and Barron, however, showed that Paul had carried Tucson by a large margin. Paul and his supporters immediately began investigating the balloting at

George Hand, left, and Eugene O. Shaw in 1880. Hand was Bob Paul's jailer, while Shaw's candidacy for Pima County sheriff resulted in the biggest controversy of Paul's career. Courtesy of the Arizona Historical Society/Tucson, 1483.

the county's various precincts. They found persuasive evidence that voting fraud had taken place at several polling places and that once again Bill Oury had been in the thick of it. Paul's attorneys quietly began preparing an election contest. Paul later said he was concerned that Democrats "would put up a job on [me] as they did in Tombstone in 1880 when ballots were changed . . . after the election." He approached a friend, George T. Martin, formerly the Wells Fargo agent in Tucson, and asked "whether he thought there was any danger of those fellows getting Wells Fargo's seal and tampering with the ballots as had been done in Tombstone?" Said Paul, "Martin replied he thought not, but it might be well to caution them [Wells Fargo] about their seal."[32]

Sheriff Paul later explained that he "went to Wells Fargo's office, and asked Mr. Groseclose if he remembered the package of ballots that McDermott had brought there to be sealed." When Agent Groseclose answered in the affirmative, Paul asked whether "that package had ever been brought back to be resealed," to which Groseclose replied in the negative. Then Paul cautioned him to "be careful of his seal until after the trial of the contest which [I] then intended to make." Paul would regret confiding his private affairs in George Martin.[33]

After the final balloting, Paul's barber friend Harry Barron told him that his private tally showed that Paul had received more votes than the official count. He also remarked to Paul, "You are sheriff, and if you will give me the reins, I think you can continue to be sheriff."

When Paul asked how, Barron replied, "If we can get the ballots we can fix them and demand a recount."

Paul refused, saying, "I have never done any dirty work."[34]

On December 15, as Louis Hughes, Bill Oury, and their fellow Democrats were crowing over their victory, Paul dropped a bombshell. His attorneys filed a lawsuit alleging that of the eighteen voting precincts in Pima County, there had been election fraud in three: in the Tucson precinct, where ten votes were falsely counted for Shaw; at San Xavier del Bac, where nine fraudulent votes were balloted; and at Tanque Verde, where all seventeen votes had been for Shaw, Paul charging that the precinct's election board had not been legally appointed and the votes had neither been secured nor counted until two days after the election. Tanque Verde, Spanish for "green tank," was a Hispanic settlement thirteen miles east of Tucson, at the base of the Santa Catalina Mountains. Its most prominent settler was Oury, who had established a cattle ranch there in 1858. Paul's lawsuit created a public sensation.[35]

The trial began twelve days later, just after the Christmas holiday. Because election contests in Arizona Territory were not decided by juries, the case was heard by District Judge William F. Fitzgerald, a prominent thirty-eight-year-old Republican. Fitzgerald hailed from Mississippi, where, at the outbreak of the Civil War, he had enlisted in the Confederate Army at the age of fifteen. He served with distinction, being promoted to first lieutenant at seventeen. After the war he studied law and, despite his youth, became city attorney of Jackson, then served as district attorney for seven years. At some point Fitzgerald made the unpopular decision to join the state's tiny Republican Party, and in 1881 he was the unsuccessful Republican candidate for attorney general of Mississippi. By this time he had become his party's leader in Mississippi, which led to his appointment in 1884 as district judge in Tucson. Some Arizona Democrats disliked Fitzgerald and considered him a carpetbagger. Mose Drachman maintained, "Southern Republicans at that time . . . were bitter partisans. No Democrat had any chance whatever in Judge Fitzgerald's court. . . . He was indeed a brilliant man but obviously unfair to any Democrat."[36]

The importance of the election lawsuit was underscored by the dizzying array of legal talent that lined up at the Tucson courthouse. Paul was represented by five lawyers, the most prominent being young Harry R. Jeffords, later U.S. attorney of Arizona, and C. C. Stephens, a veteran trial attorney and legislator. Shaw's four attorneys were Ben Hereford, his law partner William Lovell, Cameron H. King, who had achieved prominence in California, and James A. Anderson, a lawyer since 1847 who had served with distinction as a Confederate officer in the Civil War.[37]

The trial began in a packed courtroom on Saturday, December 27, with a recounting of the ballots for the three disputed precincts. First the packet of Tucson ballots, secured by a wax seal, was opened. W. A. McDermott testified that the seals he had put on it were intact. The ballots were then counted in open court. Instead of the official count, which had shown 611 for Paul and 495 for Shaw, the packet was found to hold 618 for Paul, 487 for Shaw, and one for Ben Hereford. This was an increase of 7 votes for Paul and a loss of 9 votes for Shaw. Next the votes for San Xavier were recounted. The official count had shown Shaw with 29 and Paul with 11; the new count gave Shaw 27 and Paul 13, an increase of 2 votes for Paul. Finally the returns from Tanque Verde were counted, with no change: 17 for Shaw and none for Paul. Shaw and his supporters were stunned that the Tucson recount showed a 16-vote change, enough to throw the election in Paul's favor. They jumped to the conclusion that the Tucson judges could not have made such an error and that the ballot box must have been stuffed after the election. In fact, the change of 16 votes was less than 1.5 percent of the 1,106 cast in Tucson, which is statistically insignificant and well within the typical error rate of 1–2 percent for hand-counted ballots. Shaw and his counsel recognized that if they could not disprove Paul's allegations or show that some of Paul's own votes were fraudulent, Paul would remain sheriff.[38]

The counting of votes and arguments by lawyers consumed most of the first day of trial. Under territorial law, each polling place had three judges, or inspectors of elections, and two clerks. They were important witnesses. Each had to be officially appointed by the board of supervisors or a justice of the peace and sworn in before election day. In San Xavier, J. M. Berger, a Tucson jeweler, farmer, and Paul supporter, had been one of the three inspectors in that precinct. He was also a Republican candidate for justice of the peace. The other two inspectors, both Shaw supporters, were well-known Tucson merchant Phil Drachman and Dr. F. J. Hart, the assistant Indian agent for the Papago reservation. The election clerk was Charley Kresham, a gambler who owned an interest in the Fashion Saloon in Tucson. He was a Democratic operative to whom Shaw had offered a deputy sheriff's badge if he won the election. J. M. Berger was the first to take the stand. He testified that his house had served as the San Xavier polling place. Berger swore that he had challenged two Hispanic voters, one a noncitizen and another who used a false name, both of whom had been allowed to vote for Shaw. His damning testimony concluded the first day of trial.[39]

On Monday morning, December 29, the case resumed, with Shaw's attorneys filing a new answer to the lawsuit in which they claimed that Paul had bribed fifty voters. Paul's lawyers objected, arguing that this new charge was a surprise and left them no time to respond. Judge Fitzgerald took a recess to consider the problem, then ruled, "I am going to allow the very widest latitude in probing this matter to the bottom. If there has been any fraud in this election I want it brought to light; if there has not been any fraud, no one is going to be injured by a full and free investigation. . . . I am going to allow you, if it is necessary, to adjourn from day to day for a month or two months, to get at the truth of this matter. The truth has got to come out, no matter who is hurt by it." Despite Democrats' fears that Fitzgerald was unfair, the judge was determined to uphold the rule of law.[40]

Paul's counsel then called Nicolas Sosa, who had been one of the inspectors at Tanque Verde. Sosa's testimony showed that the balloting there had been highly irregular: "William Oury appointed me inspector the day before the election. I was not sworn in. Manuel Campas, Manuel Martinez, and Ramon Gallego were judges. . . . None of the judges were sworn in. Emilio Carrillo was appointed afterward—two days after the voting. . . . The voting took place at the house of Mr. Oury." Sosa explained that the ballots were placed in a box, tied with string, and placed in a locked trunk. Because they were unfamiliar with the balloting process and were awaiting instructions from Oury, they did not count the votes until two days later, when Oury, Charlie Shibell, and a third man whom he didn't know—Charley Kresham—came to Tanque Verde to supervise the tally. Sosa testified that all seventeen of the voters were Hispanic, and all were U.S. citizens.

Next Ramon Gallego, one of the election judges, took the witness stand and testified in detail about the identities and qualifications of the seventeen voters. He explained that two days after the election, Oury, Shibell, and Kresham appeared in Tanque Verde to supervise the vote count. Gallego recalled, "Mr. Oury had told us that if we had any trouble as we did not know anything about [the] law he would assist us. . . . We took out the papers and he saw them and he saw that they were not in good condition and we counted the votes. . . . Manuel Martinez took the votes out of the box and gave them to Charley Kresham as interpreter, and he read them off. Seeing there was one judge wanting . . . Mr. Oury told us to appoint another judge." At that point Emilio Carrillo stopped by Oury's house, and they asked him to act as election judge. After the votes were counted, the tally list was certified and signed by those present.

The testimony of Sosa and Gallego, both Democrats and supporters of Shaw, was a serious blow to Shaw, as it showed that the balloting process at Tanque Verde had been contrary to the law, which mandated that inspectors and clerks be present at the voting, and then, promptly at the closing of the polls, count the ballots and certify the tally list. That plainly did not happen. Oury was furious with his Hispanic neighbors for jeopardizing Shaw's election chances. Said Gallego plaintively, "Mr. Oury told us that we had done wrong because we did not know entirely what to do. We did our best."[41]

Yet there were even more problems with the Tanque Verde vote. Miguel Andrade, who had been listed as voting for Shaw, swore that he had not been in Tanque Verde on election day and had not voted. Tomas Munguia testified that although he had been present at the polls, he had not voted either. Their signatures had been forged. Manuel Martinez, one of the judges, was sworn and revealed that during the balloting, Nicolas Sosa and Charley Kresham had read the names aloud from a tally list, not from the ballots, and the votes had then been counted. Manuel Campas, another of the judges, confirmed that the votes had been counted two days after the election. Even worse, he said that Kresham had instructed him to make several changes to other candidates' names on the tally list. The actions of Kresham, as a Shaw operative counting the votes, raised eyebrows in the courtroom.

Bill Oury attended the trial, and Paul's lawyers believed that he had tried to coax the Tanque Verde men into changing or coloring their testimony. They recalled Sosa to the stand, and although he admitted that Oury had approached him, he denied that anything improper had occurred. Paul's attorneys, having demonstrated both fraud and irregularity at Tanque Verde, now turned their attention to the Tucson precinct. They called Paul to the stand. He testified about his concern that political enemies might tamper with the Tucson vote count and his request that the ballots be sealed by the Wells Fargo agent. Of W. A. McDermott, Paul said, "I suggested that he put them in one of the bank vaults, and McDermott went one way and I came up here [to the courthouse], and that is all I know about it."

Paul went on to explain that of the three election judges for the Tucson precinct, two, McDermott and Snyder, were against him politically, and one, Charles H. Meyer, Tucson's German-born justice of the peace, was his friend and supporter. Under cross-examination Paul insisted, "I never touched the ballots in any way." He did admit, however, that J. M. Berger of San Xavier had supported him. Said Paul, "Mr. Berger was appointed a deputy of mine at his request for the purpose of arresting drunken Papago Indians. He was my deputy at the time of the election. He has never done any work in my office, and never claimed any fees." The testimony of these witnesses took up the entire day.[42]

The next morning, William J. Osborn, clerk of the Pima County Board of Supervisors, testified to the efforts by the Tucson judges to seal the ballot package with wax. Of Paul's role, he said, "Mr. Paul came in at that time and asked Mr. McDermott if he would have any objection to going down to Wells Fargo & Co.'s and have them sealed there, as an additional security. Mr. McDermott said he had not, and Mr. Paul and Mr. McDermott went off together." Next W. A. McDermott was sworn. He acknowledged that he was a Shaw supporter but denied being drunk: "There was liquor in the room when we were counting, but I took none." After

Charley Kresham, the crooked deputy sheriff, gambler, and Democratic operative. Courtesy of the Arizona Historical Society/ Tucson, 1806.

completing the tally, he celebrated: "I drank a large drink of whiskey. . . . I felt elated over the success of the ticket."[43]

Next Paul's friend, Deputy U. S. Marshal Connell, took the witness stand and related, "After the votes were counted I happened to step accidentally into the Supervisors' office and saw Mr. McDermott trying to tie up the votes. I went down the hall and saw Mr. Paul and I told him to go in and see to the sealing of the ballots. I don't think that I said anything about McDermott's condition. We returned together, and I got some sealing wax and the votes were sealed up. I did not see Mr. Paul touch the package." Justice of the peace Charles Meyer testified that as election inspector he had supervised the two-day vote count. The inspectors had stayed up the whole night counting the votes and had gotten very little sleep. George Hand, courthouse janitor and night jailer, took the stand next and twirled his hat on one forefinger as he described guarding the ballot box: "I don't think anybody touched it. If anybody had done so I would have seen them." Because Hand worked for Paul, Shaw's lawyers cross-examined him closely, suggesting that he might have tampered with the votes. Hand retorted, "I didn't have anything to do with the election or the box. I was not within ten feet of the box at any time."[44]

Paul's last witness hammered the final nail into Shaw's political coffin. Hilario Pacho, whose name appeared on the Tanque Verde list as having cast a ballot for Shaw, swore that he had not voted at all. Here Paul's lawyers rested their case. They had shown substantial evidence of fraud and irregularity. In San Xavier, two fraudulent votes had been shown; at Tanque Verde, all seventeen votes were thrown into question; and in Tucson, the inspectors had been sleep deprived and one had been intoxicated, showing that they could easily have made a sixteen-vote mistake. On the other hand, Shaw, his counsel, and his supporters were outraged. They still believed that the Tucson count had been done carefully and under the watchful eye of inspectors and clerks from both parties, and they convinced themselves that Paul's partisans had somehow altered a handful of Tucson votes to give him a majority. Shaw's attorneys now mounted a desperate defense.

First they produced ten of the Hispanic voters from the Tanque Verde precinct to demonstrate that they had in fact voted for Shaw. Paul's lawyers objected on the ground that their votes were intended to be secret and that their oral testimony should not be allowed in place of the written ballots. Judge Fitzgerald, in keeping with his earlier ruling that he would allow wide latitude in testimony, ruled that even if there were irregularities in Tanque Verde, and the inspectors were not properly appointed or sworn, there still had to be a showing of fraud to throw out the ballots. He allowed the ten Tanque Verde witnesses to testify, and each confirmed that he had in fact voted. However, there were still seven more voters from Tanque Verde whose ballots were in question. Two had testified that their signatures had been forged, while none of other five appeared in court, either because they could not be located or they did not exist.

Next Shaw's lawyers called William S. Oury to the stand. The old pioneer and veteran of the Mexican War, as well as of the San Simon frauds of 1880, admitted that the Tanque Verde board had not been properly appointed or sworn in and that they had not followed his instructions regarding the proper way to run the polling pace. On cross-examination, Oury was unable to explain why Shibell and Kresham had gone with him from Tucson to Tanque Verde two days after the vote. "I did not enquire on what business Shibell and Kresham had there," he said. "I wanted to go out and they took me out. I don't know whether Shibell and Kresham took any part in the counting or not." It was obvious that the three Democrat operatives had gone to Tanque Verde to salvage its irregular votes. Oury's vague and misleading testimony was hardly helpful to Shaw.

Dr. F. J. Hart, the assistant Indian agent for the Papagos at San Xavier and a political enemy of Paul, had been one of the poll inspectors. He testified that he and J. M. Berger were the only persons living in San Xavier who spoke English. Insisting that the first count had been correct, he admitted that Charlie Shibell had been at the San Xavier polls. "He took no part in the counting. I saw him putting down marks opposite names, I should judge for his own use." Hart said that Berger had objected to one voter, not two, and that the man had been allowed to vote even though Berger had questioned his identity. Phil Drachman also testified that the first San Xavier count was correct. He admitted being a friend of Shaw, but insisted, "I read off the votes and am positively sure that I did not make any mistake." Other testimony offered by Shaw showed that after the election, Berger kept the votes in a cigar box in his house and that he had had several visitors in the days after the election. The implication was that someone could have accessed the box and changed the ballots.

Charley Kresham testified on behalf of Shaw and likewise claimed that the San Xavier tally list was correct. He admitted that Berger had challenged one Hispanic, but claimed that the voter was a Republican: "I saw the ticket. It was a Republican ticket." Yet Kresham could not explain why Berger, a Paul supporter, would challenge a man who was trying to vote for Paul. Kresham then recounted a remarkable tale: "Silas Waters came down to vote and Mr. Berger took his ballot and opened it and Waters jumped and caught him by the hand and cursed him. Mr. Berger told me that he [Waters] had received a certain amount of money to vote a certain way and he was very anxious to see whether he did or not." Kresham's claim that Berger would admit bribery to a political adversary was particularly hard to believe. None of the numerous witnesses who testified about the San Xavier balloting had said a word about the incidents that Kresham described, and Silas Waters was never produced by Shaw's lawyers to testify that he had been bribed. Much of Kresham's testimony was not credible.[45]

Judge Fitzgerald was determined to complete the trial without any delay. Witness after witness took the stand in a grueling process that lasted all that day and throughout the night. Shaw's counsel introduced a self-described handwriting expert, Charles M. Strauss, a Tucson banker and former mayor, whom one newspaper referred to as an "egotistical blunderer." He claimed that his examination of the Tucson ballots showed that five were signed in a "disguised hand," and nine more were forgeries, for a total of fourteen fraudulent votes. Assuming that Shaw's allegation of seven fraudulent votes for Paul was true, it was evident that Strauss had made a mistake as to seven of the ballots he had examined. And if he was wrong about seven signatures, the judge was entitled to believe that he erred as to all fourteen. The testimony of Strauss, instead of helping Shaw, damaged his case. Judge Fitzgerald, in giving broad leeway to both sides during the trial, had allowed Strauss to testify without first proving he was a handwriting expert. Now the judge allowed Paul's attorneys to call, out of order, a number of rebuttal witnesses. Since most of the questioned ballots had been cast in Tucson by railroad employees, superintendent John Muir and his clerk took the stand and produced a list of employee signatures, showing that they matched those on the ballots. When Shaw's lawyers attacked Muir's credibility, he admitted, "I am a warm supporter of Mr. Paul," but then added something that few in the courtroom believed: "He was not supported by the railroad. He was supported by me personally." In addition to Muir, several other railroad men testified that they had seen the questioned voters at the polls.

Now Shaw's lawyers resumed their case, calling Manuel Vasavilbaso, who swore that he had seen young Horace Appel give two dollars to a prospective voter, Arcadio Castro. Appel's mother was Hispanic, and he spoke Spanish fluently. Vasavilbaso said he did not know why Castro had received the two dollars or whether Castro had voted. Pedro Pellon, however, was able to supply the missing link. Pellon, who was prominent in the Old Pueblo, testified that he had seen young Appel escorting Castro down Court Street. "Mr. Appel had hold of Castro by the arms. Castro stopped and said, 'I don't want to vote,' and Appel said, 'Then why did you receive money?' And Castro said, 'Two dollars is very little.' Then Appel gave him two dollars more, and the man took the money, and Appel took him by the arm and brought him inside the courthouse."[46]

A similar charge was made by Harry Holey, who swore that he had been approached by one M. M. Dodge, who offered him five dollars to vote for Paul and three dollars if he would not vote at all. One of the most prominent citizens to be called by Shaw's attorneys was Sam Hughes, a respected pioneer, former territorial treasurer, Republican politician, and Paul supporter. Ironically enough, he was also the older brother of Louis C. Hughes. When asked whether he had given two Hispanics five dollars each to vote for Paul, Hughes answered sharply, "I did not do it. I could have got plenty of votes for two dollars if I wanted to buy. A man named Vasquez told me if I would give him $40 he would give me twenty votes to vote as I pleased." It was hardly a ringing endorsement of the Pima County electoral process.[47]

Arizona pioneer Nathan B. Appel, Bob Paul's loyal friend and deputy. Courtesy of the Arizona Historical Society/Tucson, 1846.

By now the grueling testimony had gone all night long, and by daybreak on December 31, Judge Fitzgerald ordered a one-and-a-half-hour recess. Then he promptly started up again. Shaw's lawyers presented a line of witnesses who claimed that various Republican voters appearing on the tally lists either were not registered or were out of the county on election day. Without doubt, the witness that rankled Paul the most was his former deputy, Charles Vosburg. Vosburg claimed that Paul's friend James Speedy, a noted lawman on the border, was a resident of Mexico and not qualified to vote. Later in the day, however, Speedy's wife took the stand and explained that although Speedy ran a saloon in Mexico, his home was in Nogales.

Shaw's attorneys produced Douglass Snyder, who owned the general store where the Tucson votes were stored. He had served as an election officer and admitted being a Shaw supporter. Although Snyder insisted that the Tucson vote count had been accurate, he was unable to otherwise further Shaw's case. He described how the ballots had been slipped onto a string to prevent tampering, adding, "As far as I was concerned a person could have slipped a ballot off and put another one on." But that was rank speculation, and his testimony did nothing to help Shaw.

Constable Martin W. Brady was then called as an adverse witness and questioned about whether he had bribed any voters. Brady admitted to being active around the polls but angrily insisted, "I did not give any person any bribe or reward on election day." Brady was the last witness called by Shaw. It was New Year's Eve, and everyone was eager to finish the trial by the end of the day. Paul's lawyers now called various rebuttal witnesses to confirm that those who had cast questioned ballots had in fact voted. William Lucas, whom Paul had appointed a special deputy to keep order at the polls, testified that had been in the courthouse, where he had witnessed an angry exchange. "During the last night of the count I heard Mr. Snyder offer to bet against Paul. He was standing up with his hand on the box and his foot on a chair, and he was having words with someone. I think it was Mr. Brady. He said, 'You may get all the money you can, but I will bet you any money Paul don't get there.'"

Two more special deputies testified that there was no chance for anyone to have tampered with the ballots during the vote counting. Charles Meyer, Tucson's veteran justice of the peace, confirmed their accounts, saying, "After the count the tickets were placed in the box and fastened up, and was afterwards carried into the office of the Board of Supervisors. There was no opportunity to tamper with the ballots." He added, "I asked Mr. McDermott two or three days after the count where the ballots were, and he said they were down in Snyder's safe." The final witness was W. A. McDermott, who was recalled to explain that Douglass Snyder had insisted on a fair count, and he also swore that he had kicked one of Paul's special deputies out of the office because he thought he should not be present during the tallying.[48]

That ended the testimony. Judge Fitzgerald ordered a one-day recess, and the exhausted participants and spectators went home to enjoy New Year's. On January 2, 1885, after the lawyers made their closing arguments, Fitzgerald retired to consider the case. True to his word, the judge wasted no time in making a decision. The next morning, in a courtroom overflowing with spectators, he read a long, detailed ruling from the bench. Focusing on the voting at Tanque Verde, Fitzgerald did not mince words, and he found that the count "reeked with rottenness." He ruled that the Tanque Verde officers had never been appointed by the board of supervisors, but instead "were selected and appointed by one William S. Oury . . . and that said Oury had no authority or color of authority to make any such appointments." He found that "Charles Kresham, who was not and never claimed to be an officer of said election . . . proceeded to make a pretended count of the votes" and that Oury and Kresham "made out a false and fraudulent pretended tally list" that gave all seventeen votes to Shaw. Nonetheless, Fitzgerald allowed the votes of the ten Tanque Verde men who testified that they had in fact voted for Shaw. The judge threw out the other seven Tanque Verde ballots.

Fitzgerald, also highly suspicious of Kresham's actions at San Xavier, ruled that the recount showed that Paul had received two additional votes there, and he threw out two of Shaw's votes as fraudulent. As for the Tucson precinct, he accepted the count done in open court, which showed that Paul had gained seven votes and Shaw had lost nine. Fitzgerald then turned his attention to claims that Paul's supporters had committed fraud. "I want to say now that if there had been the slightest evidence that R. H. Paul had bribed or offered to bribe any voter, I should have annulled this election and sent it back to the people. . . . It is true there was evidence in this case, and I believe it to be true, that young Mr. Appel bribed a voter, paid him money, and dragged him like a dog to the polls, but there was not the slightest evidence going to show whom Mr. Appel was supporting or whether what he did was known by Mr. Paul." Fitzgerald specifically rejected the testimony of Charles Vosburg, owing to the former deputy's obvious animus toward Paul. The judge found that the final count was 863 for Paul and 843 for Shaw. Paul had won the election by a mere twenty votes.[49]

Fitzgerald announced that he would order the next grand jury to investigate the Tanque Verde fraud. To appease Democrats, the judge added, "I wish to say . . . there has not been a particle of evidence showing or tending to show that this contestee, Mr. Shaw, had the slightest knowledge or was in any way connected with these glaring and infamous frauds which were perpetrated in his behalf by some of his overzealous friends." Shaw and his supporters, especially Louis C. Hughes, were outraged. They howled that Paul's men had stuffed the ballot box in Tucson, but there was no proof, only wild allegations. Shaw's friends announced an indignation meeting that night, and they threatened to burn Sheriff Paul and Judge Fitzgerald in effigy. But as one newspaperman reported, "Wiser counsels have prevailed, and thus serious trouble has been avoided."[50]

That same day an elated Bob Paul was sworn in for his third term as sheriff of Pima County. Commented a friendly newspaperman, "Paul, seemingly, has had the last laugh, and he is entitled to a loud and long guffaw." He had been victorious in the two most important and hard-won election trials in the history of Arizona Territory.[51]

CHAPTER FIFTEEN

"I Am Sheriff of Pima County"

The Papago Indians, also known as the Tohono O'odham, were deadly enemies of the Apaches and were friendly toward the whites. They adopted the Catholic faith of the Spanish missionaries, spoke Spanish, and subsisted by raising crops and cattle. Although the Papagos received very little aid from the federal government, in 1874 a reservation for the tribe was created on their ancestral lands south of Tucson. In 1881 a new Indian agent, Roswell G. Wheeler, was appointed. His headquarters were in the Papago village at San Xavier del Bac, ten miles south of Tucson on the Santa Cruz River. Wheeler, who was accused of corruption by the Arizona press, was determined to rid the reservation of its Hispanic settlers, and in 1882 he began ejecting them. That same year Bob Paul's friend J. M. Berger and his Mexican American wife, Maria Martinez, settled on her family's seventy-five-acre farm surrounded by reservation land a mile south of San Xavier. The land had been granted to Maria's father, Jose Maria Martinez, by the Mexican government in 1846, long before the reservation was established. She had been born on the little rancho in 1850 and inherited the land after her father died in 1868 from wounds he received in a battle with Apaches. Although the Martinez family had worked this plot for decades with the consent of the Papagos, Agent Wheeler disputed the Bergers' right to possession. The U.S. surveyor general's office investigated and found that the Bergers' land title was valid.[1]

Nonetheless, Agent Wheeler continued his efforts to move the Bergers off the reservation. He claimed that they had made improvements to the property without his permission and had blocked access to the Santa Cruz River. In January 1885, backed by a squad of soldiers from the Fourth Cavalry, Wheeler forcibly ejected the couple, instructing a party of Papagos to empty the house and carry its contents off the reservation. Their possessions were dumped in the road more than a mile from their house and were later carried off by the Indians. Berger and his wife went into Tucson and immediately filed a lawsuit against Wheeler, seeking an injunction to stop the eviction. On January 22 Judge W. F. Fitzgerald issued the injunction, which was given to Sheriff Paul for service. Wheeler was in Tucson, and Paul served him before he could leave town. Paul, accompanied by Maria Berger and her attorney, Cameron King, drove out to San Xavier to put Maria in possession. They found the Berger farmhouse occupied by a sergeant and five soldiers, who refused to let them in. Wheeler had not yet returned from Tucson, so Paul looked up the agent's assistant, Dr. F. J. Hart, and handed him the injunction. Dr. Hart, protected by a band of armed Papagos, refused to obey the court's order and told Paul "he had no business on the reservation." The sheriff then returned to the Berger place and served the injunction on the sergeant, but he also refused to recognize it.[2]

Paul drove back to Tucson, where Judge Fitzgerald issued warrants for the arrest of Dr. Hart and the sergeant for contempt of court. Hart was convicted and sentenced to five days in jail and a $500 fine. The furious judge gave Dr. Hart a well-deserved tongue-lashing: "I want to impress upon you, sir, and upon all your sort, that the officer or citizen who willfully disregards the process of this Court, it matters not who they are, or what their rank or station in life maybe be, will receive the condign penalty of the law."[3]

Now the case went back to the courts, where the Bergers won a writ of restitution that restored their right to the property. On March 8, Paul again drove out to the Berger place in a buckboard. He was met by Corporal Jewell and seven soldiers, who stood behind the Bergers' fence, covering him with their rifles. Paul announced, "I have come to serve a process of the court."

"Tell the court to go to hell with his orders," one of the soldiers exclaimed, adding, "Don't you get out of that wagon."

Ignoring the command, Sheriff Paul climbed down and declared, "I am sheriff of Pima County, and represent the court, whose orders I serve."

"If you go further we will shoot," retorted Corporal Jewell.

Paul replied calmly, "I wish you to listen to a writ of the court I am about to read." Stepping toward the fence, he read the writ aloud and demanded possession of the premises. At that, the soldiers advanced with their rifles leveled at him. Pointing at the fence, Jewell ordered, "You must not cross that line!"

It was a tense confrontation, which Paul quickly defused by climbing into his buckboard and heading back to Tucson. There he served the writ on Colonel George A. Forsyth, who was in command of the Fourth Cavalry. The sheriff also brought charges against the soldiers for contempt of court and resisting an officer. Before the situation could deteriorate any further, the Bergers' lawyers telegraphed secretary of the interior Lucius Lamar in Washington, who ordered that the troops be withdrawn. The Bergers returned to their farm and, in the end, made peace with the Papagos. In 1890 J. M. Berger was appointed Indian agent at San Xavier, a post he held for twenty years.[4]

Less than a week later Sheriff Paul encountered troubles of a different type. One of the prisoners in the county jail was an indigent woman named Isidora Summers. When her mental condition deteriorated, she was moved to the county hospital. There doctors determined that she was four months pregnant, and upon being questioned, she told them that the father was one of Paul's jailers, named Trowbridge. As the Pima County Board of Supervisors investigated, the county physician recommended that she be released to the care of her family in Boston. The supervisors interviewed Trowbridge, who naturally denied the charges. The board concluded that "taking into consideration the mental defects of the woman and the attending circumstances . . . this Board exonerates Mr. Trowbridge from the charges made." Nonetheless, the case was yet another embarrassment for Tucson's sheriff.[5]

Early in May Paul was called to the mining camp of Harshaw to quell a deadly feud. A Texas badman named James Claiborne held a longstanding grudge against a local miner, "Chloride Bill" Covington. Allied with Chloride Bill were "Old Man" Salcido and his sons, Gabriel and Tomas. The Salcidos had rented a house to a barkeeper named Lewis, who used it for a saloon. When they filed a lawsuit to cancel the saloon lease, Lewis turned over the business to Claiborne, a deadly enemy of the Salcidos. On the night of April 30, Claiborne met Old Man Salcido in the street and berated him in loud and profane terms. Tomas Salcido came to his father's defense, and their shouting attracted the attention of Chloride Bill. Chloride Bill ducked into James Jamison's saloon, grabbed a Winchester rifle, stepped into the street, and opened fire. A .44 caliber ball struck Claiborne in the face and tore out the back of his head, lifting him into the air and killing him instantly. Then Chloride Bill rushed back into Jamison's saloon and vanished. At daylight more trouble started when Pat Ryan, a friend of the dead Claiborne, opened fire on Gabriel Salcido, but missed his mark. A wire was sent to Sheriff Paul, but by the time he arrived in camp, Chloride Bill, the Salcido boys, and Jamison had all fled to Mexico. Warrants charging them with murder were issued, and a month later the four were all captured in Sonora, with Paul arresting Chloride Bill in Magdalena. Chloride Bill was tried in Tucson eight months later and acquitted. In the rough ethic of that era, the jurors concluded that the Texas badman got what he deserved.[6]

But it was trouble with Papago Indians that would continue to plague Paul. Elijah Dobbs, a well-known pioneer, ran a stage station near Coyote Wells, forty-nine miles west of Tucson on the road to Quijotoa. Water in that parched desert was scarce and fetched the exorbitant price of two to three dollars per forty-gallon barrel. A thousand yards from Dobbs' Station was a natural spring, Coyote Wells. Although it was not located on the Papago reservation, the Indians had used the well for hundreds of years. In the spring of 1885 Dobbs dug his own well nearby, set up a windmill, and ran pipes to supply water for his station. As a result, the Indians' well dried up. In May a Papago named Jose Ignacio and several of his tribesman choked Dobbs's well with rocks and tore down his windmill. Dobbs came into Tucson and swore out a warrant against Jose Ignacio, charging him with malicious mischief. On the morning of May 16, 1885, Paul boarded the Quijotoa stage to serve the warrant. After meeting Dobbs, the two got into a buckboard and drove out to the Indian village, known as Coyote, located three miles west of the station, at the north end of the Baboquivari Mountains. Several hundred Papagos lived in the village, headed by a chief named Howlatoxome.[7]

Paul had no trouble locating and arresting Ignacio. After ironing his hands in front of him, he placed his prisoner on the front seat of the buckboard. As Dobbs took the reins, the sheriff, as was his custom, sat behind to guard the prisoner. Halfway back to Dobbs' Station, a gust of wind blew off the Indian's sombrero. Paul ordered Dobbs to stop, then got out to retrieve the hat. At that, Ignacio leaped from the buckboard and fled toward his

Dobbs' Station in 1884. Elijah Dobbs is second from the right. Courtesy of the Arizona Historical Society/Tucson, 40898.

village. Despite middle age and physical bulk, Paul managed to catch up with the prisoner, who put up a violent struggle. Ignacio was a large, powerful man—fully a match for Paul. Clenching both fists, Ignacio struck the lawman over the head with his handcuffs. Sheriff Paul returned the blow, slugging the Papago in the head with a pair of leg irons. With Dobbs's assistance, Paul managed to overpower the prisoner and iron him securely, hand and foot.

The commotion spooked the horses, which raced back to Dobbs' Station with the empty buckboard, leaving the trio afoot. By now a band of twenty-five armed Indians had come out from the village. They surrounded Sheriff Paul and demanded that he release the prisoner. Though Paul had sympathy for the impoverished Papagos and their claim to water, it was not in his nature to back down from a fight. At the same time, he had no desire for bloodshed and fully realized that the Papagos had been longtime friends of the white settlers. With his pistol in one hand and prisoner in the other, he tried to parley with them. But the Papagos circled around, covering him with rifles, bows, and arrows. Though he was legally entitled to use deadly force, his cool judgment prevailed. Paul pulled out his keys, unlocked the shackles, and released Ignacio. Instead of being mollified, the angry Indians circled closer. Paul tried to break out, but one Indian seized him from behind, pinioning his arms, and another wrestled away his six-gun. A young Papago drew back his bow to shoot. Paul, with a Herculean effort, broke loose, seized one Indian, and held him close.

Using the Papago as a shield, the sheriff continued to parley with the Indians and finally managed to talk them into returning his pistol and letting him go. He and Dobbs returned to the stage station, where Paul sent a message for help via the next Tucson-bound coach. News of the confrontation caused wild excitement in the Old Pueblo. Recalled one pioneer, "The white hotheads around Tucson wanted to dash out that night, but saner minds prevailed." At daybreak Deputy Sheriff Nathan Appel started out with a posse of ten armed men. Constable Martin W. Brady spent the day putting together a larger posse of twenty-two volunteers, with weapons, ammunition, supplies, and wagons for transportation. According to Herbert Brown of the *Citizen*, who accompanied the posse, "Among the hastily raised volunteers were some of the best men of the city, but unfortunately considerable riffraff was gathered up at the same time." They left Tucson at five o'clock and arrived at Dobbs' Station at three in the morning. Among the posse was Charles T. Etchells, a Tucson pioneer and veteran of the Camp Grant Massacre, who had long been a friend of the Papagos.[8]

Meanwhile, a Papago messenger rode to San Xavier and told the assistant Indian agent, Dr. F. J. Hart, about the trouble. Hart's political enmity toward Paul, coupled with the sheriff's successful actions in restoring the Bergers to their property two months earlier, led to, as the *Tucson Citizen* described it, "personal animosity existing between Dr. Hart and the Sheriff of Pima County." Hart's dislike of Sheriff Paul resulted in his sending a warning to the Papagos that a sheriff's posse would soon be coming to the Coyote village. Hart foolishly advised the Indians to flee into the hills instead of cooperating with Paul. The doctor then sent a letter to Louis Hughes describing what he purported to be the Papagos' version of the trouble.[9]

The *Star*'s editor had a field day reporting the affair. The newspaper's May 17 headline read, "CAPTURED. Acting Sheriff Bob Paul Arrests a Papago Indian without Stating Cause and Maltreats Him." Owing to his belief that Eugene Shaw had been cheated of the title, Hughes had taken to calling Paul "acting sheriff." He provided a garbled account of the affair, claiming that Paul "arrested a Papago Indian and after binding him hand and foot, beat him over the head so that he bled badly" and "exercise[d] a degree of brutality open to the severest censure, if not punishment under the law." He then quoted at length the letter from Dr. Hart, who wrote, "A messenger just arrived from the Coyote, saying that Sheriff Paul had been there this day and arrested a Papago man. The man did not resist Paul. After Paul had tied him hands and feet, he then beat him about the head and limbs with a revolver, sufficient to cause the flow of blood. He then took him to Mr. Dobbs'. . . . A number of Indian men . . . went to the house of Mr. Dobbs, and asked Paul for what offense the man was arrested. In answer, Paul did not tell them the offense, but said: 'I come for any one when I like.' The Indians were not satisfied with this, and seeing that the prisoner had been beaten, they released him, and detained Mr. Paul, until he should tell them the offence which the man had committed." The fact that Hart's account was flagrantly false did not trouble Hughes in the least, and when the correct story later surfaced, he never retracted Hart's version.[10]

At daybreak, May 18, 1885, Sheriff Paul and his thirty-two-man posse headed for the Indian village. He was grimly determined to uphold the law and bring to justice Jose Ignacio and the Indians who had freed him. The sheriff was just as determined to avoid bloodshed, and he ordered his possemen neither to provoke the Papagos nor to fire on them unless they were shot at first. As the posse neared the village, which was located on a high mesa, Paul divided his men into two groups. He sent one, led by Constable Brady, into a deep arroyo where the Papagos had their ponies tied, to prevent their escape. Then Paul, Appel, and the others entered the village. At Paul's orders, the possemen waved white bandannas as a token of peace. The Papagos paid no heed, and the women and children poured out of their wickiups and fled in a panic to the hills west of the village. The men, heavily armed, followed slowly behind, brandishing their weapons. Deputy Appel, who spoke Spanish fluently, ran the length of the village, calling to the Indians "to stop and talk, as the whites had not come against them as enemies, but as friends."[11]

Paul followed the band of Indians west to the end of a brush-choked arroyo. Here the Papagos made a stand, as reported by Brown of the *Citizen*: "[They] made many threats to shoot, and dared the posse to follow them into the hills. At this juncture, several shots were heard at the upper end of the town, about one-quarter of a mile distant from where Paul and his posse were standing." The shooting had started when Constable Brady's men approached several Indians, waving their white bandannas. One Papago shouldered his rifle and pulled the trigger, but the gun misfired. Two possemen opened fire, sending five shots after the Indian, who scrambled to safety.

Sheriff Paul ordered his men to stay a hundred yards away from the Indians. Then he instructed Deputy Appel and Charles Etchells to approach the Papagos, but their efforts to negotiate were unsuccessful. Finally, according to Herbert Brown, "After much parleying they were induced to listen to peaceful overtures that were continually being made to them. Their chief orator was a naked-limbed individual who stood, Winchester in hand, and held himself as good against all comers. He said that his people in their present action were influenced by Dr. Hart, who had previously notified them of Paul's coming, and had advised them to take to the hills and avoid arrest. They accused Dobbs of having appropriated their well and refused for a while to believe that no injury was intended to them." Brown added, "Speaking in Spanish, he derided the whites, upbraided them for their poor marksmanship, and defied them to cross the canyon and enter the brush."[12]

After more haggling, however, the village chief, Howlatoxome, finally agreed to turn over the wanted Indians, provided that Sheriff Paul and his posse would withdraw to Dobbs' Station. Paul immediately agreed to this. Leaving Appel, Etchells, and several others behind to bring in the prisoners, Paul led his posse back to the station. After a wait of two hours, the wanted Papagos still had not been produced, and Paul sent an interpreter to negotiate further with the Indians. Now, however, the Papagos refused to surrender the men. Sheriff Paul had the foresight to bring along a telegraph operator, who tapped into the wires and sent a message to district attorney Ben Hereford in Tucson, asking for horses and a troop of cavalry. Hereford's response was that he could not get the soldiers without the approval of the secretary of war in Washington, D.C., which would take much too long. Instead, Hereford met that night with Indian agent Roswell Wheeler, who agreed to arrange a meeting with Chief Howlatoxome.

The next day, May 19, the Papago chief rode into Tucson and met with District Attorney Hereford, Agent Wheeler, and several other prominent Tucsonans. Once assured that his tribesmen would be treated fairly, he agreed to turn them over. Chief Howlatoxome returned to Coyote, where he ordered Jose Ignacio and eight other Papagos to follow Paul into Tucson. There the sheriff lodged them in the county jail. Although they could have been charged with felonies, punishable by long terms in the territorial prison, the Papagos were treated leniently by a sympathetic district attorney, judge, and jurors. A week later Ignacio was the first brought to trial. The *Star* reported that the Papago held "his arm in a sling, and showed some other traces of his late combat with Paul." He was charged only with malicious mischief, and the jurors were divided as to how to decide his case. After six ballots, they found him guilty and recommended clemency. The

Coyote village, also known as Pan Tak, in 1894. Here Sheriff Paul had a dangerous encounter with Papago Indians in 1885. University of Arizona Libraries, Special Collections.

judge sentenced Ignacio to ten days in jail and a ten-dollar fine. A few days later six more Papagos were tried for "forcibly assisting a prisoner to escape from Sheriff Paul." They received similarly lenient sentences: ten days in jail and twenty-five-dollar fines. The last two were let off with a warning from the district attorney.[13]

The editor of the *Arizona Mining Index* lambasted the *Star* for its false reporting and commented, "We all appreciate the friendship of the Papagos practically manifested in the past; but this cannot and should not operate to sanction their ignoring of the laws of this Territory.... The sheriff had nothing to do with any dispute between Mr. Dobbs and the Indians. He was not there to settle the water rights but to arrest an Indian against whom a warrant had been procured." Paul, who prided himself on his physical prowess, was no doubt deeply embarrassed by his experience at Coyote. For the first time in his long career, he had been overpowered and disarmed. Yet despite the anger he must have felt, his judgment prevailed over his ego. Paul understood the Papagos' unique position in frontier Arizona, and as a result, he had exercised great restraint and went to extraordinary efforts to avoid gunplay. Like most Tucsonans, Paul sympathized with the Papagos and recognized that without water they were doomed. His tactful desert diplomacy resulted in all the culprits being brought to Tucson without bloodshed.[14]

At home, Bob and Margaret Paul brimmed with pride when their oldest son, John, age twenty-one, graduated with honors from Santa Clara College on June 3. One of the top students in his class, he was the commencement speaker and received a bachelor of science degree. John liked Tucson and immediately returned home. His parents undoubtedly wanted him to pursue a career in business, but John was active and energetic and did not like deskwork. Much to Margaret's chagrin, John was interested in law enforcement and prevailed upon his father for a job. Paul appointed him a deputy sheriff, a position that John would hold for the next year.[15]

The same day that Paul took his posse into Coyote, fifty Chiricahuas led by Geronimo left the reservation near Fort Apache and headed south. Telegraph wires throughout the territory hummed with the news: "The Apaches are out!" With U.S. troops in pursuit, Geronimo fled across the border into Mexico. That summer his followers made numerous raids into southern Arizona, stealing livestock and killing settlers, and the army was kept busy chasing small bands of renegades. On June 10, 1885, Paul's friend Billy Daniels, former Cochise County deputy sheriff and now a mounted U.S. customs inspector, followed an Apache trail six miles from Bisbee. Daniels was ambushed and murdered by hostiles; his two possemen managed to escape. These raids created a national uproar, and Louis C. Hughes led an editorial campaign that demanded that the Apaches be removed from Arizona. But, as one authority has pointed out, "Similar outrages, of course, were perpetrated upon the red men by the whites, but these naturally were not reported."[16]

On July 24, Paul received a brief telegram from Harshaw, sent via the telegraph office at Crittenden: "R. H. Paul, Sheriff: F. M. Peterson was killed and the mail robbed six miles from here yesterday, at 2 o'clock P.M." Two days later Paul was in Crittenden, investigating the murder. He found that Frank Peterson, a Swede who had been married less than three weeks, had been driving the U.S. mail wagon from the train depot in Crittenden to Harshaw, eight miles distant. He was found dead near his buckboard, the mail pouches rifled and his horses gone. Peterson had been a principal witness to the killing of James Claiborne in Harshaw and had testified against Chloride Bill Covington in the preliminary hearing. Townsfolk in Crittenden told Sheriff Paul that Peterson feared he would be killed by partisans who supported Chloride Bill in that feud. Others believed that the killers were Apaches, and still more settlers suspected Mexican bandidos.[17]

Sheriff Paul learned that James Finley, a mine owner in Harshaw, had returned after leading a short manhunt for the killers. Paul recruited Finley and a local rancher, Lew Gormley, and after some difficulty in getting horses, they left Harshaw the next morning. At the murder site, Finley had found moccasin tracks, as well as the hoofprints of two unshod horses, showing that the killers were undoubtedly Apaches. They picked up the trail near the Elgin railroad station. Here there were far more tracks than Finley had seen earlier, suggesting that a troop of cavalry was already trailing the Indians. Sheriff Paul and his posse followed the tracks to the base of the Mustang Mountains, arriving the following day, July 28, where they were joined by the prominent cattleman Walter Vail and two of his cowhands. The trail led through the west pass of the Mustangs, then northeasterly to Mescal Springs in the Whetstone Mountains. This was not far from the spot where Wyatt Earp had killed Curly Bill Brocius.

At Mescal Springs Paul found a lieutenant and fifteen infantrymen in camp. The army's strategy was to post guards at the desert springs, knowing that the Apaches would have to get water at one or more of them. The lieutenant told Paul that Captain Henry Lawton, the noted soldier who would later bring in Geronimo, had left the springs the day before with a troop of cavalry in pursuit of the Indians. The Apaches had already killed a Mexican woodcutter and had stolen several of Walter Vail's horses near the springs. Paul searched the ground and saw the same unshod hoof-prints that he had found at the Frank Peterson murder scene. After the posse watered their horses, Vail returned to his ranch while Sheriff Paul and the rest pressed on. The trail meandered north, then turned south and headed across the Babocomari River, two miles from the McLaury brothers' old ranch, then owned by William Land. Paul and his men spent the night at the ranch, and at daylight they made a hot, exhausting, fifty-five-mile ride south before making camp for the night. The next day they struck the road between Babocomari and Charleston, then followed the meandering tracks to within two miles of Charleston. Here they found the trail of the cavalry and followed it to Crystal Springs. From there they rode south to Roberts' ranch, three miles north of the border, where they found two stolen horses, one of which had belonged to Peterson's team. It was now the night of July 30, and the Apaches had plainly crossed over into Mexico. Sheriff Paul believed that the raiding party consisted of four warriors from

Mexico, who had made a weeklong, horseshoe-shaped raid, driving forty stolen horses to their refuge south of the border. Captain Lawton had better luck than Paul. On the night of July 27 he captured twenty Apaches and four stolen horses in the Whetstones. But neither Paul nor Lawton were able to track down the raiders who murdered Frank Peterson.[18]

Bob Paul would soon have troubles far different from, and in many ways more difficult than, tracking elusive Apaches. His friend George T. Martin had been Wells Fargo's agent in Tucson since 1883. In June 1884 Martin fell from a runaway express wagon, suffering head trauma that caused psychiatric troubles. When he was able to return to work, his company books were audited, and they came up $2,000 short. He was also accused of mis-appropriating private funds that had been deposited in Wells Fargo's safe. The company fired Martin and sued him for damages, and in turn he filed his own lawsuit against Wells Fargo for money due him. In January 1885, soon after Paul's election trial, Martin approached Eugene Shaw and Louis Hughes and showed them an affidavit he had signed that contained an astounding revelation: he claimed that a few weeks after the election, at Paul's request, he had obtained the wax sealer from Wells Fargo's office and had given it to the sheriff. He did not know what Paul did with the seal, but the implication was that the lawman used it to reseal the Tucson ballots. Martin readily admitted his motive for making the affidavit: "I wrote to L. F. Rowell, an officer of Wells Fargo & Company in San Francisco, stating that the Wells Fargo Company had robbed me, and that I would show them up and reveal all their participation in the Paul-Shaw election case."[19]

Paul got wind of this when Superintendent John A. Muir of the Southern Pacific showed him a letter he had received from Wells Fargo detective Jim Hume, dated January 13, 1885. Wrote Hume, "Supt. Rowell received an offensive and threatening letter from your friend George T. Martin in which, among other things, he says as follows: 'Don't blame me if I expose your hand in the controversy of the Paul and Shaw affair in which your name and Hume's will appear and the good credit of the company assailed.' What does the fellow mean? Rowell saw Paul only once while we were in Tucson in December, and that was in my presence, and the subject of the contest for sheriff was not mentioned. I saw Paul once prior to this, but we had no conversation about any contest, nor expected contest." On receiving Hume's letter, Muir asked George Martin why he wrote the letter to Rowell, and Martin replied "that Wells Fargo & Company had robbed him" and that he "intended to get even with the company, through Paul." Muir said that Martin told him "that if Paul would pay him . . . three thousand dollars for said affidavit, that Martin would give Paul the affidavit and leave the country." Martin said that Shaw's supporters had offered him even more money, in promissory notes, but he wanted cash. Superintendent Muir told Martin that "he would not be a party to any such scheme."[20]

On hearing this, Paul asked Southern Pacific detective Len Harris to talk with Martin. Harris did so and reported that Martin "did not know any thing wrong against Paul, but he thought he could make Wells Fargo & Co. settle with him." Paul was deeply concerned about the unstable Martin and the affidavit he had signed. Martin later claimed that one night in March, Constable Brady came to his room and said Paul wanted to meet with him. Martin and Brady walked to Pennington Street, where they met Sheriff Paul and Nathan Appel. Paul talked with him alone and demanded to know why he had signed the affidavit. "Paul added that he had always been a friend of mine," said Martin. He claimed that Paul feared that the current grand jury might look into the case. "Paul wanted me to go away until everything had blown over. He said the grand jury would only be in session a few days, and he wanted me to go to El Paso, saying that he would furnish the expenses. I said I would do so, and Paul stated that he did not have much money, and said that he would give me $50.00 to start on. I asked him to see about passes on the railroad, which he said he would do." Martin said that he was given a round-trip pass signed by Southern Pacific Superintendent Muir. Paul would later admit loaning Martin twenty-five dollars, but he and Muir vehemently denied the rest of Martin's claims.[21]

In El Paso Martin ran into Len Harris. The latter was surprised to see the former Wells Fargo agent and asked what he was doing there. "Martin replied that the grand jury was in session and he was afraid of being indicted, but did not say what for," recalled Harris. Martin spoke of his affidavit and said "there was nothing in it. . . . He denied that Paul was guilty of any fraud, that he was offered big money to do certain things, but he did not know anything to hurt Bob Paul." The sheriff soon heard a rumor that Joseph W. Evans, the one-armed deputy U.S. marshal, was investigating the election, despite the fact that no federal offense was involved. Evans had no love for Paul, whose arrival in Arizona had put an end to the deputy's part-time Wells Fargo work. Because Evans was a Democrat, U.S. Marshal Zan L. Tidball, a Republican, had come under fire for appointing him his chief deputy in 1882. Evans, an experienced detective, was also highly ambitious. With a new Democratic administration under President Grover Cleveland in Washington, Tidball was now a lame-duck marshal, and he knew that William K. Meade was favored to succeed him. In that atmosphere, Tidball did nothing to rein in Deputy Evans, who, at the behest of Shaw, Louis Hughes, and other Democratic leaders, began a criminal investigation into the alleged ballot-box stuffing in Tucson.[22]

Paul now heard that one of the witnesses whom Evans interviewed was his barber friend Harry Barron. The sheriff had loaned Barron $150 to open a barber shop in San Francisco, and on June 22 Paul wrote to him: "I understand that J. W. Evans, Deputy United States Marshal, has been in California having interviews and getting affidavits from several parties and among the names mentioned yours was one of them. Is there any truth in it? These affidavits are for the purpose of bringing something concerning the last election before the next Grand Jury. If you know anything about it let me know."[23]

Barron's response, if any, is unknown. The sheriff's fears increased on July 8, when President Cleveland appointed Paul's bitter enemy, William K. Meade, as U.S. marshal of Arizona Territory. Meade, a thirty-four-year-old Virginian, had drifted about the Southwest before settling in Arizona in 1876. He prospected for silver, served one term in the territorial legislature, and came to Tombstone in 1880. Meade was energetic and ambitious and found politics more rewarding than mining. He made his permanent home in Tombstone and had been serving another term in the legislature when he received the marshal's appointment. While Arizona's Democrats were pleased that a local man had been appointed, Republicans correctly pointed out that Meade was a politician with no law enforcement background. Meade's lack of detective experience would be offset by his partisan political skills.[24]

One of Meade's first tasks was to select a U.S. grand jury. Under federal law, the U.S. marshal was required to submit the names of prospective grand jurors, and their names were drawn from a box at random by the court clerk and U.S. commissioner. Bob Paul later charged that Meade had packed the grand jury with Democratic partisans in order to indict him and other prominent Republicans. The claim was not without merit, for Meade appears to have exercised broad discretion in procuring names. The new grand jury contained some of the most notable Democratic Party leaders in southern Arizona. Among its nineteen members were the extraordinary frontiersman, trader, and Indian agent Tom Jeffords, a longtime

William Kidder Meade, politician and U.S. marshal. Bob Paul called him "my personal and political enemy." Author's collection.

Democrat famous in Arizona as the blood brother of Cochise; former sheriff Johnny Behan; Richard Rule, Tombstone newspaper editor and bitter foe of Paul and the Earps; the prominent Democrat William J. Ross, who had been Charlie Shibell's undersheriff and captain of the ill-fated Tucson Rangers; and Thomas E. Farish, a leader of the so-called spoils section of the Democratic Party, which sought federal patronage jobs for its party members.[25]

While Marshal Meade busily picked a grand jury in September, Paul was sick in bed, probably from one of his occasional bouts with malaria. He got two letters from Harry Barron, asking about the grand jury and begging for money. On September 25 the sheriff penned a quick reply: "There is no use of talking about anything till next month as I have not got it and will not have it till then." In response to a question about Nathan Appel testifying against them, Paul answered that "there is nothing in it. Appel knows nothing about me that I am afraid the world to know and as to the new Judge opening the [civil] case up again is all bosh."[26]

Judge Fitzgerald swore in the new grand jury on September 29, 1885. Some of its investigations were nonpartisan, including those of violations of polygamy laws by Arizona Mormons, smuggling across the border, and civilian complaints of the military's handling of Apaches. But its other actions were either blatantly partisan or entirely outside its jurisdiction. Jeffords, Behan, Rule, and the others wasted no time in issuing criminal indictments against three of Arizona's most prominent Republicans: surveyor general Royal A. Johnson; Lewis Wolfley, later governor of Arizona; and U.S. attorney James A. Zabriskie, who was responsible for giving legal advice to the very grand jury that indicted him. The charge: each had made a ten-dollar donation to a Republican campaign fund. Although such contributions were plainly protected by the free-speech provisions of the First Amendment, the Democratic operatives on the grand jury saw what they thought was an easy way to get rid of three Republican opponents. The U.S. Civil Service Act, which they relied on, prohibited federal officers from receiving bribes and gratuities and from giving gifts to their superiors. It manifestly had nothing to do with political donations. The indictments were so flimsy and blatantly political that they were later dismissed by the federal court.[27]

Next the grand jurors tackled the expenses of the current legislative assembly, which became known as the "Thieving Thirteenth" owing to its extravagant expenditures. They found that territorial legislators had violated the law by spending almost $47,000 in excess of the amount authorized by Congress. The grand jury found a federal statute that authorized territorial legislatures to spend no more than $4,000 on printing costs. Ignoring the fact that this limit applied only to printing, they concluded that all the expenses over that sum were in violation of federal law: "The outrageous appropriations . . . were the result of a venal conspiracy and . . . someone should be punished." While it was true that the legislature had violated the statute by spending almost $17,000 on printing, the rest of the expenditures were for clerical help and related expenses that did not violate federal law in the least.[28]

The grand jurors also issued a scathing criticism of the former U.S. marshal, Republican Crawley P. Dake, for purportedly canceling a $2,300 contract to purchase a large supply of firewood from a private woodcutter. They did not bother to explain what violation of federal law this constituted. In fact, this was a civil dispute entirely beyond the scope of the grand jury's authority. U.S. attorney James Zabriskie, shocked that they had indicted him, tried to counsel the grand jurors to follow the law rather than politics, but they rejected his advice. On October 19 they filed into Judge Fitzgerald's courtroom and told him that "in the opinion of this grand jury, as U.S. District Attorney Zabriskie is not in harmony with this body, he is not a proper legal advisor to guide and direct this body in the matters which it had under consideration." Judge Fitzgerald explained that Zabriskie had been "properly appointed to the position of U.S. attorney" and "it was the duty of the attorney to advise the grand jury on law points."[29]

Both Zabriskie and Judge Fitzgerald explained to the grand jurors that, as a federal body, they lacked jurisdiction over county matters. The grand jurors responded by pressing Zabriskie to resign, but he vowed to stay on and clear his name. Future governor Lewis Wolfley, one of the indicted figures, later charged that the grand jury, after indicting Zabriskie, "acted without legal advice." Now the grand jurors turned their wrath on Judge Fitzgerald. As Wolfley explained, "In the midst of the county investigation, and at the *instigation of said grand jury*, the Judge was removed by telegram, presumably, for telling them that they had no legal right to consider County matters, there being no question relating to the violation of any U.S. law." Judge Fitzgerald's suspension from office on October 23, 1885, shocked the Tucson bar. The Old Pueblo's lawyers voted unanimously to support his reinstatement, concluding, "We do not know the cause of his suspension and greatly regret it." Contrary to Mose Drachman's assertion that Fitzgerald was unfair, the newspapers commented on his impartiality. Said the *San Francisco Bulletin*, "No Arizona Justice has ever enjoyed to a greater degree the esteem and confidence of the people than does Judge Fitzgerald." Drachman later claimed that Fitzgerald left Tucson in the private railroad car of Charles Crocker, one of the Big Four who had founded the Southern Pacific. "This certainly showed the close connection between the S. P. and Judge Fitzgerald," said Drachman.[30]

Paul heard rumors that the grand jurors were now looking into the allegations of ballot-box stuffing in Tucson. On October 16 he wrote to Harry Barron in San Francisco: "The U.S. Grand Jury are in session here and Capt. Ross, Capt. Jeffords, Tom Farish, John Behan are on it, and they with Pin Head Hughes and a few others are trying to dig up some frauds in the last election and every man that I have done a favor to is in it. They have exhausted themselves here and have now gone afishing in San Francisco. . . . If they bring you before them I hope you will testify to what you told me about the mistake in the tally when you was keeping tally." Paul's last reference was to the private tally Barron had kept while the votes were counted.[31]

The grand jurors either interviewed George Martin or obtained a copy of his affidavit, for they now summoned witnesses whom Martin had identified. Several Wells Fargo employees testified that the public seal was briefly missing in November, but they could not recall on which date. Douglass Snyder and his clerk testified that the ballots were kept in his store and that one of his office keys had been misplaced. Charles M. Strauss, the former mayor who had claimed during the election trial to be a handwriting expert, now asserted that the wax found on the ballot box was a different color than that used by Wells Fargo. He offered no explanation as to how he knew this. The Wells Fargo employees, who knew what color sealing wax they used, were never asked about it. Harry Barron was also questioned, and he responded: "I swear positively without any equivocation whatever that I have never told to any person anything whatever in regard to changing any ballots . . . nor have I stated anything to any person either directly or indirectly in regard to any fraud of any kind having been perpetrated. . . . I swear further that I know of no fraud whatever having been perpetrated in connection with said election." Although the grand jury had been unable to corroborate Martin's story, they nonetheless began preparing indictments in the election case.[32]

In the meantime, President Cleveland appointed William H. Barnes, an experienced and capable Illinois attorney, as Fitzgerald's replacement. Barnes, like the new president, was a Democrat. He traveled promptly to Arizona, where, in a formal court proceeding on October 28, just five days after Fitzgerald's suspension, Barnes took over. No sooner was he sworn in than the grand jurors filed into the packed courtroom to deliver their final report. Paul was incensed, but hardly surprised, by what happened next. The grand jury announced the indictment of Harry Barron for destroying ballots and perjury, and it charged Paul, George Martin, and Constable Martin W. Brady with conspiracy. Judge Barnes had no choice but to issue bench warrants for them. Paul then suffered the supreme indignity of being arrested and brought into court, along with Barron and Brady, where they quickly posted $500 bail each and were released. Barron had no money, so Paul cosigned his bail bond. The final affront: the arresting officer was none other than the vote-rigger Charley Kresham, whom William K. Meade had recently appointed a deputy U.S. marshal. The *San Francisco Chronicle* reported, "The work of the Grand Jury attracted the attention of the entire territory. . . . When the report was made this evening the courthouse was crowded with citizens and no such event was ever witnessed in Tucson."[33]

The depth of Paul's anger can only be imagined. It was the first—and only—time in his life that he had been charged with a crime. The sheriff consulted with his lawyers, and they advised him that the indictment was without any legal basis whatsoever. First, a charge of conspiracy, standing alone, did not exist under the law. There had to be proof of a conspiracy to commit an underlying crime, such as election fraud. Regardless, at that time the federal government had no jurisdiction over fraud committed in an election of local officials. In 1894 the U.S. Supreme Court explicitly ruled that the purpose of the federal voting law was to prevent fraud that would affect the vote for representatives in Congress; it did not bring elections for state or territorial officers under the control of the federal government. Yet this distinction did not prevent the grand jury from indicting Paul. The grand jurors may well have been aware that their indictments were unsupportable. However, their investigation had allowed them to interview witnesses secretly, under oath, and to exert pressure on Harry Barron, something that would soon give Bob Paul no end of trouble.[34]

CHAPTER SIXTEEN

Politics and Perjury

In mid-November 1885, Sheriff Paul got a tip that Frank Morton, the long-missing murderer who had escaped in the big Tucson jailbreak, was hiding out in Sonora. He headed south to Mexico and disappeared for four weeks while hunting the fugitive. Reported the *Star*, "The long absence . . . causes some uneasiness among Paul's friends as to his safety." For her part, Margaret was heartsick with worry. But her husband returned safely, without Morton. The killer vanished, finally surfacing in 1892 in Los Angeles, where he was arrested for burglary under the name Fred Morgan. Nathan Appel, by then a Los Angeles police officer, recognized him as the fugitive murderer. The Los Angeles chief of police notified Paul, who presumably turned the report over to the Pima County sheriff. That official took no steps to return Morton to Tucson to face homicide charges. Morton ended up serving three terms in San Quentin prior to his final release in 1904, and he was never sent back to Arizona. His fate is unknown.[1]

Upon Sheriff Paul's return from Mexico, he found three anxious letters from Harry Barron, expressing concern about the criminal charges. On December 14 Paul replied: "All my lawyers tell me there is nothing in those indictments—and in fact the lawyers on the other side say the same thing. The whole object of the action of that Grand Jury was to get evidence to try to reopen the Contest Case again. . . . Do not give yourself any trouble over the indictments for they cannot amount to anything. . . . You know very well that a certain gang has been saying that they would have me in the [Yuma prison] Hole for the last three years, they know they deserve it themselves and that I know all about them."[2]

By this time the normally healthy Margaret found herself feeling unwell. Soon the reason for her mysterious illness became evident: at age forty, she was two months pregnant. Her morning sickness was so troublesome that Paul arranged to send her by train to San Jose after Christmas. There she could be cared for by son Robert, then a senior at Santa Clara College, and daughter Agnes, a student at Notre Dame College. Paul knew she was in good hands, for her sisters in San Francisco were also nearby if help was needed. He also understood that Margaret's worrying about his safety, coupled with the stress caused by the criminal charges against him, made a change of scenery better for her emotional health. After seeing Margaret off at the railroad depot, Paul turned his attentions back to the election fight.[3]

The preliminary hearing in federal court on the charges against Paul, Harry Barron, Constable Brady, and George Martin was scheduled for January 1886. Barron had no money for train fare from San Francisco, and Sheriff Paul was eager for him to return and respond to the charges. On January 5 Paul wired Barron seventy-five dollars to pay his expenses to Tucson. Once there, on January 21, a terrified Barron met secretly with Eugene Shaw's lawyers. In hope of making a deal, he signed an affidavit in which he claimed that the night after the election returns had been released, he, Paul, and Brady had closely examined them. He provided a different version of his conversation with the sheriff. According to Barron, Paul said to him, "I am beat."

"How is that?" Barron asked.

"Come in here and look and count for yourself," Paul replied. Barron counted the returns, and saw that Paul was short. He told Paul, "You are sheriff, and if you will give me the reins, I think you can continue to be sheriff."

When Paul asked how, Barron replied, "If we can get the ballots we can fix them and demand a recount."

Paul responded, "That is something I do not like to do, for I have never done any dirty work." According to Barron, "The matter was dropped then, and Paul said he would think over it, with the understanding that if the work was to be done, I would be the one to do it."[4]

Harry Barron claimed that a week later he and Constable Brady got the key to Snyder's store and surreptitiously entered late at night, removed the sealed package of ballots from a drawer, and took them to the sheriff's office. There, in the presence of Paul, they opened the package and scratched off Shaw's name, replacing it with Paul's, on enough ballots to alter the election. Barron said that Brady used a coin to impress a wax seal on the inner package, and a wax sealer "similar to those used by Wells Fargo & Company's Express" to affix a seal to the outer package. Then he and Brady returned the packet of ballots to Snyder's store.[5]

This affidavit was exactly what Shaw and his attorneys had hoped for, and they promptly began preparing a motion for a new trial of the election lawsuit. Barron also told them that he had numerous letters from Paul that proved the sheriff's guilt. He said that the letters were in his San Francisco home. Barron hoped to use them as leverage to make a deal: if the Democrats would get the indictment against him dismissed, he would produce the supposedly incriminating correspondence. Then Barron, fearful of what Paul might do when he found out, departed immediately for San Francisco. Shaw was desperate to get Barron's letters, and he asked for help from one of the barber's Tucson friends, Eli B. Gifford, the gambler and owner of the Fashion Saloon. Gifford—the same man who had run against Paul in the Republican primary—was happy to aid Shaw. He wrote to Barron to convince him to turn over the letters. On February 1, Barron responded without mentioning the letters, but telling Gifford, "I suppose there is hell poping [sic]. Giff, I am satisfied when Paul finds out what I have done he will go off my bonds and have me sent for and put me in jail."[6]

Early in February detective Len Harris was in San Francisco on railroad business and looked up Harry Barron, who later described the meeting to Gifford: "Len Harris was here to see me. He wanted to know what got into me for making those affidavits. Says he, did you not make them. I told him yes. He says has not Paul been your friend. I told him things looked very blue for me. I would look out for myself and try and get out of this trouble. . . . I want to wash my hands from the case and tend to my business. He says I was foolish to let the other side pull the wool over my eyes. He says they had no case and Paul would get away with it. He says Paul will be here in a few days with a crazy man and he is coming to see me. He will get as much satisfaction as Harris got. The work is done and that settles it. I suppose Bob will give me hell. But I think I can stand him off."[7]

A few days later Paul came to California by train, dropping off a prisoner at the state insane asylum in Stockton, which by contract housed the mentally ill from Arizona. Then he continued on to San Francisco, where he met with Harris and Frank Rhodes, a Sacramento saloonkeeper, gambler, and Republican boss who supported the Southern Pacific. They found

Southern Pacific Railroad detective Len Harris. He was one of Bob Paul's closest friends. Author's collection.

Barron in Chris Buckley's saloon. Buckley, the notorious "Blind Boss," never held political office but ran Democratic politics in San Francisco in the 1880s until he was indicted for bribery in 1891. The noted gunfighter Dave Neagle, former police chief of Tombstone, was in Buckley's saloon, along with Big Ed Burns, then a San Francisco deputy sheriff but infamous in the West as a crooked gambler and hardcase. Barron feared Paul's wrath and sought Buckley's protection. As Barron told it, Paul was furious and felt betrayed: "Paul told Buckley that I had made those affidavits for money. I told him that was not so. He is hurt. He says to me well you gave it to me. I told him yes, I had to protect myself." But Sheriff Paul was peaceable, as Barron recalled: "I thought Paul would do me up here the way he started to talk with me. But there happened to be a great many friends of mine in Buckley's at the time, among them Dave Nagle [and] Big Burns and they have no love for Bob."[8]

After describing the encounter in a letter to Gifford, Barron said of Paul, "He told me in presence of Buckley that everything will be alright. If everything will be alright what is he so worried about." Barron then asked Gifford to enlist the aid of Cameron H. King, a prominent Democrat and one of Shaw's lawyers: "I wished Cameron King would write a few lines to Buckley showing Buckley what a hard box I was in and that I will be protected through him. Buckley is my friend and wants to see me get out alright. A letter from King to Buckley would be some benefit to me and show Buckley that Paul lies to him." In his reply, Gifford continued to press Barron to give him the Paul letters. On March 6, 1886, a reluctant Barron responded, "In regard of those letters, I will write to you again in a few days. I want to get some advice and I may send them either to you or Shaw or may be advised to send them to King. But I will hold them and let you know in my next [letter]. I met Harris here yesterday, the 5th. He says Paul is all right and everything will be dismissed, but I ought to send those letters to Bob. I told him I would keep them to protect myself with."[9]

While Gifford continued to write to Barron, pestering him to release the letters, Shaw's attorneys turned up the heat on George Martin to produce another affidavit. What methods they used are unknown, but on February 6, 1886, he signed a long declaration, repeating his claim that he pilfered the Wells Fargo sealer and charging that Superintendent Muir of the Southern Pacific was present when he gave it to Paul. According to Martin, Muir announced that Wells Fargo's Jim Hume had offered to procure a Tucson sealer from the main office in San Francisco. Martin did not explain why Hume offered to do this, nor why a sealer for the Tucson office would be in San Francisco. Martin also gave a detailed description of how Paul, Len Harris, Muir, and Muir's assistant, W. W. Booth, had obtained free railroad passes for him to leave town.[10]

Two days later Shaw filed a motion for a new trial, with the affidavits of Barron and Martin as his main evidence. Louis Hughes published the two affidavits in full in the *Star*, creating a public sensation. Democrats were ecstatic, for they believed they had solid evidence of fraud. But Hughes failed to mention in his columns that Martin and Barron had serious—virtually fatal—credibility issues: Martin was pressing a lawsuit against Wells Fargo and had offered to sell his testimony to the highest bidder, and Barron had previously sworn before the grand jury that no fraud had occurred. Paul's lawyers promptly filed affidavits signed by Paul, Muir, Constable Brady, and others denying the charges in great detail. W. B. Groseclose, the

Wells Fargo agent, also signed a detailed declaration showing that it was impossible for Martin to have pilfered the company's wax sealer. Hughes, of course, neglected to publish any of Paul's affidavits.[11]

In the meantime, Gifford continued his entreaties, but Barron still would not send him the letters. Barron continued to hope that he could get the charges against him dismissed in exchange for turning over the correspondence. On March 12 he wrote Gifford:

> You must not think hard of me because I did not send them letters. My wife and children begged me not to do so and my friends and several attornies [sic] told me not to part with them. I am surprised at Paul making those affidavits swearing that he and Brady were not present and that he never saw any ballots and that the ballots were not removed. My letters will show with his own signatures that he knew all about it and got the key for me and gave Katz $1,000.00 for the key and that he was there and help[ed] and that he gave Berger $500.00 . . . for Berger to give me the ballots of San Xavier. I brought them to the sheriff's office and changed 1 ballot and returned the ballots to Berger and then he sealed them up in a large envelope. . . . I got $50.00 from Berger for doing what I did. Brady, Paul and Ricabaugh [sic] was present when we made the agreement. . . . I could never have done what I did if Paul did not tell me to.[12]

Barron's claims about the San Xavier poll were false. The San Xavier ballots were kept in a cigar box and were still enclosed in it when they were delivered to court; they were never "sealed up in a large envelope." His new claims of cash bribes to J. M. Berger and store clerk Marcus Katz and of changing one San Xavier ballot were never mentioned in his court affidavit. He appears to have invented additional details in the hope that he could use them to negotiate a dismissal of the federal charges. On March 16 Barron finally produced two telegrams and twelve letters he claimed to have received from Paul. None of them confirmed his claims to Gifford.

Sheriff Paul readily admitted writing both telegrams and most of the letters. They consisted of his correspondence with Barron about the grand jury investigation, his responses to Barron's requests for a $250 loan, and his arrangements to pay for Barron's trip to Tucson to testify. None of those pieces of correspondence were remotely incriminating. Three of the letters, however, contained damaging statements. Unlike the others, they were undated, not written on the sheriff's official letterhead, and penned in a strange hand. One of them read, "Harry: You think I am a son of a bitch. I will tell you the truth. I am in hell's hole and may have to go to the wall. I cannot send you any money at present. . . . All I ask of you is to give me a little time and you will not regret it." Another said, "Your letter is received, there is no use of talking about five hundred at present. I will send you two hundred when I hear from you again. I think you should be satisfied with that. Nothing can be got out of Martin. He has quit. He is all right." Paul, on seeing the letters, prepared an affidavit in which he pronounced the last three to be forgeries. Existing copies of the three letters in the court file show plainly that they were written in different handwriting from the rest. Barron, recognizing that the authentic letters contained nothing damaging to Paul, evidently prepared the other three himself.[13]

Meanwhile, on March 11, 1885, Eugene Shaw's motion for a new trial was heard in Judge Barnes's packed courtroom. Paul's lawyers argued that there was no legal basis to reopen the case, but Judge Barnes ruled against him. The hearing was resumed on March 22, and for the next week the attorneys read into the record the numerous affidavits and letters that both sides had gathered. Shaw presented a declaration in which he swore that he neither promised nor gave money to Barron or Martin for their testimony. Nonetheless, the *Citizen* repeatedly charged that the two had been bribed. Final arguments were made on the 29th, and Judge Barnes took the matter under advisement. On April 3 he issued a detailed ruling, summarizing the evidence against Paul and finding that the affidavits presented by each side were in conflict. He said, "It is at best an unsatisfactory method to try a question of fact by affidavits. . . . The witness cannot be subjected to cross examination." Ruled Judge Barnes, "Society has the right to demand that no stone be left unturned to ascertain the real truth. . . . In the hope that another trial may make clear the real truth in this case, I conclude that a new trial be ordered."[14]

Judge Barnes had little choice but to order the new trial. The anti-Paul affidavits, if true, were so inflammatory and struck so directly at the heart of the democratic process that it was incumbent upon him to get at the truth. Paul's lawyers immediately filed an appeal to the Arizona Supreme Court. Appellants in civil cases are often required to provide a bond to pay the judgment against them in case they lose their appeal. Judge Barnes ordered Paul to post a bond of $5,000 or, in lieu of that, a $3,600 cash deposit to cover his sheriff's salary while the appeal was pending. The reason for this was that if Paul lost, he would be forced to pay his wages back to the county. Paul should have been able to deposit the cash with the court, for during five years in office he had earned at least $40,000 and perhaps as much as $100,000, a fortune in that era. But as usual, Paul had spent most of his income and was forced to seek out friends to act as sureties on his appeal bond. Shaw's supporters understood that if Paul could not post the bond, his appeal would be dismissed. They systematically contacted Tucson's prominent businessmen in efforts to dissuade them from going on Paul's bond or loaning him any money. But the sheriff's friends were loyal, and he was finally able to post $3,600 in cash. Commented the *Tombstone Epitaph*, "Sheriff Paul has thus won a significant victory over a gang of political boycotters who have attempted to frustrate every endeavor he has made to obtain sureties upon his bond."[15]

Bob Paul had little time to ruminate over his court difficulties, for politics in Tucson meant little to the Mexican bandidos who preyed along the border. Procopio's gang was still active, and according to the *Citizen*, one of them, Gregorio Alvarez, "is known throughout Arizona and Sonora as the worst desperado yet unhung." He had been captured in December near Tubac and jailed for horse theft. The witnesses against him were three Mexicans who, when subpoenaed, skipped to Mexico for fear of testifying against Alvarez. With no evidence against him, the outlaw was released. On the night of April 14, 1886, Paul was handed a warrant for the desperado, charging him with selling a stolen horse in Calabasas. Paul learned that Alvarez was believed to be hiding out at the Salazar ranch, twenty miles south of Tucson. With his son and deputy, John, driving, Paul headed south in a buggy, arriving at Salazar's at daybreak. Paul found the desperado trying to mount his horse to escape. The burly sheriff quickly overpowered Alvarez and clapped him in irons. Then he and John brought their prisoner to the county jail.[16]

In the meantime Shaw's attorney Cameron King made a settlement offer to Paul: if he would drop his appeal and step down by June 15, they would allow him to keep $1,000 of the salary due for that quarter. Paul's lawyers rejected the offer outright. Then gambler Lou Rickabaugh, a friend of both Paul and Shaw, intervened, telling Shaw "it would be better for both to settle it." Shaw's counsel subsequently offered Paul $1,500, which he also rejected. Finally Shaw's lawyers proposed that Paul would keep the salary that he had earned thus far and would be paid back the $3,600 deposit if he would turn the sheriff's office over to Shaw. Louis C. Hughes was present at the meeting when this offer was made.[17]

Paul was under tremendous pressure to settle. On one hand, he and his lawyers recognized that Shaw's case was exceedingly weak. It was based almost entirely on the testimony of Martin and Barron, whose credibility was nearly worthless. But Paul and his lawyers were concerned about the fairness of Judge Barnes, who would be the sole trier of fact. As Lewis Wolfley later said, they believed that Barnes, as a newly appointed Democrat, "was required to make a political decision" in favor of Shaw. Under Arizona law, if Paul lost the election trial, he would be forced to pay back the income he had earned for that term. His earnings for the year and a half he had served were more than $11,000, the loss of which would be a financial disaster. It was a risk he could not afford to take. On June 14, 1886, Paul accepted Shaw's last offer and signed a written settlement agreement that provided that Paul would drop his appeal and Shaw would take over on July 9.[18]

To Arizona Democrats, the settlement was a huge victory. Crowed Louis Hughes, "Good-bye Mr. Paul. Welcome Mr. Eugene O. Shaw to the office to which you was honestly elected by the people!" Democrats believed that they had been vindicated and that Paul had been forced out of office. Before long, Hughes would begin to rewrite history. Even though he had been present during the settlement discussions, he would claim that Paul "was ousted by the judge. On the new trial the fraud was so completely exposed that [Shaw] was reinstalled in the office to which he had been elected." But no judge had ousted Paul, and there had never been a new trial. Unfortunately, many Arizonans would believe Hughes's outrageous fabrications, including his oft-repeated claim that Paul committed fraud at San Simon in 1880.[19]

The reality is that Paul's decision to settle was entirely financial. What he had done with his substantial sheriff's income can only be guessed at. No doubt he spent significant sums for Margaret and the children to spend summers in San Francisco and for John, Robert, and Agnes to attend private colleges in California. Yet that can account for only a fraction of his expenditures. He must have lost some of his money in risky mining ventures. In any event, Paul's foolish investment strategies left him without the funds to fight to clear his name and protect his reputation. Had the case proceeded to trial, Paul would almost certainly have prevailed. His lawyers' fears about Judge Barnes proved groundless; the jurist later wrote that he believed Paul had done nothing wrong. Even Shaw's own attorneys, Anderson, Hereford, and Lovell, subsequently expressed misgivings about the case. Paul's decision to avoid a trial was the biggest miscalculation of his professional life. The *Paul v. Shaw* case would leave an almost indelible black mark on an exemplary career.[20]

Did Harry Barron tell the truth about stuffing the ballot box at Paul's request? The answer to this question can be found in events that took place some years later in San Francisco, where Barron ran a barbershop and worked as a ward heeler for the Republican Party. His political connections got him appointments with both the fire and street departments. He lost his fireman's job in 1888 for unspecified "irregularities" and was fired by the street department in 1889 after he was prosecuted for a scheme to steal paving blocks. During the 1890s he obtained political appointments as a San Francisco deputy county clerk and then as a health inspector. As deputy clerk he was denounced for unlawfully attempting to influence a justice of the peace, and as health inspector he was accused of accepting a bribe. By 1908 Barron was running a saloon and illegal gambling hall in San Francisco's Tenderloin district, and in 1913 he was arrested for forging thousands of names on a petition to overturn a red-light abatement law. Barron's conflicting statements and production of forged letters in the *Paul v. Shaw* case, coupled with the dishonesty and unscrupulousness he later displayed in San Francisco, answer the question quite plainly.[21]

There was one bright spot for the Paul family that spring. Margaret, now forty-one, was staying with her sisters in San Francisco. Paul jumped at the chance to visit his pregnant wife when James Mugan, a fugitive Tucson embezzler, was located in San Francisco on May 2. The sheriff boarded a train for the city, where the next day he and police detective Ben Bohen arrested Mugan in front of a Bush Street saloon. He stayed with Margaret the rest of May, while unsuccessfully seeking to return the embezzler to Arizona. Paul appeared repeatedly in court with his requisition papers, but Mugan was politically connected to "Blind Boss" Buckley, and he hired good lawyers who managed to create one delay after another. Finally Paul received a telegram urging him to return to Tucson. Apaches were again on the warpath, pursued both by the army and by a civilian militia from Pima County. The sheriff went back to Tucson on June 1, too late to take part in the Apache hunt.[22]

Now he started to wrap up his affairs as sheriff. But Paul was to handle one more murder case as the county's top lawman. On June 13 he got word that a Papago Indian named Benancio Rios, a relative of Chief Ascension Rios, had murdered a girl at the Mission San Xavier. It was first reported that Rios had killed his wife for being unfaithful. Paul went to San Xavier, where he learned that Rios, in a drunken brawl, had stomped to death an Indian girl aged only twelve or fourteen. Paul learned from Chief Ascension that the girl was not his wife, but his cousin, and that the killing was entirely without justification. He arrested Rios and brought him to jail in Tucson to face the grand jury. It was his last arrest as sheriff of Pima County.[23]

On July 2, 1886, Margaret gave birth to a healthy boy, Edgar Havlin, in San Francisco. The happy news was promptly wired to her husband in Tucson, and it must have relieved some of the stress of the election litigation. A journalist who saw him wrote, "Noticing a peculiarly humorous twinkle in Bob Paul's eye this morning, a *Citizen* reporter inquired the cause of it, and was informed that the cause was of the masculine gender, which weighed twelve pounds, with a voice that weighs anywhere in the neighborhood of a ton or so."[24]

Eugene Shaw took over as sheriff on July 9, soon appointing as deputies his younger brother Matthew and vote-riggers Charley Kresham and Pedro Pellon. Paul, after closing his sheriff's accounts, returned to San Francisco on July 15. He sorely needed to escape the bitter recriminations in Tucson. His reunion with Margaret must have been a joyful one, matched only by his delight in their new baby boy. The couple spent a month in the city, until Margaret felt well enough to travel, then left for their Tucson home on August 17. Their son John, now also unemployed as his father's deputy, returned to work for Wells Fargo. He spent a year as a cashier at the Wells Fargo offices in Stockton and San Diego, California, and the following year as a messenger in Mexico City. Returning to Arizona, he served in several of the company's offices before being appointed Wells Fargo agent in Nogales.[25]

Paul had made an excellent record as Pima County sheriff. Irrespective of the constant criticisms of Louis Hughes, he had enforced the law aggressively and impartially. But did he treat Pima County's large Hispanic population fairly? In 1883 *El Fronterizo*, Tucson's Spanish-language newspaper, had criticized Sheriff Paul for failing to publish the county's delinquent tax list in Spanish. The editor argued that by failing to print the list in Spanish, Mexican Americans would not know whether they owed back taxes and might thereby lose their property by a tax sale. That criticism was entirely misplaced, because appearing on the list was not the process by which a delinquent taxpayer could lose his property. Instead, Arizona law required that the district attorney had to bring a lawsuit against a delinquent taxpayer—and win it—before he could sell the taxpayer's property to collect back taxes. County publishing contracts were rich plums for newspapers, and in Paul's case he gave his patronage to the Republican journal, the *Citizen*, and, for a time, to the *Arizona Mining Index*. *El Fronterizo*'s real complaint was that Sheriff Paul gave the printing contract to the *Citizen* and not to it.[26]

Examination of Tucson's newspapers failed to reveal any other reports of unfair treatment of Hispanics by Sheriff Paul. Given Louis Hughes's antipathy toward Paul, he would have readily published any such complaints. Paul and his deputies did arrest Hispanics for a myriad of offenses. The sole surviving Pima County jail register from Paul's three terms as sheriff shows a total of 154 prisoners from April 15, 1881, to September 9, 1882. Of these, one was black, four were Indian, four were Chinese, seventy had Spanish surnames, and the balance was Anglo. Though it is not possible to determine which prisoners were arrested individually by Paul or by his deputies, constables, or the Tucson police, of the total arrests by Pima county lawmen, 45 percent of those arrested were Hispanic. At that time, the population of Pima County was roughly one-half Spanish surnamed, which means that Sheriff Paul and his fellow lawmen arrested Hispanics in proportion to their numbers in the overall county population. It can therefore be concluded that Paul did not unfairly target Hispanics as criminal suspects.[27]

Bob Paul brought a significant level of diplomacy, professionalism, and fairness to the sheriff's job. He established new techniques in tax collecting and even aggressively pursued collection efforts against his own patron, the Southern Pacific. He employed Spanish-speaking deputies and established a close working relationship with the authorities of Mexico. He endeavored to hire men of good character and sound judgment. Incidents of trigger-happy policing were all but unknown during his administration. He taught officer safety to his deputies and ordered his jailors never to handle prisoners alone. He strove to arrest the most dangerous criminals without violence. Even in his gunfights with the Red Jack gang, he gave the outlaws a chance to surrender before killing them. And he led by example. Despite a wide reputation for ironhanded fearlessness, he was a quiet family man, a devoted husband and father, and a prominent and influential civic leader.

Not all of Paul's efforts to improve diplomacy and professionalism were successful. Without his personal leadership, the Tucson Rangers had violated Mexican sovereignty and caused a significant diplomatic incident. He had hired an incompetent and dishonest jailer, George Cooler, who was responsible for one of Tucson's biggest jailbreaks. Another of Paul's jailers may have impregnated a female prisoner. His personal and political friendship with Wyatt Earp clouded his judgment, and consequently he never sought to arrest Earp on the Frank Stilwell murder warrant.

On balance, however, Paul's record as sheriff was an extraordinary one. He resisted lynch mobs, tracked Apaches, and brought in scores of cattle thieves, killers, and highway robbers. Over and over again, journalists commented on his coolness and courage in the face of extreme danger. Though subjected to persistent and even vicious personal attacks by his political enemies, he never retaliated or abused his official authority in revenge. No doubt Paul's easygoing personality reinforced his knack for evenhanded enforcement of the law. As exemplified by his confrontation with the Papagos at Coyote village, he was able to set aside his feelings of anger and humiliation to defuse a crisis fraught with the potential for explosive violence.

With what remained of his sheriff's salary, Paul bought a large smelting plant at the Columbia copper mine near Arivaca in the Santa Rita Mountains. It had a thirty-ton water jacket, boiler, engine, and blast furnace and could handle up to eighty tons of copper ore a day. For the next year he worked assiduously at running the smelter with a crew of workmen. But the Columbia mine was not a rich one, and Paul struggled to make his expenses. In the meantime, he remained active in politics. That fall Eugene O. Shaw was a candidate for reelection. Paul supported the Republican challenger, rancher Lewis H. Gormley. Republicans were not shy about accusing Democrats of fraud. The *Citizen* charged that Shaw's new deputies, Charley Kresham and Pedro Pellon, "were very industriously at work naturalizing Mexicans who did not understand the nature of their acts in swearing an allegiance to the United States." One of the new citizens confessed that he was underage and that Pellon had offered him blankets and clothing for his vote. Soon afterward Kresham and Pellon were accused of releasing from jail Hilario Urquides, a politically connected saloonkeeper, in exchange for his vote.[28]

The *Citizen* next reported that the Tanque Verde precinct was once again the subject of ballot fraud. In the 1884 election, seventeen votes had been polled there, but now forty-nine voters—more than its population of voting-age adults—had registered in the precinct. The newspaper printed several affidavits from Tanque Verde residents listing names of voters who were either fictitious or resided elsewhere. The *Citizen* also charged that settlers on the San Pedro River in Cochise County had been induced to register in Pima County and that the main beneficiary of the fraud would be Sheriff Shaw. "By acquiescing in this method Mr. Shaw himself becomes a party to the fraudulent schemes," said the *Citizen*, "and he is therefore as guilty of the outrages as any of his foul associates."[29]

Another method by which Tucson's political bosses then ran election campaigns was explained by lawman Jeff Milton to his biographer, J. Evetts Haley: "The 'good politicians' made a habit of corralling blocs of Mexican voters the night before election. The Democrats herded theirs into Goodwin Hall, kept them liberally supplied with whiskey until morning, then handed them a registration receipt and a ticket apiece, and flanking them with a squad of guards marched them down to the polls to cast their free and democratic choice of office for a dollar a head." Sheriff Shaw also came under severe Republican criticism for overcharging fees and failing to collect certain taxes. But the charges of fraud and mismanagement changed very little in Pima County. In the election on November 6, 1886, Shaw was elected for a two-year term.[30]

Paul was especially irritated that Eli B. Gifford and other Republicans had once again supported Sheriff Shaw. That, coupled with the strain of the election lawsuit and his anger at Democratic voting fraud, embroiled him, uncharacteristically, in an altercation soon after the election. Recalled Mose Drachman, then a sixteen-year-old clerk for his uncle, Sam Drachman:

> In the election of 1886, when Shaw defeated Gormley, Paul and the S. P. gang tried in every possible way to defeat him and were much incensed because they lost out. They were particularly sore against the Republicans who helped elect Shaw. One evening, I was standing in front of the Fashion Saloon, talking with E. B. Gifford when Bob Paul came by. I think he was intoxicated, which was strange for him—he was usually a very temperate man and it was the only time I ever saw him in such a condition. He came up to Gifford and said in a threatening manner:

"You told So and So that if I ever drew a gun on you, you'd take it away from me," following the statement with a string of oaths. Gifford, in a very quiet way replied:

"Mr. Paul, I never said such a thing, and furthermore, I have always said you are a brave man. If any one told you that, they told you a lie."

It was only a few minutes before a large crowd gathered, supporters of both sides; for a few minutes it looked as though there would be a shooting affair. The Chief of Police was a small man named [Matthew] Johnson—a fearless fighter in his day but an old man at this time. He was a bitter opponent of Paul. The Constable, named Brady, was a staunch Paul partisan, and naturally, Johnson and Brady were enemies. Johnson appeared on the scene, anxious for a fight, and desirous of showing his authority as Chief of Police. He shouted to Paul and his friends, "Here, clear the sidewalk!" and with that, Brady picked Johnson up and threw him across Congress Street—of course it was a narrow street in those days, but it was quite a toss. I ran into my uncle's cigar store and hid under the counter. I didn't know what was going to happen next. In the midst of this turmoil, E. O. Shaw came on the scene. He was a big man and towered above the crowd. He spoke in a calm voice and everybody cooled down in a hurry. It was only a minute or two before everything was serene but for a while it certainly looked bad.[31]

This was the only documented instance of Bob Paul taking part in a public, personal quarrel. The relentless political attacks had plainly taken their toll. Accordingly, after the election he disappeared from public life. His enemies thought that he was finished with politics and that his law enforcement career was over. They could not have been more mistaken.[32]

CHAPTER SEVENTEEN

Manhunt in Old Mexico

Not far from Tucson, on a clear spring night in 1887, a band of daring outlaws pulled off Arizona's first train robbery. It set off a chain reaction of extraordinary events that would take Bob Paul deep into Mexico for the bloodiest exploit of his long career. Train holdups in the far West were then quite rare. There were two in Nevada in 1870, one in California in 1881 and another in 1888, one in Utah in 1883, and two in New Mexico in 1883 and 1884. During the late 1880s they became increasingly common and violent, reaching epidemic proportions in the 1890s. Between 1890 and 1903 there were 341 actual and attempted train robberies in the United States, which resulted in the deaths of ninety-nine persons.[1]

On the night of April 27, 1887, a westbound Southern Pacific train entered the Cienega Creek wash, midway between Pantano and Papago Stations and seventeen miles southeast of Tucson. Three outlaws were waiting there. The leaders of this youthful bunch were Jack "Kid" Smith and John "Dick" Maier, a hardcase pair of former railroad brakemen who had met in El Paso, Texas. There they ran with the notorious "Cowboy Bob" Rennick and established a bloody record. On January 4, 1886, Smith and Rennick had robbed and murdered a merchant, Jules Boisselier, across the line in Paso del Norte (now Ciudad Juarez). On July 9, Smith, Rennick, and an accomplice held up the famous Gem Saloon in El Paso, shooting and wounding three patrons. On March 15, 1887, Kid Smith shot down and badly wounded an El Paso police officer. The next day, Smith, Maier, and gang members J. M. "Doc" Smart and George Green made arrangements to flee to Arizona, where they intended to rob a train. With the help of two railroad friends, brakeman William Skidmore and freight conductor Alfred Syndor, they stowed away on a Southern Pacific train scheduled to leave for Tucson. But Doc Smart got cold feet and failed to show up, so Smith, Maier, and Green departed El Paso without him.[2]

The trio spent several weeks in Tucson, obtaining supplies and scouting a good location for the holdup. Finally they headed out of town on foot to Cienega Creek and made camp in the Rincon Mountains. Cienega Creek is a dry wash up to a half mile wide, and it was often subject to flash floods. The railroad followed along the north side of the streambed, the tracks supported here and there by rickety trestles, the victims of frequent washouts. On the evening of April 27, Smith, Maier, and Green piled railroad ties on the track and set a red signal lantern on top. Then the outlaws took up positions on the embankment above the tracks. As the passenger train neared, the engineer spotted the red warning light and halted the train. Smith, masked and with a pistol in each fist, clambered aboard the engine cab. Then he and Maier marched the engineer and fireman to the express car. There Wells Fargo messenger Charles F. Smith was ordered to get out, but instead he slammed the side door shut and bolted it. At that, the other two bandits on top of the embankment opened fire, and a half dozen pistol balls tore though the walls and roof of the car. But still Messenger Smith refused to give up. Then the robbers handed the engineer a stick of giant powder, ordering him to light it and place it beneath the express car. The engineer and fireman pleaded with Smith to surrender, and finally, after hiding $3,500 in the stove, he opened the door.

The desperadoes searched Smith, taking the key to the safe. Then they uncoupled the mail and express cars from the rest of the train, climbed onto the engine, and headed toward Tucson. En route they leisurely rifled the express and mail cars, taking $3,000 from the Wells Fargo safe and another $3,000 from the mail car, but missing the $3,500 in the stove. Then the robbers took the locomotive to the outskirts of Tucson, put it into reverse, and jumped off. The engine continued several miles down the track until it ran out of steam. Then Maier walked into Tucson, undetected in the darkness. Smith and Green hiked into the foothills of the Rincons, buried some Mexican silver coin, and joined Maier the following night in Tucson. After spending two days in a lodging house, they met their crooked railroad friends, Al Syndor and William Skidmore, who gave all three a free return

Cienega Creek wash in 1888. It was the scene of the train robberies of April 27 and August 10, 1887. Courtesy of the Arizona Historical Society/Tucson, 6945.

trip to El Paso in their caboose. On the ride back, Smith and Maier described the holdup to Syndor and Skidmore. "That was pretty slick done," the railroaders remarked. "Any ordinary sucker could hold up a train on that road."[3]

By daylight, news of the daring robbery had hit the telegraph wires, featuring prominently in newspapers throughout the country. Messenger Smith was widely praised in the press for his stove ruse. Deputy Sheriff Matthew Shaw and Undersheriff Charlie Shibell, with Papago Indian trailers and a troop of cavalry from Fort Lowell, searched for the bandits in vain. Wells Fargo and the Southern Pacific offered rewards of $1,000 each for the robbers. Wells Fargo officials asked Bob Paul to take up the case, but he was busy with his copper smelter and could not help. Instead, company detectives Jim Hume and John Thacker rushed to Tucson. Hume immediately recognized that the bandits, unlike most Arizona desperadoes, were not cowhands. Their ability to uncouple the cars and operate the engine stamped them as railroad men. For three months local officers, augmented by express and railroad detectives, as well as U.S. Marshal William K. Meade, ran down leads. A number of suspects were picked up in the massive dragnet, but all were released for lack of evidence.[4]

During the spring and summer of 1887, Sheriff Eugene Shaw was gone from Tucson. Soon after starting his term as sheriff, he fell seriously ill and took a trip to California to recuperate. He returned to Tucson in March, but became so sick he could not get out of bed. On April 9 Shaw obtained a leave of absence and went back to his old family home in North Carolina to regain his health. Charlie Shibell served as acting sheriff in his absence. The exact nature of Shaw's illness was mysterious. According to the *Tombstone Epitaph*, he suffered from "glandular trouble"; another newspaper said it was lymphoma. Louis C. Hughes claimed—predictably—that his sickness was brought on by "the terrible mental and nervous strain he endured in making a contest for the people which will be forever memorable in the history of Arizona." A recent writer concluded that he suffered from severe cirrhosis of the liver brought on by a long history of alcoholism. His condition deteriorated, and in August Shaw sought a promise that his younger brother and deputy be appointed in his place. He soon resigned by telegram, and on September 7, 1887, Matthew F. Shaw, twenty-eight, was appointed sheriff. A month later, on October 9, Eugene Shaw died at age thirty-seven and was buried in North Carolina. After all the political battling, litigation, and personal acrimony, he had acted as sheriff of Pima County for only eight months.[5]

Paul remained busy with his smelting works, but he was in desperate financial straits. After realizing that the Columbia mine did not produce enough copper ore to keep the smelter operating full-time, he decided to move the smelter to Tucson. The city had no smelting works, and local ore had to be shipped out of state for extraction. Paul believed that if the smelter was brought to Tucson and set up near the railroad, it could handle copper and lead from mines all over southern Arizona. This was an expensive proposition, one that he could not afford on his own. It would cost $5,000 to dismantle the huge smelter, transport it to Tucson, and reassemble it. In September, in an effort to drum up public support, he and his workmen shipped a ton of copper ore into Tucson. Paul reported to the newspapers that he had another thirty-five tons ready to ship. On October 21 he held a public meeting in Tucson to raise the $5,000 for the project. Interested businessmen pledged $1,500 that night, and Paul sought other subscribers. Each signed a contract in which Paul agreed to repay the money at the rate of one dollar for each ton of ore smelted. By late November he had raised the money. He and a crew of workers took down the smelter and hauled it into Tucson, where they erected it near the railroad tracks a mile north of town. Paul had great hopes for this new venture. He ran newspaper advertisements for his Tucson Smelting Company, offering to "treat all kinds of lead and silver ores." But like all of his other mining schemes, it would prove a dismal failure.[6]

Meanwhile, the train robbery investigation was still under way when Kid Smith and Dick Maier brazenly returned to Tucson. Once again they left town on foot and made camp in the Rincon Mountains above Cienega Creek. This time their hideout was the large cave system now known as Colossal Cave, as well as a much smaller cave about five hundred yards distant. They also camped a mile south at Mountain Springs House, an abandoned stage station. On the night of August 10, 1887, Smith and Maier set up an ambush in Cienega Creek, at a switch a mile east of the site of the first robbery. They set up a red signal lantern and placed track torpedoes on the rails. Just in case that did not stop the train, they opened the switch a short distance down the tracks. At 9:40 P.M. the Southern Pacific train approached. The engineer, warned by the red light and the track torpedoes exploding as the wheels struck them, opened the sand valves and set his air brakes. But the train was moving too fast to stop, and it swerved through the open switch and careened onto a gravel side spur. As the locomotive lurched onto its side, the engineer and fireman leaped to safety.

The outlaws, thinking the train and its crew had tried to escape, became enraged and unloosed a volley of pistol and rifle fire into the engine cab and express car. The fireman, seeing a man in the darkness and thinking he was the engineer, asked, "Are you hurt?"

His reply was a pistol shot that tore away half of his mustache. "You damned son of a bitch, you are not dead yet?" demanded a bandit. "Why didn't you stop the train when I told you to?"

Then the outlaws approached the express car, once again guarded by messenger Charles F. Smith, who was accompanied by Wells Fargo route agent A. M. Gault. Again Smith refused to open up. The holdup men placed a stick of giant powder under the side door, lit the fuse, and blew a hole in it. Then they ordered the mail clerk to crawl inside and persuade Smith to give up. Smith finally agreed, and as he climbed down from the car, one of the masked men immediately recognized him. Striking Smith over the head with his revolver, he growled, "You damned son of a bitch, you won't play us any more tricks by hiding money in the stove." According to another account, the bandit's words were, "Smithy, the stove racket don't go this time."

While one of the robbers guarded the train crew, the other searched the express car and emerged with $2,000 in U.S. currency and $1,000 in

Mexican coin. Then they left on foot and vanished into the blackness. At daybreak another huge manhunt began. It was obvious to Bob Paul that the same men committed both holdups. Wells Fargo officials, unhappy with the result of the prior investigation, asked him to take over the case. But once again Paul declined, saying that he was too occupied with his smelting works. Undoubtedly another reason he refused was the animosity between him and Sheriff Shaw and Marshal Meade, neither of whom would have welcomed his help. A small army of peace officers and manhunters was soon on the case, among them Wells Fargo's Hume and Thacker, Len Harris, Marshal Meade, Deputy U.S. Marshal Will Smith, Charlie Shibell, Jesus Maria Elias, and, from California, Virgil Earp and the Southern Pacific's chief detective, Fred T. Burke. Competing posses trailed the fugitives to Mountain Springs House, then to the small cave, then to Colossal Cave, and they finally lost the trail in the Rincon Mountains. The outlaws were on foot, making tracking almost impossible. Exhaustive efforts to run down the outlaws proved fruitless. After hiding for a few days in the Rincon Mountains, the bandits boarded an eastbound freight train and returned to El Paso.[7]

Two Cochise County lawmen, Sheriff John H. Slaughter and Constable Fred Dodge, suspected that the train robbers were a band of tough livestock thieves from the Stein's Pass area in New Mexico, near the Arizona line. Three of them had stolen a pair of horses from a ranch near Willcox and had headed east toward Stein's Pass. The most notable of this bunch was "Red Larry" Sheehan, who, with his pal Jimmy Hughes, the notorious Sweetheart of the San Simon, had been members of the gang of John Kinney, New Mexico's "King of the Rustlers." Sheehan's close friend was Thomas J. "Dick" Johnson, a saloonkeeper at Stein's Pass who had formerly ridden with Presley "Toppy" Johnson, a noted New Mexico livestock thief. On August 27, 1887, two weeks after the train robbery, a posse led by Sheriff Slaughter and Constable Dodge descended on the Stein's Pass area and rounded up four desperadoes: Larry Sheehan, Dick Johnson, Si Blunt, and Joseph T. Brooks. Their compadre Jimmy Hughes managed to escape on horseback. The suspects were bundled into a westbound train conducted by Sam Gillespie, who had been in charge of the last train robbed. Larry Sheehan and Dick Johnson, who were colorful, loud mouthed, and exceedingly reckless, began ribbing Gillespie, telling him that they "had the money buried, and as soon as they had done their time they would hold him up again."[8]

At Tucson all four were lodged in the county jail. Si Blunt was quickly released on grounds of mistaken identity, as he had been confused with his brother, Jack Blunt. The others, however, were held on federal charges of attempting to rob the U.S. mail. At a preliminary hearing a few days later, Larry Sheehan was held to appear before the grand jury, but Dick Johnson and Joseph Brooks were released due to lack of evidence. In fact there was little evidence against any of them. The only strike against Larry Sheehan was that when he was arrested, the ejector rod was found to be missing from his six-gun, and a matching ejector rod had been found in the train robbers' camp near Colossal Cave. It was much too thin to hold Sheehan, and the grand jury refused to indict him. On October 5 he was released. Dick Johnson was waiting for him, and as the two left the Tucson courthouse, Johnson remarked sarcastically to Sheriff Matthew Shaw, "We have never robbed any trains yet, but as long as we have been accused, we are going to get busy and rob one for luck."[9]

Johnson's words would prove prophetic. But in less than ten days, the fact that they were innocent of train robbery would be conclusively, and violently, proven. On the night of October 14, 1887, the eastbound Galveston, Harrisburg, and San Antonio train pulled out of El Paso. Kid Smith and Dick Maier swung aboard and concealed themselves in the coal tender. The train was a mile out of town when they climbed over the coal, covered the engineer with six-shooters, and ordered him to stop at a crossing now called Alfafa, three miles east of El Paso. Wells Fargo messenger J. Ernest Smith refused to open the express car, and he blew out the lights. While one of the bandits guarded the train crew, the other blew open the express car door with dynamite.

This messenger Smith was made of even tougher stuff than Charles F. Smith. He crawled out the rear platform door, leaving his Colt six-gun on the floor. Kid Smith climbed up and at gunpoint ordered him to go back into the car and light the lamps. Messenger Smith obeyed, but as he entered the car he snatched his revolver, whirled around, and shoved the barrel into the bandit's chest. The messenger exclaimed, "Die, damn you!" and fired once. Kid Smith dropped dead with a bullet in his heart. Dick Maier snapped a quick shot at the messenger, narrowly missing his head. The Wells Fargo man ducked inside the blackened car and grabbed his sawed-off shotgun. At the same time Maier ordered the engineer and fireman to pick up Kid Smith's corpse and carry it to the engine. Apparently he intended to escape in the locomotive, as they had done in the first holdup. Messenger Smith watched carefully from the shattered express car and waited until he had a clear shot at the masked bandit. He fired one barrel, and Maier reeled, a lone buckshot striking him in the artery above the heart. Maier staggered off down the tracks and vanished in the darkness.

The train raced back into El Paso, and by daylight a large posse was at the scene. A quick search produced the dead body of Maier fifty yards away. J. Ernest Smith was the hero of the hour. The grateful citizens of El Paso bought him a new suit of clothes and a $100 medal encrusted with jewels. He was paid $7,000 in rewards from the government and the express and railroad companies. The bodies of Kid Smith and Dick Maier were soon identified by George Green's mother, with whom they had roomed in El Paso. George Green was quickly arrested and made a full confession, admitting his involvement with Smith and Maier in the first Arizona train holdup. He revealed that Doc Smart had helped plan the holdups and that they had been transported to and from Tucson by Syndor and Skidmore, the crooked conductor and brakeman. George Green, Doc Smart, and the two railroad men were all extradited to Arizona and held for trial in the Pima County jail. Their trial on federal charges of mail robbery began in Tucson in January 1888. Green pled guilty and testified against the others. Smart was convicted as an accessory; the railroad men, with a stroke of luck, were acquitted. Green received a five-year term, and Smart got life. This result was unfair, as Green was an actual robber and Smart was not. Probably for that reason, Smart was pardoned in 1890.[10]

This result fully exonerated Larry Sheehan and Dick Johnson. Instead of rejoicing, they began carrying out the threat they had made to Sheriff Shaw. In late January 1888 the pair boarded a train at Stein's Pass and got off in El Paso. There they met Dick Hart, a hardcase pal from Stein's Pass country. The three bought horses and rode 225 miles south to Chihuahua, Mexico. A city of about fifteen thousand people, it was the capital of the Mexican state of Chihuahua, a center for mining and fruit growing, famous for its apples and peaches. A few days later Sheehan ran into Wells Fargo detective John Thacker, whom Sheehan and Johnson knew well from their sojourn in the Tucson jail. Thacker was in Mexico, investigating the recent holdup of a train at Mapula, south of Chihuahua. Thacker was dumbfounded to find that Sheehan and his saddle partners were in Mexico, and he asked what they were doing there. Sheehan told him sarcastically, "We came down to see the folks and eat peaches."[11]

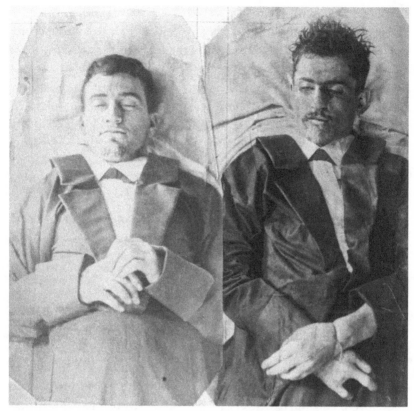

Jack "Kid" Smith, left, and Dick Maier, wearing cheap undertaker's suits. They were slain by Wells Fargo messenger J. Ernest Smith in a train robbery near El Paso, October 14, 1887. Author's collection.

On February 8, 1888, the three rode north, heavily armed and leading a packhorse. In less than three days they arrived at the pueblo of Casas Grandes, two hundred miles away. Here the outlaws stopped at the ranch of an American, George Dowling, who had formerly lived in Tucson, and they stayed with him for several days. From Dowling the trio bought a deerskin from which they made moneybags. While visiting a nearby rancho, they offered to buy it from its Mexican owner, and he agreed. The desperados told him they were headed to the United States and would soon return with the purchase money. They rode on, and ten miles north of Janos, at the Rancho la Palotada, Sheehan traded his jaded horse for a fresh one. To make sure that the animal was not gun-shy, he fired his six-shooter into the ground. The horse bucked wildly, and Sheehan's pistol accidentally discharged, inflicting a flesh wound to his leg. Since Sheehan was now unable to ride, Johnson and Hart left him behind in care of the ranchero, and they started toward the border. On the night of February 22, 1888, they left their horses in a nearby canyon and stole onto a westbound passenger train at Stein's Pass. Kicking two tramps off the front platform of the express car, the outlaws climbed into the engine cab. The engineer, William Harper, had been in the first Pantano robbery. He later recalled: "We were pulling out of Stein's Pass when I saw a man jump on the steps of the car back of the tender. I slapped the air [brakes] on and turned to find the cold muzzle of a Henry rifle touching my cheek."

The bandit exclaimed, "Put her on, you son of a bitch."

Harper continued to apply the brakes, telling the robber, "We've a heavy train, my friend, and you must give us time to stop."

"All right," the outlaw answered. "Do what I tell you and you won't get hurt."

A year earlier, a law had been enacted in New Mexico that made train robbery a capital offense, so the bandits ordered Harper to stop in what they thought was Arizona, just beyond the New Mexico line. But in the darkness they could not tell that they were actually still in New Mexico. Ordering the crew to uncouple the engine and express car from the rest of the train, they had Harper proceed a mile down the tracks. Firing three rifle shots to cow the passengers, Johnson and Hart ordered Wells Fargo messenger Stanley to open up. Unlike the previous messengers, he promptly complied, opening the safe as well. The bandits emptied its contents, about $2,000, plus some diamonds and opals, into a sack. Recalled Harper, "It was a beautiful moonlit night, and after stepping from the car the nervy highwayman placed the sack on the ground, shook hands cordially with each one of us, bade us a cheerful good night, and walked off with the treasure on his back." At Stein's Pass, Johnson and Hart recovered their horses and rode south to meet up with Sheehan at the Rancho la Palotada.[12]

Word of the holdup was immediately telegraphed to Tucson, where U.S. Marshal Meade quickly raised a posse and made arrangements for a special train to take them to Stein's Pass. Not surprisingly, Meade's plans did not include his old enemy. By this time it was clear to Paul that his smelter was a failure. Very little ore was being shipped to Tucson, and the smelter was now mostly idle. He had lost all of his money and was, in his own words, "dead broke again." Once again the old lawman was desperately in need of paying work. He later recalled:

A friend of mine came to my house and woke me and told me of the robbery about ten o'clock and said there was a posse being made up and asked me why I did not go as I had a good horse, saddle, and bridle and arms and everything necessary for such a trip. I told him to go tell the railroad special officer Mr. L. [Len] Harris if he wanted any men I would like to go. He did so and Mr. Harris said yes, I would like for him to go. On learning this I started to get ready and asked my friend who was going. He told me and said Marshal Meade seems to have charge of affairs. I then told my friend to go tell Mr. Noble the R. R. Superintendent if he and Mr. Harris wanted me to go I would be there in half an hour with horse and everything necessary for the trip. Mr. Noble told Mr. Meade I wanted to go and Mr. Meade said *no*, we have men enough and do not want to wait for anyone. My friend said, you will not have to wait for him for he will be here before you can load your horses. Mr. Meade replied, we have men enough. This all happened before 11 P.M. and they did not leave till 2 A.M. There was not one of the posse that had horses and Meade could not get saddle horses enough here for his posse and was forced to telegraph to Willcox for horses.[13]

When the special train left the depot, it carried U.S. Marshal Meade; his deputy, Will Smith; Sheriff Matthew F. Shaw and his undersheriff, Charlie Shibell; Southern Pacific detective Len Harris; W. G. Whorf, a volunteer; and four Papago Indian trackers from San Xavier. After stopping at Willcox, the train's boxcars carried their horses, saddles, and firearms sixty miles to Stein's, arriving at dawn. The lawmen unloaded their animals and saddled up, with the Papago trackers walking and running in front of and flanking the posse. The Indians quickly cut the robbers' trail. Johnson and Hart had fast horses, plenty of food, and they knew the country. The officers, on the other hand, carried little food or supplies. Meade, knowing that the bandits were Americans, assumed that their trail would go north, where the posse could easily be supplied in Lordsburg. Instead, the outlaws' tracks led due south in a circuitous route for three days and one hundred miles to the old Mike Gray ranch, located about ten miles north of Cloverdale in New Mexico's Animas Valley. The posse, starved of food and water, underwent great hardships on the long ride. In four days they ate only one meal. At the Gray ranch, posseman Whorf gave up and started for home, while the others stayed for a day to eat and rest themselves and their horses.

From here the trail led south into Mexico. In the mountains the posse met with snow and freezing weather, and the ill-prepared lawmen had no blankets or warm clothing. Finally, on February 28, 1888, after an exhausting 175-mile ride, the possemen arrived at the Rancho la Palotada. They learned that the outlaws had stopped there on the way north and that Larry Sheehan had waited at the rancho for his partners. Two of the desperadoes had returned the day before, spent the night, and then all three had set off again to the south. In the morning Sheriff Shaw, Len Harris, and two of the Papago trackers left the posse and turned back. Harris was sixty years old and could not stand the hard riding. Although Paul was very friendly with Harris, he had little respect for the horsemanship, stamina, or manhunting skill of the other possemen. He also believed that they did not know the terrain, saying, "Marshal Meade knew that neither he nor any of his posse had been ten miles off the line of the R. R. in the vicinity of the robbery, and the result was three of his men gave out . . . and returned."[14]

Harris, who had worked cases south of the border, may have been concerned that they had entered Mexico without its government's permission. For Harris, the decision to turn back was a fortuitous one. With a guide from the Rancho la Palotada, the balance of Meade's posse set off south, following the bandits' sign in a meandering course for twelve miles toward Janos. Situated thirty-five miles south of the border, Janos was an adobe village that had grown up around a seventeenth-century Spanish presidio, or fort, and it was the first town on their route. Once they reached Janos, Marshal Meade intended to report his presence to the Mexican customs authorities and seek permission to continue the manhunt.

That afternoon Meade, Charlie Shibell, and Will Smith, with the two Papagos running alongside, rode into Janos in a drizzling rain. At the customs house, Meade contacted Lieutenant J. M. Martinez, the officer in charge, telling him of their mission and requesting assistance from his command and permission to continue the pursuit. Instead, Martinez, backed by a platoon of troops, placed the Americans under arrest for entering Mexico as an armed body and without a permit. The dismayed lawmen were lodged in the Janos calaboose. Meade, beside himself with anger and frustration, called their imprisonment a "high-handed outrage." While the marshal and his possemen spent two weeks languishing in the Janos jail, Sheehan, Hart, and Johnson escaped south into the mountains of Chihuahua.

Sheriff Matthew F. Shaw, brother of Eugene Shaw, took part in the ill-fated manhunt in Mexico for the Larry Sheehan gang. Author's collection.

For more than a week no one in Arizona knew Meade was in jail; the public assumed that his posse was on the bandits' trail deep in Mexico. Finally an American arrived in Lordsburg from Janos on March 9 and reported the posse's arrest. The story hit the wires immediately, making national news and creating a diplomatic incident. Surprisingly, Marshal Meade was castigated in the eastern press. The *New York Times* commented, "There is no doubt that the recent arrest of . . . Meade and his posse . . . was entirely justifiable." Even Arizona's Democratic governor, C. Meyer Zulick, criticized Meade in an official report, charging that his precipitous entry into Mexico was prompted by lust for rewards and that the marshal "could not expect any better treatment than that which he received." Meade and his men were finally released, and they made their way back to the United States, minus their horses and firearms. The governor of the Mexican state of Chihuahua, Lauro Carrillo, assured the U.S. press that he had acted promptly to secure the Americans' release, but that Janos was isolated and communication was slow. He said that President Porifirio Diaz had ordered him to free the prisoners, "but not to return their arms." Nonetheless, the actions of the Mexican authorities were foolish in the extreme. While the Janos troops were certainly within their rights to detain Meade's posse, they made no effort to continue the pursuit of the train robbers. Meade had explained to them that he was less than a day behind the fleeing bandits. Plainly blinded by their distrust of gringos, the Mexican authorities kept good men in jail and allowed bad men to escape.[15]

Meanwhile, Bob Paul had been conducting his own investigation for the Southern Pacific into the Stein's Pass train robbery. He later explained that the day after the holdup, "General Superintendent J. A. Fillmore telegraphed from San Francisco to [Division Superintendent] Noble to send me after the train robbers." Paul immediately boarded a train for Stein's Pass, arriving late the same day, after Meade's posse had left. Then, after obtaining permission to enter Mexico, Paul spent a week south of the border trying to intercept the robbers. He returned to the United States on March 6 and went to Deming, New Mexico, a railroad town, where he may have hoped to pick up pointers on the fugitives. There Paul received word that Len Harris, after giving up the manhunt, had been transferred to Los Angeles and that he had been appointed in Harris's place as Southern Pacific detective for Arizona and New Mexico. Paul was still in Deming on March 9 when the news of Meade's arrest came over the telegraph wires. The old manhunter did not waste a moment. He boarded the next train for El Paso, where he met with J. E. Lindberg, superintendent of the Galveston, Harrisburg, and San Antonio Railroad. Crossing the border to Paso del Norte, Paul and Lindberg met with the American consul and asked him to make every effort to get Meade and his posse released. Paul, hearing that Governor Lauro Carrillo happened to be in town, called on him. "I went to the governor," explained Paul, "and he was very nice and very courteous. He told me I might have all the horses and men needed to pursue the robbers, and I went back to my hotel to fix my plans."[16]

Carrillo instructed Paul to meet with the acting governor, Juan Zabrian, in the capitol city of Chihuahua. Paul quickly boarded the Mexican Central Railway for Chihuahua, 230 miles to the south. Arriving on the morning of March 12, he immediately sought an audience with Zabrian. Paul recalled that Zabrian "was quite sharp and short with me" and that the official declared, "You Americans come down here and want everything. How do I know that you are what you say you are?"

The veteran lawman was stunned when Zabrian positively refused to help. Zabrian complained that he had been "imposed upon" in the recent investigation of the Mapula train robbery. Evidently John Thacker and two lawmen from Texas, working for Wells Fargo, had failed to adequately cooperate with Mexican officers in the Mapula case. Undaunted, Paul first consulted with Nicholas F. Pierce, detective for the American-controlled Mexican Central Railway, then sent a telegram to Governor Carrillo, asking him to overrule Zabrian. Carrillo replied the next day, ordering Zabrian to cooperate with the American detectives. Said Paul of the chastened official, "He sent for me, and was very nice. He offered me all the men and horses I wanted." Zabrian assigned an orderly sergeant, a second sergeant, and four privates to assist in the manhunt, and he put them under Paul's supervision. They were provided with good horses and provisions, and on the morning of the 14th, Paul, Nick Pierce, and the six soldiers rode out of Chihuahua.[17]

Paul's thirty years of manhunting experience now became abundantly evident. He suspected that the outlaws could be found in the Sierra Madre mountains west of Chihuahua, because that was the route that they had taken on their ride north. Paul decided to follow their old trail north, anticipating that they would return south by the same route. He astutely recognized that the Sheehan bunch were strangers to Mexico and would probably follow the trail they knew best. Paul and his posse rode twenty-one miles north to Rancho El Fortin, where they camped for the night. Here the soldiers made inquires and found that Sheehan, Hart, and Johnson had indeed passed through a month earlier on their northward ride. This was a hopeful sign, and in the morning they pressed on, riding all day and fifty-seven miles in a circuitous route to Carretas. The next day the trail took them south another fifty-eight miles to Casa Colorada, high in the Sierra Madre and just west of the present-day city of Cuauhtémoc. A mile and a half before reaching Casa Colorada, they passed a large L-shaped adobe with a big stone corral. Unknown to Bob Paul, Larry Sheehan, Dick Hart, and Dick Johnson were inside, stopping for the night with a Mexican family. Just as Paul suspected, they had backtracked toward Chihuahua. The outlaws watched Paul's posse ride by, but they suspected nothing wrong.

At Casa Colorada the soldiers made their usual inquiries and were gratified to learn that three heavily armed gringos matching the fugitives' descriptions were stopping at the big adobe. The Americans were bearded, weather beaten, and ragged from their long flight southward. Night was falling, and Paul decided not to wait until daylight, but to try to capture them immediately. He recruited six volunteers from Casa Colorada and started for the big adobe, but on the way three of the locals got cold feet and disappeared. Paul and Pierce, with the six soldiers and three volunteers, now quietly took up positions in the brush a short ride from the adobe, which was a typical Mexican hacienda with a thatched roof and four large rooms that housed an extended family of about two dozen men, women, and children. The windowless adobe rooms had been added on as the family grew. There were no doorways between each room; the front doors of the rooms opened into an outdoor patio in the angle formed by the structure. The patio was covered by a ramada of brush and tree branches.

One of the volunteers lived in the adobe, and Paul told him to scout the house. He soon returned and told Paul that the robbers were eating dinner in the kitchen, at the north end of the adobe. He said that they had left their rifles in the bedroom at the opposite end. Paul asked him if he would try to get the bandits' rifles, and the man agreed. He silently entered the room, found two Winchester rifles, ducked back out, and brought them to Paul. Now the Mexican returned to locate the third rifle. After some searching, he found it resting on a shelf. As he picked it up, Sheehan, Johnson, and Hart, having finished their supper, suddenly stepped inside. They angrily demanded to know what he was doing with the rifle, and the startled Mexican made an excuse and put the weapon down. The three outlaws suspected trouble and refused to let him leave.

After a long delay, Paul became alarmed that the Mexican might have met with foul play. He and his posse mounted up and rode quickly to the adobe, taking positions across the angled patio to guard its four doors. The outlaws slammed their door shut and frantically searched for their Winchesters. They demanded that the Mexican return their rifles, but he denied any knowledge of them. Bob Paul, Nick Pierce, and the Mexican troops were still on horseback, facing the patio. Paul and Pierce dismounted and yelled for the outlaws to surrender. There was no reply. The Mexican second sergeant grew impatient. Leaping from his horse, he ordered one of his men to follow him as he charged the door of the bedroom. As he smashed it open with the butt of his rifle, the outlaws unleashed a volley of fire. The sergeant dropped dead with a bullet in his heart. As Paul explained later, "It was a foolish thing to do. . . . There must have been twenty shots gone over our heads and some of them through the soldier. That ended him."[18]

From the doorway the three bandits sent a blistering fire with their six-shooters, and the soldier who had followed the sergeant fled in a hail of lead. The kitchen and adjacent room, which formed the right angle of the adobe, were filled with twenty-one women and children, who began

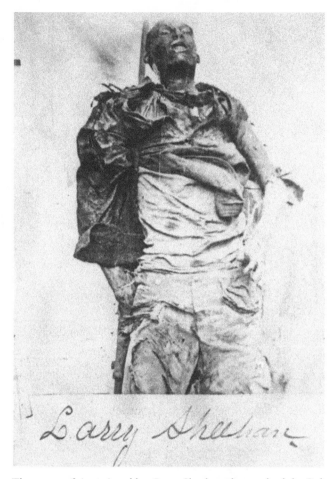

Larry Sheehan

The wages of sin: train robber Larry Sheehan, shot to death by Bob Paul's posse in the gunfight at Casa Colorada, March 17, 1888. His hair and beard were burned off and his clothing was scorched by the raging fire. Author's collection.

screaming hysterically. Some of them ran outside and then back into the center room, next to the kitchen. Paul ordered the soldiers to tell them to come out. Several did, but the outlaws fired at them from the doorway, and they rushed back inside. Paul yelled at his men to hold their fire so that innocent people would not be killed. The outlaws dragged the sergeant's body inside, barred the door, and settled in with their hostages for a siege.

Bob Paul recognized a pending disaster and decided to get help. He sent one of the Mexicans on horseback to the nearest town, Cusihuiriachi, fifteen miles to the south. Cusihuiriachi, now virtually deserted, was then a prosperous silver-mining town of three thousand people and large enough to have an *alcalde*, a combination mayor and judge. Later that night the alcalde arrived with a half dozen armed reinforcements. Now Paul had enough men to surround the entire adobe and stone corral. After stationing each man about ten feet apart, he and Pierce took up positions on top of the structure to prevent the bandits from escaping through the roof.

In the meantime the alcalde ordered several of his men to dig a hole through the back wall of the kitchen, the room farthest from that held by the bandits. The women and children, half-crazed from fright, escaped through the hole. The alcalde's men then entered and dug another hole into the adjacent room and released the rest of the women and children. The outlaws, hearing the digging, ordered their Mexican hostage to help them carve a hole in the bedroom wall. From there they crawled into the first middle room, then dug another hole through the opposite wall. Sheehan and Hart scrambled through it into the kitchen just in time to see the last of their hostages escaping though the hole in the back wall. They opened fire at close range at the fleeing women and children. Their muzzle flashes set one girl's dress on fire. Recalled Paul, "One discharge grazed across the back of that girl, and of all the screaming and yelling you ever heard, she did it." She fled toward the posse in flames, but they seized her and smothered the fire. "She was not much hurt," said Paul.[19]

The possemen maintained their positions all night. Every ten minutes Paul would call out, "Are you awake?" Each time he received the same answer down the line of sentries: "Despierto, senor" ("I am awake, sir").

At first light, March 17, Paul again demanded that the outlaws surrender. They refused with a defiant yell, shouting that they would never be taken alive. Dick Johnson was positioned in the bedroom at the far left, giving him command of the entire patio area. Larry Johnson and Dick Hart were still in the kitchen at the opposite end of the adobe. One of them watched the patio, while the other guarded the hole in the back wall. Paul decided to blast them out, and he instructed one of the Mexicans to go back to Cusihuiriachi to get a supply of giant powder from the mines. By late morning the Mexican had not returned, so Paul climbed onto the kitchen roof for a closer look. He found that under the adobe bricks was a patchwork of brush supported by wooden *vigas*, or beams. He began scraping away the adobe, then set fire to the brush underneath. After several attempts he managed to get a fire started, and he jumped down from the roof. Soon the flames spread, and smoke poured out the doors. The fire began to roar like a furnace, and Sheehan and Hart struggled desperately to put out the flames. Finally, almost overcome by smoke and heat, they drew their pistols and made ready for a last stand. In a scene out of a Hollywood film, they burst out the door, six-shooters belching lead.

"They came out calling us sons of bitches and shooting, a gun in each hand," recalled Paul. "We let them have it in return." Paul and the men in front of the patio opened up with a terrific volley of rifle and pistol fire. Dick Hart reeled, sieved by bullets that killed him instantly. Larry Sheehan, desperately wounded, staggered back into the room, collapsed upright on an adobe bench, and died. Soon the inferno spread to the opposite bedroom. When Dick Johnson could stand the smoke and heat no longer, he too charged headlong at the posse, clutching a six-gun in each fist and firing as fast as he could thumb the hammers. He made it ten feet before the guns of Bob Paul and the possemen brought him face down. With a Herculean effort, Johnson struggled to his knees, fired both pistols, then fell forward, dead, riddled with bullets.

Bob Paul stepped forward and searched Johnson's body. In his pockets he found $595 in cash, a pair of diamond earrings, and twenty-one opals, all stolen in the train robbery. He then turned to Hart's body and searched it. Paul later said that he "found poor picking. The soldiers had got there first." Paul thought it was "just as well to say nothing about it, as the loot obtained by the troops would encourage them to give willing and efficient aid" in the future. When the flames died down, Paul had Larry Sheehan's body brought outside. Sheehan was severely burned; the flames had singed off his hair and beard and disfigured his face.

Bob Paul and Nick Pierce accompanied the alcalde to Cusihuiriachi, where Paul sent a wire to the Southern Pacific superintendent: "Our posse found the Stein's Pass robbers, Sheehan, Hart, and Johnson, about one hundred and twenty miles west of Chihauhua, on the night of the 16th. We called on them to surrender and they took refuge in an adobe house where they were attacked by us. They killed one man; [we] burnt them out after 18 hours fight. All three men were killed fighting. The bodies were brought here and we recovered about $600 and jewelry. Can not say when I can leave here. The inquest will be held to-day. Will advise you later. R. H. Paul."[20]

The dead sergeant was buried in Cusihuiriachi with military honors. Paul had a local photographer take postmortem images of all three outlaws,

Postmortem photograph of outlaw Thomas J. "Dick" Johnson, slain in the shootout with Bob Paul at Casa Colorada in the Sierra Madre Mountains of Mexico. Author's collection.

who were then unceremoniously buried in the local cemetery. Armed with these photographs as proof of his successful manhunt, Paul made the long trip back to the United States, arriving at his home in Tucson on March 23, 1888. By that time news of his exploit had been published in newspapers throughout the country. Then the *San Francisco Examiner* issued a lengthy report based on information from Deputy U.S. Marshal H. J. Burns, a San Francisco friend of Paul's who had gone to Arizona to participate in the manhunt. The *Examiner's* account, graphically headlined, "Robbers Roasted Out. How Sheriff Paul Cooked the Three Outlaws of Stein's Pass," was picked up by wire services and reprinted nationwide. It

Train robber Dick Hart, dead. Bob Paul had this image, and those of Larry Sheehan and Dick Johnson, taken in Cusihuiriachi, Mexico, on March 17, 1888. Author's collection.

criticized Meade and praised Paul: "While the U.S. Marshal of Arizona and his deputies were getting themselves locked up in a Sonora jail for crossing the frontier without permission, [former] Sheriff Paul took the precaution of applying to the Governor of Chihuahua for extradition papers and permission to hunt the robbers on Mexican territory." The *Examiner* included illustrations as well as a diagram of the adobe and gave

Paul the entire credit for tracking down the bandits and organizing the successful siege.[21]

Paul's success was the culmination of three decades of experience. He used every skill he had acquired in his long career: his capability of speaking Spanish and his good relations with the Mexican government, coupled with his ability to track like an Indian, outthink his quarry, organize his men, and outshoot and defeat a desperate foe. Paul's exploit in Old Mexico firmly cemented his reputation as one of the greatest manhunters on the western frontier. For William K. Meade, his ill-fated expedition was one of the most humiliating events of his life. For him and Sheriff Shaw to be bested by their bitter enemy was a bitter pill to swallow. However, their travail was not without recompense. As a Southern Pacific detective, Bob Paul was not eligible to collect the railroad rewards. Instead, the bounty was divided between Meade and the Mexican soldiers who had served in Paul's posse. For his part, Paul thought little of Meade's efforts, snorting to a reporter that "had not Marshal Meade's posse been detained at Janos they would have been ambushed and killed." Paul's close working relationship with the Mexican government and his long experience in hunting wanted men had spelled the difference between him and Meade.[22]

In the end, Sheehan, Johnson, and Hart believed that they had no choice but to fight to the death. Had they surrendered and returned to New Mexico, they would have faced the death penalty for train robbery. And once they killed the Mexican sergeant, they surely would have faced a firing squad in Chihuahua. But the editor of the *Tucson Citizen* could not help but admire the outlaws' courage, and he provided their only epitaph: "However bad their calling or desperate their cause, they died like brave men, with their boots on—a manner that befitted their lives."[23]

CHAPTER EIGHTEEN

U.S. Marshal

Bob Paul was now the Southern Pacific's full-time railroad detective, or special officer, for the Tucson division. His jurisdiction included the entire line from Arizona to El Paso. While his most important responsibility was investigating holdups and train wrecks, such incidents were comparatively rare. Most of his duties were much more mundane: guarding railroad payrolls and investigating boxcar burglaries, track obstructions, and civil claims by persons who had been injured in railcar accidents. During one of Paul's less exciting duties, guarding the pay car that delivered wages to railroad workers on the route between Los Angeles and El Paso, a reporter who met him in Los Angeles in 1888 provided a sketch: "Paul is a typical looking frontiersman, with brown, honest face and costume such as one mentally associates with the wilds of Arizona. He is possessed of considerable humor, and looks what he is, a man that law-breakers would do well to steer clear of."[1]

Paul always packed a pistol, but now, instead of carrying his six-shooter in a holster and cartridge belt, he needed an unobtrusive way to conceal his weapon. For advice, he turned to his friend from San Francisco, Deputy U.S. Marshal H. J. Burns, a champion sharpshooter and California militia officer. In April 1888, *San Francisco Examiner* reporter Allen Kelly, later a noted author and outdoorsman, interviewed Deputy Marshal Burns for a pair of feature articles about gunfighters and gunfighting techniques. Kelly reported that Burns had devised a unique way to carry his pistols. "He has two patch pockets sewed on the outside of his corduroy trousers half way between the waist and the knee, one on each leg. In these he carries two revolvers. . . . When his arms hang by his side at full length his hands are just on a level with the pistol butts and within two inches of them. To seize and draw them is no trick at all, and as soon as they are out of the pockets the guns are in position for active service." Kelly explained that Burns's friend Paul now wore his weapon the same way. "Ex-Sheriff Paul of Tucson, now employed by the Southern Pacific to trail train robbers and guard express cars, has adopted the Burns patch pocket, which is coming into favor among men in that line of business."[2]

Immediately after his appointment as Southern Pacific detective, Paul encountered more trouble with Marshal William K. Meade. Paul later explained:

> It has always been customary for the special officer to be a deputy U.S. marshal, to give him authority to make an arrest when necessary, but with the understanding that it is for R. R. business alone, unless specially called upon. A few days after my return from Chihuahua from the pursuit of the Stein's Pass R. R. robbers, Supt. Noble told me to ask Marshal Meade for a deputyship so I would have authority to make arrests when necessary for the R. R. Co. I asked him the first time I met him and he very pleasantly said yes, he would do so. A short time after I had occasion to make an arrest and did so. About four months after asking Marshal Meade for the deputyship I had another occasion to make an arrest on a charge of stealing from the R. R. and came very near having some trouble. I then told Superintendent Noble that the next time I went to New Mexico I would get a deputyship there, as I might get into trouble making arrests without any authority. Mr. Noble was quite displeased and said in the presence of a friend of Marshal Meade's that if Marshal Meade did not want to grant the R. R. Co. that favor then perhaps the R. R. Co. might curtail some of the favors he was receiving. A few days after that I received the appointment.[3]

The favors Paul spoke of were gratuities that the Southern Pacific routinely handed out to local officials. Just as it had done so successfully in California, the Southern Pacific gave legislators, judges, and other officials free railroad passes, hotel rooms, campaign contributions, and special shipping rates. In turn, the railroad expected, and got, preferential treatment. The Southern Pacific bribed newspapers to procure favorable coverage, and it wielded extraordinary political power until 1910, when Progressive leader Hiram Johnson was elected governor of California on a platform "to kick the Southern Pacific out of politics," something that he and his party largely did.[4]

It was not long before Paul was knee deep in yet another train robbery investigation. On the night of May 11, 1888, a train on the Sonora railroad left Nogales, southbound for Mexico. At 10:00 P.M. it stopped to refuel in Agua Zarca, twelve miles south of the border. Five robbers—an American, Jack Taylor, and four Mexicans, Geronimo Miranda, Federico Duran, Nieves Duran, and Manuel Orozco Robles—were lying in wait. With no warning they opened fire on the engine, killing the fireman, John Forbes. The engineer leaped from the cab and took cover, saving his own life. The bandits immediately surrounded the express car and shot and wounded Wells Fargo messenger Isaac Hay with bullets in the head and right shoulder. The conductor, Louis Atkinson, stepped from the baggage car and was mortally wounded by a bullet in the stomach. W. H. French, a passenger who poked his head out of a coach, was shot in the arm. The bandits entered the express car, where Messenger Hay played dead. They rolled him over, took his keys, and tried to open the Wells Fargo safe, a small iron box. But, as Paul later explained, "they were so excited that they could not open the box, so they carried it off with them and after breaking it open and extracting the coin, threw it into the brush." Paul described their spoils: "Exactly $139.75 in Mexican silver, all that was in Wells Fargo's box." For that paltry sum they had engineered one of the bloodiest train robberies of the Southwest.[5]

The train backed up with its wounded and dead and returned to Nogales. There a posse of local men was organized and returned by the same train to Agua Zarca. They followed the tracks a short distance, where they discovered the emptied safe and, next to it, the bandits' masks. Here they foolishly abandoned the trail, which led north toward the border. In the meantime, news of the holdup was telegraphed to Wells Fargo's Jim Hume in San Francisco, who later explained, "I sent a telegraphic request to R. H. Paul, special officer of the Southern Pacific Railway Company, to go to Agua Zarca by the first train, if he can possibly be spared by the railroad company." Paul quickly arrived in Nogales and, on learning of the short-lived pursuit, immediately went to the scene with local officers. He tracked

Jack Taylor, train robber and murderer. He was captured by Bob Paul
in Nogales, Arizona, in 1888. Author's collection.

the outlaws north and on the trail found a brown felt hat, which he realized
was their best clue. Continuing on to Nogales, Paul and the other officers
soon learned that the hat belonged to Jack Taylor, a hardcase teamster and
wagon maker well known in Tombstone. A French Canadian, his true name
was reportedly Jean J. Tallier. Paul later described how they connected
Taylor to the bloody holdup:

> It is rather a good story about the way he was caught. He used to
> keep a wagon-making shop at Willcox, A. T., and left there with
> another fellow's wife for Nogales, where they appeared as mar-
> ried folk. He owed money to a man in Willcox named Rawlings

[Conrad Rohling], who went on Taylor's track, and located him in his Nogales home. He arrived there on the morning of the 11th of May, and on rounding up Taylor that individual said, "I haven't got any money now, but I will let you have it in the morning." Taylor left the house at four o'clock that same afternoon, with four Mexicans who had been in his employ and did not return until the following morning, when he paid Rawlings up in Mexican silver dollars. When we were tracking toward the thieves we found a hat that was afterwards identified as Taylor's, and this with Rawlings' statement gave us a clear statement against him.[6]

Paul arrested Taylor the day after the holdup. Rohling was captured in Huachuca, while Geronimo Miranda fled toward Contention. Taylor first claimed that Rohling had led the robbers. A week later, however, he made a full confession, exonerating Rohling but implicating Geronimo Miranda and the three other Mexicans. Taylor was jailed in Tombstone and on June 6 was turned over to Mexican officials in Nogales. Rohling was released, but soon after he was rearrested and also delivered to Mexican authorities. A few days later, Cochise County Sheriff John Slaughter and his deputy Burt Alvord tracked a portion of the gang into the Whetstone Mountains. In a pitched gunfight, they killed Nieves Duran and Guadalupe Robles, brother of Manuel. Federico Duran was later captured and lodged in jail in Guaymas, Mexico, with Jack Taylor. The gang's decision to rob a train south of the border was exceedingly foolish, as one newspaper pointed out: "In Mexico train robbery is a capital offense, and where murder follows the robbery, there is rarely a trial." In December 1889, Jack Taylor and Federico Duran were executed by firing squad in Guaymas. Geronimo Miranda committed several murders and numerous stage robberies before he was finally slain resisting arrest near Benson, Arizona, in June 1891. After being freed from a Mexican prison, the last of the gang, Conrad Rohling, returned to Arizona and was shot dead in a gunfight in Willcox in 1894.[7]

By this time Paul's good friend Nathan Appel was a Los Angeles police officer, and probably through his influence the old manhunter was offered a job as a city policeman. Perhaps at the urging of Margaret, who liked California much better than Arizona, he accepted the position in December 1888. On New Year's Day 1889 he proudly posed for a local photographer, his burly figure uniformed in the blue tunic and distinctive "series one" badge of the Los Angeles police. But for unknown reasons, his career as a city policeman was extremely short, and within a few weeks he was back in Tucson working for the Southern Pacific.[8]

Paul had greater ambitions than being a police patrolman. In the presidential election of 1888, Benjamin Harrison, a Republican, defeated the incumbent Democrat Grover Cleveland. Harrison took office in March 1889 and began appointing loyal Republicans to federal offices. For governor of Arizona Territory he chose Paul's friend Lewis Wolfley, who turned out to be an inept, bitterly partisan politician who made as many enemies in his own party as he did among Democrats. Wolfley was sworn in on April 8 and promptly nominated Paul as U.S. marshal to succeed Meade, whose four-year term expired on June 30. Wolfley offered Paul the highest praise: "I know by personal knowledge that Arizona owes more to Mr. Paul for her present law abiding condition than to any other person. His excellent executive ability is only equaled by his personal courage, and the two combined make him the best man in Arizona for the position." Paul received prominent support. Declared the *Los Angeles Times*, "Mr. Paul's name is familiar from San Francisco to El Paso, and down into Mexico, as that of a fearless man and a gallant officer. It would be difficult to make a better or more popular selection for the office." On May 30 the *Tombstone Epitaph* reported that it expected "to hear any day of the appointment of Paul as Marshal."[9]

But it was not to be. A few weeks earlier a gang of bandits had robbed a heavily guarded army payroll escort in one of the bloodiest and most celebrated crimes in Arizona's violent history. The Wham Paymaster Robbery, in which soldiers guarding an army payroll were brazenly attacked in broad daylight, would consume Marshal Meade and his deputies for almost a year, halting any replacement of Arizona's chief federal lawman. The Wham robbery had been carefully planned and daringly executed. Its ringleader was Gilbert Webb, a fifty-one-year-old patriarch of the Mormon community in the Graham County village of Pima. Webb had a checkered past. As a young man he was rumored to have participated in Utah's infamous 1857 Mountain Meadows Massacre, during which Paiutes and Mormons disguised as Indians attacked a wagon train and slaughtered 120 men, women, and children. Webb's family was prominent in the Mormon church; his sister, the beautiful Ann Eliza Webb, had become one of Brigham Young's many wives in 1868, and she left him in a sensational 1873 divorce case. Five years later Webb fled from Utah to Arizona to escape charges of livestock theft. By 1889 Webb was well known and respected in Graham County but heavily in debt, and he began planning an elaborate raid on a U.S. Army paymaster.[10]

Bob Paul in his Los Angeles police uniform, January 1, 1889. Courtesy of Pat French.

The Mormon community had long suffered religious discrimination, and its practice of polygamy often brought it into conflict with the U.S. government. Since Mormons had a contentious relationship with federal authority, it was not difficult for Webb to persuade some of them to steal government money. He recruited at least a dozen Mormon followers, among them his son Wilfred; three hardcase brothers, Wall, Lyman, and Ed Follett; and cowhands Mark Cunningham, Tom Lamb, and David Rogers. Cunningham was the only non-Mormon in the bunch. Their target, the army payroll, was regularly carried on the road from Fort Grant to Fort Thomas, guarded by Buffalo Soldiers, or African American troopers. Webb and his men considered the black soldiers cowards and believed they would not fight. At an isolated spot later known as Bloody Run, located fifteen miles west of Pima, Webb and his band erected rock fortifications on a ridge above the road. Tom Lamb rode into Fort Grant to determine when the paymaster, Major Joseph W. Wham, would leave for Fort Thomas.

The next morning, May 11, 1889, Major Wham started out with $28,000 in gold and silver coin. He traveled in an army ambulance, the gold locked in a strongbox, with his clerk, a driver, and a nine-man escort of mounted Buffalo Soldiers. At Bloody Run they were halted by a large boulder that had been rolled onto the roadway by the highwaymen. As the soldiers struggled to move it, Webb and his men, hidden behind the rock fortifications, opened fire. The black troopers, caught in the open, fought valiantly. In a desperate thirty-minute gun battle, eight of the soldiers were badly wounded, forcing them to withdraw to cover in a nearby ravine. Webb and his men, after driving off Major Wham and his bullet-riddled escort, climbed down from the ridge, broke open the strongbox, and escaped with their booty. The heroic actions of noncommissioned officers Sergeant Benjamin Brown and Corporal Isaiah Mays during the attack resulted in both being awarded the Medal of Honor.[11]

News of the brazen ambush created an uproar. A massive manhunt, led by U.S. Marshal Meade and including local lawmen and hundreds of soldiers, was soon under way. The robbers had not worn masks, and Major Wham and several of his troopers had recognized Webb and his son Wilfred, as well as Cunningham, Lamb, Rogers, and Lyman and Warren Follett. Within a short time, ten suspects were behind bars. They were soon moved to the jail in Tucson to face federal charges of robbery. The arrests caused a sensation in Arizona. Some of these men, such as Gilbert Webb, were prominent and respectable, and most had friends in Pima County. The public was unwilling to accept that the bandits were not shadowy desperadoes from the Mexican border, but instead were well-known local farmers and cattlemen. Soon supporters began working to influence witnesses and prejudice the jury pool.

Meade and his deputies labored feverishly to gather evidence against them, but the marshal knew he needed an expert detective on the case. Paul was eager to assist. Meade, however, had no interest in asking his hated enemy for help. As Paul later recalled:

> At the time the Wham robbery occurred I was on the [rail]road between here [Tucson] and El Paso, my headquarters being at Tucson. Marshal Meade knew this, and sent to the R. R. Co. at San Francisco to ask them to send Mr. Will Smith down here to help him to work up the Wham case. Mr. Smith holds the same position in the R. R. Co. that I do, with headquarters at Los Angeles. If Marshal Meade had wanted any of my assistance he could have asked the R. R. Co. for it as easily as he did for Mr. Smith, and if he had said he wanted Mr. Smith and I, he knew he could have got us both by asking for us. I have seen Mr. Meade every few days since the Wham robbery. I have been on trains with him when we were traveling and he has never once spoke to me about the Wham robbery. He knows me well enough to know I would only be too glad to assist him in any way in my power if he would only meet me half way.

Referring to Meade's earlier refusal to let him join the ill-fated posse that pursued the Larry Sheehan gang, Paul said, "I did not think it my place to offer my services the second time, especially as I was a candidate to succeed him, as I felt that he and his deputies would think I would only be working for personal motives."[12]

Will Smith arrived from Los Angeles on May 21, 1889, and immediately set to work on the Wham case. Smith, though a highly capable detective and manhunter, was obnoxious, argumentative, and strongly disliked by many fellow lawmen. Paul, who put law enforcement before politics and worked closely with officers of both parties, was infuriated by Marshal Meade's partisanship and wanted him out. Meade's supporters lobbied furiously to keep him in office, arguing that a sudden change in the marshalship would irreparably damage the Wham case. Louis C. Hughes, who was now U.S.

court commissioner in Tucson as well as editor of the *Star*, pressured
W. H. H. Miller, the Republican attorney general in Washington, to retain
Meade. Hughes was motivated, in large part, by his bitter hatred of Paul.
Meade, to his great credit, conducted an aggressive investigation in the face
of opposition by many who sympathized with the accused robbers, and
he developed a strong case against Webb and the other defendants.[13]

Their trial began in federal court in Tucson in November. It lasted a
month, and the government's case was proved beyond any reasonable doubt.
Prosecutors presented in painstaking detail a mountain of evidence against
seven defendants: the Webbs, the Folletts, and Cunningham, Lamb, and
Rogers. All of them were placed at the scene of the crime. The Buffalo
Soldiers identified a number of the defendants whom they knew personally. Other witnesses testified that several of the accused, including Gilbert
Webb, who had been broke, suddenly began paying their debts in gold
coin; one farmer even described watching Webb dig up the stolen loot
after the robbery. The defense, for its part, showed that the soldiers had
misidentified two suspects who had been subsequently released. The defendants also benefited from Major Wham's blunder in claiming he could
identify the stolen gold coins but in failing to do so when challenged in
court. Finally, numerous friends and relatives of the accused provided them
with alibis, evidence that was extremely suspect and would normally have
been rejected by a jury. But things were not that simple in frontier Arizona.
The jurors were blinded by racial prejudice, and they chose to ignore the
compelling testimony of the Buffalo Soldiers. After listening to witnesses
for thirty-three days, they deliberated just two hours before acquitting
all of the defendants. Strong distrust of the federal government, combined
with blatant bigotry, had won the day for the defense. Although in popular
myth the acquitted men were persecuted innocents, there can be no serious
doubt of their guilt. A year before his death in 1938, Wilfred Webb boasted
to a newspaper reporter, "I've never denied or affirmed that I was in on
[the robbery]," adding, "We all might have been guilty as hell."[14]

While the Wham investigation was going on, Paul simultaneously attended
to his railroad duties and lobbied for appointment as U.S. marshal. He
continued to receive powerful support. In late May he and Margaret visited
San Francisco and stayed at the Grand Hotel. In addition to visiting Margaret's family, Paul evidently met with Leland Stanford, the powerful U.S.
senator and president of the Southern Pacific. Two weeks later Stanford
penned a personal note to President Harrison from his office in San

Francisco: "I earnestly recommend Mr. Robert H. Paul for the position of United States Marshal for the Territory of Arizona. I have been acquainted with Mr. Paul for many years. He was formerly sheriff in one of the counties of this State, and was a most efficient and reliable officer." Soon Arizona newspapers were publishing false rumors that Paul had received the appointment. The *Citizen* called for Meade to be replaced, pointing out that "Bob Paul . . . has had more experience in handling the criminal element in one week than the present marshal has had in his life time." But Meade's supporters continued their successful lobbying of the Republican administration to keep him in office until the Wham case was concluded.[15]

Meanwhile, at 11:30 P.M. on August 12, 1889, westbound Southern Pacific passenger train no. 20 left Benson and headed up a low grade two miles from town. The engine was straining when it struck a deliberately loosened rail and careened off the tracks. Steam hissing and twisted metal groaning, the locomotive rolled over as it plunged down the twenty-foot embankment, followed by the mail car, which folded onto the engine. The passenger coaches fortuitously stayed on the tracks. Although the locomotive was completely destroyed, the engineer and fireman miraculously escaped injury. The Southern Pacific promptly offered a $1,000 reward for the train wreckers, and Bob Paul quickly arrived at the scene, where he was later joined by Cochise County Sheriff John Slaughter. Footprints led from the wreck up the embankment to a telegraph pole, where several horses had been tethered. Would-be train robbers had removed the four bolts on a fishplate joint, which held the end of the rails together. Then they pried loose seven spikes and two rail braces, ensuring that the weight of a passing train would spread the rails and wreck the engine. The train crew found a crowbar at the scene, which the officers determined had been stolen in a burglary of the railroad tool house in Benson. Evidently, as the *Citizen* remarked, "those who planned it lost their nerve when the time for action came." Paul and Sheriff Slaughter, with a Papago trailer, made an unsuccessful hunt for the train wreckers. The lawmen suspected that "the parties doing the train wrecking . . . were Mexicans and that they are in Tucson by this time." Paul was never able to capture the train wreckers.[16]

By the end of the year it was becoming increasingly evident that Meade's days as U.S. marshal were coming to an end. The *Tombstone Epitaph* reported, "Now that the Wham robbery case has been disposed of there is no longer any excuse for further postponing the appointment of a United States Marshal for Arizona. The *Epitaph* has private information that the fight has narrowed down to Mr. A. L. Grow, of Tombstone, and Mr. R. H. Paul, of Tucson." Artemus L. Grow was a mining superintendent with political influence, but he had no police experience whatsoever. In the end, Bob Paul's long record prevailed. On January 6, 1890, President Harrison formally nominated him for the office and sent his name to the Senate for confirmation. But Meade was not willing to give up quietly, and his supporters lobbied feverishly on his behalf, even charging that Paul "was in sympathy with the Wham robbers." The old lawman was furious, and in a lengthy letter to attorney general W. H. H. Miller in Washington, he explained his long feud with Meade and his spurned offer to help in the Wham investigation. Paul concluded, "I have always said that the parties arrested were part of the men who committed the Wham robbery, but I believe there were others in it. . . . If I succeed in getting to be the U.S. Marshal of this territory, I will satisfy you before another year rolls around that I am no sympathizer of the Wham or any other robbers."[17]

Letters both supporting and opposing Paul poured into Washington. Charles T. Dunavan, Meade's chief deputy, wrote: "I have known Mr. Paul for about ten years and from a personal knowledge know him to be thoroughly corrupt; he (Paul) was twice defeated for sheriff of this County (Pima) by getting possession of the ballots . . . personally assisted in changing a sufficient number of ballots to give himself a majority." Dunavan had even repeated the outrageously false claim, published by Louis C. Hughes and believed by many newcomers to Arizona, that Paul had committed the ballot fraud in the 1880 election. Meade's strongest supporter was the influential Brewster Cameron, Arizona cattleman, district court clerk, and nephew of U.S. senator J. Donald Cameron of Pennsylvania. In January 1890 Brewster Cameron entrained for Washington to lobby on behalf of Meade. At the same time Governor Wolfley, with a delegation of Arizona Republicans, also arrived in Washington to lobby for Paul and other Republican candidates. They found that President Harrison was eager to replace Arizona's Democratic holdovers. Meanwhile, Paul continued to receive strong support from other Arizonans. In a telegram to the chairman of the Senate Judiciary Committee, Nathan O. Murphy, later governor of Arizona, and numerous other prominent territorial officials urged Paul's confirmation, saying that he "is the right man for the place. His services would be invaluable while his defeat would be a public calamity. He is thoroughly qualified and worthy beyond question."[18]

Paul's strongest support came from Judge William H. Barnes, who bitterly disliked Meade. The marshal had been instrumental in having Judge Barnes removed from the bench during the Wham case. When Barnes read a news report of Brewster Cameron's Washington visit, he was incensed and fired off a letter to Washington in support of the former sheriff:

> I have known Bob Paul four years. . . . I regard Paul as one of the ablest men among those who serve society in hunting down criminals and crime. There has been an attempt to attack him by what grew out of a contested election for the office of Sheriff in 1885. That case came before me on motion for new trial and affidavits was filed of what was offered as newly discovered evidence. There [*sic*] truth was denied by Paul. In granting the new trial, I said that an issue of fact could not be satisfactorily tried by affidavit and I granted a new trial that the witnesses might come face to face, be cross-examined and the truth arrived at if possible. The case was afterwards compromised. . . . This was politics. In such cases you know much feeling was engendered, but take it all together, there is nothing in the record which should cause any hesitation in confirming Mr. Paul. Paul is a consistent Republican and I am a bourbon Democrat, but I could under the circumstances cheerfully vote for his confirmation, and I hope it will be done.

Governor Wolfley also forwarded to Washington letters of support from Eugene Shaw's own attorneys, Anderson, Hereford, and Lovell, "all to show, just as Judge Barnes says, 'This was politics.'" One of the lawyers, J. A. Anderson, whom Wolfley termed an "ultra Democrat," wrote that "there was nothing in the Paul-Shaw case that in any way reflected on Mr. Paul's integrity and character as a man." Even the powerful Democratic congressman and later U.S. senator Marcus A. Smith agreed: "I know of no reason why Mr. Paul should not be confirmed. His experience in that line of business undoubtedly fits him for the place." Smith was a political enemy of Meade, which no doubt led him to support Paul.[19]

Attorney General Miller was particularly concerned by the allegations of voter fraud. Governor Wolfley submitted a lengthy, point-by-point rebuttal of the charges, also forwarding a transcript of the supporting testimony from the trial. He emphasized the fact that the Tucson ballot seals had never been broken and that at all times the ballots had been in possession of Paul's political opponents. Miller was perplexed by the varying accounts he received of the *Paul v. Shaw* case, but in the end he was swayed by the arguments by one of Paul's friends, U.S. attorney Harry Jeffords. The Tucson lawyer gave Paul the highest praise, saying that "his detective ability is miraculous in its character, and the great strength of physique enables him to run down and trace any trail which he might strike." On February 28, Miller responded to Jeffords, "It is because of my confidence in you that I have concluded not to withdraw Mr. Paul's name." In the end, Bob Paul was confirmed by the U.S. Senate, and on March 17, 1890, he was sworn in as U.S. marshal of Arizona Territory. It was the pinnacle of his law enforcement career.[20]

The appointment could not have come at a better time. Paul was in desperate financial straits. His smelter had proved a complete failure. Tucson was in an economic slump, and very little ore was shipped in for smelting. As a result, the smelter was rarely operated. Even worse, an old civil case had come back to haunt him. During his first term as sheriff, Tucson's leading mercantile firm, Lord & Williams, had failed, and Paul had attached and sold $35,000 in goods that, as it turned out, had previously been sold to Henry Cullum. Cullum had sued Paul for the $35,000, and the sheriff lost the case in district court. Paul's lawyers appealed to the Arizona Supreme Court, which upheld the lower court's ruling. Finally, in desperation, Paul had appealed to the U.S. Supreme Court. In December 1889 the country's highest tribunal ruled that Lord & Williams's original assignment of the goods to Henry Cullum had been valid, that Cullum was the rightful owner, and that Paul owed Cullum $35,000. How Paul satisfied the judgment is unclear, but it was probably paid partly by his bondsmen and partly by him personally. Either way, it was a financial disaster for the old lawman. Most of the money and investments he had accumulated were now gone.[21]

The new marshal appointed his eldest son, John V. Paul, as chief deputy. Now twenty-six, John was Wells Fargo's agent in Nogales, where he had been living with his twenty-three year old sister, Agnes, who suffered from tuberculosis. The two moved back to Tucson so that John could begin his new duties. Bob Paul retained Marshal Meade's bookkeeper, Isidor Neustatter, who was temperamental but highly experienced. Marshal Paul also appointed resident deputies in Prescott, Phoenix, Florence, and other communities. Due to low pay, it was difficult to find good deputies, and there

John V. Paul, Bob Paul's eldest son, as he appeared when serving as chief deputy marshal under his father in 1892. Courtesy of the Arizona Historical Society/ Tucson, 1892 Arizona Republic Special Edition.

Robert J. Paul, known as Bob Paul, Jr. Robert G. Paul collection.

was regular turnover. Bob Paul's second son, twenty-three-year-old Robert J., popularly known as Bob Paul, Jr., was also interested in law enforcement and a year earlier had been appointed a mounted customs inspector on the border. In Nogales young Bob Paul worked with fellow customs inspector Vernon C. "Vic" Wilson. Marshal Paul thought highly of the former Texas Ranger and recommended him as his Southern Pacific replacement. In April Vic Wilson was named railroad detective for Arizona and New Mexico. Wilson's new job would prove a fatal one. Two years later he would be murdered in California by the notorious train robbers Chris Evans and John Sontag.[22]

Procuring reliable deputies was never easy. One applicant, Dell M. Potter, wrote to Marshal Paul, advising that he had recently moved to Clifton and asking for appointment as resident deputy. On the surface, Potter looked like a good candidate. He had been a deputy under New Mexico's U.S. Marshal Trinidad Romero and Grant County Sheriff Harvey Whitehill. But Potter did not wait for a reply from Paul before sending telegrams to New Mexico, identifying himself as a deputy U.S. marshal. Cipriano Baca, a noted New Mexico lawman, learned of this and wrote Paul to dissuade him from making the appointment: "Dell Potter was put out by our Marshal on account of dirty work. Potter is considered a crook and I know him perfectly well to be nothing but a pimp and low down gambler. He has a family here and treats them like a dog. Any one in our territory can testify to that." Baca added that he intended to have Potter charged with impersonating an officer. Although Paul never hired Potter, the latter would later become a wealthy Arizona mine owner and prominent civic booster.[23]

Paul's most dangerous deputy was undoubtedly John H. "Jack" O'Neil of Fort Thomas. O'Neil had long been a saloonkeeper there, serving at times as constable and Graham County deputy sheriff. In March 1881 John Ringo, Cactus Bill Graham, Jimmy Hughes, Joe Hill, and some of the other Cowboys delivered a herd of cattle to the San Carlos Indian reservation. They rode into Fort Thomas to celebrate, meeting fellow Cowboy Dick Lloyd in O'Neil's saloon. Lloyd was drunk, and after quarreling with Ed Mann, a former justice of the peace, he shot and dangerously wounded him. Then Lloyd mounted his horse and, six-gun blazing, tried to ride into O'Neil's saloon. O'Neil shot the Cowboy dead. Despite his rough reputation, Bob Paul was very fond of O'Neil, calling him a "good deputy." O'Neil seems to have performed adequately for Marshal Paul. The same could not be said of his subsequent career. In January 1896 O'Neil quarreled in his saloon in Geronimo with a patron, F. B. Grannis, and shot him to death. O'Neil finally met his end in December 1901, when he was slain in a gunfight with a cowhand, Bill Oglesby.[24]

As was his custom, Paul rarely gave newspaper interviews, at least not while an investigation was ongoing. On May 1, 1890, the *Tucson Citizen*, in reporting that he had returned home after an official trip, remarked, "He is as usual noncommittal as to where he has been, or to what he has been doing. Of these matters the public know[s] nothing until they see the results." Evidently Marshal Paul had been looking into the Wham robbery case. The day before, April 30, he had been in Solomonville, where he boarded a southbound stage to the railroad station at Bowie. With him were Constable McCarty of Solomonville and Mark Cunningham, the Gentile member of the Wham robbers. Presumably, Paul had contacted Cunningham to discuss the Wham holdup. About halfway to Bowie, Paul's stage driver spotted a pair of armed Mexicans following them on horseback. When the riders got close enough to see that there were male passengers aboard the coach, they got cold feet and turned off the road. At Bowie, Paul boarded the train for Tucson. The next day the two Mexicans held up the stagecoach at the same spot. It later developed that they were train robber Geronimo Miranda and his partner, Guadalupe Redondo. Their decision to leave Paul alone was a wise one.[25]

Many Arizonans expected that Marshal Paul would aggressively investigate the Wham robbery and bring additional suspects to justice. The *Star* pressed Paul to do exactly that. But those who expected him to crack the case were sorely disappointed. As one historian has pointed out, "Bob Paul's surviving files contain few references to the Wham case, and he expended no special energy in searching for new suspects." Paul evidently believed that because the ringleaders had already been acquitted in the trial, any effort to convict additional accessories would be equally fruitless. While Paul undoubtedly had Mormon friends—religion and ethnicity were indifferent to him—he was certainly not in sympathy with the robbers, as his enemies alleged. Probably because Paul believed that further investigation was a waste of time and money, Arizona's new U.S. attorney, Thomas F. Wilson, hired a Tucson private detective, Lyman Smith, Jr., to work up the Wham case. A brother-in-law of Sheriff Matthew Shaw, Smith was young and inexperienced. Wilson and Smith conducted a bungled, yearlong investigation, deliberately keeping Paul in the dark. They identified a list of new suspects, but there was no real evidence against any of them. Paul was hardly surprised when their investigation fizzled out in 1892.[26]

Marshal Paul evidently believed that his humble adobe on Pennington was not a suitable dwelling for an important federal official. He and Margaret acquired a large, single-story, flat-roofed adobe situated at 297 Main Street, at the corner of Franklin Street. It had been built in the 1870s, had thick mud-brick walls, and was square in shape. The Pauls wanted a home that reminded them of New Bedford, and they had the adobe remodeled in New England style. They added a veranda that surrounded the entire house, as well as a second story with a high-pitched gable in the front, topped off by brick chimneys and a railed widow's walk on the roof. The rooms inside had high ceilings, opening into a center hallway that led to a garden in the rear. Any New Bedford whaleman would have been proud to own such a house. This spacious, elegant home is still standing, beautifully restored as El Presidio Inn, a popular bed and breakfast. As soon as the remodeling was completed, the Paul family moved in and rented out the Pennington adobe. Many other fine houses were built on Main Street, and it soon became Tucson's most desirable neighborhood, later nicknamed Snob Hollow.[27]

During the 1890s train robberies became increasingly frequent in the United States. Paul may have anticipated that due to its remoteness, Arizona would see its share of railroad holdups. At least one Arizonan, however, believed that Paul's fearsome reputation discouraged train bandits in the territory. William Harper, the engineer in two of the Southern Pacific robberies, declared, "Bob Paul is a holy terror to lawbreakers and it is not probable that there will be any attempt at train robbery in his jurisdiction while he holds his present position." Harper's words were prophetic, for no train holdups took place in Arizona while Paul was U.S. marshal.[28]

Paul quickly found that one of his first and most onerous duties as marshal was enforcement of the Chinese Exclusion Act. This flagrantly racist law had been passed by Congress in 1882 to prevent cheap Chinese labor from entering the country. Until 1913 it was the duty of U.S. marshals to enforce it. Two months after his appointment, Paul publicly complained of the difficulty: "It is a practical impossibility to prevent the smuggling of Chinese across the border from Mexico with the present force at our disposal. They come from San Francisco to Guaymas, and then make their way into Arizona. For a long time past . . . it was the practice for them to come up the railroad as far as Santa Ana, from which point they were taken in

The Bob Paul house on Main Street, Tucson, in the 1890s. Author's collection.

covered wagons over the old trail that crossed the border near the Gunsight mine." He explained how lightly guarded the border was: "From Yuma
to the New Mexico line, a distance of about 400 miles, there are four men
only who are expected to watch the whole length of the border. Of course
this is a physical impossibility. The first of these is at Fort Yuma, and there
is no other man for 200 miles when La Osa is reached. The next man is
at Nogales, sixty miles from La Osa. These men ... can patrol the territory
only near their stations. To keep out the Chinese effectually, the border
must be patrolled much more closely, and I am heartily in favor of strength-
ening the patrol."[29]

Based on information he had received from Mexico, Paul predicted,
"One hundred and twenty-five Chinese landed at Guaymas this week and
all will come over the line." His words proved prophetic. Early in June
1890, his son Robert and treasury agent James C. McCoy arrested two
dozen Chinese who had crossed the border near Nogales. The Chinese
had been smuggled into the United States in an elaborate scheme. They had
first arrived in San Francisco by steamer in mid-April, then they transferred in the bay onto a Mexico-bound steamship. They landed in Guaymas
and made a meandering journey to the border by wagon and horseback.

Paul went south to Nogales with his deputies, loaded the Chinese into two wagons, and brought them to jail in Tucson. In a federal court hearing, Marshal Paul was ordered to take them to San Francisco for deportation back to China. A lawyer for the Chinese appealed by a writ of habeas corpus, which was denied.[30]

Paul, his son John, Agent McCoy, and two assistants brought the Chinese by train to California. During a stop in Los Angeles, Bob Paul was served with a writ by Horace Appel, Nathan's son, who was now a California lawyer. Appel argued that one of the Chinese was a legal U.S. resident, but he was unable to prove it in court. The hearing caused a delay, and Paul finally arrived in San Francisco on July 12. The marshal promptly put his hapless charges aboard the China-bound steamer *Gaelic*. Before the ship could depart, however, lawyers for the Chinese filed a petition for a writ of habeas corpus in San Francisco federal court. Their lawyers argued that the Chinese Exclusion Act required that they be returned to the country from whence they came, which was Mexico, not China. Paul, who was present for the hearing, must have been incensed, for if that happened, they could easily reenter the United States. He was determined not to leave San Francisco until the Chinese were deported. On July 23, he was in court when Judge Lorenzo Sawyer ruled that the original court order from Arizona was final, and the Chinese had to be deported to their homeland. The *Tucson Arizona Star*, abandoning its enmity for Paul, praised him for sticking with the Chinese until the final decision was rendered.[31]

But the question of whether Chinese should be deported to Mexico or China caused further trouble for Marshal Paul. Federal court orders were not uniform; some judges ordered Paul to deport immigrants to China, others to Mexico. Early in September John Paul deported two Chinese to Sonora, near the Nogales customs office. George Christ, the newly appointed collector of customs, fired off an angry letter to the young officer, accusing him of secretly deporting them at 4:00 A.M. and of failing to notify him. Christ also complained that although the law required that the Chinese be photographed before deportation, John Paul had neglected to do that. Christ's complaint was passed on to Washington, and Attorney General Miller chastised Bob Paul and his son for what he termed a "clandestine" procedure. Marshal Paul came to his son's defense, telling Miller that John had traveled twenty-four hours by buggy in a driving rainstorm, arriving in Nogales exhausted at 4:00 A.M., upon which he promptly sent his prisoners across the border and retired to bed. Bob Paul said that he had shown Christ's letter to both the U.S. attorney and to Louis C. Hughes, now U.S. commissioner. "They both told me that my deputy had done his duty and was right in paying no attention to Mr. Christ's letter." An angry Paul explained that he had gone to great lengths to enforce the Chinese Exclusion Act: "I have had several conversations with Mr. J. C. McCoy, Special Agent of the Treasury Department . . . and at his request I have appointed three special deputies, who live near the Mexican line, to watch for Chinese. All the deputies have special instructions to assist the Customs Officials in every way they can legally do so, and there had been perfect harmony . . . up to the time Mr. Christ took possession of the collector's office." Eventually Arizona marshals were ordered that all Chinese violating the act were to be returned to China.[32]

So-called timber trespass prosecutions were even more contentious than immigration cases. U.S. law prohibited the cutting of timber on most federal lands. This statute was hugely unpopular, for early Arizonans generally believed that government land was there for public use. Paul and his deputies made many arrests for violation of the timber trespass laws. Late in September 1890 Marshal Paul arrested Daniel D. Ross, owner of a sawmill in the Chiricahua Mountains. The criminal charge was cutting three million board feet of timber, valued at $93,000, on government land. Ross had sold most of the timber to the Copper Queen Mining Company in Bisbee. Paul brought Ross into Tucson for arraignment, and he was released after posting a $10,000 bond. At first the U.S. grand jury in Tucson failed to indict Ross. Thereupon the district court clerk complained to Attorney General Miller in Washington, claiming that of the thirty potential grand jurors summoned by Marshal Paul, twenty-six were from Bisbee and under the influence of the Copper Queen. Paul's response was a documented statement proving that not a single grand juror was from Bisbee. At the same time the federal government filed a civil lawsuit against Ross and the Copper Queen for the loss of the timber. The timber trespass case wound its way through the courts for years, finally reaching the U.S. Supreme Court in 1902. The high court upheld the right of Ross and the Copper Queen to the disputed timber.[33]

That fall Marshal Paul ran afoul of the prominent Tucson merchant William Zeckendorf. Zeckendorf filed a lawsuit against him, alleging that on election day in November 1890, he was quietly watching the courthouse polls when one of Paul's deputies ordered him to leave. When he refused, Marshal Paul stepped up and repeated the command. Zeckendorf charged that an angry exchange took place between him and Paul until the election officers demanded that they stop. Zeckendorf then left the courthouse yard, but soon attempted to return, and Paul prevented him. His voting rights lawsuit, which demanded $25,000 in damages from Paul, quickly came to trial in December. It didn't take long. The testimony showed that Paul and Sheriff Shaw had arranged for voters to pass through one gate in the courthouse yard to the polling place, then exit another gate. When a deputy tried to prevent Zeckendorf from reentering, the merchant pushed him aside. At that, Marshal Paul stepped forward and ordered him out. The jury deliberated only a few minutes before rendering a judgment in Paul's favor. One newspaper called the lawsuit "one of those political prosecutions . . . of which Arizona Territory is so prolific."[34]

In April 1891, Benjamin Harrison became the first President to travel across the United States entirely by train. He covered ten thousand miles in forty days and made 140 impromptu addresses on his way from Washington, D.C, to the West Coast via Texas. On the evening of April 21 Harrison arrived in Tucson amid great fanfare. A crowd of five thousand, including a large band of Papago Indians, was at the station to greet him. The depot was bedecked with flowers and illuminated with outdoor lights. A cannon salute was fired, and every church bell in town pealed its song. The reception committee consisted of three dozen dignitaries, Paul among them. Harrison gave a short speech and to great cheers told the throng that he supported statehood for Arizona. Tucsonans were disappointed that the president's whistle-stop appearance lasted but thirty-five minutes. Statehood for Arizona would remain a distant dream.[35]

Meanwhile, desperadoes continued to ride the Arizona deserts. One of the most notorious stage robbers of the Old West was Ham White. After a checkered career of stagecoach holdups in Texas and Colorado, he landed in Arizona in 1888. On November 23 of that year he robbed a stage near Casa Grande and was arrested the next day. Under the alias Henry Miller he was sent to Yuma prison for twelve years. White managed to wangle a pardon in 1891. He went to California and in March tried to stop the Weaverville–Redding stage, but was driven off by gunfire from Wells Fargo's shotgun messenger. A few weeks later he successfully robbed the same coach, but was soon captured in Los Angeles. Instead of holding him on the California charges, authorities returned White to Arizona to stand trial for robbing the U.S. mail in the Casa Grande holdup. He was convicted in the federal court in Florence and sentenced to ten years in

San Quentin, which then housed Arizona's federal prisoners. On June 10, 1891, John V. Paul and Pinal County Sheriff William Truman took Ham White and a Mexican prisoner to Casa Grande to await the next day's train to California. They spent the night in a house near the depot. Deputy Paul slept in a cot in the same room with the prisoners, while Sheriff Truman slept outside, and a local constable acted as guard. Sometime after midnight, while Paul and Truman slumbered, White saw that the constable was dozing. Wrapping a sheet around his leg irons to muffle the noise, he crept silently to Sheriff Truman's cot and lifted his watch and pocket-book. Then he slipped outside, and with a sledgehammer from a black-smith shop he broke his chains and headed into the desert. After a day of wandering, half-crazed with thirst, White was captured and brought into Florence. From there, Bob Paul, taking no chances, took the bandit to San Quentin himself. Wire reports of this incident first claimed that White had escaped from Bob Paul. The fact that the embarrassment happened to his son could not have been much comfort to the old lawman.[36]

One of Marshal Paul's close friends was Dr. John C. Handy, chief surgeon for the Southern Pacific Railroad. Handy was a prominent figure in Tucson, beloved by the poorer classes, especially Hispanics, for caring for those without the means to pay. But he was a Jekyll-and-Hyde character, with a furious temper and vengeful nature, who habitually brutalized his young wife. When she finally sued him for divorce, Handy feared that his spousal abuse would become public knowledge, and he threatened to kill any lawyer who took her case. That was a challenge readily accepted by Francis J. Heney, a young, ambitious, and fearless Tucson attorney. Paul was also friendly with Heney and his brother, Ben, a Republican who supported him politi-cally. Just before the trial of the divorce case, Marshal Paul learned that Dr. Handy had hired his old deputy George McClarty as a bodyguard. Fearing there might be trouble, he warned the U.S. attorney, who in turn cautioned Heney: "I don't want to alarm you, Frank, but Bob Paul, who is a friend of Handy's, told me to warn you that the Doctor has employed McClarty to help him. McClarty is to hang around the court room. If you make a break Handy will shoot you and McClarty will look after Ben."[37]

Perhaps due to Paul's timely intervention, no violence occurred at the trial, but Handy continued to threaten and bully Heney every chance he got. All Tucson was agog, wondering when bloodshed would occur. Finally, on September 24, 1891, the two men encountered each other on the corner of Church and Pennington Streets. After an exchange of angry words,

Handy began beating the much smaller Heney, who pulled a revolver. The two struggled desperately for the weapon before Heney pulled the trigger, sending a fatal bullet into Dr. Handy's intestines. After a lengthy court hearing, Heney was ruled to have acted in self-defense. From Tucson he went on to pursue a brilliant legal career, becoming nationally famous as chief prosecutor in the San Francisco graft cases that followed the great earthquake and fire of 1906. But Heney first achieved prominence for his part in "the most notorious shooting in Tucson's early history."[38]

As deputy U.S. marshal, John V. Paul made frequent trips to Florence to attend the federal court. On one such trip he met an attractive young woman, Mary "Mamie" Cullen, stepdaughter of a local businessman. The relationship blossomed, and on John's twenty-eighth birthday, December 29, 1891, they were married in the Catholic church in Florence. John's brother Robert served as best man. After the ceremony a banquet was held in the home of the bride's parents. As was the custom, her mother baked two wedding cakes. The guests included the entire Paul family and well-wishers from as far away as California. After the reception, John and his bride left by buggy for the train station at Casa Grande, where they were serenaded by a group of happy friends. They spent their honeymoon sightseeing in California. John and Mamie's marriage would be short and tempestuous.[39]

Other marriages in the territory were likewise complicated, and Marshal Paul and his deputies received frequent complaints of violation of the Edmunds Act, which prohibited polygamy and cohabitation of unmarried couples. An 1892 letter signed by fifteen Anglo and Hispanic residents of Ehrenberg was more descriptive than grammatic: "there a case of pallegme here by the James Maxey and a woman Susan Leard they been living to gether 12 month he has got her with a child and he want to brought on the world without any home and the paple want you to attend at wonce." In another case, Paul made a long trip into the desert sixty miles south of Kingman to arrest a couple that had been indicted for cohabiting. When he got there, he was surprised to find that the woman of the house was dressed as a man—an apparent attempt to avoid detection. To preserve her dignity, Paul took her into Yucca so she could obtain women's clothing before bringing her to jail.[40]

Paul must have taken some satisfaction when, on February 26, 1892, he was called on to arrest his old rival, former sheriff Matthew F. Shaw, on charges of smuggling cattle from Mexico and evading the customs duty.

Marshal Paul brought him into court in Tucson, and the ex-sheriff was released on bail. At Shaw's hearing the next week, a U.S. commissioner found that there was insufficient evidence and dismissed the charges. The *Tombstone Epitaph* complained about the case, pointing out that Shaw's stock grazed on ranges on both sides of the border, crossing at will. "This has always been the custom among cattlemen along the line on both sides," said the editor, "and the arrest was merely another instance of the enforcement of petty authority." The *Epitaph* referred to prior instances of Paul's deputies making unpopular arrests of settlers for setting up fences and cutting timber on government lands.[41]

Examiners from the Department of Justice in Washington made routine annual visits to audit the books of the various marshals. The examiner who visited Tucson in 1890 found Paul's office in good order. At that time his office deputy was the erratic but efficient Isidor Neustatter, who had served as Marshal Meade's bookkeeper. When Neustatter quit, Paul's accounts fell into disarray. In April 1892 examiner Sam Kercheval found that Paul "is not . . . a successful businessman," a conclusion that surprised neither the marshal's friends nor his enemies. Much more troubling was Kercheval's finding that Paul "manages . . . to successfully manipulate the business of office . . . to make his maximum fees." Kercheval discovered that Paul made duplicate charges and charged fees for attending court on days in which no court business was done. Paul's motivation was evident. His fees and expenses were paid quarterly, averaging from $750 to $1,000, resulting in an annual income of $3,000 to $4,000. In addition, he received 25 percent of the sums paid to his deputies, which could amount to another $2,000 a year. In 1890, for example, he earned $6,534. Although this was a substantial income for that era and one that would provide a very comfortable living, it was still a fraction of the amount he had earned as sheriff and was barely enough to pay off his debts.[42]

Kercheval also skewered Paul for his jury-selection methods. He charged that Paul's jury panels consisted of "loafers, bar-room bums and the 'ragged reubens' of the community, especially about Tucson where the marshal resides." He found critics of Paul who claimed that the marshal put smugglers on jury panels in smuggling cases and selected Mormons for jury panels trying fellow Mormons. That criticism was misplaced. The marshal only selected those trial jurors whom he could locate; it was up to lawyers and judges to pick a fair and impartial jury from that pool. One of Paul's deputies, George E. Brown, insisted that the marshal had directed him to summon as jurors only the "best citizens . . . without regard to creed, clique or party." And finding responsible jurors was not easy. On one trip Paul took to Tombstone to investigate a sheep-smuggling case, local merchants got wind that the marshal was in town and took cover. The amused editor of the *Epitaph* reported that "the way our business men . . . got up and dusted would have paralyzed a group of soldiers when trying to get away from two or three harmless Indians. They thought the Marshal was after another invoice of jurors, and some of them haven't got over their scare yet and are probably still running."[43]

The low pay of his deputies was also a recurring problem. For the year 1892, B. B. Denure, his deputy in Phoenix, earned less than $1,200. On one occasion Denure complained to Paul that he had received a notice to pay his back rent or move. "If you can send me $25.00 by return mail, it will help me out very much," Denure pleaded. Citizens wrote letters to Paul complaining that they had provided money or provisions to his deputies and asking the marshal's help in getting repayment. Protested one exasperated merchant, "You employ deputies to go over the country contracting debts on the strength of the official position which they never intend to pay." To make ends meet, deputy marshals were always looking to collect rewards. In 1892 Deputy Denure wrote to his boss, "Is there a reward offered in California for a man with a bullet hole through his ear? If so, how much and where and what is his occupation?" Denure even wrote Paul asking if he knew of any other work "that will return a fair salary" and begging Paul to "exert your influence in my favor."[44]

During Paul's tenure as marshal, Arizona's most infamous and elusive fugitive was the Apache Kid. He had been an Apache scout, serving under the famous Al Sieber, and he took part in various campaigns against Geronimo in the 1880s. In 1887 he killed a fellow Apache, and when he surrendered, a melee broke out in which Sieber was shot in the foot. The Kid and three of his band were later convicted in Globe of the attempted murder of Sieber and sentenced to seven years each in Yuma prison. On November 2, 1889, while en route to the prison by stagecoach, they killed Gila County Sheriff Glenn Reynolds and a deputy near Riverside Station. In the years that followed, the fugitive Apache Kid was accused of many raids and murders. On May 17, 1892, he killed an Indian woman on Black River and made off with her daughter. Two weeks later, on May 30, he appeared with the girl at a ranch house in the Superstition Mountains, thirty miles north of Florence. While ransacking the house, he shot and killed a

thirteen-year-old boy, Charlie Dobie. As a troop of soldiers unsuccessfully hunted the Kid, Marshal Paul went to the scene to investigate. He
concluded that "it was the work of Kid, the renegade Apache." Neither Paul
nor the army ever captured the Apache Kid, whose fate remains in dispute.[45]

In addition to his marshal's duties, Bob Paul remained active in Republican politics. At the party's Pima County convention in 1892, he acted
as chairman and was elected a delegate to the territorial convention. That
year he acquired an ownership interest in the *Phoenix Republican*. In November the Democrat Grover Cleveland won a second term as president. This
meant a new slate of Democratic appointees in Arizona, and Paul knew
his days as marshal were numbered. Cleveland took office in March and
again nominated William K. Meade, who received the formal appointment on May 8, 1893. Meade was formally sworn in at Phoenix on May 26.
That night Meade left for Florence, where the federal court was in session.
The next day Paul vacated his Tucson office. His thoughts and feelings
were unrecorded, but turning the marshal's office over to his arch-foe
was surely one of the most distasteful duties of his long career.[46]

Both Republican and Democratic newspapers lauded Paul's performance
as marshal. When the Democratic editor of the *Prescott Courier* commented,
"United States Marshal Paul is highly thought of by the Territorial press,
regardless of party," the editor of the *Phoenix Republican* exclaimed that the
compliment "is the stronger when one considers that the *Courier* is the
most red hot Democratic paper in the Territory." History, however, is not
so kind. As marshal, Paul had performed adequately but not exceptionally.
Given his experience, ability, and skill, Arizonans had high—perhaps unrea-
sonably high—expectations. Many had anticipated that he would crack
open the Wham case—a tall order considering that the principal culprits
had already been tried and acquitted. He had fought smuggling and attempted
to secure the Mexican border, an impossible task. And he had faced new
challenges, such as enforcing antipolygamy statutes, unpopular timber trespass laws, and the Chinese Exclusion Act. He had performed those duties
well. Despite complaints that he had overcharged fees, his office was free
from scandal. He had enforced the law in a steady and evenhanded manner.
But as U.S. marshal, Paul captured no infamous outlaws, led no great manhunts, and solved no major criminal cases. His duties were routine and
unspectacular. It is a great irony that although the U.S. marshal's position was the most important one Bob Paul ever held, the work he did as
Arizona's chief federal lawman was the least significant of his career.[47]

CHAPTER NINETEEN

The Last Trail

Bob Paul's sudden unemployment could not have come at a worse time. During 1893 the nation was in the throes of one of its worst depressions. Arizona was especially hard hit, as the territory suffered a devastating drought, and cattle died by the thousands. Silver prices plummeted, and many mines closed. Unemployment rose, as business and commerce suffered. Paul had saved a little money, enough to hold over his family during the hard times that year. On February 9 they celebrated the wedding of son Robert to Annie Finley, the nineteen-year-old daughter of Paul's friend, Harshaw mine owner James Finley. A few weeks later, on March 29, the Paul family celebrated the twenty-fifth birthday of daughter Agnes in the big house on Main Street. For ten years she had suffered from tuberculosis "with the greatest patience and without a complaint." Although Margaret and Bob paid for the best medical attention, there was no cure. Her family knew her condition was terminal, but they little realized she had less than three months to live. On the evening of June 12, Agnes talked of going for a buggy ride, and seemed strong enough, but she decided to forego the pleasure. At 2:00 A.M. she suddenly called to her brother, "Bob, I believe I am dying." Her parents and siblings rushed to her side, but there was little they could do. Three hours later she was gone. For the Pauls, memories of that horrible time in Visalia must have flooded back. They had funeral invitations printed so that friends could attend the wake in their home two days later, followed by a Mass at the Catholic church. Agnes, frail, gentle, and kind, had always been a bright spot in their lives.[1]

By late 1893 Paul was again in financial trouble. His big smelting furnace in Tucson was mostly idle, as the *Citizen* later reported: "It never proved a success, owing that there was no money with which to buy ore." Paul had leased it out, but other operators were also unable to make a profit. The smelter, worth at least $15,000, was sold at a sheriff's auction for just $1,205.75. It would have cost a small fortune—which Paul did not have—to move it to a better location. In November, to make ends meet, Paul borrowed $870, the loan secured by a mortgage against the Pennington Street house. Once again, Paul began looking for law enforcement work. That same month his old friend Len Harris was shot and killed while attempting to arrest a bandit in California. Newspapers reported that Billy Breakenridge, the Southern Pacific detective in Arizona, would take Harris's place in California, and Paul would be reappointed special officer for Arizona. But Breakenridge remained in Arizona, and Paul did not get the job.[2]

He still had aspirations to regain the sheriff's office, and in August 1894 his friends floated his name as a possible candidate. He received the support and then the nomination of the Republican Party. The ever-loyal *Citizen* provided its unqualified endorsement: "Indomitable of will, large and strong of frame, he has ever been a terror to the evil doers of the country, more of whom he has brought to the bar of justice, it can safely be said, than any other man in Arizona." Reported the *Citizen* optimistically, "A very partial canvass of the County demonstrates that in the race for Sheriff there was practically but one man, Mr. Paul, and seeing this the opposition knowing itself defeated has begun to distort facts in the foolish hope of being able to draw from some of his friends." The *Star*, for once, refrained from attacking Paul. His opponent was Robert N. Leatherwood, a livery stable owner and former mayor of Tucson. Leatherwood was very popular, and the *Citizen* had been too optimistic about Paul's chances. In the November 6 general election, Paul polled 660 votes to Leatherwood's 765. He had made a respectable showing, but Leatherwood was Pima's new sheriff.[3]

Paul was not discouraged, for soon a new mining opportunity presented itself. Through his railroad connections, he secured a position with the Pacific Improvement Company, the Southern Pacific's construction arm, to search for coal deposits in Graham County. Paul had never lost the mining fever that had seized him a half century before. He reckoned that since there was coal in New Mexico, adjacent Graham County was also

The most frequently published image of Bob Paul. It is taken from the 1899 group photograph that appears on page 397. Author's collection.

a good prospect. In January 1895 he was in Solomonville with G. B. Reynolds, general manager of the Pacific Improvement Company, and G. B. Fox, a railroad engineer. They secured a wagon and two weeks' supplies and set off to explore the country between Bonita Creek and the San Carlos Indian reservation. The trio spent ten days prospecting and found promising signs of coal. Commented the editor of the *Solomonville Bulletin*, "The gentlemen of the Southern Pacific are supposed to be experts and will know when they discover anything valuable. . . . The discovery of coal in sufficient quantity in this section would not only be a great bonanza for the railroads but would add materially to the prosperity of the people of this valley."[4]

Soon Paul located traces of coal on the Gila River, nine miles north-west of Solomonville. Coal mining was an expensive proposition, and the Pacific Improvement Company paid for the heavy drilling equipment and diamond bits needed for test boring. Paul supervised the workers and helped operate the diamond drill. Seven bore holes, each up to three hundred feet deep, were drilled into the strata beneath. After a year of work, no large coal deposits had been found. Characteristically, Paul remained optimistic and regularly traveled back and forth between his home in Tucson and the coal-boring works near Solomonville. However, by August 1896 he despaired of striking coal, giving up his position at the coal camp and returning to Tucson.[5]

His son Robert had left the customs service and established a cattle ranch on Arivaca Creek in the southern part of Pima County. Father and son ranged cattle together on the ranch. In 1897 Robert received an accidental gunshot wound, taking a full charge of birdshot in the chest. Doctors were unable to remove all of the shot, which caused him to suffer from inter-mittent lung infections. The old lawman's favorite nephew, Robert E. Paul, the son of Thomas, had grown up in San Francisco and had moved to Tucson as a young man. He followed in his uncle's footsteps and worked as a Tucson constable and police officer during the 1890s. In 1894 he was appointed Tucson's city marshal, a position he held for two years. His career ended prematurely when he suddenly took ill at the end of 1896, dying two weeks later on January 10, 1897, age thirty-five.[6]

In the meanwhile Paul's old enemy, Louis C. Hughes, had suffered a massive defeat. Hughes had been appointed Arizona governor in 1893—the pinnacle of his career. Paul had strenuously opposed the appointment and, according to the *Tombstone Epitaph*, had furnished the majority of the papers filed against Hughes. Seven months after Hughes's appointment, Paul submitted to Washington a detailed affidavit accusing Hughes as editor of the *Star* of soliciting bribes to support Republican candidates and of charging the territorial government "grossly extortionate" printing fees. As governor, Hughes's strong support of prohibition made him unpopular with Ari-zonans, but his main failing was an inability to cooperate with his own party. Still bitterly partisan and uncompromising, he was accused of working against a Democratic nominee for Congress and of exerting undue influence on legislators to ensure passage of bills. Although the long-married Hughes painted himself as scrupulously honest, opponents within his own party accused him of price gouging on a county printing job and again of consorting with prostitutes. Complaints against him flooded into Washington. The final straw came when he opposed President Grover Cleveland by supporting a bill that placed restrictions on the use of certain public lands in Arizona. On March 23, 1896, Hughes was notified that the president wanted his resignation.[7]

Characteristically, Hughes refused to step down, and President Cleveland removed him from office. Hughes, in a combination of arrogance, disbelief, and stubbornness, hung on for several days before he finally vacated the governor's office. Paul must have grinned broadly when he read the Phoenix newspaper reports of the ensuing celebration: "Wooden barrels filled with flammable material were placed on the corners of the principal streets of the city and as soon as it was dark they were lighted, while the brass band played lively tunes around the flames. All the small boys that could be found were furnished with fish horns and the night was made hideous with the noise from them." It was a spectacular and ignominious downfall for Paul's most bitter enemy.[8]

But it was mining, not politics, that forever ran deep in Paul's blood. He needed money, and before long he was back at the coal camp. Paul told reporters that he planned to drill one thousand feet deep and had "great hopes for success." But the rock proved extremely hard, and the diamond drill he used had trouble penetrating it to any great depth. In December 1896, following almost two years of fruitless work, the drilling was temporarily suspended, but still Paul was unfazed. A newspaperman who interviewed him wrote, "There is nothing, however, to discourage the hope of ultimately striking coal, and Mr. Paul is only awaiting the arrival of an experienced man from New York to take charge of the work and resume boring." A few weeks later the new engineer arrived, and the newspapers reported, "The work in sinking for coal will begin in earnest in a few days at the camp above Solomonville." A well-boring machine made in San Francisco was shipped to Solomonville and brought up the Gila River to the coal camp.[9]

By March of 1898, after more than three years of labor, coal deposits had still not been discovered. A reporter who visited Paul found him ever confident, explaining, "California capitalists are associated with him in the enterprise. Should they succeed in finding coal it will revolutionize copper mining about Clifton, Morenci, and Globe, and greatly cheapen the cost of reducing other ores in that region." But the coal-mining venture remained a complete failure, and in September it was abandoned. The next year Paul and a partner purchased mining property at Las Guijas, a small camp in the southwestern corner of Pima County. But that too failed to pan out. The unrepentant forty-niner finally began to recognize that his prospecting days were over. He and Margaret had been forced to vacate their big house on Main Street, which they rented to boarders. They moved back into the adobe house at 146 East Pennington Street. Their finances were always precarious. On one occasion he and his son Robert mortgaged their entire herd of horses and cattle, situated on the latter's Arivaca Creek ranch, for $2,900. But Paul and his son struggled to make the installment payments.[10]

Despite Bob Paul's financial failures, his old friend Wyatt Earp saw him as a successful mining man. Earp himself had struggled to eke out a living as a racehorse owner, mining speculator, and prizefight promoter. In 1896 Wyatt recalled his old comrade fondly to a San Francisco newsman: "Lucky Bob Paul! In fancy I see him, his always well-nourished frame endowed with 'fair round belly with fat capon lined,' overseeing his smelting works in Tucson, and telling a younger generation about the killing of Bud Philpott." But in fact, perhaps in deference to his wife, Paul rarely spoke of his hair-raising exploits or committed them to print. One of the few times he did was in 1898, when he read an inaccurate account of the Earp-Clanton troubles in the *Citizen*. Paul wrote a long letter to the editor, correcting the errors and explaining his role in those dramatic events.[11]

By this time the normally happy Paul household was thrown into turmoil by the stormy relationship between John V. Paul and his wife, Mamie. They lived in a rented house in Tucson, where John now worked as a fireman, and later as an engineer, on the Southern Pacific. The couple had three children, Vincent, born in 1892, Alfred, born in 1893, and Charles, born in March of 1896. These were the first grandchildren of Bob and Margaret, and they doted on them. Mamie, by her own admission, was "of a nervous and hysterical temperament" and believed that Margaret hated her. According to Mamie, her husband was "wholly dominated by and controlled by his mother." Margaret was strong willed and sharp tongued and undoubtedly did influence her son. In January 1894, John and Mamie's first son, fourteen-month-old Vincent, died of illness. John's marriage, unlike that of Bob and Margaret, was not strong enough to survive the tragedy. During 1896 John and Mamie quarreled frequently. On December 17, John returned home from work to find his house empty. Mamie had sold all of the furniture and had taken both boys to Indiana to live with her father. Finally she returned to her stepfather's home in Florence, where she filed for divorce in September 1897. The case was a long and bitter one. Mamie claimed that John had driven her out of the home, had failed to support her, and had neglected the children. After a trial in Florence in December 1899, the judge found that none of her allegations were true. He ruled that Mamie "did abandon her said husband and did desert him." The judge granted sole custody of the two boys to John, with reasonable visitation by Mamie. John could not raise the boys on his own, so he and his sons moved in with Margaret and Bob in the little adobe on Pennington Street. The adobe had room for both grandchildren, for by this time Walter, now eighteen, and Edith, sixteen, were living with their aunts in San Francisco, where they attended school.[12]

By the fall of 1898 Paul was sixty-eight and showing his age. His huge frame was now slightly bent, and he was slowing down. He had no money, no pension, no prospects, and was in desperate need of paying work. In the general election that November, Paul's friend Lyman Wakefield was elected sheriff of Pima County. Wakefield was a prominent cattle rancher and Republican Party leader. It was a godsend when Wakefield offered to appoint him as undersheriff. Wakefield took office on January 1, 1899, and immediately announced his choice of staff. L. C. Hughes, perhaps humbled by his downfall and mollified by the passing of the years, forgot all about their old enmity, commenting in the *Star*: "The appointment of R. H. Paul as under sheriff, places one of the most experienced executive officials of Pima County in a place which he understands well. Sheriff Wakefield shows good judgment in associating experience with the duties of the most responsible office in the county. Under Sheriff Paul will be a most valuable aid in the administration of the office." The veteran lawman must have taken great satisfaction in praise from the journalist who had repeatedly savaged him over the years.[13]

Sheriff Wakefield was a good horseman and tracker and had been toughened by encounters with Apaches twenty years earlier. But he had never held a law enforcement position of any type, and he sorely needed Paul's expertise. Due to Paul's advancing age, his primary duties were running the jail, handling the books, and managing the sheriff's civil business. But from time to time he would serve in the field. Just two days after his appointment, Undersheriff Paul rode out into the desert to investigate a dead body hanging from a tree near Red Rock. He found that it was a young man who had committed suicide. Paul and a justice of the peace held an inquest, then cut the body down and buried it on the spot.[14]

Pima County officials in front of the Tucson courthouse, 1899. Standing at far left is Undersheriff Paul. Back row, third from the left, is Charlie Shibell. Sheriff Lyman Wakefield is seated, center. Courtesy of the Arizona Historical Society/Tucson, 28913.

Paul booked his most famous prisoner into the Pima County jail on the morning of June 20, 1899. Her name was Pearl Hart, and she had achieved instant national notoriety as Arizona's "lady bandit." Pearl dressed in men's rough clothing, smoked cigars, talked tough, and enjoyed posing with guns in widely published photographs. Withal, Paul saw her as a petite and pretty, though troubled, young woman. A great deal of fictional nonsense has been written about Hart, much of it based on interviews she gave to gullible reporters. She claimed to have been born in Canada, saying that she had turned to stagecoach robbery to get money to visit her poor and dying mother. In fact, her true name was Caroline Hartwell, and she had been born in 1871 to a respectable family in Toledo, Ohio. She had a wild streak and loved outdoor sports, horseback riding, and target shooting. After completing high school she eloped with a youth, Dick Baldwin, who was actually Daniel E. Bandman, a talented piano player. By Pearl's own account, her husband abused her, and she left him in 1893, drifting west to Trinidad,

Colorado. She recalled, "I was good-looking, desperate, discouraged, and ready for anything that might come. I do not care to dwell on this period of my life."[15]

In 1896 Pearl Hart arrived in Phoenix, where she became a well-known madam and prostitute. She preferred men's clothing and was often seen in male attire on the streets. She also became addicted to opium and morphine, a habit engaged in by many prostitutes of that era. In Phoenix Pearl took back her husband, Dan Bandman, and later said that they then had two children together. Bandman, an opium addict who was reduced to playing piano in gambling houses, again began mistreating her. She left him once more and sent their children to be cared for by her mother in Toledo. Pearl's account of her troubled marriage is undoubtedly true. Bandman later worked as a musician in Tucson, where he remarried in 1901. His second wife sued him for divorce three years later on the grounds of extreme cruelty and his addiction to opium.[16]

By 1899 Pearl Hart was in Globe with a male companion and fellow morphine addict known only by his alias, Joe Boot. Destitute, they planned a stage robbery to feed their morphine habits. On May 29, Hart and Boot held up a stagecoach on the route between Globe and Florence, taking a little more than $400 from the three passengers aboard. Pinal County Sheriff William Truman took to the saddle and trailed the bandits to their camp north of Benson, where he arrested them on June 4. They were lodged in the county jail in Florence, where reporters rushed to interview Pearl. Their stories hit the wires, and within days she was nationally famous. Pearl loved the publicity, and she described to reporters the holdup and her other adventures. "I don't care what the world does with me," she said defiantly. "I'd do it all over again if I had the chance." Puffing furiously on a cigarette, she expressed scorn for Joe Boot's manliness: "Why, the fellow hadn't an ounce of sand. While I was going through the passengers his hands were shaking like leaves, and he a-holding the guns, too. Why, if I hadn't more nerve than that, I'd jump off the earth."[17]

The Florence lockup had no cells for women, so Pearl was transferred to the Tucson jail to await trial in November. Sheriff Truman brought her by train from Florence, turning her over to Wakefield and Paul. She was still wearing her preferred men's work clothing: trousers, white shirt, suspenders, knee boots, and a slouch hat. Sheriff Truman had provided her with morphine, but his supply ran out, and she was now in the throes of opiate withdrawal. Paul and Sheriff Wakefield lodged her in a comfortable private room, which was used for female prisoners, located on the second floor of

Pima County sheriff's office in the courthouse, 1899. Left to right, Sheriff Lyman Wakefield, Bob Paul, and Alfred Wakefield, the sheriff's brother and deputy. Robert G. Paul collection.

the courthouse, above the recorder's office. Pearl Hart sprawled on a sofa, tossing and writhing in pain. The officers summoned the jail doctor, and he recommended that she be given morphine twice a day. Although shocking to modern sensibilities, morphine was then legal, and Undersheriff Paul saw to it that Pearl got a dose every morning and evening.[18]

Paul seems to have been amused by the female desperado, and he treated her well. Somewhere she had picked up a pet wildcat cub, and Paul let her bring it into the jail. However, he would not allow Pearl to wear men's clothing and instead got her a stylish new outfit: a willowy white dress and belt, checkered blouse, cravat, and a white straw hat decorated with flowers. When a writer for *Cosmopolitan* magazine requested an interview, Paul and Wakefield not only complied, they allowed her to don her men's clothes so that she could be photographed. The lawmen even supplied Pearl with a pistol belt, two revolvers, and a Winchester rifle, and she posed for several now iconic images in the jailyard. Later Paul fully relented and allowed her to wear pants whenever she wished. To reporters, Pearl Hart claimed suffragette sympathies and declared that she "would never submit to the trial under laws neither she nor her sex had in making."

Paul would regret his lenient treatment of Arizona's lady bandit. When not basking in publicity, Pearl found time to seduce the jail trusty, Ed Hogan. He was serving a term for drunk and disorderly conduct, and she later boasted that he was in love with her. The room Pearl occupied was not secure. Its walls were built of lathe and plaster, and its wooden door was locked at night from the outside. Hogan was given freedom to work around the jail during the day, and he was kept in his cell at night. But when the jail was locked up on the night of October 11, 1899, Hogan was missing. He was hiding nearby, and after midnight the trusty returned to the courthouse and entered through an unlocked door. The stairway to the courthouse tower passed behind Pearl's room, and Hogan quickly scraped away the plaster and cut a small hole in the wood wall. Pearl held up her bed sheet to catch the falling plaster so the noise would not wake anyone. Then, with Hogan's help, she squeezed through the hole.[19]

The pair walked to the depot just as an eastbound freight train was leaving. They swung aboard, hiding between two cars. At daybreak Sheriff Wakefield, Paul, and the other deputies discovered the escape and immediately began a fruitless manhunt. The escapees beat their way to Deming, New Mexico, where Pearl found work in a brothel. She was soon spotted in town by George Scarborough, one of the most able lawmen of the Southwest. Scarborough knew Pearl Hart had escaped jail and recognized her from the photographs in *Cosmopolitan*. Instead of arresting her, he wired Sheriff Wakefield for instructions. Wakefield told him to try to capture both Hart and Hogan. Scarborough kept watch on the bordello, and early in the morning of October 20 he barged into Pearl's room and found her and Hogan undressed. She unleashed a torrent of oaths, but Scarborough handcuffed both and brought them to Tucson.

By this time, Undersheriff Paul was no longer amused by Pearl, and he took no more chances with her. She was transferred back to the Florence jail. At her robbery trial a month later, she flirted with the all-male jury and pleaded for mercy. Despite conclusive evidence of her guilt, they acquitted her. The furious judge ordered Pearl rearrested, and she was promptly retried and convicted of stealing a revolver from one of the stage passengers. The judge sentenced her to five years in Yuma. Joe Boot, who had been jailed and was awaiting trial, pled guilty and received extremely harsh punishment: thirty years' confinement. Pearl was pardoned in 1902. She moved to Kansas City, where she ran a cigar stand for some years, then disappeared from history.[20]

Pearl Hart, America's best-known woman stage robber. This photograph is one of several taken in the Pima County jailyard in 1899. Author's collection.

Although Pearl Hart had been the most infamous prisoner in Paul's jail, she was hardly the most dangerous. That dubious honor fell to Luis Chavez, whom the *Arizona Republican* called "one of the most fiendish criminals that Arizona ever knew." Chavez was a miner from Sonora, Mexico. After murdering his wife and beating a fellow miner to death with a shovel, he fled north across the border. In 1897 he killed a Chinese brickmaker known as "Crazy John" in the little mining camp of Rollin. Chavez fled back into Mexico and escaped punishment. In December 1898 he was working for the New Mexico and Arizona Railroad, building fences on the right-of-way near Sonoita, fifty miles south of Tucson. On the morning of December 12, Chavez quarreled with the section foreman, E. A. Shepard, over $1.25 in past-due wages. Jerking a long knife from under his serape, Chavez plunged it into Shepard's chest, a mortal wound. Shepard died that night, and Chavez was lodged in the Pima County jail on a charge of murder.[21]

At the same time that Pearl Hart had been locked in her private room, Chavez had been awaiting trial, kept under close guard in a cell on the ground floor. Ed Hogan's trusty status had been revoked, and he was kept in a cell next to Chavez. On the morning of November 27, 1899, the jailer, J. S. Hopley, unlocked the cells and released Chavez, Hogan, and two smugglers, Jesus Preciado and Agustin Bran, into the inner corridor. Bob Paul, standing guard at the corridor gate, sent a trusty into the cells to empty the night buckets. As the trusty walked down the corridor with the buckets, Undersheriff Paul unlocked the grated door to let him out. Suddenly Chavez sprang forward and shoved the wicket open. Paul, still possessing great strength despite his sixty-nine years, slammed the door shut, but one of the buckets caught on the jam and stopped it from closing. Chavez seized Paul, and the two engaged in a deadly struggle inside the corridor. At the same time, prisoner Jesus Preciado grappled with Jailer Hopley. Then prisoner Agustin Bran seized a piece of firewood and struck Hopley a terrific blow on the head, knocking him unconscious. Paul, who was a much bigger man than Chavez, had got the better of him, throwing him to the floor and holding him down. Preciado, Bran, and Ed Hogan dragged Hopley into a cell and locked the door. Then they turned on Bob Paul. One of the desperadoes picked up the firewood club and struck the old lawman a vicious blow to the head. But Paul dodged the blow, swinging up his left arm, and the force shattered the cap of his elbow. Dragging Paul off of Chavez, all four of them overpowered the officer, dragged him into another cell, and locked him inside.

The desperadoes rushed out of the corridor and into the jail office, where Hogan grabbed Hopley's pistol. Hogan, adding insult to injury, also stole Paul's hat. Then the escapees passed through the courthouse and slipped outside unseen. They headed south on foot. Paul raised the alarm, and soon Sheriff Wakefield and a posse were hunting the fugitives, without success. Paul was angry and humiliated. When one newspaper reported that Chavez had thrown him down and overpowered him, he contacted reporters about the error. Despite his age, Paul still had great pride in his physical prowess, as one journal reported in its correction: "With three men over him it could not otherwise be expected than that they should overpower Mr. Paul

On the left in irons is Luis Chavez, the most dangerous prisoner in Bob Paul's jail. On the right is the notorious bandido Agustin Chacon. Courtesy of the Arizona Historical Society/Tucson, 29909.

and lock him up, as they did Hopley. The break might be repeated and men of even greater strength than Hopley or Paul be placed in the predicament in which they were found. . . . Neither of the officers has the slightest tinge of cowardice in his composition, as all who know them can attest."[22]

Despite a broken elbow and bruises to his body and his ego, Undersheriff Paul returned to duty immediately. Four days after the break, on

December 1, a Hispanic boy came to the jail and told the officers that he had seen Chavez a day earlier at Tanque Verde, thirteen miles east of Tucson. Paul was in no condition to take part in a manhunt, so Sheriff Wakefield set off alone on horseback. He tracked Chavez from Tanque Verde across the Rincon Mountains where he learned that the fugitive was headed to Greaterville, a small mining camp about forty-five miles south of Tucson. Wakefield quickly boarded a train for Crittenden, where he hired a horse and arrived in Greaterville the following evening, December 2. There a Mexican told him that he had spotted Chavez in the brush outside of town. Wakefield caught up with Chavez five miles east of Greaterville. The desperado was afoot, sixty yards ahead of him, when the sheriff called on him to throw up his hands. Chavez was still carrying Jailer Hopley's revolver. As he jerked the pistol, Sheriff Wakefield swung up his shotgun and fired. A full charge of buckshot slammed into the outlaw's chest, killing him instantly. A coroner's inquest was held the next day, then Luis Chavez was buried under a tree near the spot where he died.[23]

The following year Bob Paul had more notorious outlaws in his jail. Burt Alvord and Billy Stiles, both former lawmen who went bad, had organized a bandit gang that robbed two trains in Cochise County. Eventually most of the band was captured, and several of them, including Alvord, Stiles, Matt Burts, and William Downing, were placed in the Pima County jail for safekeeping. In October another jailbreak embarrassed Paul and Wakefield. Four Hispanic prisoners managed to cut through the outer brick wall; three of them were promptly recaptured. When the *Citizen* laid the blame on the county board of supervisors for not paying for proper upkeep and an additional jailer, Sheriff Wakefield immediately accepted personal responsibility.[24]

By now Paul—undoubtedly at Margaret's urging—recognized that at age seventy he was too old to safely perform a lawman's duties. He decided to make a run for one of the two posts of justice of the peace in Tucson. In the general election of November 1900, he polled 402 votes but was defeated by a Democratic candidate. Lyman Wakefield ran for reelection and also lost. On the morning of January 2, 1901, Sheriff Wakefield formally turned over his office to the Democratic challenger, Frank Murphy. As the *Citizen* reported, "Mr. Paul is busy today closing the accounts of the old sheriff and Manuel Drachman will take Mr. Paul's place as undersheriff and jailer."[25]

It was the last law enforcement duty Bob Paul would ever perform. Still active and apparently healthy, a few days later he was elected one of the trustees of the Tucson Building and Loan Association. Two weeks after that he suddenly fell gravely ill from stomach cancer and Bright's disease, today known as acute nephritis, which causes the kidneys to fail. Coincidentally, that was the same illness that had claimed his brother Tom thirty years earlier. Except for his occasional bouts with malaria, it was the first serious illness of Bob Paul's life. He was bedridden in his humble adobe on Pennington Street, tended to by Margaret and his youngest son, Edgar. The *Citizen* commented, "The best medical attention is provided in his case and the physicians fear that the disease has gotten an upper hand of the patient." But the old pioneer was still tough and strong, and he rallied so much that in a week the doctors believed he would recover. It was a false hope. He began to steadily fail, and on March 23 the *San Francisco Call* ran a prominent headline, "Noted Peace Officer Is Dying at Tucson," and reported, "The once powerful man has wasted away until there remains but a mere semblance of his former self."[26]

His son Robert and daughter-in-law Annie rushed to his bedside from their Arivaca ranch. Soon John, who came from Los Angeles, and Walter and Edith, who came from San Francisco, joined them. Margaret, ever the devout Catholic, made sure that a priest visited the house and administered the last rites. On the morning of March 26, 1901, the old lawman's suffering ended, and he died in his home, surrounded by friends and family. His body was embalmed and placed in an open casket in the front room. His grandson Alfred Paul, then seven years old, recalled being lifted up to view the body, and that "all the while many friends of the family sat in chairs arranged about the walls of the room keeping the long, quiet vigil of a typical Irish wake." The funeral was the next afternoon, and a large procession followed his casket to the Catholic cemetery.[27]

Paul's obituary was published widely in California and the Southwest and even prominently in the *National Police Gazette*. The *San Francisco Examiner* called him "one of the most noted characters of the southwest" and proclaimed that "his life was one long tale of peril and adventure. . . . As sheriff it was a notable fact that all of the hardest work of the office was done by him, and that he never sent a deputy where he would not go himself. He seemed to have no fear of man or devil, and was as willing to go after the quickest and nerviest gun man in the Territory as he was after a petty criminal." Eulogized the *San Francisco Call*, "He was known over the southwest as one of the bravest officers. . . . In the pursuit of bandits, Apaches, and 'bad' men he never faltered, and at the risk of his life many desperadoes have been brought to justice." To that the *Tucson Citizen* added, "As an officer ever working for the suppression of outlawry in the southwest, the character of Bob Paul stands unique, fascinating in its many thrilling memories—a life which was not spent in vain. Knowing not fear, never for a moment feeling the impulse of hesitancy when duty confronted him, brave Bob Paul spent the best years of his life in protecting the lives, the homes and the property of his fellow men." The *Phoenix Gazette* declared, "The territory is largely indebted to him for its law abiding character today; more to him than to any other one man the territory has ever called citizen."[28]

But perhaps Paul would have been most pleased with the eulogy published in the *Star* by Louis C. Hughes, who ran a laudatory sketch of the adventurous life of "this old and fearless pioneer of the coast." Proclaimed Hughes, "Sheriff Paul . . . was always equal to the task. He was considered a brave and fearless man, a good peace officer. . . . Mr. Paul was appointed United States Marshal for Arizona, and he filled the office with credit to himself and the public service. . . . The deceased was a man of wonderful physical power and endurance. Few men could have passed through the experiences he met and overcame and survived. In many ways he was a remarkable man and filled a large place in the history of Arizona's development and civilization."[29]

A month after her husband's death, Margaret Paul sold the big house on Main Street for $3,500. Later that year she rented out the adobe on Pennington and moved with Walter, Edith, Edgar, and her grandchildren to San Francisco. By family tradition, one of her last acts was to toss Paul's guns down the well behind her adobe house. They represented the part of his life that had most caused her worry and distress. Margaret lived in San Francisco until her death in 1915. To visiting friends, she proudly displayed her collection of newspaper articles chronicling her husband's adventurous career. Her son Robert remained behind in Tucson with his wife and daughter. He died there in 1902, age thirty-six, from a lung abscess caused by his old gunshot wound. John V. Paul, after his divorce, moved to Canada to work for the Canadian Pacific Railroad. After 1902, none of the Paul family was left in Tucson.[30]

During the years after Paul's death, his political enemies in Tucson gave accounts of the 1884 election to newspapers and magazines. Their versions placed him in the worst light possible. With his family gone and many of his closest friends dead, there were few left to defend him. In newspaper interviews, former sheriff Matthew Shaw was especially critical of Paul. Until his death in 1935 Shaw served in various Tucson law enforcement positions, spending his final fourteen years as night watchman at the county courthouse. As late as 1931 Shaw gave an interview to the *Star* in which he charged that in the 1884 election, "Paul had some of his henchmen obtain the box and change the ballot count." Mose Drachman, prior to his death in 1935, compiled his reminiscences, which also gave an anti-Paul account of the election. Copies of both memoirs were filed with the Arizona Historical Society and have been relied on by almost every subsequent writer who has described Paul's career in Arizona. Modern historians and writers repeated the election-fraud myth so often that stories of Paul's exploits are sometimes overshadowed by false claims that he was a dishonest official and a ballot-box stuffer.[31]

In the end, however, history bears out the judgment of the contemporary journalists who penned his obituaries. The truth is that Paul's honesty and integrity were unimpeachable. He also had one of the longest, most colorful, and most significant careers of any western lawman, spanning a half century on two of the toughest frontiers of the Old West. From his service as a young constable and deputy sheriff in the gold rush, to his years riding shotgun for Wells Fargo, to his career as sheriff and U.S. marshal in Arizona, he had taken part in some of the most exciting events on the western frontier. He saved seven men from lynch mobs but never flinched from his duty in the legal hangings of eleven murderers in California and Arizona. He led posses that killed five of the most dangerous outlaws of the Southwest. He rubbed shoulders with some of the West's most noted gunfighters and frontiersmen: Mike Tovey, Al Sieber, the Earp brothers, Doc Holliday, Bat Masterson, Buckskin Frank Leslie, Lou Rickabaugh, Dave Neagle, and Jim Leavy. He counted as friends some of the West's most capable lawmen: Charlie Clarke, Ben Thorn, John Boggs, Jim Hume, John Thacker, Sam Deal, Len Harris, Pete Gabriel, Dan Tucker, and John H. Slaughter. He came to Arizona a seasoned lawman and was fifty-one years old—an age at which many modern police officers retire—when he took office as sheriff of Pima County. But his power, energy, and endurance were those of a young man, and his utter fearlessness was the stuff of legend.

By nature Bob Paul was a hunter: of whales, mineral wealth, and wanted men. It is a great irony that he became a lawman only by default. In pursuing his ambition to be a wealthy mine owner, he made and lost several

The Paul family in front of the Pennington Street adobe in Tucson, circa 1900. Bob Paul is seated at right, and wife Margaret is standing in the doorway. To right of the door, standing, are son Edgar and daughter Edith. Robert G. Paul collection.

fortunes. Each time he failed in business, he turned to what he did best—enforcing the law. And as a lawman he had few equals and no betters. In size, strength, and temperament he was born to deal with danger, violence, and death. Yet he never became hardened or cynical. To his final months he was a firm and unrelenting lawman, yet at the same time he was friendly, good humored, and kind. As a parent, he was stern but caring; as a friend, steadfast and loyal. With women, in particular, he was, as his grandson once said, "as gentle as a kitten." He was a faithful and constant companion to Margaret, and despite his poor financial acumen, Paul provided well for his family and sent his sons and daughters to the finest colleges on the West Coast. As a businessman, he was a marked failure. Though he died on the brink of poverty, few men on the frontier lived a life so rich.[32]

A true pioneer of American law enforcement, Bob Paul was crucial in establishing law and order on two frontiers. His career both mirrored and exemplified the creation and development of modern American policing. It began at a time when professional law enforcement was in its infancy. By determination and dedication Paul taught himself the intricacies of police work: investigating crime, assisting prosecutors in court, cultivating informants, interrogating suspects, communicating by telegraph and telephone, issuing wanted notices, writing reports, supervising and training subordinates, balancing a budget, managing jails, and performing a plethora of related tasks. He was no dime-novel gunfighter, but because his career encompassed an era of extraordinary violence, he became adept at resisting mobs, executing condemned men, and shooting down criminals who resisted arrest. It is no exaggeration to say that he helped invent law enforcement in the American West.

A century later his story remains relevant, its lessons still to be learned. The challenges he faced—violent crime, youth gangs, ethnic violence, racial discrimination, police-minority relations—are as important today as they were in his lifetime. The great controversies of his career—electoral corruption, Mexican-U.S. diplomatic relations, illegal immigration, and border security—still await resolution. A close look at Bob Paul's turbulent life and times can help show us from whence we came, and where we might go.

Today he is largely forgotten, the story of his deeds as hushed as the silent walls of Tucson's crumbling adobes and the played-out placers of old Calaveras. There is no monument to him anywhere in Arizona or California, and even his grave is long lost. And yet, unlike Ozymandias, he left to the deserts of the Southwest something more substantial than marble or stone. The very week he died the territory's first state police, the Arizona Rangers, was created in an eventually successful effort to stamp out lawlessness and pave the way for statehood, which was finally achieved in 1912. It is a legacy Bob Paul would have been proud to claim.[33]

Notes

PREFACE AND ACKNOWLEDGMENTS

1. Waters, *Earp Brothers of Tombstone*, 127.

2. A note on ethnic terminology is appropriate. I use the term "Mexicans" in referring to natives of Mexico; "Mexican Americans" in referring to Arizonans of Mexican heritage; and "American Indians" or "Indians" in referring to Native Americans. Often, however, the historic record is not clear as to the nativity of a Spanish-speaking person, and in such cases I refer to them as "Hispanic." I also employ the widely used term "Hispanic" in a generic sense for Spanish-speaking residents of the Southwest. For the same reason, I use the term "Anglo" to refer to the white, English-speaking population, though it included Irish and many others of non-English European heritage.

3. Undated Tucson newspaper clipping, Robert H. Paul scrapbook.

CHAPTER ONE

1. Robert H. Paul family genealogical records; "List of Persons Composing the Crew of the Ship Majestic, 1842," New Bedford Whaling Museum; seamen protection papers for John Paul, New Bedford Free Public Library; *Phoenix Arizona Republican*, special edition, August 1892; *Lowell Directory*, 46. Some Paul family sources show Bob Paul's middle name spelled "Havelin." However, in his application for membership in the Society of California Pioneers, completed in his own hand, he spells it "Havlin."

2. Carlton, *History and Problems of Organized Labor*, 30; *New Bedford Directory* (1836), 72; *New Bedford Directory* (1838), 91. There is no record of the John Paul family in the vital records of Lowell. Stuart M. Frank to the author, May 4, 1996.

3. Chickering, *Statistical View*, 58; *Cincinnati Daily Gazette*, August 19, 1840.

4. Melville, *Moby Dick*, 36–37.

5. *New Bedford Directory* (1839), 107 (listing Mary Paul as a widow for the first time); seaman protection papers for John Paul; ship registers of New Bedford, 1:171, New

Bedford Whaling Museum; Wood, abstracts of whaling voyages, 1:261, New Bedford Whaling Museum.

6. *Phoenix Arizona Republican*, special edition, August 1892; Paul, biographical sketch of Robert H. Paul, Arizona Historical Society.

7. Philbrick, *In the Heart of the Sea*, 2.

8. Wheeler, *History of Newport*, 414; "List of Persons Composing the Crew of the Ship Majestic, 1842"; *Tucson Daily Citizen*, July 21, 1895.

9. Log of the *Majestic*, August 10, 1846, New Bedford Whaling Museum; "List of Persons Composing the Crew of the Ship Majestic, 1842"; ship registers of New Bedford, 1:194.

10. Log of the *Majestic*, July 22–August 5, 1842; Creighton, *Rites and Passages*, 60–61.

11. *Whale Fishery of New England*, 39.

12. Log of the *Majestic*, August 6–11, 1842; Nordhoff, *Whaling and Fishing*, 122–29.

13. Nordhoff, *Whaling and Fishing*, 129.

14. Log of the *Majestic*, September 6, 1842; Nordhoff, *Whaling and Fishing*, 131–32.

15. Log of the *Majestic*, September 7–10, 1842; Creighton, *Rites and Passages*, 9, 29, 141.

16. Log of the *Majestic*, October 2–11, 1842; *New Bedford Register*, April 26 and July 4, 1843; *New Bedford Mercury*, May 12, 1843; *New York Spectator*, May 8, 1844; Wood, abstracts of whaling voyages, 1:208. The *Majestic's* log ends abruptly on October 11, 1842.

17. *Adelaide South Australian Register*, September 23, 1843.

18. Wood, abstracts of whaling voyages, 1:208; *New Bedford Mercury*, June 7, 1844; undated newspaper clipping, Robert H. Paul scrapbook. The *Majestic* experienced an ignominious but honorable demise as part of the stone fleet during the first year of the Civil War, when she was filled with stones and sunk as an obstruction in the Charleston harbor.

19. *New Bedford Directory* (1845), 128; *New Bedford Directory* (1849), 126; *New Bedford Directory* (1852), 137; *New Bedford Directory* (1856), 136; ship registers of New Bedford, 1:100; Wood, abstracts of whaling voyages, 2: 242; *Boston Daily Atlas*, October 1, 1844; *San Francisco Examiner*, March 31, 1901.

20. "List of Persons Composing the Crew of the Ship Factor, 1843"; whalemen's shipping paper, ship *Factor*, New Bedford Free Public Library; Wood, abstracts of whaling voyages, 2:242; *New Bedford Register*, January 21, 1845.

21. Heflin, *Herman Melville's Whaling Years*, 187–88; Daws, *Shoal of Time*, 166–67; Goodman, "1849 Gold Rush Fleet," 315.

22. *Tucson Daily Citizen*, March 26, 1901; undated newspaper clipping, Robert H. Paul scrapbook; Waters and Gilchriese, "Story of Bob Paul," 4.

23. *Honolulu Friend*, November 1, 15, 1845; Wood, abstracts of whaling voyages, 2: 242.

24. *Sydney Morning Herald*, August 8, 1846; *Boston Courier*, October 23, 1846; Wood, abstracts of whaling voyages, 2: 242; "List of Persons Composing the Crew of the Ship Factor, 1843"; Hoskins, *Sydney Harbour*, 81–82.

25. *Sydney Morning Herald*, September 21, December 25, 1846, February 17, 18, 1847; *Sydney Shipping Gazette*, February 6, 1847; *New Bedford Mercury*, June 4, November 5, 1847; Wood, abstracts of whaling voyages, 2:242.

26. *Honolulu Friend*, August 26, 1847; undated newspaper clipping, Robert H. Paul scrapbook; Dodge, *Islands and Empires*, 72; Dolin, *Leviathan*, 180.

27. *New Bedford Whaleman's Shipping List and Merchants' Transcript*, November 2, 1847; *New Bedford Mercury*, May 3, July 26, August 2, October 25, 1850.

28. Ship registers of New Bedford, 1:228; Parker, *Herman Melville*, 251–53.

29. Log of the *Nassau*, October 11–24, 1847, March 20–April 12, June 9–30, 1848; Wood, abstracts of whaling voyages, 1:483; R. H. Paul dictation, circa 1885, Bancroft Library; *Honolulu Friend*, May 1, December 1, 1848. One early account claimed that Paul

retired from whaling "after gaining the rank of captain in 1849." He would have been a mate; he certainly was not captain of the *Nassau*. See *Arizona and Its Resources*, 57.

30. *Honolulu Friend*, July 1, December 1, 1848.

31. Carson, *Recollections*, 10.

32. *Honolulu Friend*, January 1, 1849; Paul, application for membership, Society of California Pioneers; Waters and Gilchriese, "Story of Bob Paul," 2–3.

33. On the January 18, 1849, triple lynching in Placerville, see Boessenecker, *Gold Dust and Gunsmoke*, 26–28.

34. *Sonora Herald*, December 21, 1850, quoted in Lang, *Early Justice*, 12.

35. *Phoenix Arizona Republican*, special edition, August 1892; Waters and Gilchriese, "Story of Bob Paul," 4.

36. Paul dictation, Bancroft Library; *Phoenix Arizona Republican*, special edition, August 1892; *History of Yuba County*, 84; Waters and Gilchriese, "Story of Bob Paul," 4.

37. Goodman, "1849 Gold Rush Fleet," 316; *Phoenix Arizona Republican*, special edition, August 1892; Waters and Gilchriese, "Story of Bob Paul," 4–5. Shubael Hawes died on June 3, 1856, in Calcutta, India, while on a merchant voyage. Wheeler, *History of Newport*, 414.

38. *Sacramento Daily Union*, December 20, 1851. Campo Seco should not be confused with another camp of the same name situated near Jamestown in Tuolumne County.

39. *San Francisco Daily Alta California*, November 24, 1851, January 26, 1852. Joaquin Murrieta was later accused of this crime; his involvement seems doubtful. See Varley, *Legend of Joaquin Murrieta*, 23–24.

40. *Sacramento Daily Union*, February 24, April 8, 1852; *Baltimore Sun*, May 18, 1852; Boessenecker, *Gold Dust and Gunsmoke*, 23–37.

41. *San Francisco Daily Alta California*, August 3, September 13, 20, 1852; *San Francisco Daily Placer Times and Transcript*, September 9, 21, 1852; Ayers, *Gold and Sunshine*, 106–07; Stellman, *Mother Lode*, 105–06; Limbaugh and Fuller, *Calaveras Gold*, 120. Waters and Gilchriese ("Story of Bob Paul," 5) claim that Paul was involved in the both the French war and the Chilean war, both of which took place in Calaveras County. If this were true, his involvement would have been entirely against his character, for these mining disputes resulted in ethnic disturbances with large-scale Anglo mistreatment of Frenchmen and Chilenos. In addition, the Chilean war occurred in December 1849 and the French war in April 1851, when Paul was in the northern mines. Since Paul did not arrive in Calaveras County until October 1851, his participation was impossible. On the Chilean war, see Boessenecker, *Gold Dust and Gunsmoke*, 47–51, and Limbaugh and Fuller, *Calaveras Gold*, 114–17. On the French war, see *San Francisco Daily Alta California*, May 1, 1851, and Limbaugh and Fuller, *Calaveras Gold*, 101–03.

42. Boessenecker, *Gold Dust and Gunsmoke*, 86–91.

43. A great deal of fictional nonsense has been written about Murrieta. For factual accounts, see Secrest's biography of Harry Love, *Man from the Rio Grande*; Thornton, *Searching for Joaquin*; Varley, *Legend of Joaquin Murrieta*; and Boessenecker, *Gold Dust and Gunsmoke*, chap. 5.

44. *Phoenix Arizona Republican*, special edition, August 1892.

45. The Paul quotation is from the *Denver Rocky Mountain News*, May 22, 1882.

CHAPTER TWO

1. *Phoenix Gazette*, March 28, 1901; *Fresno Republican*, quoted in *Phoenix Arizona Republican*, September 18, 1891.

2. Paul dictation, Bancroft Library. On Mark McCormick, see *A Volume of Memoirs and Genealogy of Representative Citizens of Northern California*, 702–03.

3. *San Andreas Independent*, March 3, 1860. On the statewide homicide rates for 1854 and 1855, see Boessenecker, *Gold Dust and Gunsmoke*, 324–25. The compilation of Calaveras County homicides is from the author's examination of digitized San Francisco, Sacramento, and Stockton newspapers of the period. No doubt additional murders that escaped the author's search took place. Historian Clare V. McKanna compiled homicides for seven California counties of the nineteenth century. He found that Calaveras County experienced forty-three homicides in the decade between 1850 and 1860. To obtain this figure, he consulted coroner's reports, court files, and prison records. McKanna, *Race and Homicide*, 6–8; McKanna, "Enclaves of Violence," 400. McKanna's count is, if anything, far too low. Between 1854 and 1859 alone there were at least sixty-five homicides in the county. Many more took place between 1849 and 1854. Records of indictments and coroner's inquests can be helpful in determining gold rush homicide rates; however, many murders took place after which no one was arrested nor any inquest performed, thus no official record of these homicides were made. Coroner's records are often incomplete or nonexistent for the gold rush period. Gold rush newspapers are one of the best sources for measuring homicide rates, for murders were newsworthy and usually reported. Nonetheless, McKanna's conclusion—that the California communities he studied were excessively violent—is incontrovertible. Historian Robert R. Dykstra, on the other hand, has consistently maintained that western frontier communities were not excessively violent. See, for example, his "Overdosing on Dodge City," 505–14; "Body Counts and Murder Rates," 554–63; and "Quantifying the Wild West," 321–47. However, during the past decade numerous studies of frontier communities have established that most had excessively high homicide rates. See Roth, "Guns, Murder, and Probability," 165–75.

4. Johnson, *Policing the Urban Underworld*, 12–40; Prassel, *Western Peace Officer*, 24–30; Friedman, *Crime and Punishment in American History*, 67–71.

5. Boessenecker, *Gold Dust and Gunsmoke*, 280–82; Ethington, "Vigilantes and the Police," 197–227.

6. *San Francisco Call*, April 17, 1881. On Charles A. Clarke (1821–63), see *Stockton Daily Independent*, February 9, 1863; O'Meara, "Story of the Mier Prisoners," 470–71.

7. *Sacramento Daily Union*, February 6, 1854, February 11, 1861. This jail was evidently burned in the massive fire of August 20, 1854, and rebuilt on the same spot.

8. *Outline History of the California National Guard*, 1:60; O'Hare, Berry, and Silva, *Legal Executions in California*, 19.

9. *San Francisco Daily Alta California*, November 13, 1854; *Sacramento Daily Union*, November 13, 1854.

10. *San Francisco Daily Placer Times and Transcript*, March 27, June 25, November 19, 1855; *San Francisco Daily Alta California*, April 5, 1855; *Sacramento Daily Democratic State Journal*, June 27, 1855; *Stockton San Joaquin Republican*, November 24, December 22, 1855; *San Francisco Bulletin*, December 13, 1855, September 27, 1856.

11. *Sacramento Daily Union*, March 28, 1855, August 11, 1856; *San Francisco Daily Alta California*, April 1, 1855, August 20, 1856; *San Francisco Daily Placer Times and Transcript*, March 29, 1855; *Stockton San Joaquin Republican*, March 28, 1855, June 13, 1857; *People v. Wallace Stewart*, case no. 1354, California Supreme Court Records, California State Archives.

12. *San Francisco Daily Placer Times and Transcript*, May 22, 1855; *Sacramento Daily Union*, December 25, 1855.

13. *Stockton San Joaquin Republican*, May 30, 1855; *San Francisco Bulletin*, August 4, 1856; O'Hare, Berry, and Silva, *Legal Executions in California*, 30.

14. *San Francisco Daily Placer Times and Transcript,* June 15, 18, 1855; *Stockton San Joaquin Republican,* May 10, 1856; *Sacramento Daily Union,* June 16, 1855; San Quentin prison register, inmate no. 651 (James Neal) and no. 732 (William Freeman).

15. Richard Maxwell Brown has identified two models of vigilance movements. One is the socially constructive model, such as existed in the early years of the gold rush. The other is the socially deconstructive model, exemplified by masked mobs that broke into jails at night to hang accused rapists and killers. Brown, *Strain of Violence,* 118–26.

16. The identifications of the Rancheria killers are based on the confessions of Manuel Castro and Rafael Escobar. Other reports identified the leader as Guadalupe Gamba; he was described as being light complected with gray eyes, and therefore he may have been the bandit identified by Castro as "El Huero," a common nickname for a light-skinned person. *San Francisco Daily Alta California,* August 11, 18, 1855.

17. *Sacramento Daily Union,* August 9, 10, 17, 1855; Secrest, *California Badmen,* 66–71.

18. *San Francisco California Chronicle,* August 10, September 1, 1855; Secrest, "Revenge of Rancheria," 16–18; Secrest, *California Badmen,* 72–74. A wildly inaccurate account of the Rancheria massacre and manhunt appears in the *Jackson Amador Ledger,* January 14, 21, 28, 1910. Jesse D. Mason, in his *History of Amador County,* wrote that these three men were probably innocent (85). Several writers have followed him, including the author (Boessenecker, *Gold Dust and Gunsmoke,* 54). William B. Secrest, however, has pointed out that the contemporary diary of Alfred Doten shows that two of the hanged men had items stolen from the Dynans in the raid; accordingly at least those two were probably guilty. Secrest, *California Badmen,* 72–73.

19. *San Francisco California Chronicle,* August 11, 1855; Boessenecker, *Gold Dust and Gunsmoke,* 54–55.

20. Boessenecker, *Gold Dust and Gunsmoke,* 55.

21. *Sacramento Daily Union,* August 10, 1855.

22. Mason, *History of Amador County, California,* 86.

23. *San Francisco Daily Alta California,* August 14, 1855; *Sacramento Daily Union,* August 14, 15, 1855; *Stockton San Joaquin Republican,* September 1, 1855; Secrest, "Revenge of Rancheria," 19; Buckbee, *Saga of Old Tuolumne,* 424–25.

24. *Sacramento Daily Union,* August 17, 1855; Secrest, *California Badmen,* 77–81.

25. *Sacramento Daily Union,* August 17, 1855.

26. *Sacramento Daily Union,* August 31, September 3, 1855; *San Francisco California Chronicle,* September 1, 1855; *Stockton San Joaquin Republican,* September 1, 1855; Mason, *History of Amador County,* 86–87; Enock, *Great Pacific Coast,* 170.

27. *San Francisco Daily Alta California,* September 12, 1855; *San Francisco Daily Democratic State Journal,* September 12, 1855; *Sacramento Daily Union,* September 12, 18, 25, 1855.

28. Sherman, *Fifty Years of Masonry in California,* 1:261; *Mokelumne Hill Calaveras Chronicle,* February 21, 1868. David L. Mulford was born in Saratoga, New York, in 1827 and was raised in Texas. He came to California in 1850 and served for four years as a deputy under Sheriff Charles Clarke. After serving one term as Calaveras sheriff, he moved to San Francisco, where he was appointed a U.S. customs officer. From there he went to Idaho and in 1862 became the first sheriff of Boise County. Mulford suffered from tuberculosis and returned to San Francisco, where he died from its effects at age thirty-seven on February 24, 1865. *Stockton Daily Independent,* February 27, 1865.

29. *Sacramento Daily Democratic State Journal,* June 24, 1856; *Sacramento Daily Union,* June 25, 1856. The San Quentin prison register does not show that Jose Sanchez was sent to the penitentiary, supporting the notion that he was released without charge.

30. *Denver Rocky Mountain News,* May 22, 1882.

CHAPTER THREE

1. Boessenecker, *Badge and Buckshot*, 16, 19. The Skinner brothers used the aliases Walker, Williams, and Williamson; Ned Conway was also known as Conner and Convery. Jim Smith's proper name was probably Schmidt. It should be noted that Joseph Henry Jackson's popular book *Bad Company* includes chapters on Tom Bell and Rattlesnake Dick Barter that contain many errors and have been the source of a great deal of misinformation. On Bell's remarkable resemblance to David Mulford, see *Sacramento Daily Union*, October 6, 1856.

2. *San Francisco Daily Alta California*, May 14, 1855; *San Francisco Bulletin*, October 22, 1856; *Nevada City Democrat*, October 15, 1856.

3. Boessenecker, *Gold Dust and Gunsmoke*, 226–30.

4. Moore, "Early Days in California," Wells Fargo Bank History Department, 2, 6.

5. *Stockton San Joaquin Republican*, September 20, 1856; *San Francisco Bulletin*, October 22, 1856; *Marysville Daily Herald*, October 25, 1856.

6. Boessenecker, *Gold Dust and Gunsmoke*, 232–34.

7. *San Francisco Bulletin*, October 22, 1856.

8. *San Francisco Bulletin*, June 21, 1856; *Stockton San Joaquin Republican*, July 12, 1856; *Sacramento Daily Union*, July 14, 1856; *San Francisco Daily Alta California*, July 21, 1856.

9. *San Francisco Bulletin*, June 21, July 10, 1856. On James Cusick (1824–90), see the *New York Times*, July 11, 1890. Cusick was best known as the trainer for bare-knuckle champion John C. Heenan. There is an ongoing debate about the motives of the San Francisco vigilantes. The best evidence is that they rid San Francisco of political ruffians and cleaned up its government. See Ethington, *Public City*, 92–105, 112–27, 130–34. Others have argued that the rise of vigilance in 1856 was caused by anti-Irish sentiment, anti-Catholic sentiment, and class conflict between the city's mercantile elite and its Irish working class. Focusing on the undeniable influence of the city's merchants in the committee, proponents of this view have argued that economic reasons rather than electoral fraud led the vigilantes to target scapegoats under the guise of law and order. See, for example, Lotchin, *San Francisco*; Brown, *Strain of Violence*; Decker, *Fortunes and Failures*; and Senkewicz, *Vigilantes in Gold Rush San Francisco*. The weakness in this argument is that its proponents tend to overlook the character of the men whom the vigilantes blacklisted. The vast majority were notorious political criminals—ballot-box stuffers, shoulder strikers, and ward heelers—whose violent exploits inflamed public sentiment against them; each richly deserved the punishment meted out by the vigilantes. See Boessenecker, *Against the Vigilantes*, 32–36, 165n77.

10. *Sacramento Daily Union*, July 29, August 4, 1856. On the flume and ditch works in Calaveras County, see Limbaugh and Fuller, *Calaveras Gold*, 148.

11. *Stockton San Joaquin Republican*, August 2, 1856; *Sacramento Daily Democratic State Journal*, July 29, 1856.

12. Quoted in the *Sacramento Daily Union*, August 4, 1856; *Sacramento Daily Democratic State Journal*, July 31, 1856.

13. *Sacramento Daily Union*, August 4, October 6, 1856; *Sacramento Daily Democratic State Journal*, July 29, 30, 1856; *San Francisco Bulletin*, July 29, 1856.

14. *Stockton San Joaquin Republican*, June 14, 1856; *San Francisco Daily Alta California*, July 28, 1856; *Sacramento Daily Union*, August 4, 1856; *People v. Williams* (1856) Cal. Reports 206.

15. *Sacramento Daily Union*, August 4, 1856; *San Francisco Call*, April 17, 1881.

16. *San Andreas Independent*, September 24, October 18, 1856; *Tombstone Epitaph*, October 2, 1884.

17. *Auburn Placer Herald*, October 4, 1856, February 28, 1857; Moore, "Early Days in California," 7.

18. Boessenecker, *Badge and Buckshot*, 17–19; Boessenecker, *Gold Dust and Gunsmoke*, 235–38.

19. *Sacramento Union*, October 6, 1856; *San Andreas Independent*, November 29, 1856.

20. Boessenecker, *Gold Dust and Gunsmoke*, 238–40.

CHAPTER FOUR

1. *San Andreas Independent*, November 29, 1856. On Ben Thorn (1829–1905), see Boessenecker, *Badge and Buckshot*, chap. 3. Thorn's honesty later came into question. He would be accused of embezzling tax money and of securing perjured testimony to obtain a reward in a murder case. Ibid., 72, 81–83.

2. *San Francisco Bulletin*, October 27, 28, 29, November 11, 1856; *Sacramento Daily Democratic State Journal*, October 27, 31, 1856; *Sacramento Daily Union*, November 5, 1856; Waters and Gilchriese, "Story of Bob Paul," 5; Boessenecker, *Gold Dust and Gunsmoke*, 199–201.

3. *San Andreas Independent*, November 22, 1856; *Auburn Placer Herald*, February 28, 1857.

4. *Stockton San Joaquin Republican*, June 20, 27, 1857; Boessenecker, *Badge and Buckshot*, 66; O'Hare et al., *Legal Executions in California*, 35–36.

5. Quoted in *Sacramento Daily Union*, August 10, 1857.

6. *Stockton San Joaquin Republican*, July 4, 1857; *San Andreas Independent*, September 5, October 10, 1857.

7. *Sacramento Bee*, March 2, 1858; *San Andreas Independent*, March 6, 1858.

8. *Sacramento Daily Union*, April 24, May 6, October 18, 1858; *San Francisco Bulletin*, August 31, 1858; *San Andreas Independent* October 23, November 20, 1858.

9. *San Francisco Bulletin*, November 29, 1858.

10. *People v. Pedro Ybarra* (1860) 17 Cal. 166; *People v. Ybarra*, case no. 2606, California Supreme Court Records, California State Archives; *San Andreas Independent*, October 23, 1858, September 24, October 22, 1859; *San Francisco Bulletin*, April 19, 1864; *Sacramento Daily Union*, February 9, May 22, 1878.

11. *San Francisco Herald*, January 15, 1859; *San Andreas Independent*, January 15, 1859; *Sacramento Daily Union*, January 13, 1859; San Quentin prison register, inmate no. 1600 (Louis Cortez [sic]).

12. *Sacramento Daily Union*, August 25, 1862; Browne, *Resources of the Pacific Coast*, 55.

13. *Sacramento Daily Union*, June 15, 1859.

14. Johnston, "Wade Johnston Talks to His Daughter," 9–10. Joseph K. Doak (1827–99) later became prominent in Stockton, serving as the city's mayor from 1872 to 1876. *History of San Joaquin County*, 492.

15. *San Andreas Independent*, June 18, 1859; *Sacramento Daily Union*, May 12, June 17, 1859; *Stockton San Joaquin Republican*, June 25, 1859; Johnston, "Wade Johnston Talks to His Daughter," 9–10.

16. *San Andreas Independent*, September 24, 1859; *San Francisco Daily Alta California*, September 21, 1859; *San Francisco Bulletin* September 17, 1859.

17. *San Andreas Independent*, September 17, 1859. On dueling during the gold rush, see Boessenecker, *Gold Dust and Gunsmoke*, chap. 10. The written articles for this duel are preserved in the Bancroft Library.

18. Indenture, William H. Badgley and wife to R. H. Paul, October 19, 1859, Calaveras County Archives.

19. *San Francisco Daily Alta California*, February 22, 1858; *People ex rel. Attorney General v. Squires* (1859) 14 Cal. 12; Laws of California, Article 2402, sec. 10 (Fees of Sheriffs), Article 3085, sec. 111 (Revenue), in Wood, *Digest of the Laws of California*, 438–39, 638; *Volume of Memoirs and Genealogy of Representative Citizens of Northern California*, 506. Paul's income as sheriff has been estimated by a comparison of the fees earned by the sheriff of Sacramento County, which were $9,393 in 1861 according to the *Sacramento Daily Union*, March 15, 24, 1862. The economies of the two counties were similar, though Calaveras had 67 percent of the population of Sacramento County, with 16,299 residents in 1860 compared with Sacramento County's 24,157. If we assume that sheriffs' fees were similarly proportional, it can be estimated that Paul earned a salary of $6,293 in 1861.

20. *Sacramento Daily Union*, November 4, 1861; Boessenecker, *Badge and Buckshot*, 69.

21. *San Andreas Independent*, July 14, December 15, 1860, January 26, 1861; *San Francisco Bulletin*, December 13, 17, 1860; *San Francisco Daily Alta California*, December 16, 1860; Boessenecker, *Badge and Buckshot*, 69–71.

22. *San Andreas Independent*, February 9, 1861; *Sacramento Daily Union*, February 11, 1861.

23. *Sacramento Daily Union*, March 25, 1861, November 4, 1861; *Stockton Daily Independent*, November 8, 1861.

24. *Ninth Census of the United States*, 14; McKanna, "Enclaves of Violence," 399–400.

25. U.S. Census Population Schedules, Calaveras County, 1860, National Archives; *New Bedford Directory* (1859), 138; *Stockton San Joaquin Republican*, June 23, 1860.

26. On the county jail inmates charged with murder, including five Chinese charged with killing a countryman, see *San Andreas Independent*, June 30, 1860; *Sacramento Daily Union*, July 3, 1860; *San Francisco Bulletin*, September 3, 1860; *San Francisco Daily Alta California*, October 17, 1860.

27. *San Andreas Independent*, February 11, 1860, March 23, 1861; *Sacramento Daily Union*, March 20, 25, 1861; *Los Angeles Times*, March 5, 1899; Boessenecker, *Badge and Buckshot*, 71–72.

28. On the Big Break, see Boessenecker, *Bandido*, chap. 6.

29. *Mokelumne Hill Calaveras Chronicle*, September 7, 1861, quoted in *Sacramento Daily Union*, September 9, October 12, 1861; *Stockton Daily Independent*, October 11, 1861, February 9, 1863.

30. Index to births in New Bedford, 30, New Bedford Free Public Library; Marriages solemnized in New Bedford, 89, 107, 108, New Bedford Free Public Library; *Calaveras Chronicle*, December 29, 1861; U.S. Census Population Schedules, New Bedford, Mass., 1860; Waters and Gilchriese, "Story of Bob Paul," 6–7.

31. Marriages solemnized in New Bedford, 89, 107, 108; *New Bedford Directory* (1859), 80, 138.

32. *Phoenix Arizona Republican*, August 21, 1891.

33. *Census Bulletin*, 5; *Mokelumne Hill Calaveras Chronicle*, March 8, 1862. On courtship, marriage, and gender imbalance in 1860s California, see Hurtado, *Intimate Frontiers*, 75–77, 98–99.

34. Boessenecker, *Badge and Buckshot*, 133.

35. Boessenecker, *Gold Dust and Gunsmoke*, 219–24; Buchanan, *David S. Terry of California*, 124–25.

36. *San Francisco Bulletin*, April 17, 1862; Hittell, *History of California*, 4:300–301.

37. *San Francisco Bulletin*, April 29, 30, 1862; *Sacramento Daily Union*, April 30, May 1, 3, 1862.

38. *San Francisco Bulletin,* August 27, 1862.

39. *San Francisco Bulletin,* May 5, 6, 1862; *Official Report of the Proceedings, Testimony, and Arguments in the Trial of James H. Hardy,* 203–05, 240–43; Stewart, "Impeachment of James H. Hardy," 61.

40. Assessment list of Township 6, 1863, Calaveras County Archives; *Stockton Daily Independent,* July 23, September 5, 1863.

41. Indenture, J. C. Gebhardt and Augustus Gebhardt to R. H. Paul, February 9, 1863, Calaveras County Archives; *San Andreas Register,* February 27, 1864; *Sacramento Daily Union,* March 9, 1863; *Stockton Daily Independent,* February 25, 1864; *San Francisco Daily Alta California,* February 26, 1864; *San Francisco Bulletin,* February 26, 1864; *Mokelumne Hill Calaveras Chronicle,* December 24, 1864.

42. Robert H. Paul family genealogical records; *Stockton Daily Independent,* January 5, March 15, 1864; Assessment list of Township 6, 1864, Calaveras County Archives.

CHAPTER FIVE

1. Mining notice of R.H. Paul et al., August 4, 1863, Calaveras County Archives; Assessment list of Calaveras County, Calaveras County Archives; *San Francisco Daily Alta California,* December 7, 1864; *Sacramento Daily Union,* March 24, 1865, March 25, 1867; *San Francisco Bulletin,* July 22, 1867.

2. U.S. Census Population Schedules, Calaveras County, Township 6, 1870; *Mokelumne Hill Calaveras Chronicle,* December 1, 1866; Robert H. Paul family genealogical records.

3. *Calaveras Chronicle,* May 15, August 21, 28, 1869; *Sacramento Daily Union,* May 28, 1869.

4. Deed, R. H. Paul and others to John T. Carr, April 1, 1870, Calaveras County Archives; U.S. Census Population Schedules, Calaveras County, Township 6, 1870; Robert H. Paul family genealogical records; Holy Cross Cemetery records, interment no. 19873; *Mokelumne Hill Calaveras Chronicle,* July 9, 1870, April 29, 1871, April 20, 1872; *Sacramento Daily Union,* September 19, 1870.

5. *Sacramento Daily Union,* July 26, September 11, 1871; *San Andreas Calaveras Weekly Citizen,* September 9, 1871; *Phoenix Arizona Republican,* special edition, August 1892; *Los Angeles Times,* July 8, 1896; *San Francisco Call,* December 25, 1896; Santa Barbara *Morning Press,* October 25, 1907. A geologist who visited the Bob Paul Claim later commented that it "had not proved of special commercial importance." Lindgren, *Tertiary Gravels,* 208.

6. *Phoenix Arizona Republican,* June 18, 1893. On Lee Matthews at San Quentin, see *Sacramento Daily Union,* November 21, 1871; *San Francisco Bulletin,* December 4, 1872; *San Francisco Daily Alta California,* November 30, 1875. On wages in 1880, see Long, *Wages and Earnings in the United States,* 26, 28.

7. On James B. Hume (1827–1904), see Dillon, *Wells Fargo Detective.* On John Thacker (1837–1913), see Boessenecker, "John Thacker," 14–19.

8. *San Francisco Call,* February 5, 1885; Chandler, "Wells Fargo: 'We Never Forget!,'" 7; Frank Q. Newton, Jr., to author, October 23, 1996. The late Frank Newton was *the* authority on the western express and stage business, and especially Concord stagecoaches.

9. An extraordinary amount of myth and misinformation has been circulated about Wells Fargo shotguns. See, for example, Christian, "Riding Shotgun," 94–96, 132–33, which has been widely posted on the Internet. Most of the historical statements made in the article are wrong. Authentic Wells Fargo shotguns are exceedingly rare today and are highly prized by collectors. Due to their rarity and value, dishonest gun dealers often cut the barrels down on worthless old shotguns and stamp them with Wells Fargo markings. At

least 98 percent of all Wells Fargo shotguns offered for sale today are counterfeits. Fortunately, these fakes are laughably bad and are easily detected by an expert. Nonetheless, even experts can be fooled. In the otherwise excellent reference work by Louis A. Garavaglia and Charles G. Worman, *Firearms of the American West, 1866–1894,* twelve Wells Fargo firearms (rifles, shotguns, and revolvers) are illustrated. Five of them are phonies.

10. *San Francisco Examiner,* August 9, 1896.

11. Wells Fargo & Company's Express, *Messengers Instructions,* collection of Don Gordon. This publication lists fifty-seven different instructions.

12. *San Francisco Daily Alta California,* December 22, 1885; Roberts, *Great Understander,* 274; *Phoenix Arizona Republican,* June 18, 1893; *Calaveras Chronicle,* April 29, 1871, April 20, 1872.

13. Sonnichsen, *Billy King's Tombstone,* 216; Waters and Gilchriese, "Story of Bob Paul," 5.

14. *Calaveras Chronicle,* April 10, 1875; *Denver Rocky Mountain News,* May 22, 1882.

15. *Calaveras Chronicle,* December 2, 1876; Wells Fargo cash book, 451, Wells Fargo Bank History Department; Brent, "Brief Review of the Service of John Brent," Wells Fargo Bank History Department. On Tovey, see Boessenecker, *Badge and Buckshot,* 79–81.

16. Boessenecker, *Bandido,* 271–74, 389–91.

17. *Sacramento Daily Union,* June 14, 1876. In *Robbers Record,* James B. Hume incorrectly identified Santos Sotelo as Chico Lugo. This has caused confusion, since both William B. Secrest in *Perilous Trails, Dangerous Men* (198ff) and R. Michael Wilson in *Wells, Fargo & Company's Report of Losses from 1870 to 1884* (185ff) followed Hume and made the incorrect identification. Several contemporary newspaper accounts correctly identify Francisco Sotelo as Chico Lugo, including the following: *Sacramento Daily Union,* April 28, July 13, 1877; *Los Angeles Star,* July 10, 1877; and *Los Angeles Herald,* July 10, 1877 (based on an interview with Los Angeles police detective Emil Harris). Additionally, Chico is a nickname for Francisco, not Santos. In the Latin American custom, the mother's name is last; hence the full name, Francisco "Chico" Lugo Sotelo.

18. *Sacramento Daily Union,* September 6, 1876; *San Francisco Bulletin,* September 1, 4, 1876; *Los Angeles Herald,* July 10, 1877; *Independence Inyo Independent,* January 13, 1877; Secrest, *Perilous Trails, Dangerous Men,* 197–99; Hume and Thacker, *Wells Fargo Robbers Record,* 49, 59. Red Rock Canyon is now a California state park and was the location for numerous western films, including *The Big Country* (1958). Robert M. Briggs (1816–86) had been a prominent political figure in Amador County, later serving as land register of Inyo County and superior court judge of Mono County. Coincidentally, his son, N. C. Briggs, as district attorney of San Benito County, prosecuted Tiburcio Vasquez for murder in the Tres Pinos raid, for which the bandit leader was hanged in 1875. *Hollister Free Lance,* December 24, 1886.

19. *Ventura Weekly Free Press,* January 27, 1877.

20. *Los Angeles Weekly Star,* February 3, March 17, 1877; San Quentin prison register, inmate no. 7463 (Jose Tapia).

21. *Independence Inyo Independent,* February 10, 1877. Francisco Sotelo was arrested under the name Francisco Lugo.

22. *Bakersfield Weekly Gazette,* February 24, March 3, 1877; *Independence Inyo Independent,* February 17, 1877; *Winnemucca (Nev.) Daily Silver State,* February 19, 1877. Balch, at the coroner's inquest, testified, "I saw but two men, but it was so dark I could not tell whether they were Mexicans or Americans, but it is my belief they were Americans. . . . After shooting they cried 'stop' several times in good English voice." However, the Sotelo

brothers, as Californios who were born and raised during the American period, spoke English as well as Spanish and were certainly capable of saying "stop" in good English. Oliver Roberts, in his memoirs, published posthumously as *The Great Understander*, claimed that he knew who the killers were and that they were Americans (74–76, 268–73). However, he does not name the killers or explain how he knew who they were. Roberts also claimed that he and the noted Wells Fargo messenger Aaron Y. Ross had investigated the case; but it was Paul who investigated, not Ross. Roberts's book contains a number of demonstrably false "recollections" (such as his claim to have been an eyewitness to Tiburcio Vasquez's 1874 raid on the Coyote Holes stage station) and often cannot be accepted at face value.

23. *Independence Inyo Independent*, February 17, 1877; *Darwin Coso Mining News*, quoted in *Sacramento Daily Union*, February 22, 1877.

24. *Bakersfield Courier-Californian*, March 1, 8, 1877; *Bakersfield Weekly Gazette*, March 3, 1877; *Visalia Weekly Delta*, March 3, 1877.

25. *Bakersfield Courier-Californian*, March 8, 1877; *Bakersfield Weekly Gazette*, March 10, 1877; *Los Angeles Herald*, July 10, 1877.

26. *Sacramento Daily Union*, April 28, 1877; Secrest, *Perilous Trails, Dangerous Men*, 202–03.

27. *Phoenix Arizona Republican*, special edition, August 1892.

28. *Bakersfield Weekly Gazette*, July 28, September 22, 1877; *Los Angeles Star*, July 10, 1877.

29. *Visalia Weekly Delta*, June 23, 30, 1877; *Mokelumne Hill Calaveras Chronicle*, June 30, 1877; undated newspaper clippings in Robert H. Paul scrapbook; Edwards, "Three Unmarked Graves," 2.

30. *Coso Mining News*, August 4, 18, September 13, November 10, 1877.

31. *Visalia Weekly Delta*, February 15, 1878; *San Francisco Bulletin*, December 21, 1875, February 20, 1878; *Los Angeles Herald*, February 22, 1878; Chalfant, *Story of Inyo*, 274–75.

32. *Mokelumne Hill Calaveras Chronicle*, April 20, 1878; Robert H. Paul family genealogical records; Edwards, "Three Unmarked Graves," 2.

33. *Phoenix Arizona Republican*, June 18, 1893.

CHAPTER SIX

1. John J. Valentine to R. H. Paul, August 30, 1878, George A. Brown papers, Arizona Historical Society. Brown was the Wells Fargo agent in Florence, Arizona. The dead bandit was Bill Brazelton, slain by a Tucson posse on August 19, 1878. John and Lillian Theobald, in *Wells Fargo in Arizona Territory*, 60–61, claim that Paul had been in Arizona as a Wells Fargo messenger for several years prior to 1878, which is incorrect. They also erroneously state that Paul and Jim Hume arrested two Arizona stage robbers in early September 1878 and that Paul was therefore already in Arizona when Valentine sent him the August 30 letter. That is also a mistake; the arrests the Theobolds describe took place in late November 1878.

2. On Joseph W. Evans (1851–1902), see *A Historical and Biographical Record of the Territory of Arizona*, 441–42.

3. Theobald and Theobald, *Wells Fargo in Arizona Territory*, 8, 15–17, 51.

4. Ball, *United States Marshals*, 108–09; Wilson, *Encyclopedia of Stagecoach Robbery in Arizona*, 101–02, 217. The latter volume is particularly useful and describes most stage robberies in Arizona; only a few have been overlooked.

5. The Flagstaff–Prescott stage holdups took place on April 5 and 7, 1882. Sheriff Walker was the nephew of the famous mountain man Joseph Reddeford Walker. *Tucson*

Weekly Arizona Star, April 13, 1882. On Walker's demand for money, see Chandler, "Wells Fargo: 'We Never Forget!,'" 10. On Bill Brazelton, see Wilson, *Encyclopedia of Stagecoach Robbery in Arizona*, 105–08, 172–73.

6. A common misconception is that most western lawmen were professional gamblers and gunfighters. This myth was fostered by popular writers of the 1930s and '40s who focused on and extrapolated from the careers of Wyatt Earp, Bat Masterson, Ben Thompson, and Wild Bill Hickok, all of whom were professional sporting men. While it is true that many gamblers did act as lawmen in frontier boom camps, the majority of western police, sheriffs, and constables came from more traditional backgrounds. See Prassel, *Western Peace Officer*, 49–52.

7. Wells Fargo cash book. See also Chandler, "Wells Fargo and the Earp Brothers," 20–25.

8. Salas, *In the Shadow of the Eagles*, 103–05; Hietter, "Surprising Amount of Justice," 193–95; Thomas E. Sheridan, *Los Tucsonenses*, 3.

9. *Tucson Weekly Arizona Star*, August 22, 1878; Wilson, *Encyclopedia of Stagecoach Robbery in Arizona*, 103–08; L. F. Rowell to A. Willard, U.S. Consul at Guaymas, Mexico, September 24, 1878, in *Papers Relating to the Foreign Relations of the United States*, 36.

10. *Tucson Weekly Arizona Star*, August 22, September 5, 19, 1878.

11. On the murder of John H. Adams and Cornelius Finley, see Potter, "Gunfighters and Lawmen," 14, 16, 70.

12. L. F. Rowell to A. Willard, U.S. Consul at Guaymas, Mexico, September 24, 1878, in *Papers Relating to the Foreign Relations of the United States*, 36.

13. *Tucson Weekly Arizona Star*, September 26, October 31, November 21, 1878, January 30, February 13, 1879; *Tucson Weekly Citizen*, February 8, 1879; V. Mariscal to A. Willard, October 11, 1878, and related correspondence, in *Papers Relating to the Foreign Relations of the United States*, 736–41.

14. *Prescott Weekly Arizona Miner*, November 29, 1878; James B. Hume to Lida Munson, November 20, 1878, James B. Hume Papers, Bancroft Library.

15. James B. Hume to Lida Munson, November 28, 1878.

16. James B. Hume to Lida Munson, November 28, 1878; *Prescott Weekly Arizona Miner*, November 29, December 6, 1878; Wilson, *Encyclopedia of Stagecoach Robbery in Arizona*, 175–76. Neither Hume's letters nor the contemporary newspapers named the two suspects.

17. James B. Hume to Lida Munson, December 14, 1878; *Tucson Daily Citizen*, December 7, 1878.

18. On Virgil Earp in Prescott, see Chaput, *Virgil Earp*, chap. 2. On John Behan in Prescott, see Alexander, *John H. Behan*, chaps. 2 and 3. On Doc Holliday in Prescott, see Roberts, *Doc Holliday*, 115–21. In 1882 Paul said he had known Holliday for about three years; the most likely place he could have met him was in Prescott, where Holliday lived from October 1879 until he moved to Tombstone in the summer of 1880. See *Denver Rocky Mountain News*, May 22, 1882. On Paul's visits to Prescott, see *Prescott Weekly Arizona Miner*, November 29, December 6, 1878, April 18, June 13, 27, November 28, 1879; *Tucson Weekly Arizona Star*, February 5, 1880.

19. Undated newspaper clipping in Robert H. Paul scrapbook; Edwards, "Three Unmarked Graves," 2; *Phoenix Arizona Republican*, special edition, August 1892.

20. *Tucson Weekly Arizona Star*, June 23, 1881; *Directory of the City of Tucson for the Year 1881*, 101. *Phoenix Arizona Republic*, special edition, August 1892; U.S. Census Population Schedules, Tucson, Arizona, 1880.

21. *Prescott Weekly Arizona Miner*, June 27, 1879; Wilson, *Encyclopedia of Stagecoach Robbery in Arizona*, 84–85, 176–77. On Jim Stewart, see *Prescott Weekly Arizona Miner*, November 16, 1898; Pridham, "In Stage Days," 98.

22. *Prescott Weekly Arizona Miner*, June 21, July 18, 1879; *Phoenix Herald*, July 12, 1879. Blankenship recovered from his wounds and served for many years as a Phoenix lawman.

23. *Phoenix Herald*, July 16, 19, 1879; U.S. Census Population Schedules, Phoenix, Arizona, 1880; Wilson, *Encyclopedia of Stagecoach Robbery in Arizona*, 85–87; Wilson, *Wells, Fargo & Company's Report of Losses*, 340–42.

24. *Phoenix Herald*, July 16, 19, 1879; Wilson, *Encyclopedia of Stagecoach Robbery in Arizona*, 87.

25. *Phoenix Herald*, August 9, 1879; *Prescott Weekly Arizona Miner*, August 15, 1879; Dillon, *Wells Fargo Detective*, 162–63.

26. *Prescott Weekly Arizona Miner*, August 13, November 20, 28, 1879; *Tucson Daily Citizen*, November 26, 1879; Thrapp, *Al Sieber*, 211; Wilson, *Encyclopedia of Stagecoach Robbery in Arizona*, 176–78.

27. *Prescott Weekly Arizona Miner*, November 26, 1880; *Phoenix Herald*, November 26, 1880; McClintock, *Arizona*, 458.

28. *Phoenix Herald*, November 28, 1879; Wilson, *Crime and Punishment in Early Arizona*, 78–79.

29. Thrapp, *Al Sieber*, 211–12; *Tucson Daily Arizona Star*, February 4, 1880.

30. *Tucson Daily Arizona Star*, February 4, 5, 1880; *Tucson Daily Citizen*, February 3, 5, 1880; Willson, *No Place for Angels*, 111. On David Harshaw (1825–84), see *Tucson Daily Arizona Star*, October 1, 1884.

31. *Phoenix Gazette*, November 26, 1880; *Prescott Weekly Arizona Miner*, July 23, 880; *Prescott Weekly Arizona Miner*, November 29, 1880. Maurice Kildare (Gladwell Richardson) wrote a totally fictitious account of Paul's capture of Demetrio Dominguez in "The Youngest Stage Robber of Arizona," *Real West*, January 1971, 34–35, 50–52.

32. *Tucson Weekly Citizen*, January 31, 1880. On Pete Gabriel, see Boessenecker, "Gun Smoke at the Tunnel Saloon," 58–63.

33. *Tucson Weekly Arizona Star*, June 10, July 22, 1880; *San Francisco Bulletin*, July 15, 1880; *Prescott Weekly Arizona Miner*, July 16, 1880; *Phoenix Herald*, July 16, 1880. Wilson, *Encyclopedia of Stagecoach Robbery in Arizona*, 88–90, incorrectly places this robbery in Maricopa County and states that the culprits were Pony Deal and Sherman McMaster. In fact, they were not accused of this holdup, but rather the one on February 16, 1881, at nearby Dripping Springs.

CHAPTER SEVEN

1. *Prescott Weekly Arizona Miner*, June 18, 1880; *Tombstone Epitaph*, August 28, 1880; Ball, *Desert Lawmen*, 246–64, 285–88.

2. On Charles Shibell (1841–1908), see Anderson, "Posses and Politics in Pima County," 253–82.

3. Ball, *Desert Lawmen*, 67–68; Ball, *Ambush at Bloody Run*, x–xi; Brown, *No Duty to Retreat*, 39–47.

4. Wagoner, *Arizona Territory*, 76–77, 90–95.

5. On Louis C. Hughes (1842–1915), see Wagoner, *Arizona Territory*, 148–49, 310–24; Lyon, "Louis C. Hughes," 171–200; and Dill, "Removal!," 257–76. Lyon presents a complimentary view of Hughes's editorial career. The affair between Hughes and the "notorious courtesan Clara Edwards," identified as "a resident of Maiden Lane" (Tucson's red-light district), is mentioned in two clippings, circa 1885, in the Robert H. Paul scrapbook. However, by profession Edwards was a singer and actress, and one newspaper called her a

"beautiful and celebrated artiste" and an "empress of song." *Tucson Arizona Mining Index*, October 17, 1883, April 26, June 28, 1884. The same journal accused Hughes of "squandering his money on variety women" and "lallygagging . . . with bewitching actresses." *Tucson Arizona Mining Index*, May 20, June 28, 1884. A laudatory sketch of Hughes appears in McClintock, *Arizona, the Youngest State*, 3:5–8. Roosevelt's quote is in the *Tucson Daily Citizen*, July 10, 1906.

6. On John Wasson (1832–1909), see *Tucson Daily Citizen*, January 16, 1909, September 30, 1911, October 15, 1920. On the early history of the *Daily Citizen*, see *Tucson Daily Citizen*, October 15, 1920.

7. *Tucson Daily Arizona Star*, October 5, 1883. On the Mussell Slough Tragedy, see Brown, *The Mussel Slough Tragedy*, and Orsi, *Sunset Limited*, chap. 5. The latter volume presents a well-researched and thoughtfully constructed revisionist view of the Southern Pacific, painting it in a better light than previous histories.

8. For homicides between 1879 and 1880, see *Tombstone Epitaph*, October 20, 1880. The homicides for 1881 and 1882 are from the author's examination of Tucson newspapers; there were probably others that were not recorded. The 1880 census showed Pima County's population as 19,934. *Tombstone Epitaph*, August 12, 1880. Cochise County was created in February 1881 from the southeastern portion of Pima County, thus reducing Pima County's size, population, and crime rates accordingly. The territorial census of 1882 showed that the population of Pima County was 17,504, including 9,743 living in Tucson. *Tombstone Epitaph*, July 8, 1882. For the 2008 Tucson rate, see *Tucson Daily Citizen*, January 2, 2009. One scholar who studied criminal prosecutions in early Pima County concluded that rates of violent crime were low. Hietter, "How Wild Was Arizona?," 183–209. Hietter examined court records of criminal prosecutions and correctly found that the county's law enforcement system was effective and that "endemic violence and lawlessness were an exception" (208–09). Like other scholars who have examined frontier violence, Hietter points out that popular histories that deal with notable incidents, such as the Earp-Cowboy troubles or the Graham-Tewksbury feud, exaggerate the degree of violence and create "an impression of a justice system unable to combat crime." Hietter found that of all serious crimes prosecuted in Pima County, murders made up only 7.3 percent of the total. Hietter does acknowledge a weakness in his methodology: that "court cases are an inadequate measure of violent crime." The reason that scholars cannot rely on court cases as a measure is that some crimes were never reported, and many criminals were never arrested or prosecuted, especially in frontier regions. Despite this recognition, Hietter then attempts to ascertain the homicide rate by counting murder prosecutions. He concludes that "as a proportion of crime, violent transgressions were not chronic problems in Tucson or Pima County" and "the most exaggerated violent crime was murder" (198, 202). That conclusion appears to understate the murder rate. Homicide rates in 1880s Pima County were very high, just as they were in neighboring Cochise and Graham Counties, as is made plain from a close examination of the Tucson and Tombstone newspapers of that period. Because many murders in frontier regions were never solved and many killers were never brought to justice, newspaper reports are a much more reliable indicator of frontier homicide rates than court records. It is important to note that Southern Arizona, like the mining country of the California gold rush, was not a free-fire zone. Nonetheless, these regions during the periods under study were extremely violent, with homicide rates vastly higher than modern national rates.

9. *Tucson Weekly Arizona Star*, February 20, 1879; Cool, "Bob Martin," 25–28. The description of Curly Bill is from the Silver City (N.Mex.) *Enterprise*, as quoted in Young, *Pete Spence*, 15. A well-researched biography of Curly Bill Brocius is Gatto, *Curly Bill*.

10. Cool, "Bob Martin," 28–38; *Paul v. Shibell*, Pima County District Court case no. 479, reporter's transcript of testimony, Arizona Historical Society, testimony of James K. Johnson, 132–33. On Pony Deal or Diehl (his true name was Charles Ray), see Rasch, *Desperadoes of Arizona Territory*, 27–28, 33–39.

11. On Ringo, see Burrows, *John Ringo*, and Johnson, *John Ringo*.

12. Wyatt Earp claimed to have been a Wells Fargo messenger for eight months. Perhaps he did fill in for Morgan, but it was Morgan who was paid by Wells Fargo for full-time messenger duty from September 1880 through February 1881 and for part-time duty in May and June 1881. Wyatt was paid for messenger duty only in August 1881. For the service of Wyatt and Morgan Earp as shotgun messengers, see *Tombstone Epitaph*, July 29, August 28, 1880; *San Francisco Examiner*, August 2, 9, 1896; Chandler, "Wells Fargo and the Earp Brothers," 20–25; and Shillingberg, *Tombstone, A. T.*, 142. In his memoirs, published posthumously as *Under Cover for Wells Fargo*, Fred Dodge claimed that Wells Fargo president John J. Valentine had sent him to Tombstone in December 1879 as an undercover agent and that his first act for the company was to recommend that Wyatt Earp be hired as a shotgun messenger. That is incorrect; it was Bob Paul "who secured the services of the famous Earp boys for service as Wells, Fargo & Co. guards." See *San Francisco Examiner*, March 27, 1901; *San Francisco Call*, March 23, 1901; *Calaveras Chronicle*, March 23, 1901. Dodge's claim that he was sent to Tombstone by Wells Fargo as an undercover man is also untrue. At that time Wells Fargo had never been robbed in the Tombstone area. The first stage holdup on the Tombstone route took place on September 16, 1879, and only the passengers were robbed; Wells Fargo's express shipment was not touched. Therefore there was no reason for Wells Fargo to send an undercover agent to Tombstone. Furthermore, undercover officers infiltrate criminal gangs, not cities or towns. By his own account, Dodge says he associated with the Earps, who were lawmen; if he really was a secret agent, this association would have blown his cover. Wells Fargo records show that in October 1881 Dodge was paid by Wells Fargo for posse duty; if he was already on the payroll as an undercover man, the company would not pay him twice. As will be detailed later, Dodge made various other claims in his memoir that are patently false. Wells Fargo had a detective in Tombstone in 1880, and it was Paul, not Dodge. For details on Dodge's false claims, see Chaput, "Fred Dodge," 10–15; and Chandler, "*Under Cover for Wells Fargo*: A Review Essay," 83–96. As Chandler aptly points out: "Paul needed no subterfuge to hide his Wells Fargo work, why should Dodge?"

13. Young, "William Breakenridge," 7.

14. *San Francisco Examiner*, May 27, 1882, as quoted in Turner, *Earps Talk*, 102. On the Earps in Tombstone, see Marks, *And Die in the West*; Tefertiller, *Wyatt Earp*; Shillingberg, *Tombstone, A. T.*; Lubet, *Murder in Tombstone*; and Roberts, *Doc Holliday*.

15. Anderson, "Posses and Politics in Pima County," 269, 271; Shillingberg, *Tombstone, A. T.*, 131. On Shibell's inability to deal with the increase in crime after 1878 and reign in the Cowboys and other criminals, see Anderson, "Posses and Politics in Pima County," 266–68. In fairness to Shibell, it should be pointed out that his deputies arrested several of the Cowboys for violent crimes: Pete Spence in 1878 for killing William Creelon; John Ringo in 1879 for shooting Louis Hancock; and Tom Harper in 1880 for killing John Tolliday.

16. *Tucson Weekly Arizona Star*, September 23, 1880; *Tucson Weekly Citizen*, September 25, October 9, 1880; *Tombstone Epitaph*, October 9, 1880.

17. *Tombstone Epitaph*, September 29, 1880.

18. An uncritical biography by his grandson, Cornelius C. Smith, Jr., is *William Sanders Oury: History Maker of the Southwest*. Unfortunately it contains little on Oury's political

activities in Tucson. In an 1874 application for a military pension from the state of Texas, Oury described his service during the war for Texas independence, but said nothing about being at the Alamo. William S. Oury to comptroller of the state of Texas, August 26, 1874, in William S. Oury file, Texas State Library and Archives. What may be the first public mention of Oury at the Alamo appears in an article that Cornelius C. Smith wrote in the *Tucson Daily Citizen*, September 30, 1912. But in 1921, when Smith prepared a biographical sketch of his grandfather's life, he made no mention of any service at the Alamo. *Tucson Daily Citizen*, February 20, 1921.

19. *Paul v. Shibell*, testimony of John Magill, 294–96. The San Simon Cienega is now dry. The following account of the San Simon election frauds is based primarily on the original trial transcript from the Arizona Historical Society library. Although it had apparently been long in the collection, it was not cataloged and was only recently located by historian Steve Gatto. Robert Palmquist and Casey Tefertiller kindly provided the author with a copy. Previous accounts of this case contain numerous errors because the transcript was not known to exist.

20. On Joe Hill (1849–84), see Johnson, "Alias Joe Hill," in Boardman, *Revenge!*, 115–29. On Nicholas Hughes, see Anderson, *History of New Mexico*, 2:743–44. On A. H. Thompson, see Walker, "Retire Peaceably to Your Homes," 11.

21. *Tombstone Epitaph*, October 14, 1880; *Tombstone Daily Nugget*, October 17, 19, 1880.

22. *Paul v. Shibell*, 24–25; see also the testimony of William S. Oury, 581–82.

23. *Paul v. Shibell*, exhibit E, abstract of Great Register, Precinct 27.

24. *Paul v. Shibell* transcript, testimony of James K. Johnson, 168–78. William C. Davis was a prominent merchant, mine owner, and politician. See *Tucson Daily Citizen*, August 12, 1902, and *San Jose Mercury News*, August 12, 1902.

25. *Tucson Daily Citizen*, April 9, 1901; *Globe Arizona Silver Belt*, April 14, 1907. A transcript of Hancock's account is in the Arizona Historical Society and was published in the *Phoenix Arizona Republican*, April 1, 1927. These stories seem to have had their origin in the following report, which appeared in the *Tombstone Epitaph*, November 7, 1880, just five days after the election: "At the recent election 104 votes were cast at San Simon precinct, 103 of which were Democratic. The odd vote is said to have been cast by a Texas cowboy, who, when questioned why he was voting the Republican ticket, said: 'Well, I want to show those fellows that there wasn't any intimidation in this precinct.'"

26. Tefertiller, *Wyatt Earp*, 51–52; Roberts, *Doc Holliday*, 130–31; *Paul v. Shibell*, testimony of Martin S. Stiles, 268–69.

27. *Paul v. Shibell* transcript, testimony of James K. Johnson, 172–74, 182. A great deal of misinformation has been published about Bill Graham, who has often been confused with Curly Bill Brocius. The testimony at the *Paul v. Shibell* trial plainly shows that he was known as Cactus Bill Graham and that he had a brother named George who used the alias of George Ross. In the 1920s an Arizona pioneer, Melvin Jones, correctly recalled that Bill Graham had a brother named George, but incorrectly stated that Graham was the same man as Curly Bill Brocius. Melvin Jones was one of those interviewed for the hugely popular book *Tombstone: An Iliad of the Southwest* by Walter Noble Burns, who printed the misidentification on page 78. Ever since, Curly Bill Brocius has been confused with Cactus Bill Graham. Some writers have incorrectly claimed that the Bill Graham of the Graham-Tewksbury feud was Bill Graham of the Cowboys; the feudist was an entirely different person. A recent look at Bill Graham of the Cowboy gang has inadvertently muddied the waters even further. Randolph W. Farmer, in "William Henry Graham Was Not Curly Bill," suggested that one William Henry Graham from Coryell

County, Texas, was Bill Graham of the Cowboys. Again, the *Paul v. Shibell* testimony demonstrates that this William Henry Graham was not Cactus Bill Graham of the Cowboys. Nor is there any contemporary evidence that this William Henry Graham had any connection to the Cowboys.

28. *Paul v. Shibell*, testimony of James K. Johnson, 165–70, 191–92; *Paul v. Shibell*, testimony of C. F. Joy, 212; *Paul v. Shibell*, testimony of Martin S. Stiles, 255–57. Several accounts incorrectly claim that John Ringo helped run the fraudulent San Simon balloting. He is not mentioned in the trial testimony as a participant.

29. *Paul v. Shibell*, testimony of R. B. Kelly, 375–78. Randolph Benton Kelly (1845–1903) was a Civil War veteran and a surveyor by trade. He came to Arizona in about 1870 and later served for many years as a Pima County deputy recorder. *Tucson Daily Citizen*, September 8, 1903.

30. *Paul v. Shibell*, testimony of James K. Johnson, 195–96; testimony of R. B. Kelly, 391–92.

31. *Tucson Weekly Arizona Star*, December 23, 1880. Earp's quote is from Palmquist, "Election Fraud 1880," 1.

32. Lake, *Wyatt Earp*, 245. For discussions of Wyatt Earp's account of this bargain, see Palmquist, "Election Fraud 1880," 22–23; and Tefertiller, *Wyatt Earp*, 54, 350n40. On the Earp brothers' election support of Paul, see *Tucson Daily Arizona Star*, November 13, 1880; Shillingberg, *Tucson, A. T.*, 168.

33. *Paul v. Shibell*, testimony of James K. Johnson, 163–64. For the court testimony regarding the $250 loan, see testimony of Johnson, 201–04, and testimony of R. H. Paul, 576–80. On Curly Bill's preliminary hearing, see the *Tucson Weekly Arizona Star*, January 1, 1881, and Gatto, *Curly Bill*, chap. 5. Paul's agreement is evidently what Louis Hughes referred to when he complained that Curly Bill was allowed to go free for the killing of Marshal White "by a pretext and a political bargain." *Tucson Weekly Arizona Star*, February 3, June 23, 1881.

34. R. H. Paul to W. H. H. Miller, January 16, 1890, Arizona Historical Society. Richard Gird (1836–1910) was one of the discoverers of silver at Tombstone. See Shillingberg, *Tombstone, A. T.*, chap. 2.

35. *Paul v. Shibell*, complaint, December 18, 1880; Palmquist, "Election Fraud 1880," 6–7. Charles G. W. French was born in Berkeley, Massachusetts, on August 22, 1820. He graduated from Brown University in Rhode Island, became a lawyer, and joined the California gold rush in 1850. He practiced law in Sacramento County until 1875, when he was appointed chief justice of Arizona by President U.S. Grant, serving until 1884. He died in San Francisco on August 13, 1891. *San Francisco Call*, August 14, 1891; *Sacramento Record-Union*, August 15, 1891; *Phoenix Arizona Republican*, August 15, 1891.

36. *Tucson Weekly Citizen*, December 11, 1880; Cool, "Bob Martin," 38–42; Shillingberg, *Tombstone, A. T.*, 189; *Paul v. Shibell*, memorandum of costs, 1. On Behan's statement that he asked Virgil Earp for the location of the Clanton ranch, see Turner, *O.K. Corral Inquest*, 152. The same statement appears in the *Tombstone Epitaph*, November 5, 1881, but identifies Morgan Earp as the man that Behan asked.

37. *Paul v. Shibell*, testimony of James Johnson, 199–200. Horace Greeley ran for president in 1872.

38. *Paul v. Shibell*, testimony of R. H. Paul, 305–08.

39. *Tucson Weekly Arizona Star*, January 20, 1881.

40. *Paul v. Shibell*, testimony of R. B. Kelly, 366–89; testimony of Leslie F. Blackburn, 412–49. On Leslie Blackburn, see Young, *Cochise County Cowboy War*, 13.

41. Testimony of Marshall Williams, *Paul v. Shibell*, 543–64.

42. *Paul v. Shibell*, 569–76; *Tucson Weekly Arizona Star*, November 25, 1880.

43. *Paul v. Shibell*, testimony of R. H. Paul, 578–80.

44. *Paul v. Shibell*, testimony of W. S. Oury, 583–90, 599–602. Jim Johnson accidentally shot himself in Galeyville in May 1881 and died of the wound. *Salt Lake City Tribune*, June 18, 1881.

45. *Paul v. Shibell*, testimony of William Soule, 615–31; *Paul v. Shibell*, testimony of Hugh Haggerty, 635–41; *Paul v. Shibell*, testimony of R. H. Paul, 643–45; *Paul v. Shibell*, testimony of Isaac Brokaw, 647–49; *Paul v. Shibell*, testimony of A. S. Hooker, 651–53; *Paul v. Shibell*, testimony of A. O. Wallace, 667–90.

46. *Paul v. Shibell*, decision of Judge C. G. W. French, 743–53.

47. *Paul v. Shibell*, memorandum of costs, 3; R. H. Paul genealogical record.

CHAPTER EIGHT

1. *Tucson Weekly Arizona Star*, February 3, 17, March 10, 1881; *Prescott Weekly Arizona Miner*, February 25, 1881; *San Francisco Bulletin*, February 15, March 7, 8, 31, April 2, 1881. Joseph Goldwater's older brother, Mike, was the grandfather of U.S. Senator Barry Goldwater. On Joseph Goldwater, see Smith, *Goldwaters of Arizona*, chap. 7.

2. *Tombstone Epitaph*, March 17, 1881; Wilson, *Encyclopedia of Stagecoach Robbery in Arizona*, 36, 57; Cool, "Escape of a Highwayman."

3. Rasch, "They Tried to Hold Up the Tombstone Stage," 17. According to tradition, the coach Bob Paul rode that day is the so-called Modoc Stage, which is on display in the Sharlot Hall Museum in Prescott. However, in an 1892 newspaper article, the stage was identified as the Grand Central, named after the Tombstone mine, and that name was painted on the side of the coach. *Phoenix Arizona Republican*, June 26, 1892. It is unclear whether these are two different coaches or whether the name "Modoc" was later over-painted onto the Grand Central coach. However, according to the late Frank Newton, an authority on western staging and express, the Modoc Stage in the Sharlot Hall Museum was not the one used on the Tombstone–Benson route in 1881. Frank Q. Newton, Jr., to author, August 16, 1998. At the time, Tombstone had two competing stage lines: Kinnear & Co. and that of Charles "Sandy Bob" Crouch. Numerous accounts state incorrectly that it was the Sandy Bob coach that was attacked at Drew's Station.

4. *San Francisco Bulletin*, June 26, 1877; *Napa Register*, March 19, 26, 1881; *Phoenix Arizona Republican*, June 26, 1892; U.S. Census Population Schedules, Calistoga, Calif., 1880. Eli P. Philpott, born in Illinois on June 5, 1853, was the son of a farmer who settled with his wife and children near Calistoga in Napa County. As a youth Eli, known as Bud, worked in a local stage company's livery stable and later became a driver. His brother-in-law was fellow stage driver Charley Foss, the son of Clark Foss, one of California's most famous whips.

5. Young, "William Breakenridge," 7. Breakenridge disliked Holliday and the Earps, which may have motivated him to repeat this yarn. See Roberts, *Doc Holliday*, 144.

6. *San Francisco Examiner*, August 9, 1896; *Tombstone Epitaph*, March 16, 17, 1881; *Tucson Weekly Arizona Star*, March 17, 24, 1881; *Tucson Daily Citizen*, March 20, 1881; *Phoenix Arizona Republican*, June 26, 1892. The *Arizona Republican* account contains many details about the Benson stage robbery that are not found elsewhere. From its reporter's reference to "Bob Paul, now stopping in this city," some writers have concluded that the entire article is based on an interview with Paul. The same conclusion was reached by the editor of the *Tombstone Epitaph*, who, in the issue of June 28, 1892, described the *Arizona Republican's* account and said it "was furnished by Bob Paul." However, the article contains so many

errors, including a garbled account of the subsequent manhunt with the possemen killing Leonard and Head, that either Paul was misquoted or else he only supplied the information related to the history of the stagecoach itself (see note 3 above) and the actual holdup. The reporter incorrectly claimed that Bat Masterson was aboard the stage, that one of the bandits was Doc Holliday, and that the Earp brothers knew beforehand of the planned holdup. These statements certainly did not originate with Paul, who never alleged any involvement by Doc Holliday and the Earps. Bat Masterson joined the pursuing posse in Tombstone and thus could not have been on the stage. In addition, in his later years as a newspaperman, Masterson wrote about many of his experiences in the West, but according to his biographer, Robert K. DeArment, Bat never mentioned being on the coach. The *Republican's* reporter seems to have obtained some of his information from Paul and then augmented the account with common rumor and vague recollections. There is another false story connected to this incident. Numerous writers have claimed that Bud Philpott had taken ill and that he had switched places with Paul, who actually drove the stage; and further, that the bandits intended to kill Paul but shot Philpott by mistake. This yarn had its origins in an account in the *Tucson Weekly Arizona Star*, August 25, 1881, in which it was claimed that Jim Crane told a friend that Paul and Philpott had switched places. This scenario is not borne out by contemporary newspaper accounts and is most improbable. The correct location of Drew's Station was ascertained by Tombstone historian Nancy Sosa in 2010. She consulted railroad maps and assessor's records and was kind enough to lead the author and other historians on a tour of the site. Today, nothing is left but part of the slate foundation of the stage station and one adobe corner of Drew's house, located two hundred feet north of the station.

7. *Tombstone Epitaph,* March 16, 1881.

8. *San Francisco Examiner,* May 28, 1882, as quoted in Palmquist, "Arizona Affairs," 70.

9. On Curly Bill at the Redfield ranch, see the statement of Redfield's nephew, Frank Carpenter, in the *San Francisco Bulletin*, September 5, 1883.

10. *Tucson Daily Citizen,* March 27, 1881; *Tucson Weekly Arizona Star*, March 24, 1881; *Tombstone Epitaph*, March 22, 1881; Lake, *Wyatt Earp*, 256–62. Lake's popular book, when first published, was considered a masterpiece of western biography. It elevated Earp to folk-hero status and was the basis for several Earp films and the popular television series of the 1950s. By that time, however, its flaws were becoming apparent. Researchers learned that Lake had exaggerated the number of contacts he had with Earp, that most of the Wyatt Earp quotations in the book had been invented by Lake, and that Earp had many human failings and was not the superhero whom Lake had portrayed. Some researchers and writers felt duped and betrayed, and soon the Lake biography fell under severe criticism. For more than thirty years it has been considered a "fictionalized biography" or a "biographical novel." In recent years, however, a new generation of Earp enthusiasts has delved deeply into the events of Earp's life and discovered that Lake's book, although having serious failings, nonetheless was based upon extensive research, contains a wealth of accurate data about Earp's life and times, and, if used carefully, can be a valuable source.

11. *Sacramento Daily Union,* March 19, 1881.

12. *Tombstone Epitaph,* April 2, 1881; Palmquist, "Arizona Affairs," 70.

13. Wells Fargo reward poster, March 23, 1881, copy in author's collection. Fred Dodge claimed that another of the Cowboys, Johnny Barnes, later confessed to him that he had taken part in the stagecoach attack. No contemporary source confirms this. Dodge, *Under Cover for Wells Fargo*, 24.

14. Breakenridge, *Helldorado*, 122.

15. Ibid., 123.Virgil Earp said that the ranch where they were misdirected was Barlow and Pierce's ranch in the San Simon Valley. *Tombstone Epitaph,* April 2, 1881.

16. Breakenridge, *Helldorado,* 123.

17. *Tombstone Epitaph,* April 2, 1881; *Tucson Weekly Arizona Star,* April 7, 1881. Numerous writers, beginning with Stuart Lake, named Wyatt Earp as the leader of the posse. However, the Tombstone and Tucson newspapers referred to the posse as "Detective Paul's party." James B. Hume called it "agent Williams' and detective Paul's posse." Roberts, *Doc Holliday,* 263.

18. Palmquist, "Arizona Affairs," 72; Wells Fargo cash book. See also Chandler, "Wells Fargo and the Earp Brothers," 20–25.

19. Palmquist, "Arizona Affairs," 72.

20. *Paul v. Shibell,* order dismissing appeal, April 12, 1881; Palmquist, "Election Fraud 1880," 19–20.

21. *Tucson Weekly Arizona Star,* April 14, 21, 28, 1881.

22. *Tucson Weekly Arizona Star,* April 28, 1881; C. A. Shibell to Board of Supervisors, May 2, 1881, Pima County documents, University of Arizona Library, Special Collections; *Winnemucca (Nev.) Daily Silver State,* May 9, 1881.

23. *Directory of the City of Tucson for the Year 1881,* 26. Jim Coleman served in Benson as Cochise County deputy sheriff. *Tombstone Epitaph,* July 23, 25, 1882. Ike Brokaw served as jailer until his death from pneumonia on January 11, 1882. On Brokaw, see *San Francisco Bulletin,* November 29, 1870, November 10, 1875; *Tucson Weekly Arizona Star,* January 12, 1882.

24. On Nathan B. Appel (1828–1901), see *Los Angeles Times,* December 12, 1897, January 6, 7, 1901. On Thomas D. Casanega (1853–1934), see Hart, "Arizona Cattle Baron," 50–57. His correct last name was Kazanegra, Americanized into Casanega. On James Speedy (1846–97), see *Phoenix Arizona Republic,* special edition, August 1892, and *Phoenix Weekly Herald,* March 25, 1897. Frederick Russell Burnham (1861–1947) claimed to have worked as a deputy for Paul. Burnham, later a noted scout for the British army in Africa, wrote many wild yarns about his purported adventures on the Arizona frontier. This author has been unable to authenticate any of them. Burnham, *Scouting on Two Continents,* 49.

25. R. H. Paul, "Statement of Sheriff of Property in His Possession Belonging to the County of Pima," Pima County documents, University of Arizona Library, Special Collections.

26. On the Arizona sheriffs' duties as assessor and tax collector, see Ball, *Desert Lawmen,* chap. 12.

27. *Tucson Weekly Arizona Star,* May 5, June 2, 1881.

28. *Southern Pacific Railroad Company v. R. H. Paul, Sheriff and Ex-officio Assessor and Tax Collector of the County of Pima* (1882), Pima County District Court case no. 705; *Tucson Daily Citizen,* July 31, 1882.

29. Harlow, *Duties of Sheriffs and Constables,* 13–14, 128–30. Harlow was undersheriff of Alameda County, California, from 1875 to 1904. His book, first published in 1884, was the standard tome for western sheriffs and constables.

30. *New York Times,* October 27, 1881; *Tucson Weekly Arizona Star,* January 5, 1882; *Paul v. Cullum,* 132 U.S. 539 (1889); Sonnichsen, *Tucson,* 94, 105.

31. *Tucson Weekly Arizona Star,* May 26, 1881. Modern yarns that contend that there was telephone service between Tucson and Tombstone in 1881 are false. Long-distance telephone lines from Tucson to Tombstone and other communities in southern Arizona were not even proposed until 1901 and not completed until after 1903. *Tucson Daily Citizen* July 16, August 10, 1901, October 26, 1903. On Adolph Buttner (1847–85), see Hogan "Adolph George Buttner," 26–31.

32. Tefertiller, *Wyatt Earp*, 86–87, 100; Roberts, *Doc Holliday*, 154–57, 170–71, 263. Kate Elder's charges got some traction in 1960 when Frank Waters released *The Earp Brothers of Tombstone*, the memoir of Virgil's wife, Allie. However, in Allie's original manuscript no such claims are made; they are a fabrication by Waters. See Wheat, "Waters Travesty"; Tefertiller, "What Was Not in Tombstone Travesty"; and Roberts, "Allie's Story."

33. Although the Wells Fargo reward was for the arrest of the murderers, L. F. Rowell, the company's assistant superintendent in San Francisco, wired its Tombstone agent that "we will pay rewards for them dead or alive." Roberts, *Doc Holliday*, 150–51.

34. *Tombstone Epitaph*, June 18, 1881; Young, "Other Ike and Billy," 24–30.

35. *Tucson Weekly Arizona Star*, April 7, 1881; Tefertiller, *Wyatt Earp*, 84–85. On Luther King as Sandy King, see Myers, *Last Chance*, 226; and Thrapp, *Encyclopedia of Frontier Biography*, 2:783.

CHAPTER NINE

1. Tefertiller, *Wyatt Earp*, 4–5, 284–305, 314–16; Erwin, *Truth about Wyatt Earp*, 22–27; Jay, "Peoria Bummer," 46–52; DeMattos, *Mysterious Gunfighter*, 32–34; *Dallas Morning News*, March 17, 1899; Brand, "Wyatt Earp, Jack Johnson, and the Notorious Blount Brothers," 45. Regarding Wyatt's arrest for illegally entering the Ozark Saloon at night in Hot Springs, Arkansas, to mark and switch a faro dealer's cards, see the *Peach Springs Arizona Champion*, March 21, 1885; *Cleveland Plain Dealer*, December 17, 1896; *Dallas Morning News*, March 17, 1899; and *New Orleans Times-Picayune*, March 18, 1899.

2. Undated 1888 Tucson newspaper clipping, Robert H. Paul scrapbook.

3. Masterson, "Famous Gunfighters of the Western Frontier," 22.

4. *Denver Rocky Mountain News*, May 22, 1882; *Denver Daily Tribune*, May 20, 1882. The *Rocky Mountain News* quoted Paul as saying, "The so-called Earpp [*sic*] gang, or faction if you please, was composed entirely of gamblers who preyed upon the cowboys, and at the same time in order to keep up a show of having a legitimate calling was organized into a sort of vigilance committee, and some of those including Holliday, had United States Marshal's commissions. . . . The feeling is . . . very strong, especially among the more respectable citizens who have been terrorized for years by the cowboys and the Earpp gang and justice will no doubt be meted out to Holliday and his partners." However, Paul never alleged at any time that the Earps preyed upon the Cowboys or that the Earps had terrorized the citizenry; he also knew that they were not organized into a vigilance committee and that Doc Holliday never held a deputy U.S. marshal's commission. The *Rocky Mountain News* account was also internally inconsistent. It quoted Paul as saying both that Holliday was "a terror to the criminal classes" and that Holliday and the Earps had "terrorized for years respectable citizens." Its reporter either misquoted or misunderstood Paul's statements.

5. Earp is quoted in Roberts, *Doc Holliday*, 388. The only biography of Behan is Bob Alexander's *John H. Behan: Sacrificed Sheriff*. It is a spirited defense of the sheriff. Many, including Paul, thought that Behan lacked courage. That was not correct, as was demonstrated by a forgotten incident that took place when Behan was superintendent of Yuma prison. On the night of June 13, 1888, a convict, Joseph Porter, escaped and somehow obtained a Winchester rifle. In the morning Behan, who was ill, discovered the break. Despite his weak condition, he started on Porter's trail with Indian trackers. The convict crossed and recrossed the Gila River, finally taking to the brush, where Behan could not follow on horseback. Behan was taking the lead into a dense thicket when suddenly Porter opened up with his Winchester. Behan returned the fire and kept advancing until he managed to disarm and capture the escapee. *Tucson Weekly Citizen*, June 16, 1888.

6. *Tombstone Epitaph*, June 23, 1881; *Baltimore Sun*, July 11, 1881. A somewhat different account of this murder is in the *San Francisco Bulletin*, June 24, 1881. The old convent is long gone, but the ruins of Warner's Mill can still be seen on the west side of Mission Road, near its junction with Mission Lane.

7. *Tucson Weekly Arizona Star*, July 14, 1881.

8. *Tucson Weekly Arizona Star*, September 23, October 21, 1880, July 14, 1881; *Tombstone Daily Nugget*, July 10, 1881; Wilson, *Crime and Punishment in Early Arizona*, 86–87. There is no truth to the popular yarn that Thomas Harper is buried in Boot Hill Cemetery in Tombstone. In order to attract tourists, many of the Boot Hill gravesites are falsely marked, and fictitious claims of burials have been made by the cemetery's various operators over the years.

9. R. H. Paul to Mexican Consul at Tucson, June 30, 1881, Arizona State Library and Archives.

10. John J. Gosper to James G. Blaine, September 20, 1881, Arizona State Library and Archives.

11. James G. Blaine to Manuel de Zamacona, November 10, 1881, in *House Documents, Otherwise Publ. as Executive Documents: 13th Congress* (1883), 627–29. The authors of a revisionist history write that Blaine "based his conclusion entirely on the testimony of the local sheriff, R. H. Paul." Carrigan and Webb, in Cole and Parker, *Beyond Black and White*, 55–56. In their zeal to establish anti-Mexican racism on the part of both the vigilantes and lawmen, the authors (unaware that the lynchers were mostly Hispanic) suggest that "local officials"—presumably Paul—were members of the mob. Daniel S. Margolies, in *Spaces of Law in American Foreign Relations*, goes further, saying Paul "was involved in the hanging" (157). Not a whit of evidence supports this conclusion.

12. *Tombstone Epitaph*, September 10, 1881; *Tucson Weekly Arizona Star*, September 22, 1881; *Prescott Weekly Arizona Miner*, September 16, 1881; Cool, "Escape of a Highwayman," 2–13. Some writers have described this telegram to Marshall Williams as an example of Paul's bias in favor of Wells Fargo, and Paul's reporting to Virgil Earp as an example of his mistrust of Sheriff Behan. However, Sheriff Paul undoubtedly sent the wire to Marshall Williams because he believed that was the fastest way to get it to City Marshal Earp. And Paul notified Virgil Earp because he, not Behan, had jurisdiction in the city of Tombstone.

13. Roberts, *Doc Holliday*, 177–80; Tefertiller, *Wyatt Earp*, 111–12. On Pete Spence, see Young, *Pete Spence*.

14. *Tucson Weekly Citizen*, October 16, 1881; *Tombstone Epitaph*, October 15, 1881; Rasch, "Jerry Barton," 37–39; Nelson, "Trailing Jerry Barton," 36–42; Breakenridge, *Helldorado*, 106–07; Martin, *Tombstone's Epitaph*, 63–66; Cool, "Salt War Sheriff," 26. Jerry Barton was not punished for any of his misdeeds until 1887, when he killed another man with his bare fists and was sent to Yuma prison for three years. After his release, Barton ran a succession of saloons and stayed out of trouble. He died in Tucson on June 4, 1904. *Tucson Daily Citizen*, June 7, 1904; *Phoenix Arizona Republican*, June 12, 1904.

15. Tefertiller, *Wyatt Earp*, 113; Roberts, *Doc Holliday*, 182.

16. A full recounting of the street fight in Tombstone is beyond the scope of this book. The literature is enormous. Among the most informed and reasoned treatments are Marks, *And Die in the West*; Tefertiller, *Wyatt Earp*; Shillingberg, *Tombstone, A. T.*; and Roberts, *Doc Holliday*. A number of recent writers have argued that the Clantons and McLaurys were not livestock thieves. But in an 1897 interview, even Sheriff Behan admitted that they were: "The Clanton brothers and the McLowrys [*sic*] were a tough lot of rustlers who were the main perpetrators of the rascality rife in that region." In the same interview, Behan

gave his skewered version of the Earp-Clanton troubles: "Between them and the Earps rose a bitter feud over the division of the proceeds of the looting. The Earp boys believed they had failed to get a fair divide of the booty and swore vengeance. They caught their former allies in Tombstone unarmed and shot three of them dead while their hands were uplifted." *San Francisco Call*, December 7, 1897.

17. On the preliminary hearing, see Turner, *O.K. Corral Inquest*, and Lubet, *Murder in Tombstone*.

18. On Turkey Creek Jack Johnson, see Brand, "Wyatt Earp, Jack Johnson, and the Notorious Blount Brothers." Federal possemen acted under the authority of U.S. marshals pursuant to the Posse Comitatus Act and served for short periods for a limited purpose. Ball, *United States Marshals*, 12–14.

19. *Florence Weekly Enterprise*, September 8, 1883; *San Francisco Bulletin*, September 5, 1883; Rasch, *Desperadoes of Arizona Territory*, 35.

20. *Phoenix Arizona Republican*, March 3, 1898. The most detailed accounts of Frank Stilwell's death are found in the coroner's inquest testimony in the *Tucson Weekly Citizen*, April 2, 1882, and Young, "Assassination of Frank Stilwell," 16–29. Stilwell came from Tombstone to Tucson, arriving on the westbound train from Benson on the morning of March 19, the day before he was killed. *Tucson Weekly Arizona Star*, March 23, 1882. Paul was in Tucson at the time of the Stilwell killing, having returned from a manhunt in Mexico after an embezzler, Julius Craine, on March 13. *Los Angeles Times*, March 14, 1882.

21. *Phoenix Arizona Republican*, March 3, 1898. David Butler Neagle (1847–1925) was a noted lawman, gambler, and miner. He served as chief of police of Tombstone in 1882, and in 1889, while bodyguard for Justice Stephen J. Field of the U.S. Supreme Court, he shot and killed the famous dueling judge David S. Terry when Terry attacked Field. The resulting murder case, *In Re Neagle*, was a groundbreaking U.S. Supreme Court decision that expanded federal power and found that local authorities could not prosecute a federal officer for an act performed in the line of duty. *In Re Neagle* 135 U.S. 1 (1890).

22. Breakenridge, *Helldorado*, 178; Johnson, *John Ringo*, 251. It was later reported that Florentino Cruz was the same man as Florentino Sais, one of the killers of ex-sheriff John H. Adams and Cornelius Finley in 1878. *Tucson Weekly Citizen*, April 2, 1882. This was disputed by a letter writer to the *Tucson Daily Arizona Star*, March 31, 1882.

23. *Phoenix Arizona Republican*, March 3, 1898.

24. *San Francisco Chronicle*, March 25, 1882; *Tombstone Epitaph*, April 3, 1882; Roberts, *Doc Holliday*, 251–55, 473n; Tefertiller, *Wyatt Earp*, 237–40. Since 1882, there has been an ongoing debate whether Wyatt Earp killed Curly Bill. The weight of evidence suggests that he did. For a contrary view, see Gatto, *Curly Bill*, chap. 11. The site of the Earp–Curly Bill shootout has long been debated. Mescal Springs has often been identified as the location, but it does not match the description in Earp's memoirs. Cottonwood Springs, located a mile and a half west of Mescal Springs, is a close match and is the probable location. The author is indebted to Bill Evans of Sierra Vista, Arizona, who has thoroughly researched this issue and has led groups of visitors to both sites.

25. Tefertiller, *Wyatt Earp*, 252–53; Walker, "Retire Peaceably to Your Homes," 1–18.

26. *Los Angeles Times*, April 2, 1882. In that issue the *Times* stated that its article about the Cowboys was based on an interview "with a gentleman just in from Arizona," and elsewhere it noted Sheriff Paul's arrival. Much of the article deals with the negative effects on mining caused by the violence, and the information and opinions contained in the story make it evident that Paul was the source. The author is indebted to Don Chaput for providing a copy of the article and for pointing out that it must have originated with Paul.

27. On the San Francisco vigilance committees, see Mullen, *Let Justice Be Done*, and Boessenecker, *Against the Vigilantes*. On the Roach-Belcher feud, see Boessenecker, *Bandido*, chap. 4. On Henry Plummer and vigilantism in Montana, see Allen, *Decent Orderly Lynching*. For the Lincoln County War, see Utley, *High Noon in Lincoln*; Nolan, *Lincoln County War*; and Jacobsen, *Such Men as Billy the Kid*.

28. *Tucson Daily Arizona Star*, May 18, 1882; Boessenecker, "Lawman Bob Paul's Doc and Wyatt Connection," 44.

29. *Denver Republican*, May 22, 1882. The Masterson quotation is from Roberts, *Doc Holliday*, 300.

30. *Tucson Weekly Arizona Star*, June 1, 1882.

31. *Denver Rocky Mountain News*, May 31, 1882. On Dan Tucker, a noted New Mexico lawman, see Alexander, *Dangerous Dan Tucker*.

32. Requisition for John H. Holliday, signed by F. A. Tritle, May 16, 1882, Arizona State Library and Archives; *Denver Daily Tribune*, May 30, 1882. Louis C. Hughes argued that Governor Tritle's requisition was defective, saying, "the Governor's certification could not legally rest in the body of the requisition, but must form a separate verification attached to the indictment. This Governor Tritle failed to do." *Tombstone Epitaph*, June 10, 1882. As authority, Hughes cited sec. 5728 of the *Revised Statutes of the United States*, as well as the opinion of a "prominent lawyer" of Tucson. Hughes was wrong. Sec. 5728 merely provided that a copy of the indictment be produced and be "certified as authentic by the governor or chief magistrate of the state or territory from whence the person so charged has fled." Governor Tritle's requisition complied fully with the law.

33. *Tucson Daily Arizona Star*, June 1, 1882; *South Pueblo News*, May 31, 1882; Roberts, *Doc Holliday*, 284–310; Tefertiller, *Wyatt Earp*, 255–62. Some writers have posited the theory that Tritle deliberately prepared defective extradition papers. That is improbable, first because they were not defective, and second because the papers were drafted by Tucson attorney C. C. Stephens, not by Governor Tritle himself. Stephens publicly accepted responsibility for any drafting errors. *Tucson Weekly Arizona Star*, June 1, 1882.

34. *Denver Rocky Mountain News*, May 31, 1882; undated Denver newspaper clipping, Robert H. Paul scrapbook.

35. *Tucson Daily Arizona Star*, June 1, 1882.

36. Requisition for John H. Holliday, signed by H. M. Van Arman, June 9, 1882, Arizona State Library and Archives; *Prescott Weekly Arizona Miner*, June 9, 1882; *Tombstone Epitaph*, June 17, 1882; McClintock, *Arizona, the Youngest State*, 2:482.

37. *Sacramento Daily Union*, May 17, 1882; *Los Angeles Times*, May 17, 1882; *Tucson Daily Arizona Star*, May 18, 1882; *Tucson Weekly Arizona Star*, June 8, 1882; *Tombstone Epitaph*, May 16, June 1, 1882.

38. From *The Life and Legend of Wyatt Earp*, which appeared on ABC television from 1955 to 1961.

CHAPTER TEN

1. Thrapp, *Conquest of Apacheria*, 6–9, 79–94. Jesus Maria Elias (1829–96) was seen as a hero to both Anglos and Mexicans. *Tucson Daily Citizen*, January 10, 1896. Camp Grant was moved in 1872 to the present-day location of Fort Grant. On the Camp Grant Massacre, see Colwell-Chanthaphonh, *Massacre at Camp Grant*, and Jacoby, *Shadows at Dawn*.

2. *Papers Relating to the Foreign Relations of the United States* (1883), 435–37; Thrapp, *Conquest of Apacheria*, 231–50; Debo, *Geronimo*, chap. 8.

3. On William J. Ross, see Thrapp, *Encyclopedia of Frontier Biography*, 3:1243–44.

4. *Papers Relating to the Foreign Relations of the United States*, 428–32. The list of Tucson Rangers appears in a May 1882 newspaper clipping in the Robert H. Paul scrapbook.

5. Bernardo Reyes (1850–1913) served first as a general under Porfirio Díaz, then as governor of the state of Nuevo Leon. Considered to be one of the potential successors of Díaz, he was slain during the Mexican Revolution.

6. *Tucson Weekly Arizona Star*, June 22, July 6, 1882; Thrapp, *Conquest of Apacheria*, 251–53; *Papers Relating to the Foreign Relations of the United States*, 430–31. It was incorrectly reported that the Tucson Rangers had killed thirty-seven Indians on June 2 near Casas Grandes. What actually happened was that on May 26, Mexican troops attacked a band of Apaches led by Chief Juh near San Diego, Chihuahua, killing thirty-six and capturing ten. *Papers Relating to the Foreign Relations of the United States*, 436.

7. *Tucson Weekly Arizona Star*, May 25, 1882; *Tombstone Epitaph*, May 25, 1882.

8. *Tucson Weekly Arizona Star*, March 30, 1882; *Tucson Daily Arizona Star*, May 18, 1882; *Tombstone Epitaph*, May 27, 1881; *Arizona Mining Index*, July 19, 1884. Paul's brother-in-law, Thomas Drady, died in San Francisco on June 1, 1884. *San Francisco Bulletin*, June 2, 1884.

9. Secrest, "Jim Levy," 24–26, 56–58; Secrest, "Quick with a Gun," 14–15; DeArment, *Deadly Dozen*, 82–95; Lake, *Wyatt Earp*, 158, 164. Stuart Lake has been often accused of inventing quotations by Earp, and this one sounds suspiciously like that of Frank Wilstach, who wrote, "Jim Levy was the top-notcher of them all, except Wild Bill." Wilstach, *Wild Bill Hickok*, 268. While contemporary newspaper accounts generally used the phonetic spelling, Levy, both court and property records show that he spelled his name Leavy. Gary L. Roberts to the author, June 20, 2010. Based on the "Levy" spelling, numerous writers have concluded that he was Jewish, which is probably incorrect.

10. *Tucson Weekly Arizona Star*, April 14, 1881; *Tucson Daily Arizona Star*, June 10, 1882.

11. *Tucson Daily Arizona Star*, June 6, 8, 10, 11, 1882; *Tucson Weekly Citizen*, June 11, 1882, December 15, 1883; DeArment, *Deadly Dozen*, 96–101.

12. *Tucson Daily Citizen*, July 5, 1882; *Tucson Daily Arizona Star*, July 18, 1882.

13. *Tucson Daily Citizen*, July 11, 1882.

14. *Tucson Daily Citizen*, July 10, 21, 1882; *Tucson Weekly Arizona Star*, July 13, 1883.

15. *Tucson Daily Citizen*, July 10, 17, 21, 1882.

16. *Tucson Daily Citizen*, July 19, 1882, April 16, 1884; *Tucson Weekly Citizen*, April 19, 1884.

17. *Tucson Daily Citizen*, July 19, 21, 22, 1882; Rockfellow, *Log of an Arizona Trail Blazer*, 50–52. Lorenzo D. Walters, in *Tombstone's Yesterday* (263), also refers to this incident, but incorrectly states that the man Paul saved from lynching was Tim Hurley.

18. *Tucson Daily Citizen*, July 22, 1882. On Paul's manhunt into Mexico for a San Francisco forger, Julius Crane, and the assistance he received from Governor Ortiz, see *Sacramento Record-Union*, March 14, 1882; *Los Angeles Times*, March 14, 1882; and *Tucson Weekly Citizen*, March 19, 1882. For examples of other Paul manhunts in Mexico, see *Tucson Weekly Citizen*, December 25, 1881, March 19, 1882, September 1, 1883, and June 6, 1885.

CHAPTER ELEVEN

1. *Tucson Weekly Arizona Star*, March 24, 1881, August 24, 1882.

2. *Tucson Daily Citizen*, July 25, 1882. Frank Morton was prosecuted under the name James A. Morton.

3. *Tucson Weekly Arizona Star*, August 24, 1882; *Tucson Daily Citizen*, August 18, 1882.

4. *Tucson Daily Citizen*, August 24, 25, 1882.

5. *Tucson Daily Arizona Star,* August 29, 1882; *Tucson Daily Citizen,* August 31, September 1, 1882.

6. Affidavit of R. H. Paul, *R. M. Wilkin and Richard Starr v. Paul Jernicke* (1882), Pima County District Court case no. 825, Arizona State Library and Archives. This case was filed when the seller, Paul Jernicke, failed to pay the real estate agents' commission. Prior to 1884 the address of the Paul home was 637 East Pennington Street; then the address numbers were changed, and 637 became 146 East Pennington.

7. Paul, biographical sketch of Robert H. Paul.

8. Advertisements for John Paul's express business appear in the *Tucson Daily Citizen,* July 12, 13, 17, 24, August 1, 1882. His education is set forth in a biographical sketch appearing in the *Arizona Republican,* special edition, August 1892; see also *Tucson Weekly Citizen,* June 16, 1883.

9. *Tucson Weekly Arizona Star,* March 24, May 12, 1881, September 8, 1882; *Tucson Daily Citizen,* September 8, 12, 13, 1882. The building was demolished in the 1920s, and in 1928 the current Pima County courthouse was erected on the same spot.

10. *Tucson Daily Citizen,* September 12, 13, 1882; George Cooler biographical sketch, Arizona State University Library.

11. *Tucson Daily Citizen,* September 8, 1882.

12. *Tucson Daily Arizona Star,* September 9, 1882.

13. *Los Angeles Times,* September 20, 21, 1882; *Tucson Daily Citizen,* September 20, 26, 1882.

14. *Tucson Weekly Citizen,* October 22, 1882; *Tucson Weekly Arizona Star,* May 5, 1882; *Tucson Daily Arizona Star,* October 14, 1882.

15. Affidavit of R. H. Paul, March 11, 1886, in *Paul v. Shaw,* Arizona State Library and Archives; *Tombstone Epitaph,* March 12, 1886; *Tucson Daily Arizona Star,* March 12, 1886; *Tucson Weekly Arizona Star,* March 13, 1886.

16. *Tucson Daily Arizona Star,* October 24, 31, 1882; *Tucson Daily Citizen,* October 24, 27, 1882; O'Dell, "Joseph Casey," 22–23; Carmony, *Whiskey, Six-guns and Red-light Ladies,* 230.

17. *Tucson Daily Arizona Star,* October 28, 1882; *Tucson Daily Citizen,* November 1, 1882; *Tucson Weekly Citizen,* June 9, August 4, 1883.

18. *Tucson Daily Arizona Star,* November 21, 1882.

19. *Globe Arizona Silver Belt,* December 22, 1883; *Tombstone Daily Republican,* December 28, 1883; *San Francisco Bulletin,* September 5, 1883; *Los Angeles Times,* July 12, 1902; Wilson, *Encyclopedia of Stagecoach Robbery in Arizona,* 58–59.

20. *Tucson Daily Citizen,* November 18, 1882. Several accounts incorrectly state that Joe Casey was captured by El Paso City Marshal Dallas Stoudenmire. That is impossible, for Stoudenmire was shot and killed more than a month before Casey escaped the Tucson jail.

21. *Tucson Weekly Citizen,* November 26, 1882; *Tucson Daily Arizona Star,* October 11, 1887.

22. Boessenecker, *Bandido,* 133–35, 146–49, 174–75, 386–87. Tomas Procopio Bustamante was born circa 1842 to Tomas Bustamante and Vicenta Murrieta of Hermosillo, Sonora, Mexico. His mother was the sister of Joaquin Murrieta.

23. *Tucson Weekly Citizen,* January 7, 1883, February 4, February 25, 1883.

24. *Tucson Weekly Citizen,* December 31, 1882; *San Francisco Chronicle,* December 26, 1882; San Quentin prison register, inmate no. 10890 (Francisco Lopez).

25. *Tucson Weekly Citizen,* February 4, February 25, November 10, 1883; *Los Angeles Times,* November 7, December 1, 1883; *Tucson Daily Arizona Star,* March 20, 1886; Secrest, *Dangerous Trails,* 130–32; Boessenecker, *Bandido,* 387.

26. *Tucson Weekly Citizen,* December 24, 31, 1882, June 9, October 13, 1883.

27. *Tucson Weekly Citizen*, January 7, 14, 1883; Carmony, *Whiskey, Six-guns and Red-Light Ladies*, 231.

28. *Tucson Daily Citizen*, January 25, 1883; *Tucson Daily Arizona Star*, January 26, 1883.

29. *Tucson Weekly Citizen*, February 11, June 16, 23, 1883, April 19, 1884; *Tucson Weekly Arizona Star*, April 17, 1884. Gladwell Richardson, under his penname of Maurice Kildare, wrote an account of Joe Casey, "The Mysterious Gunman," *West* 6, no. 1 (December 1966): 20–21, 60–62, and another under his own name, "Mystery Outlaw of the Border," *Westerner* 1, no. 5 (November–December 1969): 22–25, 56–59. Like many of Richardson's writings, most of these two stories is utter fiction. Richardson, who had a penchant for publishing phony photographs of western outlaws, even used an image of lawman Bill Tilghman to represent Joe Casey.

30. *Tucson Weekly Citizen*, May 5, 1883.

31. *Tucson Daily Citizen*, April 16, 1884.

32. *Tucson Daily Arizona Star*, May 1, 1883; *Tucson Daily Citizen*, May 1, 1883, April 16, 1884; *Tucson Weekly Citizen*, June 16, 1883.

33. *Tucson Daily Arizona Star*, May 1, 1883.

34. *Tucson Daily Arizona Star*, May 1, 1883; *Tucson Daily Citizen*, May 1, 1883, April 16, 1884; *Tucson Arizona Mining Index*, August 30, 1884; O'Dell, "Joseph Casey," 23–24. Although Andrew Holbrook was the first Pima County deputy sheriff killed in the line of duty, the first lawmen slain in Pima County were Deputy U.S. Marshals John H. Adams and Cornelius Finley, murdered by bandidos in 1878. Thomas Cordis was undersheriff from 1883 to 1884. Prior to that, Cordis had served as an internal revenue collector for twelve years. He died in Tucson in 1916. *Tucson Daily Citizen*, February 2, 1916.

35. *Tucson Weekly Citizen*, May 12, 1883.

36. *Tucson Weekly Citizen*, June 16, 23, 30, 1883. Harry Sinclair was pardoned after serving fewer than five years of his life term. *Tombstone Epitaph*, March 31, 1888.

37. *Tucson Weekly Citizen*, July 28, August 4, 1883; *Tombstone Daily Republican*, December 28, 1883.

CHAPTER TWELVE

1. *Tucson Weekly Citizen*, October 6, 1883; reward circular for Red Jack Almer and Charley Hensley, issued by Sheriff A. J. Doran, copy in author's collection. According to an account by Harry L. Doney, a California constable, in 1879 Red Jack drifted into the mining camps of Shasta County in Northern California. He labored in the mines and lived in a cabin on Squaw Creek just above its confluence with the Sacramento River. Doney believed that Red Jack was responsible for several stage robberies that took place on the roads outside of Redding between 1879 and 1881. Doney's memoir about Red Jack Almer was written in 1906, kept by his family, and published in the Woodland (Calif.) *Democrat* in 1961. The holdups Doney described, which took place in October 1879, September 1880, and October 1881, have all been attributed to Charles E. Boles, better known as Black Bart, who later admitted to them. Doney said he reported his suspicions about Red Jack to Jim Hume of Wells Fargo, but Hume never looked into them, probably because the evidence was strong that Black Bart was the culprit. Based on his suspicions, Doney claimed that Red Jack Almer, not Boles, was actually Black Bart, which is impossible. Given that L. J. Moore of Willcox testified that he had known Red Jack for five years prior to 1883, and given Frank Carpenter's statement that he had also known Red Jack in Arizona since 1878, Doney's account seems even more improbable. See Collins and

Levene, *Black Bart*, 230–31. L. J. Moore's statement appears in *In the Matter of the Inquest Held on the Body of Chas. Hensley and Jack Elmer*, Cochise County District Court records, Arizona State Library and Archives. Frank Carpenter's statement is in the *San Francisco Bulletin*, September 5, 1883.

2. *Tucson Daily Arizona Star*, October 5, 1883; U.S. Census Population Schedules, Pinal County, 1880; U.S. Census Population Schedules, Tulare County, Calif., 1870, and Pima County, Ariz., 1880; *Memorial and Biographical History of the Counties of Fresno, Tulare and Kern, California*, 291, 647; McClintock, *Arizona*, 248. Leroy J. Redfield died in Tulare County in 1897. *Visalia Weekly Delta*, June 24, 1897.

3. *Tucson Daily Arizona Star*, July 16, 1944; U.S. Census Population Schedules, Pinal County, Ariz., 1880. William C. Davis's recollections of Len Redfield are in the *Los Angeles Times*, July 12, 1902. He purchased Len Redfield's ranch, where he discovered the smelter.

4. *Globe Arizona Silver Belt*, September 8, 1883.

5. *Phoenix Herald*, August 13, 1883; *Visalia Weekly Delta*, September 7, 1883; *Tucson Weekly Citizen*, September 8, 1883; Brown, "Reminiscences of George A. Brown," Arizona Historical Society; Rasch, "Riverside Stage Robbery," 14–17; Wilson, *Encyclopedia of Stagecoach Robbery in Arizona*, 114–16. There is no truth to the inane yarn that Red Jack boarded the stage wearing women's clothing.

6. Red Jack and Hensley told L. J. Moore that Redfield had shot the stage horse. See Moore's testimony, *In the Matter of the Inquest Held on the Body of Chas. Hensley and Jack Elmer*.

7. *Los Angeles Times*, July 12, 1902; Brown, "Reminiscences of George A. Brown"; Wilson, *Encyclopedia of Stagecoach Robbery in Arizona*, 116–18.

8. *San Francisco Bulletin*, August 17, 1883; *Florence Weekly Enterprise*, August 10, 1883.

9. *Tucson Daily Citizen*, August 24, 26, 1882; *Tucson Weekly Citizen*, September 8, 1883; *Visalia Weekly Delta*, September 7, 1883; Rasch, "Riverside Stage Robbery," 16–17.

10. *Tucson Weekly Citizen*, September 8, 1883; *Visalia Weekly Delta*, September 7, 1883; *Florence Weekly Enterprise*, September 8, 1883; Rasch, "Riverside Stage Robbery," 16–17. For arguments that Len Redfield was innocent, see McKelvey, "Riddle of the Redfield Robbers," 24–25, 30–33. Contrary to McKelvey's assertions, many of them based on insufficient and inaccurate information, there can be no reasonable doubt of Redfield's guilt. Hank Redfield, due to the resulting notoriety, sold his ranch in 1884 to the Republican politician and mine owner William C. Davis and moved his family to the new settlement of Benson, on the railroad, where he ran a livery stable. He committed suicide in 1886. His son, Leonard D. Redfield, served as postmaster of Benson from 1896 to 1940, the longest-serving postmaster in the United States. In old age he gave many interviews about his life on the Arizona frontier, but he never mentioned his family's former notoriety. *Sacramento Daily Union*, August 16, 1886; *Tucson Daily Arizona Star*, September 26, 1937, March 26, 1940, July 16, 1944.

11. *San Francisco Bulletin*, September 5, 1883.

12. *San Francisco Bulletin*, September 14, 1883; *Tucson Weekly Citizen*, September 15, 29, 1883; *Clifton Clarion*, September 26, 1883.

13. *Tucson Weekly Citizen*, September 29, October 6, 1883; *Tucson Daily Citizen*, October 8, 1883; *Sacramento Daily Union*, September 29, 1883; Rasch, "Riverside Stage Robbery," 17.

14. Casanega, "Life History of T. D. Casanega," 4, Arizona Historical Society.

15. *Tucson Weekly Citizen*, October 6, 1883; Casanega, "Life History of T. D. Casanega," 5.

16. Casanega, "Life History of T. D. Casanega," 5.

17. *Tucson Weekly Citizen*, October 6, 1883; *San Francisco Daily Alta California*, October 6, 1883; *Tombstone Epitaph*, quoted in the *St. Louis Globe Democrat*, October 12, 1883; Casanega, "Life History of T. D. Casanega," 5–6; *In the Matter of the Inquest Held on the Body of Chas. Hensley and Jack Elmer*. A popular account of the Red Jack gang is J. A. Long (a pseudonym for prolific Arizona writer Gladwell Richardson), "How Red Jack Died," *West* 1, no. 5 (October 1964): 46–47, 54–56. Like many of Richardson's writings, it contains numerous fictional elements and is wildly inaccurate. Richardson illustrated it with a purported photograph of Red Jack Almer, which is actually the image of a New York sneak thief that he copied from Thomas Byrnes, *Professional Criminals of America* (New York: Cassell & Co., 1886), 265.

18. R. H. Paul to L. F. Rowell, October 12, 1883, copy in author's collection.

19. Brown, *No Duty to Retreat*, 39–47, 69.

CHAPTER THIRTEEN

1. *San Jose Mercury News*, August 28, 1885, April 22, 30, 1886, July 19, 1887; *Tucson Weekly Citizen*, January 2, December 25, 1886; undated newspaper clipping, Robert H. Paul scrapbook.

2. *Tucson Arizona Mining Index*, undated 1884 clipping, Robert H. Paul scrapbook; Eppinga, "Law and Order in Graham County," 22; *Prescott Weekly Journal-Miner*, October 23, 30, 1889; Ball, *Ambush at Bloody Run*, xvii–xv, 90. *Tucson Daily Citizen*, January 17, 1906. Clifton is now located in Greenlee County, which was created in 1909 from the eastern portion of Graham County. George Stevens disappeared, but in 1906 he was found to be running a saloon and gambling house in Victoria, British Columbia.

3. *Dallas Weekly Herald*, June 2, 30, 1881, March 23, 1882, February 28, 1884; Miller, *Bounty Hunter*, 132–34. John Heath's name is frequently misspelled Heith.

4. *San Francisco Bulletin*, January 18, 1884; *Tombstone Republican*, February 19, 1884. DeArment, "Outlaws of Clifton," 35; Alexander, *Lynch Ropes and Long Shots*, 34–35; Kelley, *I Don't Propose*, 1; Breakenridge, *Helldorado*, 194–95. On Shoot-'Em-Up Dick, see Rasch, *Desperadoes of Arizona Territory*, 156–59. John C. Delaney (1848–1915) was reportedly the youngest soldier in the Civil War. Active in Pennsylvania politics, he was awarded the Medal of Honor in 1894 for bravery in 1865. *Wilkes-Barre (Pa.) Times*, April 16, 1915. Yorky Kelly's first name is recorded as Daniel in some accounts.

5. Clifton *Clarion*, August 29, 1883; *Tucson Daily Arizona Star*, May 1, 24, 1883; *Tucson Weekly Citizen*, September 1, 1883; Miller, *Arizona Story*, 133–35; Ball, *Ambush at Bloody Run*, xii, 123.

6. Undated 1890 newspaper clipping, Robert H. Paul scrapbook; *Los Angeles Times*, September 6, November 20, 1883; *San Francisco Bulletin*, September 11, November 20, 1883; *Tucson Weekly Citizen*, September 29, October 6, 1883; Clifton *Clarion*, September 26, 1883; Ball, *Ambush at Bloody Run*, xiv. Kid Lewis's true name was reportedly James Bartlett. On lawlessness in Clifton, see *Tucson Weekly Citizen*, December 1, 1883. For criticisms of Sheriff Stevens, see *Tucson Weekly Citizen*, October 13, 1883; *Tombstone Prospector*, October 12, 1890. Although the Bisbee Massacre has been retold countless times in books and magazines, prior authors have overlooked most details of the outlaws' backgrounds and criminal careers. Some uninformed writers have even suggested that the John Heath gang had not committed any previous crimes.

7. *Tucson Weekly Citizen*, December 29, 1883. The notorious Gage train robbery, in which the engineer, T. C. Webster, was murdered, was committed by Kit Joy, Mitch Lee,

George Cleveland, and Frank Taggart. A well-researched and detailed account of the Gage train holdup and resulting manhunt is Alexander, *Lynch Ropes and Long Shots*. On the Bisbee killers as suspects in the Gage robbery, see *Tucson Weekly Citizen*, December 15, 22, 1883; Alexander, *Lynch Ropes and Long Shots*, 45–48; and Dillon, *Wells Fargo Detective*, 217–18.

8. Many garbled or otherwise unreliable accounts of the Bisbee Massacre have been published. I have used the detailed accounts in the *Tombstone Republican*, March 28, 1884, and the trial testimony from the *Tombstone Epitaph*, February 10, 12, 17, 19, 1884.

9. *Tombstone Epitaph*, February 10, 12, 17, 19, 1884; *Tucson Weekly Citizen*, December 15, 1883. On William A. Daniels, see Thrapp, *Encyclopedia of Frontier Biography*, 4:128.

10. *Tucson Weekly Citizen*, December 15, 1883; *Tombstone Epitaph*, March 28, 1884; Kelley, *I Don't Propose*, 11–15.

11. J. B. Hume to R. H. Paul, December 11, 1883, James B. Hume Papers, Bancroft Library. On railroad detective Len Harris (1827–94), see Secrest, *Lawmen and Desperadoes*, 168–72.

12. J. B. Hume to R. H. Paul, December 11, 1883, James B. Hume Papers (emphasis in original). On Pete Spence and other suspects being arrested on suspicion of the Gage robbery, see Alexander, *Lynch Ropes and Long Shots*, 23. Long Neck Charlie Lazure was a notorious cattle thief in Arizona and New Mexico. *Tombstone Epitaph*, August 30, 1885.

13. *Tucson Weekly Citizen*, December 22, 1883; *Sacramento Daily Union*, December 15, 1883. On Paul in the Bisbee manhunt, see LeBaron, "Bisbee's Five Black Ghosts," 56; Traywick, *Hangings in Tombstone*, 2–3; Thrapp, *Encyclopedia of Frontier Biography*, 4:150.

14. *Tucson Weekly Citizen*, December 15, 22, 1883; *Tombstone Epitaph*, March 31, 1888.

15. Dillon, *Wells Fargo Detective*, 162, 218.

16. *Sacramento Daily Union*, January 3, 1884; *Peach Springs Arizona Champion*, January 19, 1884.

17. *Tucson Daily Arizona Star*, January 1, 1884, March 27, 1926; *Tucson Weekly Citizen*, January 5, 1884.

18. *Tombstone Republican*, January 7, 1884; *Tucson Weekly Citizen*, December 22, 1883, January 19, 1884; Kelley, *I Don't Propose*, 15–18. Deputy Sheriff Cesario Lucero was slain while in pursuit of bandits on August 12, 1888. Dodge, in *Under Cover for Wells Fargo* (45–55), provided a great deal of incorrect information about the Bisbee massacre. Some of it can be attributed to a poor memory, but other statements are rank fabrications. He adds a fictitious murder victim, one "Indian Joe," and states that Dan Dowd (whom he calls Jack Dowd) had worked as a teamster in Cochise County (true) but that the massacre was his first crime (false). Dodge places himself at the forefront of the manhunt and says that he accompanied the Bisbee posse, which included John Heath. That would have been impossible. Although Dodge had accompanied a six-man posse from Tombstone to Bisbee, by the time they got to Bisbee Deputy Daniels and his posse had already left in pursuit of the gang. See Chisholm, *Brewery Gulch*, 38. Dodge also claims that he used field glasses to watch a deputy sheriff arrest Heath while they were on the manhunt. Not only was Dodge not present, but Heath was not arrested until the next day, when he returned to Bisbee. Dodge also asserts that Deputy Daniels arrested Billy Delaney at the Minas Prietas mine before Dowd was captured; in fact, Dowd was arrested two weeks before Delaney. Most egregiously, however, Dodge claims that he captured Big Dan Dowd in Mexico, a flagrant falsehood.

19. *Tombstone Republican*, February 10, 18, March 28, 1884. Several authors have incorrectly claimed that John Heath made a full confession in jail. In fact, none of the Bisbee killers ever confessed, and all insisted on their innocence until their dying breaths. A grave

for John Heath is prominently marked in Boot Hill Cemetery; countless photographs of it have been published in books, magazines, and newspapers. Like many of the Boot Hill markers, it is a blatant phony. Heath's body was returned to his estranged wife in Terrell, Texas, and was buried there in Oakland Cemetery. *Kaufman (Tex.) Sun*, February 28, 1884.

20. On Jerome L. Ward (1833–1913), see *Prescott Weekly Arizona Miner*, May 11, 1872, March 8, 1873; Thrapp, *Encyclopedia of Frontier Biography*, 1511; and especially Ellis, "Sheriff Jerome L. Ward," 315–42.

21. *Tombstone Republican*, March 28, 1884.

22. *Tombstone Epitaph*, March 29, 1884.

23. *Tucson Daily Citizen*, March 29, 31, 1884; *Tucson Daily Arizona Star*, March 29, 1884; *Tombstone Republican*, March 28, 1884; *Tombstone Epitaph*, March 29, 1884. Billy Daniels, who had been so instrumental in the case, ran against Bob Hatch for sheriff and was defeated. He continued to serve as a lawman until he was slain by Apache Indians on June 10, 1885. Thrapp, *Encyclopedia of Frontier Biography*, 4:128. At least one writer has claimed that the Bisbee killers were innocent. Maurice Kildare [Gladwell Richardson], "The Bisbee Massacre Hangings," *Real West* 14, no. 95 (August 1971): 16–19, 54–56. Like most of Richardson's writings, his account is larded with fiction, and his conclusions are totally preposterous.

24. *Tucson Daily Citizen*, April 8, 1884. Judge A. W. Sheldon died while visiting San Francisco on January 30, 1884, reportedly from an old Civil War wound. William F. Fitzgerald was appointed on March 11, 1884. Both served simultaneously as district trial judge and as associate justice of the Arizona Supreme Court.

25. *Tucson Daily Arizona Star*, April 9, 1884; *Tucson Daily Citizen*, April 8, 1884.

26. *Tucson Weekly Citizen*, April 19, 1884.

27. *Tucson Weekly Citizen*, April 12, 1884; *Tucson Arizona Mining Index*, undated clipping from April 1884 in Robert H. Paul scrapbook.

28. *Tucson Arizona Mining Index*, undated clipping from April 1884 in Robert H. Paul scrapbook.

29. *Tucson Daily Citizen*, April 15, 16, 1884; *Tucson Weekly Citizen*, April 19, 1884; *Tucson Daily Arizona Star*, April 15, 1884; *Tucson Weekly Arizona Star*, April 17, 1884.

CHAPTER FOURTEEN

1. Undated Tucson newspaper clipping, Robert H. Paul scrapbook.

2. *Tucson Daily Arizona Star*, April 26, 30, October 7, 1884; *Globe Arizona Silver Belt*, May 9, 1885; undated newspaper clipping, Robert H. Paul scrapbook. Dave Gibson stayed in Florence and was stabbed in the leg by Joe Phy after he was shot in his fatal gunfight with Pete Gabriel in 1888. Boessenecker, "Gun Smoke at the Tunnel Saloon," 63.

3. *Tucson Weekly Citizen*, May 17, November 1, 1884. On Martin W. Brady, see *Los Angeles Times*, November 3, 1887. On Horace H. Appel (1862–1922), see *Tucson Daily Citizen*, March 15, 1905; and *Who's Who in the Pacific Southwest*, 15.

4. *Tucson Weekly Citizen*, June 21, 1884.

5. *San Francisco Daily Alta California*, September 24, 1884; *Tucson Weekly Citizen*, July 5, 1884; *Tucson Arizona Mining Index*, July 5, 1884.

6. *Tucson Weekly Citizen*, October 11, 1884; *Tucson Arizona Mining Index*, October 25, 1884.

7. *Tucson Weekly Citizen*, November 8, 1884. The Cababi mining district was located seventy miles southwest of Tucson.

8. *Tucson Weekly Citizen*, November 1, 1884.

9. *Tucson Daily Arizona Star*, August 30, 1884.

10. *Tucson Weekly Citizen*, October 18, 1884; *Tucson Arizona Mining Index*, July 11, 1885; 1884 *Tucson Daily Citizen* clipping, Robert H. Paul scrapbook; *Revised Statutes of Arizona*, secs. 428, 1987; Ball, *Desert Lawmen*, 246–64, 285–88, 339n41. The *Star* later reported that Paul's fees for the second quarter of 1885 were $2,499.46; quoted in the *Kingman Mojave County Miner*, August 23, 1885. At that rate, his income for 1885 would have been about $10,000.

11. On property owners' right to appeal assessments, see Ball, *Desert Lawmen*, 248.

12. *Tucson Weekly Citizen*, August 30, October 4, 11, November 1, 1884; *Tucson Daily Arizona Star*, October 7, 1884; *Tucson Arizona Mining Index*, October 11, 1884.

13. *Tucson Arizona Mining Index*, August 30, 1884; *Nogales Express*, quoted in *Tucson Arizona Mining Index*, September 13, 1884.

14. *Tucson Weekly Citizen*, August 30, September 6, October 16, 1884. On Eli B. Gifford, see *Tucson Daily Citizen*, October 14, 16, 18, 1882; and DeArment, *Knights of the Green Cloth*, 115, 131.

15. Drachman, "Reminiscences," 70, Arizona Historical Society.

16. *Tucson Daily Arizona Star*, August 31, 1884; *Tucson Arizona Mining Index*, September 6, 1884. Gifford's brother Miles had previously worked for Paul as a jailer. Mose Drachman (1870–1935) was the son of Tucson's prominent Jewish merchant Philip Drachman. John A. Muir (1850–1904) had joined the Central Pacific as a telegrapher in 1870 and worked his way up to division superintendent, serving in Arizona until 1893, when he was sent to Los Angeles as division superintendent for Southern California. At the time of his death he was general manager of the Los Angeles Railway Co. *Tucson Daily Citizen*, April 3, 1886; *San Francisco Call*, January 9, 1904; Busbey, *Biographical Directory of the Railway Officials of America*, 267.

17. *Los Angeles Times*, December 10, 1899; *Tucson Weekly Citizen*, October 11, 1884; *Tucson Arizona Mining Index*, October 25, 1884; *Tucson Daily Arizona Star*, October 23, 1884.

18. *Tucson Weekly Citizen*, September 6, November 8, 1884.

19. *Tucson Arizona Mining Index*, September 20, 1884.

20. *Tucson Weekly Citizen*, October 11, 18, 1884; *Tucson Daily Arizona Star*, October 7, 1884; *San Francisco Daily Alta California*, October 8, December 11, 1884; *Globe Arizona Silver Belt*, October 11, 1884; *Tombstone Prospector*, March 22, 1887; Ayres, "San Rafael Ranch," 2–3; Traywick, *That Wicked Little Gringo*, 80–82.

21. *Tucson Daily Arizona Star*, October 18, 1884.

22. *Tucson Arizona Mining Index*, October 25, 1884; *Tucson Weekly Citizen*, November 1, 24, 1884; *Tucson Daily Arizona Star*, November 1, 1884.

23. *Tucson Daily Arizona Star*, October 31, 1884.

24. *Tucson Daily Arizona Star*, October 22, 1884.

25. *Tucson Arizona Mining Index*, undated 1884 clipping in Robert H. Paul scrapbook.

26. *Los Angeles Times*, December 10, 1899; *Tucson Daily Arizona Star*, November 4, 1884; William S. Oury to Lola Oury Smith, October 18, 1884, papers of the Oury family, University of Arizona Library, Special Collections.

27. The author is indebted to Gary Roberts for background information on Harry Barron. Gary L. Roberts to the author, March 28, 2009.

28. *Los Angeles Times*, December 10, 1899. The *Tucson Weekly Citizen* (January 3, 1885) printed the trial testimony in detail. Charles T. Connell served as a deputy U.S. marshal under Zan L. Tidball from 1884 to 1885 and in numerous other official capacities for many years thereafter. *Portrait and Biographical Record of Arizona*, 344–45.

29. *Tucson Weekly Citizen*, January 3, 1885. Snyder's store was located at the corner of Congress and Meyer Streets.

30. *Tucson Weekly Citizen*, November 22, 1884, January 10, 1885.

31. William S. Oury to Lola Oury Smith, November 15, 1884, papers of the Oury family.

32. *Tucson Arizona Mining Index*, December 27, 1884; affidavit of R. H. Paul, March 6, 1886, *Paul v. Shaw*.

33. Affidavit of R. H. Paul, March 6, 1886, *Paul v. Shaw*. William B. Groseclose was the Wells Fargo agent in Tucson from November 1884 to 1886 and agent in Nogales from 1886 to 1888. Theobald and Theobald, *Wells Fargo in Arizona Territory*, 105, 179, 186.

34. Affidavit of R. H. Paul, March 6, 1886, *Paul v. Shaw*.

35. *Tucson Weekly Citizen*, November 24, January 3, 1885. There were then twenty-three voting precincts in Pima County, but only eighteen were used in the 1884 election.

36. *Tucson Weekly Citizen*, April 12, 1884; Shuck, *History of the Bench and Bar of California*, 688–91; Drachman, "Reminiscences," 71.

37. Harry R. Jeffords was elected Pima County district attorney in 1886; in 1889 President Harrison appointed him U.S. attorney. He died in Tucson in 1891, only thirty-six years of age. *Phoenix Arizona Republican*, April 4, 1891. Columbus Cecil Stephens, born in 1840, had a long career as a criminal attorney in Arizona and California, dying in Los Angeles in 1894. *Los Angeles Times*, September 8, 1894. On James A. Anderson (1826–1902), see McGroarty, *Los Angeles*, 325. Benjamin H. Hereford practiced law in Tucson from 1876 until his death in 1890. The town of Hereford, Arizona, is named after him. On Cameron H. King, see *Master Hands in the Affairs of the Pacific Coast*, 45.

38. On the modern error rate for hand-counted ballots, see *Minneapolis Star Tribune*, August 22, 2006. A 2000 Caltech/MIT study calculated the average error rate for hand-counted ballots at 2 percent. Howard, "In the Margins."

39. Charles Kresham was born in Brunswick, Germany, in 1852. He claimed to have been a stage driver on the old Santa Fe Trail and an express rider for Wells Fargo. In 1880 he shot a watchman at the Tucson train depot; the grand jury refused to indict him. He was first a salesman and merchant in Tucson, and he later served in minor political positions and acted as a deputy sheriff under the Shaw brothers. By 1895 he had moved to Colorado, where he ran a saloon, then operated hotels, first in Alamosa and later in Pueblo. He died in Pueblo at the age of fifty-one on February 25, 1904. *Tucson Weekly Arizona Star*, August 19, 1880; *Tombstone Epitaph*, October 5, 1880; *Tucson Weekly Citizen*, September 16, 1882, March 17, 1895; *Akron (Colo.) Weekly Pioneer Press*, March 4, 1904.

40. *Tucson Weekly Citizen*, January 3, 1885.

41. Ibid.

42. Ibid.

43. Ibid.

44. Ibid.

45. Ibid.

46. *Tucson Arizona Mining Index*, October 4, 1884; *Tucson Weekly Citizen*, January 3, 1885. Pedro Pellon (1850–1911), a native of Spain, came to Tucson in 1875, where he was a saloonkeeper, policeman, and political leader in the Hispanic community. *Tucson Daily Citizen*, February 25, 1911.

47. *Tucson Weekly Citizen*, January 3, 1885. On Sam Hughes (1829–1917), see *Tucson Daily Citizen*, June 20, 1917; Farish, *History of Arizona*, 2:210–11.

48. *Tucson Weekly Citizen*, January 3, 1885.

49. *Tucson Weekly Citizen*, January 10, 1885.

50. *Tucson Weekly Citizen*, January 3, 1885; *San Francisco Call*, January 4, 1885. A short article entitled "Who Was Elected Sheriff?" appeared in the *Arizona Sheriff Magazine* for February 1949 (11). A copy is on file in the Arizona Historical Society Library and has been relied on by many writers. As a result, its garbled and inaccurate account of the *Paul v. Shaw* election case has, unfortunately, been often repeated.

51. Undated 1884 newspaper clipping, Robert H. Paul scrapbook.

CHAPTER FIFTEEN

1. *Tucson Daily Citizen*, July 29, 1882, August 22, 1911; *Tucson Arizona Mining Index*, January 26, 1884; *Sacramento Daily Union*, January 23, 1885; Bancroft, *History of Arizona and New Mexico*, 550–52.

2. *Sacramento Daily Union*, January 23, 24, 1885; *Tucson Weekly Citizen*, January 24, February 7, 1885; *Tucson Arizona Mining Index*, January 24, 31, 1885.

3. *Globe Arizona Silver Belt*, January 31, 1885.

4. *Tucson Daily Arizona Star*, March 8, 1885; *Globe Arizona Silver Belt*, March 14, 1885; *Los Angeles Times*, March 10, 1885; *Salt Lake City Tribune*, March 12, 1885; *Tucson Daily Citizen*, May 7, 1890. Colonel George A. Forsyth (1837–1915) was a famous frontier soldier known for his heroism at the Beecher Island fight of 1868.

5. *Tucson Daily Citizen*, March 17, 1885.

6. *Tucson Weekly Citizen*, May 9, December 19, 1885; *Tombstone Epitaph*, May 27, 1885; *San Francisco Daily Alta California*, June 7, 1885. Tomas Salcido was probably the same man who was slain in a Fairbanks brothel in July 1887. Whether James Claiborne was related to Billy Claiborne of OK Corral notoriety is unknown.

7. Some accounts spelled the chief's name as Howlatoscom.

8. *Tucson Weekly Citizen*, May 23, 1885; *Bisbee Daily Review*, November 5, 1907; newspaper clipping dated April 13, 1921, Robert H. Paul biographical file, Arizona Historical Society. This latter source, entitled "Desert Diplomacy Proves Valuable in the Early Days," is based on a pioneer's memoir, contains many errors, and fails to give Sheriff Paul credit for defusing the Papago trouble. Herbert Brown (1843–1913) was publisher of the *Tucson Daily Citizen* for fifteen years in the 1880s and 1890s. *Tucson Daily Citizen*, May 14, 1913; October 15, 1920.

9. *Tucson Weekly Citizen*, May 23, 1885.

10. *Tucson Daily Arizona Star*, May 17, 1885.

11. *Tucson Weekly Citizen*, May 23, 1885.

12. *Tucson Weekly Citizen*, May 23, 1885; *San Francisco Bulletin*, May 19, 1885; *Bisbee Daily Review*, November 5, 1907.

13. *Tucson Daily Arizona Star*, May 27, 1885; *Tucson Arizona Mining Index*, May 23, 1885; *Salt Lake City Tribune*, May 28, 1885; *San Francisco Bulletin*, May 22, 29, June 8, 1885; *Sacramento Daily Union*, May 19, 21, 1885; *Boise Idaho Statesman*, June 4, 1885.

14. *Tucson Arizona Mining Index*, May 23, 1885.

15. *San Francisco Bulletin*, June 3, 1885; *Phoenix Arizona Republican*, special edition, August 1892.

16. *Tucson Weekly Citizen*, June 13, 1885; Thrapp, *Conquest of Apacheria*, 326.

17. *Tucson Weekly Citizen*, August 1, 1885.

18. *San Francisco Bulletin*, July 25, 1885; *Tucson Daily Citizen*, August 2, 1885; *Philadelphia Inquirer*, July 29, 1885. Walter Vail (1852–1906) owned the vast Empire Ranch and the Total Wreck Mine, founded the town of Vail, Arizona, and served in the territorial legislature.

James Finley was a tough mine owner. In Harshaw in 1889 he shot and killed a man who attacked him with a Bowie knife. He later served in the territorial legislature and died in Tucson in 1899. His daughter Annie married Paul's son Robert J. in 1893.

19. Lewis Wolfley to George F. Edmunds, January 15, 1890, National Archives; affidavit of R. D. Ferguson, March 24, 1886, *Paul v. Shaw*; *Tucson Daily Arizona Star*, February 9, 1886. George T. Martin was injured on June 17, 1884. For several weeks he was unable to work, and Martin claimed that any financial losses occurred while he was off the job. In 1886 a Tucson jury agreed with Martin, awarding him about $1,800 in damages. But a month later Wells Fargo won its own lawsuit against Martin, and the company was awarded almost the same sum from Martin. *Sacramento Daily Union*, June 19, 1884; *Tucson Weekly Citizen*, June 21, 1884; affidavit of Ferguson, *Martin v. Wells Fargo & Co.* (1889) 3 Arizona Reports 57; *Martin v. Wells Fargo & Co.* (1892) 3 Arizona Reports 355. John and Lillian Theobald, in *Wells Fargo in Arizona Territory* (187), confuse George T. Martin with Dr. George Martin (1831–1907), an early Arizona pioneer and druggist. They were different men.

20. Affidavit of J. A. Muir, March 6, 1886; J. B. Hume to J. A. Muir, January 13, 1885, *Paul v. Shaw*.

21. *Tucson Daily Arizona Star*, February 9, 1886; affidavit of R. H. Paul, March 6, 1886, *Paul v. Shaw*.

22. Affidavit of Len Harris, n.d., *Paul v. Shaw*; *Tucson Daily Citizen*, September 11, 13, 1882.

23. Robert H. Paul to Harry Barron, June 22, 1885, *Paul v. Shaw*.

24. *Historical and Biographical Record of the Territory of Arizona*, 508–09; *Prescott Weekly Journal-Miner*, October 9, 1889.

25. On Paul's claim that Meade packed the grand jury, see R. H. Paul to W. H. H. Miller, January 16, 1890. On Thomas J. Jeffords, see Thrapp, *Encyclopedia of Frontier Biography*, 2:723–24; and Sweeney, *Cochise*, 291–96. He was no relation to attorney Harry Jeffords. On selection of federal grand jurors, see sec. 808 of the *Revised Statutes of the United States* and *Agnew v. United States* (1897) 165 U.S. 36.

26. R. H. Paul to Harry Barron, September 25, 1885, *Paul v. Shaw*.

27. *Tucson Weekly Citizen*, October 10, 1885; *Tombstone Epitaph*, January 28, 1886; *San Francisco Bulletin*, April 20, 1886. The grand jury relied upon the Civil Service Act set forth in the *Revised Statutes of the United States*, apparently secs. 1781 and 1782, which prohibited receiving bribes and gratuities, and sec. 1784, which prohibited federal employees from giving gifts to their superiors. These statutes were part of the early attempts to stop the political spoils system. James A. Zabriskie (1843–1904) was a prominent attorney. He attended West Point and served in the Civil War. As a district attorney in West Texas in 1878, he prosecuted Curly Bill Brocius and Bob Martin for attempting to rob a U.S. Army ambulance near El Paso. That same year he came to Tucson, where he represented Charlie Shibell in the 1881 election fraud case. A noted orator and active in Republican politics, he was U.S. attorney for Arizona from 1882 to 1885. *Tucson Daily Citizen*, April 21, 1904.

28. The grand jury's report is published in the *Tucson Daily Arizona Star*, November 1, 1885. The federal statute in question is sec. 1887 of the *Revised Statutes of the United States*, which limited spending on printing only. The other statute cited by the grand jury, sec. 1886, provides no dollar limitation whatsoever. On the "Thieving Thirteenth," see Wagoner, *Arizona Territory*, 208–14, 218–21. Wagoner mentions the grand jury's findings but does not recognize its legal errors and misuse of the law.

29. *Tombstone Epitaph*, October 21, 1885; *Tucson Daily Arizona Star*, November 1, 1885.

30. *Tucson Weekly Citizen*, October 17, 1885; *San Francisco Bulletin*, October 23, 24, 1885; *Tombstone Prospector*, October 23, 1885; Lewis Wolfley to George F. Edmunds, January 15, 1890, National Archives (emphasis in original); Drachman, "Reminiscences," 72. Owing to political turnover, two other Arizona judges were removed at the same time.

31. *Tucson Daily Arizona Star*, March 31, 1886; R. H. Paul to Harry Barron, October 16, 1885, Arizona State Library and Archives.

32. Affidavit of Richard Rule, n.d.; affidavit of James N. Mason, March 6, 1886; affidavit of John A. Black, March 6, 1886; all *Paul v. Shaw*.

33. *Tucson Daily Arizona Star*, November 1, 1885; *Tucson Daily Citizen*, November 2, 1885; *San Francisco Chronicle*, November 1, 1885. On Judge William H. Barnes (1843–1904), see *Phoenix Arizona Republican*, November 11, 1904; and *Portrait and Biographical Record of Arizona*, 27–28.

34. Paul was indicted for violation of sec. 5440 (conspiracy) of the *Revised Statutes of the United States*. On election fraud, see secs. 5511–15 of the *Revised Statutes of the United States*; *Blitz v. United States* 153 U.S. 308, 313 (1894). The law later changed. The National Voting Rights Act of 1965 allowed for federal oversight of elections in states with a history of discriminatory voting practices.

CHAPTER SIXTEEN

1. *Tucson Daily Arizona Star*, December 5, 1885; J. M. Glass, chief of police, Los Angeles, to R. H. Paul, August 27, 1892; San Quentin prison register, inmate nos. 15090, 15626, and 18310 (Frank Morgan, alias Frank Smith).

2. *Tucson Daily Arizona Star*, March 31, 1886; R. H. Paul to Harry Barron, December 14, 1885, *Paul v. Shaw*, Arizona State Library and Archives.

3. R. H. Paul to Harry Barron, December 14, 1885, *Paul v. Shaw*; *Tucson Weekly Citizen*, January 2, 1886.

4. Barron's affidavit is missing from the *Paul v. Shaw* case file, but was published in the *Tucson Daily Arizona Star*, February 9, 1886.

5. *Tucson Daily Arizona Star*, February 9, 1886.

6. Harry Barron to E. B. Gifford, February 1, 1886; affidavit of E. O. Shaw, March 22, 1886, *Paul v. Shaw*.

7. Harry Barron to E. B. Gifford, February 8, 1886, *Paul v. Shaw*.

8. Harry Barron to E. B. Gifford, February 16, 1886, *Paul v. Shaw*. On Chris Buckley, see Bullough, *Blind Boss and His City*. It is, unfortunately, a somewhat uncritical biography and fails to deal adequately with Buckley's corruption. On Big Ed Burns (sometimes spelled Byrnes) as a Democratic politician and deputy sheriff in San Francisco, see *San Francisco Bulletin*, March 25, 1886, and *Tombstone Epitaph*, June 2, 1888.

9. Harry Barron to E. B. Gifford, February 16, 1886, *Paul v. Shaw*.

10. The affidavit of George Martin is not in the *Paul v. Shaw* file, but is published in the *Tucson Daily Arizona Star*, February 9, 1886.

11. *Tucson Daily Arizona Star*, February 9, 1886; affidavits of R. H. Paul, John A. Muir, M. W. Brady, and W. B. Groseclose, *Paul v. Shaw*.

12. Harry Barron to E. B. Gifford, March 12, 1886, *Paul v. Shaw*.

13. *Paul v. Shaw*, affidavit of Henry Barron, March 16, 1886, exhibits 1–14. The letters were also published in the *Tucson Daily Arizona Star*, March 31, 1886.

14. Affidavit of E. O. Shaw, March 22, 1886, order granting new trial, April 3, 1886, *Paul v. Shaw, Tucson Weekly Citizen,* March 27, April 3, 1886; *Tucson Daily Arizona Star,* March 12, 26, 30, April 4, 1886.

15. *Shaw v. County of Pima* (1888) 18 Pacific Reporter 273; *Tombstone Epitaph,* April 9, 11, 1886; *Tucson Daily Citizen,* April 3, 1886.

16. *Tucson Weekly Citizen,* April 17, 1886; *Tombstone Epitaph,* April 16, 1886.

17. The negotiations over the *Paul v. Shaw* case became an issue between Cameron King and Harry Jeffords when both men were candidates for Pima County district attorney in 1886. In a public debate, they spelled out details of the negotiations. *Tucson Weekly Citizen,* October 9, 1886.

18. Lewis Wolfley to George F. Edmunds, chairman of Judiciary Committee, January 15, 1890, National Archives; *Arizona Revised Statutes* (1887), secs. 1750-1751.

19. *Tucson Daily Citizen,* July 9, 1886; *Tucson Weekly Citizen,* July 24, 1886; *Tucson Daily Arizona Star,* July 10, 1886, October 11, 1887.

20. William H. Barnes to C. W. Wright, January 24, 1890; Lewis Wolfley to W. H. H. Miller, January 31, 1890; Lewis Wolfley to George F. Edmunds, January 15, 1890.

21. *San Francisco Chronicle,* January 15, June 9, 1888, November 1, 2, 1892, April 25, 1894, May 5, 1898, September 13, 1899, December 9, 10, 11, 1913, plus undated *Chronicle* clipping from 1889 in Robert H. Paul scrapbook; *San Francisco Call,* November 1, 1894. During the Abe Ruef graft prosecution in 1908, Francis J. Heney identified Harry Barron as the same man who had lived with several brothers in Tombstone and had been mixed up in the Tucson ballot-box-stuffing case. *San Francisco Call,* September 23, 1908.

22. *San Francisco Chronicle,* October 13, 14, November 10, 1887; *Tombstone Epitaph,* June 5, 1886. Years later Paul's friend Charles T. Connell, who penned a long series on the Apache wars for the *Citizen,* incorrectly recalled that Paul had helped lead the civilian militia in the Apache hunt. *Tucson Daily Citizen,* July 10, 1921. The Tucson volunteers returned on May 24, 1886, while Paul was still in San Francisco. *Tucson Daily Citizen,* May 25, 1886.

23. *Tucson Daily Citizen,* June 15, 1886.

24. Undated newspaper clipping in Robert H. Paul scrapbook; *Tucson Weekly Citizen,* July 10, 1886.

25. *Tucson Daily Citizen,* July 25, 1886; *Tucson Weekly Citizen,* November 26, 1887; *San Francisco Chronicle,* November 10, 1887; *Visalia Tulare County Times,* August 22, 1889; *Phoenix Arizona Republican,* special edition, August 1892.

26. In *Los Tucsonenses,* Thomas E. Sheridan describes this incident and argues that Paul's failure to published the delinquent tax list in a Spanish-language newspaper was the result of racial discrimination: "Sheriff R. H. Paul apparently attempted to subvert this [legal] process. . . . In essence, he was denying the Mexican population the knowledge they needed to fulfill their public obligations and protect their property" (89). That analysis misapprehends Arizona law. On the law regarding publication of the delinquent tax list and the requirement of lawsuits and due process to enforce tax liens, see *Compiled Laws of Arizona,* secs. 32–41.

27. Pima County jail register, 1877–82, Arizona Historical Society; Hietter, "Surprising Amount of Justice," 211. Hietter concludes that Arizona's justice system was generally fair and that Mexicans and Mexican Americans received equal treatment until they got to jury trial and were convicted at higher rates than Anglos.

28. *Tombstone Epitaph,* October 8, 1887; *Tucson Daily Citizen,* October 30, 1886, September 8, 1905; *Tucson Weekly Citizen,* November 5, 1887; undated 1886 newspaper clipping

in Robert H. Paul scrapbook. On Hilario Urquides, see Sheridan, *Los Tucsonenses*, 115–17. Gormley is the same man who accompanied Paul on his manhunt for Apaches in 1885.

29. *Tucson Daily Citizen*, October 30, 1886.

30. *Tucson Arizona Mining Index*, October 9, 16, 1886; Haley, *Jeff Milton*, 195.

31. Drachman, "Reminiscences," 73. Matthew Johnson (1831–1928) was chief of police of Tucson for one term starting in 1886. *Tucson Daily Citizen*, June 28, 1921. Martin W. Brady was no longer a constable, having resigned in July; Nathan Appel was appointed to replace him. Brady went to Colorado, then to Los Angeles, where he was appointed a police detective in 1887. His wife obtained a divorce from him in Tucson during his absence. *Tucson Daily Citizen*, July 15, 19, 1886; *Tucson Arizona Mining Index*, December 4, 1886; *Los Angeles Times*, November 3, 1887.

32. In its issue of January 10, 1894, the *Prescott Weekly Arizona Miner* claimed that Paul and district attorney Calvert Wilson of Yuma County had a "scrap" in Tucson a few days earlier. However, no such incident was reported either in the *Citizen* or the *Star*. Had it actually happened, the *Star* would have provided prominent coverage.

CHAPTER SEVENTEEN

1. Boessenecker, *Badge and Buckshot*, 200.

2. *San Francisco Bulletin*, January 5, 1886; *Tucson Daily Arizona Star*, January 19, 1888. On Smith and Maier, see Burton, *Western Story*, 17–24; and Burton, *Constable Dodge and the Pantano Train Robbers*, 20–22.

3. *Los Angeles Times*, April 29, 1887; *New York Times*, April 29, 1887; Rasch, "Train Robbery Times Four," 35; Burton, *Constable Dodge and the Pantano Train Robbers*, 10–11, 22. George Green was also known as George Wills. He later confessed in court; his testimony appears in the *Tucson Daily Arizona Star*, January 19, 1888. A full account of the four train robberies between Tucson and El Paso in 1887–88 is beyond the scope of this book. Jeff Burton's recently published *Western Story* is an exhaustive and painstakingly researched account of this neglected episode of southwestern outlawry. This chapter was first written before the publication of *Western Story*. I concur with Burton on most details, but disagree with some of his conclusions.

4. *Tucson Daily Citizen*, August 13, 1887; Burton, *Constable Dodge and the Pantano Train Robbers*, 11–13; Dillon, *Wells Fargo Detective*, 234–35.

5. E. O. Shaw to Board of Supervisors, April 9, 1887, Pima County documents, University of Arizona, Special Collections; *Tombstone Epitaph*, September 3, 1887; *Tucson Daily Arizona Star*, September 8, October 11, 1887; *Tucson Weekly Citizen*, September 10, 1887; Eppinga, *Arizona Sheriffs*, 70; Burton, *Western Story*, 46, 107, 112n23, 176.

6. *Tucson Weekly Citizen*, September 10, October 29, November 5, 26, 1887, September 6, 1888; *Tucson Daily Arizona Star*, October 22, 1887; *Tombstone Epitaph*, October 8, 1887; *Phoenix Arizona Republican*, July 20, 1890.

7. *Tucson Daily Arizona Star*, August 12, 14, 16, 20, 1887; *Tombstone Epitaph*, August 20, 1887; Burton, *Constable Dodge and the Pantano Train Robbers*, 13–15; Rasch, "Train Robbery Times Four," 35. In *Western Story*, Burton suggests that Smith and Maier were probably, but not definitely, the culprits in the second holdup (178, 295). In this writer's opinion, there can be little doubt that they robbed both trains. Burton also argues that they did not escape by train. Given the fact that the bandits were on foot, no other scenario makes sense. Fred Dodge, in *Under Cover for Wells Fargo* (78–94), placed himself at the forefront of the manhunt. However, in both *Constable Dodge* and *Western Story*, Burton has established in great

detail the inaccuracy, and even outright falsity, of many of Dodge's claims. While Dodge's faulty memory does not inspire confidence in his accuracy, his flagrant fabrications—generally placing himself in important roles in manhunts or other events—tend to cast a pall of suspicion over other parts of his memoir. This is most regrettable, for there is ample evidence that after 1890 Dodge was a highly active and competent Wells Fargo detective and was at the forefront of numerous train robbery investigations. Even in retelling those later adventures, however, Dodge cannot resist his grandiose impulses. For example, he states that prior to the Dalton gang's bloody 1892 raid on Coffeyville, Kansas, he had sent a warning to the town (172, 174–75). In fact, no warning was ever sent, and the citizens were taken completely by surprise. See Smith, *Daltons!*, 201–07. Smith discusses Dodge's phony claim on 204.

8. *Los Angeles Times*, August 30, 1887; *San Francisco Bulletin*, August 29, 1887; Burton, *Western Story*, 14, 154–64; Dodge, *Under Cover for Wells Fargo*, 95–99. Stein's is pronounced "Steen's" by locals.

9. Burton, *Constable Dodge and the Pantano Train Robbers*, 16–19; Southern Pacific Company, "History of Train Robberies on the Southern Pacific Company's Pacific Lines," 29, copy in the author's collection. Lorenzo D. Walters, in *Tombstone's Yesterday*, evidently obtained a copy of the latter source, for he copied it almost verbatim on 183–89. Jack Blunt, or Blount, was probably not the same Jack Blount as Wyatt Earp's friend Turkey Creek Jack Johnson. Peter Brand to author, November 1, 2008. On Turkey Creek Jack Johnson, see Brand, "Wyatt Earp, Jack Johnson, and the Notorious Blount Brothers."

10. *Tucson Weekly Citizen*, October 22, 1887; *Express Gazette*, 205; Rasch, "Train Robbery Times Four," 36; Burton, *Constable Dodge and the Pantano Train Robbers*, 20–23; Burton, *Western Story*, chap. 11; Dillon, *Wells Fargo Detective*, 237–38. On Doc Smart's presidential pardon, see Washington, D.C., *Critic-Record*, December 2, 1890.

11. *Tucson Daily Arizona Star*, March 6, 1888. The Mapula train robbery took place on January 10, 1888. *Los Angeles Times*, January 12, 1888.

12. *Tucson Daily Arizona Star*, February 24, 1888; *Tucson Daily Citizen*, February 23, 1888; *Phoenix Herald*, February 25, 29, 1888; *San Francisco Daily Alta California*, February 24, 1888; *Tombstone Prospector*, February 25, 1888; *Tombstone Epitaph*, March 24, 1888; *St. Paul (Minn.) Daily Globe*, August 10, 1890; Burton, *Constable Dodge and the Pantano Train Robbers*, 24–25; Burton, *Western Story*, 223–26.

13. R. H. Paul to W. H. H. Miller, U.S. attorney general, January 16, 1890, copy courtesy Larry Ball.

14. R. H. Paul to W. H. H. Miller, January 16, 1890.

15. *Tucson Daily Arizona Star*, March 20, 1888; *Tucson Daily Citizen*, March 24, 1888; *Tombstone Prospector*, March 15, 1888; *New York Times*, March 13, 1888; Southern Pacific Company, "History of Train Robberies on the Southern Pacific Company's Pacific Lines," 29–32. On Marshal Meade's travail, see Ball, "This High-Handed Outrage," 219–32; Ball, *United States Marshals*, 174–75; and Edwards, "Trouble in Mexico," 26–35. According to Will Smith, Meade was allowed to organize a Mexican-only posse in Janos, but when they arrived in Casas Grandes, fifty miles south, they were ordered to desist, even though the outlaws were only nine miles ahead of them. *Tombstone Epitaph*, March 24, 1888.

16. R. H. Paul to W. H. H. Miller, U.S. attorney general, January 16, 1890; *Phoenix Herald*, March 7, 1888; *Tucson Daily Citizen*, February 25, 1892. Although the Southern Pacific contended that Len Harris's transfer to Los Angeles was a promotion, it seems evident that part of the reason for the move was that he could no longer handle desert manhunts. *Tucson Weekly Citizen*, March 10, 1888. Scott Noble took over the Yuma division after

John A. Muir was promoted to superintendent of the Southern Pacific's Los Angeles division. *Tucson Daily Citizen*, April 3, 1886.

17. *Tucson Daily Citizen*, February 25, 1892.

18. Ibid.

19. Ibid.

20. *Tombstone Epitaph*, March 24, 1888.

21. *Tucson Weekly Citizen*, March 31, 1888; *San Francisco Examiner*, April 24, 1888.

22. *San Francisco Chronicle*, September 16, 1892; *Tombstone Prospector*, March 28, 1888.

23. *Tucson Weekly Citizen*, March 31, 1888.

CHAPTER EIGHTEEN

1. *Los Angeles Herald*, undated clipping from May 1888, Robert H. Paul scrapbook.

2. *San Francisco Examiner*, April 29, 1888; Boessenecker, "Genesis of the Gunfighter," 40–50. On H. J. Burns, see *San Francisco Bulletin*, April 19, 1876, January 2, November 6, 1877, November 26, 1880.

3. R. H. Paul to W. H. H. Miller, attorney general, January 16, 1890.

4. Rolle, *California*, 458–63.

5. *Tucson Weekly Citizen*, May 19, 1888; *San Francisco Bulletin*, May 12, 14, 1888; *Sacramento Daily Union*, May 13, 14, 1888; *Los Angeles Times*, May 13, 1888; *New Haven (Conn.) Register*, May 14, 1888; *Los Angeles Herald*, undated clipping from May 1888, Robert H. Paul scrapbook.

6. *San Francisco Chronicle*, May 13, 1888; *Tucson Weekly Citizen*, May 19, 26, 1888; *Tucson Daily Arizona Star*, May 22, 1888; *Los Angeles Herald*, undated clipping from May 1888, Robert H. Paul scrapbook.

7. *Sacramento Daily Union*, May 14, June 8, 1888; *San Francisco Daily Alta California*, May 20, June 9, 1888; *San Jose Mercury News*, May 14, 19, June 7, 1888; *Tucson Weekly Citizen*, June 16, 1888; *Tombstone Epitaph*, October 2, December 11, 16, 1889, June 14, 1891, November 19, 20, 1894.

8. *Los Angeles Herald*, undated clipping from May 1888, R. H. Paul scrapbook; *Tucson Daily Citizen*, February 8, 13, April 4, 12, 1890.

9. *Tombstone Epitaph*, April 16, May 30, 1889; *Los Angeles Times*, May 27, 1889; Lewis Wolfley to W. H. H. Miller, December 16, 1889, National Archives. On Lewis Wolfley's contentious term as governor, see Wagoner, *Arizona Territory*, chap. 11.

10. Ball, *Ambush at Bloody Run*, 60–62; Schubert, *Voices of the Buffalo Soldier*, 162. On Ann Eliza Webb, see her autobiography, *Wife No. 19*.

11. Ball, *Ambush at Bloody Run*, 1–18, 61–65.

12. R. H. Paul to W. H. H. Miller, January 16, 1890.

13. Ball, *Ambush at Bloody Run*, 76–77. On Will Smith, see Boessenecker, *Badge and Buckshot*, 185–87, 191–94; Edwards, "Will Smith," 16–17 (no. 3), 12–13, 18 (no. 4).

14. On the Wham trial, see Ball, *Ambush at Bloody Run*, chaps. 7–10. For Webb's boast, see Rogers, "Bushwhacked," 44–45.

15. Leland Stanford to Benjamin Harrison, June 3, 1889, National Archives; *San Francisco Daily Alta California*, May 22, 1889; *Tombstone Epitaph*, July 26, 1889; *Prescott Weekly Arizona Miner*, July 31, October 10, 1889.

16. *Tucson Daily Citizen*, quoted in the *Tombstone Epitaph*, August 14, 15, 1889; *Tucson Daily Arizona Star*, August 14, 1889; *Sacramento Daily Union*, August 19, 1889.

17. *Tombstone Epitaph*, December 21, 1889; *Tucson Daily Citizen*, January 6, 1890; R. H. Paul to W. H. H. Miller, January 16, 1890. On Artemus L. Grow (1840–1917), see *Tombstone in History*, 38. Grow later became a U.S. customs collector on the border.

18. Ball, *Ambush at Bloody Run*, 175–76; C. T. Dunavan to Joseph Blackburn, February 17, 1890; N. O. Murphy to George F. Edmunds, February 18, 1890.

19. William H. Barnes to C. W. Wright, January 24, 1890; Lewis Wolfley to W. H. H. Miller, January 31, 1890; Lewis Wolfley to George F. Edmunds, January 15, 1890; Marcus A. Smith to U.S. Senate Committee on the Judiciary, January 14, 1890, National Archives; Ball, *Ambush at Bloody Run*, 96.

20. R. H. Paul to W. H. H. Miller, March 17, 1890, Arizona Historical Society. Jeffords's letter to Miller is quoted in Creswell, *Mormons and Cowboys*, 204. Miller's letter to Jeffords is quoted in Ball, *Ambush at Bloody Run*, 176–77.

21. *Paul v. Cullum*, 132 U.S. 539 (1889). Paul's smelter did not operate more than ten months total during the next seventeen years, and it was finally dismantled and shipped to California in 1905. *Tucson Daily Citizen*, September 8, 1905.

22. *Phoenix Arizona Republican*, special edition, August 1892; *Tucson Daily Citizen*, April 14, 1890; *Prescott Weekly Arizona Miner*, March 26, 1890, January 10, 1894; undated newspaper clipping in Robert H. Paul scrapbook; *Nogales Herald*, October 10, 1889; *Tombstone Epitaph*, October 22, 1889, April 5, 12, 1890; *San Francisco Examiner*, September 15, 1892. On the numerous deputies employed by Paul during his term, see U.S. Marshal Records, general correspondence, Arizona Historical Society. On Vic Wilson, see Boessenecker, "Buckshot for a Marshal," 35–40.

23. Dell M. Potter to R. H. Paul, March 25, 1892; Cipriano Baca to R. H. Paul, April 8, 1892; and related telegrams, U.S. Marshal Papers, Arizona Historical Society. On Delbert M. Potter, see *Notables of the West* 2:584–85.

24. Ball, *United States Marshals*, 185; Johnson, *John Ringo*, 162–64; *Globe Arizona Silver Belt*, January 26, 1896; *Phoenix Arizona Republican*, December 22, 1901.

25. *Tucson Daily Citizen*, May 1, 1890; *Tucson Weekly Citizen*, May 10, 1890. Geronimo Miranda robbed ten stagecoaches in Arizona before he was slain by a posse near Benson on June 11, 1891. *Tombstone Prospector*, June 14, 15, 21, 1891; *San Francisco Chronicle*, June 24, 1891; Wilson, *Encyclopedia of Stagecoach Robbery in Arizona*, 52–55, 64–65. The author states incorrectly that Geronimo the stage robber was not the same Geronimo who had robbed the train at Agua Zarca.

26. Ball, *Ambush At Bloody Run*, 184–89, 199.

27. The current address of the Paul house is 297 North Main Avenue. The exact date on which the Pauls acquired this property is unclear, and the transfer does not appear in the Pima County Recorder grantee or grantor index books. However, the *Arizona Republican*, special edition, August 1892, contains a photograph of the house with the improvements completed, and it identifies the house as R. H. Paul's residence. The Pauls owned the home until 1901, when Margaret sold it. Deed, Margaret A. Paul to Herbert B. Tenney, April 29, 1901, Pima County Recorder. See also Stewart, "Mansions of Main Street" (204–05, 221), which incorrectly states that Margaret Paul acquired the house in 1899. Over the years, the history of the Paul home was lost. It is now referred to as the Julius Kruttschnitt house, named after a Southern Pacific official who acquired it in 1912.

28. *St. Paul (Minn.) Daily Globe*, August 10, 1890.

29. *Phoenix Arizona Republican*, May 22, 1890.

30. *San Francisco Call*, June 13, 1890: *San Jose Daily Evening News*, May 22, 1890; *Tucson Daily Arizona Star*, June 10, 1890; *Tombstone Epitaph*, June 11, 1890.

31. *Tombstone Epitaph*, July 11, 1890; *San Francisco Bulletin*, July 15, 22, 23, 1890; *Tucson Daily Arizona Star*, July 22, 26, 1890; *Los Angeles Times*, July 12, 1890; Ball, *United States Marshals*, 171–72; Cresswell, *Mormons and Cowboys*, 204–06.

32. Ball, *United States Marshals*, 172–73.

33. *Tombstone Prospector*, September 30, November 27, 1890, November 10, 1895; *San Francisco Bulletin*, September 30, 1890; *Tucson Daily Citizen*, May 19, 1902; *United States v. Copper Queen Mining Co.* 185 U.S. 495 (1902); Creswell, *Mormons and Cowboys*, 206, 219. On the difficulty of prosecuting timber trespass cases, see Ball, *United States Marshals*, 142, 198–99.

34. *Tombstone Epitaph*, November 21, 1890; *Prescott Weekly Arizona Miner*, December 17, 1890; *Florence Weekly Enterprise*, December 13, 1890. On William Zeckendorf (1842–1935), see Sonnichsen, *Tucson*, 83, 92, 105.

35. *Tucson Daily Arizona Star*, April 22, 1891; Hedges, *Speeches of Benjamin Harrison*, 337–38.

36. *Phoenix Arizona Republican*, June 13, 1891; *Yuma Sentinel*, June 13, 1891; *Tombstone Epitaph*, June 14, 1891; *Prescott Weekly Arizona Miner*, June 17, 1891; *Tucson Daily Arizona Star*, June 19, 1891; *Tucson Weekly Citizen*, June 27, 1891. On Ham White's remarkable career, see Dugan, *Knight of the Road*. For his own account of the escape from John Paul and Sheriff Truman, see *San Francisco Call*, June 15, 1891.

37. Steffens, "Making of a Fighter," 348–51; Ben Heney to W. H. H. Miller, October 24, 1889, National Archives.

38. *Tombstone Epitaph*, September 25, 1891; Sonnichsen, *Tucson*, 130–32.

39. Undated Florence (Ariz.) newspaper clipping, Robert H. Paul scrapbook. The couple's marriage certificate shows that the bride's name was Mary F. Miller. Matthew Cullen evidently was her stepfather. Robert G. Paul to the author, August 4, 2009.

40. George Brown et al. to R. H. Paul, May 29, 1892, U.S. Marshals Records, Arizona Historical Society; *Prescott Weekly Arizona Miner*, August 12, 1891.

41. *Tombstone Epitaph*, October 13, 1890, February 29, March 3, 1892.

42. *Prescott Weekly Arizona Miner*, January 10, 1894; Ball, *United States Marshals*, 187, 272n68; abstract of marshal's fees and expenses, June 30, 1891, June 30, 1892, May 26, 1893, U.S. marshal records, Arizona Historical Society; *Account of the Receipts and Expenditures of the United States*, 304.

43. Ball, *United States Marshals*, 187; *Kingman Mojave County Miner*, June 14, 1890; *Tombstone Epitaph*, November 26, 1890.

44. B. B. Denure to R. H. Paul, March 24, March 31, April 13, 30, 1892; Frank F. Flint to R. H. Paul, August 9, 1890; J. W. Wilson to Robert Paul, December 22, 1891; L. B. Comstock to R. H. Paul, April 15, 1891; U.S. Marshal Records, Arizona Historical Society.

45. Thrapp, *Encyclopedia of Frontier Biography*, 1:29–31; *Annual Report of the Secretary of War*, 2:130; *San Francisco Chronicle*, June 8, 1892; *Prescott Weekly Arizona Miner*, June 8, 1892; *Tombstone Epitaph*, June 20, 1892.

46. Newspaper clipping dated April 3, 1892, Robert H. Paul scrapbook; *Tombstone Prospector*, December 21, 1892; *Tucson Daily Citizen*, May 8, 9, 27, 1893; *Tucson Daily Arizona Star*, May 10, 27, 1893; *Phoenix Arizona Republican*, May 24, 1893; Ball, *U.S. Marshals*, 179–80.

47. *Phoenix Arizona Republican*, August 21, 1891.

CHAPTER NINETEEN

1. Sheridan, *Los Tucsonenses*, 90–91; *Tombstone Epitaph*, June 14, 1893; *Phoenix Arizona Republican*, June 16, 1893; Robert H. Paul family genealogical records; undated newspaper clippings, Robert H. Paul scrapbook.

2. Indenture between Robert H. Paul and Margaret A. Paul and John Invancovich, November, 6, 1893, Pima County Recorder; *Phoenix Arizona Republican*, July 20, 1890; *Tombstone Prospector*, May 21, 1894; *Tucson Daily Citizen*, September 8, 1905. In 1953 Paul's grandson Alfred Paul (1893–1969) supplied a statement about the lawman's life to the Arizona Historical Society. It contains some inaccurate information, including the claim that in 1893 "he retired on account of illness" and "went into retirement from active life" due to an eight-year struggle with Bright's disease. In fact Paul's health was excellent throughout the 1890s.

3. *Phoenix Arizona Republican*, September 20, 1894; *Tombstone Prospector*, August 20, 1894; *Prescott Weekly Journal-Miner*, August 22, October 10, 1894; *Tucson Weekly Citizen*, October 29, November 3, 1894; *Tucson Weekly Arizona Star*, November 15, 1894.

4. *Solomonville Bulletin*, January 13, February 1, 1895.

5. *Tombstone Epitaph*, September 22, 1895; *Phoenix Herald*, March 5, 1896; *Solomonville Bulletin*, August 21, 1896. The exact location of the mining activity is unknown. The Graham County Recorder has no record of the mining claims of Paul or the Pacific Improvement Company. Wendy John to the author, September 16, 2008.

6. *Tucson Daily Citizen*, August 14, 1902; *Tucson Weekly Citizen*, February 10, April 14, 1894; *San Francisco Call*, January 15, 1897; *San Andreas Calaveras Prospect*, January 30, 1897.

7. *Tombstone Epitaph*, April 5, 1893; *San Francisco Chronicle*, December 10, 1893; Dill, "Removal!," 257–76. A summary of charges against Hughes, including those brought by Paul, is in the *New York Herald*, June 17, 1895.

8. *Phoenix Herald*, April 2, 1896.

9. *Prescott Weekly Arizona Miner*, July 21, September 15, 1897, March 30, 1898; *Phoenix Weekly Herald*, October 21, 1897; *Solomonville Bulletin*, July 16, September 3, 17, 1897.

10. *Prescott Weekly Arizona Miner*, March 30, 1898; *Tombstone Prospector*, September 12, 1898; *Phoenix Arizona Republican*, November 16, 1899; *N. W. Bernard v. R. H. Paul and R. J. Paul* (1905), Pima County District Court case no. 3805, Arizona State Library and Archives.

11. *San Francisco Examiner*, August 9, 1896. Earp's Shakespeare quotation was undoubtedly added by the reporter. Paul's letter to the *Citizen* was reprinted in the *Phoenix Arizona Republican*, March 3, 1898.

12. *Mamie Paul v. John V. Paul*, Pinal County District Court, Arizona State Library and Archives; *Tombstone Prospector*, January 28, 1894; *Phoenix Herald*, July 21, 1898; undated newspaper clipping, Robert H. Paul scrapbook.

13. *Tucson Daily Arizona Star*, January 1, 4, 1899. Lyman Willis Wakefield (1855–1919) later served as Pima County assessor and U.S. land register in Tucson. *Tucson Daily Citizen*, September 30, 1919.

14. *Tucson Daily Arizona Star*, January 4, 1899.

15. Pearl Hart's background was ascertained by the Toledo, Ohio, correspondent of the Chicago *Inter Ocean* and reprinted in the *Omaha World Herald*, December 28, 1902. Her own account is in *Cosmopolitan: A Monthly Illustrated Magazine* 27, no. 6 (October 1899): 673–77.

16. *Phoenix Herald*, June 8, 1899; *Los Angeles Times*, June 5, 11, 1899; *Tucson Daily Citizen*, July 5, 1901, January 20, February 27, 1904.

17. *Los Angeles Times*, June 1, 1899. An oft-repeated myth is that Pearl Hart's holdup was the last stage robbery in the West; in fact, there were dozens of holdups of horse-drawn stagecoaches after 1900.

18. *Tucson Daily Citizen*, June 22, October 13, 1899.

19. *Grand Forks (N.Dak.) Herald*, October 13, 1899; *Tucson Daily Citizen*, October 13, 1899; *Tucson Daily Arizona Star*, October 13, 1899, May 19, 1904.

20. *Albuquerque Citizen*, October 23, 1899; *Tucson Daily Citizen*, October 22, 1899; *Phoenix Arizona Republican*, November 16, 1899; *Los Angeles Times*, November 23, 1899; DeArment, *George Scarborough*, 219–21. Various accounts list Boot's term as three, seven, and thirty years, but the Yuma prison register in the Arizona State Archives shows that it was thirty years. A popular story that Pearl Hart returned to Arizona as Pearl Bywater, dying there in 1955, is improbable.

21. *Phoenix Arizona Republican*, December 7, 1899; *Los Angeles Times*, December 14, 1898; *Tombstone Prospector*, December 14, 1898; Cady, *Arizona's Yesterday*, 112–13.

22. *Tucson Daily Citizen*, November 27, 1899; *Phoenix Arizona Republican*, November 30, December 7, 1899; *Prescott Weekly Arizona Miner*, December 6, 1899; *Los Angeles Times*, December 5, 1899. J. S. Hopley served in the U.S. Cavalry from 1870 to 1885, was city marshal of Tucson from 1902 to 1909, and was undersheriff of Pima County from 1909 to 1914. *Tucson Daily Citizen*, October 26, 1914.

23. *Phoenix Arizona Republican*, December 7, 1899.

24. *Tucson Daily Citizen*, October 18, 20, 22, November 21, 1900, February 11, 1901. On Alvord and Stiles, see Chaput, *Odyssey of Burt Alvord*.

25. *Tucson Daily Citizen*, January 2, 1901. Several accounts in the files of the Arizona Historical Society state incorrectly that Paul was elected justice of the peace and that he held that post at the time of his death. Emanuel Drachman (1872–1933) was a younger brother of Mose Drachman.

26. *Tucson Daily Citizen*, January 4, 21, 1901; *San Francisco Call*, March 23, 1901; Robert H. Paul, death certificate, Arizona State Library and Archives.

27. Paul, biographical sketch of Robert H. Paul; *Tucson Daily Arizona Star*, March 27, 1901.

28. *San Francisco Examiner*, March 31, 1901; *San Francisco Call*, March 27, 1901; *Tucson Daily Citizen*, March 26, 27, 1901; *National Police Gazette*, July 30, 1901; *Phoenix Gazette*, March 28, 1901.

29. *Tucson Daily Arizona Star*, March 27, 1901.

30. Deed, Margaret A. Paul to Herbert B. Tenney, April 29, 1901, Pima County Recorder; *Tucson Daily Citizen*, August 14, 1902; Paul, biographical sketch of Robert H. Paul. Margaret Paul sold the Pennington adobe in 1905 for $1,500. Deed, Margaret A. Paul to B. M. Mariner and wife, June 12, 1905, Pima County Recorder. She died in San Francisco on July 18, 1915. *San Francisco Chronicle*, July 20, 1915. Paul's youngest son, Edgar, was the only one to make a lasting career in law enforcement. He joined the San Francisco Police Department in 1922 and retired in 1950. A shotgun purportedly owned by Paul is on display at the Woolaroc Museum in Bartlesville, Oklahoma. It is a Colt double-barrel hammer gun, and it is marked "Bob Paul, Tombstone, A.T." and "Wells Fargo Express No. 15." Unfortunately, the style of the engraving is not of the type used by Wells Fargo, Paul never lived in or was based in Tombstone, and the shotgun was manufactured in 1883, two years after he stopped working as a Wells Fargo messenger. Its authenticity is especially dubious.

31. *Tucson Daily Arizona Star*, January 2, 1931, June 24, 1935; Drachman, "Reminiscences," 70–73. Shaw's account of the 1884 election was the basis for the oft-quoted article "Who Was Elected Sheriff." Matthew Shaw's bitterness was evident in his 1920s retelling of the deaths of the Stein's Pass train robbers in Mexico. Shaw gave the credit to Mexican soldiers, not Paul. See Southern Pacific Company, "History of Train Robberies on the Southern Pacific Company's Pacific Lines," 32. In *Tombstone's Yesterday* (186–89), Lorenzo D. Walters copied this account almost verbatim. Walters, who interviewed Shaw in Tucson prior to 1928, wrote, "Shaw stated that he did not mind the misfortunes of the five days'

travel or the twelve days' confinement, but to think that Bob Paul should come along after they had located the outlaws for him, and get into a fight and then worst of all collect the reward for the killing of the gang was a little too much" (189). Yet, as we have seen, the rewards were paid to Marshal Meade and the Mexican soldiers, not Bob Paul. And Shaw's statement that his posse had located the outlaws for Paul is outrageously false.

32. Paul, biographical sketch of Robert H. Paul.

33. The Catholic cemetery, where Paul was buried, consisted of the eastern half of the old Court Street Cemetery and was located between what is now Speedway Boulevard on the north, East 2nd Street on the south, North 11th Avenue on the west, and North Stone Avenue on the east. Due to development needs, the cemetery was closed in 1907. Family members could have their loved ones reinterred in Evergreen Cemetery for a fee, but few did. In 1915 newspapers announced a thirty-day deadline for the last bodies to be moved. Presumably Margaret Paul never knew that the cemetery was being moved. Buildings and other developments were placed on top of the old cemetery, and in later years numerous graves were uncovered by accident. Paul's final resting place is now lost. Callender, "Tucson's Early Cemeteries," 29–30; Callender, "All Cemeteries Are Not Created Equal," 161–63.

Bibliography

ARCHIVES AND UNPUBLISHED MATERIALS

Arizona Historical Society

Abstract of marshal's fees and expenses, June 30, 1891, June 30, 1892, May 26, 1893. U.S. marshal records.

Cipriano Baca to R. H. Paul, April 8, 1892. U.S. marshal correspondence.

George Brown et al. to R. H. Paul, May 29, 1892. U.S. marshal correspondence.

George A. Brown, "Reminiscences of George A. Brown," 1929.

Thomas D. Casanega, "Life History of T. D. Casanega." Unpublished manuscript.

L. B. Comstock to R. H. Paul, April 15, 1891. U.S. marshal correspondence.

B. B. Denure to R. H. Paul, March 24, March 31, April 13, 30, 1892. U.S. marshal correspondence.

Moses Drachman, "Reminiscences."

C. T. Dunavan to Joseph Blackburn, February 17, 1890. U.S. marshal correspondence.

Frank F. Flint to R. H. Paul, August 9, 1890. U.S. marshal correspondence.

Alfred L. Paul, biographical sketch of Robert H. Paul, October 14, 1953.

Robert H. Paul biographical file.

Paul v. Shibell, Pima County District Court case no. 479.

Pima County jail register, 1877–82.

Dell M. Potter to R. H. Paul, March 25, 1892. U.S. marshal correspondence.

John J. Valentine to R. H. Paul, August 30, 1878. George A. Brown papers.

J. W. Wilson to Robert Paul, December 22, 1891. U.S. marshal correspondence.

Arizona State Library and Archives

N. W. Bernard v. R. H. Paul and R. J. Paul (1905), Pima County District Court case no. 3805.

In the Matter of the Inquest Held on the Body of Chas. Hensley and Jack Elmer, Cochise
    County District Court records.
John J. Gosper to James G. Blaine, September 20, 1881.
Robert H. Paul, death certificate.
Mamie Paul v. John V. Paul, Pinal County District Court.
R. H. Paul to Mexican Consul at Tucson, June 30, 1881.
R. H. Paul v. E. O. Shaw, Pima County District Court case no. 1192.
Requisition for John H. Holliday, signed by F. A. Tritle, May 16, 1882.
Requisition for John H. Holliday, signed by H. M. Van Arman, June 9, 1882.
*Southern Pacific Railroad Company v. R. H. Paul, Sheriff and Ex-officio Assessor and Tax
    Collector of the County of Pima* (1882), Pima County District Court case no. 705.
R. M. Wilkin and Richard Starr v. Paul Jernicke (1882), Pima County District Court case no. 825.

Arizona State University Library

George Cooler biographical sketch.

Bancroft Library

James B. Hume Papers.
R. H. Paul dictation.

John Boessenecker Collection

J. M. Glass, chief of police, Los Angeles, to R. H. Paul, August 27, 1892, copy.
Reward circular for Red Jack Almer and Charley Hensley, copy.
Southern Pacific Company, "History of Train Robberies on the Southern Pacific Com-
    pany's Pacific Lines," copy.
Wells Fargo reward poster, March 23, 1881, copy.

Calaveras County Archives

Assessment list of Calaveras County, 1868–69.
Assessment list of Township 6, 1863.
Assessment list of Township 6, 1864.
Deed, R. H. Paul and others to John T. Carr, April 1, 1870.
Indenture, William H. Badgley and wife to R. H. Paul, October 19, 1859.
Indenture, J. C. Gebhardt and Augustus Gebhardt to R. H. Paul, February 9, 1863.
Mining notice of R. H. Paul et al., August 4, 1863.

California State Archives

People v. Wallace Stewart, case no. 1354, California Supreme Court Records.
People v. Ybarra, case no. 2606, California Supreme Court Records.
San Quentin prison register.

Correspondence

Wendy John to the author, September 16, 2008.
Frank Q. Newton, Jr., to the author, October 23, 1996.

Frank Q. Newton, Jr., to the author, August 16, 1998.
Robert G. Paul to the author, August 4, 2009.
Gary L. Roberts to the author, March 28, 2009, June 20, 2010.

Don Gordon Collection

Wells Fargo & Company's Express, *Messengers Instructions*, 1884.

Holy Cross Cemetery

Interment record no. 19873.

National Archives

Department of Justice year files:
   William H. Barnes to C. W. Wright, January 24, 1890.
   Ben Heney to W. H. H. Miller, October 24, 1889.
   N. O. Murphy to George F. Edmunds, February 18, 1890.
   R. H. Paul to W. H. H. Miller, January 16, March 17, 1890.
   Marcus A. Smith to U.S. Senate Committee on the Judiciary, January 14, 1890.
   Leland Stanford to Benjamin Harrison, June 3, 1889.
   Lewis Wolfley to George F. Edmunds, January 15, 1890.
   Lewis Wolfley to W. H. H. Miller, January 31, 1890.
U.S. Census Population Schedules, 1860, 1870, 1880.

New Bedford Free Public Library

Index to births in New Bedford, 1847–60.
Marriages solemnized in New Bedford, 1848–61.
Seamen protection papers.
Whalemen's shipping paper, ship *Factor*, 1844.

New Bedford Whaling Museum

"List of Persons Composing the Crew of the Ship Majestic, 1842."
Log of the *Majestic*.
Log of the *Nassau*.
 Ship registers of New Bedford, vol. 1.
Wood, Dennis. Abstracts of whaling voyages, vol. 1, 1831–61.

Robert G. Paul Collection

Robert G. Paul family genealogical records.
Waters, Frank, and Gilchriese, John D., "The Story of Bob Paul," typescript.

Robert H. Paul Collection

Robert H. Paul family genealogical records.
Robert H. Paul scrapbook.

Pima County Recorder

Deed, Margaret A. Paul to Herbert B. Tenney, April 29, 1901.
Deed, Margaret A. Paul to B. M. Mariner and wife, June 12, 1905.
Indenture between Robert H. Paul and Margaret A. Paul and John Invancovich, November 6, 1893.

Society of California Pioneers

Robert H. Paul, application for membership.

Texas State Library and Archives

William S. Oury file.

University of Arizona Library, Special Collections

Papers of the Oury family.
R. H. Paul, "Statement of Sheriff of Property in His Possession Belonging to the County of Pima," Pima County documents.
E. O. Shaw to Board of Supervisors, April 9, 1887, Pima County documents.
C. A. Shibell to Board of Supervisors, May 2, 1881, Pima County documents.

Wells Fargo Bank History Department

Brent, John. "Brief Review of the Service of John Brent." Unpublished memoir.
Moore, B. F. "Early Days in California." Unpublished manuscript dated October 4, 1892.
Wells Fargo cash book, general salary, 1876. Abstract prepared by Dr. Robert J. Chandler.

Court Records

Agnew v. United States (1897) 165 U.S. Supreme Court Reports 36.
Blitz v. United States (1894) 153 U.S. Supreme Court Reports 308.
In Re Neagle (1890) 135 U.S. Supreme Court Reports 1.
Martin v. Wells Fargo & Co. (1889) 3 Arizona Supreme Court Reports 57.
Martin v. Wells Fargo & Co. (1892) 3 Arizona Supreme Court Reports 355.
Paul v. Cullum (1889) 132 U.S. Supreme Court Reports 539.
People ex rel. Attorney General v. Squires (1859) 14 Cal. Supreme Court Reports 12.
People v. Charles Williams (1856) 6 Cal. Supreme Court Reports 206.
People v. Pedro Ybarra (1860) 17 Cal. Supreme Court Reports 166.
Shaw v. County of Pima (1888) 18 Pacific Reporter 273.
United States v. Copper Queen Mining Co. (1902) 185 U.S. Supreme Court Reports 495.

Newspapers

Adelaide South Australian Register
Akron (Colo.) Weekly Pioneer Press
Albuquerque Citizen
Auburn Placer Herald

Bakersfield Courier-Californian
Bakersfield Weekly Gazette
Baltimore Sun
Bisbee Daily Review
Boise Idaho Statesman
Boston Courier
Boston Daily Atlas
Cincinnati Daily Gazette
Cleveland Plain Dealer
Clifton Clarion
Dallas Morning News
Dallas Weekly Herald
Darwin Coso Mining News
Denver Daily Tribune
Denver Republican
Denver Rocky Mountain News
Florence Weekly Enterprise
Fresno Republican
Globe Arizona Silver Belt
Grand Forks (N.Dak.) Herald
Hollister Free Lance
Honolulu Friend
Independence Inyo Independent
Jackson Amador Ledger
Kaufman (Tex.) Sun
Kingman Mojave County Miner
Los Angeles Herald
Los Angeles Star
Los Angeles Times
Marysville Daily Herald
Minneapolis Star Tribune
Mokelumne Hill Calaveras Chronicle
Napa Register
National Police Gazette
Nevada City Democrat
New Bedford Mercury
New Bedford Register
New Bedford Whaleman's Shipping List and Merchants' Transcript
New Haven (Conn.) Register
New Orleans Times-Picayune
New York Herald
New York Spectator
New York Times
Nogales Herald
Omaha World Herald
Peach Springs Arizona Champion
Philadelphia Inquirer
Phoenix Arizona Republican
Phoenix Gazette

Phoenix Herald
Prescott Weekly Arizona Miner
Sacramento Bee
Sacramento Daily Union
Sacramento Record-Union
Salt Lake City Tribune
San Andreas Calaveras Prospect
San Andreas Calaveras Weekly Citizen
San Andreas Independent
San Andreas Register
San Francisco Bulletin
San Francisco California Chronicle
San Francisco Call
San Francisco Chronicle
San Francisco Daily Alta California
San Francisco Daily Democratic State Journal
San Francisco Daily Placer Times and Transcript
San Francisco Examiner
San Francisco Herald
San Jose Daily Evening News
San Jose Mercury News
Santa Barbara Morning Press
Solomonville Bulletin
South Pueblo News
St. Louis Globe Democrat
Stockton Daily Independent
Stockton San Joaquin Republican
St. Paul (Minn.) Daily Globe
Sydney Morning Herald
Sydney Shipping Gazette
Tombstone Daily Nugget
Tombstone Epitaph
Tombstone Prospector
Tombstone Republican
Tucson Arizona Mining Index
Tucson Arizona Star
Tucson Citizen
Ventura Weekly Free Press
Visalia Tulare County Times
Visalia Weekly Delta
Wilkes-Barre (Pa.) Times
Winnemucca (Nev.) Daily Silver State
Yuma Sentinel

Books and Articles

Alexander, Bob. *Dangerous Dan Tucker*. Silver City, NM: High-Lonesome Books, 2001.
———. *John H. Behan: Sacrificed Sheriff*. Silver City, NM: High-Lonesome Books, 2002.

————. *Lynch Ropes and Long Shots*. Silver City, NM: High-Lonesome Books, 2006.

Allen, Frederick. *A Decent Orderly Lynching*. Norman: University of Oklahoma Press, 2004.

An Account of the Receipts and Expenditures of the United States. Washington, D.C.: Government Printing Office, 1893.

Anderson, George B. *History of New Mexico: Its Resources and People*. Los Angeles: Pacific States Publishing Co., 1907.

Anderson, Mike. "Posses and Politics in Pima County: The Administration of Sheriff Charlie Shibell." *Journal of Arizona History* 27, no. 3 (Autumn 1986).

Arizona and Its Resources. Los Angeles: Reuck & Rich, 1899.

Ayres, James E. "The San Rafael Ranch." *Glyphs: The Monthly Newsletter of the Arizona Archeological and Historical Society* 56, no. 12 (June 2006).

Ayers, James J. *Gold and Sunshine: Reminiscences of Early California*. Boston: Richard G. Badger, 1922.

Ball, Larry D. *Ambush at Bloody Run: The Wham Paymaster Robbery of 1889*. Tucson: Arizona Historical Society, 2000.

————. *Desert Lawmen: The High Sheriffs of New Mexico and Arizona*. Albuquerque: University of New Mexico Press, 1992.

————. "This High-Handed Outrage: Marshal William Kidder Meade in a Mexican Jail." *Journal of Arizona History* 17, no. 2 (Summer 1976).

————. *The United States Marshals of New Mexico and Arizona Territories, 1846–1912*. Albuquerque: University of New Mexico Press, 1978.

Bancroft, Hubert H. *History of Arizona and New Mexico*. San Francisco: History Company, 1889.

Boardman, Mark, ed. *Revenge! And Other True Tales of the Old West*. Lafayette, Ind.: Scarlet Mask, 2004.

Boessenecker, John, ed. *Against the Vigilantes: The Recollections of Dutch Charley Duane*. Norman: University of Oklahoma Press, 1999.

————. *Badge and Buckshot: Lawlessness in Old California*. Norman: University of Oklahoma Press, 1988.

————. *Bandido: The Life and Times of Tiburcio Vasquez*. Norman: University of Oklahoma Press, 2010.

————. "Buckshot for a Marshal." *Real West* 26, no. 189 (February 1983).

————. "Genesis of the Gunfighter: Two Accounts from the 1880s." *Wild West History Association Journal* 1, no. 1 (February 2008).

————. *Gold Dust and Gunsmoke*. New York: John Wiley & Sons, 1999.

————. "Gun Smoke at the Tunnel Saloon." *Wild West Magazine* 23, no. 3 (October 2010).

————. "John Thacker, Train Robbers' Nemesis." *Real West* 147, no. 19 (September 1976).

————. "Lawman Bob Paul's Doc and Wyatt Connection." *Wild West* 16, no. 2 (August 2003).

Brand, Peter. "Wyatt Earp, Jack Johnson, and the Notorious Blount Brothers." *Quarterly of the National Association for Outlaw and Lawman History* 27, no. 4 (October–December 2003).

Breakenridge, William M. *Helldorado*. Boston: Houghton Mifflin Co., 1928.

Brown, J. L. *The Mussel Slough Tragedy*. Published by the author, 1958.

Brown, Richard Maxwell. *No Duty to Retreat: Violence and Values in American History and Society*. New York: Oxford University Press, 1991.

————. *Strain of Violence: Historical Studies of American Violence and Vigilantism*. New York: Oxford University Press, 1975.

Browne, J. Ross. *Resources of the Pacific Coast*. New York: D. Appleton & Co., 1869.

Buchanan, A. Russell. *David S. Terry of California: Dueling Judge*. San Marino, Calif.: Hunting-
ton Library, 1956.

Buckbee, Edna Bryan. *The Saga of Old Tuolumne*. New York: Press of the Pioneers, 1935.

Bullough, William A. *The Blind Boss and His City: Christopher Augustine Buckley and Nineteenth-
Century San Francisco*. Berkeley: University of California Press, 1979.

Burnham, Frederick Russell. *Scouting on Two Continents*. Garden City, N.Y.: Doubleday,
Page & Co., 1926.

Burns, Walter Noble. *Tombstone: An Iliad of the Southwest*. Garden City, N.Y.: Doubleday,
Page & Co., 1927.

Burrows, Jack. *John Ringo: The Gunfighter Who Never Was*. Tucson: University of Arizona
Press, 1987.

Burton, Jeffrey. *Constable Dodge and the Pantano Train Robbers*. Published by the author, 2006.
———. *Western Story*. Published by the author, 2008.

Busbey, T. A. *Biographical Directory of the Railway Officials of America*. Chicago: Lakeside
Press, 1893.

Cady, John H. *Arizona's Yesterday: Being the Narrative of John H. Cady, Pioneer*. Published by
the author, 1914.

Callender, Joanne. "All Cemeteries Are Not Created Equal." *Copper State Journal* (Winter 2001).
———. "Tucson's Early Cemeteries." *Copper State Journal* (Spring 1999).

Carlton, Frank Tracy. *The History and Problems of Organized Labor*. New York: D. C. Heath
& Co., 1920.

Carmony, Neil, ed. *Whiskey, Six-guns and Red-light Ladies: George Hand's Saloon Diary, Tucson,
1875–1878*. Silver City, N.Mex.: High-Lonesome Books, 1994.

Carson, James H. *Recollections of the California Mines*. Stockton, Calif.: San Joaquin Republican, 1852.

Census Bulletin, no. 322. Washington, D.C.: United States Census Office, 1890.

Chalfant, W. A. *The Story of Inyo*. Published by the author, 1933.

Chandler, Robert J. "*Under Cover for Wells Fargo*: A Review Essay." *Journal of Arizona History*
41, no. 2 (Spring 2000).

———. "Wells Fargo: 'We Never Forget!'" *Quarterly of the National Center for Outlaw and
Lawman History* 11, no. 3 (Winter 1987).

———. "Wells Fargo and the Earp Brothers: The Cash Books Talk." *California Territorial
Quarterly*, no. 78 (Summer 2009).

Chaput, Don. "Fred Dodge: Undercover Agent or Con Man?" *National Association for
Outlaw and Lawman History Quarterly* 25 (January–March 2000).

———. *The Odyssey of Burt Alvord*. Tucson: Westernlore Press, 2000.

———. *Virgil Earp: Western Peace Officer*. Encampment, Wyo.: Affiliated Writers of America, 1994.

Chickering, Jesse. *Statistical View of the Population of Massachusetts, from 1765 to 1840*. Boston:
Little and Brown, 1846.

Chisholm, Joe. *Brewery Gulch*. San Antonio: Naylor Co., 1949.

Christian, Chris. "Riding Shotgun." *Popular Mechanics* 181, no. 6 (June 2004).

Cole, Stephanie, and Alison M. Parker, eds. *Beyond Black and White: Race, Ethnicity, and
Gender in the U.S. South and Southwest*. Arlington: University of Texas Press, 2004.

Collins, William, and Bruce Levene. *Black Bart: The True Story of the West's Most Famous
Stagecoach Robber*. Mendocino, Calif.: Pacific Transcriptions, 1992.

Colwell-Chanthaphonh, Chip. *Massacre at Camp Grant: Forgetting and Remembering Apache
History*. Tucson: University of Arizona Press, 2007.

Compiled Laws of Arizona. Detroit: Richmond, Backus & Co., 1875.

Cool, Paul. "Bob Martin: A Rustler in Paradise." *Western Outlaw History Association Journal* 11, no. 4 (Winter 2003).

———. "Escape of a Highwayman: The Riddle of Sherman McMaster." *Western Outlaw Lawman History Association Journal* 9, no. 2 (Summer 2000).

———. "Salt War Sheriff: El Paso's Charles Kerber." *Quarterly of the National Association for Outlaw and Lawman History* 27, no. 1 (January–March 2003).

Creighton, Margaret S. *Rites and Passages: The Experience of American Whaling, 1830–1870.* New York: Cambridge University Press, 1995.

Creswell, Stephen. *Mormons and Cowboys, Moonshiners and Klansmen.* Tuscaloosa: University of Alabama Press, 1991.

Daws, Gavan. *Shoal of Time: a History of the Hawaiian Islands.* Honolulu: University of Hawaii Press, 1968.

DeArment, Robert K. *Deadly Dozen,* Vol. 3. Norman: University of Oklahoma Press, 2010.

———. *George Scarborough: The Life and Death of a Lawman on the Closing Frontier.* Norman: University of Oklahoma Press, 1992.

———. *Knights of the Green Cloth.* Norman: University of Oklahoma Press, 1992.

———. "The Outlaws of Clifton, Arizona Territory." *Quarterly of the National Association for Outlaw and Lawman History* 27, no. 1 (January–March 2003).

Debo, Angie. *Geronimo: The Man, His Time, His Place.* Norman: University of Oklahoma Press, 1976.

Decker, Peter R. *Fortunes and Failures: White Collar Mobility in Nineteenth-Century San Francisco.* Cambridge, Mass.: Harvard University Press, 1978.

DeMattos, Jack. *Mysterious Gunfighter: The Story of Dave Mather.* College Station, Tex.: Creative Publishing Co., 1992.

Dill, David B., Jr., "Removal!: The Political Downfall of Louis Hughes." *Journal of Arizona History* 29, no. 2 (Autumn 1988).

Dillon, Richard H. *Wells Fargo Detective.* New York: Coward-McCann, 1969.

Directory of the City of Tucson for the Year 1881. San Francisco: H. S. Crocker & Co., 1881.

Dodge, Ernest S. *Islands and Empires: Western Impact on the Pacific and East Asia.* Minneapolis: University of Minnesota Press, 1976.

Dodge, Fred. *Under Cover for Wells Fargo: The Unvarnished Recollections of Fred Dodge.* Edited by Carolyn Lake. Boston: Houghton Mifflin Co., 1969.

Dolin, Eric Jay. *Leviathan: The History of Whaling in America.* New York: W. W. Norton & Co., 2007.

Dugan, Mark. *Knight of the Road: The Life of Highwayman Ham White.* Athens, Ohio: Swallow Press, 1990.

Dykstra, Robert R. "Body Counts and Murder Rates: The Contested Statistics of Western Violence." *Reviews in American History* 31 (2003).

———. "Overdosing on Dodge City." *Western Historical Quarterly* 27 (Winter 1996).

———. "Quantifying the Wild West: The Problematic Statistics of Frontier Violence." *Western Historical Quarterly* 40 (Autumn 2009).

Edwards, Harold L. "Three Unmarked Graves." *Los Tulares: Quarterly Bulletin of the Tulare County Historical Society,* September 2004.

———. "Trouble in Mexico." *Old West,* Spring 1995.

———. "Will Smith: A Study in Controversy." *Quarterly of the National Association for Outlaw and Lawman History* 12, nos. 3–4 (Winter–Spring 1988).

Ellis, George M. "Sheriff Jerome L. Ward and the Bisbee Massacre of 1883." *Journal of Arizona History* 35, no. 3 (Autumn 1994).

Enock, Charles Reginald. *The Great Pacific Coast: Twelve Thousand Miles in the Golden West.* New York: Charles Scribner's Sons, 1910.

Eppinga, Jane. *Arizona Sheriffs: Badges and Badmen.* Tucson: Rio Nuevo Publishers, 2007.

———. "Law and Order in Graham County." *Arizona Sheriff* 9, no. 1 (Spring 1990).

Erwin, Richard. *The Truth about Wyatt Earp.* Carpinteria, Calif.: OK Press, 1993.

Ethington, Philip J. *The Public City: The Political Construction of Urban Life in San Francisco.* New York: Cambridge University Press, 1994.

———. "Vigilantes and the Police: The Creation of a Professional Police Bureaucracy in San Francisco, 1847–1900." *Journal of Social History* 21 (Winter 1987).

Express Gazette 12, no. 11 (November 1887).

Farish, Thomas E. *History of Arizona.* San Francisco: Filmer Brothers, 1915.

Farmer, Randolph W. "William Henry Graham Was Not Curly Bill." *Wild West History Association Journal* 2, no. 1 (February 2009).

Friedman, Lawrence M. *Crime and Punishment in American History.* New York: Basic Books, 1993.

Garavaglia, Louis A., and Charles G. Worman. *Firearms of the American West, 1866–1894.* Albuquerque: University of Mexico Press, 1985.

Gatto, Steve. *Curly Bill: Tombstone's Most Famous Outlaw.* Lansing, Mich.: Protar House, 2003.

Goodman, John B., III. "The 1849 Gold Rush Fleet: The Ship *Harriet Rockwell.*" *Southern California Quarterly* 67, no. 3 (Fall 1985).

Haley, J. Evetts. *Jeff Milton: A Good Man with a Gun.* Norman: University of Oklahoma Press, 1948.

Harlow, William S. *Duties of Sheriffs and Constables.* 3rd ed. San Francisco: Bancroft Whitney Co., 1907.

Hart, Mary Nicklanovich. "Arizona Cattle Baron, Pioneer and Lawman Thomas David Casanega." *Serb World USA* 17, no. 1 (September–October 2000).

Hedges, Charles. *Speeches of Benjamin Harrison, Twenty-Third President of the United States.* New York: United States Book Co., 1892.

Heflin, Wilson. *Herman Melville's Whaling Years.* Nashville: Vanderbilt University Press, 2004.

Hietter, Paul T. "How Wild Was Arizona? An Examination of Pima County's Criminal Court, 1882–1909." *Western Legal History* 12, no. 2 (Summer–Fall 1999).

———. "A Surprising Amount of Justice: The Experience of Mexican and Racial Minority Defendants Charged with Serious Crimes in Arizona, 1865–1920." *Pacific Historical Review* 70, no. 2 (May 2001).

A Historical and Biographical Record of the Territory of Arizona. Chicago: McFarland & Poole, 1896.

History of San Joaquin County. Chicago: Lewis Publishing Company, 1889.

History of Yuba County, California. Oakland: Thompson & West, 1879.

Hittell, Theodore Henry. *History of California.* San Francisco: N. J. Stone & Co., 1898.

Hogan, William F. "Adolph George Buttner, Tucson's First Chief of Police." *Journal of Arizona History* 5, no. 2 (Summer 1964).

Hoskins, Ian. *Sydney Harbour: A History.* Sydney: University of New South Wales Press, 2009.

House Documents, Otherwise Publ. as Executive Documents: 13th Congress. Washington, D.C.: Government Printing Office, 1883.

Howard, Philip N. "In the Margins: Political Victory in the Context of Technology Error, Residual Votes, and Incident Reports in 2004." Center for Communication and Civic Engagement Working Paper 2005-1, University of Washington, 2005.

Hume, James B., and John B. Thacker. *Robbers Record.* San Francisco: H. S. Crocker & Co., 1885.

Hurtado, Albert L. *Intimate Frontiers: Sex, Gender, and Culture in Old California*. Albuquerque: University of New Mexico Press, 1999.

Jackson, Joseph Henry. *Bad Company*. New York: Harcourt, Brace & Co., 1949.

Jacobsen, Joel. *Such Men as Billy the Kid*. Lincoln: University of Nebraska Press, 1994.

Jacoby, Karl. *Shadows at Dawn: A Borderlands Massacre and the Violence of History*. New York: Penguin Press, 2008.

Jay, Roger. "The Peoria Bummer: Wyatt Earp's Lost Year." *Wild West* 16, no. 2 (August 2003).

Johnson, David. *John Ringo: King of the Cowboys*. Denton: University of North Texas Press, 2008.

Johnson, David R. *Policing the Urban Underworld*. Philadelphia: Temple University Press, 1979.

Johnston, Effie Enfield. "Wade Johnston Talks to His Daughter." *Las Calaveras: Quarterly Bulletin of the Calaveras County Historical Society* 18, no. 1 (October 1969).

Kelley, Troy. *I Don't Propose to Walk into Anybody's Graveyard: The Story of the Bisbee Massacre*. Published by the author, 2004.

Lake, Stuart N. *Wyatt Earp: Frontier Marshal*. Boston: Houghton Mifflin Co., 1931.

Lang, Margaret Hanna. *Early Justice in Sonora*. Sonora, Calif.: Mother Lode Press, 1963.

LeBaron, A. D. "Bisbee's Five Black Ghosts." *True West* 7, no. 6 (July–August 1960).

Limbaugh, Ronald H., and Willard P. Fuller, Jr. *Calaveras Gold: the Impact of Mining on a Mother Lode County*. Reno: University of Nevada Press, 2004.

Lindgren, Waldermar. *The Tertiary Gravels of the Sierra Nevada of California*, Washington, D.C.: Government Printing Office, 1911.

Long, Clarence Dickinson. *Wages and Earnings in the United States, 1860–1890*. Princeton: Princeton University Press, 1975.

Lotchin, Roger W. *San Francisco, 1846–1856: From Hamlet to City*. New York: Oxford University Press, 1974.

Lowell Directory. Lowell, Mass.: Thomas Billings, 1832.

Lubet, Steven. *Murder in Tombstone: The Forgotten Trial of Wyatt Earp*. New Haven, Conn.: Yale University Press, 2004.

Lyon, William H. "Louis C. Hughes: Arizona's Editorial Gadfly." *Journal of Arizona History* 24, no. 2 (Summer 1983).

Margolies, Daniel S. *Spaces of Law in American Foreign Relations: Extradition and Extraterritoriality in the Borderlands and Beyond, 1877–1898*. Athens: University of Georgia Press, 2011.

Marks, Paula Mitchell. *And Die in the West: The Story of the O.K. Corral Gunfight*. New York: Simon & Schuster, 1989.

Martin, Douglas D. *Tombstone's Epitaph*. Norman: University of Oklahoma Press, 1997.

Mason, Jesse D. *History of Amador County, California*. Oakland: Thompson & West, 1881.

Master Hands in the Affairs of the Pacific Coast. San Francisco: Western Historical and Publishing Co., 1892.

Masterson, W. B. "Famous Gunfighters of the Western Frontier: Wyatt Earp." *Human Life* 4, no. 5 (February 1907).

McClintock, James H. *Arizona, the Youngest State*. Chicago: S. J. Clarke, 1916.

McGroarty, John Steven. *Los Angeles: From the Mountains to the Sea*. Chicago: American Historical Society, 1921.

McKanna, Clare V. "Enclaves of Violence in Nineteenth-Century California." *Pacific Historical Review* 73, no. 3 (August 2004).

———. *Race and Homicide in Nineteenth-Century California*. Reno: University of Nevada Press, 2002.

McKelvey, Nat. "Riddle of the Redfield Robbers." *True West* 5, no. 3 (January–February 1958).

Melville, Herman. *Moby Dick*. New York: Harper & Brothers, 1851.

Memorial and Biographical History of the Counties of Fresno, Tulare and Kern, California. Chicago: Lewis Publishing Company, 1892.

Miller, Joseph. *The Arizona Story*. New York: Hastings House, 1952.

Miller, Rick. *Bounty Hunter*. College Station, Tex.: Creative Publishing Co., 1988.

Mullen, Kevin J. *Let Justice Be Done: Crime and Politics in Early San Francisco*. Reno: University of Nevada Press, 1989.

Myers, John Myers. *The Last Chance: Tombstone's Early Years*. New York: E. P. Dutton & Co., 1950.

Nelson, Scott L. "Trailing Jerry Barton." *Quarterly of the National Association for Outlaw and Lawman History* 26, no. 1 (January–March 2002).

New Bedford Directory. New Bedford, Mass.: J. C. Parmenter, Printer, 1836.

New Bedford Directory. New Bedford, Mass.: J. C. Parmenter, Printer, 1838.

New Bedford Directory. New Bedford, Mass.: J. C. Parmenter, Printer, 1839.

New Bedford Directory. New Bedford, Mass.: Henry Howland Crapo, 1845.

New Bedford Directory. New Bedford, Mass.: Henry Howland Crapo, 1849.

New Bedford Directory. New Bedford, Mass.: Henry Howland Crapo, 1852.

New Bedford Directory. New Bedford, Mass.: Henry Howland Crapo, 1856.

New Bedford Directory. New Bedford, Mass.: Henry Howland Crapo, 1859.

Ninth Census of the United States: Statistics of Population. Washington, D.C.: Government Printing Office, 1872.

Nolan, Frederick. *The Lincoln County War: A Documentary History*. Norman: University of Oklahoma Press, 1992.

Nordhoff, Charles. *Whaling and Fishing*. New York: Dodd, Mead & Co., 1855.

Notables of the West, Being the Portraits and Biographies of the Progressive Men of the West. New York: International News Service, 1915.

O'Dell, Roy. "Joseph Casey, Arizona Escape Artist." *Quarterly of the National Association for Outlaw and Lawman History* 12, no. 2 (Fall 1988).

Official Report of the Proceedings, Testimony, and Arguments in the Trial of James H. Hardy. Sacramento: Benjamin P. Avery, 1862.

O'Hare, Sheila, Irene Berry, and Jesse Silva. *Legal Executions in California: A Comprehensive Registry*. Jefferson, N.C.: McFarland & Co., 2006.

O'Meara, James. "The Story of the Mier Prisoners." *Californian* 5 (January–June 1882).

Orsi, Richard J. *Sunset Limited: The Southern Pacific Railroad and the Development of the American West, 1850–1930*. Berkeley: University of California Press, 2005.

Outline History of the California National Guard. Sacramento: State Printing Office, 1950.

Palmquist, Robert F. "Arizona Affairs: An Interview with Virgil Earp." *Real West Annual*, Spring 1984.

———. "Election Fraud 1880: The Case of *Paul v. Shibell*." Unpublished manuscript, April 10, 1986.

Papers Relating to the Foreign Relations of the United States. Washington, D.C.: Government Printing Office, 1880.

Papers Relating to the Foreign Relations of the United States. Washington, D.C.: Government Printing Office, 1883.

Parker, Hershel. *Herman Melville: 1819–1851*. Baltimore: Johns Hopkins University Press, 1996.

Philbrick, Nathaniel. *In the Heart of the Sea: The Tragedy of the Whaleship* Essex. New York: Viking Penguin, 2000.

Portrait and Biographical Record of Arizona. Chicago: Chapman Publishing Co., 1901.

Potter, Pam. "Gunfighters and Lawmen." *Wild West* 16, no. 2 (August 2003).

Prassel, Frank Richard. *The Western Peace Officer: A Legacy of Law and Order.* Norman: University of Oklahoma Press, 1972.

Pridham, William. "In Stage Days." *Wells Fargo Messenger Magazine* 3 (February 1915).

Rasch, Philip J. *Desperadoes of Arizona Territory.* Stillwater, Okla.: Western Publications, 1999.

———. "Jerry Barton, A Noted Desperado." *Real West,* February 1986.

———. "The Riverside Stage Robbery." *Real West,* August 1986.

———. "They Tried to Hold Up the Tombstone Stage." *Real West,* October 1984.

———. "Train Robbery Times Four." *Real West,* June 1982.

Revised Statutes of Arizona. Prescott: Prescott Courier Print, 1887.

Roberts, Gary L. "Allie's Story: Mrs. Virgil Earp and the 'Tombstone Travesty.'" *Western Outlaw Lawman History Association Journal* 8 (Fall 1999).

———. *Doc Holliday: The Life and Legend.* New York: John Wiley & Sons, 2006.

Roberts, Oliver. *The Great Understander: True Life Story of the Last of the Wells Fargo Shotgun Express Messengers.* Aurora, Ill.: William W. Walter, 1931.

Rockfellow, John A. *Log of an Arizona Trail Blazer.* Tucson: Acme Print Co., 1933.

Rogers, W. Lane. "Bushwhacked: The Wham Payroll Robbery." *True West* 42, no. 7 (July 1995).

Rolle, Andrew F. *California: A History.* New York: Thomas Y. Crowell Co., 1969.

Roth, Randolph A. "Guns, Murder, and Probability: How Can We Decide Which Figures to Trust?" *Reviews in American History* 35, no. 2 (June 2007).

Salas, Miguel Tinker. *In the Shadow of the Eagles: Sonora and the Transformation of the Border during the Porfiriato.* Berkeley: University of California Press, 1997.

Schubert, Frank N. *Voices of the Buffalo Soldier.* Albuquerque: University of New Mexico Press, 2003.

Secrest, William B. *California Badmen: Mean Men with Guns.* Sanger, Calif.: Word Dancer Press, 2007.

———. *Dangerous Trails: Five Desperadoes of the Old West Coast.* Stillwater, Okla.: Barbed Wire Press, 1995.

———. "Jim Levy: Top-Notch Gunfighter." *True West* 25, no. 6 (July–August 1978).

———. *Lawmen and Desperadoes.* Spokane, Wash.: Arthur H. Clark Company, 1994.

———. *The Man from the Rio Grande.* Spokane, Wash.: Arthur H. Clark Company, 2005.

———. *Perilous Trails, Dangerous Men.* Clovis, Calif.: Word Dancer Press, 2001.

———. "Quick with a Gun: The Story of Dave Neagle." *True West* 42 (June 1995).

———. "Revenge of Rancheria." *Frontier Times* 42, no. 5 (August–September 1968).

Senkewicz, Robert. *Vigilantes in Gold Rush San Francisco.* Stanford, Calif.: Stanford University Press, 1985.

Sheridan, Thomas E. *Los Tucsonenses: The Mexican Community in Tucson, 1854–1941.* Tucson: University of Arizona Press, 1986.

Sherman, Edwin A. *Fifty Years of Masonry in California.* San Francisco: George Spaulding & Co., 1895.

Shillingberg, William B. *Tombstone, A. T.: A History of Early Mining, Milling, and Mayhem.* Spokane, Wash.: Arthur H. Clark Co., 1999.

Shuck, Oscar T. *History of the Bench and Bar of California.* Los Angeles: Commercial Printing House, 1901.

Smith, Cornelius C., Jr. *William Sanders Oury: History Maker of the Southwest.* Tucson: University of Arizona Press, 1967.

Smith, Dean. *The Goldwaters of Arizona.* Flagstaff, Ariz.: Northland Press, 1986.

Smith, Robert Barr. *Daltons! The Raid on Coffeyville, Kansas.* Norman: University of Oklahoma Press, 1996.

Sonnichsen, C. L. *Billy King's Tombstone.* Caldwell, Idaho: Caxton Printers, 1942.

———. *Tucson: The Life and Times of an American City.* Norman: University of Oklahoma Press, 1982.

Steffens, Lincoln. "The Making of a Fighter." *American Magazine* 64, no. 4 (August 1907).

Stellman, Louis J. *Mother Lode: The Story of California's Gold Rush.* San Francisco: Harr Wagner Publishing Co., 1934.

Stewart, Frank M. "Impeachment of James H. Hardy, 1862." *Southern California Law Review* 28 (1954–55).

Stewart, Janet Ann. "The Mansions of Main Street." *Journal of Arizona History* 20 (Summer 1979).

Sweeney, Edwin R. *Cochise: Chiricahua Chief.* Norman: University of Oklahoma Press, 1991.

Tefertiller, Casey. "What Was Not in *Tombstone Travesty.*" *Western Outlaw Lawman History Association Journal* 8 (Fall 1999).

———. *Wyatt Earp: The Life behind the Legend.* New York: John Wiley & Sons, 1997.

Theobald, John, and Lillian Theobald. *Wells Fargo in Arizona Territory.* Tempe: Arizona Historical Foundation, 1978.

Thornton, Bruce. *Searching for Joaquin: Myth, Murieta and History in California.* San Francisco: Encounter Books, 2003.

Thrapp, Dan L. *Al Sieber: Chief of Scouts.* Norman: University of Oklahoma Press, 1964.

———. *The Conquest of Apacheria.* Norman: University of Olahoma Press, 1967.

———. *Encyclopedia of Frontier Biography.* Glendale, Calif.: Arthur H. Clark Co., 1988.

Tombstone in History, Romance, and Wealth. Tombstone, Ariz.: Daily Prospector, 1903.

Traywick, Ben T. *The Hangings in Tombstone.* Tombstone, Ariz.: Red Marie's Books, 1991.

———. *That Wicked Little Gringo.* Tombstone, Ariz.: Red Marie's Books, 2001.

Turner, Alford E., ed. *The Earps Talk.* College Station, Tex.: Creative Publishing Co., 1980.

———. *The O.K. Corral Inquest.* College Station, Tex.: Creative Publishing Co., 1981.

Utley, Robert M. *High Noon in Lincoln.* Albuquerque: University of New Mexico Press, 1987.

Varley, James F. *The Legend of Joaquin Murrieta.* Twin Falls, Idaho: Big Lost River Press, 1995.

A Volume of Memoirs and Genealogy of Representative Citizens of Northern California. Chicago: Standard Genealogical Publishing Co., 1901.

Wagoner, Jay J. *Arizona Territory, 1863–1912: A Political History.* Tucson: University of Arizona Press, 1980.

Walker, Henry P. "Retire Peaceably to Your Homes: Arizona Faces Martial Law, 1882," *Journal of Arizona History* 10, no. 1 (Spring 1969).

Walters, Lorenzo D. *Tombstone's Yesterday.* Tucson: Acme Printing Co., 1928.

Waters, Frank. *The Earp Brothers of Tombstone.* New York: Clarkson N. Potter, 1960.

Whale Fishery of New England. Boston: State Street Trust Co., 1915.

Wheat, Jeffrey. "The Waters Travesty." *Western Outlaw Lawman History Association Journal* 8 (Fall 1999).

Wheeler, Edmund. *The History of Newport, New Hampshire.* Concord, N.H.: Republican Press, 1879.

Who's Who in the Pacific Southwest: A Compilation of Authentic Biographical Sketches of Citizens of Southern California and Arizona. Los Angeles: Times-Mirror Printing and Binding House, 1913.

"Who Was Elected Sheriff?" *Arizona Sheriff Magazine* 8 (February 1949).

Willson, Roscoe G. *No Place for Angels*. Phoenix: Arizona Republic, 1958.

Wilson, R. Michael. *Crime and Punishment in Early Arizona*. Las Vegas: Stagecoach Books, 2004.

————. *Encyclopedia of Stagecoach Robbery in Arizona*. Las Vegas: RaMA Press, 2003.

————. *Wells, Fargo & Company's Report of Losses from Stagecoach and Train Robbers, 1870 to 1884*. Las Vegas: Stagecoach Books, 2007.

Wilstach, Frank J. *Wild Bill Hickok, the Prince of Pistoleers*. Garden City, N.Y.: Doubleday, 1926.

Wood, William H. R. *Digest of the Laws of California*. San Francisco: S. D. Valentine and Son, 1857.

Young, Ann Eliza. *Wife No. 19; or, The Story of a Life in Bondage*. Hartford, Conn.: Dustin, Gilman & Co., 1875.

Young, Roy B. "The Assassination of Frank Stilwell." *Wild West History Association Journal* 1, no. 4 (August 2008).

————. *Cochise County Cowboy War*. Apache, Okla.: Young and Sons Enterprises, 1999.

————. "The Other Ike and Billy: The Heslet Brothers in Grant County, New Mexico." *Western Outlaw-Lawman History Association Journal* 15, no. 2 (Summer 2006).

————. *Pete Spence: Audacious Artist in Crime*. Apache, Okla.: Young and Sons Enterprises, 2000.

————, ed. "William Breakenridge Tells the Story of the Earp Faction and the Cowboy Rustlers in the Palmy Days of Tombstone." *Western Outlaw-Lawman History Association Journal* 15, no. 1 (Spring 2006).

Index

CPSIA information can be obtained
at www.ICGtesting.com
Printed in the USA
LVHW041753280220
648534LV00002B/194